Four Decades of Distance Education in India

Reflections on Policy and Practice

Four Decades of Distance Education in India

Reflections on Policy and Practice

Edited by
Suresh Garg
V. Venkaiah
Chambi Puranik
Santosh Panda

Viva Books
New Delhi | Mumbai | Chennai | Kolkata
Bangalore | Hyderabad | Kochi | Guwahati

First Published 2006
Reprinted 2010

VIVA BOOKS PRIVATE LIMITED

- 4737/23 Ansari Road, Daryaganj, New Delhi 110 002
  E-mail: vivadelhi@vivagroupindia.net, Tel. 42242200
- 76, Service Industries, Shirvane, Sector 1, Nerul, Navi Mumbai 400 706
  E-mail: vivamumbai@vivagroupindia.net, Tel. 27721273, 27721274
- Jamals Fazal Chambers, 26 Greams Road, Chennai 600 006
  E-mail: vivachennai@vivagroupindia.net, Tel. 28290304, 28294241
- B-103, Jindal Towers, 21/1A/3 Darga Road, Kolkata 700 017
  E-mail: vivakolkata@vivagroupindia.net, Tel. 22836381, 22816713
- 7, Sovereign Park Apartments, 56-58, K. R. Road, Basavanagudi, Bangalore 560 004
  E-mail: vivabangalore@vivagroupindia.net, Tel. 26607409, 26607410
- 101-102 Mughal Marc Aptt., 3-4-637 to 641, Narayanguda, Hyderabad 500 029
  E-mail: vivahyderabad@vivagroupindia.net, Tel. 27564481, 27564482
- First Floor, Beevi Towers, SRM Road, Kaloor, Kochi 682 018, Kerala
  E-mail: vivakochi@vivagroupindia.net, Tel: 0484-2403055, 2403056
- 232, GNB Road, Beside UCO Bank, Silpukhuri, Guwahati 781 003
  E-mail: vivaguwahati@vivagroupindia.net, Tel: 0361-2666386

www.vivagroupindia.com

ISBN : 978-81-309-1430-5

Published by Vinod Vasishtha for Viva Books Private Limited, 4737/23, Ansari Road, Daryaganj, New Delhi - 110 002. Printed and bound by Sanat Printers, Kundli - 131 028.

CONTENTS

Foreword ix
Preface xi
Contributors xiii

SECTION I. POLICY, PLANNING AND MANAGEMENT **1-50**

1. Tracing the Historical Developments in Open and Distance Education
   Santosh Panda, V. Venkaiah, Suresh Garg and Chambi Puranik 03

2. National Education Policies vis-à-vis Distance Education
   V.C. Kulandaiswamy 24

3. Management of Open and Distance Learning Systems
   Madhulika Kaushik, Suresh Garg and H.P. Dikshit 39

SECTION II. DISTANCE TEACHING AND LEARNING RESOURCES **51-178**

4. Changing Role of Distance Teacher: March towards Multi-Skilling
   Suresh Garg and J.M. Parakh 53

5. Profile of Distance Learners
   Manjulika Srivastava and N.S. Ramegowda 65

6. Taking Education to the Disadvantaged: IGNOU Experience in KBK Region
   Kameshwari Moorthy 80

7. Empowering Differently-Abled Through Distance Education: Issues and Challenges
   J.P. Singh and J.S. Grewal 88

8. Changing Nature of Academic Programmes at a Distance: The Indian Perspective
   V. Venkaiah, Chambi Puranik and R.R. Rausaria 96

9. Models of Course Design and Development
Santosh Panda and Suresh Garg 107

10. Agriculture Education Through Distance Mode
Panjab Singh and M.K. Salooja 127

11. Health Education Through Distance Mode
A.K. Agarwal and T.K. Jena 142

12. Regional Languages and Distance Learning
Renu Bhardwaj 153

13. Legal Education Through Distance Mode
N.R. Madhava Menon 169

SECTION III. MEDIA AND TECHNOLOGY **179-274**

14. Emergence of Distance Education Media Networks
Abdul Waheed Khan and H.P. Dikshit 181

15. Audio and Radio
Kiron Bansal and V. Rama Rao 195

16. Teleconferencing
Zeba Khan and Santosh Panda 206

17. Interactive Radio
Sohanvir S. Chaudhary 219

18. Globalisation, e-Learning and Development
Ram Takwale 230

19. Knowledge Revolution Through Satellite Based Education
H.P. Dikshit 244

20. Tamil Virtual University: Some Experiences
V.C. Kulandaiswamy and M. Ponnavaikko 263

SECTION IV. INSTRUCTIONAL DELIVERY AND QUALITY ASSURANCE **275-402**

21. Networked and Decentralised Learner Support
S.R. Jha, C.K. Ghosh and P.K. Mehta 277

22. Monitoring Learner Support Services
Sanjeev Pandey and Masood Parveez 290

23. Online Learning Support
V.S.P. Srivastava, Shashi Bhushan and Bhupesh Khatri 305

24. Continuous Assessment in Open Education
Anuradha Deshmukh 315

25. Computers Hands-on and Lab Practicals in Distance Education
Akshay Kumar and Jyotsna Dikshit 328

26. Quality Assurance of Distance Education
V.S. Prasad 342

27. Promotion and Coordination of Distance Education: Role of National Open University
C.L. Anand and Suresh Garg 349

28. Best Practices in Open and Distance Learning
Ranjan Welukar 362

29. Quality Assurance in Distance Education: DEC Initiatives
Suresh Garg and Madhulika Kaushik 370

30. Cost of Dual Mode and Single Mode Distance Education
Ruddar Datt and Ashok Gaba 380

31. Cost and Quality of Distance Education
C.G. Naidu 392

SECTION V. STAFF DEVELOPMENT AND RESEARCH **403-472**

32. Human Resource Development for Distance Education
Santosh Panda, Sanjaya Mishra and C.R.K. Murthy 405

33. Non-Teaching and Professional Staff Development
C.R.K. Murthy and R. Satyanarayana 420

34. 'Education for All' and Professional Development of Education Functionaries
Sohanvir S. Chaudhary, Kiran Mathur and Santosh Panda 430

35. Research on Indian Distance Education
Lokesh Koul 448

SECTION VI. COLLABORATION, NETWORKING AND INTERNATIONALISATION **473-542**

36. Institutional Networking and Resource Sharing
M.M. Pant and D.C. Pant 475

37. National, Regional and Global Collaborations
S.R. Jha, Sanjay Gupta and Suresh Garg 484

38. Globalisation, Internationalisation, GATS and Cross-Border Distance Education
K.B. Powar 499

39. International Offer of Distance Education Programmes
Ved Goel 507

40. International Agencies and Distance Education in India
Usha Vyasulu Reddi 521

41. Entry of Foreign Universities in India: Issues and Implications for the ODL Systems
Sunil Kumar 531

SECTION VII. OPEN SCHOOLING AND ICT **543-603**

42. Evolution of the Open School System
Onkar Singh Dewal and Gopa Biswas 545

43. Instructional Development and Delivery
Sushmita Mitra and Anita Priyadarshini 559

44. National Consortium for Open Schooling
V.J. Williams and Savita Kaushal 581

45. ICT-Enabled School Education: Some Experiences
Jyotsna Dikshit and Santosh Panda 592

FOREWORD

The founding fathers of the Republic of India had a clear vision that education is a pre-requisite for regeneration of society, empowerment of people, national integration and international understanding. This led to rapid growth in demand for higher education and concerns about the access and equity began to pose challenges. In 1961, Kothari Committee recommended creation of educational provisions through correspondence courses on pilot basis at Bachelors degree level in liberal arts. The experiment was pioneered by the University of Delhi in 1962 and met with remarkable success. It marked the beginning of an alternative system of education in the form of correspondence education, suited for meeting the educational requirements of large numbers.

Enthused by wider acceptability, the Education Commission (1964-66) recommended correspondence and own-time education as a viable option to offer quality education, including professional education, as widely as possible. The commission suggested that gifted teachers should be engaged to develop study materials and communication technologies should be extensively used to optimally utilise intellectual and infrastructural resources for the new and cost-effective system of education. It was well appreciated and spread gradually during the decade of 1970s. However, the student support in the system was based mainly on providing print materials. Even these did not incorporate the principles of educational technology, or curriculum design and development. No study whatsoever was made on the learning habits and needs of self-learners with the result that serious concerns began to emerge to improve the quality of support by ploughing back resources generated by it rather than milking it to support the mainstream system of education. In fact, correspondence courses began to lose parity of esteem and by 1980s were relegated as 'poor cousin' of conventional system, though about 8% students in higher education were enrolled by it by the time first open university—Andhra Pradesh Open University, now known as Dr. B.R. Ambedkar Open University—was established at Hyderabad in 1982. It was a defining moment in the history of development of distance higher education in India. It marked the beginning of the Open Era in the country and played a crucial role for the establishment of Indira Gandhi National Open University (IGNOU) in 1985. IGNOU came into existence by an Act of Parliament as a resilient, responsive, innovative and flexible institution to not only take education to the deprived but also work towards expansion and regulation of open system of education in the country.

As a system leader, IGNOU has led a silent revolution in extending educational provisions at a distance. As of now, one National Open University, 11 State Open Universities (SOUs) and 106 Correspondence Course/Distance Education Institutes (CCIs/DEIs) are components of the Open and Distance Learning (ODL) system of the country. In 2004-05, nearly 2.5 million students were enrolled in the ODL system, which means that one out of four students in higher education was being catered to by this alternative system of education. It uses flexible, constructivist, learner-friendly and multi-perspective approaches to teaching-learning, so essential for nurturing creativity, leadership, scholarship and integrated development of human personality.

To reflect on the policy and practice of four decades of distance education in India, I am happy to note that a very serious attempt has been made to involve most of those who have been associated with it as insiders. Their pro-active response is a measure of their great insight and interest in the development of the ODL system. The Book has been very meticulously organised; it is spread over seven sections, each referring to an important issue: *Policy, Planning and Management*; *Distance Teaching and Learning Resources*; *Media and Technology*; *Instructional Delivery and Quality Assurance*; *Staff Development and Research*; *Collaboration, Networking and Internationalisation* and *Open Schooling*. I would like to congratulate the Editors, who are very senior academics and have been very closely associated with the developments of ODL system for a long time, for bringing out this much needed volume. I am sure that it will act as a very useful reference and prized possession for everyone connected with distance education in the years to follow.

H.P. Dikshit
Vice Chancellor, IGNOU

PREFACE

Education is an organic entity; it evolves to meet emerging societal needs. In the agrarian society, education was considered an art and in industrial societies, it became craft-oriented. The emergence of information era in the later part of the second half of 20th century ushered in 'distance education'. The UKOU heralded the arrival of technology in imparting education and training through distance mode. In our perspective, education at a distance has a larger socio-economic relevance as it has capacity to impart education to all those who desire to learn and participate in the evolution of knowledge society.

The genesis of this volume is in the realisation that authentic documentation of best practices and policies in respect of different generations, forms and formats of distance education should help identification of certain core principles for quality assurance and standardisation, issues and challenges to be addressed, and roles and responsibilities of practitioners focused towards the learner. It should also help us to analyse our strengths and weaknesses, consolidate our areas of core competences and reflect on how contemporary technological advancement and political developments can influence its future directions. In India, distance education, in its initial incarnation as correspondence education, has its origin in the decisive recommendation of Kothari Committee in 1961 and its implementation by the University of Delhi in 1962 as 'a step designed to expand and equalise educational opportunity, as it aimed at providing additional opportunities for several thousand students who wished to continue their education and the persons who had been denied these facilities and were in full-time employment or were for other reasons prevented from availing themselves of facilities at college.' Today, we have reached the fifth stage of evolution characterised by an all pervasive web-based platform environment and can impart very enriching learning experience.

The journey of Four Decades of Distance Education in India from print-based correspondence education to web-based intelligent-flexible learning has been arduous but exciting; from being just acceptable to some parity of esteem, to showing promise, to being seen as the possible solution to universal education. Distance education has evolved in a very complex socio-politico-economic environment as a vastly organised, vibrant and dynamic system endowed with capabilities of bringing high quality education to millions at low costs but superior learning experience. Some experts are of the view that in future, educational institutions may evolve as 'educational grids'.

In quantitative terms, distance education has, as of now, grown into twelve open universities and 106 DEIs catering to 2.5 million students, which account for every fourth student in higher education. This certainly is a significant strength and it is only logical to introspect at this stage to guide future course of development. We have endeavoured to present, within a single volume of reasonable expanse, a critical review of strengths and weaknesses of distance education in collaboration with those who have been associated with the system and contributed to its growth. To that extent, it is an unique insiders perspective. It is however likely that some experiences may not have been recorded. We leave these for future endeavours of similar kind.

The Book has been spread over seven sections, each referring to an important core issue: *Policy, Planning and Management*; *Distance Teaching and Learning Resources*; *Media and Technology*; *Instructional Delivery and Quality Assurance*; *Staff Development and Research*; *Collaboration, Networking and Internationalisation* and *Open Schooling*. These sections are spread over 45 Chapters.

We are indebted to all our contributors who, in spite of their serious engagements and pre-occupations, accommodated our request in their schedules. To avoid repetitive arguments, the Editors have taken the liberty of making minor changes, wherever considered absolutely necessary. We are extremely grateful to Prof. H.P. Dikshit, Vice Chancellor, IGNOU and Chairman, Distance Education Council for supporting this initiative intellectually and administratively.

Any publication of this size and that too on the eve of an International Conference, requires the support of several committed colleagues, who remain unseen. We would like to put on record our most sincere appreciation for Dr. Manjulika Srivastava, Dr. Sanjaya Mishra, Dr. P. Satyanarayana, Dr. Masood Parveez and Dr. Salil Mishra for carefully going through the manuscript and helping us at pre-print stage. Pro-active decision of a publisher helps in translating the vision on to paper. We are grateful to Sh. D.P. Sapru and his team at M/s. Viva Books Private Limited. Thanks are also due to Sh. B.H. Somayajullu and Sh.Gopal Krishan Arora for secretarial support.

We hope that this volume shall find an appropriate place in the reference collections of every serious distance educator the world over. Although every effort has been made to present it as per International Standards on the latest developments, the gaps, if any, only reflect the limitations of the editors. We look forward to constructive comments and suggestions to enrich our experiences.

Suresh Garg
V. Venkaiah
Chambi Puranik
Santosh Panda

CONTRIBUTORS

A.K. Agarwal
Abdul Waheed Khan
Akshay Kumar
Anita Priyadarshini
Anuradha Deshmukh
Ashok Gaba
Bhupesh Khatri
C.G. Naidu
C.K. Ghosh
C.L. Anand
C.R.K. Murthy
Chambi Puranik
D.C. Pant
Gopa Biswas
H.P. Dikshit
J.M. Parakh
J.P. Singh
J.S. Grewal
Jyotsna Dikshit
K.B. Powar
Kameshwari Moorthy
Kiran Mathur
Kiron Bansal
Lokesh Koul
M. Ponnavaikko
M.K. Salooja
M.M. Pant
Madhulika Kaushik
Manjulika Srivastava
Masood Parveez
N.R. Madhava Menon
N.S. Ramegowda
Onkar Singh Dewal
P.K. Mehta
Panjab Singh
R. Satyanarayana
R.R. Rausaria
Ram Takwale
Ranjan Welukar
Renu Bhardwaj
Ruddar Datt
S.R. Jha
Sanjay Gupta
Sanjaya Mishra
Sanjeev Pandey
Santosh Panda
Savita Kaushal
Shashi Bhushan
Sohanvir S. Chaudhary
Sunil Kumar
Suresh Garg
Sushmita Mitra
T.K. Jena
Usha Vyasulu Reddi
V. Rama Rao
V. Venkaiah
V.C. Kulandaiswamy
V.J. Williams
V.S. Prasad
V.S.P. Srivastava
Ved Goel
Zeba Khan

SECTION I

POLICY, PLANNING AND MANAGEMENT

1

Tracing the Historical Developments in Open and Distance Education

Santosh Panda, V. Venkaiah, Suresh Garg and Chambi Puranik

Introduction

The Indian sub-continent during the British rule included the present Pakistan and Bangladesh, and any educational developments during and subsequent to the rule are excluded today in describing the educational status of independent India. As a federal system comprising 29 states and 6 union territories, India is the second largest democracy and the second most populous country in the world. A multi-cultural and multi-linguist country, with 18 constitutionally recognised languages and as many as 1652 spoken dialects, the Indian system of education is also one of the largest and most difficult to manage in comparison to many such large systems in the world.

Starting from 17 universities and above 400 colleges at the time of independence, India today has 329 universities, nearly 16,885 colleges (including 1798 women's colleges), over 10 million students, nearly 0.45 million teachers and one of the largest higher education systems in the world (GoI, 2005). While more than 88% of the students study undergraduate programmes, 5% and 3.5% respectively study engineering and technology, and medicine; and about 1.5% of students are pursuing courses in agriculture. About 40.22% of the students are women, and the percentage of students from disadvantaged communities has not gone beyond 12. Since independence, the system has grown 14-fold in terms of number of universities, and 33-fold in the number of colleges; and its successful socio-economic planning through the Five Year Plans facilitated transition from an elitist system of education of the British era to a mass system of education subsequently. The Constitution of India guarantees free and compulsory elementary education up to grade VIII (age of 14); and, in 2002, India constitutionally guaranteed its citizens 'education' as a fundamental right. Though there is tremendous expansion in terms of numbers and access to education as briefed in Table 1 (upto 2003-04), only 6% of the relevant age group study in higher education; there is about 5% annual growth of student enrolment in conventional higher education; and nearly 40 million children are out of the provision of schooling.

Table 1: Growth of Indian education

Levels	Institutions (thousands)		Students (millions)		Teachers (thousands)	
	1950-51	**2003-04**	**1950-51**	**2003-04**	**1950-51**	**2003-04**
Primary	210	638	0.19	114	538	>1,900
Upper primary	13.6	206	0.31	42.8	86	>1,500
Secondary and senior secondary	7.4	126	0.15	27.6	127	>1,800
Higher education	27U[a] 590C[a]	304U[a] 13,500C[a]	-	10.5 (C + U)	-	350 (C + U)

[a] *Actual figures (not in 000s); U = university, C = college*
Source: *Panda (2005)*

However, in contexts of international comparison, Indian education system, like its economy, is one of the fastest growing systems in the world. The pressure of the graduates from schools, opening up of the economy, liberalisation and liberal policies for mass literacy and education, need for continuing professional development, commitment towards greater access and equity especially for the disadvantaged and minority sections of the society, tremendous indigenous developments in science and information and communication technology - all had their varying shares in contributing to significant policy decisions to go for alternative schooling, non-formal education, and open and distance learning in the country. Like the system of education in general, its distance education system is one of the fastest growing systems globally; the Indian system of distance education is the second largest in the world, and definite plans of action have contributed to this tremendous growth. It will be interesting to examine historically the growth and expansion of such a huge system. While critical reflection on the past and present experiences has been recorded elsewhere (Panda, 2005), we shall in this chapter trace and examine the historical developments in ODL in India.

Genesis

Distance education in its earlier form of correspondence education started in the West in the middle of the 19th century, though distance education in India began almost a century later in the form of postal correspondence education. The origin of postal education in India however can be traced to the educational activities of commercial institutions. The International Correspondence Schools (ICS) and the British Institutes (BIET) are the prominent institutes of postal courses, based in Bombay (now Mumbai), which offered a variety of postal courses in areas of engineering, management, architecture, interior decoration, dress making, journalism, beauty care, photography, cartooning, commercial arts, radio, transistor, refrigeration, among others (Chib, 1977).

At the time of Independence from the colonial rule in 1947, India did not have a comprehensive 'National Policy of Education'. The only policy or developmental plan was 'Post-War Educational Development in India: 1948-84' drawn by the then British rulers, though due to its narrow objectives it was not accepted by the Indian leaders. One such objective of the Five Year Plan was its advocacy for selected system of secondary and higher education and limited provision for technical and vocational education. Independence brought with it hopes for radical reforms in education. People in general felt that transformation of cducation, which thc Indian leaders pleaded for during the 'freedom struggle'; should be initiated as early as possible. Specifically no plea was made for introduction of distance education as a component of new India's education policy and programmes. But the general feeling was that the radical reorganization of the education system was one of the important national priorities. The need for the change was sufficiently expressed in the following words (Naik, 1975):

> The first and the most important step would be to abandon our exclusive reliance on the traditional system of formal education and to move in the direction of providing life-long education for all for creating a learning society. From this point of view:
>
> - education should cease to be considered as a one-shot affair meant for children and youth;
> - all three channels of education æ full-time, part-time, and own-time æ should be developed in every sector of education and given equal status;
> - education should cease to be looked upon as a school process, it should be a social process covering all learning that takes place, whether in or outside the school;
> - education should cease to be the delegated responsibility of a profession and should become the direct social responsibility in which every individual is involved, both as a teacher and as a student;
> - the right to learn should be assured to every individual without any discrimination and with full equality of opportunity, and he should also receive all the support and facilities necessary for its effective exercise through his life; and
> - the non-formal sector which has been neglected in the past should be developed and blended with the formal sector in an integrated fashion to create a new system of education which will have the advantages of both the sectors and to eliminate the weaknesses which arise when these sectors are developed in isolation.

In the late 1950s and the early 1960s in the Independent India, the planners thought of correspondence education as a supplementary method to meet the growing demand for higher educational opportunities. The Planning Commission of the country in The Five Year Plan made the following observation:

> With the expanding base at the elementary and secondary education, the demand for higher education has greatly increased over the past... The rapid expansion in the

> number of the universities and colleges in recent years has led to a number of problems. These have been reviewed in the report of the University Grants Commission for 1959-60...The Commission has stressed that if deterioration is to be avoided, increase in the number of students should be accompanied by corresponding expansion of physical and other teaching facilities ... In addition to the provision in the Plan for expansion of facilities for higher education, proposals for evening colleges, correspondence courses and the award of external degrees are at present under consideration.

Government Policy Initiatives

The Central Advisory Board of Education (CABE) in its meeting held in January 1961 noted the observations of the Planning Commission and recommended that a detailed study of 'correspondence courses' be made by a small committee before arriving at a decision to start them (Satyanarayana, 1995). Accordingly, The Union Ministry of Education constituted an Expert Committee under the Chairmanship of D.S. Kothari, the then Chairman of the University Grants Commission. The Members of the Committee included two vice chancellors, two university professors, one college principal, two educational consultants and three educational advisors to the Ministry of Education. The Committee suggested that it would be desirable to proceed slowly as correspondence education was new to India. It considered the kind of educational and administrative problems that might arise from the opening of an alternative channel of education in which there would be no regular classroom contact between the teacher and the student. Drawing on the experience of the other countries like the erstwhile Soviet Union, Australia, UK, USA, and the Scandinavian countries, the Committee felt that it would be possible to maintain high standards in education and achieve economy. The Committee observed and suggested the following (Singh, 1978):

1. The correspondence method provides for greater flexibility than classroom education, particularly in the combination of subjects.
2. Since many items of expenditure in the regular system of education can be eliminated in the correspondence method, it should be possible and essential to achieve results with economy.
3. Academic standards are determined by general factors such as admission standards, well-prepared instructional materials, easy to understand texts, ample exercises in the applica tion of knowledge, pre-tested and constantly revised courses, careful correctional and in structional service etc.
4. Correspondence courses could provide opportunities for persons who have been denied these facilities and are at present in full-time employment or are, for other reasons, prevented from availing themselves of facilities at colleges.
5. For correspondence courses leading to the first degree, there should be a personal contact between the teacher and the taught for about three weeks in a year, preferably on a tutorial rather than lecture basis.

6. To maintain educational standards, it should be necessary to associate top-ranking scholars and teachers in the preparation of courses and text books.
7. The success of the entire scheme of correspondence courses will depend upon the compe tence, resourcefulness and dedication of the staff that runs correspondence courses.

University Level Correspondence Education – The Beginning (First Decade)

All the essential conditions for making correspondence education an effective alternative channel i.e. flexibility, well written materials, training of staff, contact programmes, provision of study centres, etc were perceived and underlined by the Committee. It did not, however, take into account the difficulties involved in operating a new system within the framework of the existing conventional university system whose rules, regulations, methods, processes, techniques and organizational structures were set by and geared towards face-to-face education (Satyanarayana, 1995). The Committee's suggestion that only a pilot project of correspondence education be started at the University of Delhi was accepted by the central government. Accordingly, the University of Delhi agreed to the proposal and appointed a Sub-Committee to go into the details of its operation. On the basis of the Sub-Committee's Report and the subsequent concurrence of the UGC, the University of Delhi established the School of Correspondence Courses and Continuing Education (SCCCE) in 1962 and started BA courses in selected subjects with 112 students in the first year; later on B.Com was offered in 1970 onwards. Thus, the first correspondence course at the university level began in India. Sh. K.L. Shrimali, the then Union Minister of Education, while inaugurating the programme, highlighted three main objectives of correspondence education (Chib, 1977):

1. to provide an efficient and less expensive method of educational instruction at a higher level in the context of the national development of India;
2. to provide facilities to pursue higher education to all qualified and willing persons who had failed to join regular university courses due to personal and economic reasons or because of their inability to get admission to a regular college; and
3. to provide opportunities of academic pursuit to educated citizens to improve their standards of knowledge and learning through correspondence instruction without disturbing their present employment.

Within a year, the UD æ first dual mode university in India æ attracted a good number of students. In 1969-70, the B.Sc course was started but was discontinued in 1973-74 on account of lack of demand for it. A B.Com course was introduced in 1970-71 and subsequently postgraduate courses were also introduced in the university.

In 1964, the Government of India appointed an Education Commission under the Chairmanship of Dr. D.S. Kothari to advise the government on the national pattern of education and on the general principles and policies for the development of education at all stages and in all aspects. The Commission noted that one of the major weaknesses of the existing educational system was its exclusive reliance on full-time instruction and non-development of the two other channels of part-time education and private study or own-time education. The Commission recommended opportunities like evening colleges for part-time education and correspondence education for own-time education. The Commission dispelled any apprehension that correspondence courses are an inferior form of education than what is given in regular schools and colleges. The Commission further recommended:

i) In order to bring education to those who are unable even to attend part-time courses, widespread organisation of correspondence courses should occur.
ii) Students taking correspondence courses should be provided opportunities to meet the teachers occasionally.
iii) Correspondence courses should be supported by well-coordinated radio and television programmes.
iv) Correspondence courses should not be confined to preparing students for the university degrees but should also provide agricultural, industrial and other workers such special courses of instruction as would help them to improve production.
v) Correspondence courses should be made available for those who desire to enrich their lives by studying subjects of cultural and aesthetic value.
vi) Correspondence courses should be developed for the teachers in schools to keep them abreast with new knowledge as well as with new methods and techniques of teaching.

To get benefited by the experience of the erstwhile Soviet Union in correspondence education, the UGC sent a delegation to the country in 1967 to study correspondence education in that country. The delegation consisted of representatives of the Union Ministry of Education, the Faculty of Education & Psychology of M.S. University (Baroda) and the NCERT. The delegation after studying correspondence education in the erstwhile USSR strongly favoured it for India, particularly for the expansion of teacher education. The delegation stated "it is our considered opinion that the system of correspondence courses for teacher training can be profitably adopted in our own country..." (Singh, 1978).

Considering the recommendation of the Education Commission 1964-66, the Planning Commission, the UGC delegation and the satisfactory progress of the pilot project of the University of Delhi, the UGC appointed a committee to consider the question of expansion of correspondence courses in universities. The committee suggested that correspondence courses should be started only in a selected number of well established universities with strong faculty strength, and provided very meaningful guidelines for the expansion of correspondence courses. Besides the other things, the committee suggested study centres for contact classes for students, use of the laboratory and library facilities of conventional colleges by the correspondence students, and preparation and availability of quality instructional materials. Had the UGC and the universities followed these guidelines in the subsequent expansion of correspondence courses in India, the quality of dual mode university correspondence courses would have been different from that of today (Satyanarayana, 1997).

In the light of the recommendations of the Education Commission 1964-66 and the UGC Committee on the expansion of correspondence courses, the UGC decided to extend the scheme of correspondence courses to other universities. Punjabi University, Patiala was the second university in the country which was allowed to set up a full fledged Directorate of Correspondence Courses in 1968 with the offer of pre-university and BA courses in English and Punjabi. The university was the first to offer pre-university correspondence course with an enrolment of 2,400 students.

In 1968 another delegation comprising the principal of the SCCCE, University of Delhi and a representative of the UGC visited the erstwhile USSR. The delegation felt that although there was much in common between India and the USSR in regard to the objectives of correspondence courses, yet for historical and social reasons, it would be neither feasible nor appropriate for India to emulate the Soviet system, though India could be benefited by the Soviet model in increasing the operational efficiency of correspondence education. The delegation specifically emphasized the academic character of correspondence courses and de-emphasized the commercial character of the courses. Further, the delegation stressed the need for compulsory contact programme for the students, submission of assignments by students, and a wider coverage of course subjects including professional areas (Singh, 1978).

In 1971 the third delegation comprising the directors of correspondence courses of Punjabi University and Rajasthan University again visited the erstwhile USSR. The delegation made a detailed study of the Soviet system of correspondence education and made several important suggestions on the expansion, diversification, coverage of adult education, use of media, teachers, production of self-instructional materials, and others.

As a follow up measure to the recommendation of the third delegation to the erstwhile USSR, the Standing Committee for Part-time Education and Correspondence Courses of the UGC held a special meeting in September 1972 to consider a proposal to set up a National Institute of Correspondence Courses. The meeting, besides other things, favoured the establishment of NICC as a forerunner of the fulltime national correspondence university to be an affiliating and/or independent body for all the correspondence courses in the country. The UGC at its meeting in December 1972 agreed in principle with the suggestion of setting up a NICC and constituted a planning committee consisting of 6 members (Rais Ahmed, M.V. Mathur, J.N. Kapur, Bhakhshish Singh, D.V. Urs and P.C. Mukherji). The first meeting of the committee was held in April 1973 which discussed the details of the proposed national institute. Thereafter, though nothing happened. The main reason for the indecision seemed to be the idea of the union government to set up an open university, which might perform the functions of the earlier proposed national institute (Singh, 1978).

During the first decade of correspondence education (1962-72), the following 13 correspondence units of conventional universities were set up which offered different graduate, postgraduate and certificate level courses (Anand, 1985):

i) School of Correspondence Courses and Continuing Education, University of Delhi (1962).
ii) Directorate of Correspondence Courses, Punjab University (1968).
iii) Institute of Correspondence Studies and Continuing Education, University of Rajasthan (1968).
iv) Institute of Correspondence Courses and Continuing Education, University of Mysore (1969).

v) Institute of Correspondence Courses and Continuing Education , Meerut University (1969)

vi) Institute of Correspondence Courses and Continuing Education, Madurai Kamaraj University(1971)

vii) Directorate of Correspondence Courses, Himachal Pradesh University (1971).

viii) Directorate of Correspondence Courses, Punjab University (1971).

ix) Directorate of Correspondence Courses, Bombay University (1971).

x) Department of Extension Education, Punjab Agricultural University (1971).

xi) Institute of Correspondence Courses, Sri Venkateshwara University (1972).

xii) School of Correspondence Courses, Andhra University (1972).

xiii) Central Institute of English and Foreign Languages (1972).

Correspondence Education at School Level

The idea to start correspondence courses at the school level originated in 1964 when the Conference of Boards of Secondary Education (COBSE) in India recommended that the state boards of secondary education (BSE) should start correspondence courses to improve the academic standards of private students. As a consequence, the BSE of the state of Madhya Pradesh started correspondence course for intermediate students in 1965. The Patracher Vidyalya followed suit in 1968. The BSEs of states of Rajasthan, Orissa and Uttar Pradesh later initiated correspondence courses at school level for private candidates only. These institutions followed the same courses as were prescribed for the formal school children and held common year-end examinations.

In 1979, the Central Board of Secondary Education (CBSE) set up an Open School at the secondary level for the learners of 14 years age and above, who for a number of reasons, were unable to continue their studies in formal schools. The Open School aimed at providing education at home to out-of-school learners – school dropouts, working adults, housewives/homemakers, learners from disadvantaged sections of society and those living in remote areas of the country. The objectives were:

a) to offer bridge and preparatory or foundation courses to those whose achievement level corresponded to class VI to VIII level so that the learner may successively take up secondary school level course;

b) to offer secondary, senior secondary, technical, vocational and life enrichment courses; and

c) to promote an open distance learning system of education through research, publication and dissemination of information.

Open schooling was experimented from 1978 to 1989 as a project of the CABE and was amalgamated with the National Open School (NOS) and now called National Institute of Open Schooling (NIOS), an autonomous organisation set up in November 1989 by the Ministry of

Human Resource Department, Government of India. NIOS has supported the establishment of the largest number of open schools compared to any other country in the world. Besides NIOU, state open schools have been set up in Haryana, Madhya Pradesh, Punjab, Tamil Nadu, West Bengal, Karnataka, Kerala and J&K with NIOS collaboration and assistance. Andhra Pradesh and Rajasthan have set up their own state open schools. During the 10th Plan more state open schools are likely to come up. For a detailed study on this, Panda and Garg (2003) and the section on school education in this volume should be useful.

University Level Correspondence Education (Second and Third Decades)

By the end of the first decade (i.e. 1972), correspondence education in India gained considerable recognition and acceptance. The findings and suggestions of various committees and delegations and the practices of CCIs motivated many educators to meet periodically to discuss the problems and prospects of correspondence education provided by the conventional universities through their separate schools/institutes/directorates/departments. The Indian Association for Continuing Education, formed during this period, acted as a catalyst for periodic meetings of the (correspondence) educators to promote academic climate in favour of correspondence education.

IACE's first major contribution was the organisation of the first national seminar on correspondence education at Mysore in October 1972 in collaboration with the Mysore University. Later, three more national seminars were held in 1976, 1979 and 1982 at Patiala, Chandigarh and Trivandrum respectively. The first national seminar was significant in terms of rich discussions and valuable recommendations. It created an opportunity for the representatives of the participating universities to assess developments in the newly emerging sectors of education and to develop a perspective for the coming years. The seminar envisaged the possibility that correspondence education could become an effective agent of change in regard to the quality of higher education at the first degree level and beyond. It further recommended that a Joint Committee of the UGC and the Inter-University Board (now Association of Indian Universities) should guide the Universities in promoting correspondence education (Satyanarayana, 1995).

The UGC which had all along been concerned with the development and streamlining of the scheme of correspondence courses convened in October 1974 at Delhi a conference of the CCIs with a view to asses the functioning and to discuss their problems and make suggestions for their improvement. Satish Chandra, the then Vice Chairman of the UGC, in his address urged for the introduction of new courses of innovative character which can bring education nearer to the problems of the country. The observations and recommendations of the conference may be classified under five heads:

- Scope of correspondence education in India
- Preparation of reading materials
- Future of correspondence education and the role of the state

- Organisational and administrative set up in a directorate of correspondence courses
- Ancillary services such as radio talks, TV presentations, etc.

The UGC's Standing Committee for Part-time and Own-time Education took stock of the deliberations of the conference and after detailed discussion evolved a set of guidelines for correspondence courses which were approved by the UGC in March 1975. The guidelines helped some universities in giving serious thought to the quality aspect of their correspondence courses, but by and large they were not taken seriously. Some universities saw the correspondence courses as money spinners and not as agencies for widening the access to higher educational opportunities. This attitude of the university disturbed the heads and teachers of CCIs of the universities as well as the correspondence students which was reflected in the deliberations of the conferences and seminars on correspondence education organised later on. But on the one hand the old situation continued and on the other hand the number of CCIs increased year by year.

The 11th World Conference of the International Council for Correspondence Education (ICCE) was held in November 1978 at New Delhi. Some of the CCIs participated in the conference highlighted the need for strengthening of correspondence education. They reaffirmed the earlier proposal to establish a central organisation to promote and strengthen correspondence education and to serve as a watch dog of the working of correspondence courses of different universities in the country. In spite of the acceptance of the proposal by the UGC as early as in 1972 and the continuous demand by the CCIs, no central organisation could be established for streamlining, strengthening and monitoring correspondence education until the establishment in 1985 of IGNOU which was given the additional role of coordinating and maintaining standards in distance education in the country.

Correspondence education in India now upgraded to distance education, in spite of its long journey continued to be of poor quality like many other countries overseas. Before the emergence of the open university system in the country, correspondence education was criticised by educationists and conventional university teachers for its ineffectiveness and inefficiency. Some of the limitations which contributed to the ineffectiveness of correspondence education in India are (IGNOU Project Report, 1985; Mulay, 1986; Ram Reddy, 1985; Satyanarayana 1995; Prasad & Venkaiah, 2005):

- Most of the correspondence institutes do not have competent and adequate staff. Best of the teachers are not posted to work in these institutes. As a result, they have low degree of motivation.
- More than one university in a state started correspondence courses thereby duplicating efforts resulting in low enrolments in many universities.
- Lessons (course units) are prepared in a hurry with no regard to the principles of self-instruction.
- Not much attention is paid to student assignments; they are not evaluated, corrected and returned to the students in time.

- Most of the correspondence courses do not have 'study centres' and personal contact programmes are organised by only a few institutions and that to only a few times in a year.
- Too much reliance is placed on the printed material, and information & communication technology is hardly made use of.
- There is considerable delay in the despatch of course lessons to the students.
- Bodies charged with the running of these institutions are not organised properly.
- The system has the same rigidities in the courses offered as in the formal system, compelling the students to opt for the same courses and appear for the same examinations as the regular students.
- Rarely laboratory and library facilities are provided, and where they exist they are much below the standard.
- They do not have identity of their own as they work within the parent university structure and statutory provisions.
- Rarely efforts are made to evaluate and check the standard of these correspondence courses. Therefore, their growth and style of working are haphazard leaving much room to be im proved.

In spite of several limitations, correspondence education continued to spread rapidly in the university system. Fast expansion, meagre student support services and lack of innovativeness of flexibility in course structure caused alarm among educational planners, and intensified their desire to reform the system.

The original guidelines issued by the UGC in 1975 were later modified to conform to the changes in the expectations of the correspondence education system. The revised guidelines clearly stated:

> Distance education is essentially based on the supply of instructional material but has to be supported and supplemented by personal contact programmes, student responses, library facilities, study centres, radio programmes and audio-visual aids, etc. A well conceived programme of distance education can be as effective and meaningful as regular day-time instruction in a college or a University department and every possible effort must be made to make it so effective.

The UGC prescribed minimum standards of instruction for the grant of the first degree through non-formal distance education in the faculties of arts, humanities, social sciences, sciences and commerce. Some CCIs tried to follow the UGC guidelines while many failed to understand the spirit of new guidelines.

By the time the idea of an open university was gaining ground, 34 dual mode universities were offering correspondence courses, and the student enrolment in correspondence courses was 6.16% of the total higher education enrolment (Table 2).

Table 2: Enrolment in higher education vis-à-vis correspondence education

Year	Universities/ colleges (number)	(%)	Distance education institutions (number)	Distance education institutions (%)	Total enrolment (number)
1975-76	2,426,109	97.42	64,210	2.58	2,490,319
1976-77	2,431,563	96.83	79,718	3.17	2,511,281
1977-78	2,564,972	95.56	119,163	4.44	2,684,135
1978-79	2,618,228	95.15	133,459	4.85	2,751,687
1979-80	2,648,579	95.10	136,699	4.90	2,785,278
1980-81	2,752,437	94.30	166,428	5.70	2,918,865
1981-82	2,952,066	93.84	193,691	6.16	3,145,757

Source: Various UGC Annual Reports; Yadav & Panda (1999)

Idea of an Open University

In India, the first proposal for establishing an open university was made in the early seventies. The Ministry of Education and Social Welfare in collaboration with the Ministry of Information & Broadcasting (Government of India) and the UGC organised a seminar in December 1970 as part of a programme for the observance of International Education Year. Inaugurating the seminar, V.K.R.V. Rao, the then Union Education Minister, first mooted the idea of establishing an open university in India and observed:

> ...It must cover not only the comparatively limited number of university students, but should cover much larger number of students who drop out from the school at various points, the neo-literates, and eventually all adults who desire to avail these programmes of continuing education... The new interesting programmes of instruction, based on modern science-oriented educational technology for students of higher education studying in the Open University should be made available to this much larger body of population which remains outside the so-called University system.

As a result of these suggestions the Government of India appointed a Working Group with Mr. G. Parthasarathi, the then Vice Chancellor of Jawaharlal Nehru University, in 1971 to examine the feasibility of establishing an open university in India. This Working Group in its Report submitted in 1975 stated:

> In a situation of this type, where the expansion of enrolments in higher education has to continue at a terrific pace and where available resources in terms of men and money are limited, the obvious solution, if proper standards are to be maintained and the demand for higher education from different sections of the people is to be met, is to adopt the Open University System with its provision of higher education of part-time or own time basis.

The Group recommended that an open university be established under an Act of Parliament with jurisdiction over the entire country. This Act was to be enacted after consultation with state governments both in respect of jurisdiction as well as the possibility of drawing upon the resources of the existing institutions furtherance of the objectives of the open university. The functions suggested for such an open university were to:

a) offer courses similar to university programmes for the working population and others who are unable to join regular university courses;
b) offer continuing education for the work force including government functionaries, professionals and other members in the form of special programmes depending upon the requirement of each category;
c) organise special programmes, for housewives, of general education, home-making, nutrition, maternity, child care, population education, etc.; and
d) carry out certain catalystic functions for universities involving non-formal programmes of higher education.

The proposed open university was to carry out almost all the functions which were prescribed for the NICE. The recommendations of the Working Group did not draw much attention of the educationists and planners. The idea of a national open university remained on shelf till 1985 when IGNOU was established.

In 1982, a Committee to Enquire into the Working of the Central Universities, appointed by the University Grants Commission under the chairpersonship of Dr. (Mrs) Madhuri R Shah made the following observations:

> To satisfy existing thirst for knowledge as well as degrees, admission to formal courses on the basis of merit requires that opportunities for off-campus studies should be created on a large scale, for a great variety of courses of high quality. We already have a number of Universities offering correspondence courses; we need to utilise and coordinate this expertise and infrastructure to create an effective system of distance learning. Mass media, such as radio and television, which are already beginning to be used to greater potential is being created through the satellites, should be employed in a systematic manner to enlarge the scope and enrich the quality of distance education. We could create with available know how in software and hardware a highly proficient and attractive system of education for the whole Country of which the present correspondence institutes could become focal points. Courses in new fields, particularly in science and some in technology could also be started, perhaps using college laboratories in off-hours and some of the best teachers could be involved in delivering lectures, libraries of audio and video cassettes could be created to enrich both formal and non-formal education.

The committee recommended that practical steps for creating a national open university of distance education be taken up without delay.

The Open Universities – A New Era

The debate at the national level on the open university system stimulated thinking on the subject in various states. In Andhra Pradesh, a proposal was made to start an open university as early as in 1978. In that year Ram Reddy, the then Vice Chancellor of the Osmania University was requested by the then Education Minister of Andhra Pradesh to visit the British Open University and submit a rReport. In the report, he commended the role of the unique institution and suggested a similar institution for Andhra Pradesh to strengthen non-formal education in the state. The Education Minister liked the suggestion and proposed an open university, though the proposal did not bear fruit. About the same time, Osmania University made a proposal for starting an 'open education college' (OEC) to strengthen distance education. The college was to have full autonomy but the degrees were to be awarded by the Osmania University. At about the same time the OEC was to be set up, B. Venkataram, who as the Education Minister had requested G. Ram Reddy to submit a report on the British Open University in 1978, became the Chief Minister of the state. During the early days of his short tenure, the new Chief Minister revived the interest in the open university system. In 1982 the Government of Andhra Pradesh decided to establish an open university to provide "access to higher education to the adult population of the State, for upgrading their functional capacities and improving quality of their life in context of broader social and political objectives and equalisation of educational opportunities and the emergence of a new concept of life long education". To give shape to this policy, the government appointed a committee under the chairmanship of G. Ram Reddy, the then Vice Chancellor of Osmania University and, based on the Committee's report, the Andhra Pradesh Open University (APOU) was established in 1982. The first full fledged and totally public funded distance teaching university in India. The open university formally came into existence on August 26, 1982, and was later renamed as Dr. B.R. Ambedkar Open University (BRAOU) in 1992. The course of distance education in the country would have been different, had this open university not been set up.

Realising its importance and immediate relevance the Government of India decided to establish a National Open University in the early part of 1985. The then Prime Minister, late Shri Rajiv Gandhi, in his first broadcast to the nation on January 5, 1985, spelt out the new government's policy relating to education and announced the establishment of a national open university. He observed "...Steps are being taken to establish an open university to bring higher education within the easy reach of all". The Indira Gandhi National Open University (IGNOU) named after the late Prime Minister Indira Gandhi was set up on September 20, 1985. The idea of a national open university initiated in early 70s, thus, became a reality after fifteen years. Interestingly, the founder Vice Chancellor of the first Open University, G. Ram Reddy, became the first Vice Chancellor of the National Open University. The credit of setting up and shaping the future of two major open universities in the world, as Sidharth Ramphal, the then Secretary General of the Commonwealth acclaimed in his address to the first convocation of IGNOU in 1989, goes to Ram Reddy.

Soon after its establishment, IGNOU was entrusted with the responsibility, besides acting as a national (open) university and as a national resource centre for distance education, of promoting and coordinating the open learning and distance education system in the country as well as monitoring and determining their standards. It focused its attention on the problem of correspondence education provided through Institutes of CCIs and organised a seminar in January 1986 on the 'problems of distance education in Indian universities' to which all the heads of CCIs were invited. The seminar was attended by 23 representatives of Institutes of CCIs and a representative of Andhra Pradesh Open University (APOU). The seminar discussed and debated several issues including the nature and scope of relationship between IGNOU and the SOUs, IGNOU and CCIs and between the latter two. In the light of the problems posed and possible solutions suggested at the seminar, IGNOU convened a meeting of Vice Chancellors and Officers-on-Special Duty of SOUs in May 1986. The Vice Chancellor of APOU, Special Officers of proposed SOUs in the Maharashtra and Kerala attended the meeting. The meeting mainly discussed the pattern of academic programmes, networking of courses, standards of instructional materials and the relationship between IGNOU and SOUs.

In October 1990, the UGC organised a conference of Vice Chancellors to discuss the coordination and maintenance of standards in distance education. A theme paper was developed by the UGC for the Conference through a Committee comprising the Vice Chancellors of IGNOU, SOUs and a few others. After discussing the theme paper, the conference constituted four groups for making recommendations for strengthening distance education. The four groups made valuable suggestions. On the basis of the recommendations of the groups, the UGC and IGNOU evolved an organisational frame and procedures to coordinate and maintain standards in distance education.

Till the establishment of Distance Education Council (DEC) by IGNOU in 1990, the efforts of IGNOU to coordinate and strengthen distance education in the country confined to the system of SOUs, and the UGC continued to look after the correspondence education offered through the conventional universities.

DEC has three roles: the promotional role, the role of coordination and maintenance of standards, and the role of financial support. The activities of DEC have expanded over time. The DEC extends financial support to distance education institutions for development of infrastructure, institutional reforms, academic improvement, staff development and training, student support services, computerisation and networking of institutions for improvement of quality of education.

By 1994-95, 62 dual mode universities and 7 open universities were offering distance education to nearly 0.8 million students comprising above 13% of the total higher education enrolment (Table 3).

Present Status

The comprehensive institutional growth of distance can be discerned from Table 4 and Table 5. Higher institutional growth is a phenomenon of the nineties; and as shall be seen from Table 4 the duration 2001-05 has seen establishment of three open universities and 36 dual-mode university distance education centres.

Table 3: Enrolment in higher education and distance education (1982-83 to 1994-95)

Year	Universities/ colleges (number)	(%)	Distance education institutions (number)	(%)	Total enrolment (number)
1982-83	3,133,093	94.07	197,555	5.93	3,330,648
1983-84	3,307,649	n.a.	n.a.	n.a.	n.a.
1984-85	3,404,096	n.a.	n.a.	n.a.	n.a.
1985-86	3,570,897	90.96	3,55,090 (27,629)	9.04	3,925,987
1986-87	3,681,870	91.14	357,791 (28,745)	8.86	4,039,661
1987-88	3,814,417	90.45	402,720 (36,448)	9.55	4,217,137
1988-89	3,947,922	89.68	454,243 (77,748)	10.32	4,402,165
1989-90	4,246,878	88.84	533,441 (66,265)	11.16	4,780,319
1990-91	4,425,247	88.72	562,814 (75,417)	11.28	4,988,061
1991-92	4,611,107	87.12	678,063 (122,531)	12.82	5,289,170
1994-95	5,310,753	86.86	803,176	13.14	6,113,929

Source: Various UGC Annual Reports; figures in parentheses indicate the enrolment in the open universities;
n.a. = not available. Yadav & Panda (1999)

The policy of the Government of India is that each state shall have to establish an open university and an open school to cater to the increasing educational and training needs of the students and citizens. Above all, access and equity have so far been the prime focus, and shall remain so in the future (Panda, 2005). There is a definite federal government mandate that the enrolment in distance education must reach 40% of the total higher education by the end of the Tenth Plan period (i.e. by the year 2007). The expansion of the open university so far as given in Table 5 suggests that institutional growth and achievements have been tremendous, and are poised to grow in the future.

Table 4: Institutional growth of distance education

Year	Open universities	Conventional university distance education centres	Cumulative
1962-75	-	22	22
1976-82	1	12	35
1983-85	1	04	40
1986-90	3	08	51
1991-00	4	24	79
2001-05	3	36	117
Total	12	106	117

Table 5: Open universities in India

Sl. No.	Open University	Year of establishment
1.	Dr. B.R. Ambedkar Open University	1982
2.	Indira Gandhi National Open University	1985
3.	Vardhaman Mahaveer Open University	1987
4.	Nalanda Open University	1987
5.	Y C Maharastra Open university	1989
6.	Madhya Pradesh Bhoj Open University	1991
7.	Dr.Baba Saheb Ambedkar Open University	1994
8.	Kamataka State Open University	1996
9.	Netaji Subash Open University	1997
10.	U P Rajasri Tandan Open University	1998
11.	Tamil Nadu Open University	2002
12.	Pandit Sundarlal Sharma Open University	2005

Source: Information Base on Distance Higher Education in India DEC, IGNOU, 2004

As of today there are 12 open universities and 106 dual mode university distance education institutes/centres in the country, offering above 2.8 million students 429 academic programmes and 3817 courses through a network of 105 regional centres, 4229 study centres, and 62270 tutors/counsellors (see Table 6). In the Tenth Plan period (2002-07), the 29 states in the country are expected to have one Open University each, and the distance education system is expected to cater for the educational needs of at least 50% of the additional student enrolment. Today it takes care of above 25% of the total student enrolment in higher education. If we consider the Tenth Plan proposal of increasing student enrolment in higher education from the present 6% to 10% of relevant age group of 18-23, in absolute terms this implies an additional student enrolment of above seven million. Though the distance education system may not be able to take on 50% of this load, the enrolment within distance education is expected to increase at the most to 30% (i.e. up to about four million in total, with 50% sharing for IGNOU at 1.95 million students) by the end of this plan period.

Table 6: Status of open universities (2003-04)

Indicators	IGNOU*	BRAOU	VMOU	NOU	YCMOU	MPBOU	BAOU	KSOU	NSOU	UPRTOU	TNOU	Total
Programmes	101	25	33	22	78	77	17	19	8	38	23	441
Courses	900	332	255	148	355	611	140	n.a.	29	562	231	3863
Students ('000)	366.1	190.2	5.9	1.8	102	192.2	13.8	19.5	14.7	8	9.3	923.7
On Rolls('000)	1311	190.2	5.9	8.4	800	199.2	68.8	33.1	225.2	22.1	9.3	2873
RCs and SRCs	54 23	6	—	8	10	3	6	1	—	—	—	111
SCs	1257[1]	149	52	7	1425	1070	78	186	76	65	23	4388
ACs	33,366	5344	2465	452	8949	8000	979	1050	2473	885	875	64,838
Audio	1293	127	—	—	345	19	9	77	207	227	—	2304
Video	1792	121	—	—	333	6	16	7	13	—	—	2288
Staff	1369	565	525	46	277	240	84	419	16	71	65	3577

IGNOU=Indira Gandhi National Open University (* data for 2004-05); BRAOU= Dr. B. R. Ambedkar Open University; VMOU = Vardhman Mahavir Open University; NOU=Nalanda Open University; YCMOU= Yashwantrao Chavan Maharastra Open University; MPBOU=MP Bhoj Open University; BAOU= Babasaheb Ambedkar Open University; KSOU= Karnataka State Open University; NSOU=Netaji Subhash Open University; UPRTOU= UP Rajarshi Tandon Open University; TNOU = Tamil Nadu Open University.

RC= regional centre; SRC = sub-regional centre; SC = study centre; AC = academic counselor or tutor; n.a. = not available; 1 = includes 22 tele-learning centres and 35 overseas centres.

Source: DEC (2004); IGNOU (2005) compiled by Santosh Panda

The tremendous developments in the indigenously developed media capacity housed/handled by IGNOU as given in Table 7 reflect the growing importance given to multiple media education and media networking for distance learning.

Table 7: National media capacity (of IGNOU)

Media and technology	Number
Satellite transponder	1
Teleconferencing centres	790 (to increase to 2000)
National TV channels	6 (including the teleconferencing channel)
All India Radio stations	186 (interactive radio counselling)
Tele-learning centres	22
FM radio stations	17 (to increase to 40)
Satellite	1 (EduSat)

Source: Panda (2004); IGNOU (2005)

The ODL system has to collaborate and cooperate without reinventing the wheel. Therefore it is necessary to provide space to innovation in diversity. There is a need to encourage competition in collaboration and one of the ways would be to create a pool of best materials so that these are available off the shelf with due recognition to the contributing institutions. Moreover moving towards elearning and creating national digital repositories will enable us to compete globally in consortia mode. Open universities are likely to be established in the states of Assam and Uttaranchal soon. Orissa, Haryana and Kerala are also reportedly evaluating the benefits likely to accrue to their populations through state open universities. Moreover, OUs have to develop capabilities to using interactive multimedia and EduSat to break learner isolation. Similarly, CCI/DEIs have to march towards second/third generation models of distance education and transform their materials using rigorous principles of curriculum and instructional design.

Attracting talent and nurturing it for scholarship through research should be accorded high priority on the agenda of each institution because ODL learning has transformed from art to science. The role of distance teacher has to be re-evaluated and reassessed as a multi-skilled accomplished professional capable of communicating impressives through print and multimedia. Therefore, appropriate professional development strategies need to be put in place.

Conclusion

The distance education system in India has emerged as an alternative as well as complementary channel of education and training in India. It has already established its credibility and recognition. The growth of distance education, both quantitatively and qualitatively, has been phenomenal during the last two decades, particularly after the introduction of the single mode open universities in the country. Further, the application of ICTs gave a major fillip to the accelerated development of distance education. The role of distance education is going to be more and more predominant in the coming decades. The process of convergence between distance education and conventional education is becoming faster and the convergence will continue to be necessarily fast in the future. There is an immediate need for the planners and policy makers to formulate necessary policies and strategies so as to enhance the quality of distance education in India. The detailed reflections on policies and functional themes by various authorities and authors are in order in the subsequent chapters.

References

Anand, S. (1979). *University Without Walls: Correspondence Education in India*. Vikas Publishing House, New Delhi.

Chib, S.S. (1977). *Teaching by Correspondence in India*. Light and Life Publishers, New Delhi.

Distance Education Council (2004). *Information Base on Distance Higher Education in India.* New Delhi: DEC, Indira Gandhi National Open University.

Educational Consultants India Limited (1985). *IGNOU Project Report*. New Delhi.

Government of India (1966). *Report of the Education Commission 1964-66; Education and National Development*. Ministry of Education, New Delhi.

Government of India (2005). *Annual Report 2004-05.* New Delhi: Ministry of Human Resource Development, Government of India, New Delhi.

IGNOU (2005). *Sixteenth convocation: Vice-chancellor's report* (March 5). New Delhi: Indira Gandhi National Open University.

Mallick, S.P. (1987). Distance Education in India in *Distance Education*. Vol. 2, Asian Development Bank, Manila.

Muley, V. et al., (1985). *Correspondence Education in Indian Universities: A Review*. University Grants Commission, New Delhi.

Naik, J.P. (1975). *Equality, Quality & Quantity*. Allied Publishers, Bombay.

Panda, S. (2004). Section 2: Media and technology developments and use at IGNOU. In *Handbook 7*, Staff Training & Research Institute, Indira Gandhi National Open University, New Delhi. (forthcoming)

Panda, S. (2005). Higher education at a distance and national development: reflections on the Indian experience. *Distance Education*, 26(2), 205-225.

Panda, S. and Garg, S. (2003). Distance learning in India with open schools. In Bradley, J. (ed.), *The Open Classroom.* London: RoutledgeFalmer.

Prasad, V.S. & Venkaiah, V. (2005). *India's First Open University: Experience of Two Decades*. Dr. B.R. Ambedkar Open University, Hyderabad.

Ram Reddy, G. (1985). *IGNOU: Its Role in Higher Education*. A Paper Presented at the International Seminar on Distance Education: Experience of Open Universities, 20-22, November, New Delhi.

Satyanarayana, P. (1995). *Distance Education in India: A Developmental Spectrum* (Unpublished), IGNOU Regional Centre, Hyderabad.

Singh, Bakhshish (1978). *Correspondence Education in India.* National Council of Correspondence Education, New Delhi.

Singh, Bakhshish et al., (1994). *Correspondence/Distance Education in India: An in-depth Study covering the year 1989-90.* IGNOU, New Delhi.

Yadav, M.S. and Panda, S. (1999). Open and distance higher education: policy and development. In Panda, S. (ed.), *Open and Distance Learning: Policies, Practices and Quality Concerns.* New Delhi: ABI.

Professor Santosh Panda is Director, Staff Training & Research Institute of Distance Education; and Coordinator, Inter-University Consortium, Indira Gandhi National Open University, New Delhi.
Email: spanda@ignou.ac.in

Professor V. Venkaiah is Executive Director, G. Ram Reddy Academy of Distance Education, Dr. B.R. Ambedkar Open University, Hyderabad, India.
Email: vvenkaiah@hotmail.com

Professor Chambi Puranik is Former Dean (Academic), Karnataka State Open University, Mysore, India.
Email: mita@sancharnet.in

Professor Suresh Garg is Pro-Vice Chancellor, Indira Gandhi National Open University, New Delhi.
Email: scgarg@ignou.ac.in

2

National Education Policies vis-à-vis Distance Education

V.C. Kulandaiswamy

A New Stage in the Evolution of Education

The industrial age dawned in the late 18th century. Industrial economy meant replacement of craft by technology, which in turn meant increased productivity. Since the inception of industrial revolution, productivity increased in every area of activity except teaching essentially because the academics all over the world are in their own field conservative. Consequently till about the middle of the last century, teaching remained a craft. However, emergence of distance education heralds the introduction of technology in instruction. In the scale of evolution of education, it marks the third stage, the other two being the Gurukul System and the Classroom System.

All over the world distance learning started as correspondence education. The system had an early beginning in advanced countries and progressed in parallel with technologies and graduated into multimedia instruction.

Suggestions in Five Year Plans

The founding fathers of Indian Five Year Plans visualised the need for increasing the opportunities for higher education outside the formal system. They have made a reference in the 1st Five year Plan (1951) itself to:

> ...facilities of private study through correspondence courses and radio talks organised as far as possible by the various universities and allowing students to take the various examinations privately (GOI, 1951, p.540).

However, those in charge of implementing the Plan did not formulate any policy, nor did they develop any strategy to translate these rather vague but far-sighted observations into action during the first two plans. Only in the Third Five Year Plan (1961), the problem of rising numbers was considered and after discussing various alternatives like diverting students to vocational courses and professional education, the planners stated that:

> in addition to the provision in the plan for expansion of facilities for higher education, proposals for evening colleges, correspondence courses and the award of external degrees are at present under consideration (GOI, 1961, p. 589).

The CABE Recommendation

The Central Advisory Board of Education, the highest policy making body in India for education, took cognizance of the observations in the Third Five Year Plan and in its 28th meeting held in January 1961 took a decisive step and recommended the establishment of a committee to study the introduction of correspondence education system in India (CABE, 1961). Accordingly, the Ministry of Education, GOI, constituted a Committee under the chairmanship of Prof. D.S. Kothari, the then Chairman, UGC to formulate proposals for the establishment of correspondence education in India. The Committee after due examination of the need for expanding educational opportunities at the tertiary level, observed that the correspondence course is:

> a step designed to expand and equalise educational opportunity, as it aimed at providing additional opportunities for several thousand students who wished to continue their education and the persons who had been denied these facilities and were in full-time employment or were for other reasons prevented from availing themselves of facilities at college (GOI, 1963).

The Beginning

The recommendation of Kothari Committee marked a watershed and the opening of a new portal to the world of higher education in India. The Committee, however, was extremely cautious and wanted to proceed by stages. It restricted the programme offerings to BA degree in the fields of Arts, Commerce and Social Sciences. The Committee also recommended that the programme might be introduced as a pilot study in the University of Delhi with the restrictions stipulated above.

The University of Delhi introduced necessary amendments to the University Act and started the first ever course in correspondence education in India in 1962. This was the beginning of a new system of education and the materialisation of the expectations of the authors of the First Five Year Plan.

Education Commission, 1964-66

The next major development in the promotion of distance education was the recommendation of the Education Commission (1964-66) headed by Prof. D.S. Kothari. This report has been a landmark document covering all aspects of education and guiding the educational policies and programmes till 1986 when the National Policy on Education 1986 was re-formulated. The Education Commission expressed the view that the pilot project at the University of Delhi was a success and recommended as follows (GOI, 1966):

> 12.21. At present, a student at the undergraduate stage must either be admitted on a full-time basis or go without education altogether. This creates a great demand for full-time seats in colleges and leads to a deterioration of standards as the resources to provide all the seats needed are not available. One solution to this is to keep full-time seats strictly limited on the basis of resources available and to institute correspondence courses, part-time courses, evening courses, etc., for those who aspire to a university degree but are not able to get admission to the regular courses. This device is being increasingly used in many countries such as the USA, the UK, the USSR and Japan. The correspondence courses recently started by the Delhi University as a 'pilot project' have proved to be a promising experiment and are producing satisfactory examination results.
>
> 12.25. We recommend that the opportunities for part-time education through programmes like evening colleges, and for own-time education through programmes like correspondence courses, should be extended as widely as possible and should also include courses in science and technology (either at the degree or diploma level). There need be no fear that they will lead to a deterioration of standards, especially if due care is taken to maintain personal contacts with the students receiving correspondence education by organising academic programmes during vacations and holidays. We suggest that by 1986 at least a third of the total enrolment in higher education could with advantage be provided through a system of correspondence courses and evening colleges.

National Policy on Education, 1968

The progress of correspondence courses at the University of Delhi and the favourable observations of the Education Commission created an atmosphere highly conducive to the growth of correspondence education during the fourth Five Year Plan and the successive Plans in the seventies and eighties. The next important document is the National Policy on Education (GOI, 1968). The National Policy, by and large, endorses the recommendations of the Kothari Commission recommendations and states:

> (13) Part-time Education and Correspondence Course: Part-time education and correspondence courses should be developed on a large scale at the university stage. Such facilities should also be developed for secondary school students, for teachers and for agricultural, industrial and other workers. Education through part-time and correspondence courses should be given the same status as full-time education. Such facilities will smoothen transition from school to work, promote the cause of education and provide opportunities to the large number of people who have the desire to educate themselves further but cannot do so on a full-time basis.

It is pertinent to observe here that while all the earlier documents have looked at correspondence education only as a means of supplementing the opportunities for higher education system and helping the students who could not afford full time study, the National Policy 1968 has visualised an expanded role. It has envisaged among the target groups, school teachers, agricultural, industrial and other workers which highlights the concept of continuing education, continuous professional development and life-long learning for those already employed. The document has also emphasised *parity* between the correspondence education and conventional classroom based education. Unfortunately, even now distance education faces this problem in the case of many functionaries and institutions.

Growth of distance education institutions

The nineteen sixties and seventies have been the periods of expansion of correspondence education in the country. The University of Delhi, which was the only institution to offer the correspondence education programme, established a Directorate of Correspondence Education and offered opportunities for undergraduate education in arts, commerce and social sciences. It was towards the end of the sixties that a few other universities introduced correspondence courses; for instance Dibrugarh University, Assam (1965), University of Calicut, Kerala (1968), Gujarat Vidyapeet, Ahmedabad (1968), Punjabi University, Patiala (1968), Meerut University, Uttar Pradesh (1969) and Mysore University, Karnataka (1969). The programme picked up in the 1970s; the trend continued in the eighties and towards the end of eighties, there were 46 universities and deemed universities offering correspondence education programmes.

Open University: Parthasarathy Working Group 1974

When we move to the 1980s, we find the emergence of open universities. India was one of the earliest countries that applied their minds to the concept of open education following the remarkable success of U.K. Open University. The Ministry of Education and Social Welfare, in partnership with the UGC and the Indian National Commission for Collaboration with the UNESCO, organized in December 1970, a seminar on open universities. The seminar was in favour of India setting up an open university and recommended that the Govt. of India should set up a committee to go into the financial and other aspects. Later, perhaps in pursuance of this recommendation, the ministry of Education set up an eight member working group (1974) under the chairmanship of G. Parthasarathy, the then Vice Chancellor of Jawaharlal Nehru University.

The following statement of the Prime Minister in the Rajya Sabha on 28 February 1972 reflected the mind of the Government on issues concerning higher education, growing numbers, equity, social justice and maintenance of quality:

> Now most educational experts in the world are for the curtailment of university education. But we know that in this country it poses a special problem for us. Those people who have not had the opportunity of university education for all these centuries, naturally feel that such a curtailment will affect them and that therefore education will continue to have a kind of class bias. Surely we do not want that. We have to find a balance in which there can be some changes without shutting off a single opportunity from a person or a family who, for the first time, is in a position to avail himself of this. So, any problem which another country or even eminent educationists think of, has to be looked at in the circumstances which we obtain in our country. We have no guidelines in this. We have no examples which we can follow. We have to follow our own path step by step. It can only be done if we think more deeply about all these matters and again if we are willing to make experiments.

The working group surveyed the world scene and took note of the progressively growing demand for opportunities in higher education in India and decisively advocated the establishment of an open university in the following words:

> In a situation of this type, where the expansion of enrolment in higher education is to continue at a terrific pace and where available resources in terms of men and money are limited, one obvious solution, if proper standards are to be maintained and the demand for higher education for different sections of the people is to be met, is to adopt the open university system with its provision of higher education on a part-time or own-time basis. The Group therefore recommends that the Government of India establish, as early as possible, an open university by an Act of Parliament. The university should have jurisdiction over the entire country so that when it is fully developed, any student, even in the remotest corner of the country can have access to its instruction and degrees (GOI, 1974).

Though the recommendation of the working group was categorical and there were already examples in other countries, the Government of India was delaying action either due to hesitation or lack of serious application of their mind.

The UGC Committee on Central Universities 1982

In 1982, the University Grants Commission appointed a Committee under the chairmanship Dr. Madhuri R. Shah, Chairperson, UGC to enquire into the working of the Central Universities. The Committee applied its mind to off campus education and recommended as follows:

> 1.167. To satisfy existing thirst for knowledge as well as degrees, admission to formal courses on the basis of merit requires that opportunities for off-campus studies should be created on a large scale, for a great variety of courses of high quality. We already have a number of universities offering correspondence courses; we need to utilize and coordinate this expertise and infrastructure to create an effective system of distance learning. Mass media, such as radio and television, which are already beginning to be used in conjunction with correspondence education, and for which a greater potential is being created through the satellites, should be employed in a systematic manner to enlarge the scope and enrich the quality of distance education.
>
> 1.168. There is a great opportunity here to spread first rate education while at the same time save the universities from the great rush for admissions which leads to serious problems of discipline as well as of standards. The Government of India had set up a committee under the chairmanship of G. Parthasarathy to report on the setting up of an "Open University". The committee had submitted its report in 1974 strongly endorsing the idea. We recommend that practical steps for launching a national university of distance education be taken up without delay.

Open University: A Beginning in A.P., 1982

In this process, the Government of Andhra Pradesh took a bold decision and set up an open university at Hyderabad in 1982 as A.P. Open University. Later, the name was changed to Dr. B.R. Ambedkar Open University. The University had a good beginning and was modelled after U.K. Open University. The progress of Dr B.R. Ambedkar Open University was a source of encouragement and motivation for the State Governments to venture into the establishment of open universities.

The Beginning of a Mega University, 1985

The Govt. of India, by an Act of Parliament, established the Indira Gandhi National Open University (GOI, 1985). It is a unique institution which combines in it the functions of a regular university and a national body to promote, co-ordinate and determine the standards of distance education in the country. The mature recommendation made by the working group under the chairmanship of G. Parthasarathy, a decade ago, materialized in 1985.

While moving the bill for the establishment of IGNOU in Parliament, Sh. K.C. Pant said,

> We are awakening at the dawn of a new educational order. The old system of education has become rigid and centralised ... We are therefore in search of a system that would be capable of resilience, responsive to the changing needs of tomorrow. There is today an increasing stress on **education for all** as also on life-long **education**

> … there is sharp focus on educating those sections of society which have remained for long neglected or ignored. It is being increasingly realised that in the long run, it would cost our society heavily if we do not attend to the needs of the **weaker** sections and of the **disadvantaged**." (author's emphasis)

Notwithstanding the belated start, IGNOU has progressed fast, grown up in all dimensions and has emerged as one of the largest mega-universities of the world by providing equality of educational opportunities to all and throwing ivory towers open. As of now, about 1.3 million students have access to a learner-centric, collaborative networked environment. The profound impact of IGNOU has led one to believe that small is beautiful but big is more beautiful.

National Education Policy, 1986

A major development after the Education Commission report, headed by Prof. Kothari, was the preparation of the National Educational Policy 1986. A countrywide discussion and debate preceded the preparation. The policy document and the programme of action prepared for implementing the policies have attached considerable importance to the role of distance education to meet the educational needs of India. The National Educational Policy 1986 looks at distance education as an effective instrument for democratisation of education. It is recorded in the document under Open University and Distance Education as follows (GOI, 1986):

> 5.35. The open learning system has been initiated in order to augment opportunities for higher education, as an instrument of democratising education and to make it a lifelong process. The flexibility and innovativeness of the open learning system are particularly suited to the diverse requirements of the citizens of our country, including those who had joined the vocational stream.
>
> 5.36. The Indira Gandhi National Open University, established in 1985 in fulfilment of these objectives, will be strengthened. It would also provide support to establishment of open universities in the States.

Distance Education Council

The IGNOU has been contemplated as an apex body for Distance Education and is unique among the universities in the country. Section 5(2) of the Act states as follows:

> 5(2) Notwithstanding anything contained in any other law for the time being in force, but without prejudice to the provisions of sub-section (1), it shall be the duty of the University to take all such steps as it may deem fit for the promotion of the Open University and distance education systems and for the determination of standards of teaching, evaluation and research in such systems, and for the purpose of performing this function, the University shall have such powers including the power to allocate

> and disburse grants to Colleges, whether admitted to its privileges or not, or to any other university or institution of higher learning, as may be specified by the Statutes.

In order to fulfil the mandate stipulated in section 5(2), IGNOU has by an appropriate resolution of the Board, set up a body under the designation Distance Education Council (DEC). It was a bold and imaginative step and DEC has in it the potential of blossoming into a national institution of great importance.

Programme of Action, 1986; 1992

The Programme of Action 1986 was updated in 1992. The 1992 version of POA deals with distance education at length and is the first document, approved by the Indian Parliament, that refers to the Distance Education Council to fulfil the mandate given to IGNOU to promote and determine standards of distance education. The following excerpts from POA 1992 are pertinent to the present discussion (GOI, 1992):

> 12.2.3. The IGNOU has set up a Distance Education Council as a statutory body for the promotion, coordination and determination of standards of the open university/distance education system.
>
> The Distance Education Council will take steps for networking the State Open Universities and other distance education institutions, for sharing courses and programmes, and developing a pattern and structure for the open university programmes that would facilitate student mobility among programmes as well as institutions.
>
> The open university/distance education programmes would be structured on a modular pattern with provision for transfer of credits. Students will have the facility of registering for courses of their choice which, in appropriate combinations, will enable them to obtain certificates, diplomas or degrees.
>
> The Distance Education Council will encourage joint development of programmes and courses by IGNOU, State Open Universities and the Directorates of Correspondence Education of conventional universities.
>
> It will also recommend financial assistance from IGNOU to state open universities for their development and for undertaking specific projects.
>
> 12.2.4. The Distance Education Council will ultimately assume the responsibility for developing the existing correspondence education programmes on a selective basis and converting them into distance education programmes of an acceptable quality. However, for the time being, the responsibility for the development of distance education programmes in the conventional universities will remain with the UGC. There would be close consultation between the UGC and the IGNOU in the development of such programmes.
>
> 12.2.7. The recommendation of the Central Advisory Board of Education (CABE) that each State should establish an open university will be pursued with the State Governments for implementation during the Eighth Plan. The IGNOU will provide

> technical and consultancy support to the State Governments for this purpose. The Distance Education Council will prepare guidelines for providing financial support to State Open Universities for their development. Such assistance will include support to develop new programmes and courses. The course materials already produced by the IGNOU and other open universities would be made available to new State Open Universities which could offer them through the languages of the region so that access to Open University programmes is widened.

Tenth Five year Plan

There is a brief discussion on distance education in the tenth plan document. The emphasis is more on covering backward regions and disadvantaged sections. The following obscrvation (GOI, 2002) gives a glimpse of the main thrust:

> the coverage of open universities would, therefore need to be expanded to the backward regions, remote inaccessible tribal areas of the north east and some of the eastern states.
>
> During the Tenth Plan, IGNOU would set up Open Universities in states where none exist at present, expand the activities of Gyan Darshan and Gyan Vani. The target is to extend the coverage of the open learning system to the backward regions, remote inaccessible areas of the northeast and low female literacy blocks in some eastern states.

This document sets an ambitious target of about 40% of the total students in higher education to be enrolled in open and distance learning institutions by 2007.

Growth of OUs and DEIs

Consequent to the approach of the Govt. of India to support and promote distance education, and the recommendation of the committee set up by CABE that every state should set up an open university, distance teaching institutions witnessed a steep growth in the form of open universities and distance education institutions (DEIs) in conventional universities. After the AP Open University and IGNOU, ten more State Open Universities have been set up, the last one being Pt. Sundar Lal Sharma Open University (2004) in Chhattisgarh. It is reliably learnt that State Govt. of Assam and Uttaranchal are also likely to set up open universities soon.

As per the provision in POA 1992, the UGC transferred the statutory responsibility of co-coordinating and funding the centres for correspondence institutions to the Distance Education Council of IGNOU in 1996-97. With this the full responsibility of fulfilling the mandate contemplated in section 5(2) of IGNOU Act devolved on DEC. This development has imparted a new momentum to the emergence of new DEIs and OUs. In the period from 2001 to 2004, both the years included, 34 new DEIs and 2 new OUs have been established. The growth of OUs and DEIs is given in Table 1 (Garg, 2004).

Table 1: Growth of OUs and DEIs

Year	OU	DEI	DTI*
1962	—	1	1
1975	—	22	22
1982	1	34	35
1985	2	38	40
1990	5	46	51
2000	9	70	79
2004	11	104	115

* DTI – Distance Teaching Institution

In Fig. 1 is given the growth of DEIs and in Fig. 2 the growth of OUs.

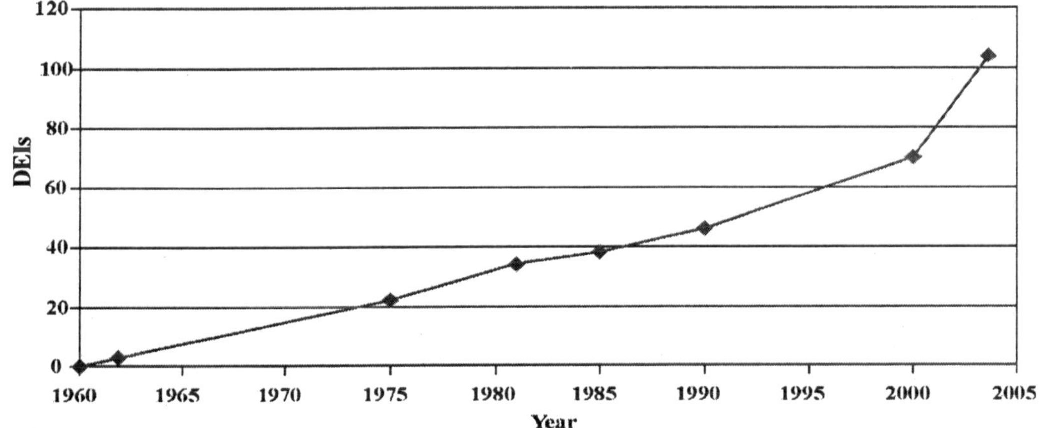

Figure 1: Year vs. number of DEIs

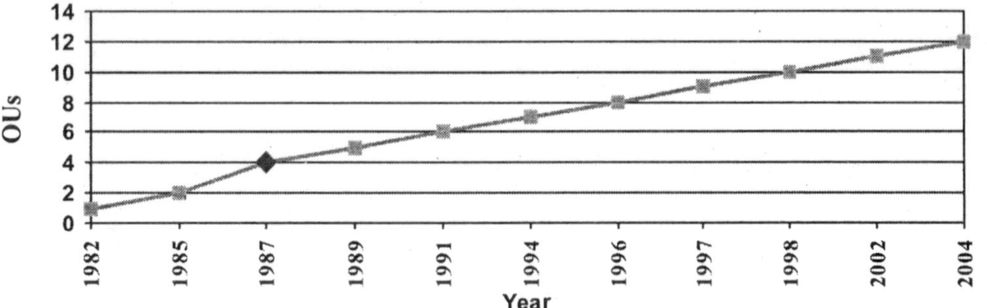

Figure 2 : Year vs number of OUs

The 115 DTIs consisting of 11 OUs and 104 DEIs cater to the educational and training needs of about 2.5 million students, constituting 24% of the total number (Garg, 2004) in higher education. The growth in DTIs as well as enrolment in DE as percent of total has been steep in the period after 1985, the year of establishment of IGNOU (Table 2).

Table 2 : Enrolment in DE as % of total*

Year	% of Total Enrolment
1971	2.1
1976	2.6
1981	5.7
1991	11.5
2002	24.0
2007	33.0[estimated]

* Sources: i. UGC (1990) Theme Paper. Conference of Vice Chancellors, Ahmedabad, October 1990. Part1, p.3.
ii. POA 1992.
iii. VC's Report. 16th Convocation of IGNOU, 2005

The growth in enrolment in DE as % of the total is given in Fig.3. The growth in terms of number of institutions, strength of enrolment, diversity of programmes offered, and the disciplines covered has been quite satisfying. The rate of growth in every aspect has been reasonably steep, especially since 1985. The establishment of open universities especially the IGNOU and DEC, has given the distance education a fillip as well as a new status, a new pedestal and a benchmark.

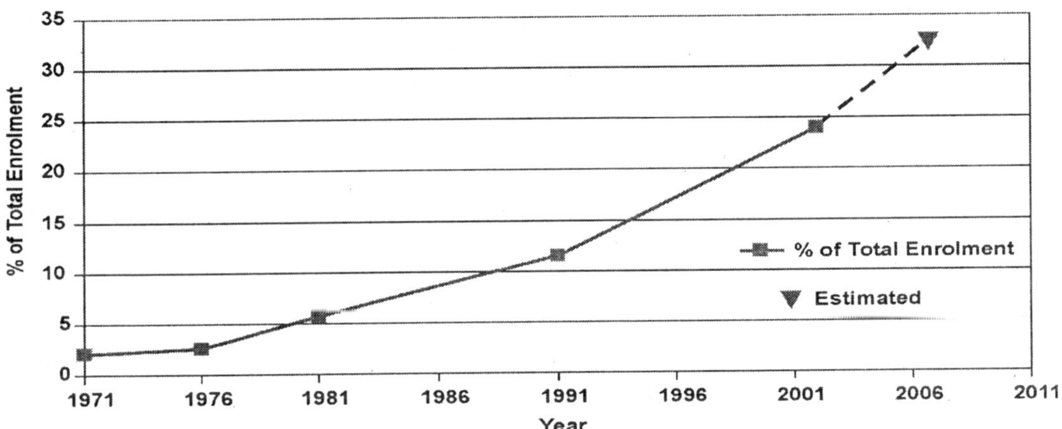

Figure 3 : Year vs. % of total enrolment

Conclusion

The progress and development in distance education in the last four decades may be assessed in terms of four aspects:

i) Programmes
ii) Target groups
iii) Quality
iv) Accessibility

The programmes in distance education, started with extreme caution in the softest of disciplines have, in steady steps earlier and fairly fast later, travelled very far and have in the last fifteen years blossomed as plants in spring. The programmes cover a wide spectrum, from auditing courses to research degrees, comprising certificate, diploma, advance diploma, bachelor's, master's, M.Phil. and Ph.D. awards. The subjects cover arts, humanities, sciences, engineering, paramedical, agriculture, home science, technology, law and numerous vocational areas. Prof. Dikshit (2005) in his VC's report at the 16th convocation of IGNOU has stated that distance education institutions in the country offered nearly 300 academic programmes and 2230 courses. That is an impressive record indeed.

The target groups now range from craftsmen to research workers and consist of individuals employed and unemployed, professionals and para professionals who want to update, upgrade and broaden their knowledge and training and such groups of men and women as are disabled and disadvantaged, socially constrained, geographically inaccessible and even sections of people abroad in the developing world. The categories catered to are impressive; the numbers are large in absolute terms but may appear modest considering the vast population.

When we come to the quality of distance education, we touch the weakest link in the chain. Educational programme at the tertiary level, in general, consists of instruction and self-learning. This is valid both for the conventional system and distance education system: in the former, instruction component is predominant; in the latter, the most important is self-learning. Consequently, the instruction material is extremely important in distance learning. Technology, whatever its advancement, only tends to restore as far as possible the classroom situation and improves communication. Instruction material is basic and cannot be replaced especially in a system where self-learning is dominant. Many of the DEIs are yet to prepare the learning materials which meet the requirements expected of them. In terms of multimedia instruction, many of the DEIs have not yet reached the third generation level; many have not moved beyond the second generation stage. Some of the Open Universities thrive on instruction material borrowed or adapted from IGNOU. They are yet to prepare instruction material of their own comparable to IGNOU material in the case of subjects where IGNOU could not come to their help.

The stepping in of IGNOU offering assistance through DEC with insistence on maintaining quality, seems to have brought about a new awareness and quality consciousness. The massive advances made in IGNOU in the form of Gyan Vani, FM radio stations, Gyan Darshan, interactive radio counselling, tele-conferencing and internet have vastly changed the distance education environment in the country. The EduSat introduced in Sep. 2004 has immense potential: the OUs and the DEIs should equip themselves to be able to make optimum use of EduSat and derive benefits from collective wisdom. It may be mentioned here that the accessibility improves with the progress made by the DTIs in technology application.The fact remains that many conventional universities started the distance education programmes with no greater objective than creating surplus funds to meet the deficiency in the conventional system. They must outgrow this culture and set to themselves the task of developing a distance education institution, as an integral part of their educational programme. It will be desirable for the DTIs in each state to form a consortium and study the ways and means of pooling the resources available with them and making maximum use of the nationally available resource in technology application.

As of now, DEC has been treading cautiously, perhaps because of limited authority, and concentrating on promotion. However, it appears necessary for the DEC to initiate a detailed study of each DEI, assess its present level of development, performance, inadequacies in instruction material, infrastructure, student services, etc. and set a time limit for meeting the minimum requirement. A comprehensive directory of all the DEIs with a complete report on present status of each and a road map to meet the minimum requirements must be prepared. It is well within the powers of the DEC to undertake an exercise of this nature.

The DEC, as contemplated, is both a funding and an accrediting institution. Its present status as an overseeing body, created by the Board of Management, presided over by the VC, IGNOU, who is in the same rank as other VCs, carries with it certain uncomfortable and embarrassing responsibilities. Exercising even a semblance of authority over one's equal creates, in practice, delicate situations. It is absolutely necessary to bring about a change in the statutory status of DEC.

The DEC must find a place in the IGNOU Act itself and its composition must also be specified in the Act with VC, IGNOU as Chairperson whose status and emoluments must be at par with the Chairperson UGC or AICTE. If this is not considered satisfactory or acceptable for any reason, the DEC must be constituted as a parallel body to the UGC with its jurisdiction over all institutions, fields and processes associated with self-learning. Any one of the two alternatives is urgently needed for improving the present position and to safeguard the future of distance education in the country.

As stated in the beginning, distance education had its beginning in 1962 in the form of a pilot study in the University of Delhi. In the last four decades, it has grown into twelve open universities, 104 DEIs catering to about 2.5 million students which accounts for 24% of the total enrolment. It is envisaged that by the end of the tenth plan, the coverage will be at least a third of the total enrolment. That certainly is a significant strength, considering that the conventional system has nearly 150 years of history. Even after independence, many commissions, committees and working groups have gone into the working of the conventional higher education system in India. Strangely, distance education which will soon be completing its golden jubilee has so far evolved mainly on its own and no committee, much less a commission, has gone into the working of the Distance Education System in the country. It is my considered opinion that a comprehensive study of the strengths and weaknesses of the system, the present stage of development and the future vision must be made by a high power Commission and a report must be made available for guiding the future course of development of distance education in India, especially in view of the explosion of opportunities ushered in by the technological revolution and the knowledge space developed by the convergence of ICT and learning.

References

Government of India (1951). *First Five Year Plan*. New Delhi: Planning Commission, Government of India.

Government of India (1961). *Third Five Year Plan*. New Delhi: Planning Commission, Government of India.

Central Advisory Board of Education (1961). 28th Meeting (January 1961). New Delhi: Ministry of Education and Social Welfare, Government of India,

Government of India (1963). *Report of the Committee on Correspondence Course*. New Delhi; Ministry of Education and Social Welfare, Government of India.

Government of India (1966). *Report of the Education Commission*. New Delhi: Ministry of Education and Social Welfare, Government of India.

Government of India (1968). *National Policy on Education*. New Delhi: Ministry of Education and Social Welfare, Government of India.

Government of India (1974). *Report of the Working Group on Open University*. New Delhil: Ministry of Education and Social Welfare, Government of India.

Government of India (1986). *National Policy on Education*.New Delhi: Ministry of Education and Social Welfare, Government of India.

Government of India (1985). *The Indira Gandhi National Open University Act 1985 (No.50 of 1985).* New Delhi: Ministry of Education, Government of India.

UGC (1990). Theme Paper Conference of Vice Chancellors, Ahmedabad, October 1990. Part 1, p.3.

Government of India (1992). *Programme of Action.* New Delhi: Ministry of Human Resources Development, Government of India.

Government of India (2002). *Tenth Five Year Plan.* New Delhi: Planning Commission, Government of India.

Garg, Suresh (2004). Role of Distance Education in Widening Access: the Experience of IGNOU. Paper presented in Second Global Forum on International Quality Assurance, Accreditation and the Recognition of Qualifications: Globalistion and Higher Education, held at UNESCO, Paris.

Dikshit, H.P. (2005). *VC's Report at the 16th Convocation of Indira Gandhi National Open University (March 5).* New Delhi: IGNOU.

Professor V.C. Kulandaiswamy has the rare distinction of being the Vice Chancellor of three universities, including IGNOU. He has been decorated by the GOI with the award of Padma Shri and Padma Bhushan for his scholarly contributions to Tamil Literature, enriching Civil Engineering discipline and administrative capabilities par excellence. He is a prolific writer and very effective communicator. As a former President of Association of Indian Universities and Chairman, Distance Education Council, he has made very significant impact in the area of management of higher education.
Email: vck99@hotmail.com

3

Management of Open and Distance Learning Systems

Madhulika Kaushik, Suresh Garg and H.P. Dikshit

Introduction

From an alternative second choice to an educational solution in its own right, often the only one available to vast segment of our population, open and distance education has travelled a long and arduous path. From the days of Eklavya, where denial of teacher led face-to-face learning opportunity prompted the learner to adopt conscientious self-study, to the era of technology supported education, where advances in information and communication technology have virtually eliminated the concept of distance, Open and Distance Learning (ODL) has spanned several generations of evolutionary developments. The present ODL institutions represent large, organized, vibrant and dynamic systems, bringing higher education within the reach of millions of aspirants. Some of the essential managerial challenges of maintaining affordability for the masses, creating access with equity for all those desirous of being educated and to do so with the highest possible standards of quality of both process and output, have remained as relevant for the ODL systems as ever .The repertoire of the available solutions, the "toolkit" at the disposal of those who manage the ODL system, has become far more varied and evolutionary in nature as the international experience pool grows and applications proliferate.

Higher education, ODL included, however, has to fulfil the mandate of constantly remaining relevant to a fast changing and dynamic world of the knowledge society, where knowledge is not only the most critical and central factor of development, but also the constantly renewable resource that can compensate for the deficit in other resources and enable nations to emerge with a competitive advantage most visibly translable in the development of their people. This is well illustrated by the emergence of Japan, as an economic super power in the 1980s.

As the aspirants for higher education in the knowledge society multiply, the expectations, needs and requirements of present and potential stakeholders (students, parents, practitioners and planners) vis-à-vis ODL are bound to undergo a vast change since the system has capacity and capability to provide contemporary, high quality cutting edge competencies to the large numbers it attracts, consistently and equitably. Such aspirations on the one hand and the need to manage large, organised and dynamic systems on the other, present unique management challenges for ODL systems. In this chapter we address the key issues in the management of the present day ODL systems and identify the directions of action in pursuance of some of these challenges. The areas identified for discussion include management of administrative systems, financial resources, academic human resources, technical and infrastructure support systems, learner support systems, quality of education, and more importantly managing leadership, change and transition. Other issues under discussion include institution building, organisational culture and leadership challenges. Though the treatment of issues has been kept generic in nature, specific institutional examples have been used to illustrate.

Management of Academic Human Resources

Having emerged from the conventional higher education system to more effectively respond to the issues of access and equity, high productivity, cost-effectiveness, continual relevance, learner flexibility and quality management, ODL systems have to innovate to cater to unreached target groups and explore newer areas to avoid more of the same. Since credibility of a system is, to a large measure, decided by the quality of academic inputs and outputs, the faculty plays the most crucial role. Therefore, attracting exciting talent, nurturing it and retaining it in the system are the foremost challenges in managing the academic human resource. The academic sub-system in an open university has to be sensitised to be far more attentive towards their responsibility to target groups and adherence to organisation priorities and management system. Since the work of the academics is always open to public scrutiny, be it their print material or their communication on the public media, particularly television and radio, their job profile demands acquisition of additional skills in instructional design to produce study materials, managerial skills to coordinate and liase with outside members of course teams working with multiple media in both broadcast and live interactive modes, behavioural skills to interact meaningfully with students or their parents at HQ and RCs and conventional peers involved in delivery of programmes at SCs. As the open universities climb the evolutionary path, from print based learning to integrated multiple media packages and Interactive Multimedia learning, academics in the open university have had to constantly evolve, reskill and re-engineer. According to Takwale (1996), "The management of academic subsystem balancing between academic autonomy on the one side and the needs of the customers and production targets on the other hand, is a delicate exercise".

The main challenges in the management of academic human resources, in addition to the 'balancing act' are:

- *Attracting the best academic resources*: The ability of an institution to attract the best possible academic resources is directly proportional to its perception of being the preferred employer. While in terms of providing opportunities for self-development, relatively faster career progression, facilities provided to discharge responsibilities, healthy work culture and conducive environment, open universities present better options. Relatively longer working hours, greater demands on academic and management skills, continuous professional development (retrain and reskill) to keep pace with fast changes, parity with conventional universities, force many bright minds to view the open university less favourably as an employer. Due to the forces of liberalisation and globalisation, universities no longer are the preferred destinations of bright young minds. It is becoming increasingly difficult to attract highly motivated, dedicated and exciting academic resources at all levels, particularly in open universities. This is specially true of professional disciplines like IT, management, engineering, health care, law, education, etc. where private sector is a major attraction for talent.
- *Retaining the talent:* The search for increasingly better solutions to the problems of learner access, effective delivery and quality have led open universities to adopt emerging technologies, necessitating continuous training and retraining of academic resources. In its formative years, the National Open University trained all new teachers in methodologies of open learning by inviting experts from UKOU for periods ranging from one to two weeks. Academics were also deputed to UKOU for larger durations. To keep pace with developments, this exercise has now been upgraded to training in Interactive Multimedia CD-ROM development of up to three weeks duration. Training is a worthwhile investment in quality of academic resources, though it may not be directly translable in measurable outputs in the short term. It also requires the time-constrained, deadline-bound open university academics to take time off from routine schedule, often at the cost of falling back in their assigned responsibilities.
- *Academic motivation and institutional ownership:* Like all tenured position situations, academics at the open universities can also be classified in the categories of the self-motivated with deep sense of institutional belonging, the situationally motivated and those who may require organisational incentives to put in extra effort. The challenge for the system is in raising the proportion of the first category in comparison to the other two, by strategically involving academics in challenging responsibilities and assignments with authority to decision-making, enlarging job profiles and enriching job descriptions. Different institutions have worked out varied solutions ranging from challenging project based assignments to evolving participative decision making structures and higher levels of academic autonomy. The success has been in direct correlation with institutional work culture, and ethical and professional practices. While it has in general worked in formative years, deformities crept in with aging and other 'extraneous' influences generated by personalities, egos and aspirations. This issue however should be seriously addressed if the ODL institutions are to manage the twin objectives of productivity and quality.

- *Research:* Since academics entering the ODL system predominantly continue to be products of conventional system, the years of their training drive them towards discipline-based research and in search of excellence in it. Probably, the inertia factor makes them feel less confident in venturing into unknown/little known areas, which obviously is a limitation of our training. The importance of discipline-based research cannot be undermined for any reasons and all institutions have been supportive of it. Mechanisms have been put in place in the form of study leave, research grants, travel grants, etc. However, systemic research has been accorded higher priority, and probably rightly, because this area is fast developing, almost unexplored and provides opportunities to be pioneers and innovators rather than doing more of the same with limited chances to emerge in the front because there 'space is crowded' and to that extent elusive. Above all, systemic research shall not only satisfy the quest of the individual to contribute to new knowledge, it will also bring benefits to the system (learners as well as the institution).

Management of Administrative Subsystem

Most DE institutions today represent large systems with far larger learner populations than ever envisaged. The need to create access far and wide, in domains unreached, for target segments left unserved, and to do so with learner-friendly, learner-supportive and learner-responsive systems, both in terms of quality and speed of response requires enthusiastic, dedicated individuals capable of working in a team situation. This work force is the second segment of human resources in the open universities that helps in furthering the institutional goals for community welfare. The volume of work has resulted in development of a fairly bulky and varied administrative system compared to the conventional higher education system. The teacher to non-academic ratio is 1:6 in ODL system against 1:3 in conventional system. The conversion of former correspondence course institutions into open universities, as in case of KSOU and VMOU has also not helped the cause. Though it is true that nature of operations in the two systems have significant fundamental differences, yet no serious effort seems to have been made at any time by any pay/administrative reform commission to lay down uniform job description, promotional policies, ethical code and the like. And wherever it has been attempted, it has been cold-shouldered for 'pragmatic' reasons based on administrative convenience and political expediency/exigency. This has resulted in adhoc piece-meal intra-institutional solutions on case to case basis leading to far greater problems with the result that a useful resource is not being used optimally. Moreover, the legacy of conventional work culture, which permeated the DEIs, has begun to defuse into OU which is not doing any good and requires application of mind, before it is too late! Probably, conducting short-term continuous professional development courses could provide a forum to sensitise them towards their responsibilities to the learner and how intimately growth, efficiency and reputation of the system is linked to their own.

ODL systems with national and/or state level jurisdiction result in multi-location, dispersed regional administrative offices, which in turn look after district level learner support systems in the cascade model. The development of administrative policy is usually a centralized activity, with participation from regional offices, while the implementation of such a policy is a multi-level coordinated exercise, building upward from the learner support centre to the headquarter via the regional centres and culminating in overall central monitoring and control. Obtaining details on financial expenditure at the end of financial year from each centre for finalisation of accounts, due to diverse spread, also presents itself as a major challenge at times. Use of technology to sensitise all functionaries to work within given time limit seems to be the only option.

The institutions of open and distance learning however have been functioning by and large under organisational structures and prescribed administrative positions, notwithstanding the fact that these were designed for conventional higher education systems and are not ideally suited to the requirements of ODL systems (Reddy, 2003). The ODL system derives a lot of its operational strengths from and relies heavily on IT support infrastructure. To handle such operations professionally in industrial mode, what is required is a multi-skilled workforce rather than an army of office assistants, senior assistants, section officers and the like. Any attempt to modify the cadres to incorporate the requirements of the system are either strongly resisted by the stakeholders or met with long delays at the hand of the approving mechanisms. As a result, open universities are saddled with cadres that they have little use for, and are denied the human resources that they require to make the systems more responsive and effective with lower reaction times and high response rates. The dead-wood not only resists change but also vitiates work ethics and institutional morale. As a result, institutions tend to cope with short term, casual appointments, which are essentially adhoc solutions to a lasting problem with potential of far greater danger, including litigation. It is therefore imperative for the growth and success of the system that DEC and UGC evolve norms in consultation and under guidance of MHRD for uniform implementation in the country; piece-meal solutions are not likely to take us very far.

Owing to the fairly industrialized nature of its operations like admissions, registration, material delivery and the declaration of results involving hundreds of thousands of learners, speed, reliability and efficiency become essential determinants of the quality of output of the ODL system. The existing hierarchical staff structures need to be apprised of the consequences of loss of quality of output vis-à-vis systemic credibility and acceptability; special needs and requirements and what incentives can bring growth to them in terms of career progression. Staff training and development policies have to be put in place and implemented for gainful participation of this segment of human resource of the system. As system leader and role model, IGNOU has to provide technical as well as academic expertise to support the initiative for continuous professional development and enhancement in their capabilities so as to work in flat, individually accountable administrative system. A comprehensive, pre-active and holistic analysis of the administrative requirements of the institution operating in networked environment, aided by technology based communications systems and information flows, should be undertaken from time to time for a candid reassessment of staff requirements for optimal growth to realise institutional vision. Other administrative challenges include devising strategies for effective work culture and coordination of various academic, professional, service and support Divisions within as well as with funding, regulating and supporting organisations/agencies from outside. An extremely important challenge is in managing public perception of an institution about quality education and practicing of moral values collectively in its march towards self-sustainability.

Management of Financial Resources

Indian ODL system comprises one national open university, eleven state open universities and 106 dual mode institutions. While the initial outlay for establishing the state open universities has been met by respective state governments, the national open university, was funded directly by the Ministry of Human Resource Development (MHRD), GoI. Like any other central university, however, the pattern of funding of the national open university, in the 9th Plan had been on a net deficit basis in the sense that the central government met the net deficit in the expenditure, after accounting for the income of the University from all sources through grants released directly. Having envisaged that the effectiveness of the open learning system would be strongly dependent pon the quality of its technical and professional capabilities, substantial financial investments have been made in the capital infrastructure. This helped IGNOU to grow fast and create a wide base (Kulandaiswamy, 2002). While the development grants as part of the Plan funds were discontinued as soon as the university began to generate sufficient revenue and became self-sufficient in financial year 2002-03, it is now contributing for creation of national facilities out of its own resources. This became possible due to excellent financial management practices. YCMOU also achieved self-sufficiency within ten years of its existence.

Though the capital costs of setting up an open university are high, it is now a well researched fact that per capita costs of ODL systems in Asia are about one-fourth of those in conventional higher education systems. It has been observed that with annual intake about 50,000 students and more, an ODL institution can generate enough funds from student fee, DEC grants and government to support new initiatives. The financial management of such institutions, in view of their size, dynamism, aspirations and requirements presents some unique challenges. These include:

- *Changing capital requirements:* The dynamic technology upgradation needs of the ODL systems require frequent investments in newer and more effective technologies to enhance their effectiveness in reaching and serving their diverse and dispersed learner populations. The life cycle of available technologies is getting shorter with proliferation of innovations in technologies, especially ICT. While open universities may not like to sub-optimize their technology infrastructure by working with less than the latest, adoption and replacement are capital intensive decisions and official approvals take a lot of time. Mobilising resources for rapid technology adoption is a key financial challenge. Innovative solutions like depreciation funds, developmental corpus are still at experimental stages in the open universities and any reliance on government funds is likely to affect the speed with which the institution may want to move.
- *Activity costing:* Since ODL institutions use available infrastructure for various activities and pool academic and administrative resources, it is difficult to calculate rationally and scientifically the actual per unit cost of academic output and activities at the level of costing of a programme. While generalizations using some formulae can always be made, these at best remain approximations in the absence of precise costing techniques applied to teamwork

based academic output. Activity costing remains an area of academic and research inquiry in open and distance learning systems which merits serious attention.

- *March towards self-sustainability:* The ODL system has been thought to be in possession of magical powers to educate and empower masses without much demand on funds. There are success stories of efficient financial management that has driven a few institutions towards self-sufficiency. The operational costs at an ODL institution include the costs of development, production and despatch of study material, cost of delivering learner support services including registration and evaluation, and institutional overheads. According to reliable estimates, almost 80-90% of budget in the conventional systems is spent on the salary component. This leaves very little scope for innovation and development. But in the ODL system, while the salary forms only a small part of the total costs; the learner support system forms a very large part of such costs. In IGNOU, the latter expenditure is about 60% of total recurring expenditure and salary component is less than 5% of total costs. If the operational costs are to be realised out of the student fee, the challenge lies in keeping it at a level that would enable the institution to absorb all its operational costs and yet be affordable for the vast majority of its learners.
- *Issue of cross-subsidisation:* ODL institutions often have to reconcile to the requirement of a socially desirable but low enrolment programme, which could lead to higher costs but would need to be offered at a low fee, looking at the socio-economic profile of the target learners. Economies of scale in operations, implementing cost economies in internal operations and cross subsidization of fee between professional and other programmes offering and sponsored programmes with financial commitment from the agency concerned for design and development of material are some of the strategies that have been successfully used. For instance, BDP and B.Tech programmes of IGNOU are grossly subsidised. Similarly, several government departments (Ministry of Agriculture, Ministry of Food Processing, Directorate General of Shipping, MHRD, Ministry of Health & Family Welfare,) international agencies (UNESCO, World Bank, WHO, ComSec COL, Ed-Excel) other corporate houses (Hero Honda), national/international agencies have met programme development costs. Similarly, KSOU, NSOU, BRAOU, BAOU and other institutions have signed MoUs with multinational/private houses to offer programmes in IT, agriculture, fashion design, etc. essentially to generate funds. Constant search for solutions for streamlining operations, more cost-effective technology enabled learner support, and cost sharing through networking are some options for continuous march towards self-sustainability.
- *Allocation of financial resources:* Institutional priorities, academic requirements and desire for offering new courses, quest for diverse technology solutions and greater learner facilitation compete for their respective share of allocation from the funds available to an institution in a given Plan period. Prioritizing these demands in view of their long term impact on the institution as well as organisational culture is a managerial challenge that has to be grappled with. Participative planning often goes a long way in enabling balanced allocations and optimum utilisation, though it is often difficult to satisfy all constituencies adequately.

Management of the Learner Support Systems

Learners in the ODL systems are spread all over the country/state (in case of SOUs/DEIs) in varying densities. As quite a substantial proportion of these learners are working adults, the institutions have also to deal with the problem of mobile populations. In pursuance of their goal of creating equitable access to the services of the institution, open universities strive to create and implement fairly standardised norms of learner support infrastructure and services throughout their jurisdiction. What however has emerged as a key challenge is the variability in availability and standards of the academic resources used as academic counsellors or mentors. The problem gets more severe in case of master level or professional programmes where the availability and the willingness of the desirable quality of resource persons to involve themselves in counselling activities become key constraints in managing effective programme delivery at distant locations. Counsellor training and constant monitoring of the quality of counselling being provided to all learners across all programmes and centres represents another managerial challenge for large and diverse open learning systems.

In addition, while the open university may desire to extend its access to areas far and wide in its bid to reach unreached populations, the enrolment in different programmes activated at the centres may not financially justify the viability of such centres or at least all the programmes at the centre. The dilemma of reach versus viability on the one hand and providing full complement of learner support services for programmes with very limited enrolments in remote centres is a real one and often fraught with compelling arguments on both sides.

For most programmes at the open universities, attending counselling sessions at the study centres is not a mandatory requirement. Managing learner participation in these sessions is again a challenge in view of the huge allocations being made for learner support services and the possibility of the benefit of these investments not reaching the learner.

Managing Quality Assurance

Quality, accountability, strategic planning etc. have been corporate concepts that have found applications in ODL systems in recent years. The Bureau of Indian Standards defines quality as the totality of features and characteristics of a product/service that bear on its ability to satisfy stated and implied needs (BIS, 1988). Quality perceptions in the context of distance education vary considerably across institutions, so also its definition. Quality has been viewed in terms of fitness of purpose, perfection, conformance to standards, value for money, consistency, and relevance (Green and Harvey, 1993). ODL systems add the criteria of access and flexibility to the quality requirements, a good quality open learning system brings higher education within reach of target population and should be flexible enough to provide for their occupational, personal and professional exigencies of time, place and pace. In addition, quality in ODL systems has to be responsive to the requirements of life long learning (L3), to keep the human resource pool of the country at the cutting edge of competitive excellence. In the era of globalization and consequent internationalization of education, quality assurance for ODL systems is no longer an option. It has become the essential survival tool in the competitive scenario of the post-GATS world order.

The industrial nature of its operational processes necessitates setting up of quality benchmarks for most of the output parameters in an open university. Standardization of credit worth for all levels of programs, design parameters to be followed in instructional design of material, formalized requirements for approval to be met by Schools intending to offer programs, insistence on participation of broad based national level expertise in course development are all examples of basic quality assurance parameters being followed at the National Open university in pursuance of quality of its course material. What is more difficult to manage is the quality of ongoing support services to the learners across the country as mentioned earlier. Benchmarks for other aspects of service delivery like timeliness and accuracy in material dispatch schedules, timely reflection of grades for both continuous and in term end assessment, high levels of responsiveness to learner queries are some of the other desirable facets of quality assurance that could be implemented in the ODL systems.

Managing Technology Infrastructure

The growth of ODL has received a major impetus with the developments in information and communication technologies, which together created a formidable array of alternatives to bridge the gap between the teacher and the taught, such that the notion of distance has become a non-barrier in conducting real time teaching learning transactions across geographical distances. Technology support and education alternatives are now used to widen access to education, improve the quality of access through interactivity and learner participation and bring in transformational changes in the processes of registration, learner support and evaluation. While technological infrastructure today offers a multitude of options to the educational planners, the choices have to be made through very serious deliberations on account of following factors:

a) Technology infrastructure selection decisions usually are capital intensive and long term, binding the university in relatively long term commitments. The cost of a wrong decision is thus very high in both financial and temporal terms.
b) Technology and selection decisions affect almost every aspect of the university's processes and related infrastructure decisions.

Today, choices of appropriate technology by the university have to be made at several levels .To take a simple example in educational delivery, choices have to be made at the level of the ideal media mix i.e. whether the programme delivery should be through print, radio, television, computer supported learning, multimedia CD based learning or a combination of some or all of these. At the next level, in the context of audio-visual or computer supported instruction, choices have to be made on the mode: broadcast, narrowcast or interactive. Then the institution has the choice of creating infrastructure through outright purchase, lease, hire or sharing of common infrastructure by entering into institutional collaborations. If the decision is to create proprietary structures through ownership, choices need to be made at the level of product, brand, make and supporting technology alternatives. Finances are important but should not be the sole criterion defining technology choices. Perraton (2004), in his paper on technology selection has outlined four criteria governing the choice of technology for ODL institutions. These include

a) *Availability and convenience:* Easy availability of technologies like the Internet as a factor has to be balanced with acceptability of technology in question by potential users i.e. the learners. Direct to home television option is highly accessible and convenient but the institution has no direct control over the creation and implementation of the receive infrastructure as these are issues of user discretion.
b) *Local and national constraints:* There are often local variations in the way technologies can be utilized in different locations. While open universities with large enrolments may find satellite technology to be very appropriate for reaching large numbers of students, local constraints like availability of power may severely constrain the actual utility of the technology. Supporting infrastructure in the form of generator sets would mean extra costs of equipment and supporting human resource.
c) *Curriculum:* While the availability of a given, new technology may be exciting, the starting point for the choice of technology should be the curriculum and its target audiences rather than the multiple features displayed by the technology. The understanding that technology is only the enables of better access and value addition, the curriculum delivery is fundamental to the overall perspective within which technology solutions have to be evaluated.
d) *Cost:* Finance is among the most visible and seemingly objective criteria that are applied to evaluation of alternative technology solutions. The relevant costs in this case however should be costs per learner reached by the given option or cost per teaching-learning transaction.

In addition to all the above, the capacity of a given technology to enhance the learning experience, or to add to the efficacy of the teaching processes as evinced from the feedback received through stakeholders like students, peers, mentors counsellors, teachers should form an important guiding post in facilitating technology choices.

There are critical issues in the administration of the technology infrastructure, which relate to the people handling technology. Policy makers often find resistance to adoption of new technology, especially when it involves major changes in the way people are accustomed to work. Examples are switching over from SIM development to multimedia instructional development or from broadcast based teaching to online interactive teaching. Reactions to new technologies range from doubts to detraction and outright rejection. The touchstone to guiding support to a given option can only be found in how it benefits the essential constituency of students and influences the quality of the teaching learning transactions.

Management of Leadership, Change and Transition

As large, dynamic and socially responsive institutions, open universities present unique challenges of leadership, management of change and transition. Like all universities, the open universities cater to different disciplines and diverse learner groups, their chosen constituency of catering to lifelong learning has made their learner segments far more than varied and with customized requirements in relation to this respective occupations and professions. The prime leadership challenge is that of remaining relevant to all these diverse requirements at the same time, without compromising any of quality parameters discussed earlier in the paper. In the context of being a large organisation, the other leadership challenge is to keep significant proportions of the academics and administrators in the university in a state of highly motivated work teams, which has often been managed by involving the different cadres in the organisation's broader mission and specific objectives at a given point of time.

Open universities often grapple with the problems of centralisation versus delegation. The industrial nature of some of its operations like planning of academic schedules, material printing, distribution, evaluation and certification, and the need of standardise these force a certain degree of centralisation of decision making. The multi location presence of organisational units like the regional and the learner support centres necessitate some degree of delegation and decentralisation. Decentralisation of operations brings with it the challenges of effective monitoring and good governance.

Today, in a bid to enrich their offerings and enhance their relevance, conventional systems are adopting several of the tools used in open learning system. For example, audio visual and online support, interactive counselling, etc. While open universities are enhancing the incorporation of face-to-face interaction in some of the programmes which demand it. The availability of enabling technologies and the constant desire to enrich programme offerings as well the quality of teaching learning is blurring the distinction between the two systems. The ODL systems have always tried to synergise the benefits of the knowledge and experience pool available with the conventional system. One of the leadership challenges in ODL system has been to manage the convergence under several types of conventional systems, without sacrificing in any way the openness and flexibility aspects. The effort has taken the universities on path of different types of collaborations which has paid ample dividends both in terms of enriching their product portfolio and bring in recognition across conventional peers. Due to its inherent capacity to absorb change, ODL systems have gone through various developmental paths, commonly referred to as five generations of distance learning, ranging from print-based, correspondence mode to the present days intelligent flexible open learning. While the national open university demonstrates the existence of all five generations, the distance education institutes in conventional universities continue to practice the first generation DE. Several State Open Universities offer good examples of being in the second, third and fourth generations. It would normally be assumed that these would be sequential stages and at any point of time, an ODL institution, could be neatly categorised as being in one of the five generations. Leaders in ODL institutions however are faced with the situations where all generations seem to co-exist simultaneously, cach moving at its own respective pace and with compelling justification for its continuance. The leadership challenge is to identify whether inertia or territory protection mask the overt arguments of learner suitability or the varying requirements and profiles of different learner segments that necessitate these varying "generational" approaches to programme design and delivery. Resistance to change is a natural phenomenon and academic freedom a cherished prerogative, which often means that leaders in steering policy initiatives have to be sensitive to the requirements of different generations of ODL; in the same institution all at once and manage them on their respective merits.

Some of the strategic issues which have been raised in the context of governance of ODL institutions include the following:

a) Is the policy basis for governance of the open universities adequate to address all its diverse cadres, sections and stakeholders?
b) Is the policy basis clearly understood and well documented, is it transparent and fairly implemented?
c) Are the arrangements for good governance dynamic enough to meet the various transitions in the university from time to time in relation to policy procedures, technologies, etc.?
d) Within the university, its governance structures are the responsibilities of stakeholders clearly defined?

Owing to their success in reaching marginalised and unreached learner populations, open universities have attracted the attention of governments, both at the centre and state levels, in terms of their capacity to lend support to achievements of developmental goals. The leadership in open universities has had to rise to the challenges of meeting societal requirements and balance the same with academic priorities of the institution. The challenge has often translated in insightful allocation of responsibilities within and managing accountability under tight deadlines outside.

References

Bureau of Indian Standards (1988). *Quality Standards.* BIS, GOI Publication.

Green and Harvey (1993). *The Essence of Quality Management.* New Delhi: PHI.

Kulandaiswamy, V.C. (2002). *Education for Knowledge Era: Open and Flexible Learning.* New Delhi: Kogan Page.

Perraton, H. (2004). Policy for open and distance learning. In Perraton, Hilary and Lentell, Helen (eds.), *Policy for Open and Distance Learning.* London, New York: RoutledgeFarmer.

Reddy, U.V. (2003). Resources for best practices. In Prasad, V.S. (ed.), *Best Practices in Open and Distance Education.* Hyderabad: BRAOU.

Takwale, R.G. (1996). Managing paradigm shift in parameters and benchmarks for best practices in open and distance education. In Prasad, V.S. (ed.), *Best Practices in Open and Distance Education.* Hyderabad: BRAOU.

SECTION II

DISTANCE TEACHING AND LEARNING RESOURCES

4

Changing Role of Distance Teacher: March Towards Multi-Skilling

Suresh Garg and J.M. Parakh

Introduction

Education is an organic entity; it evolves to meet emerging societal needs. In the agrarian society, education was considered an art and in industrial societies, it became craft-oriented. The emergence of information era in the later part of the second half of 20th century ushered in 'distance education' and classroom instruction changed from craft to technology. In the history of classroom transaction, distance education marks the third stage of development, the first two being the 'Gurukul System' and the 'Classroom System' (Kulandai Swamy, 2002). The UKOU heralded the arrival of technology in imparting education and training at a distance. Distance education has a large socio-economic relevance as it has capacity to impart education to all those who desire to learn and are in pursuit of knowledge.

In India, establishment of the Andhra Pradesh Open University (APOU), now renamed as Dr. B.R. Ambedkar Open University (BRAOU), in 1982 at Hyderabad was a defining moment in the history of development of distance higher education in India. It marked the beginning of the Open Era in the country and played a crucial role for the establishment of Indira Gandhi National Open University (IGNOU) in 1985. IGNOU came into existence by an Act of Parliament in search of a resilient, responsive, innovative and flexible institution to not only take education to the deprived but also work towards expansion and regulation of open system of education in the country. It marked the beginning of a new educational system.

In the initial years, IGNOU was viewed with some skepticism, even ridicule, for its capability to impart quality education. This was essentially because the mode of delivery of education and its objective to relate education for the well-being of our society using technology was a new concept for conventional peers. Therefore, the initial challenge before the distance teacher was to establish identity, esteem and parity of the educational processes as well as the products. This was a Herculean task but the synergy with the conventional system helped remove misplaced apprehensions; the system began to bloom soon and received national character and credibility. By the turn of the 20th century, it experienced exponential growth and major transformations catalysed by revolutionary changes in information and communication technologies. Today, IGNOU is catering to about 1.3 million students in 30 countries through an efficient network of 57 Regional Centres, six sub-Regional Centres, about 1300 Study Centres, three parallel 24 hour TV Channels supported by the Satellite Earth Station on its campus, 17 FM radio stations commissioned all over the country and EduSat supported network of 131 Satellite Interactive Terminals. We are now offering programmes such as community cardiology and nautical sciences which require most sophisticated skills and are now preparing ourselves to impart tele-education to 53 countries of the African Union. Our journey is an unparallel success story in the history of Indian education.

IGNOU is leading a silent revolution in education through the distance mode. As of now, one National Open University, 11 State Open Universities (SOUs) and 106 Correspondence Course/ Distance Education Institutes (CCIs/DEIs) have come into existence. In 2004-05, nearly 2.5 million students were enrolled in the ODL system, which means that one out of every four students in higher education in India was being catered to by this alternative system of education.

In less than four decades, open learning has been universally accepted as a philosophy of education and has graduated through five generations of development—from print-based correspondence model to ICT supported intelligent-flexible model, which facilitates teacher-taught interaction in cyber space. Different media tend to support self-directed, individualised as well as collaborative learning and add new dimensions to the transaction of course curriculum (Horgan, 1998). This has brought the learner and his study room/work place in the centre-stage and moved away from the teacher and the institution of instructions. This transformation obviously implies a change in the role and responsibilities of all those engaged in the design, development and delivery of education at a distance. This is particularly true of a teacher, who should now be seen as a facilitator rather than repository of knowledge, an agent for knowledge management to catalyse creation of wealth for social good through innovation, in addition to being conscience-keeper of society. In this chapter, we have discussed issues related to this paradigm shift.

Distance Teaching Practice

The structures and practices of the ODL system use conventional resources and it is expected that there would be some similarities in the educational provisions and roles of educators in both the systems. However, the industrial nature of operations and evolution of delivery mechanisms in the ODL system have introduced some significant differences; the most important being substitution of the conventional teacher by multiple media instructional package with limited role for face-to-face teacher-learner interaction. Major deviations have been brought in by the underlying philosophy and methodology:

- designing innovative curriculum and developing self-instructional materials by building the teacher into the text for parity, quality and acceptability;
- developing e-content and making live presentations/interactions through tele/videoconferencing; and
- devising delivery mechanisms for ensuring learner-friendliness for diverse groups.

The basic responsibilities of a conventional teacher are:

- teaching through classroom lectures;
- taking practical classes for hands-on training, wherever applicable;
- participate in conduct of examination and evaluation, revision of syllabus, and corporate life of the institution; and
- research for extending the frontiers of knowledge.

A conventional teacher draws knowledge from various sources—Internet, books, lectures/seminars given by reputed experts, and research journals—assimilates it and delivers to students in face-to-face (F2F) situation. Experience shows that not many teachers take research as primary responsibility, except some of those in Post Graduate University Departments and specialised institutions, such as IISc, IITs and IIMs. That is why the net output, i.e. the quality of publications as judged by citations and recognition conferred by international agencies has gone down considerably in recent years. Moreover, as far as classroom teaching is concerned, one feels inconvenienced even at the mention of a change in time honoured routine, which has been without much innovation. 'Chalk and talk' continue to be the mainstay in most of the leading universities; technology continues to stay out of the classroom. Some teachers even use their notes prepared once for lifetime.

On the other hand, a distance teacher is always in a state of flux; s/he has to simultaneously handle different tasks; has to be a teacher, a trainee, a trainer, a public relations person and above all an agent for change. In concrete terms, to discharge his/her responsibility effectively, a distance teacher has to respond to the changes in technology while undertaking development of self-learning materials as well as designing delivery strategies. These involve academic, administrative and technical activities and require such expertise.

When the correspondence courses were introduced in the early sixties, the basic responsibility of a teacher was to get study materials prepared with the help of conventional peers. The system was well appreciated for its cost-effectiveness and enhancing reach during the decade of 1970s. However, print continued to be the only support for learners and unfortunately even it had little input of instructional design and curriculum development. Moreover, no capacity building training was available with the result that the teacher was relegated into the background and ultimately landed up in academic wilderness, participating in activities other than academic. Also, there was not enough learner support; the system completely obscured the requirements of self-learners. The rigidities of conventional system complicated the issue further; it did not encourage deep learning and serious doubts were raised about the quality of education imparted, with the result that the system was considered a weaker option and for the rejects of the conventional system.

With the beginning of open era, technology of education and technology in education began to enter curriculum transaction. This system laid greater emphasis on quality, learner support and blending technology for systemic improvement. For instance, multimedia supported methodology of course writing based in rigorous principles of curriculum development and instructional design, initially developed by UKOU, was adopted by the open universities in India. It appeared simple but was very challenging and time consuming. Some of the illustrative salient features of self-instructional print materials (SIMs) are (Kumar and Garg, 1998):

- a well thought out plan for presentation of the matter;
- clear defining of scope and depth of study;
- use of easy-to-comprehend, simple and conversational language;
- statement of learning objectives and skills to be mastered;
- well structured (self-directed) content, which emphasises concept building;
- logical development of topics starting from basics and known situations;
- provision of an opportunity to learners to relate new ideas/information to what they already know;
- no gaps in explanations so that the text is self-sufficient and a learner does not need much outside support;
- built-in exercises interspersed for self-assessment;
- reinforcements at regular intervals;
- application to life-situations in the surroundings of the learner;
- extensive use of solved examples and diagrams, preferably in colour;
- simulating situations that make learners to think and develop problem-solving habits, i.e. promote learner participation;
- summarisation of important points for quick recapitulation;
- answers for in-text and review exercises; and
- precise and unambiguous advice for the student so as to find their way into the text, skills required for a particular course, pre-requisites and co-requisites, etc.

Obviously producing such materials is lot more difficult task than lecturing in the class. Even gifted and experienced teachers had to be trained in the instructional design methodologies. Moreover, since all study material is open to public scrutiny, the following ingredients are most essential in a distance teacher:

- sound knowledge of the subject;
- excellent command over language and communication skills;
- good understanding of principles of instructional design and pedagogy;
- capacity to work long hours as producing materials needs greater effort than teaching in the class;
- familiarity with copyright/IPR provisions, copy editing, proof reading and other skills in preparation and production of quality materials;
- comprehensive idea of the prospective learners as teacher and taught are at a distance;

- good public relation skills as one has to deal with a variety of experts - artists, course writers, editors, presenters/instructional designers; and
- patience to work in a team and take every one along.

There are some responsibilities which also help distance teachers in discharging their responsibility towards nation building. Highlighting these while delivering the 16th Convocation address at IGNOU, His Excellency, Dr. A.P.J. Abdul Kalam said, "... For participating in the nation building tasks, the capacities required to be built among the students by the faculty members are: the capacity for research and inquiry, the capacity for creativity and innovation, particularly the creative transfer of knowledge, the capacity to use high technology, the capacity for entrepreneurial leadership and the capacity for Moral Leadership."

We therefore have to also aim at character building through our act and expression because human values enhance our capacity to innovate. Moreover, a distance teacher has to do more with less rather than more of the same. We have to create Education India and cater to one billion people with multidimensional heterogeneity at multilevels and encourage innovation in diversity without reinventing the wheel. We have to prepare ourselves for inescapable realities of GATS era. This requires dynamism and as teachers we have to be informed and remain alert.

Search for Identity

Use of multimedia in curriculum delivery was a completely new experience for most distance educators, who came from conventional training system/background. It posed immense challenge in initial years and required well thought out plans to enable them to perform their tasks effectively in the ODL system. Though we in India have kept A/V as an add-on component in view of socio-economic conditions of our learners, unlike UKOU, where it has been integrated into the study materials, yet a necessary condition for all distance educators was to train them in principles of A/V production. Both these aspects demanded fairly exhaustive training, i.e. the teacher was initiated into the system as a trainee. And once programmes were developed and launched, the trainee teacher transformed into master trainer, who oriented academic counsellors highlighting finer requirements of the programme/system; a significant shift—from trainee to content developer to master trainer—occurred in the role of distance teacher. However, since instructional designers, media experts and teachers collectively participate in development of learning materials, a need was felt for defining the status of such staff. The same holds true for the staff engaged in delivery at RCs who were initially appointed as teachers but actually did not participate in developing learning materials.

IGNOU fraternity deliberated the question very seriously for quite some time. The Takwale Committee highlighted this aspect vividly for the first time. It argued, "The role of a teacher in the distance education system is considerably different from that of a teacher in the conventional system. A clear perception of this difference is very essential to understand the range of functions performed by academics in the distance education system. In distance education, the role of an academic cannot be conceived only in the context of the methodology and technique associated with classroom teaching. A distance education teacher is not just a scholar or specialist in his discipline. He has to be distance educator in the first place, while also, being a subject specialist or an experienced professional. This change in the role should get reflected progressively in the qualifications, methods of recruitment and the professional development of the academic in the distance education system" (IGNOU, 1991). It enlisted the academic tasks in detail to be performed by the teachers. These tasks were listed under following sub-headings:

- preparation of courses/programmes;
- maintenance of courses;
- bringing out revised version of courses;
- bringing out revised edition.

"All these tasks are performed by the Schools of Studies to which most of the teachers of the University are assigned", observed the report. "Other Academic Tasks" to be performed in the ODL system were enlisted in the following sub-headings:

- preparation and production of Audio/Video programmes;
- delivery of services to students;
- evaluation of student performance;
- system development;
- programme evaluation;
- planning; and
- other functions such as language editing, translation and library and documentation service.

If we analyse the above tasks, we can see that these involve a mix of academic, professional and/or administrative expertise to varying degrees. For example, recording, editing and duplication of the audio-video is a technical task but the input for the content in any such educational programme is an academic task and can come only from a teacher, which suggests that a good and effective audio/video programme needs team effort. Similarly, programme evaluation involves research and administration and so on. The committee accordingly identified the category of staff with the nature of tasks. This however continued to be opposed by the teacher association, which believes that those associated with design, development and delivery should be treated as teachers. Moreover, there ought to be a provision for the mobility of the teachers in the field to the schools of studies and vice versa in the form of exchange programme, so as to get the feedback and integrate it in the programme development process.

As of now, the University has categoriesed its academic staff as teacher—Professors, Readers and Lecturers — and academics — Regional Directors, Assistant Regional Directors, Analysts, Research Officers, Producers — working with Regional Services Division, Electronic Media Production Centre, Planning and Development Division and Academic Coordination Division. But for producers, the issue seems to be settled as far as management is concerned. However, teacher association has been of the considered opinion that this nomenclature is not strictly as per the requirements of the tasks performed, as also statutory provisions, which envisage that a person imparting instruction, giving guidance and rendering assistance to students pursuing a course are teachers. Since academics at Regional Centres (RCs) perform multifarious activities, including participation in Interactive Radio as well as face-to-face (F2F) counselling, they qualify to be termed teachers. Moreover, their service conditions, mode of recruitment, etc. are also almost the same as those of teachers. The argument that functions and responsibilities should define the category seems to be valid.

In case of producers, the issue remains blurred essentially because high power committees appointed from time to time have submitted contradictory recommendations. On the recommendations of Kidwai Committee (1991), producers were designated as professionals and the cadre of editors was merged with producers, without caring for their professional degrees and the Cadre Review Committee (1999) designated even graphic artists and cameramen as academics. The lack of understanding on the part of the affected constituency has added to the confusion; they wish to avail the benefits applicable to teachers and academics without subjecting themselves to the rigorous provisions guiding their service conditions. Moreover, similar recruitment policy for such staff in the formative years of the University and promotion policy thereafter has also not helped in resolving this issue.

Since IGNOU is mandated to coordinate, promote and regulate distance education system in the country, it has to act as role model for other institutions. It will do the system good to lay down unambiguous guidelines on issues such as appointment of full-time faculty, their role, status, service conditions and work ethics to help SOUs in formulating their policies.

Staff Development Initiatives

The ODL programme delivery is characterised by multiple media instructional package. Sharma and Garg (2005) have described education media strategy employed in India in the past forty years. Their analysis shows that except for Nalanda Open University, all OUs are imparting multimedia-based education of different generations. However, most CCIs are at the first generation and some are now stepping into second generation. It is important to realise that visual medium involves huge costs and has its own nuances. A distance teacher, to coordinate the production of audio-video programmes, has to ensure that the script highlights fundamental concepts and processes which are difficult to explain in F2F mode. Moreover, it is important to avoid duplication and material has to be presented in a manner that it engages the learner actively. Therefore, a teacher is required to make judicious choice of the presenter, format of the programme, visuals to be included, etc. That is, a distance education has to acquire capabilities of a media expert. To facilitate this, IGNOU devised a well thought capacity building strategy and organised training programmes at different levels from time to time for its own as well as other universities; it has succeeded in equipping distance teachers with both essential and desirable skills for production of print as well as A/V materials; structured training has been imparted through orientation programmes, and refresher courses conducted initially by experts from UKOU and subsequently by in-house faculty. A few faculty/professionals were even sent on attachments/secondments abroad. Others acquired these competencies on-the-job.

With rapid developments in information and communication technologies, distance teacher gained access to a wide range of additional media—radio, television, tele/video-conferencing—and tools—CD-ROMs, Internet and satellite supported networks—for synchronous or asynchronous interaction. The adoption and usage of the most appropriate media forced acquisition of new dimensions in the persona of distance teacher. IGNOU has created Inter-University Consortium for Technology Enabled Flexible Education and Development. Several extended duration (three week) national and international workshops, focused on scripting and instructional design for interactive multimedia, web-based teaching, software and authorware and transportation of content to the web, were organised to train teachers in the development of integrated multiple media content. It enabled them to gain skills for strengthening and enriching various existing and upcoming programmes and share experiences with peers in sister organisations in the developing world. It facilitated significant improvement in their communication skills and competencies and enabled them to develop comprehensible and creative content using animation, graphics and other innovative uses of IT. In emerging areas where expertise is limited, a distance teacher has to devise alternative strategies such as video-recorded lectures of eminent educators and upload these in the website. In fact, distance educators are expected to be professionals who can efficiently create and maintain new knowledge infrastructure, enhance productivity and create wealth for the nation to improve the quality of life of its people.

The point we wish to make is that emergence of open era transformed a distance teacher from being a coordinator arranging meetings and somehow putting materials together for print to a far more accomplished and multi-skilled professional, who could create print and multimedia rooted in sound principles of instructional design and curriculum development.

Issues and Concerns

The delivery of education, programme evaluation, planning, human resource development for the ODL system in India has been discussed in focussed papers in this volume and we will not go into these details. However, it is sufficient to mention here that the practices have been as varied as the institutions the world over. For example, for delivery of education, UKOU has established the concept of Regional Centres as academic centres and posted its teachers for counselling and assignment evaluation. The University of South Pacific deputes its teachers for a specified period, without uprooting them permanently, from the main campus to its RCs for organising counselling sessions. IGNOU has created its RCs as academic-administrative entities to act as intermediaries between the Headquarters and Study Centres. The academics posted in the RCs monitor the work of Study Centres and share information with them as well as the learners. There is a strong view that for effective monitoring and learner support, it would be worthwhile to post at least one full time academic per school so as to support programmes of that school. It is an acknowledged fact that regular full-time faculty is important so as to effectively service a course/programme. Therefore, every SOU must appoint teachers on regular pay rolls.

It is true that compared to conventional system, the salary component in the expenditure of an open university is much less, and is partly responsible for cost-effectiveness, it is also important that distance teachers get time for self-study to develop and undertake research rather than being burdened so much that s/he begins to lose initiative. Unless systemic research on success and retentivity of learners and their acceptability by the employers is accorded high priority, the growth of the system could be influenced adversely. Let us examine it quantitatively. At present the total student population in all open universities, including IGNOU, is about 27.3 lakh and the total strength of teachers/academics is 644. It means that, on an average, the student teacher ratio is 4000:1. This ratio was 3400:1 for IGNOU as on March 31, 2005. If we add equivalent of 35,000 part-time conventional peers engaged as counsellors/course writers/editors/experts, this ratio will drop down to about 250:1. Even this is an order of magnitude higher than that in F2F setting. For state open universities, this ratio is about 4600:1 (DEC Database, 2003-04).

In 2004-05, IGNOU with 161 teachers produced 12 new academic programmes, 80 new courses and maintained 89 academic programmes. IGNOU has normally 4 to 8 credit courses. On an average we can say that these 80 new courses are equal to 400 credits (IGNOU Annual Report, 2004-05). It means each teacher was associated with courses worth 2.5 credits, apart from maintaining courses worth 25 credits in a year. A 2.5-credit course entails 10 to 12 units. Writing a unit means that a teacher will have to spend about 100 to 150 hours. As per DEC norms (1999), a teacher should spend 1200 working hours on an average in a year. It means that if a teacher writes materials worth 2.5 credits, there may not be time left for any other work. But we know that everyone maintains courses worth up to 25 credits, which requires an effort equivalent to 240-400 hours. Moreover, every teacher has to participate in the planning and designing of the curriculum, translation, radio counselling and tele-conferencing, which have now become a regular feature due to availability of EduSat. Since we outsource course writing, content and language editing activities, the faculty manages a judicious mix of various tasks. However, there is a lurking fear that some faculty, because of outsourcing and non-initiative, may ultimately reduce to an academic manager, whose primary function would be to launch an academic programme in a given timeframe and maintain it even without requisite expertise in that field. Obviously it is not desirable and needs to be discouraged.

In case of academic staff at RCs, on an average, 5 academic staff, including one Regional Director, supervises 40 study centres (IGNOU Annual Report, 2004-05). It means that one ARD is responsible for monitoring 10 study centres (and serve about 10,000 students) for conduct of counselling and evaluation of assignments of 70 programmes spanning 750 courses. Additional administrative work related with admission, conduct of Term End Examinations, entrance tests, evaluation of project reports and conduct of viva throughout the year leaves very little time for academic work at regional centres in present scenario. It is just impossible for them even to monitor the academic tasks at study centres effectively without being stressed. Similarly, the basic responsibility of the EMPC staff has changed from production of high quality educational A/V programmes to managing Radio/TV telecast; they are busy in commissioning Gyan Vani stations/SITs or organising the tele/videoconferencing/radiocounsellings. These functions require little academic input. The point we wish to make is that due to expansion, all categories of academic staff are shouldering much greater administrative and/or managerial responsibilities. Though essential, it leaves very little time for serious analysis of the impact of these facilities and could be a cause of concern for all, unless addressed immediately.

Table 1 shows the growth of the University since 2000 in brief. When we compare the growth in terms of the number of teachers/academics, we find that in 2000-01, 765 students registered per regular academic/teacher but in 2004-05, 1270 students registered per regular academic/teacher. That is 66% growth has been registered in student strength per teacher/ academic without commensurate growth of faculty.

Table 1: IGNOU in brief

Head	2000-01	2001-02	2002-03	2003-04	2004-05	% of growth
Programmes on offer	50	62	72	89	101	102
Courses on offer	604	673	854	820	900	49
Regional centres	26	44	46	48	48	84.6
Study centres	504	626	765	1098	1251	148.2
Academic Counsellors	20000	20364	20500	30745	35266	76.3
Teachers	151	148	145	164	161	6.6
Academics	106	121	120	112	114	7.5
Technical	168	168	248	181	174	3.5
Administration	875	874	812	893	879	0.45
Students registered	196650	291360	298987	334315	366161	86.1
On Rolls	561167	750873	804271	1187100	1311145	133.6
Awarded degrees	53298	62369	76704	74603	71299	33.7

Source: IGNOU Annual Report, 2004-05.

Our experience reveals that we cannot fulfil our responsibility of course preparation with the help of external Course Writers and experts alone. Our core faculty has to put in a lot of hard work to carry out the responsibility of the development and delivery of useful educational materials to the students. Moreover, such a task cannot be fulfilled only by a Course Coordinator/Course Manager/ Course Director as implied in the TCR. Admittedly, the role of coordination is essential in an open university like ours. Though it has been widely debated, our view is that a good Coordinator should first and foremost be a subject-specialist; otherwise he/she cannot function effectively and coordinate the courses, or direct the course team.

The perception that 'the nature of teaching work in open universities is, in its essence, similar to other institutions of higher learning and specific job requirements of teachers in the Open University System however have relatively larger operational components' may not be fully justifiable. In our view, the core function of the teacher should continue to be development of teaching-learning materials and research; it should at no cost be shadowed by and reduced to coordination and delivery, which are related to logistics. Though it is at variance with the recommendations of Takwale Committee, it has been recognised by DEC (1999) when it decided that 'Every teacher shall perform the core function pertaining to the discipline i.e., dissemination and advancement of knowledge as decided collectively by all the members of the discipline/unit/ division etc. as the case may be.' It further incorporated the collective wisdom of teachers while advising on evolving annual work plans: 'In preparing the work plan of the discipline it would be desirable to integrate a core component of teaching (e.g. unit writing or such other work) in the work plan of each individual member of the discipline.' In quantitative terms, of the total 1200 working hours, about 20% time should be spent on research and self-development. Its faithful implementation should help improve the quality of education. However, the system will require more regular teaching/academic staff at School of Studies, RCs and EMPC and its implications should be examined academically rather than financially/administratively only. It may be worth considering to appoint at least one teacher of school based disciplines as regular staff at RCs so that s/he can not only monitor the counselling and assignments but also participate in it. Also, writing a minimum number of units in a year should be mandatory for every teacher/academic and lecturers/readers at Headquarters should be provided mobility through placement at RCs and vice versa.

Conclusion

A distance educator has to undertake multifarious activities which require inter-personal, communication and organisational skills, apart from proactive attitude towards change. The emergence of open era has, through training, enabled us to create far greater accomplished and multi-skilled distance teachers who can teach using latest methodologies and technologies. However, systemic research remains an area of serious concern and we need to address it adequately so that the distance teacher is not left behind as far as contribution to new knowledge is concerned.

References

Annual Reports of IGNOU from 2000-01 to 2004-05.

DEC (1999). *Work Norms for Teachers of Open Universities*. Distance Education Council, IGNOU.

DEC-Database (2003-2004). *Information Base on Distance Higher Education in India*. IGNOU.

Horgan, B. (1998). Transforming Higher Education using Information Technology: First Step. Available: http://horizon.unc.edu/TS/default.asp/show=article &id=490.

IGNOU (1991) *28th Meeting of the Board of Management*. IGNOU.

IGNOU (1999). *Cadre Review Committee for Electronic Media Production Centre*. IGNOU.

Kalam, A.P.J. (2005). *16th IGNOU Convocation Address delivered on 5th March*. IGNOU: New Delhi.

Kidwai, A.J. (1991) *Norms Committee Report on Communication Division*. IGNOU.

Kulandai Swamy, V.C. (2002). Open and distance learning and concerns of access and equity. In Dikshit, H.P. et al. (eds.), *Access & Equity: Challenges for Open and Distance Learning*. New Delhi: Kogan Page.

Kumar, N. and Garg, S. (1998). Undergraduate science textbooks: Why and how to improve them? *Staff and Educational Development International*, 2(1), 49-61.

Sharma, R.C. and Garg, S. (2005). Educational media strategy at Indira Gandhi National Open University, India. In Reddy, U. and Mishra, S. (eds.), *Perspectives on Distance Education: Educational Media in Asia*.Vancouver: COL.

Professor Suresh Garg is Pro-Vice Chancellor, Indira Gandhi National Open University, New Delhi.
Email: scgarg@ignou.ac.in

Professor J.M. Parakh is Director, School of Humanities, Indira Gandhi National Open University, New Delhi.
Email: jmparakh@ignou.ac.in

5

Profile of Distance Learners

Manjulika Srivastava and N.S. Ramegowda

Introduction

The perceived need for an alternative system of education that had given to enhance equitable access to higher education to the eligible age group, led to the concept of distance education in India in 1961. At that time the objectives were to provide cost-effective education to empower the youth to derive benefits of the education facilities to those who had missed the opportunity to acquire knowledge, skill and training for social and economic reasons (Government of India, 1963). Thus, the first distance education institutions came into existence in the 1960s, as sub-systems within conventional universities. Encouraged by their success, more conventional universities transformed themselves into dual-mode universities (DMUs), offering conventional classroom based education as well as correspondence education. It was in the third decade that the open university (OU) system was adopted with the establishment of Andhra Pradesh Open University (in 1982), later renamed as Dr. B R Ambedkar Open University; and the Indira Gandhi National Open University (in 1985). The beginning of the OU system significantly changed the paradigm of higher education. There was a shift in the emphasis from expanding the conventional education system to democratizing higher education by providing access to large segments of the population; particularly the disadvantaged groups, such as those living in remote and rural areas, including working people, women, scheduled caste and scheduled tribes and other adults who wished to acquire and upgrade their knowledge and skills. The OUs, with their flexibility, provided a means for continuing and lifelong education for enriching the lives of the people. In any case the advantages of being a distance learner were many. It appealed to those who were unable or unwilling to attend an educational institution on a regular, scheduled basis.

It also offered opportunities to those in remote locations who did not have access to more conventional forms of educational provision. Thus, what began as an alternative form of education is now becoming an important component of mainstream education

Spatial Distribution of Distance Education (DE) Institutions

DE has experienced dramatic growth during the four decades of its existence. There were barely 10 DE institutions in 1972. A decade later there were 22 in 1981, of which majority were in the northern region (45.5%) and the least in the eastern region, only one (4.5%). The situation had changed in the 1990s.The southern region dominated with 16 institutions as compared to the northern region which was reduced to 13 institutions, 8 in central and western regions and 4 in the eastern region. In 2003-04 the southern region continued to dominate with 42 institutions followed by 31in the northern region, 22 in the central and western regions and 20 in the eastern region. In fact the southern and northern regions dominate as together they account for 63.5% of the total number of institutions in the country (Table 1).

Reasons for the concentration of DE institutions across southern and northern Regions could be the following:

- high literacy (particularly in the Southern States and in the State of Delhi and all Union Territories) and also due to a large number of feeder secondary education institutions;
- lesser number of institutions offering higher education and therefore availability of limited number of seats;
- awareness about the value for education particularly higher education.

Table 1: Spatial distribution of distance education institutions in India

	1981	1992	2003-04
Southern region			
Andhra Pradesh.	4	6*	15*
Karnataka	1	2	8*
Kerala	1	2	4
Tamil Nadu	2	6	15*
Subtotal	8	16	42 (34.84 %)
Northern region			
Delhi	1	2*	3*
Haryana	-	2	3
Himachal Pradesh	1	1	1
Jammu & Kashmir	2	2	2
Punjab	2	2	6
Rajasthan	2	1*	6*

Uttar Pradesh	2	3	7*
Uttranchal	-	-	3
Subtotal	10	13	31 (39.03 %)
Central & western region			
M.P.	1	1*	9*
Maharasthra	2	5*	8*
Gujarat	-	1*	2*
Chattisgarth	-	-	1
Goa	-	-	1
Jharkhand	-	-	1
Subtotal	3	8	22 (22.54 %)
Eastern region			
Bihar	-	2*	5*
Orissa	1	2	6
W. Bengal	-	-	5*
Assam	-	-	2
Tripura	-	-	1
Meghalaya	-	-	1
Subtotal	1	4	20 (3.59 %)
Grand Total	**22**	**41**	**115 (100 %)**

* idicates Open Universities

Figures given in parenthesis indicate the distribution of student enrolment (%)

Source: Compiled by Manjulika Srivastava from: Manjulika and Reddy (1996) and DEC (2004).

Growth of Student Enrolment in Distance Education

During the first decade or so (1962-75) the student enrolment increased from 1112 students in 1962 to 64210 students in 1975-76 (UGC, 1990). It substantially increased during the next two decades to 355090 students in 1985-86 and 803176 in 1994-95 (Manjulika and Reddy, 1996). At the turn of the century, in 1999-2000, there were 1580275 students studying through distance mode that has further gone up to 2.8 million students in 2003-04. In the words of Prof. H.P. Dikshit's, Vice Chancellor, IGNOU that this is "a silent revolution in education" happening through distance mode (Dikshit, 2005. p4). It is heartening to note that the share of DE in the total enrolment in higher education has increased from 0.15 % in 1962-63 to 2.6 % in 1975-76 and about 24 % in 2005 (Manjulika and Reddy, 1996; Dikshit, 2005). It may also be noted that the number of institutions offering DE programmes/ courses has also multiplied. For details refer Tables 1 and 2.

In 1987-88 there were 3 OUs and 50569 students enrolled at these OUs which was 9.3% of the total enrolment in DE in the country. In 1991-92 the number of OUs went up to 5 and the enrolment to 116957 which was 12.6% of the total enrolment in DE. Today (2003-04), it is 32%

of the total enrolment in DE and 7%of the total enrolment in higher education in the country (Refer Table 2). IGNOU alone accounted for 37.5% of the total enrolment of all OUs put together. Being OUs, they follow a flexible policy with regard to entry and exit and therefore attract such large numbers. Also the programmes they offer are more suited to the requirements of the changing times that are more responsive to industrial demands and societal needs or in other words to the 'world of work' Their unique design of materials and planned instruction through multiple media and convenient learner support system, are other factors that have contributed to the popularity of this system of education.

With the decision of the Central Advisory Board on Education to set up one OU in every state a number of OUs are already in the pipeline. Enrolment in DE would further increase and it would not be difficult to meet the 40% mark as envisaged by the Planning Commission during the Tenth Plan period (Government of India, 2002).

Table 2: Student enrolment in DE system vs. conventional education system

Year	Conventional system	DE system (OUs + DMUs)	Share of OUs in total enrolment in DE	Share of OUs in total enrolment in HE
1962-63	752095 (99.85%)	1112 (0.15 %)	NIL	-
1967-68	137026 (99.38 %)	8577 (0.62 %)	NIL	-
1977-78	2564972 (95.1 %)	119163 (4.9 %)	NIL	-
1987-88	3910828 (90.7 %)	402720 (9.3 %)	50569 (12.6 %)	1.2 %
1991-92	4611107 (87.4 %)	664572 (12.6 %)	116957 (17.6 %)	2.2 %
1994-95	5310753 (86.84 %)	803176 (13.14 %)	200939 (28.0 %)	3.3 %
2003-04	9953506*	2800000* (22.0 %)	892745 (32.0 %)	7.0 %

* Estimated

Source: Compiled by Manjulika Srivastava, from: DEC (1995), DEC (2004), UGC (2005), UGC (1968) and Manjulika and Reddy (1996).

In 2003-04, of the total 115 institutions, 11 were OUs and the remaining 104 DMUs. However, only 4 OUs were enrolling more than 100000 students per year whereas the remaining OUs were enrolling less than 20000 students annually. These OUs with such huge annual intakes include IGNOU, followed by MPBOU in Madhya Pradesh, BRAOU in Andhra Pradesh and YCMOU in Maharashtra.

In the case of DMUs, there were only 5 DMUs that had an annual enrolment of over 45000 students in 2003-04. Interestingly majority of these DMUs are located in the southern state of

Tamil Nadu, namely Annamalai University and Madras University; followed by Delhi University at Delhi, Andhra University in Andhra Pradesh; Mumbai University in Maharashtra and Maharishi Dayanand University in Haryana.

Stage-wise enrolment in DE

The enrolment position in the academic year 2003-04 reveals that the majority of the distance learners were enrolled at the under graduate (UG) level (54.2%); 29.2% at the post-graduate (PG) level; 16% in diplomas and certificates and the remaining 0.6% in research progammes. Refer Table 3.

Table 3: Stage wise enrolment in DE 2003-04 (%)

	Research	PG level	UG level	Diploma	Certificate and others
OUs	0.06	13.99	55.36	7.83	22.76
DMUs	1.07	41.88	53.18	3.02	0.85
Total	**0.6**	**29.2**	**54.2**	**16.0***	

Source: Compiled by Manjulika Srivastava from: DEC (2004); *diploma and certificate put together.

For the purpose of analysis, 4 OUs that had enrolled more than 100000 distance learners and 6 DMUs with more than 45000 students in the year 2003-04 are being considered. These institutions not only represent the major DE institutions but also account for majority of students studying through distance mode in this country.

Data presented in Table 4 reveals that 45% of the learners of the four mega OUs were enrolled at the UG level. For example at IGNOU 47.4% and YCMOU 46.6% of the learners were enrolled in UG programmes in 2003-04. At BRAOU, where there are no certificate programmes, therefore 95.7% were enrolled in UG programmes that too mainly traditional programmes like Bachelor of Arts (BA), Bachelor of Commerce (BCom) and Bachelor of Science (BSc). This is equally true of IGNOU, YCMOU and MPBOU. Refer Table 4 for details.

Table 4: Stage-wise distribution of distance learners enrolled at mega OUs in 2003-04 (%)

	IGNOU	BRAOU	YCMOU	MPBOU
Research / Degrees	NA	0.008	0.1	0.01
PG Professional / Technical	18.4	4	2.1	7.2
PG General	7.6		0.3	
UG Professional / Technical	16.0	95.7	3.0	32.8
UG General	31.4		43.6	

Diploma	8.3	0.3	14.1	13.6
Certificate	18.2	-	36.8	46.4
Others	0.02			

Source: Compiled by Manjulika Srivastava from: DEC (2004)

Faculty (discipline-wise) enrolment in DE

In 2003-04, the bulk of the learners enrolled at OUs were mostly in UG level programmes, who were mostly pursuing general programmes like BA and BCom. Data presented in Table 5 reveals that 48% of the students at YCMOU; 38.8% at BRAOU; 23.7% at MPBOU and 19% at IGNOU were enrolled in the BA and BCom programmes. Another 7.7% at IGNOU and 19.7% at YCMOU were enrolled in the preparatory programme leading to BA/B.Com which is a compulsory programme for those who have no formal qualification. Therefore the figure for IGNOU would be 25.3% and for YCMOU 67.7%. More than 5000 students of MPBOU were pursuing B Ed (General) and B Ed (Special Education). At IGNOU too the number was more than 6000 which could have been much more but for the restrictions placed on the number of students to be enrolled at each Study Centre by National Council for Teacher Education. Despite there is a huge demand for school teachers all over the country.

MPBOU is the only OU that is offering a large number of programmes at the PG level but the enrolment in these programmes was hardly 7.2% and at BRAOU it was 4% (pursuing general PG level programmes) and 2.4% at YCMOU (majority pursuing MBA). On the other hand IGNOU had 26% students enrolled at the PG level and majority of them were pursuing MBA and MCA programmes. (Refer Table 4)

Both YCMOU and MPBHOU had a fairly large percentage of their learners enrolled in diplomas (14.1% and 13.6% respectively) and even larger percentage in certificate programmes (36.8% and 46.4% respectively) as compared to IGNOU (8.3% in diploma programmes and 18.2% in certificate programmes).

YCMOU is mostly offering certificate level programmes in computer operations and IT skills (13%) and preparatory programme (19.7%). At MPBOU they were enrolled for CLASS/CLAP/BCCO (41.2 %). At the diploma level only agriculture programmes offered by YCMOU attracted 6 % of the learners. In 2003-04 less than 1% were enrolled in research programmes, like M. Phil and Ph.D, which are offered by 7 out of 11 OUs.

However, there is a noticeable shift in the overall enrolment in programmes that are more closely linked to the 'world of work' i.e., professional development programmes. Majority of the learners enrolled at OUs in UG level programmes reflects the Indian mindset of being a graduate which is a stepping stone to acquiring a "white collar" status. Interestingly even those pursuing professional vocations from conventional universities, for example catering and hotel management, besides acquiring a diploma also want to acquire a BA or a B Com degree in order to earn the respectability that a UG level degree enjoys in the Indian society.

Table 5: Faculty wise distribution of students at mega OUs in programmes with more than 5000 enrolment

OUs	IGNOU		BRAOU	YCMOU	MPBOU
	2004-05	2003-04	2003-04	2003-04	2003-04
PG level					
Management Programme	45069 (12.3%)	38469 (11.5%)	1640 (23.30%)	-	-
MCA	48596 (13.3%)	58224 (17.4%)	-	-	-
MA (Eng.)	10802 (3%)	22896 (6.8%)	-	-	-
UG level					
BA	58942 (16.0%)	51946 (15.5%)	73719 (38.8%)	41095 (40.0%)	36516 (19%)
B Com	11505 (3.1%)	10353 (3.1%)	-	8184 (8.8%)	9026 (4.7%)
B Sc	10152 (2.8%)	8911 (2.7%)	-	-	21109 (11%)
BCA	38473 (10.57%)	44098 (13.2%)	-	-	-
BPP	23189 (6.3%)	25930 (7.75%)	-	20268 (19.7%)	-
BHA	7665 (2.1%)		-	-	-
B.Ed. (general & special education)	8739 (2.4%)	6865 (2.1%)	-	-	5492 (2.85%)
Diploma					
Agriculture	-	-	-	6201 (6%)	-
Certificate					
CIC / Computer Skills (13.0%)	10571 (3%)	13153 (4%)	-	13345	-
CLASS / CLAP /	-	-	-	-	79244 (41.2%)
BCCO / CIC / CTPM	5170 (1. 4%)	-	-	-	-
CIG	6022 (1.7%)	-	-	-	-
TOTAL	366161 (100%)	334415 (100%)	190230 (100%)	102642 (100%)	192230 (100%)

Compiled by: Manjulika Srivastava from: DEC (2004)

General demographics of Indian distance learners

The profile of distance learners enrolled in the DE system in 2003-04 has been presented in Table 6. The details are as follows:

- 48.75% were women as compared to 40.22% women in the conventional system (UGC, 2004). Female enrolment was higher at OUs (52.7%) as compared to DMUs (44.8%); it was particularly so at some OUs such as KSOU (52.15%), NSOU (44.82%), MPBOU (31.9%) etc.
- 16.3% of the learners were residing in rural areas. At some OUs the percentage of rural students was very high. For example at MPBOU it was 57.59%, NOU 55.18%, NSOU 50.65%, TNOU 50.21%, BAOU 49.11% and YCMOU 47.04%.
- 31.6% of the learners enrolled in the ODL system belonged to the marginalized groups of society namely Scheduled Castes (8.8%), Scheduled Tribes (3.9%) and OBC (18.9%). For an educational mode that is barely 4 decades old, this enrolment pattern is very encouraging. It also proves that the ODL system has succeeded in democratizing educational opportunities to large segment of the population, specially the deprived segments such as women, Scheduled Castes, Scheduled Tribes, OBC, people residing in rural areas, etc.

Table 6: Profile of students enrolled in the DE system (%) (2003-04)

	Male	Female	Urban	Rural	General	SC	ST	OBC	PH
DMUs	55.2	44.8	90.8	9.2	59.6	8	1.2	23.2	0.25
OUS	47.3	52.7	76.6	23.3	75.2	7.6	4.6	12.6	NA
Total	51.25	48.75	83.7	16.3	68.4	8.8	3.9	18.9	-

Compiled by Manjulika Srivastava from: DEC (2004)

Profile of distance learners enrolled at OUs

The profile of learners enrolled at the mega OUs in 2003-04 reveals the following. (Refer Tables 7, 8 and 9)

Table 7: Profile of distance learners enrolled at OUs (2003-04)

Total	IGNOU	YCMOU	MPBOU	BRAOU	KSOU	NSOU	BAOU	TNOU	UPRTOU	VMOU	NOU
Female (52.7)	37.40	33.02	39.97	34.55	52.15	44.82	32.32	38.79	27.53	23.57	24.2
Rural (23.3)	NA	47.04	57.59	42.25	NA	50.65	49.11	49.78	42.26	NA	55.18
SC (7.6)	6.70	14.88	11.86	21.31	NA	20.1	12.36	13.85	10.94	10.58	8.69

ST (4.6)	5.20	4.85	9.86	6.14	NA	4.75	5.57	0.65	0.03	6.21	3.15
OBC (12.6)	1.60	25.98	29.93	30.65	NA	-		71.77	34.38	-	38.78
PH (NA)	9.30	NA	0.007	0.006	NA	-	26.5	0.05	-	-	-

Source: Compiled by Manjulika Srivastava from: DEC (2004)

Female enrolment

There has been an increase in female enrolment absolute numbers as well as in terms of percentage from 33.5 % in 1991-92 to 52.7% in 2003-04. (Manjulika and Reddy, 1996; DEC, 2004). Women accounted for 37 % at IGNOU, almost 40 % at MPBOU and 33 % at YCMOU.

- At the PG level women were mostly enrolled in Masters of Arts, Masters of Commerce, and Masters in Library Sciences.
- At the UG level, the most popular programmes were BA, B Ed, BLIS and BSc(N).
- The most popular diploma programmes among women were those related to education, early childhood care and education, food and nutrition and health education, maternity and child health, or areas like interior design, fashion design and translation.
- Certificate level programmes were again pertaining to the same disciplines mentioned above under diplomas. Although at YCMOU, Certificate in computing and IT skills had attracted the school leaving women.
- Comparatively, the percentage of women was very low in programmes like MSc, MSc (Agriculture), MBA at the PG level, BCA, B Sc, Bachelor of Technology, Bachelor of Horticulture, Bachelor of Information Technology at the UG level, Diplomas in Marketing / Financial Management, Printing Technology, Agriculture Sciences, Geriatric Medicine, Environmental Studies and Journalism, and Certificate programme in Forestry Management. Even at the research degree level it was rather low.
- Majority of the women had opted for traditional subjects such as Arts, Humanities, Education, Nursing, Food and Nutrition, Childhood Care, Maternal and Child Health etc., that have always attracted women, as an extension of their traditional role of nurturing mother, sister or wife or that of a teacher. Science and Technology, Agriculture, and Management programmes were still mainly the preserve of men. However, Computer programmes and vocational courses are attracting women, which is an indication of the changing times and also of the fact that to survive in the 21st century women too have to be equipped with tools of the 21st century.

Rural enrolment

OUs were set up to democratize higher education to large segments of the population. State OUs like YCMOU and MPBOU have made inroads into the interiors. YCMOU boasts of 47 % and MPBOU 57. 6 % enrolment of students living in rural areas YCMOU is offering a variety of agriculture based programmes that has undoubtedly attracted rural learners.

Table 8: Programmes that attract more women at mega OUs (2003-04)

Overall % of Women	**IGNOU (37.4%) Women/Total**	**BRAOUNA NA Women/Total**	**YCMOU (33.02%) Women/Total**	**MPBOU (39.97%) Women/Total**
PG level programmes				
MBA	-	377/1640 (22.99%)	-	299/489 (61.1%)
MCA	3503 / 9951 (35.2%)	-	-	199/ 447 (44.5%)
MA	4068 / 8737 (46.6%)	1588 / 4138 (38.4%)	-	125 / 274 (45.6%)
M Com	1189 / 2518 (47.2%)	163 /396 (41.2 %)	-	18 / 39 (46.2%)
M Ed	-	-	94 / 269 (35%)	-
MLIS	1205 / 1806 (66.7%)	-	-	-
UG level				
BA	-	25757 / 73719 (34.9%)	15592 / 41095 (37.9%)	-
B Ed	2864 / 6968 (41.1%)	-	586 / 1574 (37.2%) (SC)(53.2%)	441 / 1000 (Gen) (44%) 2389 / 4492
BLIS	2299 / 3706 (62%)	138 / 346 (39.7 %)	405 / 766 (52.9%)	9 / 19 (47.4%)
B Sc (N)	1309/1455 (90%)	-	-	190 /190 (100%)
Diplomas				
PGDHE	218 / 417 (52.2%)	-	-	-
PGDMCH	310 / 578 (53.6%)	-	-	43 /994 (45.7%)
PGDT	279 / 544 (51.3%)	-	-	-
DNHE	1137 / 1770 (64.2%)	-	-	19 / 55 (34.5%)
DECE	2322 / 2421 (95.9%)	-	-	-
Diploma in Interior Design	-	-	16 / 35 (45.7%)	-

DPE	48 / 71 (67.6%)	-	-	-
DCE	534 / 981 (54.4%)	-	-	-
Diploma in Fashion Design	-	-	6 / 6 (100%)	-
Certificate programmes				
Cert. in Women's Empowerment	105 / 133 (78.9%)	-	-	-
CFN	855 / 1315 (65%)	-	-	-
CNCC	536 / 761 (74.4%)	-	-	-
CPE	8 / 13 (61.5%)	-	-	-
Preparatory programme	-	-	7059 / 20268 (34.8%)	-
Cert. in Computing	-	-	818 / 1778 (46%)	-
School learning IT skills	-	-	3408 / 8145 (41.8%)	-
Vocational courses	-	-	761 / 1684 (45.2%)	-

Figures in parenthesis denote the percentage of women enrolment to total enrolment
Source: Compiled by Manjulika Srivastava from DEC (2004).

Enrolment of the weaker sections

In terms of reaching out to the deprived sections like Scheduled Castes (SC), Scheduled Tribes (ST), Other Backward Castes (OBC) and the Physically Handicapped (OPH) the OUS have made a dent. At MPBOU, the number was more than the general category learners i.e., around 52%, it was 46% at YCMOU and 33% at IGNOU.

Table 9: Programmes with lesser women enrolled at OUs

	IGNOU	**BRAOU**	**YCMOU**	**MPBOU**
PG level				
MBA	3966 / 18094 (21.9%)	377 / 1640 (22.99%)	146 / 1578 (17%)	-
M Sc	-	-	4 / 60 (6.7%)	-
M Sc (Agriculture)	-	-	4 / 60 (6.7%)	-

UG level				
BCA	2144 / 11718 (18.2%)	-	-	-
B Sc	-	-	-	5161 / 21109 (24.4%)
B of Technology	55 / 751 (7.3%)	-	3 / 252 (1.2%)	-
B of Horticulture	-	-	27 / 253 (10.7%)	-
BIT	-	-	40 / 183 (21.9%)	-
Diplomas				
PG Dip in Geriatric Medicine	49 / 243 (20.1%)	-	-	-
PG Dip in Environmental Studies	-	6 / 24 (25%)	-	-
Dip in Computer Hardware	-	-	228 / 2871 (7.9%)	-
PG Dip in Business Finance and Marketing	-	2 / 25 (8%)	193 / 914 (21.1%)	-
Dip in Printing Technology	-	-	0/74 (0 %)	-
Dip in Agriculture Science	-	-	577 / 6200 (9.3%)	-
Research degrees				
M Phil	-	-	18 / 82 (22%)	-
Ph D	-	-	2 / 14 (14.3%)	-
Certificate level programmes				
CPFM	23 / 107 (21.5%)	-	-	-

Figures given in the parenthesis denote the percentage of women enrolment to total enrolment

Source: Compiled by Manjulika Srivastava from DEC (2004).

Profile of learners enrolled at DMUs

For the purpose of analysis, 6 DMUs (out of 104 that accounted for 57.3 % of the total enrolled in all DMUs put together) were taken into consideration (DEC. 2004). Only those DMUs that had an annual intake of more than 45000 students were selected as the majority of the DMUs had less than 10000 students and some of them less than 1000 and very few of them even less than 100. The profile of the learners enrolled at the selected 6 DMUs, namely University of

Delhi (Delhi), Madras University (Tamil Nadu), Andhra University (Andhra Pradesh), Annamalai University (Tamil Nadu), Mumbai University (Maharashtra) and Maharshi Dayanand University (Haryana) is as follows. (Refer Tables 10 and 11 for details)

Table 10: Stage wise distribution of distance learners enrolled at DMUs (with over 50,000 students) 2003-04

	University of Delhi	Andhra University	Madras University	Annamalai University	Mumbai University	MD University
Research	-	-	0.42	2.58	-	-
PG Prog	-	-	8.70	2.83	-	37.19
PG Gen	2.70	31.67	40.20	47.79	41.43	24.75
UG Prog	-	1.14	1.56	-	-	-
UG Gen	97.30	66.23	48.25	40.10	58.12	38.06
Dip	-	0.89	0.27	5.85	0.45	-
Cert	-	0.07	0.60	0.85	-	-
Others	-	-	-	-	-	-

Source: Compiled by Manjulika Srivastava from: DEC (2004)

- Majority of the learners were enrolled for the UG level and in traditional programmes like BA and BCom.
- Some DMUs like Annamalai University, Madras University and Mumbai University had a sizable enrolment in PG programmes. In fact at Annamalai University and Maharshi Dayanand (MD) University there were more students enrolled at the PG level than at UG level. For example, at Annamalai University, there were 50.62 % students at the PG level as compared to 40.0 % at the UG level. At MD University, there were 61.94 % at the PG students and 38.04 % UG students. At Madras University too the distribution is almost 50-50; 49.81 % at the UG level and 48.90 % at the PG level. Due to restricted number of seats available at the PG level in conventional universities, their Directorates of DE absorb the overflow, i.e., those who could not get admission into the regular PG level programme opts for the distance education mode.
- The enrolment in research degrees, diploma and certificate level programmes, is very minuscule. This is true for research degree programmes across all universities in the country as a very small percentage actually go for the highest degrees or for that matter are eligible for pursuing them. However, in the case of certificates and diplomas the number is small as the courses are mainly pertaining to languages specially regional languages and off beat programmes like Automation Technology, Industrial Safety, Printing, Pollution Control, etc., that are too specialised in nature. Therefore they have a limited clientele. Refer Table 10.

- Data presented in Table 11 reveals that the percentage of women was comparatively high. In some DMUs there were more women students enrolled than men, such as: Madras University (50.74 %) and Mumbai University (51.62 %).
- The data pertaining to urban and rural learners was not available at most DMUs except for MD University where the urban students dominated with 85.12 %.

Table 11: Profile of learners enrolled at DMUs with over 50000 students (2003-04)

	University of Delhi	Madras University	Andhra University	Anamalai University	Mumbai University	Maharshi Dayanand University	
Male	52.55	49.26	56.16	59.23	48.38	52.03	Grand Total
Female	47.45	50.74	43.84	40.77	51.62	47.97	
Urban	NA	NA	NA	NA	NA	85.12	
Rural	NA	NA	NA	NA	NA	14.88	
General	NA	27.76	48.28	0	84.72	65.22	
SC	NA	12.37	11.71	11.48	8.19	10.88	
ST	NA	0.38	3.85	1.21	1.30	1.55	
OBC	NA	58.41	36.16	87.31	5.79	21.65	
PH	NA	1.09	NA	NA	NA	0.80	
Total Enrolled	141649	47502	73923	98963	55558	46514	469109

Source: Compiled by Manjulika Srivastava from: DEC (2004)

- In the case of the marginalized groups like Scheduled Castes (SC), Scheduled Tribes (ST), Other Backward Castes (OBC) and Physically Handicapped (PH), some DMUs like Madras University have more OBC students (58.41%) as compared to the general category (27.76%), SC (12.37%) and ST (0.38%). Another DMU of Tamil Nadu boasts of the same, namely Annamalai University which has: 87.31% OBC, 11.48% SC, 1.12% ST and none belonging to the General Category of students. At Andhra University the ratio is almost 50:50, 36.10% OBC, 11.71% SC and 3.85% ST as compared to 48.28% general category. In the Northern part of the country like MD University the general category dominated with 65.22 % general category students. At Mumbai University too 84.72% belonged to the general category.
- The data pertaining to physically challenged was not available at most of the DMUs except for MD University where the number was really minuscule (0.80%).

Conclusion

Both OUs and DMUs are attracting large numbers of students. OUs because of their flexibility and provision for continuing and lifelong education and relevance of the programmes to the world of work. DMUs are mainly providing an alternative system to absorb the overflow from the conventional system. The conventional system because of its class room based instruction can offer only limited seats. Also the number of universities is limited. The rising literacy rate is witnessing a beeline of students opting for higher education. DE seems to be the only answer. Moreover, client satisfaction based education is gaining more currency today which the conventional universities are unable to provide. Only OUs are better suited to meet the demands of changing times. In the words of our President A.P.J. Abdul Kalam (2004) (University News, 2004) "Our education system should highlight the importance of entrepreneurship and develop such skills in the students right from the college stage, which will provide them opportunities of creativity, freedom and ability to generate wealth through setting up ventures producing marketable products." OUs are making this possible by introducing such programmes and imparting training in productive skills that are relevant to the world of work. The last decade has seen a phenomenal growth in the enrolment of distance learners as DE institutions particularly OUs have joined the bandwagon to meet the increasing demand for such type of education.

References

DEC (1995). *Open Universities in India, Academic Programmes*. New Delhi: DEC, IGNOU.

DEC (2001). *Open Universities in India*. New Delhi, DEC, IGNOU.

DEC (2004). *Information Base on Distance Higher Education in India*. New Delhi: DEC, IGNOU.

Dikshit, H.P. (2005). *Vice Chancellor's Report, 16th IGNOU Convocation*. March, New Delhi: IGNOU.

Government of India (1963). *Expert Committee Report on Correspondence Courses and Evening Colleges*. New Delhi: Ministry of Education.

Government of India (2002). *Tenth Five Year Plan*. New Delhi : Planning Commission.

Kalam, Abdul A.P.J. (2004). Challenges for a knowledge society. *University News*, 42(37), 16-18.

Manjulika, S. and Reddy, Venugopal (1996). *Distance Education in India: A Model for Developing Countries*. New Delhi: Vikas Publishing House Pvt. Ltd.

UGC (1968). *UGC Annual Report: 1967-68*. New Delhi: UGC.

UGC (1990). *Proceedings of Conference of Vice Chancellors, Ahmedabad*. New Delhi: UGC.

UGC (1992). *UGC Statistics*. Unpublished Document, New Delhi: UGC.

UGC (2005, 1993). *UGC Annual Report, 2003-04*. New Delhi: UGC.

Dr. Manjulika Srivastava is Reader, Staff Training and Research Institute of Distance Education, Indira Gandhi National Open University, New Delhi.
Email: smanjulika@hotmail.com

Professor N.S. Ramegowda recently retired as Vice Chancellor, Karnataka State Open University, Mysore.

6

Taking Education to the Disadvantaged: IGNOU Experience in KBK Region

Kameshwari Moorthy

Introduction

IGNOU, established in 1985, offered only two academic programmes with an enrolment of 4528 in 1987, and today is a mega university with 1.3 million learners and 108 programmes on offer. The IGNOU Act mentions that one of the objects of the University is to provide not only higher education to large sections of the population, but particularly to the disadvantaged segments of the society. The 'Vision' of IGNOU (www.ignou.ac.in) states: "IGNOU, the National Resource Centre for ODL with international recognition and presence shall provide seamless access to sustainable and learner-centric quality education, skill upgradation and training to all by using innovative technologies and methodologies and ensuring convergence of existing systems for massive human resources required for promoting integrated national development and global understanding". The 'Mission' of IGNOU is to advance frontiers of knowledge and promote its dissemination through sustainable ODL systems seamlessly accessible to all, including hitherto unreached, from among whom the leaders and innovators of tomorrow will emerge, the University shall (among others) (www.ignou.ac.in):

- provide an intelligent flexible system of education to meet the challenges of access and equity and work towards the development of knowledge society; and
- take education to the hitherto unreached and promote community participation for local development through life-coping skills.

Learner support centres in IGNOU, as in any ODL institution, play an important role in bridging the gap between the distance learners and the system by providing support services. It is here that the learners interact with the university through interaction with academic counsellors and peers. There are various types of learner support centres established by IGNOU, depending upon on the programmes on offer, need of the learners, geographic representation and, type and location of the host institutions. These are: Regular Study Centre, Recognised Study Centres, Programme Study Centres, Special Study Centres etc. The Special Study Centres are established to cater to learners who may be from groups such as minorities, women, prisons, differently-abled, or residents of rural and remote areas.

Provision of access to educational resources and equity to the learners is a prime concern in the university's operation and considerable and appreciable efforts have been made in this regard. This is heartening, but one must also consider whether the university reaches out to the unreached. By mid-August 2005, there were 1300 total number of study centres in the country, including all the other types of centres noted above. Among these, around 200 are Special Study Centres of IGNOU. The highest number of special study centres, i.e. 35, are in the state of Orissa. These are located in remote and rural areas to reach out to the disadvantaged population. This paper analyses the learner profile and distance learning in the most disadvantaged region in the state Orissa and probably in the country.

KBK (Kalahandi, Bolangir and Koraput) Region

Orissa is a state with 30 districts. Initially, the districts of Kalahandi, Bolangir and Koraput, situated in the southern and western parts of Orissa, comprised the KBK region. This was reorganized in 1992-93 to include another five districts. The KBK region today comprises eight districts: Kalahandi, Nuapada, Bolangir, Sonepur, Koraput, Nabarangpura, Malkangiri and Rayagada, with a total of 12104 villages. The KBK region has become the centre of attention of the Goverment of India owing to the high levels of poverty and consequent adverse effects on the quality of living conditions of its people.

Orissa occupies the tenth position among all states in India in terms of territory (1.56 lakh sq. kms). The state accounts for 4.74% of India's landmass and has a population of 36.71m people (Govt. of India, 2001), which is 3.57% of the country's population. The backwardness of the state is evident from some of the socio economic development indicators. The per-capita income in Orissa was Rs.9162 during 1999-2000 against the national per-capita income of Rs.16047. Percentage of people below poverty-line in Orissa was 47.15 % in 1999-2000 compared to all India figure of 26.10. Infant mortality rate of the state per thousand live births is 98, which is the highest for the whole country. Infant mortality rate in Bolangir district in Orissa is as high as 119 per one thousand birth. The literacy rates for Orissa in comparison to India in 2001 are given below in Table 1.

Table 1: Literacy rate in India (in percent)

India/State	Total	Male	Female
India	65.38	75.85	54.16
Orissa	63.61	75.95	50.97

Source: Census of India, 2001

As indicated at Table 1, the state of Orissa compares fairly well with respect to the literacy rates in India. However, the KBK districts have a low extent of urbanization and considerable Scheduled Caste (SC) and Scheduled Tribe (ST) population, particularly of the latter (Table 2).

Table 2: Social profile of KBK

Name of the district	Urbanization (percent)	Population of SC (Percent)	Population of ST (percent)
Bolangir	11.5	15.3	22
Kalahandi	7.5	17	29
Koraput	16.8	13	51
Malkangiri	7.2	20	58
Nabarangpura	5.8	15	55
Nuapada	5.6	13	36
Rayagada	14	14	56
Sonepur	7.4	22	10

Source: www.orissagov.nic.in

A greater cause for concern is the literacy rate in the KBK districts (Table 3).

Table 3: Literacy indicators in KBK districts, 2001

S.No.	District	Total	Male	Female
1.	Sonepur	64.07	80.30	47.28
2.	Bolangir	54.93	70.36	39.27
3.	Nuapada	42.29	58.78	26.01
4.	Kalahandi	46.26	62.88	29.56
5.	Rayagada	35.61	47.35	24.31
6.	Nabarangpura	34.26	47.37	21.02
7.	Koraput	36.20	47.58	24.81
8.	Malkangiri	31.26	41.21	21.28

Source: Census of India

The IGNOU Regional Centre in Bhubaneswar covers the operational area of IGNOU in the state of Orissa. The main type of learner support centres established by IGNOU in the KBK region, are the Special Study Centres. Because of the importance placed at the national level towards the development of the KBK region, IGNOU opened a sub-regional centre at Koraput, which has now been upgraded into a full-fledged Regional Centre. In view of the prevailing condition of education and employment sectors in the KBK, enrollment in certain programmes would be of use to the learners. Even those without formal schooling, provided they meet with the age requirements, can take the Bachelor's Preparatory Programme (BPP). These learners, on successful completion, could become eligible to enrol in any of the university's bachelor degree programmes such as: Bachelor of Arts/Commerce/ Social Work/Tourism Studies, or in any of several certificate programmes on offer. IGNOU also offers women's development programmes that are useful for the health and welfare of the entire family. These are the Certificate in Nutrition and Child Care (CNCC), Certificate in Food and Nutrition (CFN), Certificate in Women's Empowerment and Development (CWED), and Certificate in Empowering Women through Self-Help Groups (CWDL). The PG Diploma in Rural Development (PGDRD), Computer Literacy Programme (CLP) or Certificate in Computing (CIC) would also equip the learners for employment in the region. Apart from these, some of the Study Centres also have on offer the University's Master's Degree programmes in History (MAH) and Political Science (MPS).

Student Enrolment in KBK Region

Data presented in Table 4 reveals that student enrolment in the KBK region has increased from 1555 in 2003 to 2185 in 2004. The major reason for the increase in enrolment is the expansion of IGNOU's operations in the region. The number of study centres has gone up from 10 in 2003 to 25 in 2005.

Table 4: Student enrolment in KBK Region

Year	Admission Cycles	Number of Study Centres	Number of Students
2003	Both cycles	10	1555
2004	Both cycles	10	2185
2005	First cycle	25	1882

Source: IGNOU Regional Centre Bhubaneshwar Admission Data

IGNOU has two cycles of admissions in a year; in January and July. The data on programme-wise enrollment and demographics of learners has been taken from IGNOU Regional Centre records and combined for the two cycles (except for 2005 as admission data is to be finalised).

Many of the Study Centres mainly Malkangiri, Rayagada, Koraput, Bolangir and Kalahandi have been established with the backing and support of the local NGO's. These organisations with their link with the grassroots have been able to mobilise admissions. Many of them work in the area of women's welfare and their interaction and mediation is a possible reason for the presence of women among the learners of these Study Centres.

Among the IGNOU programmes, BPP appears to be a popular programme in this region as it is being offered in the local language Oriya. Other courses/programmes being offered in Oriya are:

- Foundation in Humanities and Social Sciences (a course offered in Bachelor's degree programme)

- Foundation in Science and Technology (a course offered in Bachelor's degree programme)
- Certificate in Women's Empowerment
- Certificate in Empowering Women through Self-help Group
- Certificate in Food and Nutrition
- BA (Political Science, History and Sociology)

This has been found to be beneficial both to the learners in pursuit of their studies and to the University by increasing its access to the disadvantaged.

The other programme with a noticeable enrolment, is the CWDL. The CWDL aims at enhancing women's confidence, inculcating leadership qualities, improving interpersonal relationships, providing legal literacy and acquiring access to credit resources. On successful completion of the programme, the learners can be master trainers for others in the region who are engaged in similar work and wish to set up self-help groups. There are several NGOs working in this area in Orissa. Another important reason could be the programme fee waiver, prevalent at that time that was awarded to functionaries of the Integrated Child Development Services (ICDS) project. The ICDS project of the Dept of Women and Child Development, Ministry of Human Resources Development, employs only women as its functionaries at all levels in the Block and village. The village level functionaries are the *Anganwadi* Workers, who are in close contact with the residents and could play an important role in initiating admissions in the Study Centres.

Profile of IGNOU Learners

Data of learners from among Scheduled Caste, Scheduled Tribe, and Other Backward Class, has been combined and presented as "reserved". There are thus two categories of learners: "general" and "reserved". Also the learners have been categorised according to gender as well as place of residence (Urban/Rural).

The profile of learners in Study Centres of KBK region (refer Table 5) shows a greater percentage of women students, which may be because of women's empowerment programmes. As discussed earlier, the fee waiver given to ICDS functionaries, all of who are women may be the main reason for the high representation of women learners. Another probable reason for the considerable enrolment of women learners in Koraput could be the presence of a female Coordinator at Study Centre 2145, who was also the recipient of a national award for volunteering in social services at the college level in the year 2004. The Coordinator is believed to be highly motivated and persuasive in enrolling women learners in the University's programmes.

There seems to be more learners from rural territories in most of the Study Centres.One of the Centres is at Koraput district headquarters, which may explain the greater number of urban based learners. The other Study Centre is at Semiliguda, away from the district headquarters, which caters to mostly rural residents of blocks in Semiliguda and adjoining Pottangi. The point of interest here is its proximity to the industries of National Aluminium Corporation (NALCO) and Hindustan Aeronautics Ltd (HAL), which might explain the enrolment in PGDRD, MAH, and MPS.

Table 5: Profile of learners in study centres of KBK in 2005

Sl. No.			As percentage of total fresh admissions in the Study Centre					
			Gender		*Category*		*Territory*	
			M	*F*	*General*	*Reserved*	*Urban*	*Rural*
1.	Bolangir	2107	68	32	84	16	59	41
2.	Kalahandi	2113	51	49	59	31	53	67
3.	Koraput	2123	55	45	78	22	80	20
4.	Malkangiri	2133	65	35	52	48	25	75
5.	Nabarangpura	2139	75	25	69	31	27	73
6.	Nuapada	2140	71	29	68	32	38	62
7.	Rayagada	2143	71	29	27	73	2	98
8.	Koraput	2145	33	67	47	53	19	81
9.	Bolangir	2157	62	38	71	29	7	93
10.	Kalahandi	2165	50	50	63	37	33	67
11.	Nuapada	2168	**Not Available**					
12.	Kalahandi	2169	**Not Available**					
13.	Kalahandi	2170	47	53	70	30	8	92
14.	Nuapada	2171	76	24	47	53	0	100
15.	Nuapada	2172	62	38	70	30	15	85
16.	Koraput	2173	65	35	55	45	4	96
17.	Rayagada	2175	70	30	45	55	37	63
18.	Koraput	2179	73	27	68	32	5	95
19.	Nabarangapur	2181	74	26	48	52	43	57
20.	Nabarangapur	2182	95	5	41	59	0	100
21.	Kalahandi	2183	88	12	0	100	12	88
22.	Koraput	2184	91	9	64	36	9	91
23.	Nabarangapur	2187	58	42	84	16	0	100
24.	Bolangir	2189	93	7	44	56	0	100
25.	Sonepur	2190	73	27	83	17	17	83

Recommendations and Conclusions

The inadequate infrastructure and educational development in the KBK region could be a barrier for those desirous of further studies. The initiative of the University in establishing learner support centres in rural and remote areas is appreciable, especially with programmes on offer such as the Bachelor's Preparatory Programme. This may be the reason for the largest number of learners in a support centre being enrolled in the BPP. In nearly all the centres across the three years under study (2003, 2004 and 2005), the highest percentage of the learners belong to the rural territory. With a view to increase student enrollment in the Study Centres of KBK region and reach out to more areas in the region, some of the suggestions which could be considered, are given below:

1. In view of the economic backwardness of the region, some kind of a financial consideration could be considered to attract enrolment. This could be by way of a fee waiver, or a fee concession, by the University for residents of the KBK region. Donor agencies and international organizations working in the region may be approached for this purpose.
2. The earlier practice of fee waiver for functionaries of the ICDS project who wish to enrol in CWDL, discontinued at present, may be revived. This would attract more learners, particularly those who are employed as functionaries in organizations dealing with women's health and family related issues. As the work done by them is for the benefit of the State's population, the State Government could offer to waive the fee or reimburse them.
3. Learners belonging to Scheduled Castes and Scheduled Tribes, enrolled in IGNOU, can avail of the facility of reimbursement of their fee from the Directorate of Social Welfare. However, it is likely that the residents in rural and remote areas may not be aware of either the presence of the University's Special Study Centres or the provision of reimbursement of fee. There is therefore a need for publicity about these matters in the region.
4. Translation of the course material of some of the academic programmes into Oriya has increased access of the State's population to the University. The translation of other relevant and need-baaed programmes could also be considered.
5. BPP has been found to be the most preferred programme by IGNOU learners of this region due to the inadequate educational infrastructure at the higher education level. Apart from that, those who are unable to continue the schooling and were forced to dropout may have enrolled in this programme. Successful completion of BPP would enable the learners to enrol in Certificate and some of the undergraduate programmes of the University. Many have already done so. It would be an incentive for the undergraduate learners if PG diplomas and Master's programmes were also made on offer. At present, the Special Study Centres in KBK region offer only BPP, BA and B.Com.
6. In view of the backwardness, lack of infrastructure, lack of trained manpower, and remoteness of the KBK region, many of the problems can be solved by appropriate use of ICT. The EduSat can be used effectively in this context as it is exclusively meant for serving the educational sector. It is a collaborative effort of the Ministry of Human Resource Development, IGNOU and the Department of Space, Indian Space Research Organization and reflects the country's commitment to the people in rural and remote locations.

Acknowledgements

I acknowledge the receipt of admission data from Dr. S.K. Tripathy, Regional Director (I/C), IGNOU Regional Centre, Bhubaneswar.

I am thankful to Dr. Srikant Mohapatra, Registrar, SRED, IGNOU, for his help in providing the background picture of the KBK region and in assessing the learners' profile.

References

Government of India (2001). *Census of India 2001*. New Delhi: Registrar General and Census Commissioner of India.

www.ignou.ac.in, Accessed on August 10, 2005

www.orissagov.nic.in, Accessed on August 09, 2005.

Dr. Kameshwari Moorthy is Deputy Director, Regional Services Division, Indira Gandhi National Open University, New Delhi.
Email: kmoorty@ignou.ac.in

7

Empowering Differently-Abled Through Distance Education: Issues and Challenges

J.P. Singh and J.S. Grewal

Introduction

In recent years, the term differently-abled has been widely used in the context of children with disabilities. It marks a major shift in thinking of individuals induced by collective efforts made in this direction by the United Nations and its member countries. The Universal Declaration of Human Rights (1948), International Year for Disabled Persons (1981), Convention of Rights of Child (1989), World Declaration on Education for All (1990), and Asian and Pacific Decade of Disabled Persons (1993-2002) are a few major milestones which focused the attention of stake-holders in this direction. The Government of India enacted Acts like Rehabilitation Council of India Act, 1992, Persons with Disabilities Act, 1995 and National Trust Act, 1995 to facilitate the process of bringing them into the mainstream.

The process of educating differently-abled children by the Government of India was initiated with the creation of a cell in the Ministry of Education in 1946. Prior to this, philanthropic organisations were educating/rehabilitating children as well as adults through residential schools and shelter homes for various disabilities. But impetus to these efforts was provided by the launching of scheme of integrated education in the year 1974. The scheme has so far benefited about 133,000 school children. Under District Primary Education Programme (DPEP), around five hundred thousand children with disabilities have been enrolled. The Ministry of Social Justice and Empowerment has initiated a scheme wherein financial assistance is given to special schools. As of now, nearly 3000 special schools are engaged in educating and training differently-abled children. Of these, 465 are being provided financial assistance by the Central Govt. However, in spite of all these efforts, the coverage of children with disabilities is not more than 4% and this is an area of serious concern because the latest census figures for the persons with disability show that 2.1 % of our population is suffering from one or other disability. However, a number of disabilities like dyslexia, autism and children having emotional disturbance have not been covered. If we account for such disabilities as well, the percentage of disabled population would be about 5%. That is, 50 million population is challenged. Of these, educational provisions exist for about one million children only though the rest also need immediate attention. The magnitude of challenge is huge and only planned and coordinated efforts can bring desired results.

The responsibility for education of children with disabilities and preparing them for challenges of life ahead can be given to only those who possess human touch and a humane attitude. To tap the latent potential of children with disabilities, the teacher must appreciate and understand their difficulties as well as abilities and act as facilitator in imparting the requisite knowledge and skills. However, by and large, most teachers fail to appreciate that children with disabilities have a lot of capacity and potential and can become useful and contributing members of the society, just like others. This lack of sensitivity amongst the majority of teachers poses a serious challenge to our efforts of maximising the potential of the differently-abled children. Innovative strategies have to be worked out to orient and sensitise the teachers, parents and the society in general towards this end and equip them with techniques and strategies of teaching-learning appropriate in the context of challenges faced by the differently-abled.

The Manpower Report of the Rehabilitation Council (1995) projected the requirement of 90,000 rehabilitation professionals and about 724,000 teachers by the end of 10th Plan (RCI, 1995). Turning this into a reality was a Herculean task because even with the present available infrastructure, the country can produce only 3000 qualified teachers annually. Moreover, there is lack of availability of requisite infrastructure in existing institutions in terms of practice lab, equipment, etc. However, we can choose to ignore the responsibility of reaching out to such children at our own peril. In such a scenario, technology presents itself as a viable option for training teachers using principles and methodology of open learning.

Education and Training of the Differently-Abled

Now-a-days, technology is being used extensively in almost every sector and level of education. Special education requires more of it in view of the specific requirements of the challenged children. Experts are of the view that technology has forced a paradigm shift in the mode and means of education and training. We have access to a wide range of media - print, radio, television, audio/video, teleconferencing/video conferencing - and tools - computers, CD-ROMs, e-mail and Internet. Indeed, now the focus has shifted from 'the teacher' to 'the learner' and from the 'institution of instruction' to the 'study room/work place of the learner' (Garg and Panda, 2001). The availability of such sophisticated technologies has forced silent transition in the modes of education and training; open-distance education is no exception. It has undergone immense changes spreading over five generations. The first generation was characterised by the predominant use of a single technology – print – and lecture notes were sent to the students. In general, the quality of such materials was low and there was little scope for direct interaction with the learners. Correspondence education is the typical example of the first generation DE. In India, the University of Delhi is credited for being the pioneer of correspondence education. The second generation was characterised by an integrated multimedia approach with Self instructional Materials (SIMs) specifically designed for study at a distance. The two-way interaction required the involvement of a tutor. DE has now graduated to IT-supported fifth stage of intelligent-flexible learning. It is now possible to interact with anyone anywhere, just as if they were next door neighbours. The availability of educational satellite (EduSat) has provided immense possibilities for tele-education. Several open universities, including IGNOU, are successfully using technology to offer a wide spectrum of professional programmes to reach the unreached and cater to the needs of differently-abled in collaboration with apex agencies like Rehabilitation Council of India (RCI), National Association for the Blind (NAB), etc.

The rehabilitation of the disabled has been drawing focused attention of the Government, Non Government Organisations (NGOs) and other agencies in context of the magnitude of the problem of disability. During the past one decade or so, there has been a strong realisation that lack of appropriate trained humanpower is a major constraint in providing worthwhile rehabilitation services to the disabled in the country. It is necessary for any civilized society to ensure that all people with disability receive services from qualified personnel, so that their quality of life is enhanced and they can live with dignity enjoying all the human rights, in keeping with the principle of "all human rights for all". The Rehabilitation Council of India (RCI) and other state and central agencies have taken significant steps in this regard but much remains to be done to train the teachers, instructors, rehabilitation counsellors and other functionaries, before the country can state to have achieved major gains in this context. Therefore, a greater stress than before has to be laid on special education and research in different areas of disability and distance education can serve as a useful tool towards fulfilling this objective.

Abraham Maslow, a prominent psychologist in the humanist movement, proposed that people have five basic kinds of needs, namely: (i) Physiological, (ii) Safety, (iii) Love and belongingness, (iv) Esteem, and (v) Self-actualisation. Self-fulfilment has direct bearing on the development of disabled persons. They are to be enabled in the development and promotion of whatever capacities they have. They are to be empowered for realising their potentialities through proper training. They need to grow and become all they are capable of becoming. Total self-actualisation, according to Maslow, is rarely achieved. As teachers, we can help our students, including the differently-abled, to move in this direction by making sure that their deficiency needs are at least partially satisfied. Till late nineties, the teacher training at the Diploma, Degree and Postgraduate levels was mostly organised in the formal face-to-face mode. Table 1 summarises the number of teacher training programmes organised by different institutions at different levels through the face-to-face mode.

Table 1: Special teacher education programmes at graduate and postgraduate levels

Graduate		Post-graduate	
B.Ed. (HI)	09	M.Ed. (VI)	03
B.Ed. (VH)	05	M.Ed. (HI)	02
B.Ed. (MR)	03	M.Ed. (Multicategory)	02
B.Ed. Spl. Ed. Multicategory	03	M.Ed. (LD & MR)	01
Total	**20**	**Total**	**`08**

Obviously, the number of the institutions imparting special teacher education is inadequate in the context of the target group. Around 125 institutions are conducting programmes at Diploma Level for meeting the need of special teachers at primary level. One-year Multicategory Teacher Training Programme was implemented as a result of the recommendations of NPE (1986) and Programme of Action 1992. The multicategory special teacher training was organised by the NCERT for a few years under the UNICEF assisted innovative Project Integrated Education for Disabled (PIED). Though these programmes addressed the unique special education needs of children by discussing the implications of different disabilities, only the State of Karnataka is conducting the programme. Other centres discontinued offering these programmes because the primary school teachers could not be deputed for long duration courses. Such constraints clearly point towards the need for radical changes in the mode of teacher training. In this context, technology enabled open learning presented itself as a viable option in view of its inherent learner-centric characteristics, flexibility, capacity and capability to accommodate large numbers. However, this mode of training remained untapped till Rehabilitation Council of India (RCI), in collaboration with state and national agencies took a bold decision to coordinate the development of special teacher education programmes at the Diploma (D.Ed. Spl. Ed.), Degree (B.Ed. Spl. Ed.) and Postgraduate (M.Ed. Spl. Ed.) levels. The Graduate Level Programmes included B.Ed (Spl. Ed.) in the categories of Mental Retardation (MR), Visual Handicap (VH), Hearing Impairment (HI), Multicategory, B.Sc. (Spl. Ed. and Rehabilitation), whereas Postgraduate Level Programmes were mostly available in the specialisation of Visual Impairment (VI), Hearing Impairment (HI), Mental Retardation (MR), Multi category and Learning Disability (MC&LD).

Special Teacher Training through Distance Mode

In 1992, the Indian Parliament passed the Rehabilitation Council of India Act, which was notified and became effective from June 1993. One of the important tasks assigned to the RCI is the recognition of institutions offering training programmes for professionals engaged in rehabilitation. The RCI signed a MOU with Madhya Pradesh Bhoj (Open) University (MPBOU) to develop B.Ed Diploma and Career Advancement Programmes in Special Education through distance mode. It was envisaged that in due course of time, the MPBOU will act as the National Resource Centre for Special Education and Rehabilitation Programmes. The B.Ed (SE-DE) was launched in 2001. The five programmes so far developed by MPBOU in collaboration with RCI have the following major objectives and thrusts:

- to advance and disseminate learning and knowledge by different means, including the use of communication technologies;
- to provide opportunities for higher education to a larger segment of the population and to promote the educational well-being of the community; and
- to encourage the open university and distance education institutes to offer programmes in Special Education.

A few challenges before the special teacher educators, NGOs and administrators are:

- Development of suitable methodologies and SIMs for training teachers for all twenty disabilities identified by the RCI.
- Management and net-working of institutions imparting training in different disabilities.
- Development of self-instructional materials in Regional languages.
- Development of laboratories and workshops for providing hands-on experiences to the teachers of disabled children.
- Integration of efforts of agencies engaged in Inclusive and Exclusive (Special) education.
- Inter-sectoral coordination and cooperation.
- Integrating vocational components with special teacher education being conducted in distance mode.

MPBOU conducts three teacher education programmes in special education through distance mode:

1. *B.Ed Special Education Programme [B.Ed. (SE-DE)]:* B.Ed Special Education Programme is offered through 72 Study Centres located in 31 States/UTs of the country. The duration of the programme is two years. The year-wise enrolment in B.Ed. (SE-DE) is depicted in Fig. 1. A candidate can specialize in any one disability area namely; Visual Impairment (VI); Mental Retardation (MR); Hearing Impairment (HI) and Locomotor Impairment and Cerebral Palsy (LI & CP). Besides this, they are required to study two school subjects with special focus on the disabled learners. Self-learning materials for all courses are provided to all trainees, who are required to attend three contact programmes of 58 days duration organised in three phases.

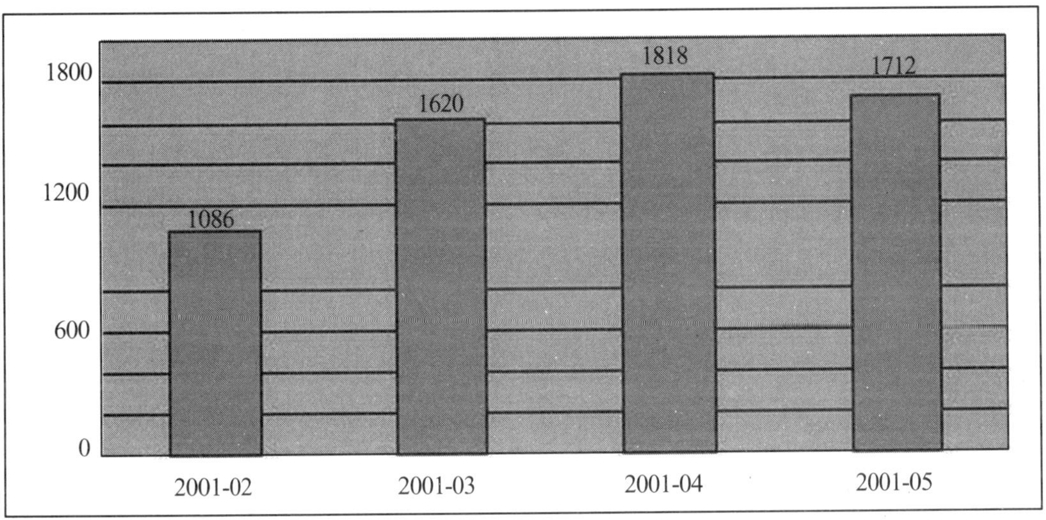

Figure 1 : Year-wise enrolment in B.Ed (SE-DE)

2. *Foundation Course on Education of Children with Disabilities (FC-SEDE):* The principal objective of this programme is to develop required competencies amongst in-service teachers and enable them to impart education effectively to students with various disabilities. This course imparts basic information in Visual Impairment, Hearing Impairment, Mental Retardation, Locomotor Impairment & Cerebral Palsy. All learners are required to attend two contact programmes at 72 Study Centres. The duration of first contact programme is two weeks while the second programme is of one week duration. This programme is also being organised in 31 States/Union Territories. The number of students enrolled batch-wise are depicted in Fig. 2.

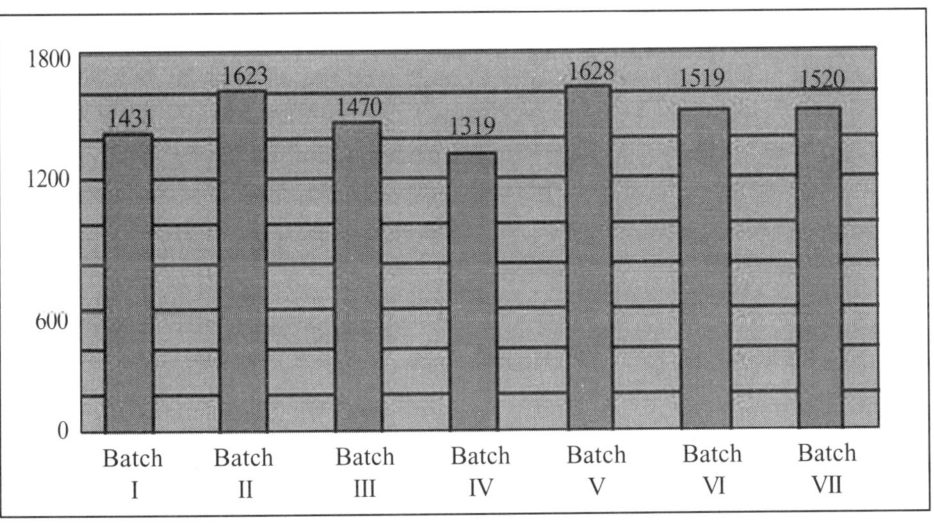

Figure 2 : Batch-wise enrolment in Foundation Course (SE-DE)

3. *Post Graduate Professional Diploma in Special Education (PGPD-SEDE)* is offered through 72 study centres located in 31 States/UTs. The target group for this programme is trained teachers, who wish to have in-depth study of anyone disability in special education.

Recently, the MPBOU and RCI have agreed to develop and implement M.Ed. Special Education. In addition, the M.P. Bhoj (Open) University has initiated research in Special Education.

Programmes Launched by Other Universities

The RCI has developed M.Ed (SE-DE) Programme based on credit system. This is being transformed into the distance mode. Encouraged by the result of the developments undertaken by the MPBOU, several other universities have come forward to develop and implement Special Education courses, especially with instructional materials in regional languages. For example, U.P. Rajarshi Tandon Open University, Allahabad, and Netaji Subhash Open University, Kolkata have translated B.Ed. (SE-DE) materials in Hindi and Bengali, respectively.

Parents have a very vital role to play in building self-confidence and positive self-concept in children with disabilities. Research in education has, time and again, confirmed that there is a close relationship between positive self-concept and a positive educational achievement. Unfortunately, many children with disabilities are the victims of negative attitudes of parents. These must be changed if the potential of children with disabilities has to be realised. The Council is launching an Awareness-cum-Training Package for Parents in collaboration with Indira Gandhi National Open University under an MoU signed to make joint efforts in promoting and implementing extension, training and education programmes for empowerment of special target groups of people with disabilities. The Package aims to bring about positive attitudinal change among parents and caregivers in particular, and the society in general, so as to provide the differently-abled a congenial, nurturing and stimulating environment to live in. The Packages will equip the parents and caregivers to provide stimulation and training to the child during the early childhood years within the home, school and community setting. These Packages shall be implemented through NGOs.

The Bangalore University is offering a course in Community Based Rehabilitation using distance mode. Similarly, National Institute of Open Schooling is offering programmes in seven disability areas but the number of beneficiaries remains low, about 1% (Sen, 2002).

RCI has signed an MoU with Manipal Academy of Higher Education for launching a Post Graduate Diploma in Disability Management for Medical Doctors. The need for such a course emerged from the demand of PHC doctors during a nationwide short term training programme undertaken by the Council focusing on prevention, early identification and intervention for people with disabilities.

Future Directions

It is said that one designs and many weave because only a few gifted can innovate. RCI has taken many steps in the right direction and initiated path breaking schemes. So far, RCI has developed resource base of professionals working in the area of disabilities, teachers engaged in education of persons with disabilities and parents of the challenged. Although sporadic efforts have been made by the Government as well as public in general, not much attention seems to have been focussed on the education and training of the disabled themselves. We need to address this, to realise the objectives of Persons with Disabilities (Equal Opportunities, Protection of Rights and Full Participation) Act 1996, and initiate concrete steps and actions to make education at all levels accessible to the differently-abled. In this context, to harness distance mode of education, programme for extensive use of technology is being worked out. With the availability of 24 hour educational TV channels under Gyan Darshan initiative of MHRD and extensive network of Gyan Vani cooperative, it should be possible to create a movement to empower the challenged and enhance their enrolment in higher education. For this, the existing instructional material will have to be transformed into convenient modes (Braille texts, audio/ videos) so as to provide individualised support services and new programmes will have to be designed to address specific needs.

References

Garg, S. and Panda, S. (2001). World Wide Web and distance education, *University News*, 39, 1-7.

RCI (1995). *Report on Manpower Development*. New Delhi: RCI.

Sen, R.S. (2002). Access and equity in context of the differently-abled. In Dikshit, H.P. et al (eds.), *Access and Equity: Challenges for Open and Distance Learning*. New Delhi: Kogan Page.

Dr. J.P. Singh is Member Secretary, Rehabilitation Council of India (Government of India), Qutub Institutional Area, New Delhi.
Email: rehabstd@nde.vsnl.net.in

Prof. J.S. Grewal is Director, Department of Multimedia Education, M.P. Bhoj (Open) University, Bhopal.

8

Changing Nature of Academic Programmes at a Distance: The Indian Perspective

V. Venkaiah, Chambi Puranik and R.R. Rausaria

Introduction

In our country demand for education at all levels has been consistently and continuously running ahead of the facilities and resources. Presently 345 Universities, either set up by an Act of Parliament or the State Legislatures, and about 18,000 colleges affiliated to the Universities are imparting higher education. Though this is a massive system, it is unable to accommodate the increasing number of new learners. It is quite costly too and the resources do not permit large scale expansion of the formal system. Realizing the important role the education plays in the overall national development, a number of Education Commissions and Committees were set up from time to time to look into the problems of education and to suggest solutions. On the suggestion of Central Advisory Board of Education (CABE), the Government of India constituted an Expert Committee in 1961 headed by Dr. D.S. Kothari, to look into the suitability of Correspondence Courses for expanding educational opportunities. The Committee recommended introduction of Correspondence Courses to expand and equalize educational opportunity. Thus, distance education (DE) in India was introduced by Delhi University in 1962.

The major objectives of DE are:

- to provide a system of student-centred self-paced learning;
- to provide a flexible, diversified and open system of education;
- to develop wider access to higher education to persons of all ages, and sex particularly to working persons and to economically or otherwise handicapped and persons residing in remote areas;

- to provide opportunity for upgradation of skills and qualifications; and
- to develop education as a life long activity so that the individual can refresh his knowledge in an existing discipline or to acquire knowledge in new areas.

The major characteristics of the distance education system are its high productivity, greater flexibility and above all its capacity to respond to varying demands. Analyses of cost incurred by the distance education system show that it can offer educational programmes of an acceptable quality at a cost which is somewhere between one-fourth and one-third of the cost incurred by the conventional education system. The growth of distance education has been exponential over the last four decades in our country beginning in 1962. Presently 12 Open Universities and 106 Correspondence Course Institutes of conventional universities are offering programmes in diverse disciplines. These Universities initiated new ways of imparting knowledge and launched new academic programmes from time to time to meet the growing needs of a wider range of learners. Distance education is a new form of education which uses cutting edge information and communication technologies in delivery of programmes. In this paper we have attempted to review the changing nature of academic programmes from early phase of correspondence education to more recently developed technology-driven distance education. We have made a concerted efforts to identify some of the important programmes commonly offered by Open Universities and Correspondence Course Institutes (CCIs)/Distance Education Institutions (DEIs) of conventional universities from 1962 to date by using the data published by Association of Indian Universities (1984,1986,1992, 1994,1996,1998,2000 and 2004), Distance Education Council Data Base (DEC, 2004), and Reports of the UGC (1998-2000) and Ministry of Human Resource Development (1998).

The Emergence of Distance Education as an Alternative System

As mentioned earlier, the correspondence courses began in India in 1962 to enable those with the necessary aptitude to acquire further knowledge and improve their professional competence with the establishment of School of Correspondence Courses and Continuing Education at University of Delhi. Subsequently in 1968, Correspondence Courses were started by Punjabi University, and University of Rajasthan. Meerut and Mysore Universities started these courses in 1969. Slowly many Universities followed them. Rapid expansion of the distance courses took place during 1970-71 and 1977-78. The advent of the Open University System in the country in 1982 brought about a qualitative change in the nature and scope of distance education. The establishment of the Andhra Pradesh Open University in 1982 and the Indira Gandhi National Open University in 1985 heralded a new era in the development of distance education in India. Establishment of three more State Open Universities followed, one each in Bihar and Rajasthan in 1987 and one in Maharashtra in 1989. Subsequently, seven more Open Universities were established. Presently there are 12 open universities and 106 dual mode universities (2005).

Changing Nature of Academic Programmes

We have examined in detail the programmes offered by Correspondence Course Institutes and Open Universities starting from 1962 to date to look into the nature and scope of programmes offered to meet the educational needs of varied learners. The growth of academic programmes offered by OUs and DEIs attached to conventional universities is given below in Table 1.

Table 1: Growth of academic programmes in Indian open universities and DEIs 2000-2004

Year	Number of Programmes inOpen Universities	Number of Programmes inDEIs
2000	222	677
2001	260	854
2002	282	990
2003	361	1264
2004	429	1428

Source: (DEC, 2004).

Initial phase: First decade 1962-63 to 1972-73 (preponderance of general programmes)

In the 1960s, undergraduate level programmes were introduced to distance mode and that too only in Arts. The first DEI (attached to Delhi University) admitted 1112 students at the B.A. level initially and in a span of five years it enrolled around 8500. It started post graduate (MA) programme from 1970-71. Out of 12 Universities that offered distance education, 10 offered B.A Courses, 5 offered B.Com courses, 1 offered B.Sc courses, 2 offered M.A Courses, 1 offered M.Ed course and 1 each offered certificate and diploma courses (AIU, 1984).

Second decade (1972-73 to 1982-83)

During 1972-73 and 1977-78, 10 more conventional universities introduced correspondence courses. Several new courses like in science and technology, law (LLB & BGL) and many other certificate and diploma courses were introduced during this period. The undergraduate level Arts courses, which were prominent in the past 10 years retained their position by being offered in 16 out of 18 Universities. Their position out of total enrolment in correspondence courses was cent percent of the first decade and 63.98% during 1972-73; and during 1977-78 their share receded to 37.46%. Next to Arts, the Commerce courses at the under-graduate level gained ground as 12 out of 18 institutions offered these courses by the year 1977-78 and they accounted for around 21% of the total enrolment of correspondence courses. A rising trend was visible in the M.A courses, as the institutions offering these courses rose from 2 during 1972-73 to 10 during 1977-78, accounting for around 28% of the total enrolment (UGC, 2000).

By 1977-78 many institutions got approval from the UGC for additional courses like B.Ed, M.Com, M.Sc, and M.A. Five dual mode universities offered B.Ed programmes to meet growing demand of untrained teachers in this decade. Surprisingly, the University of Delhi which was the only institution offering B.Sc course through distance education since 1972-73, dropped the course in 1977-78. During 1977-82 seven more Universities and institutions of higher education came forward with correspondence courses. Jawaharlal Technological University launched B.Tech programmes for in-service diploma holders. In this decade thus the programmes range included general BA, MA, M.Com, B.Com and teacher education programmes like B.Ed and technical programmes like B.Tech. Further, a few certificate and diploma programmes were also introduced (AIU, 2000).

Thus, the 1970s witnessed an increase in the number of DEIs and also many new disciplines like Science, Education, Law, etc. were brought under the fold of DE. Also, a few vocational and employment oriented diploma courses were introduced in the information sciences, journalism, tourism, management, library sciences, etc. (Manjulika and Reddy, 1996).

Third Decade – Establishment of Open Universities: New Direction in Programme Offerings

The year 1982 witnessed the establishment of APOU at Hyderabad later renamed as Dr. B.R. Ambedkar Open University. During 1982-83, the enrolment in correspondence courses rose to around 1.5 lakhs that is around 4.5% of the total enrolment in all the Universities in India. From 1977 to 1982 no new course, except the revival of B.Sc, was added to the existing ones of 1977. During 1982-83, the course position in the various Universities was, B.A 23, B.Com 17, B.SC1, B.Ed 5 (including RCEs 9), M.A 11, M.Com 6, M.SC 1, M.Ed 3, B.Lit.1, LLB 2, BGL 2 and other certificates and diploma courses. There were especially as many as 14 Arts and Social Science subjects like Political Science, Economics, English, History, Hindi and Sociology. The first MBA programme was launched by Punjabi University, Patiala, in 1985.

Indira Gandhi National Open University was established in 1985 to provide opportunities for higher education to a large segment of the population and to promote educational well-being of the community in general and to encourage the Open University and distance education systems in the educational pattern of the country. IGNOU adopted a modular approach for programmes and first launched the Diploma in Management and Diploma in Distance Education programmes in 1987. The programmes offered by IGNOU got international recognition both for their content and quality. Subsequently, it developed and started offering BA non-formal, BA/B.Com programmes in 1988. Simultaneously it also launched certificate in Rural Development and Food & Nutrition. Subsequently the Diploma in Management was upgraded to a Post Graduate Diploma and MBA by adding a few more modules. Keeping in view the demand of upcoming and new field of information technology, Diploma in Computers in Office Management and Certificate in Computing Programmes were initiated. These were followed by the launch of Nursing and Health education programmes, Master of Computer Applications and other need based programmes at Diploma and Certificate levels.

Keeping in view the demand for post graduate programmes IGNOU has now launched postgraduate programmes in Tourism, Management, English, Hindi, History, Political Science, Sociology, Public Administration, Economics, Nutrition and Dietetics. It has taken a lead and has started Ph.D programmes in Education, Economics, History, Tourism Studies, Public Administration, Sociology, Political Science, Mathematics and Physics.

In the meantime four more State Open Universities were established Kota Open University (KOU), (now renamed as Vardhaman Mahaveer Open University), in 1987, Nalanda Open University in 1987, Yashwant Rao Chavan Maharashtra Open University, in 1989 and MP Bhoj Open University in 1991. YCMOU adopted a novel approach for identification of target groups and courses relevant to them. It identified 3 broad target groups and developed courses appropriate to their levels:

(i) Illiterate, semi-literate and non-literate – Functional literacy programme based mainly on life work skills, (ii) Less educated – Vocational, Technical and Skill based programmes for income generation and better standard of life, (iii) Educated and Higher Educated – Doctoral, Postgraduate and Degree programmes in professional, vocational area and general continuing education programmes. The programmes offered by Open Universities in this decade are given in Table 2.

Table 2: Programmes offered by open universities

Sl. No.	**Name of the Open University**	**Year of Establishment**	**Courses offered**		
			Under graduate Programmes	**Post graduate Programmes**	**Certificates/Diplomas/ other Programmes**
1	**2**	**3**	**4**	**5**	**6**
1.	Indira Gandhi National Open University, New Delhi 366161	1985	B.A, B.Com, B.Sc (Phy., Chem., Maths, Life Sciences),	BCA, BSW, BTS, BIT, BLIS (Tourism Studies), B.Ed, BSC (Nursing), B.Tech (Water Resource Eng. Cons. Mgt.) MADE, MBA, MBA (Banking & Finance) Commonwealth Ex. MBA, CE-MA-Pub.Admin., MCA, MLISc, MTM, MA (Eng., Hindi, Hist., Pol., Sc.) M.Com, M.Sc (Hospitality Admin.)	**Advance Diploma in** Information Tech., Construction Mgt., Water Resource Engg. **Post Graduate Diplomas 20 programmes relating to** Management, Intellectual Property Rights, Maternal and Child Health, Hospital & Health Mgt, Geriatric Medicine, Rural Development etc. **Diplomas 11 programmes relating to** HIV and Family Education, Creative Writing in English & Hindi, Youth in Develop-

					ment Work, Early child-hood Care & Education, Management etc. **Certificate – 27 programmes relating to** Certificate in Computing, Primary Education, Tourism Studies, Women's Empowerment and Development etc. **Doctoral Programmes:** Ph. D in Education, Eco, Hist, Tourism Studies, Library & Info. Sciences, Sociology, Pol. Sc., Mathematics, Physics.
2.	Dr. B.R. Ambedkar Open University, Hyderabad 190230	1982	BA, B.Com, B.Sc (Bot., Chem., Maths, Phys, Zoology) BA (Public Rel.) B.L.I.Sc.	MBA, M.Sc (Math), MA (Public Admin., Pol. Sc., Eco, Hist., Eng, Sociology) M.Sc (LIS), M.Com	PG Diplomas In (Women Studies, Writing For Mass Media, Environmental Studies, Business Finance, Marketing Management , Human Rights **Doctoral Programmes:** Dev. Studies, Distance Education
3.	Vardhaman Mahaveer Open University, Kota 5999	1987	BA (JMC, Library) BA (Preparatory) B.Com (Preparatory), BA, B.Com, B.Ed	MA (JMC, Pol., Sc., Eco, Hist, Hindi), MBA	Advanced Diploma In Management, PG Diploma in Management programmes, Labour Law), Diploma in (Tourism & Hotel Management, Culture & Tourism, Computer in Office Management, Nutrition & Health Education, Library Science) Certificates in (Food & Nutrition, Computer Awareness, Culture & Tourism)
4.	Nalanda Open University, Bihar 1805	1987	BA (Library & Information Science)	M.Ed, MA (Hist, Pol., Sc., Psychology)	Diploma four programmes relating to Management, Journalism & Mass Communication, Youth in Development etc, Certificate in (Food & Nutrition, CBFP, CFT,

					CMAP, CHM, CLBAW, CACL, CCWR)
5.	Yashwant Rao ChavanMaharashtra Open University, Nashik 102642	1989	BA, BA (LIS), Bachelor of Horticulture, B.Com, B.Tech (Marine Engineering), B.Ed	MA (Edu and Subject Comm, distance Education, M.Com, M.Sc (Agriculture, Library Sc.,) MBA, M.Ed	Diploma 10 programmes relating to Foundation in Agriculture, Commercial, Commercial Fruit Production, Commercial Vegetable Production, Agriculture Business Management, Landscape Gardening etc. Certificate – 7 programmes School Level IT Programmes, Preparatory, Preparatory Skills in B.Sc (IT) **Doctoral Programmes** : M.Phil (Educational Communication, Distance Education, Subject Communication) Ph.D (Edu Communication, Distance Education, Subject Communication, Agriculture)
6.	MP Bhoj Open University, Bhopal 192230	1991	B.A, B.Com, B.Sc (Maths, Physics, Computer Sc., Design & Tech., enabled Services)	MBA, MCA, M.Sc (IT, Comp. Sc., Maths,) MLIS, M.Com Acc Mktg) MSW, MA (Eco, Hist., Pol. Sc., Eng., Phil., Chem, Math, Bot., Zool. Socio)	PG Diploma 10 programmes relating to (Business Information, Computer Information, Human Resource Management, Financial Management, IT Enabled Services , Advanced PG Diploma – 3 programmes Diploma – 3 programmes and Certificate–7 programmes
7.	Dr. Babasaheb Ambedkar Open University, Ahmedabad 13824	1994	B.A, B.Com, Bachelor Preparatory Programme (BPP)	M.A English, Hindi	Post Graduate Diploma In Distance Education, Diploma In English And HindiCertificates – 9 relating to Food and Nutrition, Tourism, Teaching of English etc.
8.	Karnataka State Open University, Mysore 19580	1996	B.A, B.Com, B. Lisc. B.Ed, B.Sc(IT)	Ma. (Eco, Eng, Hindi, Hist, Kannada, Pol. Sc., Sans, Socio, Urdu) M.Com, M.Ed, MBA, M.Sc (IT)	Doctoral Programmes English & Kannada M.Phil In Comm, Eco, Edu, Eng, Hindi, Hist, Kannada, Pol. Sc., Sans, Sociology, Pg Diploma – 5 Relating To Distance

					Education, Higher Education, Eng, HRM, Marketing Mgt,Diploma – 7 relating to Kannada, Journalism Tourism Certificates – 8 relating to Kannada, Environmental Studies, Guidance and Rural Development etc.
9.	Netaji Subhas Open University, Kolkata 14734	1997	B.A, B.Sc, B.Com, BCA	M.A, M.Sc, M.Com Ph.D, M.Phil, Diplomas, Certificates	
10.	UP Rajarshi Tandon Open University, Allahabad 8025	1998	B.A, B.Com, BTS, B.Sc (Phy, Chem, Maths, Zoology, Botany, MBio, Com Sc,) BCA, Bachelor of Computing & E-com, B.Lisc, B.Ed	M.A (Hindi, Pol. Sc, Socio, Hist, Eco, Eng, M.Lisc, Master of Journalism and Mass Comm, MBA, MCA	Undergraduate Arts in Single SubPG Diploma – 6 relating to Fin. Mgt, Tourism, E-Business Diploma - 10 relating to Health Education, Medical Technicians, Indian Language Certificates – 9 relating to Consumer Protection, Human Rights, Environmental Studies etc.
11.	Tamil Nadu Open University, Chennai 9361	2002	B.A (Hist, Eng, Eco, Tamil), B.Com, Bachelor of Tour. Stud, B.Ed	MBA, M.Com, M. A (Hist, Eco, Pol, Sc, Sociology, Psych, Public Admin)	PG Diploma – 6 relating to Management areas Diploma in Management Certificates – 7 relating to Environmental Studies, Food & Nutrition, Rural Dev, Teaching of Primary School Mathematics etc.

BRAOU, Hyderabad initially started in 1983 with Bachelor in Arts, Commerce and Science and after a decade launched Master programmes in Business Administration, Public Administration, Economics, History and Sociology. The Yashwant Rao Chavan Maharashtra Open University, Nashik launched BA and B.Com programmes at graduate and MA- Educational Communications, at Post graduate level and five agriculture programmes at certificate and diploma level in gardening, fruit products, vegetarian products, floriculture and landscape gardening. It started M.Phil and Ph.D programmes also. MP Bhoj Open University also offered BA, B.Com and other general programmes. The range of programme offerings increased significantly with the advent and absorption of communication technologies and its percolation to far flung areas. Management, Computer Education and Teacher Education programmes were more in demand and offered by Universities. University Grants Commission also approved offer of non-formal under graduate programme without any qualification at 10+2 and attaining an age of 21 years which was subsequently reduced to 18 years.

During the 1980s a rapid and more diversified structure of distance education programmes was developed. Several DEIs introduced science courses at the Master's level. A bold initiative was undertaken by Punjabi University, Patiala in 1991 with the introduction of an M.Phil course in English and Punjabi through this mode (Manjulika and Reddy, 1996).

The Fourth Decade 1992-93 to 2002-03: Preponderance of Computer and Management programmes

Advancement in interactive communication technologies had major impact in this decade. Both OUs and DEIs introduced a large number of programmes related to computer software and configuration at Certificate, Diploma, graduate and postgraduate levels. BCA, MCA became a main attraction. Also Management programmes in Marketing, Financial Management, Human Resource Development, Banking and Finance, Industrial Relations at certificate, diploma, Bachelor and postgraduate levels, such as BBA, MBA gained importance.

Programmes in Journalism, Mass Communication, Hospital Management, Foreign Trade, Insurance Management, Environmental Management, Human Rights, and Pollution Management were also introduced by the universities during the period 1993-2001. Programmes in Astrology and Yoga Studies were also initiated by 3 Universities. The general B.A., B.Sc., B.Com and M.A, M.Com retained their importance. Programmes of M.Sc (Computer Science) and M.Sc (IT) were also offered by a number of universities. Demand for technical and paramedical programmes started gaining increasing importance.

Table 3: Academic programmes and courses offered by Indian open universities (2004)

S1. No.	Open University	Number of academic Programmes	Number of Courses
1.	Indira Gandhi National Open University	89	820
2.	OLB.R. Ambedkar Open University	25	332
3.	Vardhaman Mahaveer Open University	33	255
4.	Nalanda Open University	22	148
5.	Y C Maharastra Open University	78	355
6.	Madhya Pradesh Bhoj Open University	77	611
7.	Dr. Baba Saheb Ambedkar Open University	17	140
8.	Karnataka State Open University	19	
9.	Netaji Subash Open University	8	29
10.	U P Rajshri Tandon Open University	38	562
11.	Tamil Nadu Open University	23	231
	Total	429	3483

Source: (DEC, 2004).

5th decade beyond 2002

The number of institutions offering programmes through distance mode has increased significantly and around 20 institutions mostly Deemed Universities have started offering B.Tech, M.Tech programmes, and Paramedical programmes such as Bachelor of Physiotherapy, Medical Lab Techniques and Radio Imaging, etc. In addition, efforts are in the direction of offering online education also. With the launch of EduSat and availability of broadband internet connectivity, it is feasible to offer online programmes in a big way in different disciplines in the years ahead.

Table 4: Level and number of academic programmes offered by open universities and DEIs of conventional universities (2004)

Sl. No.	Programme	No. of programmes offered by open universities	No. of programmes offered by DEIs
1.	Postgraduate programmes	29	91
2.	Undergraduate Programmes	23	62
3.	Postgraduate Diploma Programmes	34	57
4.	Diploma Programmes	37	62
5.	Certificate programmes	34	53

Source: (DEC, 2004).

Conclusion

To sum up, only the general programmes of B.A, B.Com and M.A, M.Com, B.Sc (Math) were offered during the first decade. This was the beginning of DE and credibility of the system was yet to be established. Several new programmes were introduced during the second decade. Teacher education (B.Ed), and first technical programmes at undergraduate level were introduced. In addition to B.A general programmes, M.A programmes in many disciplines were also introduced. A few certificate and diploma programmes were also started.

In the third decade, five OUs came into existence. OUs helped to consolidate distance education as enrolment in distance education increased to 15% of the total enrolment in higher education. OUs introduced the modular approach and started offering need based short term programmes beginning at certificate and diploma and upgrading to full graduate and master levels programmes. The management and computer education made an impact in this decade which led to diversification of programmes. Communication and information technology made a perceptive impact in this decade. Programmes in Journalism, Mass Communication, Foreign Trade, Insurance Management, Environmental Management, Hospital Management, Human Rights and Intellectual Property Rights have added new dimension and enriched the programme mix of Indian Distance Education.

The information and communication technologies had significant impact on programmes offerings in 4^{h} Decade and majority of institutions offered computer and Management programmes such as MCA, MBA, and M.Sc (IT) along with shorter duration programmes to meet the requirements of IT industry.

The authors, with their experience, feel that while planning and developing distance courses, the following questions need to be considered:

- Is there evidence of a need within the community for the proposed course?
- Is there evidence of a significant public demand for the course and objectives proposed?
- Is it clear that other agencies are not offering similar course (s)?
- Does the course offer some innovative and imaginative approach to the subject?
- Is there likely to be a continuing demand?
- Is the course capable of development by other agencies?
- Is there an opportunity for the interested target group to pursue new interest aroused by the course?

References

AIU (1984). *Handbook of Correspondence Courses*. New Delhi, Association of Indian Universities.

Association of Indian Universities (2000). *Handbook on Distance Education*. New Delhi: AIU.

DEC (2004). *Information Base on Distance Higher Education in India*. New Delhi: Distance Education Council, Indira Gandhi National Open University.

S. Manjulika and Reddy, V. Venugopal (1996). *Distance Education in India: A Model for Developing Countries*. New Delhi: Vikas Publishing House Pvt. Ltd.

UGC (2000). *Correspondence and Distance Education Courses: Enrolment Statistics 1995-96*. New Delhi: UGC.

Dr. V. Venkaiah is Director GRADE, Dr. B.R. Ambedkar Open University, Hyderabad, India.
Email: vvenkaiah@hotmail.com

Dr. Chambi Puranik is Former Dean (Academic), Karnataka State Open University, Mysore, India.
Email: mita@sancharnet.in

Dr. R.R. Rausaria is Deputy Director, Distance Education Council, Indira Gandhi National Open University, New Delhi.
Email: rrrausaria@ignou.ac.in

9

Models of Course Design and Development

Santosh Panda and Suresh Garg

Introduction

Whether universities teach at a distance or adopt online teaching, the most crucial foundation and pre-requisites to their operation are the learning packages. An equivalence to classroom teaching (the foremost role of the teacher) at the open universities is undoubtedly writing or development of (or teaching through) self-learning materials (SLMs); all other tasks centre around this main task. In tele-teaching for instance in the United States, the role combines both material development and online teaching (Gunawardena, 1992; Olcott and Wright, 1995). For single-mode open universities, distance teaching through pre-produced SLMs has been the major task; and the Course Team approach to material development, pioneered by the British Open University, has invariably been adopted by many open universities and distance teaching institutions (DTIs) in both developed and developing countries (Inglis, 1996). From the institution's point of view, the considerations of cost, time, constraints and quality output are crucial; and for the students, quality and learning effectiveness of the materials and responsiveness of learner support services are of utmost importance.

In this chapter, we describe briefly some of the course development models generally used by DTIs, and concentrate more on analysis of some of the selected models of material development in the distance education system in India — dual-mode university Distance Education Institutes (DEIs), State Open Universities (SOUs), and the National Open University — which is the second largest system of open learning in the world with about four million cumulative and about one million annual enrolment.

Course Development Models

A variety of course development models have been adopted by distance teaching universities. The most commonly adopted one is the Course Team (CT) model, followed at the Open University (UK), Athabasca University (Canada) and Deakin University (Australia). The course team model comprises academics (subject experts), radio and TV producers, educational technologists, editors, graphic designers, counsellors, student representatives, and course chairperson with varying levels of responsibilities. Because of the representation and active involvement of different categories of experts, the quality of materials thus produced are normally high. But one of the serious criticisms of this model is that it takes too long (two to three years) to produce a course, thereby making it cost-intensive and at times obsolete before being printed.

Universidad Estatal a Distancia, Costa Rica follows the Author-Contract Model (ACM); the FernUniversität, Germany, also follows the ACM, with the difference that an individual teacher takes up the overall responsibility of course development. Everyman's University of Israel also works with the same model (Rumble and Harry, 1982). Lockwood (1992, 1993, 1994) has discussed four course production models, viz. personalised training, workshop generated, text transformation, and wrap around which are considerably different from the original CT model. These are described briefly as follows:

Personalised training

In this model authors are equipped with skills and techniques that they need to use exactly at the time they decide to plan and produce self instructional materials (Lockwood, 1994). This method is suitable for producing self-instructional materials in a shorter time and with people having no previous experience in this area.

Workshop generated

In this model, the materials are generated in workshop situation, and the experts (such as subject experts, media experts, graphic experts, language editors, etc) are from different background. The time taken to produce materials is relatively shorter than that in case of other models. IGNOU developed a large portion of materials for its Certificate in Guidance programme and the B.Sc. Physics laboratory courses (Panda and Garg, 2003) through this model. This model has also been used partly to edit materials received from course writers for the M.A. (Education) and M.Ed. programmes.

Text transformation

This involves a process of transforming existing correspondence materials into self-instructional materials. In India, the DEIs have correspondence study materials which are being transformed into SIMs. The process involves organisation of workshops for the transformer-authors, as also extension of follow-up support to hasten the process of transformation.

Wrap around text

Since high quality SIM development is time consuming and cost-intensive, existing printed texts are used along with a wrap around text. The cost of developing course material through this model is as such low, but the copyright implication is a major issue in this model. At IGNOU, M.A. (Applicable Mathematics) is being developed through this model.

Educational advisor model

The educational advisors are senior subject experts with experience in educational technology. They advise and work in collaboration with the faculty within their discipline/subject area to produce course materials. This model is followed at the Murdoch University and the Darling Down Institute of Advanced Education, Australia.

Contract author-faculty model

In this model, external authors write units and the materials thus produced are vetted by internal faculty. In IGNOU, this is the usual practice, though the course is designed by a team of experts. The editor is responsible for content editing and content quality. This model, with slight variation, is also known as 'Author-Faculty-Editor Model' or 'Coordinator-Writer-Editor Model'.

Contract author-editor model

In this model, the materials developed by outside experts are vetted and edited by internal or external editors, who work on the materials as surrogate students. The courses of Master Degree in Library & Information Science and B.Tech (Civil) of IGNOU were developed in line with this model.

Seminar generated

This model of course development is useful when published literature in the subject is limited, and the subject is in the nascent stage of development. Naturally due to this, there shall be very few experts in the field. In this context, seminar turns to be a better approach to generate new ideas and thoughts, thoroughly discussed by peer groups. The papers presented in the seminar and the proceedings of the seminar become the basic material, and study guides and activities are developed and edited by internal faculty on the basis of the outcome of the seminar. Such an approach leads to faster development of course material.

A variety of individuals/agencies/institutions are involved in the use of these models for course development, and each model has its own complexities and constraints at the procedural level. We discuss below some selected models of course development and production. This is followed by a brief reflection on the changing nature of course production for distance learning in the changing context of multiple media based blended learning.

Distance Education Institutes

There are 106 dual-mode universities and institutions of higher learning in India offering correspondence courses/distance education programmes, ranging from undergraudate programmes to more skill based and professional programmes in information technology, management, agricultural sciences and electronics. We have selected three DEIs (Madras, Osmania, Kurukshetra) based on accessibility of data, for describing and analysing course development approaches adopted by them. The selected DEIs represent three different but typical course development approaches adopted in most of the DEIs in the country. It is essential to have a comparative understanding of the processes/systems, and the factors responsible for the approaches adopted by them.

ICE, University of Madras

The Institute of Correspondence Education (ICE), University of Madras was established in 1981; and till the University of Madras Act was amended in 1984, the ICE depended on university faculty for course design and development. In 1984, the state government deputed faculty against substantive posts to ICE. The planning of a programme/course starts with the Advisory Committee, which acts as the Planning Board for the ICE and comprises the VC, Director of ICE, one expert from IGNOU, two members from the university Syndicate, and the senior-most Professor from the ICE. The recommendations are placed in AC for policy decision on the desirability of a programme. The proposal is then put up to the Syndicate, Senate and the Academic Council in that order for final approval. Any proposal for a new programme passes through the Board of Studies (BOS) to go to the Syndicate. Recently, a decision had been taken to constitute a BOS (the 50th one) exclusively for ICE by amending the university Act with the approval of the Chancellor. The ICE-BOS shall act for those courses which do not exist in the university. Such approved programmes can simply be adopted by the main university Subject-BOSs for their offer in the mainstream departments.

One lesson, on an average, consists of 20 pages, and 20-25 lessons comprise a paper. Only a few lessons are in SIM format, and, except for MCA, BCA, M.Com. and MA(Eco), all the papers are offered in both English and Tamil. After approval by the AC, the DE staff or a Committee recommended by the DE Staff Committee identifies course lessons/units: sometimes, it is just a one-person committee. Lessons are written by ICE or outside faculty, who edit, proof read and prepare final CRC, vis-à-vis the DE Staff Committee (Fig. 1).

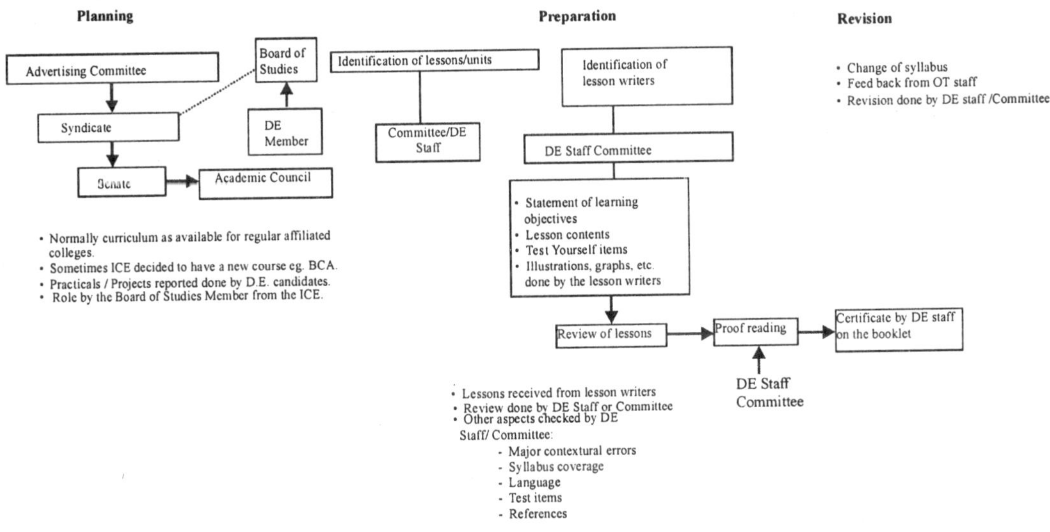

Figure 1: Process of development of materials: ICE, University of Madras (Courtesy: Prof. R. Narasimham)

CDE, Osmania University

At the Centre for Distance Education (CDE), Osmania University, (which does not have full-time faculty at the CDE), the Director of the Centre appoints (subject-wise) 'Editors' (who are usually senior faculty from the University or external consultants), and puts up the case for a new programme/course, on behalf of the CDE, to the Curriculum Development Body (Fig. 2). The CDB for DE (which is different from the CDB of formal education) comprises of BOS members, course writers, subject experts; and after detailed deliberations, the syllabus is put up to the BOS for DE (different from BOS for formal education). The CDB-DE and BOS-DE almost conform to the syllabus of their respective CDB and BOS of the formal system. The course writers and subject experts are from the formal system; and the Committee of CWs, SEs and ET organises workshops for lesson design and writing, and puts up the draft written by CWs to the BOS-DE for clearance, which then becomes the authorised draft fit for final printing. While the 'Editor' acts as the overall coordinator of the programme/course, the HOD of the parent department puts up cases to the BOS-DE for revision of courses.

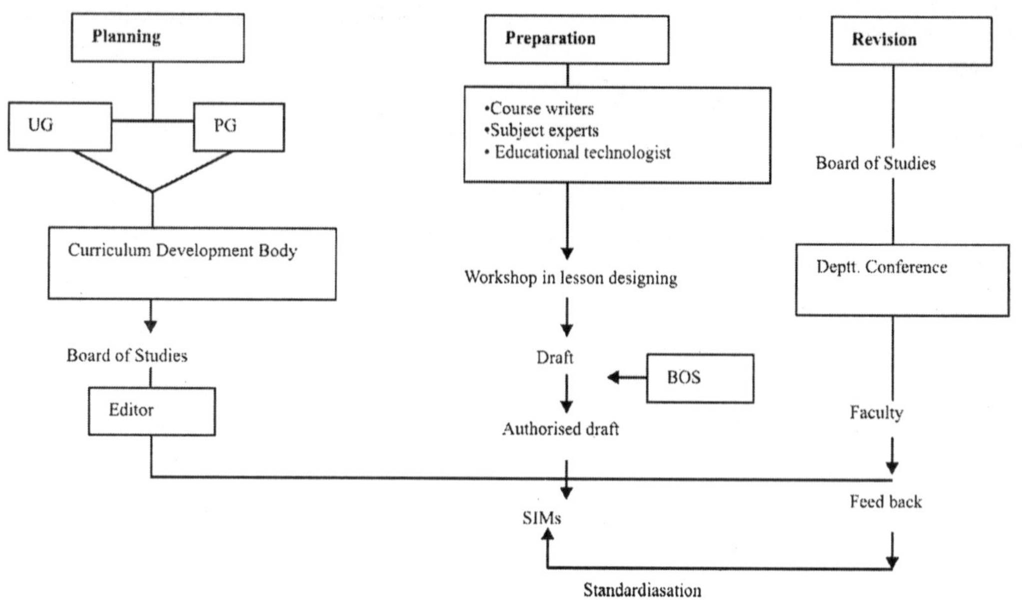

Figure 2 : Course development at Osmania University
(Courtesy: Dr. S. Prakash Rao, Dr. Indrakanth, Mr. Limbadri)

DCC, Kurukshetra University

At the Kurukshetra University (KU) (Fig. 3), the Board of Studies in the concerned discipline at the main department approves the syllabus prepared jointly by the KU and the M.D. University for ensuring parity in the state of Haryana. The Joint Syllabi Committee is chaired by the concerned HOD of KU, with members drawn from both the universities; and the JSC prepares the syllabus for approval in the BOS, followed by approval in the Academic Council of the respective university. The syllabus is adhered to by both the formal system and the Department of Correspondence Courses. In the DCC, the subject committee takes up the responsibility of planning the course development, drawing up of panel of writers and experts, and allotment of lessons to faculty members as also writers from outside the university. Vetting is done internally, so also final proof reading and clearance for printing.

State Open Universities

We discuss the case of Yashwantrao Chavan Maharashtra Open University (YCMOU) as a representative but more sophisticated case for course development in state open universities. The procedure of academic programme development adopted at the initial years YCMOU is presented in Fig. 4. Three sources - client needs, social demand, and the university authority - determine launch of a new programme. Feasibility studies are conducted, the results of which, coupled with the advice of the State-level Advisory Committee, lead to programme proposal being put up to and approved by the Planning Board and the Academic Council of the university. State-wise curriculum groups are formed, and the instructional packages are determined, followed by approval by the university Board of Management and formation of course teams. Course units, audio-visuals and practical components are developed and finalised after expert editing/ vetting/preview. Most of the course materials are in the language of the State - Marathi, and the university had also initially adopted a few courses from outside (especially IGNOU) offered mostly in English. Subsequently, the course development processes at the university have been sharpened, modified and diversified (see Fig. 5).

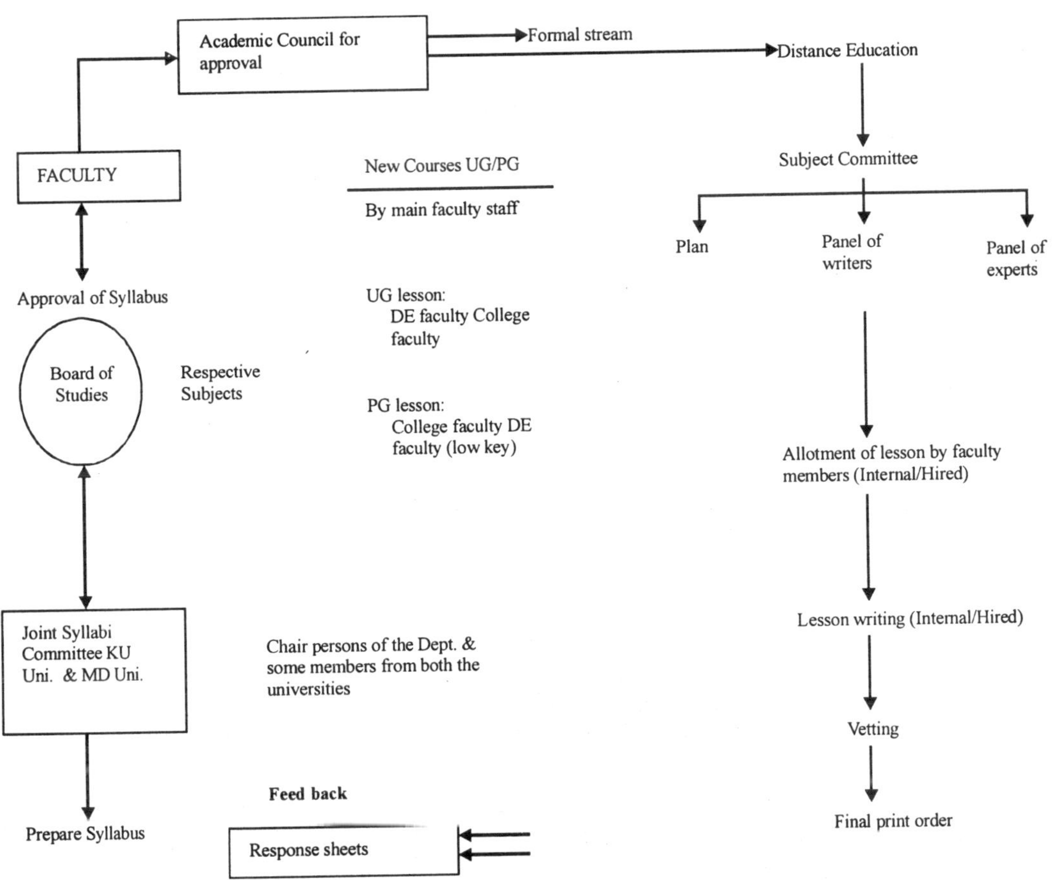

Figure 3 : Process of development of study materials at Kurukshetra University

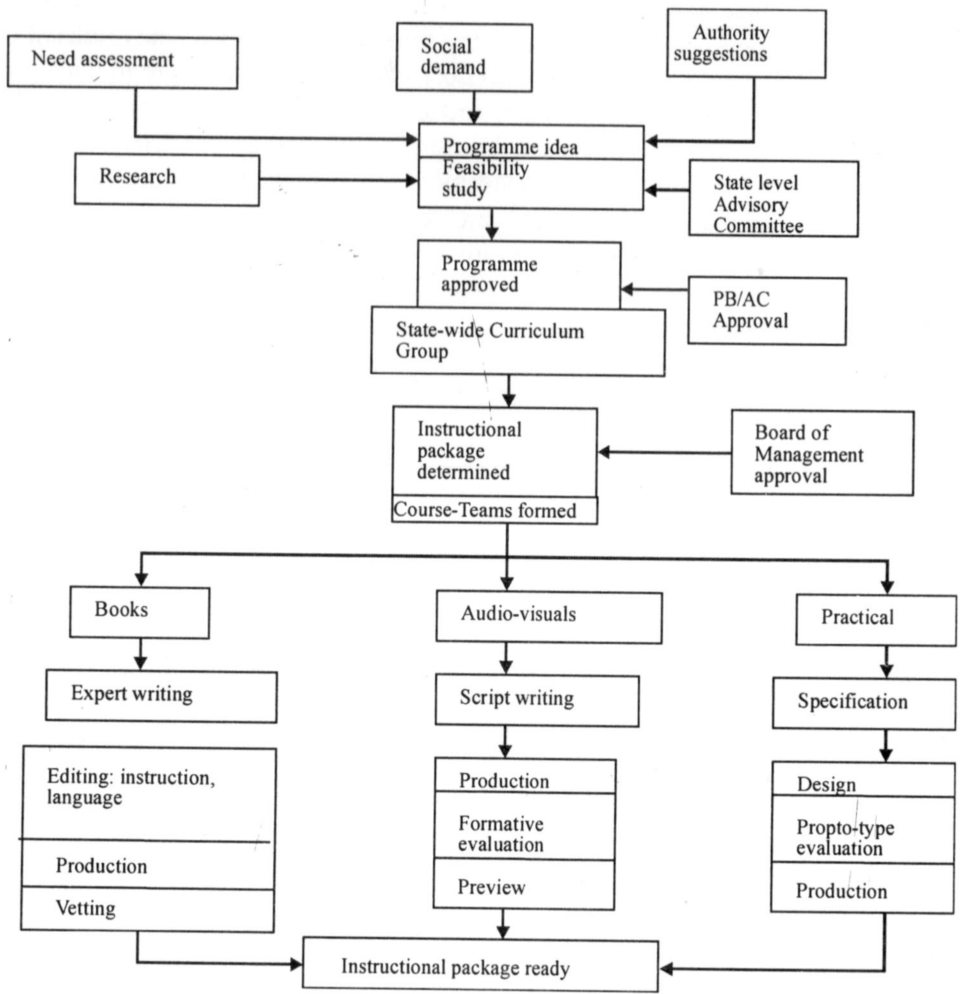

Figure 4 : YCMOU: Development of academic programmes
(Source: Deshpande, 1999)

The approach that has generally been adopted for the last few years is given in Fig. 5 and is self-explanatory. All sources of knowledge are tapped while developing the concept paper for a new programme. It is discussed and approved in the School Council, Planning Board, and Academic Council. While the SC proposes the programme, the AC approves, as it is, the resolution of the former. The Programme Advisory Committee, which is formed by the AC (by drawing experts from all over the country, but usually from within the state) designs the programme, develops framework of courses, and establishes the Course Development Committee. The CDC develops detailed structure of course units, provides instructional design support, and identifies course writers and editors. In consultation with the Director of school concerned, the Academic Services Division (IT Centre) provides orientation to writers and editors, followed by unit writing and

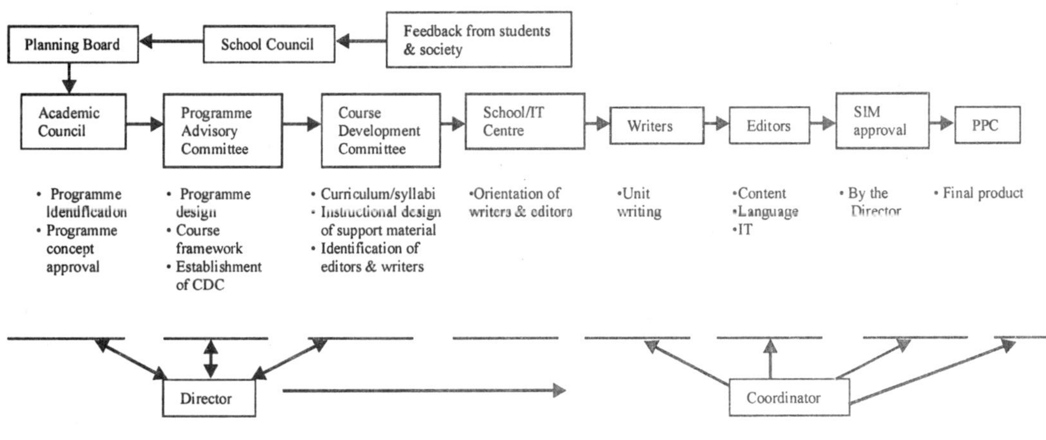

Figure 5: YCMOU - modified common model of insturctional material development (Courtesy: Prof. A.N. Joshi & Dr. Rajguru)

editing (content, language and instructional technology). While the ASD extends IT support, the school faculty have of late taken up this responsibility. The SIM is finally approved by the school Director for printing. In the process, four forms are filled up for consideration and approval of concerned authorities: Form A for PB, Form B for AC, form C for PAC and Form D for CDC. It may be noticed from Fig. 5 that the Director of the concerned School of Studies is the key person in organising and handling the process, and exercises authority in the process even if he/she does not specialise in more than one discipline within the School. Further, the Co-ordinator of the programme (i.e. the concerned faculty) is responsible for overseeing the writing and editing activities, and is responsible to the Director. Sometimes, the Co-ordinator specialising in the discipline concerned, is nominated from outside the university to carry out the tasks that an in-house co-ordinator does.

Indira Gandhi National Open University

The Indira Gandhi National Open University, the second largest mega university in the world, was established by an Act of the Indian Parliament in 1985 with dual objectives of offering need-based programmes at a distance, and coordinate and maintain standards of distance education systems in the country. A third objective, which has been functionally operative with the gradual growth of the university, concerns with acting as a regional resource centre for materials, human resources, system expertise, training and research. The university is known internationally for the quality of its academic programmes and course materials, and for the huge operation that it handles in a vast country with geographic remoteness and isolation. The university enrols about 0.3 million students annually, and has a cumulative enrolment of active students of about 1.3 million. A network of 62 regional and recognised regional centres, four sub-regional centres, 1300 study centres (study centres, programme study centres, sub-centres, work centres, web centres, multimedia learning centres, tele-learning centres, etc.) and 35 partner institutions work towards the implementation of its academic, training, research and extension programmes developed through eleven Schools of Studies and the offer of student support services.

Academic programmes

Starting from just two programmes - Diploma in Distance Education, and Diploma in Management - in 1987 with a combined enrolment of 4381 students, the university now offers 108 academic programmes comprising 980 courses at masters, bachelors, diploma, certificate and non-credit levels. Many programmes are modular in nature, and follow a credit system (where 1 credit = 30 student study hours). A certificate programme is of 12-18 credits, a diploma programme worth 24-36 credits, a bachelors degree programme of 96 credits, and a master programme of 64-72 credits. The programme areas range from bachelors degree liberal arts/ commerce/ science to professional areas like management/computer and information science/medicine and health care/engineering/services/teacher training at different levels. Other programmes relate to society and life, and continuing professional development, like rural development, maternal and child health, food and nutrition, early childhood care and education, to name a few.

Curriculum design and course development: policy and practice

In its formative years, programme identification, design and development were based on experiences of in-house faculty and the associated experts. But the University gradually developed procedures and norms for carrying out these activities. The initial curriculum identification and design processes included the following:

- The academic programmes of the university were required to conform to the objective of reaching the disadvantaged sections of society, with emphasis on secularism, and national integration.
- The University hired the services of Educational Consultants (India) Pvt. Ltd. to survey and suggest the programmes to be initiated; DDE and DIM programmes were initiated in 1987 out of this prioritised list.
- In the light of its Act, Bachelors Degree Programme (BDP) was identified for offer as the first step towards reforming and providing equal opportunity for tertiary education. It was also a bold step to design the three-year programme into foundation, elective, and application-oriented courses.

- Rural development and food and nutrition were suggested by the Union Government as prioritised areas to develop academic programmes for awareness and skill development.
- The programmes were prioritised as per the felt need, and were designed on the basis of past experiences of faculty in each discipline, and the views of outside experts involved in the course team of the respective programme. The 'faculty coordinator-writer-editor' model of course design and development evolved in this process (and which has become the mainstream course development approach in the University).
- With increasing experience, more flexibility, openness and learner-centredness were introduced. These eventually got reflected in the course design too. Relaxation of entry qualifications; increased duration for completion of the programme; addition of audio, video, teleconferencing, radio counselling into the printed course materials as either supplementary or complementar-all had implications for curriculum and course design.
- It was gradually realised that more factors need to be considered while thinking of initiating an academic programme. While financial viability and relevance currency of a programme dominate the decision making now, the needs of the prospective students, employment avenues, and the like have also been important considerations. The programme coordinators (i.e., the internal permanent faculty members) have since been concerned with: i) establishing academic credibility of programmes, ii) optimum utilisation of limited resources for programme development and implementation, iii) availability of experts in the area, iv) availability and preparedness of delivery mechanisms, and v) credibility/valuing of degrees and diplomas by other academic institutions and the prospective employers.

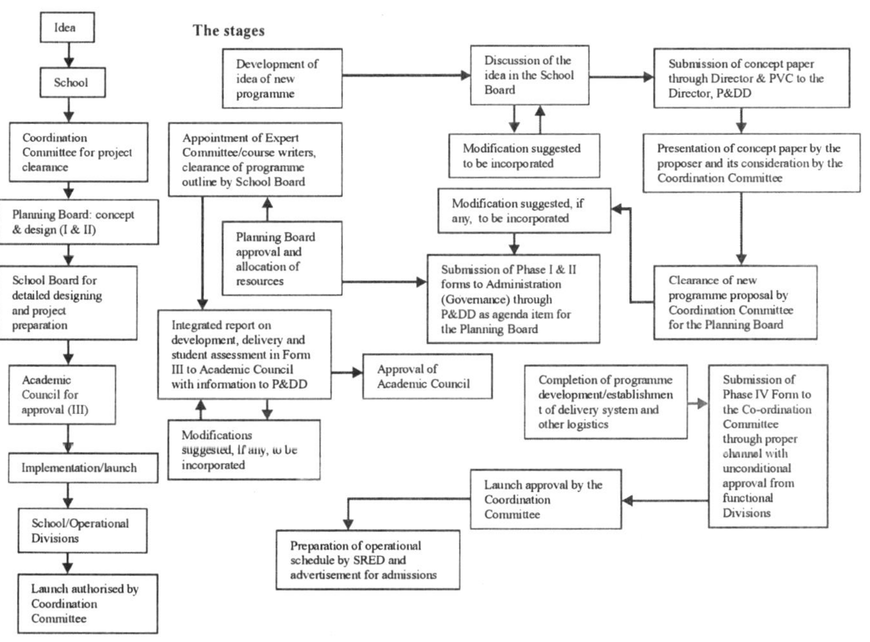

Figure 6: Procedure for approval of academic programme proposal followed till 1999

A programme can be initiated by any faculty (teacher or academic), who acts as the 'programme coordinator'. He/she has to follow well-laid down steps in the process of course design and development to finally reach the stage of printing and production of materials. The processes followed for course design and development prior to and after 1999are delineated in Figs. 6 and 7, respectively. While following the steps noted in these diagrams, the programme coordinator needs to fill up four forms - each one corroborating to certain stage/phase of course design or development. The four phases, that a programme passes through before its launch, include: programme proposal, programme concept, programme design, and programme launch.

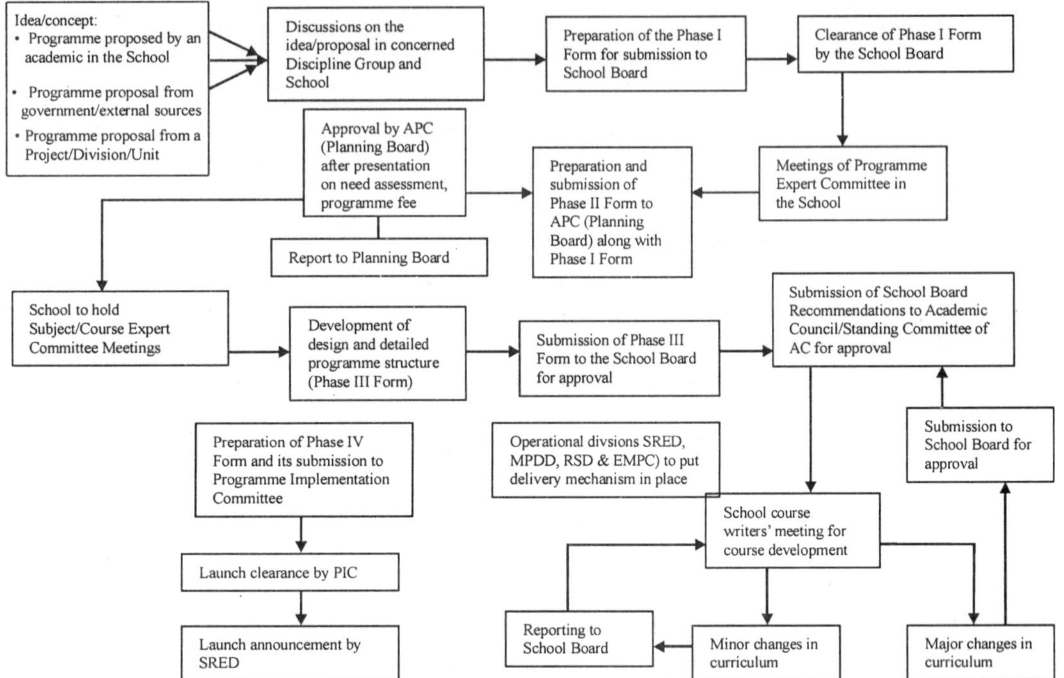

Figure 7: New programme development procedure
(Courtesy: Task Force on Student Support, IGNOU)

Programme proposal (Phase-1)

A programme proposal is initiated by the faculty based on four variables:

- need survey conducted by the faculty in collaboration with Planning and Development Division and/or outside designated agencies;
- request of the agencies/departments of the union/federal government;

- expertise of in-house faculty;
- collaboration with national and international agencies (with or without funding support).

A programme to be initiated by a faculty member is discussed in the discipline group within a school, and the phase-1 form is prepared. The proposal may be discussed in the School Council (which is optional), and is submitted to School Board for approval. Following this, budgetary approval is obtained from the competent authority for conducting a need assessment survey, external visit to discuss with experts, convening a meeting of experts for designing the programme, and the like. The programme structure is placed before the Programme Expert Committee, for guidances.

Programme concept (Phase-2)

Phase-2 proforma is submitted to the Planning Division of the University, along with the resolution of the School Board and the phase-1 proforma, for consideration of the Academic Programme Committee, a Standing Committee of the Planning Board. Once the proposal is discussed on points concerning availability of funds, fulfilment of the mission and objectives of the University, programme fee, feasibility of implementation, and the like, budgetary approval for design and development of the programme is obtained, and course-wise expert committee meetings are convened to develop detailed syllabi.

Programme design (Phase-3)

Phase-3 form, along with the Phase-1 and Phase-2 forms and the detailed course design, are placed before the School Board for approval. At this stage, the programme coordinator obtains programme and course codes from the Planning Division. Such codes are based on variables such as level of the programme (awareness, undergraduate, postgraduate, and research) designated as A,B,P,R; discipline where the programme originated from (like PH for physics, TS for tourism studies, etc.); for a laboratory course, the symbol (L) is added; the stage of preparation (new/revision) of the course/programme (new course is assigned 0, 1 for first revision, 2 for second revision, and so on till 9 for 9th revision); and the last two numerals for the number of the courses in that discipline (starting from 01 to 99). Therefore, a course code like MPH(L)001 would indicate that it is a : *"Master level Physics lab course offered for the first time"*.

This by implication also suggests that an UG course can never be a part of a PG programme, but a Certificate Course can be part of a Diploma or UG programme.

The programme, after discussion, is approved by the Academic Council or its Standing Committee (ACSC). At this stage, budgetary approval is obtained for course development and production (in print, audio, video, and digital form). On approval from AC/ACSC, the programme coordinator with the approval of competent authority, convenes the meeting of course writers for orientation and assigning course units; preparation of CRC and master copies of audio and video programmes. A programme package includes most or all of the following:

- Printed materials in the form of one or two credit blocks (or even a full course in one booklet)
- Student programme guide
- Handbooks on practicals/experiements/hands-on experience/projects
- Kits for experiments and practicals
- Audio and video programmes
- CD-ROM, multimedia materials on the Web
- Student assignments (TMAs and CMAs).

The approaches that have been adopted for development of various academic programmes at IGNOU are discussed in the next section. It is, however, worth mentioning here that curriculum and course design heavily depends on the approach adopted, and therefore, this is categorically reflected in the programme proposal by the programme coordinator (which also reflects the costs involved in course development).

Programme launch (Phase-4)

The programme coordinator submits Phase-4 form to service Divisions (Regional Services, Student Registration and Evaluation, Material Production and Distribution and Electronic Media Production), indicating their exact role in the implementation of the programme, as also alerting them in advance for their preparedness. However, submission of these forms are initiated only after 50% of the course materials (print, audio, video, etc.) are ready at hand, and that student support services (like counselling, assignment evaluation, lab experiments, practicals, teleconferencing, phone-in radio counselling, etc.) have been put in place. No programme can be put on offer without approval of Phase-4.

Models of Material Development

The 'coordinator-writer-editor' model/approach evolved in the initial stages of course development in the university due partly to the existing exigencies and partly to such a necessity. Gradually, through experience and based on course-specific needs, various other models got evolved. It is important to point out here that:

- a programme is initiated either by an in-house faculty (programme coordinator) or by the discipline group (within the school) as a whole, or even by an inter-disciplinary group;
- besides the programme coordinator, there may be course coordinators (within the programme) who may specialise in that area;
- the programme is developed by a 'course team' comprising the in-house faculty (programme coordinator/course coordinators, other faculty members), course writers drawn from outside the University, course editors drawn largely from outside the University (sometimes in-house content editors), language editor from the editing unit (sometimes by in-house discipline-based faculty and external editors) and media producers from the EMPC. In initial years,

format editor from STRIDE were also associated but as number of programmes increased and in-house faculty developed necessary expertise, the part has been abandoned.

Following the submission of Phase-3 form, a two day orientation programme of course writers is organised where the process and format of developing self-learning materials are discussed; course contents (units) are thoroughly looked into; audio and video components are concretised; and the time frame for writing course units is decided. The usual course development process involves the following steps:

- Organisation of a 2-day orientation programme by the programme coordinator, followed by writing of course units by course writers, and dispatch to the programme coordinator in a floppy/CD and also a hard copy.
- Preliminary editing and formatting by the course/programme coordinator before sending a copy each to content editor (block-wise or course-wise) for authenticity of content and its appropriateness at the given level and instructional designer from STRIDE to test comprehensive communication.
- Editing and dispatch to programme coordinator by editors.
- Correction and finalisation, and dispatch to language editors for language editing; simultaneous design of graphics, initiation of the process of audio and video programme production.
- Simultaneous or post-course development translation of units by translators of different languages (if needed).
- Simultaneous development of assignments and student handbook, and other handbooks.
- Preparation of CRC, and master copies of audio and video programmes, and their further printing/duplication, depending on expected size of enrolment.

A broader framework depicting the processes of development of an academic programme is given in Fig. 8, which depicts seven stages in the course design and development process.

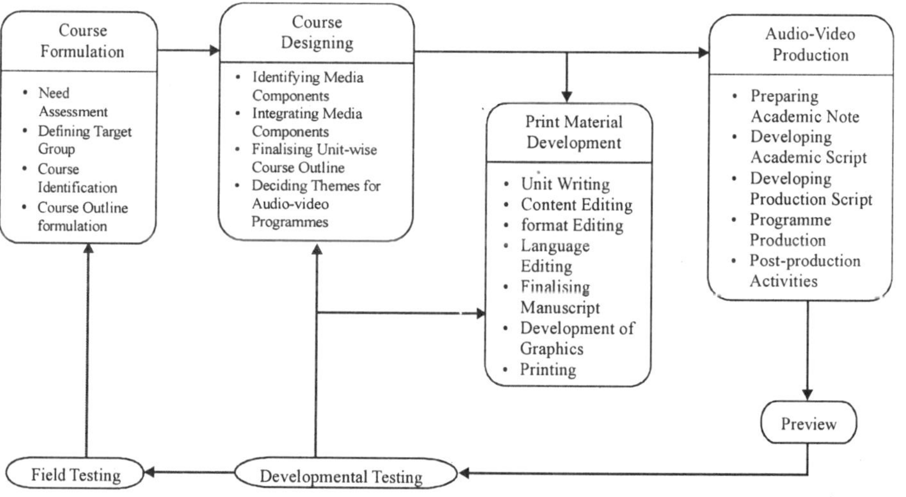

Figure 8: Course development process

While developmental testing has been tried out in a few courses, this phase needs to be built, as a regular mechanism, into design and development of all programmes.

The typical model of course (print) development process is depicted in Fig. 9. While the programme coordinator handles the entire process and is responsible for the final outcome, the 'content editor' (non-IGNOU senior academic) is largely responsible for the quality and presentation of the content. The format, language and copy editors contribute further to the readability, conversational nature, easy comprehension, etc. of the course units. Translators come in at a later stage; to translate the finalised materials, written in English, into different regional languages. While this process of translation itself has been a gigantic but satisfying task for the University to have produced authentic materials in the Indian context, there is a realisation that it is easier and more qualitative to develop/write course materials afresh in regional languages (based on existing detailed course and unit design) than translating from English. The Bachelor's Degree Programme better represents this model of course design and development.

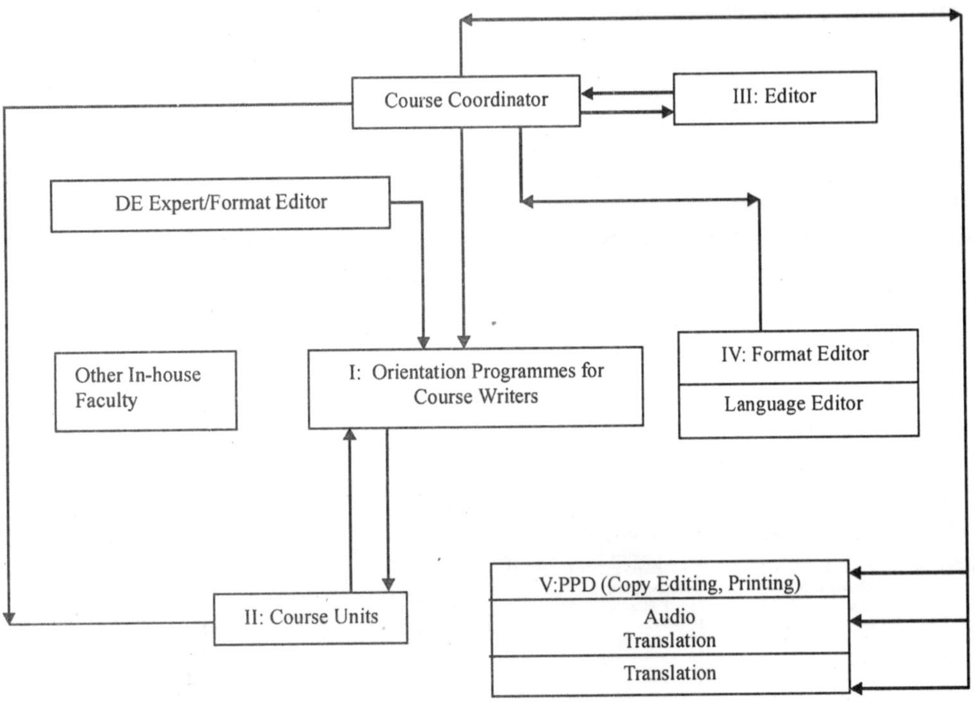

Figure 9: Coordinator-writer-editor model
(Source: Panda, 2000)

The faculty, over the years, have deviated from the established 'coordinator-writer-editor' model to approaches based on factors like nature of the programme, availability of course writers and editors, strict time schedule and the like; availability of financial resources has so far been the least important factor influencing the approach adopted. A variant is the 'non-IGNOU editor-coordinator model' (Fig. 10) in which the course editor (based in any region in the country) acts as the coordinator of the course, and course units are developed regionally with the help of experts available in the city. While the concerned faculty at the headquarters of IGNOU is responsible for organising regional orientation programmes for course writers and the editor-cum-coordinator (ECC), format and language editing and printing at the headquarters, etc. the ECC is responsible for getting course units, assignments, audio and video scripts, practical manuals, etc. written by the regional course writers, editing those, and presenting to the concerned faculty/school for further editing and compilation. Some of the good examples at IGNOU are the Postgraduate Diploma in Journalism and Mass Communication, B.Sc (Nautical Science), B.Sc (Opthalmic Techniques), among others.

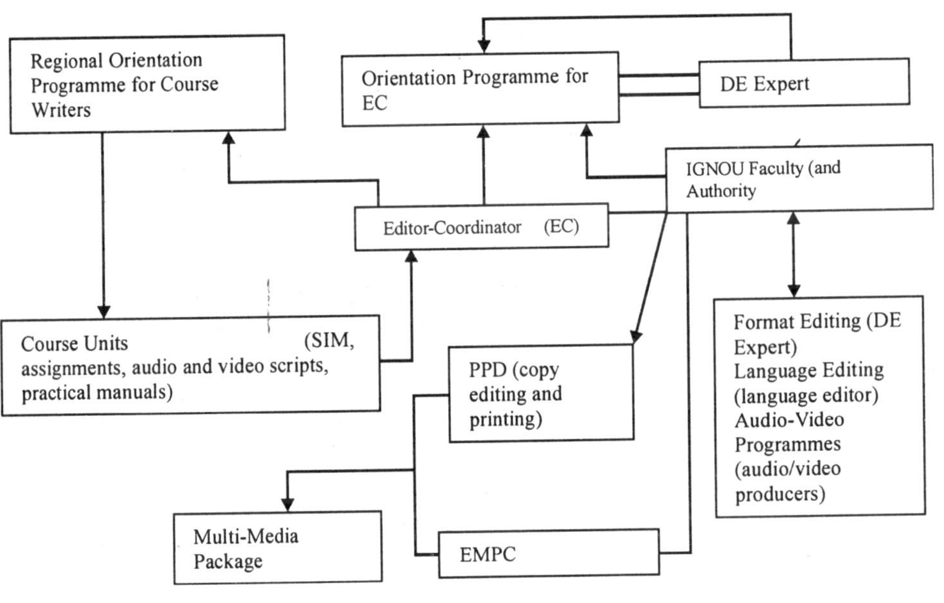

Figure 10: Non-IGNOU editor-coordinator model
(Source: Panda, 2000)

In the case of 'in-house faculty' model of course development (Fig. 11) (like the Postgraduate Diploma in Distance Education), the entire responsibility rests on the in-house faculty. The faculty members were exposed to staff development programmes in distance education, but the senior-most faculty acts as the chief editor of all the courses. Content, format and language editing were carried out in-house. Such a model is appropriate only when enough expertise is available in-house. There have been variations to the approach adopted for the PGDDE programme development in other programmes within the in-house faculty model.

A very interesting model is the development (writing and editing) of materials in a workshop mode (Fig. 12). This model have been followed in situations where a programme has been developed either in collaboration with a national or international agency (in which case the

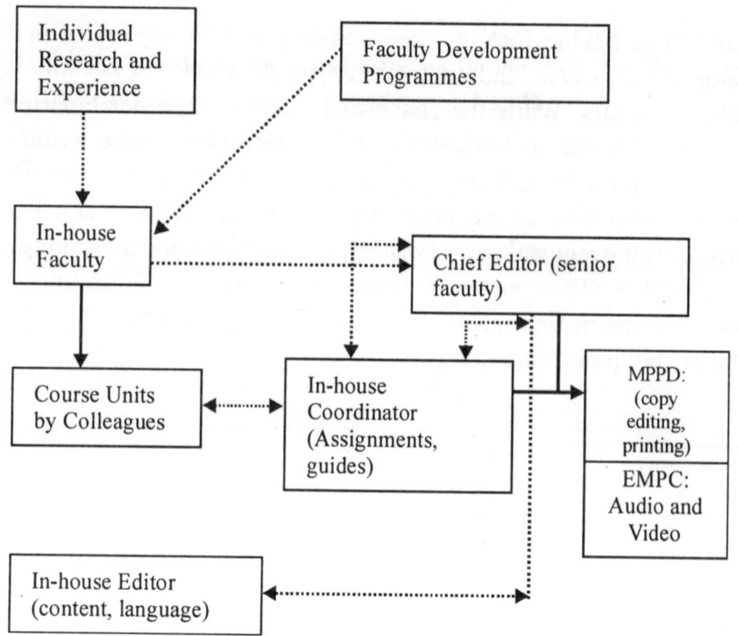

Figure 11: In-house faculty model
(Source: Panda, 2000)

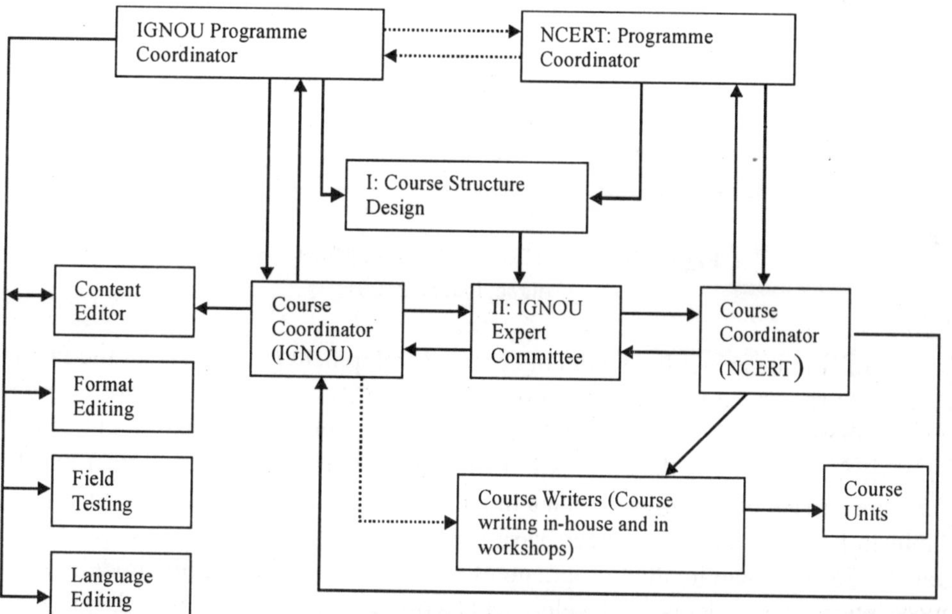

Figure 12: Collaborative workshop model
(Source: Panda, 2000)

outside agency provides content expertise for smooth implementation of the programme) or exclusively in-house (where the internal faculty feels competent and confident that quality of the programme will not be compromised if such a strategy is adopted). The Certificate in Guidance and Certificate Programme in Laboratory Techniques programme better represent the former, and lab courses in Physics within the B.Sc. programme are an example of the latter approach.

Quality Benchmarks

There have been deviations to the above models in some courses, as also within each of the models described above. However, what needs to be considered as benchmarks for adoption of an approach to course development include:

- *Time* taken to produce an academic programme.
- *Costs* involved in producing an academic programme.
- *Constraints* involved at various stages of design and development of an academic programme.
- *Quality* of the output, i.e. the self-learning package.

A recent study (Panda and Garg, 2003) conducted on the development of the physics lab courses (within the B.Sc. programme) for the three years of the programme following the workshop model analysed the above four variables. Their findings suggested that the role of the course coordinator and the in-house course team assumed greater significance in achieving course production with low cost, less time and constraints, and of high quality. In the context of these physics lab courses, the role of the course coordinator was pivotal in consideration of the parameters influencing course development, production and delivery. Studies on this area on a continuing basis are required to standardise the models, as also to reform course design and development from time to time.

References

Deshpande, P. (1999). Yashwantrao Chavan Maharashtra Open University. In S. Panda (ed.), *Open and Distance Education*. New Delhi: ABI.

Gunawardena, C.N. (1992). Changing faculty roles for audiographics and online teaching. *The American Journal of Distance Education*, 6(3), 58-71.

Inglis, A. (1996). Teaching-learning specialists' conceptions of their role in the design of distance learning packages. *Distance Education*, 17(2), 267-288.

Lockwood, F. (1992). Alternative methods of materials production. *Media and Technology for Human Resource Development*, 4(4), 233-238.

Lockwood, F. (1993). *Cost effectiveness methods of materials production*. Paper presented at the 7th AAOU annual conference 1993, Hong Kong.

Melton, R.F. (1977). Course design and development techniques used in distance teaching. *ZIFF Papiere 12*. Hagen: ZIFF.

Olcott, D. Jr. and Wright, S.J. (1995). An institutional support framework for increasing faculty participation in postsecondary distance education. *American Journal of Distance Education*, 9 (3), 5-17.

Panda, S. (2000). *Models of Course Development in Distance Education, Cost Effectiveness and Performance Indicators.* Research Report, STRIDE, Indira Gandhi National Open University, New Delhi.

Panda, S. and Garg, S. (2003). Revising distance education course development: workshop method for development of science lab courses. *Staff & Educational Development International,* 7(2), 153-163.

Panda, S., Khan, A.R. and Garg, S. (1999). Growth and development of the national open university. In S. Panda (ed.). *Open and Distance Education: policies, practices and quality concerns.* New Delhi: ABI.

Rumble, Greville and Harry, Keith (1982). *The Distance Teaching Universities*. London; Croom Helm.

Professor Santosh Panda is Director, Staff Training & Research Institute of Distance Education; and Coordinator, Inter- University Consortium, Indira Gandhi National Open University, New Delhi.
Email: spanda@ignou.ac.in

Professor Suresh Garg is Pro-Vice Chancellor, Indira Gandhi National Open University, New Delhi.
Email: scgarg@ignou.ac.in

10

Agriculture Education Through Distance Mode

Panjab Singh and M.K. Salooja

Introduction

Soon after we became free, Pt. Jawaharlal Nehru, our first Prime Minister said, "Everything else can wait, but not agriculture".

Since then, Indian agriculture has witnessed multifarious developments. The changing social and scientific context of agriculture requires a new paradigm of agriculture education, research and extension. Open and Distance learning (ODL) can play an important role in extending the access and reach of the agriculture education. The chapter analyses the present agriculture scenario, conventional agriculture education and potential of ODL in widening its access and reach particularly among the farm families and youth.

Role of Agriculture in Nation's Economy

Agriculture continues to be the backbone of the Indian economy. A strong correlation between the fortunes of agriculture sector and the overall GDP has been re-established during the mid-term appraisal of the country's 10th Five Year Plan (Table 1). In the year 2003-04, when farm output was up a whopping 9.6%, the economy grew at a solid 8.5%. In the year prior to that, when the agriculture sector shrunk a massive 7%, the GDP was up a mere 4 % (Maradia, 2005). A great concern has been shown by the policy makers in the decline of the growth rate from 3.2 per cent for the period between 1980-81 and 1995-96 to just 1.9 percent in the subsequent period. In this backdrop, the Prime Minister in the National Development Council 51st meeting of the (2005) has emphasized that "Correcting the agrarian crisis must be accorded highest priority". Agriculture constituting 22% share in the economy and 54% of the total workforce is and will be central to all strategies for planned socio-economic development of the country.

Table 1: Performance of agriculture and its impact on GDP in the last five years

	FY 05	FY 04	FY 03	FY 02	FY 01
Agriculture	1.1%	9.6%	-7%	6.3%	-0.1%
Manufacturing	9.2%	6.9%	6.5%	3.6%	7.4%
Services	7.1%	7.1%	8.7%	4.5%	3.5%
GDP	6.9%	8.5%	4%	5.8%	4.4%

FY: Financial Year; Source: (Maradia, 2005)

Achievements

The agriculture sector has made significant strides in the last six decades (about 58 years) and the country has transformed its position from the net importer to surpluses for the export. It was the result of harnessing science & technology that has heralded the Green, White, Blue, and now Rainbow revolution in the country. The visible indicators are: increase in per capita food and calorie intake, decline in vulnerability of the Indian agricultural sector to the vagaries of the monsoons, control of price fluctuations, and changing profile of agriculture from subsistence to commercialisation. The success has been attained due to commitment of researchers and policy makers and the sustained efforts of the Indian farmers.

Targets

By 2020, India's population is likely to be around 1.33 billion, and under the scenario of 5 percent growth rate in GDP, the total domestic food grains demand will be 294 million tones (mt) comprising 122 mt of rice, 103 mt of wheat, 41 mt of coarse grains and 28 mt of pulses. Similarly, during 2020, the demand will be 126-183 mt of milk, 136-181 mt of vegetables, 68-98 mt of fruits, 6.3-12.1. mt of meat and 9.5-18.3 mt of fish. To meet the estimated demand, the yield level over the base period yield (1994-95) is required to be enhanced by 136-157 percent. Considering these trends, National Agricultural Policy -2000, rightly envisages growth rate in excess of 4 percent per annum in agriculture sector. These growth targets are to be achieved against the constraints of diminishing land resources, increasing biotic and abiotic stresses, indications of decline in factor productivity, threatened loss of biodiversity, natural resource shrinkage and degradation, climate change, tightening of IPR, intensifying competition (quality and cost) in international trade, widening economic inequity besides burgeoning population.

Challenges

There is a need to bridge the yield, productivity and production gaps, and ensure sustainable improvement in food security, income, equity, livelihood security, nutrition adequacy and environmental security. Enhancing the economic value of time and labour of landless workforce by bringing about paradigm shift from unskilled to skilled work is one of the important challenges as per the Chairman, National Commission on Farmers (Swaminathan, 2005). The socio-economic changes—globalization, free trade, technological innovations in IT, communication and biotechnology, democratisation and empowerment, environment concerns, and quality and convenience add new dimensions to the challenges in the agricultural and food security system.

Indian agriculture faces promising opportunities in the production and marketing of high-value livestock products, fruits and vegetables and fishery. The second green revolution is indeed graduating from grain production to food processing and marketing, and development of vocational & entrepreneurial skills among the farmers and rural youth. Hon. President Dr Abdul Kalam on the eve of 56th Republic Day speech emphasized that the displacement of people from agriculture sector has to be facilitated through skill enabling for undertaking value added tasks in the rural enterprises so that migration to urban area is reduced. He stressed for Providing Urban Amenities in Rural Areas (PURA) and creation of knowledge networks (establishment of Village Knowledge Centres) to facilitate creation of employment in the rural areas itself thereby leading to their economic connectivity and prosperity (Abdul Kalam, 2005).

The scenario in turn forces concerned policy makers and academics to redefine agricultural education and extension to enable it to cope with the changed global situation. Its need and importance is corroborated through publication of a special issue of the *University News* by the Association of Indian Universities (2004) titled "Challenges of Higher Education in Agriculture Science and Management" and one-day workshop titled "Redefining Agriculture Education and Extension System in Changed Scenario" by the National Academy of Agricultural Sciences (2005).

Agriculture Education under the Conventional System

National agricultural education system, at the tertiary level, has developed into one of the most impressive systems in the world and is credited with the Green revolution. The major achievements in agriculture education during the 50 years of India's Independence have been compiled in an ICAR publication by Mehta and Mathur (1999). Sinha (2000) sketching the circumstances and history of development of higher education in agriculture science, which resulted in the creation of agricultural universities in the country on the pattern of land-grant system in the USA, has identified the weaknesses and advocated for a change in the system. A comprehensive profile and analysis has been reported by Katyal (2004).The aforesaid publications (AIU, 2004; NASA, 2005) also delineate issues, emerging trends and strategic alternates/interventions.

The system consists of State Agricultural Universities and their constituent/affiliated colleges, deemed to be Universities, Central Universities having agricultural faculties, Central Agricultural University and a number of private agricultural colleges (Table 1). Bachelor's degrees are offered in 11 broad disciplines of agriculture and related subjects (i.e., agriculture, horticulture, fishery, forestry, home science, sericulture, dairy science, agricultural engineering, food science and technology, agro-business including marketing, banking and cooperation) and Master's degrees is offered in 95 diverse disciplines. Compared to a total intake capacity of about 1500 students per year at the time of independence; currently, about 21,000 agricultural graduates and postgraduates (Graduates - 13,500, Post-Graduate 6,000 and Doctorate-1500) are produced every year. The qualified manpower status through institutions up to year 2000 include 1,66,200 graduates, 78,000 post-graduates and 11,400 doctorate. At School level, the agriculture education is not well structured and contribution of the vocational pass-outs at the secondary level and Sr. secondary level to the system is limited i.e. para-professional and agriculture entrepreneurs are not being developed.

Table 2: Agricultural education system in India

University	No. of Universities	No. of Colleges
State Agriculture Universities	34	200 *
Central Agriculture University	01	06
Deemed-to-be-Universities	05	10
Central Universities	03	03
Indian Institute of Technology	01	01
State General Universities	16	41
Total	60	261

* Includes nine affiliated colleges; (Source: Katyal, 2004)

Analysis

The agriculture education system has given weak human capital base and lopsided growth, i.e. 5-6 per cent of the total graduates belong to this sector and shockingly more than 43% of the agricultural graduates and 23% of the postgraduates were unemployed after completion of their degree programmes in 1999-2000. 50% of the graduates opt for the PG programmes. Proportion of educated workers (secondary and higher levels) in profession is quite low (12% male and 2% female) and ratio of para-professionals to professionals is quite low. The growth has taken place in conventional discipline and limited number are coming in emerging and application oriented courses such as agri-business management, agro-processing, bio-technology, marketing and storage, environmental science, journalism and IT. The curriculum does not impart skills required in commercial agriculture, thus restricting spread of entrepreneurship in agriculture and generate employment. There are a whole lot of new opportunities emerging which the agricultural graduates have by and large failed to take advantage of, as they lack risk taking skills mainly because of mismatch between agricultural education and the agricultural occupation.

Issues

Farming has become more knowledge intensive and technology oriented. The concerns in reference to the agricultural education system structured in three strands, i.e. policy, institutional and pedagogic are as follows:

Policy

The policy issues include: (i) mismatch between education curriculum, entrepreneur-driven skill requirement, (job-market) and employment opportunity; (ii) lack of mass awareness about ill effects from unscientific resource management; (iii) absence of mechanism to develop middle level technicians/para-professionals/extension workers, i.e. need to introduce vocational and entrepreneurial programmes; (iv) non-existence of linkages between school system and higher education; (v) absence of framework for need assessment/manpower requirements/ emerging areas to promote job oriented programmes; (vi) absence of continuing education and in-service training programmes for various stakeholders, particularly, teachers; (vii) limited budgetary allocation for education & research; (viii) ICAR serves as UGC for SAUs but with no statutory authority: and (ix) gender and environmental issues.

Institutional

Institutional issues are: (i) isolation of agricultural institutions from other multi-faculty universities of science, arts and humanities; (ii) inadequate integration and coordination among three strands, i.e. teaching, research and extension; (iii) poor accessibility and affordability of education among rural population; (iv) poor recognition to extension work for academic mobility; (v) no statutory quality control mechanism for institutions and programmes; (vi) the urban origin of agriculture students; (vii) partnership and linkages with industry and (viii) limited autonomy.

Pedagogic

The pedagogic issues include: (i) pedagogy to strengthen traditional wisdom and giving a scientific base to this wisdom and foresight, i.e. making agriculture education two way transfer of knowledge; (ii) articulating the curriculum into competency based, (iii) framework for integrating formal and non-formal mode/conventional and distance education mode; (iv) giving credit and accreditation to farmers for their experience and non-formal training programmes; and (v) availability of ICT and satellite network for pedagogical purposes.

What is Needed?

The foremost requirement for the agriculture education system is to foster a mindset among students which is analytical, technology oriented and sensitive to sociological and economic issues of farming in India. Agriculture education has so far focused on crops, dairy and livestock production in the context of food self-sufficiency. A time has come to give it a broader orientation of international competitiveness, trade and industry. The education must equip graduates to enable them to not only earn livelihood but also contribute to society development and environment protection.

The system should be such that it is easily accessible to masses especially in marginalized region and to the marginalized sector of the society, should be affordable to masses, and meet the quality standards while being relevant to the society's needs besides maintaining its flexible and innovative character.

It should aim at producing agricultural entrepreneurs who would go out proudly into the world and create a multiplying economic impact rather than look at the system to absorb them as employees. The system should aim to increase "job creators" and not "job seekers".

Indian agriculture, as a part of the world agriculture system, has to keep pace with fast and vastly changing technologies, new products and product varieties, expanding and complicated information systems, new market strategies, new services and so on. A good scope exists to improve the quality and reach of agriculture education & extension system in order to ensure efficiency, effectiveness and sustainability of production systems. The following interventions shall obviate missing links in the agriculture education system and facilitate development of para professionals and training to farmers for productive skills.

- **Accelerate the access and spread of agriculture education** to rural masses through different innovative alternative methods viz., (i) Flash card method and awareness programmes for early childhood learning, adult literacy and school drop outs; (ii) Video versions of the contents for delivery over cable TV; (iii) Multimedia forms of entire school and college curriculum for delivery over the internet. The universalization of elementary education is being revamped under *Sarva Shiksha Abhiyan* (SSA), which aims to provide useful and quality education to all children in the 6-14 age groups by 2010.The agriculture as a subject should be part and parcel of the education system at elementary and secondary level.
- **Vocational and entrepreneurial bias to agricultural programmes:** The educational programme in the present or emerging scenario either should increase the employability or ensure value addition for entrepreneurship among the youth/ to the persons. The four pillars identified under Delors Commission Report (Delors. et al, 1996) include: *Learning to know, Learning to do, Learning to live together and Learning to be. Learning to do* refers to the vocational education. In essence, education should develop every child both as a person, as a member of society, and as a person practicing a vocation. The education model

integrating vocational & entrepreneurial components is akin to the basic education philosophy advocated by Mahatma Gandhi in the late thirties. The essence of Gandhi's thinking or in *"Nai Taleem"* was education through life, work and environment. This model of integration of work with education is necessary for inculcation of productive skills among the youth and for self-reliant economy for the village. The trained manpower will facilitate in improving the productivity and quality of the system and orient the youth towards self-occupation at the village/community level. In this process, the much-needed middle level manpower/para-professionals shall also be available for transfusing the technology or to act as change agents at grass root levels.

- **Build national agriculture information delivery system:** The new century is referred as "Century of Knowledge" and the access to information shall be a key indicator for the progress. Information requirements of the farmers & rural youth are increasing and linear information flows that dominated the traditional model of technology transfer are being replaced by pluralistic information flows. The Global Agriculture Information Network (GAIN) managed by the Foreign Agricultural Services is an electronic reporting system that provides timely information to U.S. exporters and commodity analysts. This multi-commodity reporting network provides current-year estimates and next-year forecasting for food and agricultural production, supply, and distribution. It also provides information on policies and market demand that affects the sales of U.S. agricultural products worldwide. Similarly, the Agricultural Information Network (AIN) is an Internet portal enabling Thai farmers, field officers, policy-makers and government to communicate and access relevant and useful agricultural information. COL Knowledge Series on "Using ICT for Agriculture Extension" outlines the issues such as organisational, social and cultural, content and technological issues with successful examples of use of ICT in agriculture extension (Maru and Latchem, 2005).

In India too, the government supportive policy has contributed to growth of ICT based initiatives for providing information in the areas of agricultural technology, production, processing, marketing and other farm related aspects. Some of exemplar references are: (i) Kisan Call Centres, (ii) AGMARKNET, (iii) Village Knowledge Centres, (iv) Warna Wired Village Project, (v) Gyandoot project, (vi) E-Choupal, (vii) Rural Information Kiosks, (viii) I-Kisan portal, (ix) Computer on wheels, (x) Agricultural Gateway of India (xi) Help-Line services and (xii) Bhoomi project. The scope, impact and strategic issues have been discussed by Singh & Salooja (2004), Kumar (2005), Mruthyunjaya & Adhiguru (2005) and Chandrashekhar (2005).

It is essential to harness the potential of ICT. Building a National Information Delivery System (NIDS) would be an innovative step in meeting the goals set for mass education and entrepreneurship through distance mode.

There is a need to develop an integrated and network system of agriculture education and knowledge management, which may enable educational institutions to develop appropriate paradigms of development and education, and to increase coverage by serving the large number.

Open Learning Initiatives in Agriculture Education

Agriculture education through ODL will accelerate the access and spread of education to rural masses especially in marginalized regions and marginalized society through different innovative alternative methods.

International Experience

UNESCO (1997) has issued a policy document encouraging the use of distance learning, at all levels of educational systems, for purposes of development. The World Bank (1999) promotes "innovative delivery" as one of its global priorities for the educational sector. The World Health Organization (1998) promotes the use of "telematics," including distance health education, in support of its Health-for-All agenda. FAO has accumulated significant experiences in the field of distance learning. Some of the successful examples are:

a) Collaboration between FAO and the REDCAPA network. [REDCAPA is the "Network of Institutions Dedicated to Teaching Agricultural and Rural Development Policies for Latin America and the Caribbean" (Red de Instituciones Vinculadas a la Capacitacion en Economia y Políticas Agricolas en America Latina y el Caribe)].
b) The Information Network on Post-harvest Operations (INPh O): INPh O provides three basic services: i) Information and databases concerned with a range of post-harvest issues (e.g., storage, transportation, processing, marketing and food safety), ii) Interactive communication services connecting users with one another and with resource people, and iii) Links to other electronic sources of post-harvest information.
c) PG Diploma in Agriculture Development offered by Wye College of the University of London.

India

Punjab Agriculture University initiated in 1971 to start a non- formal distance education programme titled "Integrated Course in agriculture Production" by enrolling about 250 farmers who were literate enough to read and write the local languages. The salient features, curriculum structure, development of modules, evaluation of trainees, contact programmes, and programme constraints and future directions have been consolidated by Gill (2000).

Since 1973, the G.B. Pant University of Agriculture and Technology has offered a Correspondence Course Programme to farmers and rural youth in Uttar Pradesh, India. About 500 learners each year select four courses from a list of seventeen options (fourteen concern the cultivation of particular crops, and one each concern dairy production, insecticide use and fertilizer use). The Programme's delivery strategy is print-based correspondence. Each course comprises five or six lessons, written in elementary Hindi. Course scheduling is timed to coincide with the seasonal production of the various crops under study. Non-credit certificates are issued to all students passing end of term examinations in each course.

At school level, National Institute of Open Learning is offering about 12 certificate courses in agriculture and allied areas. At tertiary level under the Open and Distance Learning System (ODL), the Yashwantrao Chavan Maharasthra Open University, Nasik was the first to establish School of Agriculture and is implementing a number of agricultural programmes. The unique feature is multimedia mix and farmers support services in teaching learning process. In addition to support KVK, it has created Krishi Prayog Pariwar (15 Self Help Groups), Agri-polyclinics and Radio broadcast (Gunjal, 2000).

A Diploma programme in "Agriculture Extension Services for Input Dealers (DAESI)" through Distance Mode has been launched by the National Institute of Agriculture Extension Management, an organization of the Ministry of Agriculture (2004).

Academic programmes on offer under ODL

At present Nalanda Open University, YMCOU, Dr. B.R. Ambedkar Open University and IGNOU are offering courses in Agriculture and allied subjects as detailed below (Table 3).

Table 3: Academic programmes on offer under ODL

Institutions	Non-degree (certificate/diploma)	Bachelor's degree	Master's degree	Ph.D.
Nalanda Open University, India	Bio Fertilizer Floriculture Medicinal and Aromatic Plants Soil Management			
YCMOU, India	Gardening Fruit Production Vegetable production Floriculture & Landscaping Agribusiness management	Horticultural Agriculture	Agricultural Communication Agricultural Extension Agricultural Development	Agricultural Communication Agricultural Extension Agricultural Development
Dr. B.R. Ambedkar Open University, India			Environmental Studies	
IGNOU, * India	Participatory Forest Management Rural Development Production of Value Added Products from		Agriculture Policy	

	- Fruits & Vegetables - Dairy Technology - Meat Technology - Fish & Aquaculture - Grains, Pulses & Oilseeds Watershed Management Certificate in Sericulture Certificate in Bamboo use, technologies & enterprise development Certificate in Rattan use, technologies & enterprise development Diploma in Silkworm rearing Awareness programme - Dairy Farming Awareness programme Bamboo & Rattan Awareness programme - Fruits & vegetables			

* Except Participatory Forest Management and Rural Development, all other courses at IGNOU are currently being developed to be started from academic year 2006 onwards.

The primary concern about agriculture programmes through ODL is its limited capacity to provide farm experience and laboratory experimentations. Agriculture is an applied science and hence development in cognitive, psychomotor and affective domain is necessary to achieve quality and effectiveness in people, products and profits through agriculture per se. The effectiveness of distance agricultural education with limited access to fieldwork and laboratory work and dependency on study centres for such facilities needs serious thinking (Nimbalkar et. al. 2004). The success story of Yashwantrao Chavan Maharasthra Open University, Nasik (YCMOU) in distance education programmes has established that these inherent limitations could be obviated if the pedagogy model is appropriate.

Prospects

The conventional universities are able to meet the requirements of a small percentage of students. However, it is not possible to involve all interested people living in far-flung places, remote areas and in the (rural) countryside within the limited facilities that universities possess. To meet this requirement, Distance Education has become a most competitive system. A SWOT analysis on Distance Agriculture Education in India has been made by Nimbalkar et al. (2004). The issues and opportunities including type of courses which could be initiated have been highlighted by Sudarsan (2004) and Masood (2004). The strategic issues with regard to ODL in Agriculture Education and Knowledge Management have been delineated by Salooja (2004). The scope and opinion of eminent experts have been discussed in the recently published book titled "*Food, Health and Education for All – The Role of Open and Distance Learning*" (Powar, 2004). The report titled "Lifelong learning for Farmers (L3Farmers)" evidences a massive need to improve need to improve smallholders' knowledge and skills in the food production-market chain that cannot be met by conventional agricultural extension alone; but it can be met by employing open and distance learning/information and communications technologies (ICTs) and innovative extension methods (Latchem, Maru and Alluri,2004). The prospectus and challenges in reference to "Virtual Education in Agriculture" has been comprehensively discussed by Vijayaragavan et al (2004). The major constraints in virtual education are poor connectivity, infrastructural facilities, lack of qualified professionals to develop educational materials and assurance of quality education.

The scope and potential of the ODL can be corroborated by the recommendations made by Dr. M. S. Swaminathan committee report on education for agriculture. It has recommended that State Agricultural Universities (SAU's) should establish an independent cell for distance education develops programme for training of rural youth for imparting newer skills and agriculture and allied sciences. The committee also recommended five Agricultural Educations Media Development Center could be established to develop capsules for dissemination of knowledge in agriculture and allied sciences through television and one of multimedia as a part of distance learning. Information empowerment shall increase agricultural production through improvement in productivity.

FAO has prepared a framework which explores how distance education and training strategies could be usefully applied to the challenges of food security and rural development. It has proposed five suggestions for effective distance education and presented a logical map that depicts the pathway through which distance education and training could assist the organization to reach its target learners. The five basic suggestions include : (a) be undertaken for the right reasons, (b) be sensitive to context, (c) use existing infrastructure and have sustainable cost, (d) engage stakeholders in participatory process, and (e) be based in sound pedagogical and administrative models (McLean, 2001).

The "Consultative Group on International Agricultural Research (CGIAR)" has established the Global Open Food and Agriculture University (GO-FAU) for open distance learning and capacity strengthening that serves traditional and open universities in developing and developed countries. The university's goal is to strengthen the capacity of postgraduate students, researchers, and other working professionals in food and agriculture (including livestock, forestry, and fisheries) in order to enhance agricultural development, poverty reduction, and food security. A range of distance education technologies shall be used to fill knowledge gaps, improve existing postgraduate agriculture and natural resources degree programs in the developing world, and offer high-quality degree programs. The university would use: Web-based, CD-ROM, traditional text, and other technologies in a variety of languages so that participants from all regions of the developing world may benefit. The workshop reports on the web site provide the status of initiatives taken.

It is high time to take advantage of "flexible and learner-centric" system of education and make use of multi-media, e-journals, e-books for quality mass education and e-governance., Open and distance education will become most effective tool of imparting education to large section of society with integration of components of hand-on-training at selected study centres and face to face interaction through counselling. This requires a strong partnership among ODL imparting institutions and the institutions of conventional education system. All institutions imparting agricultural education should resort to dual and convergent mode and give place to technology mediated Open and Distance Learning (TechMODEL). It is time for agricultural universities to examine how teachers could participate in the process of change sweeping over the educational system, and utilize modern tools of communication for rapid transfer of latest academic know-how to those in need of it beyond the boundaries of university campuses. Beside, distance education for farmers and small agri-entrepreneurs need to be strengthened through multimedia component. To achieve all this we need to initiate policy dialogue for ODL in agriculture to discuss the following issues:

- Need for ODL system for meeting needs of different stakeholders
- Need for new institution to promote and support ODL for agriculture
- Restructuring and remandating existing institution to impart ODL education
- Need to redesign existing and implement new processes in institution and educational organizations for providing ODL to agricultural communities.

With the availability of an exclusive education satellite (EduSat), the time is ripe for making intense use of ICT to create an interactive virtual classroom in all our remote areas

Challenges

The challenge before ODL is to offer learning and educational opportunity for continuing and lifelong learning for all in the information society and knowledge era. The ODL may take the initiative to provide missing link in the agriculture education system, i.e. development of:

i) Vocational and entrepreneurial certificates and diplomas for creation of middle level skill manpower/technicians/para-professionals;
ii) Continuing education and in-service training programmes for teachers, technicians, managers, administrators, scientists and farmers;
iii) Competencies and qualification framework for giving recognition to non-formal sector and vertical mobility in the profession;
iv) Multimedia awareness packages;
v) Information databank, on-line project profiles and educational packages on productivity, good practices and quality aspects;
vi) Partnership and networking in agriculture;
vii) Convergence of conventional and ODL for sharing of resources;

viii) Facilitate ICT application;

ix) Virtual university and knowledge bank.

A pro-active role of ODL in the system would help improving the quality and relevance of formal education simultaneous with qualitative expansion. This would require shift from teaching to learning; shift from traditional academic to life based curriculum and value based education. Singh (2004) outlining the strategy for mass education through distance mode recommends : creation of farm school in every 'block' for development of practical skills for knowledge application, and establishment of vocational training institutes for productive skills, building the National Information Delivery System (NIDS) and effective integration and linkages at national and international level with various institutions and stakeholders.

Conclusion

Agriculture continues to be the foundation for development, hunger eradication, and poverty reduction for India. We are continuously moving towards a knowledge-based economy. The potential contribution that an individual can make in acquiring and applying knowledge for improving processes, products and services is becoming more important than physical labour. It calls upon the education system to develop the capabilities among the stakeholders of the system to operate effectively and efficiently. Strengthening their capacity through multi-media educational modules and academic programmes and using appropriate & relevant electronic, information, and communication technologies so as to reach a wide range of audience should be on top of education agenda.

The ODL can provide a range of flexible, cost effective and need based educational(particularly awareness and vocational and entrepreneurial)/continuing education programmes for farmers, extension workers, rural youth, agriculture students, scientists, administrators, planners and other stakeholders of the system. This requires a strong partnership among ODL institutions and the institutions of conventional education system. All institutions imparting agricultural education should resort to dual and convergent mode system and give place to technology mediated Open and Distance Learning (TechMODEL). It will have a synergistic effect i.e., ensure spread, reach and access necessary for sustainable use of natural resources, enhanced agricultural capacity and improved food and nutritional security in the country.

The ICT potential could be harnessed by the ODL in an effective way. A critical mass of human resource may be built up at various levels through education to masses. This will generate entrepreneurship and employment generation in different sectors viz., Agriculture, Horticulture, Animal Husbandry, Fisheries, Poultry, Farm machinery, PHT & Value added product etc. and thus raising the income of rural population. Education to masses especially in marginalized regions and to marginalize society will also tap the opportunities available in the region for sustainable productivity and livelihood security of the masses. The challenge is to develop a framework of an integrated and ICT enabled system of agriculture education.

References

Abdul Kalam, A.P.J. (2005). *Address of the President of India: Republic Day Speech on the eve of 52nd Republic Day*. New Delhi.

Association of Indian Universities (2004). Challenges of higher education in agriculture sciences and management. *University News*-Special Issue, August 30-September 05, 42(35).

Chandrashekhar, C.P. (2005). *ICT and Rural Livelihood.* Available at http://www. digitalopportunity.org/article/view/112994.

Delors, J. et al (1996). *Learning: The Treasure Within* (Report of the International Commission on Education for the twenty-first century). Paris: UNESCO.

Gill, L.S. (2000). Distance Education Programme for agricultural and rural development – PAU experience. In Dash, N.K. and Menon, S.B. (eds.), *Training of Professionals through Distance Education in South Asia.* New Delhi: IGNOU.

Gunjal, Surya S. (2000). Agriculture education and rural development through distance education in Maharashtra. In Dash, N.K. and Menon, S.B. (eds.), *Training of Professionals through Distance Education in South Asia.* New Delhi: IGNOU.

Katyal, J.C. (2004). Employment oriented agricultural education. Background paper presented at the Brainstorming session of the Workshop, National Academy for Agricultural Sciences, New Delhi, February 9.

Kumar, D. (2005). Information and communication technology (ICT) in Indian agriculture. *Effective Executive* (Feb-March, 2005). Available at: http://econwpa.wustl.edu:80/eps/get/papers/0503/0503002.pdf

Latchem, C., Maru, A. and Alluri, K. (2004). *Lifelong learning for farmers (L3Farmers).* A report and recommendations to the Commonwealth of Learning - *An open and distance lifelong learning for small-holder farmers and agricultural communities.* Available at www.col.org/programmes/capacity/l3farmers.htm.

Maradia, H.P. (2005). Pump priming agriculture. Available at: http: www.indiainfoline.com/nevi /pupr.html

Maru, A. and Latchem, C. (2005). *Using ICT for Agriculture Extension.* Vancouver: Knowledge Series, Commonwealth of Learning.

Mehta, S.L. and Mathur, B.N. (1999). *Agricultural Education in India.* New Delhi: ICAR.

Masood, Shah (2004). Distance education for agriculture and extension education. *University News,* 42(35), 85.

McLean, Scott (2001). Distance education and distance learning: A framework for the Food and Agriculture Organization of the United Nations. *Sustainable Development Dimensions* (September 2001). Available at: http://www.fao.org/sd/2001

Mruthyunjaya and Adhiguru, P. (2005). *ICT for livelihood security: a reality check.* Available at http://www.digitalopportunity.org.article/view/113295.

National Academy of Agricultural Sciences (2005). *Redefining Agriculture Education and Extension System in Changed Scenario.* A workshop report. New Delhi: NAAS.

National Development Council (2005). 51st Meeting of the NDC held on 27th June 2005 at Vigyan Bhawan, New Delhi.

Nimbalkar, S.A., Patil, V.D. and Ingle, O.P. (2004). Distance Agriculture Education: Perspectives in agricultural development in India. Paper presented in Third PAN Commonwealth Forum on Open Learning: Building Learning Communities for new Millennium: Reaching Wider Audiences through Innovative Approaches, New Zealand, July.

Powar, K.B. (2004). Building quality into distance education. In Powar, K.B. (ed.), *Food, Health and Education for All – The Role of Open and Distance Learning*. New Delhi: Anamaya Publishers.

Salooja, M.K. (2004). Role of open and distance learning in agriculture education and knowledge management. *University News*, 42(35), 76.

Sinha, S.K. (2000). Education for agriculture in India: Time for a change. *Current Science,* 79 (3), 302-310.

Singh, Panjab (2004). Sustainable agriculture and food security: Role of open and distance education. In Powar, K.B. (ed.), *Food, Health and Education for All – The Role of Open and Distance Learning.* New Delhi: Anamaya Publishers.

Singh, Panjab and Salooja, M.K. (2004). Using information and communications technology in agriculture extension: Planning issues for building a framework. *Indian Journal of Open Learning*, 13(2), 181-189.

Sudarsan, Y. (2004) Distance education in agriculture: Issues and opportunities. *University News*, 42(35), 83.

Swaminathan, M.S. (2005). Sustainable farming. *The Hindu Survey of Indian Agriculture 2005(Annual).* Chennai.

Vijayaraghavan K., Gautam R.C., Nagarajan S., and Dabas, J.P.S. (2004). Virtual education in agriculture. *University News*, 42(35), p.71.

Professor Panjab Singh is former Director, Centre for Extension Education, IGNOU, and now Vice Chancellor, Banaras Hindu University, Varanasi.

Dr. M.K. Salooja is Deputy Director, Centre for Extension Education, Indira Gandhi National Open University, New Delhi
Email: mksalooja@ignou.ac.in

11

Health Education Through Distance Mode

A.K. Agarwal and T.K. Jena

Introduction

Education through distance mode in health sector is a recent phenomenon. Though conventional education through face-to-face remains the mainstream, people have tried to adapt the new philosophy to meet their specific needs within the framework of their available resources. Developed nations like US, Canada, Australia and UK used it primarily for continuing education and training of paramedics. On the other hand, developing countries such as China, India, South Africa and Brazil adopted this tool primarily to bridge the existing gap in their health human resource needs. Indira Gandhi National Open University (IGNOU) has the unique distinction of taking pioneering steps to offer programmes in the core clinical field of medical education in the country.

Education is an organic entity and it evolves to respond to societal needs. Since the 1990s, all systems of teaching and training have undergone phenomenal transformation as a result of revolutionary technological advancement and their application for delivery of education, quest for new knowledge and emerging needs of the information knowledge society. Medical education is no exception. Usually, it is seen as the most conservative discipline because it follows very rigid and rigorous methods of training since the students ought to be fit to handle the human lives. In this era of quality consciousness, medical education cannot afford to compromise. But the fact remains that the medical education has to cope with the increasing demand for generating health professionals to meet the growing need created by population explosion. Though, it is a global phenomenon, the developing nations in particular have to look for sustainable alternatives of human resource development, while ensuring the qualitative aspect of the training system. Unfortunately not much attention has been paid to balanced growth and training of health care professionals. For instance, developing countries have more doctors than nurses and paramedical personnel, though this should be the other way around. In India, there are more than 365,000 doctors, 264,000 nurses and about 350,000 paramedical health workers. That is, there is one doctor for a population of about 2000 and three nurses for two doctors and one paramedical health worker for each doctor. Ideally, the doctor, nurse and paramedical ratio should be 1:3:9. Still worse, there is no scope for continuous professional development through knowledge updation of this vast army of health human resource. (Dutta, Jena and Panda, 1996)

Therefore, to provide best health care, the issues that need to be addressed are to create provision for:

- continuous professional development of existing human resource to keep pace with fast growth of knowledge, and
- update and upgrade medical professionals to optimum level so as to enhance access to quality health care.

Obviously, in view of resource crunch, the existing system of medical education is not enough to address these challenges and we are constrained to look for a more flexible and cost-effective system. In this scenario, the distance learning mode of training and education presents itself as a viable alternative.

Historical Perspective

Globally, there is a large spectrum of courses that covers medical, paramedical and allied health programmes. But the programmes involving core clinical subjects for doctors leading to degrees/ diplomas are few. This is essentially due to practical and ethical problems confronted in providing the facilities for hands-on-training in live situation. For example, there is lack of uniformity in standards. While some institutions offer programmes in on-line mode with facility of simulation techniques, in some others there is little scope for practical exposure. Except a few developed countries, where collaborations with medical colleges have been established to impart practical training simultaneously, health programmes are in general knowledge-based. The practical components are restricted to simulation techniques, use of models or applying the techniques on animals (e.g. teaching skin grafting through the use of animal skin).

Indira Gandhi National Open University (IGNOU), created as a single mode university by an Act of Parliament in 1985 for providing education through distance mode at low cost, initially started with the offer of programmes in food and nutrition through the School of Continuing Education. The School of Health Sciences (SOHS) was created in 1991 for launching academic programmes for various categories of health functionaries. To begin with, the School launched B.Sc. Nursing programme in 1994 for in-service diploma-holder nurses having 3-5 years of professional experience. This training programme bridged a long felt need of training nursing personnel and was developed in collaboration with Indian Nursing Council (INC) and support of the Planning Commission. The School then developed a Post-Graduate Diploma in Maternal &

Child Health (PGDMCH) for medical graduates, with financial assistance from Ministry of Health and Family Welfare, Government of India. It was launched in 1997. As of now, six health care programmes have been developed and put on offer and another five programmes are scheduled for launch in January 2006 to meet the needs of different target groups. This success acted as precursor for State Open Universities to offer health programmes based on IGNOU programme package. Over the last few years, many other open and conventional universities have started health or health related programmes through distance mode.

Present Indian Scenario

In India, the open-distance learning (ODL) system, as of now, comprises one National Open University, 11 State Open Universities and more than one hundred distance education institutions. Of these, apart from IGNOU, only five SOUs and 19 conventional universities are presently offering health related distance education programmes (Table 1). But most of these programmes are knowledge based rather than skill based. The skill based health programmes are mostly in the field of dietitics and nutrition, yoga and counselling. Though Annamalai University and Manipal Academy of Higher Education (MAHE) are offering skill based health programmes, they are put under regular streams (Jena and Dutta, 1996).

Table 1: Universities providing health programme through distance mode

Sl. No.	Name of University	Name of the Programme
1.	Vardhman Mahaveer Kota Open University, Kota	Nutrition and Health Education, Food and Nutrition
2.	Yashwantrao Chavan Maharashtra Open University, Nashik	Swasthya Mitra, Dai Prashikshan, Massage, Anganwadi, Yoga, Medical Laboratory Technology, Opthalmic Technical Assistant
3.	Madhya Pradesh Bhoj (Open) University, Bhopal	Dietetics and Therapeutic Nutrition, Maternal and Child Health, Hospital and Health Management, Physiotherapy and Nutrition, Post Basic B.Sc. Nursing.
4.	Dr. Babasaheb Ambedkar Open University, Ahmedabad	Child Care
5.	Karnataka State Open University, Mysore	Nutrition and Health Education
6.	Annamalai University (Dual mode), Chennai	Tobacco Control, Adolescent Health Care, Maternity and Neonatal Care, Acupuncture, Public Health, Medical Cosmetology, Ultrasonography, Diabetology, Family Medicine, Accident and Emergency Care, Echocardiography, Electrocardiography

7.	Manipal Academy of Higher Education, Manipal	Medical Laboratory Technology, Medical Imaging Technology, Health Information Administration
8.	University of Kerala, Thiruvananthapuram	Adolescent and Paediatrics
9.	Alagappa University, Karaikudi	Child Care and Education
10.	Bhartiar University, Coimbatore	Applied Psychology, Bioinformatics, Hospital and Health Care Management
11.	SNDT University, Mumbai	Nutrition
12.	Utkal University, Orissa	Dietetics and Nutrition
13.	Fakir Mohan University, Balasore	HIV and AIDs
14.	SP Mahila Padmavati University, Tirupati	Medical Psychology, Family and Health Counselling
15.	University of Madras Institute of Distance Education, Chennai	Medicinal Plants
16.	Jiwaji University, Gwalior	Medicinal Plants, Yoga
17.	Gurukul Kangri University, Hardwar	Yoga
18.	Kakatiya university, Warangal	Yoga
19.	Hari Singh Gaur University, Sagar	Yoga and Meditation, Psychological Counselling
20.	University of Burdwan, Burdwan	Bioinformatics
21.	University of Kalyani, Kalyani	Pesticides
22.	Indian Institute of Alternative Medicines, Kolkata	Yoga & Massage, Naturopathy, Bach Flower, Reiki Healing, Accupressure, Magnetotherapy, Medicinal Herbalism, Medical Astrology, Gem-Tele-Chromo Therapy, Electro Homoeopathy, Traditional Chinese Med, Hypnotherapy, Aroma Therapy, Radiesthesia & Radionics
23.	Sri Ramachandra Medical College and Research Institute, Chennai	Family Health, Industrial health

Besides the university system, distance mode is also being followed by different institutions and organisations to meet training need of different target groups. Indian Medical Association (IMA) is providing programmes in Family Medicine, Geriatric care etc. and National Institute of Health and Family Welfare is offering certificate programmes in Hospital management, Health and Family Welfare Management, etc. The practical component is taken care through contact sessions.

IGNOU, with core medical and nursing faculty and support of experts from all over the country, is in a unique situation to develop innovative health programmes. Most of our health programmes are not available in conventional system and are need- based. This has attracted funding organisations such as World Health Organisation (WHO), Ministry of Health and Family Welfare, Asian Heart Foundation, Academy of Hospital Administration, Association of Rural Surgeons of India (ARSI), Trained Nurses Association of India (TNAI), to collaborate with us. The list of health programmes launched by IGNOU is given in Table 2.

Table 2 : List of health programme launched by IGNOU

Name of the Programme	Target group	Duration	Launching
A) School of Health Sciences			
B.Sc. Nursing (now modified as Post-Basic B.Sc. Nursing)	GNM	3 years	1994
Post Graduate Diploma in Maternal and Child Health (PGDMCH)	MBBS	1 year	1997
Post Graduate Diploma in Hospital and Health Management (PGDHHM)	MBBS, BDS, Graduate Nurses	1 year	2000
Post Graduate Certificate in Rural Surgery (PGCRS)	Post Graduate or PG Diploma in Orthopaedics/ Surgery/O&G	1 year	2001
Certificate in Health and Environment (CHE)	12 years of schooling	6 months	2002
Post Graduate Diploma in Geriatric Medicine (PGDGM)	MBBS	1 year	2004
Post Graduate Diploma in Community cardiology (PGDCC)	MBBS	2 years	2006*
Certificate in Health Care Waste Management	12 years schooling	6 months	2006*
B. Sc. (Hons) in Opthalmic Techniques	12 years schooling	4 years	2006*
Diploma in Nursing Administration (DNA)	B.Sc. (Nursing)	1 year	2006*
Certificate in Competency Enhancement for ANM/FHW	Auxiliary Nurse Midwife (ANM)	1 year	2006*
B) School of Continuing Education			
Certificate in Food and Nutrition (CFN)	No formal qualification	6 months	1989
Certificate in Nutrition and Child Care (CNCC)	12 years of schooling	6 months	1992
Diploma in Nutrition and Health Education (DNHE)	12 years of schooling	1 year	1994
Diploma in Early Childhood Care and Education (DECE)	12 years of schooling	1 year	1995
Certificate in HIV and Family Education (CAFÉ)	12 years of schooling	6 months	2002
Diploma in HIV and Family Education (DAFÉ)	12 years of schooling	1 year	2003
M. Sc. in Dietitics and Food Services Management {M.Sc.(DFSM)}	Graduation	2 years	2005
Certificate in Food Safety (CFS)	12 years of schooling	6 months	2006*

* Advertised in 2005

Unlike the practice in distance education institutions, IGNOU has the medical and nursing professionals to design, develop, implement, monitor and evaluate the respective health programmes. This has ensured better design and implementation strategies for training through distance mode and enabling us in alienating the usual fear of quality compromise in practical components. Almost all the health programmes have more than 50% credits in practical component. Besides the term-end theory examinations, all the programmes have term-end practical component which is assessed by external examiners.

The medical faculty has pioneered in starting innovative medical programmes in medicine as well as surgery. As a departure from the conventional system, various combination of courses are developed as per the felt need of the developing countries. The hands-on training is provided by a three-tier system taking into consideration the diversity of available health infrastructure in the country. A quality monitoring mechanism has also been evolved to ensure minimum requisite inputs at all levels.

The School has also taken pioneering initiative to start super speciality training in medical field. In view of the fast growing incidences of heart-attack/stroke in semi urban and rural population, and lack of adequate cardiac expertise, it was considered necessary to develop PG Diploma in Community cardiology for practising MBBS doctors. Scheduled for offer from 2006, it is an effort in positive direction. It has been designed and developed by the best Cardiologists in the country. However, as a precautionary measure, the training methodology will be in dual mode (integrating telemedicine and residential posting), it can equally be designed as a single mode distance education programme.

Innovations

Skill training is an integral part of professional programmes, specially those related to health. Though simulation technique, animal experimentation etc. provide an idea on skills, they are not helpful to deal in a real life situation. To overcome this serious flaw, our training system provides for an inbuilt component to give exposure in real life situation. Hence, a three-tier hands-on training model has been introduced by IGNOU, which not only provides flexibility in terms of pace and place of learning but also ensures that after completion of the training process, a student can actually practice the skills with confidence in his/her own work environment. In addition, this three-tier system has integrated the pedagogy of skill learning and has ensured that the benefit of both group learning and one-to-one learning is given to the distance students (Panda and Jena, 2001).

The model

The model describes the implementation of practical component at three levels. Each level involves three steps. We first identify a tertiary level institution (Medical College) as Programme Study Centre, where renowned doctors are involved as counsellors for demonstration and discussion. The next level involves secondary level health institution (District Hospital), where subject specialists help students to hone their skills by repeatedly performing demonstrations under their supervision and guidance, i.e., practicing the skills taught in tertiary level. Finally, the primary level health set up is identified and the student performs his/her job. This could also be a clinic/health set up run by the learner himself/herself. In this case, the student practices the acquired skills without any supervision.

In IGNOU parlance, these three levels are termed as Programme Study Centre (PSC), Skill Development Centre (SDC) and Work Place (WP), respectively. For administrative purpose, every PSC is linked up with a Regional Centre (RC), which is an IGNOU establishment. The PSC acts as the nucleus for programme implementation. The Programme In-charge (PIC) is stationed at the PSC. He/she is normally a permanent faculty of the medical college with additional responsibilities of monitoring the learning process of all IGNOU students associated with his/her institution. The PIC is supported by counsellors and ministerial support staff. The learners are required to attend contact sessions in theory and practicals.

Every student has an option to select the nearest SDC. For the convenience of learners, the University has kept the option flexible. There could be as many SDCs as the number of students. At work place, the students will practice the acquired skills without supervision. This exposes him/her to enough number of patients and empower them to perfect their skills before appearing in the term-end examination for certification.

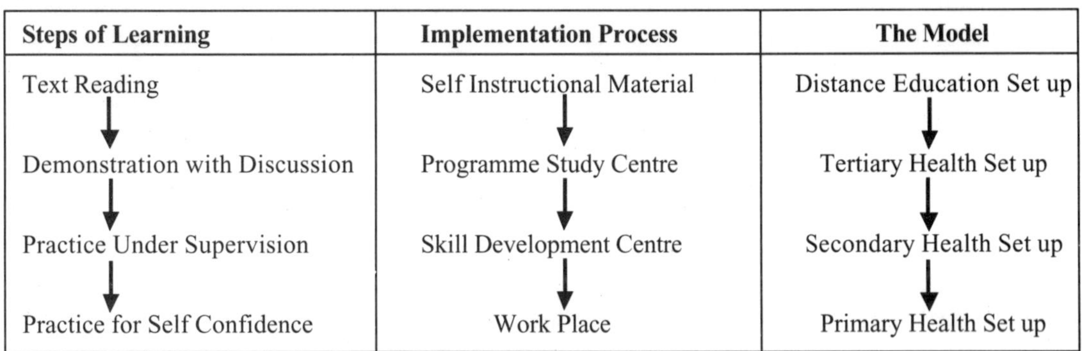

Steps of Learning	Implementation Process	The Model
Text Reading	Self Instructional Material	Distance Education Set up
↓	↓	↓
Demonstration with Discussion	Programme Study Centre	Tertiary Health Set up
↓	↓	↓
Practice Under Supervision	Skill Development Centre	Secondary Health Set up
↓	↓	↓
Practice for Self Confidence	Work Place	Primary Health Set up

Figure 1: Implementation model

Model for surgical training

For programmes like PGDMCH and PGDGM, which involve surgical training, IGNOU uses essentially the same strategy. However, since surgery involves more risks, surgical skill development needs closer and step by step supervision. Hence, the pedagogy has been divided into seven steps:

- Text Reading
- Observing Operative Procedures
- Assisting in Operation

- Performing with Assistance
- Performing under Guidance
- Performing Independently with Referral Support
- Performing Independently

This mechanism ensures acquisition of even complicated hands-on skills and training under controlled supervision and a quality product at par with the best.

These seven steps of learning surgical skills are integrated in the distance learning system as follows (Jena and Agarwal, 2003).

- Reading the text through Self Instructional Material (SIM).
- Observing operative procedures through video recorded cassettes.
- Assisting in operation and performing with Assistance could be done through hands-on-training at Medical Colleges/Tertiary Hospitals. For this, each student is associated with a counsellor for a specific period of time.
- Performing under guidance could be done at small peripheral hospitals/nursing homes, where a subject specialist could guide. This set up would train the doctors to work under limited facilities/constrains. However, such an exposure equips a surgeon to face emergency situations better.
- Performing independently with referral support is permitted at a stage where a surgeon has acquired confidence but nurses fear of casualty, though he/she is aware that a casualty could happen even in expert hands. But, before handing over knife to handle independently, some safeguard of this nature must be built-in. Hence, the best place for such activity would be own-time, own work place of the surgeon with a in-built referral mechanism.

Basic training requires reinforcement and continuity till such time that the skills get transformed into memory. Hence, the challenge of providing flexibility in learning without any compromise in quality of skill development and pedagogy demands contextualised mechanisms in implementation process in terms of geography of the location of learner and access to or availability of infrastructure facility.

Implementation of Practical Component in IGNOU Medical Programmes

Each course of all our medical programmes has a practical component. The skills that the students need to acquire and learning outcomes of each course are listed in their programme guide for the information and benefit of learners. The skill training is divided into three parts: training at PSC, training at SDC and training at Work place. The students have to maintain record for each case as mentioned in their practical manual. For all the three levels, the time budgeted for each skill has also been given in the practical manual.

At the PSC, students are demonstrated each skill. To ensure that they have understood the steps involved in each of the skills demonstrated, they are made to practice the skills on at least one sample case. If situation permits, they are given opportunities to practice the same skill on more patients. However, if they do not get sufficient chances at PSC, they are advised to practice the same procedure at their allotted SDC.

To guide students practice all the skills taught to them at the PSC, there are counsellors at SDC. Depending upon the programme, a learner has to perform the activities oneself under the supervision of the counsellor appointed and allotted by the University. The counsellors are informed in zonal meetings to ensure that the minimum of patients/activities are practiced by the learners at SDC. Similarly, a student has to do unsupervised activities at the work place.

Log book maintenance

The activities/procedures done at SDC and WP are required to be recorded in the logbooks supplied by the University. The logbooks are countersigned by the counsellors of medical college/SDC so that the learning defects of the students are identified in time and reinforcement is provided. This helps to ensure that the skill training is implemented in a standardized manner throughout the country.

The programmes where logbooks are not supplied, major headings/formats for recording the activities/case records is provided in the practical manuals. Students are required to write down the details of procedures. They have to maintain record for all the cases they perform at SDC and the work place.

In some programmes, logbooks carry 10% weightage in the final evaluation. This further enhances the regularity of maintenance of logbooks by students.

Teleconference

IGNOU has provision for interaction with learners through two-way audio, one-way video teleconferencing. For developing empathy with learners and break their isolation, teleconferencing sessions are organised regularly. Subject experts are invited to discuss different topics. While dealing with the theory component, principles/concepts dealt in different units are highlighted and the questions asked by the students are replied with the help of examples so that they could link them to practical activities.

In the practical component, important clinical examination procedures are dealt with and attempts are made to deal with rare patients and where possible, show them live or get video clips. Discussions are also generated with the help of models or with the video clips of five to ten minutes on certain procedures. Attempts are being made to make model case presentation, case discussion and simulate clinical rounds/seminars. Most of the presentations follow the format of panel discussion or lecture demonstrations.

Attempts are made to link the practical spells with the teleconference dates wherever feasible. This increases the participation of students. Some of the teleconference sessions are also recorded so that if a student misses some important sessions, he/she could acquire these cassettes and view at his/her convenience.

Monitoring

To ensure proper implementation of the programme, monitoring is done at three levels (Agarwal and Jena, 1999). Feedback from the peripheral set ups (Skill development centres) are collected by the regional consultant, who, in turn, sends bi-monthly reports to programme coordinator. Feedback at state level is taken in the Regional Health Sciences Advisory Committee (RHSAC) meeting held once or twice a year. Feedback is also collected by the faculty directly from the students and counsellors through proformas that have been incorporated in the programme guide. Feedback is also collected in structured proforma from the Programme In-charge, Regional Consultant, Regional Centres. In addition, feedback is also collected in every 4-5 years for revising and updating the programmes.

The RHSAC comprises members from State Health Departments, Medical College having the PSC, Regional Centre of IGNOU and the School of Health Sciences. When all the persons involved in the programme implementation attend these meetings, the difficulties are identified and remedial measures are taken. This committee greatly helps in streamlining procedures, particularly in the practical component at all levels.

The Regional Consultant is usually a retired medical professional who enjoys immense personal rapport at state level. He/she helps to promote the health programmes in states and win the confidence of professional colleagues as well the state governments. Health being a state subject, the Regional Consultant's personal efforts make significant impact on popularizing the programmes. The Regional Consultant, by physical supervision to SDCs in the state, ensures proper hands-on training at peripheral level.

Limitations

The model developed for implementation of complex hands-on training has a pedagogic basis. Every programme, depending upon its curriculum and the level of training, needs to adapt the implementation model. For example, a programme having training need in field components and a programme needing coronary care training will have to adopt different approaches towards training in PSCs, have different student-teacher ratio, different weightage for continuous assessment, project, TEE, components of evaluation, different monitoring and planning strategy, etc. But the basic approach of the model could still be applicable in both the situations.

For hands-on-skills in surgical programmes, students are allowed to operate as assistants. Though they may get a chance to operate independently, such opportunity to students can never be guaranteed. Though such a risk could be taken in training related to inanimate subjects, and a student could be made to pay the compensation for the damages in terms of higher admission fees. However, in case of human lives, no such mechanism could work unless the counsellor himself/herself volunteers to take this risk. Indeed, even in the conventional system of training in surgical skills, it is the teacher who hands over the knife to students at his/her own risk.

Another practical operational problem arises in monitoring the network of SDCs due to quick turnover of the counsellors, who are mostly government employees and are transferable. Countries having different type of health infrastructure (like UK or US) are able to avoid this problem.

Conclusion

Many of us would not have thought of imparting medical education through distance mode in 1980s. Even today, this is not the preferred option of medical faculties and medical schools the world over. But with the availability of video-conferencing, telemedicine, online counselling, three dimensional viewing of videos and e-models, the basic training in medical education through distance mode has become a distinct possibility. India is initiating a pilot project on telemedicine to support all countries of African Union. The professionals all over the world should take advantage of the communication technology to meet the health human resource training needs of their respective countries, and wage a war against the morbidity and mortality situations to usher in an era of healthy living - the first step for growth and prosperity of human kind.

References

Dutta P.K., Jena T.K. and Panda S.K. (1996). A plea for health manpower traning through distance education. *Med. Educ.Online (serial on line),* 1(8). Available from: URL http://www.utmb.edu/meo/

Jena T.K. and Jena T.K. (1996). Skill Training in Health through Distance Education. Paper presented at 10th AAOU Conference, Tehran, I.R. Iran, November 14-16.

Jena T.K. and Agarwal A.K. (2003). Distance education—a training tool for rural surgeons. *Indian Journal of Surgery,* 65 (1), 50-54.

Panda S.K. and Jena T.K. (2001). Changing the pattern: towards flexible learning, leaner support and mentoring. In Fred Lockwood and Anne Google (Eds), *Innovations in Open & Distance Learning.* London: Kogan Page Limited.

Agarwal A.K. and Jena T.K. (1999). Quality monitoring and quality assurance in distance professional education. *Indian Journal of Distance Education,* 123-133.

Professor A.K. Agarwal is Professor of Health Sciences (as former Director), School of Health Sciences, Indira Gandhi National Open University, New Delhi.
Email: akagarwal@ignou.ac.in

Dr. T.K. Jena is Reader, School of Health Sciences, Indira Gandhi National Open University, New Delhi.
Email: tkjena@ignou.ac.in

12

Regional Languages and Distance Learning

Renu Bhardwaj

Introduction

An ever expanding university like IGNOU with the mandate "to provide access to higher education for large segments of the population, and in particular, the disadvantaged groups such as those living in remote and rural areas" *(IGNOU Act, 1985)* for the purpose of human resource development, 'national integration' and 'educational well being of the community generally' cannot but face the multilingual challenge that so typically identifies the Indian education scenario.

Coming to the philosophy of education, it is a universally accepted fact that a child is competent to learn in the language/languages, the child is familiar with. The National Curriculum Framework for Elementary and Secondary Education (NCERT, 1992) clearly states that the medium of instruction at the primary stage should be the mother tongue or the regional language unless facilities are available for another language. It also prescribes the study of only one language i.e. the mother tongue at the primary level. As per records, as many as 1652 mother tongues are spoken yet there are only 67 languages which are actually taught in schools (Bhardwaj, 1999). Most of the mother tongues are not developed because of lack of recognition and, therefore, lack of use outside the community and home environment. Broadly speaking, the language situation in India can be grouped under the following categories:

1. Situations in which the home language is the same as the school language.
2. Situations in which the home language is similar to the school language but with some variations.
3. Situations in which the home language is very different from the school language.

4. Situations where children have to learn English from class 1 onwards and also in English without having the benefit of being exposed to the language in the environment, either at home or in school.

Such a situation results from a plethora of languages spoken in India. The issue of medium of instruction is further complicated by the fact that administratively most of the states in India have been formed on the basis of one language formula. In the administrative terms the language which is used by a majority of people in the state is defined as the mother tongue. At the same time it is also true that all major languages of India have numerous dialects. (This is true of other countries as well). But the difference between the dialect and the standard language in India is not great. Standard language is now heard in every village or habitation through radio and television with the result that the standard form of the language does not remain unknown.

The official language situation as per the Indian Constitution is as follows:

1. The official language of the Union shall be Hindi in Devanagari script.
2. Notwithstanding anything in clause (1), for a period of fifteen years from the commencement of this Constitution, the English language shall continue to be used for all the official purposes of the Union.
3. Notwithstanding anything in this article, Parliament may by law provide for the use, after the said period of fifteen years, of :
   a) the English language, or
   b) the Devanagari form of numerals, for such purposes as may be specified in the law.

The Constitution also provides for review by a commission keeping "due regard to the industrial, cultural and scientific advancement of India, the just claims and the interests of persons belonging to the non-Hindi speaking areas."

Commission and Committee of Parliament on Official Language

1. There shall be constituted a committee consisting of thirty members of whom twenty shall be members of the House of the People and ten shall be members of the Council of States to be elected respectively by the members of the House of the People and the members of the Council of States in accordance with the system of proportional representation by means of the single transferable vote.
2. It shall be the duty of the Committee to examine the recommendation of the Commission constituted under clause 10 and to report to the President their opinion thereon.
3. Notwithstanding anything in article 343, the President may after consideration of the report referred to in clause (5), issue directions in accordance with the whole or any part of that report.

Part XVII Official Language Chapter 1 – Language of the Union

The languages of indigenous groups that the Constitution recognizes as the Modern Indian languages Assamese, Bengali, Gujarati, Hindi, Kannada, Kashmiri, Konkani, Malayalam, Manipuri Marathi, Nepali, Oriya, Punjabi, Sanskrit, Sindhi, Tamil, Telugu and Urdu

Eighth Schedule (Articles 344 (1) and 351)

Irrespective of the provision provided for the education of the minorities in India, the ground reality is that English occupies a position of paramountcy in higher education just as French in Canada and its expansion in leaps and bounds brings us back to the dynamics in which languages function in a country.

The existence of English unfolds a complex web of historical, social and cultural forces at work which have shaped the destiny of modern India. Therefore, to understand the importance of English in India is nothing short of trying to understand ourselves, rather India as a nation. Several English words have seeped into Indian languages. India has a vibrant English Press, the Government owned All India Radio and Doordarshan, and all major national and international cable channels carry several English programmes, including news bulletins. It is used for a variety of official purposes, it is still used in courts and Government documents, it is used in the Indian Parliament, is the preferred language of advertising, armed forces, education and certainly higher education. It is the lingua franca of the World Wide Web and the Internet. English thrives today as the countries which use it, are together the most powerful group in the world. English fits in the bill of the shrinking global village more adequately than any other language for the following legitimate and extra literary reasons:

> One: India is the third largest English-using nation after the USA and UK which has about 35 million users of the language. This is about 5 per cent of India's population which is larger than the percentage of the users of certain scheduled languages of the Constitution. Two: English has the status of an 'associate' official language in the constitution. Three: It is the state language of four states and of most of the Union territories. Four: India has a large network of English print media with a pan-Indian circulation and is one of the world's three major book publishers in English. Five English happens to be, even if we desire otherwise, the primary language of inter-regional interaction in India and of course of India's interaction with the outside world. Six: English is fast getting assimilated into Indian languages while also assimilating them (Satchidanandan, 1999, p. 185).

It is a paradoxical situation that where as:

> English was not in the run when the linguistic rights for the linguistic minorities were decided and responsibilities listed. However, today, English has a major role in decision-making regarding language choice in education. English is replacing the mother tongue

and the regional language. Nearly 7 states in the country have opted for the introduction of English from the earliest stage, even along with the mother tongue of the student. When the language policy was debated in India decades ago, only Hindi and/or the regional language were perceived to be a threat to the place of the mother tongue in the school system. Today the situation is totally changed. At that time, there were violent protests against ignoring mother tongues, and today we see total submission in favour of English. No right bestowed by the Constitution or responsibility given by the Resolution and Recommendations of the Commissions or governments is able to shield Indian languages from the onward march of English (Mallikarjun, 2001, p. 5).

Indira Gandhi National Open University

It is no surprise, therefore that objectives such as parity with traditional formal system of education, institutional recognition and use of multi-media technology in the overall context of the paramountcy of English as the medium of instruction in higher education constrained IGNOU to initially resort to English as the language of instruction for programmes and courses other than Hindi. As the practice goes initially courses are written in English and then translated in other languages. There is also the practical aspect of resorting to course development work initially in English and subsequently translating in Hindi and other languages wherever possible. Still about 40% courses in IGNOU are offered only in English because of the technical nature of the content and terms which have not found equivalents in other languages. Such disciplines are Computer Sciences, Nursing, Medical Sciences, Engineering and Technology, Hospitality Management, to name a few.

It is also important to mention here that language study per-se and distance delivery methods constitute one of the most dynamic aspects of continuing education programmes of IGNOU. It is not a simple feat that today, a total of about 500 credit courses are either pure language based or language related courses (e.g. Literature, Practical Translation, Creative Writing, Certificate in Teaching of English, Journalism, Radio Writing etc.) Besides, language courses overboard in various programmes offered by other disciplines as well (e.g. Computers, Library Science, Nursing, Extension etc.) The number of credits will further enhance once full fledged programmes under linguistics such as Masters in Applied Linguistics and Proficiency in Languages that are in the pipeline, take off. It is not an exaggeration to say that the development of discipline based programmes in both Hindi and English have grown in leaps and bounds. The learners have an unprecedented choice of methods, media and independence levels in their study of these languages.

At the initial stage 1987-88, Foundation Course in English-1 (FEG-1) was a compulsory course for students of Bachelors' Degree Programme (BDP) across the board - Science, Commerce streams included. English is still a compulsory course for graduates of professional courses like Computer Science, Library Science, Tourism Studies, or Hospitality Management programmes. It was however, discovered that even after completing 92 credits required to get the Bachelor's degree, it was difficult for a substantial number of students to pass FEG-

1(Foundation in English) Subsequently, FEG-1 has been made optional since 1999. Now the choice is between English (FEG-1) and Hindi (FHD-2). To promote the study of Modern Indian Languages and in keeping with the linguistic versatility, a 4 credit Foundation course in any of the modern Indian languages is to be opted to complete 24 credits worth of Foundation Courses (Table 1).

The following are the Foundation Courses which are compulsory:

Table 1: Foundation courses – common to all BA/B.com/B.Sc./B.S.W (compulsory 24 credits (I year 16 credits, II year 8 credits)

Course Code	Title of the Course	Credits
FHS-1	Foundation Course in Humanities & Social Sciences	8
FST-1	Foundation Course in Science & Technology	8
FEG-1	Foundation Course in English-1	4
	Or	
FHD-2	Foundation Course in Hindi-2	4

A Foundation Course in any of the Modern Indian Languages Assamese, Bengali, English, Gujarati, Hindi, Kannada, Malayalam, Marathi, Oriya, Punjabi, Tamil, Telugu, Urdu, Sanskrit — each worth four credits is to be opted.

The Foundation courses in languages aim at improving proficiency in language by developing reading, writing, listening and speaking skills. This is done with (i) reading comprehension (ii) vocabulary, (iii) grammar and usage, (iv) writing (lessons) and (v) listening and speaking. The units on listening and speaking may accompany cassette recordings. Alternatively, students can listen to them at the study centres allotted to them.

The language skills acquisition work takes place in the form of comprehensive sequenced course designed to take the learner systematically through the elementary, intermediate and advanced levels of language study. The concerned faculties involve content experts and innovative methodologies have become key issue in curriculum planning and implementation. The instructional design in IGNOU is a multi-pronged and a mix of combinations such as print material, face to face counselling, audio cassettes, video cassettes, radio interactive counselling telecasting, Internet based delivery and Tele-counselling is resorted to. The status of enrolment and gradual increase in the option of MILs in 2003-05 admission cycles is listed below (Table 2).

Table 2: Status of students enrolled in MILs

S. No.	Course	Language	Others	Session
1.	FAS-1	Assamese	0	0103
			0	0703
			207	0704
2.	FBG-1	Bengali	0	0103
			0	0703

			0	0104
			1203	0704
			3	0105
3.	FEG-2	English		
4.	FGT-1	Gujarati		
5.	BHDF-101	Hindi		
6.	FKD-1	Kannada	0	0103
			0	0703
			0	0104
			396	0704
			3	0105
7.	FML-1	Malayalam	0	0103
			0	0703
			0	0104
			341	0704
			1	0105
8.	FMT-1	Marathi	0	0103
			0	0703
			199	0704
			2	0105
9.	FOR-1	Oriya	0	0103
			0	0703
			0	0104
			1631	0704
			1	0105
10.	FPB-1	Punjabi	0	0103
			0	0703
11.	FTM-1	Tamil		
12.	FTG-1	Telugu	0	0103
			0	0703
			0	0104
			154	0704
			1	0105
13.	FUD-1	Urdu	0	0103
			0	0703
			0	0104
			744	0704
			4	0105
14.	BSKF-1	Sanskrit	86	0704
			1	0105

The discussion so far has been restricted to formal confines of a non-formal channel of education. But if the University's objective is to go to the doorsteps of the disadvantaged and the need for continuation of education beyond formal education, the overall developmental goal has to be kept in mind. The focus, therefore, will have to be on the changing scenario of the country, amelioration of rural poverty, awareness generation and development of the minorities including women and children and the tribals. For achieving these goals regional languages can alone play a key role.

Minorities are identified with several tags such as the linguistic minorities, religious minorities, educationally backward minorities, geographically isolated minorities and so forth. Depending upon the context in which the identification is done, most of the people in India are minorities and hardly any group can be called a majority. For example, within the national context, Bengali is a minority language. But, within the context of Bengal, Bengali is a majority language. The Constitution of India under Article 29, states that the minorities with a distinct language, script or culture have the right to 'conserve the same' and that they shall not be denied admission into any educational institution maintained by the state or receiving aid from the state funds.

To meet this challenge IGNOU is playing an interventionist role. One pilot initiated by IGNOU's Regional Centre Bhubhaneshwar to catch up the rural and backward masses including scheduled tribes, scheduled castes, economically under privileged, (left out by the higher education system) the non 10+2 chunk and who have no other avenue is to offer Bachelor in Preparatory Programme in Oriya. BPP is offered otherwise, in English and Hindi only. The three Preparatory Courses under BPP are: Social Science, Commerce and Mathematics. The students can choose any two and after qualifying in these courses within a period of six months come to the mainstream Bachelors Degree Programme. The result is heartening. For the last four admission cycles, enrolment in BPP in Orissa is the highest in the country vis-à-vis others. These students would get an opportunity to do graduation in Oriya for which work of translation is going on. Bhubhaneshwar Regional Centre has brought out the entire Prospectus of IGNOU in Oriya which is a landmark.

Examples of IGNOU breaking up barrier of language in non-English and non-Hindi belts are gradually on ascent. The School of Continuing Education (SOCE) has identified certain important areas of concern and addressed them through a number of programmes such as Rural Development, Women's Development, Child Development, Disability, Youth in Development Work, Nutrition and Dietetics, HIV and Family Education, Journalism and Mass Communication and Social Work. The SOCE is in the process of preparing Masters/PG Diploma in Dietetics and Food Service Management, Bachelors in Social Work and Awareness-cum-Training Packages in the areas of Disability

Among the Continuing Education Programmes, Diploma in Early Childhood Care and Education (DECE) (Table 3) that aims to help the learners to develop the knowledge, attitudes and skills necessary for working with children up to the age of six years and equipping to organize and manage child care centres like crèches, pre-schools and day-care centres is being offered in Tamil besides English and Hindi. This has been made possible because the pre-school movement is strong in Tamil Nadu. The officials associated with the Regional Centre Chennai took a special interest also because of the availability of translators and editors. Translation, if not done properly, can kill a programme so the availability of bilingual experts is very crucial to the success of the mission.

Table 3: Session-wise – programme status
(Course: DECE)

Course	English	Hindi	Tamil	Session
DECE	1341	555	122	0103
DECE	1667	684	80	0104
DECE	1485	824	62	0105
DECE	1	0	00	0703

Source: MPDD, IGNOU

'CWDL Certificate in Empowering Women through Self-Help Groups' (Table 4) is another programme that incorporates a unique multimedia training package that helps to develop the knowledge, attitude and skills necessary for imparting training to women at the grassroots level. A unique feature of this programme is the freeships being offered by the Department of Women and Child Development (DWCD) and National Back of Agriculture and Rural Development (NABARD). The Programme is offered in English, Hindi, Tamil, Marathi, Gujarati and Braille.

Table 4: Session-wise – programme status
(Course: CWDL)

Course	English	Hindi	Gujarati	Marathi	Oriya	Tamil	Session
CWDL	151	76	103	103	676	775	0104
CWDL	68	35	129	2	317	140	0105
DECE	40	26	18	2	226	2234	0704

Source: MPDD, IGNOU

Among the awareness generating programmes Certificate in Food and Nutrition (CFN) (Table 5) holds a strong ground with the programme now being offered in Assamese, English, Gujarati, Hindi, Kannada, Marathi, Malayalam, Oriya, Punjabi, Tamil and Bengali.

Table 5: Session-wise – programme status
(Course: CFN)

Course	English	Hindi	Gujarati	Bengali	Kannada	Malayalam	Assamese	Tamil	Session
CFN	446	261	38	8	19	3	6	138	0103
CFN	307	88	19	0	1	1	9	30	0703
CFN	471	221	35	3	13	4	1	42	0104
	322	137	23	4	1	3	1	24	0704

Source: MPDD, IGNOU

The School of Education (SOE) of IGNOU has activities concentrated in two major areas:

i) the various aspects of the practice of education as a profession, and
ii) the various branches of education as an academic discipline.

Diploma in Primary Education (DPE) (Table 6) aims at improving the quality of teachers at the primary level. In fact poor teaching by badly trained or untrained teachers can be more harmful than no teaching. Therefore, keeping in view the large number of untrained teachers at the primary level in the country, particularly in North-Eastern states (where there are almost 40% untrained teachers teaching in primary schools), the School of Education, has developed this innovative teacher training programme for primary/elementary school teachers in collaboration with NCERT, New Delhi. The programme is offered in Assamese besides English and Hindi.

Table 6: Session-wise – programme status
(Course: DPE)

Year	English	Hindi	Assamese	Total
ADMS-2004	212	3	383	598
ADMS-2005	227	1	848	1076

Source: MPDD, IGNOU

Another programme of the SOE with MHRD Ministry of Human Resource Development and NCTE is aimed at the North Eastern States and Sikkim only. This programme is going to be offered in Khasi, Garo and Bengali besides English and Hindi. IGNOU has made significant strides in bringing the North Eastern region States into the mainstream of higher education in collaboration with MHRD. "10% of the 10th plan fund is proposed to be spent in the North East regions for infrastructure, translation of need based programmes into regional languages and development of job oriented courses" (IGNOU, 2004).

IGNOU after two decades of its existence has emerged as the largest open university in the Commonwealth and has been conferred the distinction of Centre of Excellence in Distance Education by the Commonwealth of Learning (COL). It is on way to transacting the distance between the teacher and the learner (EduSat: two way video-conferencing as also virtual classroom learning). To seek its objectives of democratizing higher education and catering to the needs of the disadvantaged sections, it has adopted an approach of cooperation and collaboration with both the traditional University setups and the non-formal education institutions in a holistic manner. IGNOU also aims at setting and maintaining standards in distance education in the country as an apex body. It has entered into an MoU, with the CCIs and Open Universities of the country for adaptation, purchase even translation of its self-instructional learning materials (Table 7).

Table 7: Status of the agreements processed with state open universities by the academic coordination division as on 27th Jan 2005

Sl. No.	Name of SOU	Agreement Name	Programme Name
1.	U.P. Rajarshi Tandon Open University, U.P.	Translation Rights in Hindi	DTS, ADTS, BTS, PGJMC, MBA, MCA, CES, DNHE, DECE and DCO (not translated)
2.	Dr. Babasaheb Ambedkar Open University, Gujrat	Translation Rights in Gujarati	PGJMC, PGDDE, BLIS, PGJMC, MADE, BLIS, PGDEE, BA and B.Com. BPP, CIC, CTM, Cert. in Radio Writing, MLIS, PGCMMR, PGDRD, PGDT, CTPM, CES, Cert in Consumer Protection, BTS, MTS, Cert in Women Empowerment and Development, Cert in Human Rights, B.Ed.
3.	Tamil Nadu Open University	Translation Rights inTamil	Management B.Ed., BPP, BA, BTS, B.Com., CES, CIC, CRD, CTPM, BLIS
4.	Dr BRAOU University, Hyderabad	Translation Rights in Telugu	B.Ed
5.	Maulana Azad National Urdu University	Translation Rights in Urdu	B.Ed, PGDJMC

As translation is a complex and sensitive activity, precautionary measures have been taken by IGNOU to maintain the standards required while translating from one language to another. The terms and conditions of translation have been specified in the MoUs signed with the institutions as follows:

a) The licensee shall ensure that the translated materials are authentic and that they are faithful to the original text. For this purpose, the license may provide a list of translators who could be assigned the translation work and the IGNOU will advise the licensee about the suitability of the proposed translators. The licensee shall agree to get the work done by the translators accepted by IGNOU.

b) The translated manuscript should not be printed without getting the translated manuscript approved by IGNOU. The user university may take permission as deemed to be granted in absence of response within two months from the IGNOU to the User University.
c) The license for translation shall be given for the full course material. The translation of study material in parts is not allowed.
d) The licensee, while reprinting the material shall ensure that the print quality of the materials is as per standards of the IGNOU study material in respect of quality of paper and printing, cover printing, etc.
e) The licensee, while using the printed instructional material of IGNOU, may use along with it the supportive audio-video cassettes prepared by IGNOU which are available on the sale with the agencies authorized by IGNOU.

(Source: Academic Coordination, IGNOU)

State Open Universities

IGNOU Act was aimed "to establish and incorporate an Open University at the national level for the introduction and promotion of Open University and Distance Education systems in the educational pattern of the country and for the co-ordination and determination of standards in such systems". For this purpose an apex body called the Distance Education Council (DEC) is set up. DEC is involved in coordinating the development and determination of distance teaching standards by funding and overseeing the developmental activities of the Open Universities and Correspondence Courses Institutes. A sum of 79 crores is set apart during the 10th plan period for support to State Open Universities (SOUS) and Distance Education Institutes. The status of the programmes offered through the SOUs in different languages is appended below:

Table 8: Dr. B.R. Ambedkar Open University, Andhra Pradesh

Sl. No.	Programmes	Languages
1.	Bachelor of Arts	Telugu, Urdu
2.	Bachelor of Commerce	Telugu, Urdu
3.	Bachelor of Science	Telugu, Urdu
4.	Master of Arts (Public Administration)	Telugu
5.	Master of Arts (Political Science)	Telugu
6.	Master of Arts (Economics)	Telugu
7.	Master of Arts (History)	Telugu
8.	Master of Arts (Sociology)	Telugu
9.	P.G. Diploma in Writing of Mass Media (PGDWMM)	Telugu
10.	P.G. Diploma in Human Rights (PGDHR)	Telugu
11.	Certificate in Food and Nutrition	Telugu, Urdu

Table 9: Nalanda Open University, Bihar

Sl.No.	Programmes	Language
1.	PG General	Hindi
2.	Under Graduate General (B.Com)	Hindi
3.	Inter Arts	Hindi
4.	Inter Commerce	Hindi
5.	Certificate Programmes	Hindi

Table 10: Yashwantrao Chavan Maharashtra Open University, Maharashtra

Sl.No.	Programmes	Language
1.	Master of Philosophy (M.Phil)	Marathi
2.	Doctor of Philosophy (Ph.D)	Marathi
3.	Ph.D (Agri_	Marathi
4.	Master of Arts	Marathi
5.	Master of Commerce	Marathi
6.	Master of Science	Marathi
7.	Master of Science (Agri)	Marathi
8.	Master of Library Science	Marathi
9.	Master of Education	Marathi
10.	Bachelor of Arts	Marathi
11.	Bachelor of Commerce	Marathi
12.	Bachelor of Library Information Science (B.Lib)	Marathi
13.	Bachelor of Horticulture (B.H.Sc)	Marathi
14.	Bachelor of Education	Marathi
15.	Foundation in Agriculture	Marathi
16.	Diploma in Commercial Fruit Production	Marathi
17.	Diploma in Commercial Vegetable Production	Marathi
18.	Diploma in Agricultural Business Management	Marathi
19.	Diploma in Floriculture & Land Scape Gardening	Marathi
20.	Diploma in School Management	Marathi
21.	Diploma in Journalism	Marathi
22.	Preparatory	Marathi
23.	Garden Training	Marathi
24.	Vocational Courses	Marathi

Table 11: Madhya Pradesh Bhoj (Open) University, Madhya Pradesh

Sl.No.	Programmes	Language
1.	Bachelor of Arts	Hindi
2.	Bachelor of Science	Hindi
3.	Bachelor of Commerce	Hindi
4.	Bachelor of Science (Nursing)	Hindi

5.	DNHE	Hindi
6.	PGDMCH	Hindi
7.	M.A. (AIH)	Hindi
8.	PGDTHM	Hindi
9.	B.Ed. (SE)-I	Hindi
10.	B.Ed. (SE)-II	Hindi
11.	B.Ed (SE)-III	Hindi
12.	B.Ed. (Gen)	Hindi
13.	FC (SE-DE)-I	Hindi
14.	FC (SE-DE)-II	Hindi
15.	FC (SE-DE)-III	Hindi
16.	M.A. (Economics)	Hindi
17.	M.A. (History)	Hindi
18.	M.A. (Pol. Science)	Hindi
19.	M.A. (Sociology)	Hindi
20.	B.Sc. (Hons) Mathematics	Hindi
21.	B.Sc. (Hons) Physics	Hindi
22.	BLIS	Hindi
23.	PGD (Tourism Mgt)	Hindi

Table 12: Dr. Babasaheb Ambedkar Open University, Gujrat

Sl.No.	Programmes	Language
1.	M.A. Hindi	Hindi
2.	Bachelors Preparatory Programme (BPP)	Gujarati
3.	Bachelor of Arts (BA)	Gujarati
4.	Bachelor of Commerce (B.Com)	Gujarati
5.	Diploma in Creative Writing in Hindi (DCH)	Hindi
6.	Certificate in Food and Nutrition (CFN)	Gujarati
7.	Certificate in Computing(CIC)	Gujarati
8.	Certificate in Tourism Marketing (CTM)	Gujarati
9.	Certificate in Tourism Management (CTM)	Gujarati
10.	Certificate in Child Care and Development (CCCD)	Gujarati
11.	Certificate in Personal Computer Software (CPCS)	Gujarati
12.	Certificate in Environmental Studies (CES)	Gujarati
13.	Certificate in Empowering Women Through Self Help Group (CWDL)	Gujarati

Table 13: Karnataka State Open University, Karnataka

Sl.No.	Programmes	Language
1.	Bachelor of Arts (BA)	Kannada
2.	Bachelor of Commerce (B.Com)	Kannada

3.	Bachelor of Education (B.Ed.)	Kannada
4.	Bachelor of Library Science	Kannada
5.	Bachelor of Science (IT)	Kannada
6.	Master of Education (M.Ed.)	Kannada
7.	Master of Arts (Kannada)	Kannada
8.	Master of Arts (Sanskrit)	Kannada
9.	Master of Arts (English)	Kannada
10.	Master of Arts (Urdu)	Kannada
11.	Master of Arts (Hindi)	Kannada
12.	Master of Arts (History)	Kannada
13.	Master of Arts (Economics)	Kannada
14.	Master of Arts (Political Science)	Kannada
15.	Master of Arts (Sociology)	Kannada
16.	Master of Commerce	Kannada
17.	Master of Business Administration	Kannada
18.	Master of Science (IT)	Kannada
19.	Doctor of Philosophy	Kannada

Table 14: Netaji Subhas Open University, West Bengal

Sl.No.	Programmes	Language
1.	BDP (BA, BSc, B.Com, BCA	Bengali
2.	Diploma	Bengali
3.	Certificate	Bengali

Table 15: U.P. Rajarshi Tandon Open University, Uttar Pradesh

Sl.No.	Programmes	Language
1.	Bachelor of Arts (BA)	Hindi
2.	Bachelor of Commerce (B.Com)	Hindi
3.	Bachelor of Tourism Studies(BTS)	Hindi
4.	Bachelor of Science (B.Sc.)	Hindi
5.	Under Graduate Arts in Single Subject (UGSS)	Hindi
6.	Master of Arts (Hindi English, Economics, Ancient Indian History, Medieval & Modern History, Sociology, Political Science	Hindi
7.	Master of Library and Information Sciences (MLIS)	Hindi
8.	Post Graduate Diploma in Translation (PGDT)	Hindi
9.	Post Graduate Diploma in International Marketing and E-Business (DIMB)	Hindi
10.	Post Graduate Diploma in Creative Writing in Hindi (DCWH)	Hindi
11.	Diploma in Health Education and Nutrition (DHEN)	Hindi

12.	Diploma in Tourism Studies (DTS)	Hindi
13.	Diploma in Rural Development (DRD)	Hindi
14.	Certificate in Tourism Studies (CTS)	Hindi
15.	Certificate in Child Care and Nutrition (CCCN)	Hindi
16.	Certificate in Nutrition and Food (CNF)	Hindi
17.	Certificate in Consumer Protection (CCP)	Hindi
18.	Certificate in Human Rights (CHR)	Hindi
19.	Certificate in Environmental Studies (CES)	Hindi
20.	Certificate in Labor Development (CLD)	Hindi
21.	Certificate in Disaster Management (CDM)	Hindi
22.	Diploma in Computer in Office Management (DCOM)	Hindi
23.	Certificate in Computer Course (CCC)	Hindi
24.	Bachelor of Education (B.Ed.)	Hindi

Table 16: Tamil Nadu Open University, Tamil Nadu

Sl.No.	Programmes	Language
1.	Bachelor of Business Administration (MBA)	Tamil
2.	Master of Arts in History	Tamil
3.	Master of Arts in Public Administration	Tamil
4.	Master of Arts in Economics	Tamil
5.	Master of Arts in Psychology	Tamil
6.	Master of Arts in Political Science	Tamil
7.	Master of Arts in Sociology	Tamil
8.	Master of Commerce	Tamil
9.	Bachelor of Arts in History	Tamil
10.	Bachelor of Arts in Economics	Tamil
11.	Bachelor of Arts in Tamil	Tamil
12.	Bachelor of Commerce	Tamil
13.	Certificate in Food & Nutrition	Tamil
14.	Certificate in Empowering Women through Self Help Groups	Tamil

Suggestions

A few suggestion are made to enhance visibility of MILs in various programmes:

- Translation as of now is being undertaken in a contingent manner. The offering of programmes in regional languages should become a planned, structured activity with IGNOU and focussed activity in SOUs. There is a need to establish an MIL department within the School of Humanities preferably in all open universities . The MIL faculty should oversee the work of translation which is a highly specialized activity.
- The number of courses and credits in MILs could be added at different levels.

- IGNOU along with the Central Institute of Indian Languages should promote the activity of translation and promote research in the field of Translation Studies. IGNOU should galvanize translation activity and promote informed awareness about the activity of and the academic phenomenon of translation across the country.
- A research and feedback system on the status of the translated courses should come into operation along with the launching of programmes. Feedback should become an inbuilt activity of the curriculum planning.
- As the saying goes, there is no substitute for original writing. Translation can never be a replica of the original. In the process of translation the fervor and flavour of the original text may be lost. So, OUs should not emphasise literal translation of its material. Rather the accessibility of content by bringing in local idiom, syntax, and context to build-up word – world linkages should be empahsised.
- Materials in translations often include suggested reading books as mentioned in the original texts only. The practice should be abandoned and relevant books in the translated languages should be included.

Building on the major initiatives taken by the IGNOU for promotion of regional languages to reach out to the most needy sections of society, it needs to be firmly said here that the multiplicity of languages should become a sign of strength and not of liability in the country. As an apex body IGNOU should set new standards of reaching the non-reachable through prompting education in regional languages. It has been seen in the course of two decades that IGNOU has emerged not only as an alternate albeit an improved system vis-à-vis the formal conventional system of education. The innovative nature of its programmes has accelerated the pace with which the traditional universities are now trying to vie with and catch up with IGNOU's new initiatives in various fields.

References

Bhardwaj, R. (1999). Innovative Educational Practices in Mother Tongue Language Textbooks in India. Paper presented the Second Conference on Improvement of Learning and Teaching of Language and Literature, Amsterdem, Netherlands, July 14-16.

Mallikarjun, B. (2001). Linkages for the education of the minorities. In M.S. Thirumalai (ed.), *Language in India*, 1(5).

IGNOU (2004) *Report on Development of Indira Gandhi National Open University and Open Learning System during 10th Plan Period*, IGNOU, New Delhi.

Satchidanandan, K (1999). *Indian Literature Position and Propositions.* Delhi: Pencraft International.

The Indira Gandhi National Open University Act 1985 (No. 50 of 1985). New Delhi.

Professor Renu Bhardwaj is Professor of English in School of Humanities, Indira Gandhi National Open University, New Delhi.
Email: rbhardwaj@ignou.ac.in

13

Legal Education Through Distance Mode

N. R. Madhava Menon

On Legal Education

The Bar Council of India is under a mistaken impression that professional education in Law cannot be given through distance education and open learning system. They have not realised what modern technology can accomplish, given the competent guidance of experts with high standards set by the Indira Gandhi National Open University. I believe that the Advocates Act gives authority to the Bar Councils only in matters of legal education preparing persons to practise law. And that too in consultation with universities teaching law, which under their respective statutes have full authority to determine what education they may impart and how, subject, of course, to the role assigned in higher education to the University Grants Commission. In the circumstances, it is up to individual universities to decide the best way to impart legal education and the Bar Council can only put additional qualifications, if justified, to let such graduates join the bar. This is the logic under which Indians, who had their LL.B. degrees or equivalent qualification from abroad including the so-called external LL.B. of the University of London, are being asked to take a Bar Council-administered test before being allowed to enrol in India. Therefore, IGNOU has several options with respect to the legal education agenda.

Firstly, the Bar Council may be approached to recognise the IGNOU degrees imparted through distance mode, subject to whatever reasonable condition they want to suggest. Taking into account IGNOU's special status in higher education, it shall not be treated at par with other institutions teaching through distance mode. At best, the Bar Council can say that IGNOU graduates may have to study clinical courses in a regular law school to be eligible for enrolment. In this connection it may be noted that not even one-fourth of law graduates passing out of the regular university system (which includes a large number of evening/morning colleges) every year seek enrolment with the Bar Council. Law graduates are sought in government, industry, media and civil society for a variety of jobs which are as attractive to people as legal practice. That is why there is increasing demand for law studies and an institution like IGNOU cannot ignore it, whatever the Bar Council might decide.

Secondly, IGNOU can introduce the Law degree course announcing that it is intended as part of liberal university education, in view of the importance of law education in governance, in commerce, in civil society and for responsible citizenship. It can offer courses on all the subjects the Bar Council/UGC have prescribed and more, which the changing legal market demands. IGNOU's strength lies in the quality of its study materials, its extensive network of study centres and the flexibility of its programmes. Law now touches every aspect of life and legal knowledge is essential for every profession and for civil services. In fact, if IGNOU takes the initiative on legal education through open learning, many "teaching shops", which now get recognition of Bar Council through questionable methods, will either have to improve the quality of education being imparted or close down and yield to the better learning facilities available through IGNOU.

Thirty years ago, I had argued against correspondence courses in law for purposes of enrolment; today, after seeing the popular demand of IGNOU's degrees in the field of technical and professional education and the quality of its study materials, I am convinced that there is positive good in allowing distance education in law with strict quality controls. If some section of IGNOU law graduates want to join legal practice, let the Bar Council design a scheme as they now have with respect to foreign law degree holders. This will ensure access, quality and cost-effectiveness in legal education for the future.

In addition to the LL.B. programme, there is today a felt need for people with basic knowledge and skills in law and related subjects for a variety of vocational activities. These include law clerks for lawyers and judges, law office assistants to firms and legal divisions of corporate houses, para-legals for legal aid agencies, trained mediators for dispute settlement at village level etc. There are no institutions yet imparting education for these job openings. They are fairly well paid jobs in which the LL.B. degree holders sometimes apply because their poor quality education fails to enable them to survive in an increasingly competitive profession. In the process, a lot of avoidable wastage in higher education happens. LL.B. degree itself is devalued in the legal market and the only beneficiaries seem to be those exploiting the demand through pedestrian programmes offered through the so-called law colleges, which have neither qualified faculty nor essential infrastructure facilities. In this situation, it will be a great public service if IGNOU can start law courses not only of the liberal and professional variety, but also a range of vocational diploma courses, which provide opportunities for employment to millions of talented men and women passing out of the school system.

A Vision for Legal Education in the Knowledge Society

People with vision who got the country Independence gave also a visionary document called the Constitution of India. The goals set by the Constitution initially gave the direction for all activities including legal education. Broadly speaking, the curricular goals set for legal education in Independent India reflected the Constitutional principles of democracy, pluralism, secularism, rule of law, basic human rights and social justice, which informed its content and methods. However, the structure and organization of legal education by and large continued in the colonial mould thereby creating a distance between the formal legal system and the multitude of informal legal systems, which continued at different levels of society. It was this problem of limited social relevance of formal legal education which was addressed by two important initiatives by the Bar Council of India (BCI) and the University Grants Commission (UGC) during 1980s.

The Curriculum Development Committee of the UGC, after several consultative meetings, came up with what they called a socially relevant curriculum for legal studies. It recognised the need for multi-disciplinarity and the importance of more optional courses opening up opportunities for specialisation and interface with development. Bar Council of India, on the other hand, canvassed for an integrated Five-Year LL.B. programme after higher secondary school examination to provide social context education in law. A number of social science subjects thus got into the law curriculum. Professional skills and ethics were to be imparted through experiential/ clinical learning. This improved vision of legal education was implemented initially through the National Law School sponsored by the BCI itself and later by most of the important law teaching institutions in the country.

The year 1991 marked a turning point in the country's development and system of governance. The government announced the policy of economic liberalization followed by a series of legislative and structural changes by which a new era of economic governance and changed role of the State in the economy was initiated. Simultaneously, two other developments took place in quick succession warranting fresh thinking on the role of law in society and the shape of legal education for the future. The first of these developments relate to the emergence of a globalised market economy guided by the World Trade Organization and a trade regime which, in several respects, appeared to be distinctly discriminatory against the developing world. A new jurisprudence based on the experience of the developed western countries came to occupy the legal space of the developing countries with consequences still unknown to them.

The second of these developments resulted from the amazing explosion of information and communication technology which is making established legal standards and procedures increasingly irrelevant to the changed circumstances. It is now clear that science and technology will dictate the agenda of the future, be it governance or education, administration or justice. Clearly the time has come to have a new vision for legal education in the society of the future where capacity to access, process, manage and direct all types of knowledges will determine the pace of development and the quality of governance. In short, knowledge is the key resource for progress in the emerging legal regime and dispute avoidance will as much determine the demand for legal competence as dispute resolution. The future lawyer will be called upon to access knowledge not only of the kind he is now familiar with but also what science and technology are throwing up everyday in the public domain. Judges will have to increasingly assume the role of problem solvers rather than be mere adjudicators. The adversarial style of litigation will yield to a large range of dispute resolution methods with varying skills and rules of ethics. Scientific evidence will increasingly replace conventional rules of proof. A variety of non-legal actors will enter the legal arena and law persons will have to develop the capacity to work with them in upholding rule of law and dispensing justice. Even the style of law making may undergo changes and law will become a critical input in national and international affairs.

If there is merit in some of these emerging trends identified here, it is incumbent on all those involved in legal education to envisage the scenario, let us say of 2010 and design a road map towards enabling the country acquire equal status with the developed countries so far as legal services are concerned. The legal infrastructure of the country being far less developed in comparison to others, India may have to redouble its efforts to put in place a world class legal and judicial system to support the pace of change happening around. To conceptualize this change in terms of legal education is what I would like to attempt on this occasion. I would like to do this through a two-pronged approach – firstly, narrating some insights from personal experience when I was assigned the role of restructuring legal education 25 years ago initially as a Consultant in the Bar Council of India Trust and later as Director of the National Law School of India University at Bangalore; secondly, I would like to conceptualise the legal education scenario of 2010 and suggest possible steps to prepare the legal education agenda appropriately for consideration of the legal and educational community.

Some Insights from the BCI and NLS Experience (1979-2003)

In the year 1979, I was invited by the Bar Council of India to assist the organization in shaping policies of legal education for which it has statutory responsibility under the Advocates Act, 1961. Legal education was in a shambles, despite the efforts of the Council to standardise the curriculum and to encourage universities to inculcate some degree of professionalism in the system. The initial concern of the Bar Council was to enlarge access to legal education to all sections of society and therefore allow liberally opening of new law colleges even if they are not able to provide adequate infrastructure. The demand for legal education was very high, particularly because LL.B. was the cheapest and perhaps the least difficult professional degree one could get even with less than average qualifications. The consequence of the uncontrolled expansion of part-time law teaching institutions was dilution of standards and the profession being flooded with what the Law Commission once described as "half-baked lawyers" unworthy to support the constitutional dream of a just society. The Bar Council found to its dismay that it has very little power under the Advocates Act to arrest the malaise and it must look for alternative methods to improve standards of legal education. It was in this context in late 1970s that the idea of a five-year integrated LL.B. programme and the proposal for a model national law school were evolved through a series of seminars, conferences and consultation meetings among all stake holders. It was during that period I was elected the General Secretary of the All India Law Teacher's Association, which in a conference in Delhi endorsed the idea of legal education reform and welcomed the initiative of the Bar Council, despite a section of teachers vehemently opposing the five-year integrated scheme.

As Secretary of the Bar Council of India Trust, I had the opportunity to interact with every Bar Council in the country and to create a climate to take up legal education reforms seriously. The scheme of the Integrated Five Year LL.B. Degree programme was drawn up and got adopted by the Bar Council of India in 1980. The Bar Council was persuaded to formulate a rule declaring that from the academic year 1982-83, the Bar Council would recognise for purposes of enrolment only the Five Year LL.B. Degree. Universities teaching law were to decide within a two year transition period whether they wanted to prepare students for law practice or only for improving their educational qualifications. I had the unpleasant task of popularising the scheme among universities teaching law and sorting out transitional problems to the extent possible. The politics and economics of legal education mobilised vested interests in law college management to resist the change and they eventually succeeded by winning over Bar Council members. The result was to allow the pre-existing scheme with all its inadequacies to continue indefinitely with the five-year integrated LL.B. programme and leaving the option to managements. The reform effort backfired and legal education was back to square one with division among Bar Council members and law teachers on how to go about introducing reforms.

Completing my three-year term with the Bar Council of India Trust, I returned to my parent department in 1983 to resume my regular job as Professor and Head of the Campus Law Centre, Delhi University. I was convinced that the five-year scheme is superior in academic and professional content and it was the best possible reform which could save legal education from total disaster. My belief was borne out of my experience of law teaching for over twenty years at Aligarh, Pondicherry and Delhi universities. I continued to write articles in the media advocating change and eulogising the virtues of the five-year scheme. The late Professor P.K. Tripathi, who was my Dean at Delhi Law Faculty, wrote newspaper articles opposing my views. He felt that only those with a basic degree alone are mature enough to absorb lessons in law, the argument I was not prepared to buy. The debate continued within the Bar Council and outside. The Council ultimately resolved to demonstrate the superiority of the Five Year Integrated LL.B. programme by sponsoring a model law school at the national level and secured a legislation from Karnataka Government creating a law university named the National Law School of India at Bangalore. In 1985, I was offered the job of setting up what the Council called "the Harvard of the East", a model institution to revolutionise legal education through demonstration in the field rather than by resolutions in the Council. The rest is history well recorded in the events that followed since 1986, which eventually put Indian legal education in the world legal education map and which virtually compelled State after State to set up a law university on the Bangalore model. It was the greatness of Prof. Tripathi that he did revise his assessment of the Five Year LL.B. programme after visiting the law school at Bangalore and interacting with the students.

It is not easy to capture the essence of the National Law School experiment unless one was associated with that institution, particularly in its formative years. However, it did convey to all concerned that legal education deserves immediate attention and it is possible to establish centres of excellence without big investment if there is commitment, leadership and clarity of goals. There is no alternative to hard and sustained work in pursuit of academic excellence. Existing LL.B. programmes cater largely to cognitive level of learning, which is inadequate for creativity and excellence. To assimilate fresh knowledge and to generate new knowledge, every discipline and more so Law, requires learning at affective domain, where the learner should be able to receive, evaluate, organise and respond to problems of increasing complexity and conflict. University education in law should aim at affective level learning objectives, if problem solving, social engineering and peaceful change are legitimate roles of law in society. Such a development requires capacity for strategic thinking cutting across disciplines and professions. It involves partnership and participatory processes not very common in existing campuses and institutions. The mindset of identifying law with courts and litigation has to change. Law in future will be perceived more as an instrument for development and social justice rather than a mere tool for dispute resolution and maintenance of order. 'Legal Education' will have to be transformed to 'Justice Education'. As doctors are primarily concerned with health rather than disease, lawyers will have to focus more on justice rather than dispute settlement. This transformation requires substantive and procedural reforms in law and justice, which is to become part of legal education itself.

The social justice and social engineering role of law in the development context has been the foundational idea and the organising principle of the National Law School experiment. This was translated into curricular objectives not only by integrating social sciences teaching with law, but also through a range of social context teaching methods such as socio-legal investigation of problems assigned to students as required projects in every subject, compulsory placement for two months every year with NGOs, law offices, government departments and corporate bodies, involvement in activities relating to legal aid to the poor, social audit of welfare laws, law reform initiatives on behalf of the poor etc. The emphasis has been on experiential learning, looking at law as a means to an end (that is justice) and not an end in itself. The idea was to evaluate law in terms of its impact on society and to realise that law can play multiple roles depending upon the way it is used, interpreted or organised. It was this understanding of law coupled with basic capacity to use it for constitutional goals that the National Law School curriculum attempted to give to its student body. The other value which the NLS experiment successfully inculcated in the students is ability to work hard for long hours, unlearning and re-learning from all sources of knowledge, as an essential attribute for a successful legal career. If the NLS movement made a distinctive difference in the legal world today, I can confidently assert that the work culture they imbibed at the law school is indeed largely responsible for it.

Legal Education – 2010: An Agenda for Reform

Let me now turn to few futuristic projections in the legal education scenario in the context of an increasingly globalising economy constantly pushing towards an increasingly unified and integrated legal system. Though the pace at which changes take place will depend on the events in the domestic and international policies, the direction of change appears to be clear and certain. Law in the past was considered a conservative force negotiating between status quo and change. In post-independence India, many laws were enacted questioning established practices and inducing changes, sometimes said to be far ahead of the times. This has led to non-implementation and selective implementation of the laws which brought with it several problems in the domain of rule of law and governance. Perhaps this situation might be aggravated in coming years compelling reform in the structure of laws themselves and the style of their enactment.

The trend towards decentralised administration and market-oriented regulatory systems will most probably change the structure and style of law making in future. What lessons legal education should gather from such a scenario? Alternative methods of law making through mechanisms which are democratic, participatory and experience-based will have to be explored. In fact, the role of interest groups in law making, the strength and weaknesses of existing processes of law making, the implications of these processes to equal justice under law, relevance of alternate law making arrangements, the interface between legal institutions and law making processes, the role that language and style of drafting plays in legal communication etc. must find appropriate place in the future legal education agenda. This is more important because of the pluralistic nature of society, the role "personal laws" continue to play in the lives of large sections of people and the gulf which exists between the language of the law and that of the people. The cultural lag seems to be creating tensions which make implementation difficult and institutions dysfunctional.

Equality, equity and dignity are central concepts in the human rights discourse which is likely to assume greater importance in future. Justice is explained in the Preamble of the Constitution in terms of Social, Economic and Political dimensions. Similarly, Equality is promised in terms of status and opportunity. Dignity is assured to every individual, which the Supreme Court has been clarifying in terms of a number of socio-economic rights and personal choice. Given the imperatives of economic liberalisation and globalisation of the economy, several livelihood issues of nearly half the population of India are bound to come up for legal resolution. They are primarily political and policy issues to be addressed by political processes. However, the current trend is to push them for judicial resolution. Be that as it may. For legal educators the subject of poverty and development, equity and market, equality and lack of opportunity, dignity and lack of access to basic needs, public law vs. private law, international obligations vs. domestic compulsions and a series of such value-laden questions become important across the law curriculum. Mere cognitive level learning will be inadequate to address these issues because they are value-based and apparently contradictory to the accepted notions of contemporary jurisprudence. If positivist, utilitarian approach dictated the terms of the discourse in the past, it will have to yield to a more critical, sociological dialectic in the Indian context for which legal educators have to be prepared. The balance has to be found in the Indian Constitutional framework. This requires ingenuity and comparative scholarship informed by understanding of social reality. Legal Education necessarily has to be much more inter-disciplinary and policy oriented than it is today if it were to respond to the policy challenges of the coming years.

The unprecedented and fast changing developments in science and technology, in general, and information technology in particular, have already started impacting the legal and judicial system. In coming years, it will happen in an accelerating scale. Unfortunately, the legal education system, excepting in some of the national law schools, has not absorbed even a part of the profound changes happening in the digital world. There are neither teachers equipped with cyber knowledge nor infrastructure to organise instruction on the new jurisprudence fast emerging around information and communication technology. While the rest of higher education is reaping the benefits of the digital revolution, law education continues in its nineteenth century mould. In the world of competitive excellence and trade in legal services, legal education, if not reformed, will put the legal profession in great disadvantage. It is not only a question of IT and laws relating to it. Every branch of law is affected by developments in science and technology and new laws are being enacted to cope with the situation. Lawyers and judges in future have to become critical consumers of a variety of scientific knowledges which implies that law schools should prepare them for it. Multi-disciplinarity in legal studies which today is confined to social and behavioural sciences, will have to be extended in future to physical and natural sciences in a selective and systematic way. The process is difficult and complex; but there is no alternative if the profession needs to be competent and competitive in the globalised knowledge society.

Another major challenge in the legal education agenda for the future is teaching of skills and ethics. The skills which law persons require are many and varied and are growing with the demands of the consumerist society. All of them may not be taught in the law school. However, in the Indian situation, where teaching of skills was hitherto not attempted seriously and where Bar Council would enrol every law graduate irrespective of the quality of education he had, it is dangerous for legal education to disown the responsibility for clinical legal education. Lawyers and legal educators should sit together and decide the minimum number of skills every law graduate seeking enrolment should possess and share the responsibility appropriately. It seems to me that the appropriate strategy would be for the Bar Councils to set up post LL.B. Law Practice Institutes attached with selected law schools in each State to give intensive training for few months particularly on ethics, accounting, etiquette and client relations management. These are aspects no law schools however well endowed with resources can possibly impart in adequate measure. The need for teaching mediation, negotiation, conciliation and arbitration techniques is now universally acknowledged and law schools will be well advised to provide for instruction on these subjects. In short, in future, parties will be inclined to settle disputes without litigation and legal institutions should be equipped to respond to this change.

At least major law schools in future will have to undertake an additional responsibility to provide continuing education for lawyers for which there is no regular arrangement at present. Bar Councils and the legal profession have recognised the need for continuing education and have been convening occasional workshops mainly for the junior members of the bar. The need for continuing education is for lawyers at all levels. In the absence of any institution systematically offering continuing education, it would become the responsibility of legal educators to move in that direction which would be mutually beneficial and enriching the law school activities. However, the task is neither easy nor simple. It requires research to ascertain education needs and partnership with other professions to deliver the knowledge and skills additionally required for specialised advanced learning. Without that, excellence cannot be obtained in legal services when consumer demands are going to be diverse and exacting.

Finally, to sustain a dynamic programme of legal education, the country needs legal scholars and educators of outstanding abilities constantly pursuing higher and higher levels of excellence responding to the challenges and demands. Today there is an acute shortage of law teachers even with ordinary competence and it is a tall order to expect outstanding scholars to be available in the near future. Unfortunately, there is no move from anywhere to fill this void. The crisis is slowly moving into a catastrophe with more and more national law schools being set up on the one hand, and the practising profession suddenly offering so many attractions which no law school can ever afford to give. It seems to me that the Central Government should take cognizance of the emerging paradox and adopt such measures to balance the demand and supply in respect of teachers and researchers in law.

Conclusion

I began this lecture reflecting on what distance learning can do to legal education and the role that IGNOU should play in it. While the market economy and private enterprise will hopefully shape professional legal education in association with universities and the practising profession, it is the function of open learning systems to spread public legal awareness for good governance and good citizenship. Taking the size of the population and the level of inequalities and exploitation in society, nothing but a legal education revolution can carry the message of rights-based justice and governance under rule of law to all those who are outside the system today. In this regard, IGNOU should develop a separate agenda for legal education with or without the Bar Council.

(Note: Reprinted with permission from the author, presented as Professor G. Ram Reddy Memorial Lecture, Indira Gandhi National Open University, New Delhi, July 2, 2005.)

Dr. N.R. Madhava Menon has been a member of the Legal Education Committee of the Bar Council of India and the first Secretary of the Bar Council Trust. In the past, he set up the National Law School of India in Bangalore (which later because a university as its founding Vice Chancellor, and later as the first Vice Chancellor of National University of Juridical Sciences, Kolkata. The Supreme Court of India appointed him as Director of the National Juridical Academy, Bhopal which is shaping policies and programmes for continuing education and training of superior court judges throughout the country. He was conferred *Padma Shree* by the President of India in 2003. He is now serving on the Board of Governors of the International Organisation of Judicial Trainers, and Advisor to the Commonwealth Judical Education Institute, Canada.
Email: menon_in_bhopal@sancharnet.in

SECTION III

MEDIA AND TECHNOLOGY

14

Emergence of Distance Education Media Networks

Abdul Waheed Khan and H.P. Dikshit

Introduction

A cardinal factor that distinguishes the distance education system from the traditional classroom education as well as correspondence education is the use of media in instructional design and delivery. This fact was amply recognized right at the time of conceptualizing and creating the first open university in the country in Andhra Pradesh (now called Dr. BR Ambedkar Open University) in 1982, and again while establishing the Indira Gandhi National Open University in 1985 at the national level. Evidently, the planners of the Open University system were guided by the example of the UK Open University in the aspect of using media components, as indeed in many other aspects of open and distance learning.

While print was the undisputed master medium in the self-instructional materials, audio and radio were chosen as the main components among the electronic media, to begin with. As years passed by, other media like video, television, teleconferencing networks, computers etc have gradually found place in the media-mix of the open university system. Open and distance learning institutions, which came up later on, had the benefit of making a head-start, with a richer menu of media in their academic offerings right from the beginning. Recognising the strengths of the audio-visual medium, national agencies like UGC and NCERT have also created media networks to support educational delivery for tertiary and school education, respectively.

This chapter traces the evolution of the media scenario over the years in distance education system in the country, with particular reference to the Indira Gandhi National Open University.

Media Scene at IGNOU: Early Years

The first academic offerings of IGNOU were the two PG diploma programmes in Management and Distance Education and both of them were launched with a handful of video and audio lessons as supplementary material to the printed units. The video and audio tapes were produced by outsourcing the production activity, pending the creation of departmental media facilities within the University. The video masters were produced on Low Band U-matic and audios on quarter inch spool tapes, as per the prevailing technical standards. VHS copies and audio cassettes of these masters were supplied to the study centres for the use of students during counselling sessions.

It is significant to note that the University took the conscious decision to develop the media components as an in-house activity and for this purpose a Division within IGNOU by the name 'Communication Division' was created, unlike in the case of the UK Open University, which depended solely on the British Broadcasting Corporation for producing media components. The Communication Division soon got into action for developing necessary hardware facilities on the one hand and production of the media components on the other.

To begin with, a make-shift audio studio was improvised in a rented premises of the Division (at Safdarjung Development Area) to record audio-lessons. A couple of U-matic edit suites, portable video cameras and recorders were procured for the production of video programmes. Side by side, with the help of DECU/ISRO, the Division planned for a video studio and an audio studio at the Tughlkabad Institutional Area in South Delhi, which was to be the location of the Communication Division till 1996. Despite logistical complications involved in relocating itself at short notice and carrying out the production schedules alongside the studio construction taking place in the same building, the Division was able to produce the media components for all the academic programmes as planned and complete the studio construction works by early 1988. Since the studio facility was not available during the construction phase, the production strategy adopted was total location shooting, followed by editing and post-production. Special mention may be made of the 12 videos produced for the Diploma programme in Rural Development: six of them shot in different North-Eastern states and six in the desert regions of Rajasthan, by two separate production teams of the Division with academic support from the School concerned. This was in mid 1987, when the Division was in the process of re-locating itself in the Tughlkabad complex, which was on the outskirts of the city at that time, with only one telephone line in the office, minimal equipment compliment, a single Matador van meant for shooting assignments as well as office use, meagre public transport facility and the rest of the University scattered in four other locations in different parts of the city.

Collaboration with ODA of UK

In the early years of its inception, IGNOU had the benefit of a sizable grant-in-aid from the Overseas Development Administration (ODA) of the United Kingdom and electronic media aspects formed a significant proportion of the total grant. The media part of this assistance programme, which amounted to over UK pounds 800000, covered the following aspects:

- Equipping the Tughlkabad studio complex with professional grade equipment for production of educational audio / video programmes of broadcast quality.
- On-site training of Communication Division's producers and engineers by expert consultants from UK.
- Advanced training for some select producers and engineers at the EDTV centre of the Open University, Milton Keynes / BBC's Engineering Training Centre, Evesham.
- Services of a senior media consultant (Mr. David Saligman) to help in the planning of media components and guide the Communication Division's producers on a long-term basis (around 12 months).

The equipment supplies under the ODA grant were received in two distinct instalments. The first instalment consisted of video edit suites, portable cameras, recorders, a VHS duplication plant and a set of high-speed audio cassette duplicators. They were received in 1989. The second lot were studio camera chain, control room equipment for video and audio studios, Quantel Paint Box for computer graphics, test and measuring equipment etc which came two years later, in 1991.

Training workshops held by experts from UK covered areas like educational video production techniques, video editing, television lighting, scripting for educational television and video equipment maintenance. UK-based advanced training under the ODA scheme was given to two producers and two engineers, which lasted for a duration of three to five months each. The UK-based training courses as well as in-house workshops by UK experts proved invaluable for the creative and technical personnel, who otherwise had no exposure to the nuances of educational media before joining IGNOU. Some academics too got the opportunity of receiving media training in UK under this scheme. The idea was to sensitize them to the efficacy of media inputs in the distance education methodology and how to exploit their unique strengths for pedagogical purposes. In addition to these formal trainings, periodical orientation in media for the academics and 'other academics' during orientation sessions for counsellors, coordinators, course teams etc. was a regular feature.

Collaboration with JICA

Even as the ODA scheme was underway, the Japan International Cooperation Agency (JICA) took note of the strides which IGNOU was making on the distance education front and offered their assistance to the University for the development of its media infrastructure. At that time (1988), Japan was the undisputed leader in the field of audio-video technology and an economic super power; the University saw value in their offer and agreed, despite some misgiving that there would be an overlap and possibly a conflict of interests between the ongoing ODA scheme and the new Japanese offer. And indeed it was a daunting task when it came to working out details of the equipment systems to be sought from JICA, against the backdrop of the ODA scheme in which all the hardware needs of the Communication Division had already been projected! Nevertheless, at that point of time, there was a lingering doubt that, even though the ODA scheme was in full swing, its hardware segment might suffer some pruning and delay. It was therefore felt necessary to welcome the Japanese offer and plan the equipment details under the latter with emphasis on more sophisticated and comprehensive post-production facilities, while the ODA grant would be essentially studio-centric. A degree of overlap was also built into the two schemes as a matter of caution, just in case one or the other scheme failed to materialise in full measure. More importantly, care was taken that the technical format of video recording equipment in both cases was the same (U-matic SP at that time), so that we would not end up with dissimilar and incompatible systems. In retrospect, it would be interesting and worthwhile to compare and contrast the two grant-aid schemes and how they both played a key role at a crucial juncture in the evolution of the University.

Pegged at an outlay of 110 million yen, the JICA scheme was much bigger than the ODA scheme, but was tightly focused on just one aspect viz. development of media hardware facilities. On the contrary, the ODA scheme was broad based and touched almost all facets of the University, including media hardware. A particularly gratifying feature of ODA scheme was the importance it gave to human resource development by extending many training opportunities to the University's academics and professional staff in their respective fields. The implementation calendar of the scheme was, however, very long drawn and often slipped the planned schedules. In the matter of media facilities alone, as mentioned earlier, there was an unseemly gap of over two years between the two instalments of equipment supply.

Meticulous planning and execution were the hallmark of the JICA scheme, which started later than the ODA scheme but was completed much earlier. The University had to construct a separate building on the main campus to house the equipment to be received under the JICA scheme and things were so planned that the building would be ready by the time the equipment arrived on site. The equipment came on time, but the building construction continued for another two months. During this time, the packages had to remain in the containers in lock and key. Even after that, the installation was carried out with the help of a generator, as 3-phase mains power for the building could not be made available. At the end of it all, the exercise was an eye opener to both the sides: University personnel associated with the project took a leaf from the legendary time sense, micro-planning, attention to details and discipline exhibited by the Japanese, while the latter were impressed at the fire fighting skills of Indians and their uncanny ability of pushing alternatives into place whenever things just would not happen as originally planned.

When the Post Production Centre (PPC) (as it was then called) was commissioned in 1989, it was a state-of-the-art facility unrivalled by any other facility in the country, including that of Doordarshan. This gave unprecedented credibility to the University in particular and distance education system in the country in general. There were however new problems, not the least being the sheer logistical difficulty in having the studios at one place (Tughlakabad) and the post-production activity at another. The operating personnel had to learn to use the new gadgetry mostly on job, as the JICA grant did not lay as much emphasis on training as the ODA scheme did. Despite such pitfalls, the sophisticated facilities built at the PPC as well as Tughlakabad helped in making a quantum leap in technical quality and slickness in production and eventually strengthened the University's claim for broadcast slots on All India Radio (AIR) and Doordarshan.

Foray into Broadcasting

Educational broadcasting was a stated objective and proclaimed as an important component in IGNOU's media mix right at the beginning. However, despite persistent efforts by the University in this regard, both All India Radio and Doordarshan resisted allocation of time slots for the Open University on their networks in the initial years. The University was therefore constrained to use the media components only in the non-broadcast mode of VHS and audio cassette distribution to study centres and directly to user groups by way of sale. After coming up of the studio centre at Tughlakabad and the PPC on the main campus, the University pursued the matter more vigorously with both the national broadcasters and the breakthrough came finally in 1991. IGNOU's television broadcasts on Doordarshan started with half an hour slots for three days a week on the national network. Radio broadcasts followed in close succession from AIR stations of Mumbai, Hyderabad and Shillong. The broadcast segment on Doordarshan was extended gradually to all days of the week and this has continued even after the dedicated educational channel Gyan Darshan came into being.

Teleconferencing

In a bid to overcome the one-way nature of broadcasting (both Radio and TV) and the non-broadcast mode of tape/cassette playback, the University pursued the idea of teleconferencing as an additional media component, which could provide two-way communication and live interactivity between the teacher and distance learners. The first step in this direction was taken with help of the Commonwealth of Learning in 1993 and an audio conferencing network was established, interlinking the IGNOU headquarters with all its regional centres and the State Open Universities at Hyderabad, Nashik and Kota. The system was designed to work on telephone lines and offered two-way voice interaction among all the locations. The 'audio bridge', which was the switching hub of the system, was located at IGNOU headquarters. Each location was provided with multiple mikes for group participation, external loudspeaker for community listening of the far-end voices and a hands-free listening and speaking environment.

It was a thrilling experience for the participants to use the audio conferencing system for the first time. Despite the obvious advantages the audio-conferencing mode offered in the context of distance education, the system went into disuse all too soon primarily because it was based on telephone lines at a time when the telephone system in the country was still too imperfect, rudimentary and costly on trunk calls for conferencing purposes on a regular scale. Besides, the one-way video and two-way audio conferencing system through satellite links came on the scene just around the same time and effectively submerged the audio conferencing system in its grand sweep.

Since its inception, the Development and Educational Communication Unit (DECU) of the Indian Space Research Organisation (ISRO) has been in the forefront of promoting satellite communications for educational and developmental purposes. They demonstrated use of the 'Training and Development Communication Channel' (TDCC), which is a satellite based one-way video and two-way audio communication system, in several fora for some years. TDCC shot into limelight when it was adopted by IGNOU in October 1993 for conducting the extended contact programme of PG Diploma in Higher Education through distance mode, discussions with regional centres and orientation of academic counsellors. DECU arranged a mobile satellite uplink facility on the University campus and Direct Reception Sets (DRS) at seven regional centres, while four more DRS were set up by the University at other locations. While the outbound video and audio from the teaching-end were through satellite route, the return audio from the learning-ends was through telephone lines. The ten day long experimental use of the system became an instant success and the TDC Channel became an integral part of IGNOU's instructional package ever since. The system underwent technical embellishments in later years such as better studio facilities at the teaching-end, increase in the number of nodes (DRS terminals) and was used for a variety of academic and administrative purposes by IGNOU as well as several other institutions. As of now, the University has created an impressive network of more than seven hundred DRS terminals across the length and breadth of the country, including North East and far-flung SC/ST dominated low literacy areas. The network is being used extensively for women empowerment through self-help groups, Education for All initiative of Government of India (GoI), tele-teaching, tele-lecturing, tele-induction, etc.

Electronic Media Production Centre

The successful implementation of the Post Production Centre with the help of JICA paved the way for yet another phase of collaboration and grant-in-aid from Japan under the project 'Improvement of Educational Media Production facilities at IGNOU' at an outlay of 2.2 billion yen. It was a historic step and led to the establishment of the Electronic Media Production Centre (EMPC) in 1996. The unique aspect of the project was that for the first time in the country, building construction was included in a bilateral aid programme. The project implementation was preceded by a comprehensive feasibility study during which several rounds of technical discussions between Japanese experts and University officials were held over a period of one year. The 'exchange of notes' between the Government of Japan and Government of India took place at two stages: first on the eve of the project implementation and the second after the completion of the studio building and before commencing equipment installation. The whole implementation schedule was spread over two successive financial years.

With the establishment of EMPC, all the media facilities and activities came under one roof and the erstwhile installations at Tughlkabad and PPC were integrated into the new facilities, as also the teaching-end infrastructure and mobile uplink of the TDC Channel. The Centre, has, as of now, a repository of about 1700 video programmes and more than 7000 audio programmes of its own. Many of these are available on CDs (IGNOU, 2005).

Gyan Darshan: The educational TV channel of India

Dedicated educational broadcast channels by universities, as distinct from general broadcasting, was first recommended by the Varghese Committee in 1978. Since then, several other committees appointed by the GoI from time to time voiced similar concerns; notable among them were the National Education Policy document 1986 and the Karnik Committee report of 1988. In practice, however, even securing proper time slots for the national open university on the national broadcast networks of All India Radio and Doordarshan remained an immensely difficult exercise for many years, not to speak of the utopian idea of exclusive channels for education.

The situation took a dramatic turn in 1999 when, consequent to a joint initiative of the Ministries of Human Resource Development (HRD), Information and Broadcasting (I&B), Prasar Bharati and IGNOU, the Gyan Darshan Educational TV channel was launched with the help of satellite uplink facilities established at EMPC, IGNOU. One of the C Band transponders previously allocated to Doordarshan was diverted for this purpose. The channel was inaugurated on January 26, 2000 with a modest 4 hour daily transmission. But it grew into a 24 hour channel within a span of one year. By 2003, the channel multiplied itself into a bouquet of channels with a Technology Channel (Eklavya) and Higher Education Channel (Vyas) coming under its fold. The bouquet also contains an exclusive channel for live programmes with phone-in facility. This was a phenomenal growth by any reckoning. One GD channel is likely to be put on DTH platform supported by fully dedicated educational channel EduSat.

The problem however was at the receiving end. Being a satellite-based channel on C Band, cable distribution is indispensable for receiving the channel at home. The major cable networks in the country demanded 'carriage fee', which could not be acceded to. IGNOU, on its own, set up several C Band dishes at its study centres and other institutions, but this process has its limitations and cannot obviate the need for cable distribution. On continuous persuasion and follow up, Prasar Bharati recently declared Gyan Darshan as one of its 'must-carry' channels for cable operators. However, this step can help the University to reach millions of cable-linked households, provided the programmes are interesting, informative and catch the viewers' attention, while at the same time retain their educational character. Needless to mention that the success or otherwise of the educational channel critically hinges on this all important factor.

In order to relate to the community in general and the unreached in particular, the University has added several features for their empowerment. The Bhasha Mandakini initiative to teach Indian languages is a long felt need. It is also intended to promote national interaction and composite culture through study of literature of various languages. Sanskrit teaching was initiated on Sept. 5, 2003 and Urdu teaching was added on Oct. 28, 2005. The University proposes to include teaching of Tamil, Bengali and other regional languages in due course to create awareness about our rich heritage, culture, and diversity.

Gyan Vani FM radio network

While throwing open the FM Band for private broadcasters at 40 locations across the country, the Ministry of I&B set aside one FM channel at each of these places for educational broadcasting.

IGNOU was identified as the nodal agency to set up FM educational radio stations at all these places under the name Gyan Vani. The Gyan Vani network has taken the shape of a radio cooperative with a partner institution identified by IGNOU at each place for managing the local station with the help of content generated by itself, as well as other institutions in the vicinity. Local NGOs are also encouraged to partner with Gyan Vani in promoting social welfare programmes. In addition, some content generated by EMPC is also circulated to the Gyan Vani stations for use in their local broadcasts. As of now, 17 Gyan Vani stations are on the air, while the rest are at different stages of commissioning. The programmes of common interest are shared by all stations so as to effect economy in operations and diversity in experience. This also helps to avoid more of the same being reinvented at each station. By March 31, 2005, EMPC had developed a repository of about 7000 audio-programmes, each of 30 minute duration.

It is interesting to note that while the Gyan Darshan channel is a centralized network, Gyan Vani is a distributed network; each Gyan Vani station is an autonomous entity to the extent of broadcasting programmes of local educational relevance in the regional language. With judicious software planning, the two networks can support each other in addressing the myriad educational concerns of the nation at the micro-level as well as at the macro-level.

Educational media at other institutions: Linkages with IGNOU

Almost all the State Open Universities and some Directorates of Distance Education within the conventional universities have made significant strides in using media; in some cases with the active assistance provided by IGNOU and in other cases on their own accord and initiative. The important institutions in this regard are Dr. B.R. Ambedkar Open University, Yashwantrao Chavan Maharastra Open University and MP Bhoj (Open) University. Karnataka State Open University, Netaji Subash Open University, MP Bhoj (Open) University, Andhra University, Banaras Hindu University, IIIT Allahabad, and Dr. G.R. Damodaran Educational Trust are the partners of IGNOU at Mysore, Kolkatta, Bhopal, Visakhapatnam, Varanasi, Allahabad and Coimbatore, respectively in running the local Gyan Vani services. The Tamil Virtual University is a totally Internet-based institution; unique of its kind in the whole country signed an MoU with IGNOU for language courses.

Under the aegis of the Distance Education Council, IGNOU has been supporting media related initiatives of the SOUs and other distance education institutions. In general, the support is given for establishing Gyan Darshan/TDCC dishes, computer networking facilities etc. Kota Open University (now called Vardhman Mahavir Open University) established its 'Educational Media Production Centre' with the help of technical planning and guidance provided by EMPC, IGNOU and financial support from DEC. A similar technical assistance was provided to the National Institute of Open Schooling in planning and execution of an audio/ video studio.

Media Initiatives in Conventional Institutions

Among the conventional educational institutions, the Indian Institutes of Technology (IITs) took the exemplary initiative of supporting the Technology Channel under the coordination of IIT, Delhi. The Technology Channel is a part of the Gyan Darshan bouquet. On-going class room lectures of IIT professors are recorded and these form the content for this channel, with very little editing or post-production. Many private engineering college teachers and students are said to be the beneficiaries.

IIT, Mumbai runs an interesting distance education programme (DEP) based on Ku Band satellite links using VSAT technology at the remote learning centres. Launched in 2002 with an initial student enrolment of 78, the network configuration of DEP provides for the teaching end at IIT, Mumbai, and network control through a virtual hub at HCL-Comnet, Noida and interactive VSATs at seven learning-ends. Engineering diploma courses are being taught through DEP. The popularity and success of the programme can be gauged from the fact that enrolments for the DEP registered a five-fold growth in a span of just one year (Kavi Arya et al., 2005).

The erstwhile EMRCs of the UGC network have been upgraded as 'EM^{2}RC's (Educational Multi-Media Research Centres) so that a paradigm shift in favour of production of multi-media educationalware can be brought about, in addition to their contributing to the Higher Education TV channel, as at present. The National Council for Educational Research and Training (NCERT) created Central Institute of Educational Technology (CIET) to promote mass media singly or in multimedia packages at the school level. It now has a fairly good repository of A/V programmes and partners IGNOU in Gyan Darshan.

EduSat Project

An epoch-making development in the history of educational media based on satellite communications was the launch of an exclusive geostationary satellite for education by ISRO under the 'EduSat' project on Sept. 20, 2004. The satellite has its footprints all over India and it provides for multiple beams; one national and five regional beams in Ku Band and one national beam in Extended C Band (Fig. 1). The ground facilities for the national as well as regional

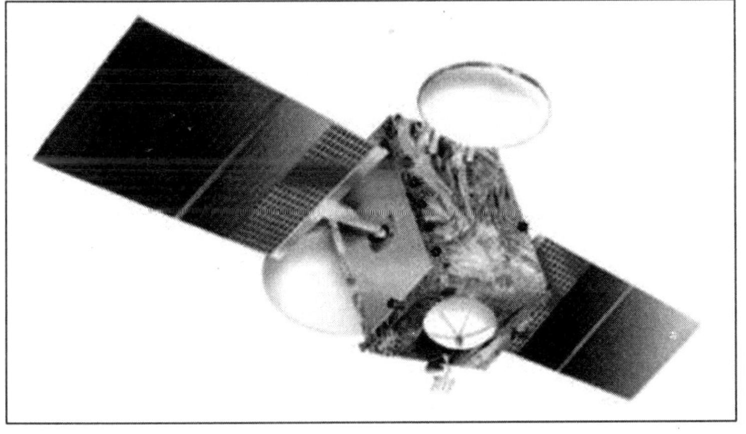

Figure 1: Satellite in extended C Band

services can be so configured as to permit interaction through one-way audio, one-way video Receive Only Terminals (ROTs) and two-way audio, or two-way video Satellite Interactive Terminals (SITs). In addition, EduSat provides for two-way computer connectivity, which can be used for creating digital library services and virtual classrooms (Fig. 2).

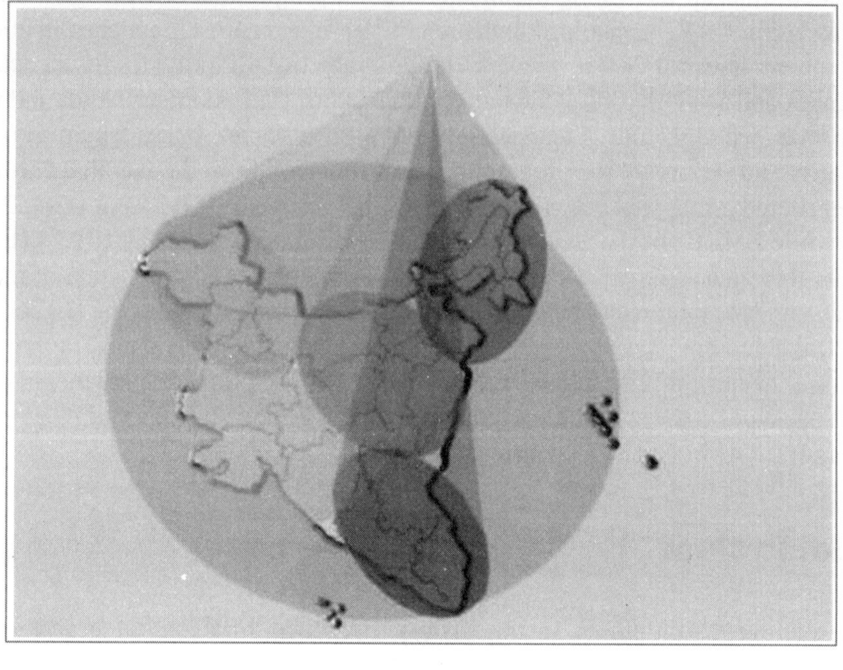

Figure 2: Connectivity within EduSat

In the first phase, IGNOU has created a network of 131 EduSat supported Satellite Interactive Terminals in collaboration with ISRO. Though option to create unlimited number of Receive Only Terminals (ROTs) exist with IGNOU, it has, as of now not exercised it. An important feature of this network is that it has provision for multi teaching-ends, ten have been planned at present so that the expertise available in and around these centre-cities can be utilised gainfully. Advanced computer strategies such as computer conferencing, online courses web-based instruction, virtual learning, interactive multimedia-composite disk (IMM-CD), etc. can be used through EduSat supported data transmission network. Understandably, IGNOU programmes are placed on the national beam of EduSat, which is regularly put to use for interactive live lessons and several other academic/administrative applications. EduSat terminals based in regional centres and some select study centres are equipped for two-way video interactivity, while the rest are confined to audio interactivity as in the case of the TDC channel.

Notable among the regional networks under the EduSat project are the APNET/Mana TV which caters to the educational and developmental needs across Andhra Pradesh with more than 2000 terminals, KARNET of Karnataka (over 200 terminals), Goa (20 terminals), Gujarat

(550 terminals), Madhya Pradesh (1350 terminals), Orissa (1434 terminals) and Tamilnadu (20 terminals) (Bhatia and Dikshit, 2005). In fact, now every state is being encouraged and motivated to participate in and create network of EduSat supported centres. NCERT has been sanctioned a network of 100 SITs for connecting Jawahar and Navodaya Vidyalayas, Kasturba Vidyalayas, and select Govt. schools. Similarly, UGC, through CEC is establishing its network by connecting leading universities and institutions. The APNET/Mana TV network in Andhra Pradesh is the fore runner to the EduSat, having been in operation since 2001 under a separate initiative of the government of Andhra Pradesh with ISRO and having the largest number of learning end terminals. With the launch of EduSat, it is now classified under the EduSat project. Thus, the EduSat project stands as a nation-wide umbrella network for distance education in the country, encompassing in its fold all the other satellite-based educational networks –existing as well as forthcoming. EduSat has tremendous capacity to take education to the unreached and bridge the gap between rural and urban societies.

One of the major weaknesses of Indian school education system is high drop out rate (~ 80%) from 1st to 12th standard. The reasons are many and varied; socio-economic, locational disadvantage, resource crunch, lack of trained teachers, lack of infrastructure, weak communication systems, etc. These grass root realities are well understood by educational planners and they are convinced that only technology can help us reach the most distant and deprived (Dikshit, 2002). Several projects have been initiated to improve the quality of school education. Computer Literacy and Awareness Studies in Schools (CLASS) initiated in early 1990s failed because of lack of enthusiasm in school teachers working in remote villages, lack of communication and transportation facilities, non-availability of appropriate software and supportive mechanisms. The lessons learnt from the failure of CLASS project made Dikshit et al (2001) to involve the community as well as motivated teachers and develop local capabilities for infrastructure maintenance. This change in strategy turned the outcome on its head; in less than a year, the challenge of connecting about 1000 schools in the interior of the State of Madhya Pradesh, predominantly inhabitated by Scheduled Tribes, was accepted and addressed.

To strengthen the quality of school education further, EduSat network can help upscale the existing virtual classroom initiatives. Recently, MHRD, ISRO and IGNOU have taken a pilot project worth US$ 3 million to connect 1200 one teacher schools in four most educationally backward districts; one each in Madhya Pradesh, Bihar, Uttar Pradesh and Chhattisgarh. For these schools, the software is being created by IGNOU following the strategy successfully adopted in HEADSTART (Dikshit et al., 2001) wherein highly motivated teachers were invited to first identify hard spots. The educational technologists then helped them to develop scripts and transformed these to create software indigenously.

Educational Media Management: Some Issues

The four decades of distance education in the country has witnessed phenomenal strides in respect of establishing media centres, media networks as well as in the variety and range of media applications, most of these having taken place in the more recent past. Nevertheless, a dispassionate observation of the educational media scene as it evolved over the years cannot but reveal that the growth has often taken place in fits and starts, in the independent spheres of major institutions and often resulted in a disproportionate attention on the new schemes, to the detriment of previously introduced schemes which needed consolidation and reinforcement. Be that as it may, the following issues are presented in the hope that they would generate some debate and discussion among policy makers, institutional authorities and educational media managers so that a concerted action would emerge for the betterment of the educational system.

- A growing mismatch is in evidence between the availability of network capacities and hardware facilities on the one hand and generation of educational media software in adequate quality and quantity on the other. Live, interactive programming is no doubt the quickest and most economical way of meeting this challenge, but parallel attention is also needed for programme production in other formats such as documentary, drama, case-studies, quiz etc to address a wider variety of educational needs at different levels. This will not only help in enhancing the quality of media components but also go a long way in sustaining viewer interest.
- Considering that India today has one of the most extensive networks of educational media production and distribution, there is a need to develop a comprehensive human resources development strategy. Rapid advances in technology demands life-long learning opportunities, not only for production and technical staff, but also for managers and support staff. Only then, we can hope to attract and retain talent in the ODL system and derive them away from the lure of multinational/corporate houses.
- The growing education media capacity requires regular flow of quality programmes. Although in-house production capacity of most media centres has increased significantly in recent years, there are still vast gaps between demand and supply of programmes. In order to make full and effective use of the existing capacity, a flexible approach including out-sourcing programme production, sharing with and acquisition of programmes produced by others, as practised by IGNOU, is essential.
- Media production is essentially team-work, requiring specialization in the subject matter, script writing, creative production technique, camera work, lighting, graphics and editing. Managing the tension between different specialists is a major challenge and may at times consume a significant part of senior managers' time and energy. Senior managers need specialized training to handle their responsibilities effectively. They ought to be given autonomy and authority for enhancing efficiency.
- Greater thrust is needed to improve the quality of school education and training of primary/secondary teachers through the EduSat network, as that is where the maximum unmet demand persists. The regional networks and the teachers themselves in particular have to play a leading role in this regard.
- From the beginning, media components are being relegated as supplementary inputs in the media-mix of distance education institutions. While this approach was understandable in the past when access to the media in the rural areas and among people in the lower strata of society was a question mark, it is no longer tenable from today's standpoint, particularly in

the context of the EduSat project. The time has now come to launch full courses on interactive networks, with print and face-to-face counselling supplementing the instructional strategy. This new paradigm will help accelerate the educational process and elevate the distance education methodology on to a higher plane of effectiveness. IGNOU is best equipped to pioneer such a paradigm shift.

- Sharing of media resources and networking of media facilities existing in different institutions is a perennial issue that is discussed at many levels and on different fora. Institutional apathy, lack of standards in production and technical formats and lack of an agreed mechanism among institutions to exchange their educational resources either on a cost basis or otherwise seem to be the main impediments in this matter. The Commonwealth Educational Media Centre for Asia (CEMCA) was established by the Commonwealth of Learning to address this need and serve as a catalyst in promoting institutional interaction. It needs to go beyond creation of a data base of media materials available with various institutions and such other developments.
- Educational media research is yet another area which deserves serious consideration. Research studies, such as they are, are undertaken either as commissioned projects with funding from the same institution, or by individual researchers who are on the pay roll of the same institution or a sister institution. In the circumstances naturally, objectivity and credibility of the research findings leave much to be desired. The situation can be remedied if educational media research is de-linked from the concerned educational institutions and put in the hands of an altogether independent body with its source of funding not even remotely connected with the former, say, a body like the Public Broadcasting Trust. Distance Education Council has been sponsoring tracer studies on the impact of Gyan Vani, Gyan Darshan, radio, TV, teleconferencing, etc. But the efforts need greater impetus and expediency.

Conclusion

In the short span of a few decades, Distance Education as an indispensable and alternative mode of education has come to stay. It has been empowered to embrace an increasing proportion of the educational sector in the coming years and so also are the media components within the instructional media mix of the distance education institutions.

It is time that the recent developments in the country for capacity building through establishment of media facilities and interactive communication networks are taken advantage of by the academic community in the interest of providing 'education for all', which is one of the cherished national goal as well as Millennium Development Goals (MDG) of UNESCO.

References

Bhatia, B.S. and Dikshit, H.P. (2005). *EduSat: A Dedicated Satellite to provide Information and Communication Networks at National and State Levels for Education*. Project Report. Indian Space Research Organisation and Indira Gandhi National Open University.

Dikshit, H.P. et al. (2001) (eds.). *Access & Equity: Challenges for Open and Distance Learning*. New Delhi: Kogan Page.

Dikshit, H.P. (2002). Multidimensional strategy and capability of ICT to reach the most distant and deprived. Paper presented at UNESCO-Learntree Asian Forum, Karlsruhe, Germany.

IGNOU (2005). *Annual Report: 2004-05*. New Delhi: IGNOU.

Japan International Cooperation Agency (1993). *Development of Educational Media Production Facilities at IGNOU.* Project Feasibility Study.

Kavi Arya et. al. (2005). Satellite based distance education programme at IIT, Bombay. In Usha Reddi et al. (eds.), *Perspectives in Distance Education: Educational Media in Asia*. Vancouver: Commonwealth of Learning.

Professor Abdul Waheed Khan, former Vice Chancellor, Indira Gandhi National Open University and Chairman, Distance Education Council, is Assistant Director General (Media), UNESCO, Paris. He also served Commonwealth of Learning as Director (Media).
Email: awkhan@col.org

Professor H.P. Dikshit is Vice Chancellor, IGNOU and Chairman, Distance Education Council. He has the rare distinction of being Vice Chancellor of four Universities: two conventional and two open. He also served as President, AIU. Currently, he is Chairman, EduSat Utilisation Committee, Government of India.
Email: hp_math@ignou.ac.in

Audio and Radio

Kiron Bansal and V. Rama Rao

Introduction

The use of communication media is an integral part of any Open Distance Learning (ODL) system. Presently, a wide spectrum of technologies is being harnessed for reaching out to the dispersed and heterogeneous groups of learners at different levels. However, despite the emergence of wide media options, audio based technologies continue to remain an indispensable choice because of their versatility, low cost and user friendliness. The inherent simplicity of technology and its ability to adapt to innovative and interactive formats have been some of its major strengths. It can invoke the imagination and promote active participation of the learner. Experience shows that new technologies add things on but they do not replace the old. Each medium reinvents itself in the context of changes in the communication environment and radio-audio is reorienting and reinventing itself to create its own 'listening space'.

Among the various audio technologies used for ODL, such as audio cassettes, audio-vision, audio-conferencing, audio-graphics and telephone tutoring; radio broadcast and audio cassettes are by and large the most commonly used media in India which will be the focus of this chapter. Before we proceed to examine their role, it will be pertinent to take a look at the growth of educational broadcasting in India to contextualize the discussion.

Growth of Educational Broadcasting

A brief look at the use of radio-audio for education reveals that even before All India Radio came into existence, educational programmes were broadcast from Bombay (Mumbai) and

Calcutta (Kolkata) radio stations. However, organised school broadcasting started bi-weekly for half an hour from Calcutta in 1937, followed by Delhi, Madras (Chennai) and other primary stations of AIR. The programmes were enrichment-based, not strictly governed by curriculum and the duration ranged from half an hour to one hour, the frequency from two to six days a week. Over a period of time, AIR made concerted efforts to make the radio broadcasts curriculum-based but due to factors such as the absence of a common syllabi and time tables as well as non-availability of radio sets in schools, these broadcasts could not make much headway (Masani, 1976).

Over the decades, educational broadcasts have been made more curriculum oriented aimed to support the school teachers. Planned by AIR in consultation with the respective state education department, the consultative panels comprise several educationists as members and the subject specialist committee comprises eminent school teachers. The programmes are of 40 minutes duration with short introduction and provision of follow-up discussion with varying frequency and language as per the requirements of the respective state.

Various institutions assisted by AIR have been engaged in planning and producing educational programmes. Prominent among them are Central Institute of Educational Technology (CIET) of NCERT and its state wings, State Institutes of Educational Technology (SIETs) for programme production for primary and secondary level students on teaching of skills in Hindi and other regional languages. In a project entitled 'Radio Pilot Project' started jointly by the Department of Education, Rajasthan, AIR Jaipur and NCERT, radio was used to teach Hindi language to the primary school children as part of the instructional package. The impact studies conducted by AIR revealed significant knowledge gain by teaching through radio. Some specialized institutions such as Central Institute of English and Foreign Languages (CIEFL) have made extensive use of audio/radio for teaching of English. The text book-based audio lessons are produced for different grades.

Audio-Radio Components in ODL System

In India, Distance Education (DE) began in 1962 in the form of correspondence education to meet the ever-growing demand for education; the School of Correspondence and Continuing Education (now campus of Open Learning) of Delhi University introduced correspondence courses. Encouraged by its success, the Education Commission (1964-66) recommended 'fuller exploitation of the method for a wide range of purposes'. The concept attracted the attention of many universities and institutes of higher learning, which established separate centres or adopted the method as a part of their regular curricula. Over a period of time ODL system has evolved greatly and as of now, we have one National Open University, 11 State Open Universities (SOUs) and 106 dual mode conventional universities offering education through distance mode.

IGNOU

The establishment of Indira Gandhi National Open University (IGNOU) on 20 September 1985 marked the beginning of a new era in open learning in India. The Project Report of IGNOU

(EdCIL,1985) outlined the objectives of the University as to 'advance and disseminate learning and knowledge by a diversity of means, including the use of any communication technology, to provide educational opportunities for higher education to a larger segment of the population and to promote the educational well being of the community'. In conformity with this objective, the instructional package of IGNOU constitutes a wide spectrum of technologies from print to multi-channel modes such as audio and video programmes, broadcasting, interactive radio counselling, teleconferencing, CD ROMs and online education though the Internet. The Electronic Media production Centre (EMPC) established with financial support from Japan International Cooperation Agency (JICA) is entrusted with the task of production, distribution and broadcast of audio-visual materials.

Audio cassettes have been found useful in the educational context as they provide flexibility and control to the learner who can stop, start, replay, rewind, and fast forward a cassette. Almost all the programmes offered by IGNOU have an audio component. These cassettes are made available at the Study Centres and can also be procured from the University at a nominal cost. Till date, a total of 1293 audio programmes have been produced for various academic programmes. The University has also produced 135 programmes comprising audio transformations of the print material for independent use by the visually challenged.

In addition to the audio cassettes in non-broadcast mode, the University has been using radio broadcast from select stations of AIR. Drawing upon its extensive reach, radio broadcast is being harnessed to serve the students from AIR-Hyderabad and AIR-Mumbai for half an hour on three and two days, respectively, in a week.

To overcome the limitation of radio as being one-way medium, Interactive Radio Counselling (IRC) sessions are being organised from 184 radio stations of AIR every Sunday for one hour in which the SOUs have a slot on every fourth Sunday.

In view of the various pressures and constraints in which the mainstream broadcasting organisations operate and the air time not freely available for educational purposes, the Project Report of IGNOU (EdCIL,1985) had envisaged that 'efforts should be made therefore to develop separate and independent educational channels on television and radio. Only then can the National Open University make use of these channels for educational purposes effectively'. In tune with the suggestion, as a joint venture, the Ministry of Human Resource Development, Ministry of Information and Broadcasting, the Prasar Bharati and IGNOU have established a network of Gyan Vani radio cooperative dedicated to education and development.

Gyan Vani is a network of FM radio stations operating from various places in the country. Launched in November 2001, Gyan Vani operates as media cooperative with the day-to-day programmes being contributed by educational institutions, NGOs, government and semi government organizations, UN agencies and Ministries. At present, 17 FM radio stations are operational at Allahabad, Bangalore, Bhopal, Coimbatore, Chennai, Delhi, Guwahati, Jabalpur, Kolkata, Lucknow, Mysore, Mumbai, Raipur, Rajkot, Varanasi, Vishakhapatnam and Shillong. Another ten FM Stations are in advanced stage of commissioning and are likely to go on air in the near future. Each station has a range of about 70 kms radius enabling it to meet the specific educational needs of the local community with programmes in their own language. The software contributed by partner institutions is supplemented by local production and acquisition of programmes from private production houses. It is important to note that these radio stations can and ought to supplement each other's efforts by sharing programmes of universal nature.

Technical considerations

Technically, radio broadcasting through FM (Frequency Modulation) stations differs radically from the Medium Wave and Shortwave broadcasts through All India Radio. Medium Wave (300 KHz to 3000 KHz) broadcasts are propagated along the ground and reach distances upto 300 km. Shortwaves (3 MHz to 30 MHz) on the contrary travel skyward, get reflected by the upper layers of the atmosphere (known as ionosphere) and reach target areas thousands of miles away. While their vast reach is a great advantage, shortwave broadcasts suffer from inconsistent reception due to fading and other vagaries of ionospheric propagation.

FM broadcasts (30 MHz to 300 MHz) are limited in their reach by line-of-sight considerations. Hence, even under favourable conditions, a typical FM station cannot reach beyond 70 km or so. Despite the limited reach, FM has become the most popular means of radio broadcasting in recent years because of better clarity and freedom from noise. While throwing open the FM band for private broadcasters in the year 2000, the Ministry of Information & Broadcasting, in consultation with the Ministry of Human Resource Development (MHRD), reserved 40 FM channels at different places across the country for the sake of the Gyan Vani network.

It is pertinent to note that Gyan Vani educational radio is a localized service from a specific place to the local community in the local language. Used properly, Gyan Vani caters to a more focused, area-specific approach to education and development.

Transition from tape to tape-less audio

Technical formats adopted for audio recording, mastering, preservation and distribution in educational institutions generally followed the trends prevalent in broadcast radio, in order to ensure interoperability among the institutions as well as between institutions and broadcast stations.

During the 1980's and earlier, the spool type quarter-inch magnetic tape was virtually synonymous with professional audio recording the world over. In the early years at IGNOU, spool tapes were used for recording, mastering, preservation and for broadcast through AIR. Duplicated copies of these master tapes on audio cassettes were the means of distribution to study centres and for sale.

In the 1990s, the DAT (Digital Audio Tape) format was introduced in the newly built EMPC setup and slowly the new format gained ascendancy over the spool tape because of its compactness, superior technical quality and overall economy. But the transition was inordinately slow, as parallel use of spool tapes was unavoidable for sending them to AIR stations for broadcast. Strange as it may seem, the country's broadcast network, barring a few major stations, was still mired in spool tapes at a time when the professional audio industry, including educational audio, took the lead to go beyond them. Audio cassettes continued as the distribution medium for study centres even after the change over to the DAT at the studio end.

Even as the DAT format was making inroads in the educational audio studios, the march of digital revolution brought in its wake tape-less audio recording techniques by way of Audio Work Stations and Audio CDs (Compact Discs). To keep pace with the latest technology, the Gyan Vani network was designed as a tape-less operation from the beginning. All studio-based recording, post production and playout activities are based primarily on the audio work station. Outdoor recordings are also carried out in a tape-less manner with the help of digital portable recorders with facility to transfer their content into the work station for post-production work. Side by side, Audio CDs are also used extensively for exchanging programmes from one station to another and for non-broadcast distribution at study centres. Audio CDs have also proved very convenient for library purposes as well because of their compactness, ability for multiple use without wear and tear, ease of replication without loss of quality and long shelf-life.

The current scenario in this respect is a composite one: with IGNOU and the Gyan Vani network on the tape-less plane with workstations and CDs, many SOUs with spool tapes or the DAT format, while the All India Radio network makes use of all the formats in varying degrees of proportion.

State Open Universities

In pursuance of its role as a national resource centre, IGNOU has provided support for the establishment of SOUs located in different states. Dr. B.R. Ambedkar Open University (BRAOU) was the first open university in India that made use of media for instructional purpose 'to enrich, support, illuminate, demonstrate or otherwise strengthen the learning experiences'. Established in 1982, and earlier known as Andhra Pradesh Open University, BRAOU has been broadcasting educational programmes since its inception, four days a week on Hyderabad 'B' station with short wave support for state wide coverage. The Audio-Visual Production and Research Centre (AVPRC) established in 1986 is engaged in production and transmission of audio-video programmes, apart from conducting training and research activities.

Among other SOUs, Yashwantrao Chavan Maharastra Open University, Nashik and Vardhman Mahaveer Open University, Kota enlist good number of audio programmes. Madhya Pradesh Bhoj (Open) University, Bhopal, Netaji Subhas Open University Kolkata, and Dr. Baba Saheb Ambedkar Open University, Ahmedabad are also gearing towards their greater use while Karnataka State Open University, Mysore lays more emphasis on audio lessons in its programme delivery (Table 1).

National Institute of Open Schooling (NIOS)

In India, open education at the school level, as at the tertiary level, had its beginnings in the correspondence model to improve the academic standards of out-of-school students (Panda and Garg, 2003). Starting from Madhya Pradesh in 1965, other centres soon came up in Delhi, Rajasthan, Uttar Pradesh, Orissa and other states. The National Open School came into existence in 1989 when the Government of India upgraded the Open School, now rechristened National Institute of Open Schooling (NIOS). NIOS provided support for the establishment of seven state open schools in Haryana, Rajasthan, Madhya Pradesh, Karnataka, Punjab, West Bengal and Kerala. Though print has been the mainstay of programme delivery, audio and video are also being used. A total of 94 audio programmes ranging from 2 minutes to longer duration have been produced with 35 at Open Basic Education (OBE) level, 43 at Secondary and 16 at Senior Secondary levels.

Table 1: Audio programmes produced by open universities

Name of the University	Audio programmes	
	2001-02	**2003-04**
IGNOU (New Delhi)	1109	1293*
YCMOU (Nashik)	298	345
VMOU (Kota)	200	-
BRAOU (Hyderabad)	500	127
KSOU (Mysore)	-	77
MPBOU (Bhopal)	27	19
NSOU (Kolkota)	23	207
BAOU (Ahmedabad)	12	9
UPRTOU (Lucknow)	-	227
TNOU (Chennai)	-	-
NOU (Patna)	-	-

Source: *Information Base on Open Universities, Distance Education Institutes and Correspondence Courses Institutions*, 2003, DEC, IGNOU, New Delhi; Panda (2005).
* Data for 2004-05.

Audio-radio in Correspondence Course Institutions (CCIs) and Dual Mode Institutions

The major difference between correspondence education and open education constitutes in the use of technology as the CCIs offer courses in the printed form only, whereas in OUs, the printed material is supplemented and complemented with audio-visual materials. According to the available data, only Punjab University has been using audio-video materials with 325 audio and 76 video programmes and Gujarat Vidyapeeth coming far behind with just one audio.

In recent years, some of the correspondence institutes have changed their names to Directorates of Distance Education and introduced the use of radio and television programmes. However, this has a limited impact as till 2003, among 57 Distance Education Institutes, only seven were using audio in their academic delivery. MG Gramodyog Vishwavidyalaya enlisted 6, Andhra University Vishakhapatnam 5 and Rani Durgavati Vishwavidyalaya, Indore enlisted 3 audios. The University of Jammu, Maulana Azad National Urdu University, Hyderabad enlisted one audio each and Kuvempu University, Karnataka not specifying the number. Recently, Anna University has established a FM radio station under the Community Radio initiative of University

Grants Commission. It is producing programmes for education as well as community empowerment.

Broadcast support for higher education is also provided by some dual mode institutions. For example, AIR Delhi broadcasts programmes for the students of the School of Correspondence Courses and Continuing Education, University of Delhi; AIR Jalandhar broadcasts programmes for the students of the Punjabi University. Similarly, AIR Trichi is producing and broadcasting programmes for Madurai Kamraj University. Some other universities are also engaged in planning, producing and utilizing radio programmes for their learners in which the schedule of lessons and the scripts are prepared by the Universities with AIR extending recording and broadcast facilities.

District Primary Education Programme (DPEP)

Apart from the institutions discussed above, radio-audio have also been used in Distance Education Programme of the MHRD (DPEP-DEP) for teaching of Language, Mathematics and Environmental Studies in its various projects. The Karnataka Radio Project (2000-01) used radio to teach the students in 4000 schools spread over 15 blocks in Gulbarga and Raichur districts. The achievement of the students of radio schools was found significant than the students of non-radio schools. In Radio Project, Vizag 380000 students of class III spread over 15250 schools in two districts were taught through radio and the positive feedback led to the extension of the programme for classes IV and V in six other districts. In both the experiments, the teachers also found the lessons useful in terms of content enrichment and teaching of the concepts. In Gyan Kalash project, radio was used for capacity building of primary school teachers without disturbing their daily classroom schedule. The programmes which initially began with 1500 teachers increased later on to 7500 and then covered the entire teaching community not only in DPEP districts but non-DPEP districts as well (DEP, 2003). An impact study found increase in listenership and popularity of the programmes among various sections leading to its replication in other districts of the state.

Audio-Radio in Distance Education: Some Issues

Among the various defining elements of DE, 'the use of technical media, usually print to carry the content' constituted one of its major characteristics. According to Bates (1984 b), broadcasting is *not* an essential feature of DE. However, television and radio being technical media, many DE institutions are using broadcasting as instructional media due to their inherent strengths. Wilbur Schramm in an attempt to categorize instructional media, termed complex and expensive media such as television and computer assisted instruction as 'big media' and the less expensive to produce and easy to use media such as slides 'little media'. According to Power (1990), with audio cassette or radio delivery modes, audio stands alone and may be categorized as 'little media'. However, when audio is combined with the varying modes of visual presentation and is delivered by expensive hardware, it can be categorised as an integrated component of big media. Within the context of DE, audio-radio can be seen as the 'big-little medium'.

Among the various strengths of radio are its vast outreach, especially among the poor and rural learners and those located in the hilly and difficult geographical terrain. The simplicity of technology and relatively low cost, both in terms of programme production and delivery, adds to its reach and accessibility. The intimate and personal nature of the medium gives the feel of the teacher's presence to the learner. Though broadcasting is ephemeral in nature, the use of audio cassettes provides the learner with the control to stop, pause and replay the programme and listen at a convenient time and place. Audio cassette thus encompasses some of the advantages of the written text and also compensates for the ephemaracy factor of radio. Rowntree (1994) lists a variety of uses of audio in DE, prominent among them are: to provide aural source material for the learners to analyse and react; breath life into ideas; talk to the learners through tasks; help them practice skills; make teaching more personal and human; say things that are not so easily expressed in print; encourage/motivate learners and influence their feelings and attitudes; let learners hear the voice of experts, users, clients and other learners; and act as a trigger for group sharing of ideas and experience.

Radio-audio being 'sound only medium' can lend itself to only those subjects that cannot include in-depth information, statistics and visuals. With creativity, this can be tapped to its advantage by selecting only those subjects that offer greater rein to imagination. Radio-audio have been specially found useful in teaching of language and mathematics. However, it needs to be emphasized that they cannot be a substitute for all kind of learning experiences. Moreover, if programmes are dull and a mere repeat of the printed text, they hold little justification.

Radio-audio have great utility among the visually challenged. Keeping this in view, the IGNOU has made audio transformation of the print material in 135 audio lessons, which are self-sufficient for independent use of the visually impaired. Such audio transformations have been found especially useful for those courses, in which the level of literacy of the target group is generally low, e.g. certificate course for tannery workers. In a few cases, the audio lessons are designed in the audio-vision format so that related visual content can be drawn from the printed material, while listening to the audio tape.

One-way nature of radio, as pointed out by renowned playwright, Bertolt Brecht used to be one of its major limitations, which has since then been overcome. Now radio is adapting itself to innovative formats and providing live two-way interactive programmes. The IRC for live counselling on academic and administrative matters have proved popular among learners as well as the general audience. If used as an alternative to face-to-face counselling at the study centres or at least as a supplement, IRC can address the issues related to variations in academic standards, higher cost and the need for dispersed students to travel long distances to reach the study centres.

Content, presentation and pedagogical effectiveness comprise some other important issues related to the use of audio which have direct bearing on learning. Bates (1984 a), however, argues that measuring educational effectiveness is not easy as many of the mental processes stimulated by educational broadcasting are not accessible. Placing emphasis on utilization, he observes that no matter what the quality of the programmes are, they need to be watched or heard to be effective. Thus the primary condition in the use of media is that for making any qualitative difference in learning, the medium should be *used* by the learner. In his comprehensive review of the research in the US, Japan, Colombia, India and Thailand, Schramm (1977, in Bates, 1984 b) showed that students using television or radio as a supplement scored higher on the various attainment tests used than students not using these programmes. A number of studies conducted in IGNOU and other institutions corroborate these findings and report an increase in achievement of the target group. However, a few studies recently reviewed by Mishra (2005) indicate 'no significant difference' in learning.

One major factor affecting the utilization pattern in the Indian DE context could be the fact that their use was hitherto confined to the supplementary and complementary modes. If the radio-audio components are integrated with the printed course material, it will be imperative on the part of the learner to use them. Such integration may not be possible as a blanket measure for all the academic programmes, nonetheless, a beginning can be made with programmes with less number of students and greater stress on media inputs.

Scheduling is yet another important issue as in the mainstream broadcasting, educational programmes generally get a low priority, resulting in scheduling of programmes at inconvenient hours. Gyan Vani radio stations, by broadcasting educational programmes in morning as well as evening slots, aim to bridge this gap. Though utilization of these broadcasts remains moderate, studies have revealed that discerning audiences, tired from the onslaught of mindless entertainment, prefer to listen to them at their time and pace for value addition. The interactive segment encourages them to participate in the programme and seek further information from the experts. It is also observed that sporadic broadcasts do not accrue long term gains. This also requires attention of the media planners with adequate planning, preparation as well as generation of software.

Digital Audio Broadcasting: A Promising Medium

The present day radio broadcasting, including the FM stations of Gyanvani, is all in the analogue domain. Advancement of digital technology has brought in Digital Audio Broadcasting (DAB) with superior capabilities and value added services as an alternative to the analogue broadcasting. DAB services are already in vogue in many advanced countries as well as in some developing countries. Prominent examples of countries with DAB services in the Asia-Pacific region are Australia, China, Japan, Malaysia and Singapore. In India, All India Radio has introduced DAB in a test transmission mode, but regular transmissions seem to be a long way off. The examples cited above are all of DAB Terrestrial, i.e. transmissions carried out by means of ground-based transmitters, each with a limited coverage area like indeed the FM transmitters of Gyan Vani. While there is no specific advantage of any increased coverage, DAB can however offer value additions like simultaneous data transmission, continuity of reception without any need for re-tuning the radio set when one is traveling, say in a car, etc. Besides this, DAB transmissions can offer CD quality sound, superior to the present day FM. The 'sound only' nature of the analogue audio/radio can be overcome by the visual dimension provided by the Digital Audio Broadcasting.

The only disadvantage of DAB receivers is that these are costly; at least 10 times more than the normal radio sets. This can be a great impediment for utilizing DAB services for distance education, despite the quality advantage and other value additions such services may be able to offer. Hopefully, this situation may improve in course of time as DAB services become more wide-spread and as the DAB receiver population multiplies, resulting in economies of scale.

A more promising alternative is DAB(S) i.e. DAB transmissions based on satellite communications. DAB(S) combines in itself the advantages of satellite communications (global reach, consistent reception independent of distance) and digital technology (high reception quality, addressability, store & forward features, electronic programme guide, variable bit rate as per content needs etc.). Some of the potential application areas of DAB(S) in the context of distance education are discussed below.

Transnational DE programmes

Many open universities across the world, the mega open universities in particular, are in the process of offering their programmes to student clientele located beyond their national boundaries and across continents. In this context, DAB(S) can provide a cost-effective medium for delivery of multi-media educational content, so that the same can be downloaded directly by the student groups or at study centres. Live counselling sessions can also be held through this medium. A similar process through satellite TV channels across the globe would be costlier by several orders of magnitude.

Joint educational offerings

Educational/training concerns of most developing countries in the Asian region have common priorities such as primary/secondary teacher training, vocational education, awareness programmes in health and hygiene, HIV Aids, Environment etc. It would be in the common interest of the countries to develop such programmes jointly and offer them on a region-wide scale, by sharing their resources and infrastructural facilities. DAB(S) can come in handy as a simple and effective delivery medium for such joint educational ventures involving multiple partners across nations.

Audio on demand

When coupled with the Internet for return channel (from the receiver to the central server), it should be possible to access a specific audio lesson/programme instantly on the DAB radio set. This means greater autonomy for the distant learner and greater utility for the audio components.

Conclusion

It can be said that as we move towards a complex media environment, audio-radio will continue to remain an important component of the instructional packages in DE. However, for claiming their rightful place in the fiercely competitive scenario, radio-audio will have to innovate with creative formats and applications, while retaining their inherent simplicity and flexibility. With the availability of EduSat, DAB(s) should provide much needed transmission quality.

References

Bates, A. (1984 a). *Broadcasting in Education: An Evaluation*. London: Constable.

Bates, A.W. (1984 b). *The Role of Technology in Distance Education*. London and Sydney: Croom Helm.

DEC (2003). *Information Base on Open Universities, Distance Education Institutes and Correspondence Courses Institutions*. New Delhi: DEC, IGNOU.

DEP (2003). *Distance Education Initiatives in District Primary Education Programme, India*. IGNOU-NCERT Collaborative Project. New Delhi.

Educational Consultants India Limited (1985). *Indira Gandhi National Open University Project Report*. New Delhi: EdCIL.

Panda, S. (2005). Higher education at a distance and national development: reflections on the Indian experience. *Distance Education*, 26(2), 205-225.

Panda, S. and Garg, S. (2003). Distance learning in India with open schools. In Bradley, Jo (Ed.), *The Open Classroom: Distance Learning In and Out of Schools*. London: RutledgeFalmer.

Power, D.J. (1990).The use of audio in distance education. In Timmers, S. (Ed.), *Training Needs in the Use of Media in Distance Education*. Singapore: AMIC.

Masani, M. (1976). *Broadcasting and the People*. New Delhi: National Book Trust.

Mishra, S. (2005). Audio, radio and interactive radio. In Reddi, U.V. and Mishra, Sanjaya (Eds.), *Educational Media in Asia*. Vancouver: Commonwealth of Learning.

Rowntree, D. (1994). *Teaching with Audio in Open and Distance Learning , An Audio Print Package for Teachers and Trainers*. London: Kogan Page.

Dr. Kiron Bansal is Senior Lecturer, Electronic Media Production Centre, Indira Gandhi National Open University, New Delhi.
Email: kiron_b@yahoo.com

V. Rama Rao is CEO, Mana TV, Hydrabad.

16

Teleconferencing

Zeba Khan and Santosh Panda

Introduction

The scenario of teleconferencing, the world over, has undergone a dramatic change over the past one and half decades. In the early seventies, when teleconferencing came into existence, it was seen to possess great potential for sharing of information at a distance. However, its use remained limited to long distance meetings and conferences of corporate world due largely to exorbitant costs involved in using a teleconferencing system. The phenomenal growth of Open and Distance Learning (ODL) systems in the 90's and the advancement in the technology of teleconferencing, coupled with fairly easy access to communication satellites, brought the system of teleconferencing to the forefront. Compared to many developing countries, India has been in the lead in using teleconferencing for nearly three decades. For instance, at the Indira Gandhi National Open University (IGNOU), teleconferencing has been one of the most viable means for reaching millions of students enrolled in diversified programmes of study and scattered all over this vast country. With a mandate to provide quality education to its dispersed students on an equitable basis, IGNOU has embraced teleconferencing as an integral part of the student support system. Realizing the unifying quality and immense reach of teleconferencing, educational institutions, state governments, and non-government organisations are coming forward in large numbers to utilise teleconferencing for formal and non-formal education, training and capacity building, decision making, and programme monitoring. While we record the developments in the applications of teleconferencing for education and development briefly in the first section, in the subsequent sections we reflect on the applications of teleconferencing for distance education and training, and the implications EduSat has for the emerging converged system of multi-media education.

Teleconferencing in the Context of Distance Education

In an educational context, teleconferencing not only facilitates two-way interaction among individuals but also brings in 'immediacy' between the teacher and the learner - a much sought after element in a distance learning environment. Watching the teacher on-screen during a teleconference helps the learner develop a rapport with the former. This ultimately contributes to the richness of the learning environment (Murrell, Boverie, Lowe, Zittle & Gunawardena, 1997). In addition to providing a platform for two-way communication, teleconferencing allows the visual presentation of objects and artefacts, so essential for the development of visual imagery and individual perception (Gay & Lentini, 1995).

The two-way video and two-way audio teleconferencing is closest to face-to-face meeting enabling participants at various sites to speak and see each other through a television screen; but, this was not very often used in distance education because of its high cost. In case of one-way video and two-way audio, the activities at the transmitting end are seen at the receiving end, but vice versa is not possible. The backward communication from the receiving ends to the transmitting end was by audio link only. This mode of teleconferencing is generally preferred in education for economic reasons. The educational satellite 'EduSat' launced in India in 2004 has been designed with special configuration for multiple digital interactive classrooms. When EduSat-supported network becomes fully operational (though significant progress has been made in this direction), the two-way video/two-way audio teleconferencing will become an affordable reality for all those involved in the ambit of education, training and development.

Teleconferencing can be conducted via a satellite, cable or a microwave network. Bestowed with the satellite footprint covering the entire country, and policies ensuring affordable access of the space technology for education and development, Very Small Aperture Terminal (VSAT) or satellite-based teleconferencing is befitting the Indian situation. What teleconferencing entails at the ground level is an 'uplink' for sending signal up to the satellite and 'downlinks' to receive the signals from the satellite. The uplinking facility coupled with a studio serves as 'teaching end' and downlinks with viewing facilities are known as 'receiving ends' or 'receiving nodes'. The set-up at each of the receiving end consists of a dish antenna which receives the signal from the satellite and passes it to a satellite receiver located indoors connected to a normal domestic TV set. To facilitate interaction, toll free STD telephone lines are provided at the receiving end for return audio link to the teaching end. Availability of fax and e-mail service at receiving ends provide better options of connectivity with the teaching end. In EduSat-based teleconferencing, the hardware of the receiving end, TV set and the STD telephone have been replaced by a PC with a microphone and a web camera. The great advantage of satellite based teleconferencing, is that after making the initial investment in infrastructure at the receiving end, the operational costs are very low.

Development of Teleconferencing in India

The origin of teleconferencing can be traced back to the development of satellite technology by the Indian Space Research Organisation (ISRO). The most important development occurred in 1975, with the beginning of a project called Satellite Instructional Television Experiment (SITE), the first of its kind in the history of development communication. The SITE project was a joint effort of an Indo-US Agreement, under which the United States loaned its Application Technology Satellite-6 (ATS-6) to India for a period of one year. Except for the satellite, all the hardware ground system was the responsibility of the ISRO. The SITE programmes were received simultaneously in 2,400 villages for target audiences who had no prior exposure to television. Apart from acquiring the technical competence of developing, testing, and managing satellite based television infrastructure, the major objectives of the project were to improve primary education, provide teacher training and create awareness in the areas of health and nutrition, population control, agriculture, general improvement in quality of life (Agrawal, 1978). The success of this experiment demonstrated the feasibility of satellite communication and opened new vistas for satellite application for education and development and interactive television ('teleconferencing' being one of them). Teleconferencing over the years has evolved as a unique delivery system to emancipate education from within the four walls of conventional classroom.

The major developments in teleconferencing in India are chronologically tabulated in the following box.

Major initiatives at a glance

1979 - ISRO and the Post and Telegraph Department, Government of India jointly organized a national seminar in teleconferencing mode for professionals assembled at Ahmedabad, Delhi, Mumbai, Kolkata and Chennai during Satellite Telecommunication Experiment Project (STEP) using Franco-German satellite SYMPHONIE's transponder (Chaudhary, 1999).

1983 - Teleconferencing technology was tested exclusively for education with ISRO's course on satellite communications for engineering students using APPLE. Apart from testing the system efficacy, the experiment also investigated the impact of teleteaching in terms of knowledge gain which was found to be significant (Agrawal & Pande, 1992).

1983 - Indian National Satellite System (INSAT), India's first geostationery satellite, was launched. The indigenous satellite facilitated broadcast of University Grants Commission's enrichment programme for undergraduate level students (CWCR) and NCERT's programmes for children (ETV).

1991 – A three day training programme for trainers of adult education in Gujarat was conducted in collaboration with Gujarat Vidhyapeeth through INSAT-1B. Trainees from rural background viewed programmes through teleconferencing as an effective approach and used talk back facility with ease.

UGC conducted talk back experiment for undergraduate students in Science, Arts, and Commerce for a six-day period in the same year involving eight receiving ends: Ahmedabad, Kolkata, Hyderabad, Imphal, Jodhpur, Madurai, Patiala and Roorkee. The question-answer sessions conducted after each programme were found to facilitate comprehension of the content. Many educational institutions showed enthusiasm to use the system (Agrawal and Pande, 1992).

1992 - Skill development training on maintenance engineering for the supervisory staff of the industries at eight locations, followed by Bhiwani Experiment for development functionaries, and Institution of Electronics and Telecommunication Engineers (IETE) experiment involving 11 locations were conducted. These experiments repeatedly endorsed the potential of teleconferencing as a "distance neutral" technology which could be used to great advantage in formal and non-formal education (Agrawal and Pande, 1992).

1993 - The ten-day long first IGNOU-ISRO teleconferencing experiment covered 525 participants. The transmission was carried out for five hours every day. It became a major landmark in the extensive and continuous use of teleconferencing for distance education and provided useful insights in organisational, managerial and technical aspects involved in the teleconferencing system. 10 regional centres were chosen as receiving ends. The success of the experiment prompted the university to include teleconferencing as a regular component of IGNOU's student support system (Chaudhary, 1999).

1995 - The Training and Development Communication Channel (TDCC) of ISRO became operational using the transponder of INSAT 2-C earmarked for the purpose to implement one-way video and two-way audio teleconferencing network on a regular basis for IGNOU and other user agencies for tele-teaching, tele-counselling, tele-training, academic seminars, and other related activities. The teaching-end facilities including studio and uplink were provided at IGNOU campus at New Delhi and at Space Application Centre (SAC) campus in ISRO, Ahmedabad. Gradually several users such as AIMA, NCERT, NIPCCD, State governments of Gujarat, Karnataka, Madhya Pradesh, Orissa and Rajasthan, NGO's like SEWA joined in to take advantage of this powerful technology on a regular basis. Later, four more teaching ends were established in Bhopal, Mysore, Gandhi Nagar and Cuttack (DECU, 2003).

2001 – Initiation of *Gyan Darshan 2* (GD-2) at IGNOU, a digital channel devoted to one-way-video and two-way audio teleconferencing enabled the University to serve its teleconferencing needs more effectively. GD-2 also extends teleconferencing service to other user agencies: NIEPA, ICAI, NCERT, RCI, National Trust, and other user agencies.

Towards EduSat – A Satellite for Education

Being a multipurpose satellite system, INSAT combined telecommunications, broadcasting and meteorology in a single spacecraft. Five transponders of INSAT are carrying educational transmission, including Gyan Darshan (comprising of GD1, GD2, GD3, GD4, GD5, with provision for stand by channel GD6), TDCC programmes, APNET-MANA TV, and ERNET (Nair, 2004). It was realized that an exclusive satellite is indispensable to meet the growing need of ICT supported education. Launched on September 20, 2004, the EduSat's space features include one national and five regional beams in Ku-band and one national beam in extended C-band to provide continuity to existing services. It is noteworthy that EduSat offers cost effective ground segment configuration, which can be used to access ICT as per requirement of the institution. There are two kinds of receiving end services; Receive Only Terminals (ROTs) and Satellite Interactive Terminals (SITs). ROTs, provided with a small dish antenna have capability of TV and data reception; these are basically meant for schools. The hardware cost for setting up an ROT is only about US$ 3,500. The SITs, besides data and TV reception, have capability of two-way video/audio teleconferencing. The hardware cost for setting up an SIT is about US$ 7500 with an additional cost of US$ 3500 for system enhancement. The clientele for SITs are higher secondary schools, colleges, professional institutions and universities (DECU, 2004). In semi-operational phase of EduSat, each beam will have at least one uplink and about 100-200 downlinks or interactive classrooms. IGNOU has taken a keen initiative by setting up 125 SITs nationwide. These terminals provide multi-point teleconferencing in two-way video/two-way audio mode. The number of SITs is likely to increase in the second phase. The teaching-end output continues to be fed on GD-2 also. It is likely that GD1/2 may be put on DTH platform soon with the result that education imparted by IGNOU shall reach millions of homes. CEC (UGC), IGNOU and NCERT are also establishing their own networks. In the next phase when EduSat becomes fully operational and ground infrastructure is fully in place, all major academic and professional institutions in the country will be interlinked with databases and digital libraries through EduSat. EduSat will equip these institutions with multicasting facilities, so that students anywhere in the country will be able to access telelectures in real time or on offline basis (Nair, 2004).

Applications

The earlier experiments and present utilization of teleconferencing bear sufficient testimony to the claim that endowed with its intrinsic interactive quality and technical capacity to integrate various media in one, teleconferencing provides optimum solutions for problems related to educational reach: remote distances, large numbers, transmission losses etc.

Tele-teaching

In any ODL system, teleteaching is a boon for its students who can see, listen and more importantly, interact with their teachers and other experts drawn from the field. For students of conventional colleges and universities, particularly those living in small towns, rural and remote areas, teleconferencing provides a rare opportunity to be benefitted by the expertise drawn from different fields. His Excellency The President of India, Dr. A.P. J. Abdul Kalam, father of Indian Missile Programme will himself deliver telelectures in interactive mode. Absolutely fantastic. What more can a student ask for! Dr. B.R. Ambedkar Open University (BRAOU), Hyderabad, Andhra Pradesh; Yashwantrao Chauhan Maharashtra Open University, Nashik, Maharashtra; M.P. Bhoj (Open) University, Bhopal, Madhya Pradesh; Goa University and several other government and privately run institutions are delivering their courseware partially through teleconferencing mode. For other institutions, teleconferencing is an important mode for extending their reach to their enrolled students.

For IGNOU, teleconferencing is a round the year activity for its academic programmes, facilitated by a strong network of downlinks at its 57 Regional Centres 4 Sub-Regional Centres and about 1300 Study Centres, all over India. For MBA, CEMPA, CEMPA, MCA, Nursing, Health Care, Intellectual Property Rights, and other professional programmes, teleconferencing has been integrated as a complementary component of the learning package. The induction programmes for new students, important announcements, review meetings, orientation of staff at Regional Centers, and convocation are other major activities of IGNOU which are carried out in teleconferencing mode.

For IGNOU, teleconferencing is a round the year activity for its academic programmes, facilitated by a strong network of downlinks at its 57 Regional Centres 4 Sub-Regional Centres and about 1300 Study Centres, all over India. For MBA, CEMPA, CEMPA, MCA, Nursing, Health Care, Intellectual Property Rights, and other professional programmes, teleconferencing has been integrated as a complementary component of the learning package. The induction programmes for new students, important announcements, review meetings, orientation of staff at Regional Centers, and convocation are other major activities of IGNOU which are carried out in teleconferencing mode.

Pedagogic support for distance students is provided through tele-teaching by the faculty, academic counsellors and coordinators. Telecast of video courseware (in stand alone mode), live interactive video lectures by distinguished teachers/eminent personalities/ other experts are other components of tele-teaching. The University also conducts tele-induction for new students. Skill oriented teaching such as demonstrations/procedural guidance, analyzing case study material/ language pronunciation drills can be very efficiently communicated using this medium of instruction.

Administrative uses of teleconferencing for ODL system comprise consultations with peers, periodic review meetings and monitoring/orientation of staff located in different parts. IGNOU is using it extensively to share new dimensions of developments, training the staff in financial and technological upgradation as well as obtaining feedback on counselling/assignment evaluation. Teleconferencing facilitates synchronous access to audio, video and text resources. It is also being used for publicity and dissemination of information pertaining to admissions, course material delivery, assignments, exams and Tele-Convocation for students.

Since 2002, BRAOU is delivering telelectures three hours a week through interactive channel of Mana TV, a Ku band channel on INSAT-3C owned by the Government of Andhra Pradesh for which the uplink is located in the University premises. BRAOU is also organizing teleconferencing on Doordarshan Kendra (DDK), Hyderabad's regional transmission five days a week ensuring deeper penetration. The response and participation in teleconferencing on DDK is very encouraging both for target viewers asking the concerned subject related questions and the secondary audience i.e. the general public asking questions and giving inputs based on their experience and knowledge (Venkaiah , 2005).

Tele-training

In a situation, 700 hundred teachers distributed across 20 locations in Madhya Pradesh had to be trained in a very short period of time. Teleconferencing was the only option left since it was not administratively possible to bring all these participating teachers at one location for want of space and equipment. Phalachandra (1997) narrates his experience of using tele-training methodology for special orientation programme for in-service primary school teachers on the subject of hard spots in Mathematics. The evaluation of the programme revealed not only significant gains in knowledge but also a high level of satisfaction and motivation among participants, who indicated their preference for interactive teleconferencing compared to conventional means.

In the conventional cascade model when large numbers have to be trained in a face-to face mode, transmission loss is a major concern by the time information and skills are passed on to those for whom training was really meant. Training by teleconferencing overcomes this problem since participants are watching, listening and interacting with the primary resource persons. *Sarva Shiksha Abhiyan* (SSA), Rehabilitation Council of India (RCI), National Trust are regularly using tele-training methodology for implementation of their all India level schemes and projects. State Bank of India and National Productivity Council also find this technology very cost-effective for training their staff located in different parts of the country.

The District Primary Education Project - Distance Education Programme (DPEP-DEP), a comprehensive national programme aimed at attaining Universal Elementary Education, is an ideal example of judicious mix of teleconferencing with other media and face-to-face components for the purpose of orientation, sensitisation and training. Teleconferencing played a pivotal role in successful implementation of the project in reaching out to more than 23,000 primary school teachers, teacher educators, and other functionaries associated with primary education in 18 states. In all, 112 teleconferences were organised at the national and state levels (DEP-DPEP, 2003). Presently DEP-SSA (Distance Education Programme - Sarva Shiksha Abhiyan) is using teleconferencing as a cost effective intervention on a much larger scale. According to DEP-SSA annual report for the period-2004-2005, DRS (Direct Reception Sets) have been installed at all DIETs (District Institutes of Education and Training) and other concerned centers to provide maximum teleconferencing connectivity. During 2004-2005, 31 teleconferences at national level and state level have been organized. In a single teleconference, "Teaching of Science through experiments" conducted for SSA in Rajasthan, approximately 1800 teachers participated. This bears testimony to the magnitude of the tasks being accomplished through this interactive technology in SSA programme.

Tele-training can be effectively used for

- training of field level functionaries;
- awareness creation among SIGs (Women, people with special needs);
- updating knowledge and skills of in-service staff;

- enrichment and community participation; and
- microteaching for village level/ block level teachers.

Application for rural development: e-governance

Jhabua Development Communication Project, a major initiative of ISRO was implemented in the tribal belt of Madhya Pradesh, from 1996 where even STD lines were not easily available. To facilitate talk back, a custom made computer called Demand Assigned Multiple Access (DAMA) was installed at each receiving node. DAMA used the same satellite link for real time talk back. Further, it overcame some other barriers to communication, such as holding time of telephone call by registering a centre in the beginning and processing the sequential asking of questions later from each centre (Trivedi, 2004). TDCC's expansion as Gramsat Pilot Projects (GPP) for different states in the country is a good example of effective use of teleconferencing for rural development. It is primarily concerned with establishment of communications networks at the state level connecting state capital to district and blocks in order to reach the villages, providing computer connectivity, data-broadcasting and TV-broadcasting facilities for applications like e-governence, besides other utilities. The GPP networks are operational in Gujarat, Karnataka, Madhya Pradesh, Orissa, Rajasthan, Andaman & Nicobar, Goa, and Himachal Pradesh (DECU, 2003). GRASAT–Northeast Region has been the recent addition, run by North East Space Application Centre, Shillong for effective e-governance of seven states of the region characterised by its difficult terrain and tribal prominence.

Issues in teleconferencing

Teleconferencing is not picture perfect. Like any other communication technology, teleconferencing has its own share of limitations, which have bearing on its usage and effectiveness. For instance, teleconferencing imposes constraint of time and place on participants; they have to assemble at a particular time on some chosen location. There are no universal solutions for such problems; organisations have to tackle them in ways suitable in their own context.

In a recent research review on teleconferencing, Chaudhary & Panda (2005) note that very few studies has been done during implementation stage of teleconferencing. On the basis of research done in the experimental stage and whatever little work has been done in the recent years, the authors have highlighted the following pattern of findings recurring across different studies:

- Significant gains in knowledge and comprehension of learners and a favourable response of participants and resource persons towards the use of teleconferencing in case of both urban and rural settings.
- Lack of production and presentation values in teleconferencing sessions, inadequate interaction time, need for improving the quality of interaction.

- Mismanagement at the learning-ends such as uncomfortable viewing conditions, poor communication links with the teaching-end and other small technical hiccups affecting the smooth flow of sessions.

Chaudhary and Panda (2005) conclude by saying "that teleconferencing is economically and technically feasible and can serve as an important educational tool, provided the snags in the system are worked out" (p. 90).

Presentation and content design

Studies investigating presentation and design of sessions reflect that in general, teleconferencing suffers from formal teaching approach. The participants find the presentations dull and boring. The use of graphics and other visual support is found to be minimal, drab and unimaginative. The participants also feel that resource persons do not come fully prepared, student queries are not well responded (Sinha, Kishore and Hashmi, 1994; Prakash and Lal, 1998; Rao and Khan, 1998; Trivedi, 2004). The tendency to use a talking head approach in a teleclass is a misuse of technology. Khan (2000) argues that presentation problems are actually mere symptoms of a much deeper contextual problem: a teacher tries to emulate classroom lecture method even in a teleclass, without realizing that the medium of instructional delivery is a technological interface, that is, a TV screen which would have its own implications. For instance, stress arises when one sees a talking head on screen for several minutes unimaginatively and without involving the listener/viewer. Pedagogic strategy should be oriented around exploiting the visual attributes of television and minimizing the negative effects of technology. Instead of long lectures, the presentations should use interactive formats. Incorporation of pictorial material, video clips, relevant graphics, illustrations, models not only reinforce the content but also makes the presentation lively and interesting. From the reactions and opinions of tele-teachers, it appears that "teachers find preparation for a teleconference difficult and cumbersome…" (Chaudhary and Panda, 2005, p. 89). Concerns and attitudes of teachers using teleconferencing, studied in other countries tend to suggest that that teachers' main concerns were their lack of experience with the technology, and self-consciousness about their performance and presentation (Tykwinski & Poulin, 1991). There is strong emphasis on the need of training resource persons/presenters for effective handling of learner queries, designing of teleconferencing sessions and in presentation skills (Reddi, 1996; Prakash and Lal, 1998; Rao and Khan, 1998).

Interactivity

Interactivity decreases with increase in the number of participants beyond a certain point. Interactivity is a highly contextualised issue. In Australian situations, every participant may get a chance to interact with the resource person as the total enrolment for a tele-course is sometimes less than a hundred. On the contrary, the number of students attending a single course may be ideally running in thousands in an Indian open-distance university. Such circumstances may have strong implications on interactivity on an equitable basis. 'Insufficient time for interaction' during a teleconferencing session is a common grievance seen in almost all studies. However it has also been observed that questions are often repeated and may not be relevant to a particular session (Mishra, 1999).

Analysing the research findings of four major teleconferencing experiments conducted between 1991 and 1995 in terms of impact on learners, Reddi (1996) finds no clear evidence to demonstrate that interaction through one-way video, two-way audio teleconferencing resulted in higher learning outcomes than non-interactive television mode. This is a important question to investigate in depth since interactivity has strong implications on all other components of teleconferencing; planning, pedagogy, management and delivery.

Participation

Rao and Khan (1998) reviewed the teleconferencing at IGNOU over a three year period and observed definite patterns of participation at the learning ends. They found that meticulously planned short term programmes were well attended; extended contact programmes, induction programmes and professional programmes fall in this category. Among the routine teleconferencing programmes, students of professional courses (Health Sciences, Management, and Computer Application programmes) are more particular about attending teleconferencing. Attendance is however not a issue in training programmes which run for limited period of time and more accountable since they have a strong monitoring mechanism. The researchers have reported lack of advance information, non-suitability of timings, deficient session design and presentation as the main demotivating factors for poor student attendance. This finds support from Reddi (1996) based on learners' reactions in experimental stage studies of teleconferencing.

Technical issues

Teleconferencing reception quality in terms of picture and sound is reported to be good in most of the studies. There are sometimes disturbances in the telephone lines. Non-functioning of telephone and fax lines affect student interaction with the resource persons (Mishra, 1999; Rao & Khan, 1998; Reddi, 1996). The smooth handling of telephone calls often poses problems. Particularly in very busy sessions, many participants have to be put on hold and resource persons are interrupted by a stream of questions from the learning ends while responding to the previous question. This affects the quality of interaction (Phalachandra, 1997). It is not difficult to develop mechanisms to streamline such bottlenecks. Non-transmission of the programme due to electricity failure is a major de-motivating factor (Trivedi, 2004). In many learning centres, power back-up is provided, and this facility should be extended to others for better learning environment. In a micro level study conducted for in-service primary teacher's training programme in the state of Maharashtra, Parmane and Gokhale (2005) found that effectiveness of teleconferencing depends on "continuous electric supply" which was made feasible by using an inverter instead of a generator, which needs switching on every time power goes off and thus breaks the flow of information. Dealing technical issues at macro- and micro-levels, both at teaching and learning-ends will contribute to overall improvement in utilization of teleconferencing.

The problems and concerns discussed above are one way or the other linked with managerial and organizational issues. Trivedi (2004) identifies: ad-hoc planning, deficient management practices, lack of training to facilitators, inadequate monitoring documentation and evaluation processes as factors impeding the optimum utilisation of such a powerful technology. Such issues can only be redressed at policy level before they manifest in a multitude of small problems creating chaos for small setups which have limited means. Smaller issues such as appropriate placement of telephone for students to ask questions need to be attended to; the onus of trouble shooting lies with the management of respective learning ends. Attention to details in planning, facilitating comfortable viewing conditions, and proper talk back links with the teaching-end enhances the quality and effectiveness of teleconferencing.

Transition from Teleconferencing to Videoconferencing

At present, technology of teleconferencing is in a state of rapid transition, from one-way video/two-way audio to two-way video/two-way audio mode. A learning-end will not only be heard but also seen at the teaching-end as well as other learning-ends. This will induce parity between teaching-end and learning-ends. EduSat objectives include providing support to formal and non-formal education and teachers' training programmes, increasing access to quality resource persons, enhancing community participation, taking education to remotest corner of the country. Teleconferencing will be the crucial means for implementation of EduSat objectives. It is safe to presume that EduSat and teleconferencing will nurture a fruitful symbiotic relationship in the years to come.

EduSat has a great deal to offer to teleconferencing. In order to understand this, it is imperative that we look at some specific features of EduSat in operational terms. EduSat supported teaching-ends would have connectivity with Central Repository and data bases, through intranet and internet. These resources including multimedia teaching aids, VCD/DVD Clippings/Graphics, illustrations, charts would be at the disposal of teacher in off-line or on-line mode for self-learning and enhancing the quality of teaching. The teaching-end would also be provided with storage facility for live lectures for reuse and editing. At the learning-end, besides two-way teleconferencing, the Satellite Interactive Terminals (SITs) will give immense control to the student for learning through automatic local storage of live lecture for reuse. A student would be able to access teaching-end in off-line mode also. That is, EduSat supported networks shall provide access to content (lectures, supplementary materials etc.) on demand.

EduSat's user-friendly technology has an in-built redress mechanism for many of the existing interrelated problems that teleconferencing is confronted today. For instance 'time' would not remain a constraint anymore with the off-line access to telelectures and other supplementary materials. Interactivity, sense of participation, and immediacy will definitely improve because the participants will also be visible. Moreover, since audio link will be through EduSat, the chances of signal break and poor audibility will be minimised. Presentation of the teleconferencing can be easily enhanced since teaching-end would have access to all resources that a teacher might need to improve her/his tele-teaching, be it updated information, interesting examples, visuals, graphics and so on. Perhaps it is easier said than done, but a teacher needs to be transformed into a tele-teacher, training is crucial for changing the mindset and for making a teacher technology savy. Work has already begun in this direction; NCTE-IGNOU collaborative national workshop in December 2004, followed by regional level workshops in various parts of the country are systematic initiatives to train teachers for use of ICT-Enabled education, which is on its way via EduSat (Dikshit, 2005).

There exists a tremendous paucity of research in the area of teleconferencing. EduSat will provide several options to users on teaching-learning continuum, a requisite variety to choose from. Systematic research efforts need to be undertaken to understand within media differences in terms of learning from different options and combinations.

The need of inter-institutional cooperation for system efficacy emphasized earlier by Trivedi (2004) becomes all the more important in EduSat oriented teleconferencing. EduSat ICT-support is based on systems approach, with the premise that all networked institutions will be one big system sharing knowledge, skills and resources through EduSat, rather than serving their own needs as small entities in isolation.

References

Agrawal, Binod C. (1978). *Television Comes to Village: An Evaluation of SITE.* Bangalore: Indian Space Research Organisation.

Agrawal, Binod C. and Pande, M. (1992). Interactive communication in distance education. Paper presented in the workshop on Distance Learning and New Communication Technologies, IGNOU, New Delhi (August 25-26, 1992).

Chaudhary, Sohanvir (1999). *Status and potential of communication technologies in India: A study.* Research Project Report, Indira Gandhi National Open University.

Chaudhary, S. and Panda, S. (2005). Educational television and teleconferencing. In Reddi, U.V. & Mishra, Sanjaya (eds.), *Educational Media in Asia.* Vancouver: Commonwealth of Learning.

DECU (2003). Development and Educational Communication Unit. Ahmedabad: ISRO.

DECU (2004). *EduSat: A Satellite Dedicated to Education*. Ahmedabad: DECU-SAC-ISRO.

DEP-DPEP(2003). *Distance Education Initiatives in District Primary Education Programme*. IGNOU-NCERT Collaborative Project, DEP-DPEP, IGNOU, New Delhi.

DEP-SSA (2005). *Annual Report, IGNOU-MHRD Collaborative Project*. DEP-SSA, IGNOU, New Delhi.

Dikshit, H.P. (2005). *Vice Chancellor's Report*. XVIth IGNOU Convocation New Delhi (March 5).

Gay, G. and Lentini, M. (1995). Communication resource use in a networked collaborative design environment. Paper presented at the Annual Meeting of the American Educational Research Association (San Francisco, CA, April 18-22, 1995.) (ED 385 226).

Joshi, H. (2004). *EduSat Utilisation: Process of Building Partnerships.* Ahmedabad: Development and Communication Unit, Indian Space Research Organisation.

Khan, Z (2000). *Application of television production techniques to teleteaching: An investigation of the effects of visual reinforcement of lesson content on student performance and attitude towards presenter and content*. Ph.D Thesis, Concordia University, Montreal.

Mishra, S. (1999). An empirical analysis of interactivity in teleconference. *Indian Journal of Open Learning*, 8(3), 243-253.

Murrell, W.G., Boverie, P., Lowe, C.A., Zittle, R.H., and Gunawardena, C.H. (1997). *Live vs. Taped: New perspectives in satellite-based programming for primary grades.* University of New Mexico, Albuquerque, (ED 407939).

Nair, G.M. (2004). Development of space programme and its impact on Education. Address of Chairman, Indian Space Research Organisation at 9th Annual Professor G. Ram Reddy Memorial Lecture (July 2). New Delhi.

Parkash, Dharam and Lal, Harmesh (1998). Using satellite technology for special orientation of primary teachers in Madhya Pradesh: a study of presentation aspects and production values of Teleconferencing. *Indian Journal of Open Learning*, 7(3), 323-330.

Parmane, S and Gokhale, Shubhada M. (2005). Improving effectiveness of training through teleconferencing at its cascading mode – A follow up study. Paper presented at National Seminar on ICT initiatives for quality improvement at elementary stage of education.(29-30th March).

Phalachandra, (1997). NCERT trains primary teachers in Mathematics through satellite. Paper presented at ICDE Conference, Penn State University, USA.

Rao, V.R. and Khan, Zeba (1998). Satellite-based interactive learning system at IGNOU: retrospect and prospects. Paper presented at International Conference on Collaborative Networked Learning, IGNOU (February 16-18), and New Delhi.

Reddi, Usha V. (1996). Lessons from the application of communication technology in higher education in India. In *Educational Technology 2000: A Global Vision for Open and Distance Learning.* Commonwealth of Learning, Vancouver, BC, Canada.

Sinha, A., Kishore, D., and Hashmi, J. (1994). Interactive communication for distance education – An evaluation study of ISRO – IGNOU experiment. Jointly conducted by DECU, ISRO, Ahmedabad and Communication Division, IGNOU, New Delhi.

Trivedi, Bela, (2004). Teleconferencing in India: rural development. In *Teleconferencing: A training kit.* NewDelhi: Commonwealth Educational Media Centre for Asia.

Tykwinski, J.R. and Pouline, R.C. (1991). *North Dakota interactive video network: a practical guide to teleconferencing and distance education.* (ED 348945).

Venkaiah, V. (2005). Educational media in Dr. Ambedkar Open University with special reference to teleconferencing. In Reddi, U. & Mishra, S. (eds.), *Educational Media in Asia.* Vancouver: Commonwealth of Learning.

Dr. Zeba Khan is Deputy Director, Electronic Media Production Centre, Indira Gandhi National Open University, New Delhi.
Email: zebakhan@hotmail.com

Professor Santosh Panda is Director, Staff Training & Research Institute of Distance Education; and Coordinator, Inter-University Consortium, Indira Gandhi National Open University, New Delhi.
Email: spanda@ignou.ac.in

17

Interactive Radio

Sohanvir S. Chaudhary

Background

Radio broadcasting started in India in 1927 with the proliferation of private radio clubs. The operations of the All India Radio (AIR) began formally in 1936, as a government organisation, with clear objectives to inform, educate and entertain the masses. When India attained Independence in 1947, AIR had a network of six stations and 18 transmitters. The coverage was 2.5 percent of the area and just 11 percent of the population. Rapid expansion of the radio network took place in the post-independence period. AIR today has a network of 215 broadcasting centres with 144 medium frequency (MW), 54 high frequency/ short wave (SW) and 139 FM transmitters. The coverage is 91.42 percent of the area, serving 99.13 percent of the people in the largest democracy of the world. AIR covers 24 languages and 146 dialects in its home services (AIR, 2005).

Radio has been perceived to be a cost-effective tool for greater learning effects at all the levels. From the very beginning, AIR started broadcasting school programmes from metropolitan cities. In 1956, it attempted to broadcast programmes for rural adults, known as 'listening-cum-discussion-cum-action group'. In 1966, programmes on agriculture and allied subjects, having immediate relevance to the farmers, were started by AIR. The use of radio in open distance learning system (known as correspondence courses at that time) started in 1965 catering to the needs of distance learners at the tertiary level. Both general and curriculum-based programmes developed by respective higher education institutions were produced and broadcast by AIR. Now many higher educational institutions are engaged in developing and broadcasting audio programmes for various target groups. Radio offers a viable way of increasing access to education for learners of all age groups. The success of broadcast led educators to use interactive mode for education in different countries, such as Radio Education for Afghan Children (REACH), Interactive Radio Instruction for Somalia (IRIS), Somalia Distance Education for Literacy (SOMDEL), etc. For some years it however remained under the shadow of television. But because of its affordable access and tremendous reach, it is becoming a preferred choice of educational institutions for teaching, learning, training and counselling purposes. The fact is that the motivated learners can learn and achieve their learning objectives through different modes of audio medium (broadcast, cassette and interactive).

Radio has come a long way in the past few years in India. It has reinvented itself in the new form: the FM Radio, when most people thought that it would be swamped by its more glamorous counterpart–television. It has now become an active/working medium for masses in general and for the youth in particular. In its new form, the radio as a mass medium has overcome a lot of its earlier limitations of technical, sound quality, clarity, access, etc. It has a lot of potential now to entertain (even when the listener is mobile), to inform (tremendous access to live current affairs all over the world) and to educate (as per the convenience and pace of the learner) masses.

The major decision of Ministry of Information & Broadcasting, Government of India in 1999 to allocate FM radio frequencies to private broadcasters led to phenomenal expansion of radio stations in the country. Indira Gandhi National Open University (IGNOU) signed an agreement with Prasar Bharti on 2nd August 2001 to set up FM radio stations for Gyan Vani cooperative initiative of MHRD. As turnkey solutions to open distance learning systems, IGNOU, in collaboration with All India Radio, is mandated to set up 40 such stations in different parts of the country in the Tenth Plan. AIR has earmarked one frequency to each station and IGNOU has, as of now, set up 17 such stations. Gyan Vani stations in Allahabad and Coimbatore became operational on 7th Nov 2001 and 14th Jan. 2002, respectively. Other stations have been commissioned at Bangalore, Bhopal, Chennai, Delhi, Guwahati, Jabalpur, Kolkatta, Lucknow, Mumbai, Mysore, Raipur, Rajkot, Shillong, Varanasi and Visakhapatnam with minimum infrastructure investments. At other 23 cities, Gyan Vani stations are being commissioned in a phased manner. To be relevant and practical, all the activities of Gyan Vani stations are entrusted to local partners: State Open Universities, conventional universities and other institutions of higher learning. Adequate resources, support, and guidance is provided by the IGNOU regularly. Some conventional universities and educational institutions have also signed memorandum of understanding with AIR in recent years as part of community radio initiative.

IGNOU started broadcasting its radio programmes in January 1991 through AIR stations at Mumbai, Hyderabad and Shillong. The programmes were aimed at serving the learners pursuing their study both through open and conventional universities. These also aimed at expanding the scope of open distance learning further to include those disadvantaged sections of society who still remained out of the reach of educational opportunities. Besides core educational topics/ curriculum-based programmes, other subjects based on the needs and requirements of the local listeners, such as career counselling, employment news, community development, adult education, women empowerment, consumer protection, health and hygiene, mother and childcare, etc., are being covered by the Gyan Vani. Some folk songs/folklore, dances, music, etc. have also been included in the transmission schedule of Gyan Vani stations for community empowerment. Gyan

Vani was also intended to cater to the entertainment, information and educational needs of local audiences, starting from primary school to tertiary level education. To make the programmes more area specific and cater to the needs of target listeners, it would be desirable to offer print supplement to the audio, and keep open the provision of value added services like downloading the texts through the internet, radio data services, etc.

Instructional Approach in IGNOU and Radio

The Indira Gandhi National Open University (IGNOU) has the mandate to reach out to all those who want to learn with the support of a variety of multiple media and multimedia and provide opportunities for lifelong/continuing education to those who want to avail the opportunity. There is a pool of technological tools from which we have to choose the most appropriate tool(s) to solve problems and achieve course objectives effectively and efficiently. What is important is an understanding of the way technology can be optimally exploited, how technology planning should be done and how technology can be implemented and managed. The multiple media and multimedia approach is aimed at bridging the massive gap between the demand and supply of education, especially for disadvantaged section of society. The multiple media approach forms an integral part of the teaching learning process in all the open learning institutions, including IGNOU. This approach includes a variety of media/information communication technologies, viz., the audio-visual broadcast, audio-video cassettes, interactive radio, teleconferencing, computer-enabled instruction, etc.

Radio, in both the modes—broadcast and cassette—is an integral part of the instructional design being followed by IGNOU and other state universities. For extensive utilization of the medium, as mentioned earlier, the IGNOU is creating a cooperative radio network/infrastructure (known as *Gyan Vani*) all over the country so that every one desirous of learning is reached and provided affordable access to educational resource as per his/her needs. The *Gyan Vani* (GV) network endeavours to bring about educational and social development of the community through radio. It seeks to empower the people, particularly the disadvantaged and physically challenged, by seeking their participation in programming, to bridge the gap between educationally privileged and deprived through special programming for lifelong learning and social development. The network is being used by other institutions/agencies at the local level.

A need assessment study conducted in Coimbatore revealed that there was a strong felt need among learners for accessing relevant information and knowledge through radio. There was high enthusiasm and expectation among both the learners and parents about the use of radio for counselling and other educational purposes. The study also revealed that there was a need for an exclusive channel on radio for education and they preferred FM channel for its superior quality of sound. This justified the launch of Gyan Vani FM radio network, a dedicated channel for education and development, in the country. This was followed by more research studies in other cities, such as Bhopal, Bangalore, Mumbai, Allahabad, and Lucknow in September/October 2002 almost a year after the launch of Gyan Vani. These studies also confirmed the earlier findings on the need for Gyan Vani channel for the learners pursuing their study through both the open-distance learning (ODL) system and the conventional institutions. The challenge of Gyan Vani lies in its ability to project itself as a reliable voice of the community and changing the existing mind set of the people. Its impact however can be measured only in a longitudinal time frame (Karnik, 2000). As per its very mandate, the Gyan Vani functions as a *bottom-up* flexible model. That is, the channel is decentralised in structure and functioning.

Interactive Radio Counselling (IRC)

Both the teachers and the learners, because of its one-way communication, criticized radio as a tool of learning. In fact, radio was treated as a passive and monotonous medium of instruction. Introduction of interactivity component in radio overcame this limitation and made it more effective tool of teaching and learning. Researchers have analysed the role of interaction in enhancing learning and satisfactorily catering to the information needs of the learners. Coupled with easy access and cost effectiveness, the interactivity raised the potential of radio by actively involving the learners in the teaching-learning process. Interactivity provided feedback to the learners on their performance in acquisition of knowledge and made open distance teaching more suited to the mental level and pace of learning of the learners. Based on feedback, the distance teacher/instructional designer/resource person can modify/improve the instructional strategy and facilitate learning. Interactivity allows the learner to ask questions or raise queries and construct their path/pace of learning. One added quality of interaction is that it humanizes the entire distance teaching-learning process by generating personal rapport with the learners. It helps break the feeling of isolation and other psychological problems of and among the distance learners. Moreover, interactivity creates awareness in the learner to control his/her learning. That is, it imparts ability to influence, direct and determine the decisions related to the teaching-learning process. The learner can exert his/her control on learning strategy, sequence of learning, and selection of content (Edirisingha, 1995).

The interactive radio counselling was based on certain assumptions pertaining to the strength and limitations of radio as a uni-sensory medium (Chaudhary & Bansal, 2000):

- Radio has inherent strength of outreach among masses and is more affordable medium for both the distance education institutions and the learners pursuing their study at a distance.
- Used at the local level, it can cater to area specific needs of the learners and involve them in the selection of problem areas for discussion.
- The decentralized approach of local broadcasting can develop a sense of intimacy and warmth between the resource persons and the learners.
- The interactive radio counselling can benefit the disadvantaged groups, poor, physically and visually challenged, and women-folk who find it difficult to attend/participate in face-to-face academic counselling sessions at the study centre.
- The use of local language for interaction can help the learners to understand difficult concepts discussed in their courses and can motivate them in pursuing their studies.

- As interactive radio counselling is designed in a decentralized way, follow-up interaction (either through face-to-face or telephonically) with the resource persons and among the learners can be strengthened. This can motivate the learners to form self-help groups to help themselves.
- Act as substitute to a teacher, in case local expertise is not available.

Interactive radio counselling (IRC) offers the benefits of live interactivity at a relatively low cost in a medium based on familiar and available technology. The learners residing within the effective transmission range of local radio station can communicate with the resource persons and the fellow learners directly, engage in discussion and provide/receive feedback. In recent years, interactive radio has emerged as a powerful medium of education. Educational institutions perceived the importance of interactive radio to emphasize greater learner activeness and their participation in teaching and learning at a distance. The medium is also being used for providing information to the learners on roll as well as prospective learners.

Considering this strength of the audio medium, the IGNOU launched a pilot interactive radio counselling service to provide support to learners who study print material, and may attend weekend tutorial/counselling sessions. For the first time, a pilot project on interactive radio counselling for the learners of Diploma in Management (DIM) and Bachelor of Preparatory Programme (BPP) was launched on May 3, 1998 from All India Radio, Bhopal. In the interactive radio counselling sessions, the experts/counsellors made their presentation followed by question-answer sessions with the learners. The objective of the pilot project was that the initiative could be replicated in other cities if it proved successful. IGNOU is now using this mode very successfully to train in-service school teachers in the State of Jharkhand as 'Mukt Samvad' as well as under Sarva Shiksha Abhiyan (EFA) in other states.

A study to ascertain the reach, access and the extent of utilization of the interactive radio counselling, assess the level of learner's participation in terms of attendance and interactivity, evaluate performance of the experts in terms of the effectiveness of their presentations and ability to respond to questions/queries of the learners, and to understand the organizational difficulties in implementing interactive radio counselling was conducted by Bansal and Chaudhary (2002). Besides questionnaire-based responses, the learners were observed during the sessions; focused group discussions with learners were also organised, in addition to interviews with academic counsellors, AIR and Regional Centre staff to obtain a comprehensive picture of the interactive radio counselling.

Feedback on the curtain raiser

The entire interaction during the inauguration function of the pilot project was punctuated with intermittent phone calls. The first call was received barely after three minutes of the beginning of the session. During the hour-long programme, a large number of calls were received. However, only ten of these could be responded. The issues raised by them were broadly related to the submission of assignments, receipt of study materials, admission procedure, term-end examinations, etc. At this stage, feedback of the participants was collected through telephonic interviews and face-to-face interaction with learners. This was followed by administration of questionnaires. Those learners who had called during the interactive radio counselling session were given a call back on the same day. Their first reaction over the launching of interactive radio counselling was of optimism. The learners appreciated the importance and utility of the interactive radio counselling and termed it a positive step in the right direction, albeit taken a bit late. They felt that the interactive radio facility gave them an opportunity to obtain much needed information and guidance from experts. Learners who feel shy in asking questions in the face-to-face counselling sessions or classroom could ask questions over telephone.

The learners hoped that interactive radio counselling would reach out to those living in remote areas. They observed that for making the interactive radio counselling sessions fruitful, the learning support service should be made receptive to the needs of learners.

Feedback on the pilot project

The main findings are as follows:

Profile of the listeners: The study revealed that the majority (78%) of listeners were males in the age group of 21-30 years. Programme-wise variations were perceptible as majority of the learners of DIM belonged to 26-30 years age group, whereas those in BPP were in 21-25 years age group. An occupation-wise break up revealed that majority of the Management listeners were engaged in business, followed by private service and government service.

Awareness and participation in IRC: A majority of the learners were aware of the interactive radio counselling. The sources of information were the IGNOU Regional Centre, newspapers and fellow learners. The level of participation of learners, however, was found low. The main reasons reported by them were their being away from the house and non-availability of radio sets at their house/workplace. The sessions however became gradually popular. The learners of DIM showed higher level of participation as compared to BPP learners.

Effectiveness and usefulness of IRC: The BPP learners were of the opinion that interactive radio counselling in Hindi (i.e. their mother tongue) was more useful to them. However, they argued that presentation could be a mix of Hindi-English for optimum results. The learners of DIM however preferred English as a medium of presentation and interaction. More than half of the learners were of the opinion that interactive radio counselling facilitated greater interaction with the experts and fellow learners. Majority of them found the content matter relevant and current, which was, supplemented with additional information through IRC vis-à-vis the printed text. They observed that adequate examples were cited and the objectives stated in the learning units were achieved through the presentations of experts and all this led to increased comprehension. Those learners who faced difficulty in understanding the content observed that frequent questioning during the presentations interrupted their learning process. Some of them suggested that the topics needed to be explained with greater clarity. On the whole, the learners found the presentations by the experts interesting and satisfactory. They observed that the experts were able to answer the queries to their satisfaction.

The listeners also suggested that the number of face-to-face counselling sessions should be reduced to accommodate interactive radio counselling sessions. Moreover, the University should ensure that there is no clash in the schedules of interactive radio counselling and face--to-face counselling sessions. To make the sessions more need-based, they suggested that before selecting the topics for counselling, they could also be consulted. One session every month should be devoted to learners' general queries related to their study. To ensure optimum utilisation of interactive radio counselling sessions, the system should be rigorously monitored.

Experiences Gained from IRC

Since 1998, IGNOU has traversed a long distance ahead in using IRC for tele-counselling. With the support of AIR and its own Gyan Vani network, it has been catering to the needs of distance learners all over the country. IGNOU uses both the national (centralized communication) and regional/local (decentralized communication) interactive radio network for tele-counselling.

Now-a-days state open universities have been allotted a chunk by IGNOU to use interactive radio counselling. Besides, these universities have produced audio programmes both for radio broadcast and in cassette mode for use at the study centres. For example, Dr. B.R. Ambedkar Open University, Hyderabad has produced 1805 radio lessons, which are being broadcast, and 244 audio lessons (cassettes), which are being used at the study centres (Venkaiah, 2005). IGNOU had produced about 7000 radio broadcast worthy programmes by March 31, 2005 (IGNOU, 2005a).

In his study Sukumar (2001) has reported that interactive radio fulfilled the real need of distance learners to interact with eminent speakers, professors and guest faculty and solve their problems. According to his findings, general public also got opportunities to interact with experts and was enriched by the latest knowledge/skills imparted during the session. The study also revealed that interactive radio is well received by the learners, and ought to be made more effective by inviting gifted teachers/ practitioners/personalities of today and yesteryears.

In a study on the use of interactive radio to discuss pedagogical and classroom management problems of primary school teachers, Pal (2001) has reported that the participating teachers found it more effective than the traditional methods of teacher orientation. Agarwal and Ganesan (2003) have found that the IRC has wider reach and attracted learners from far-flung locations. The participation in IRC was higher among general public in comparison with the learners enrolled with IGNOU. The category of general public included parents, husbands/wives, and brothers/sisters of the IGNOU learners. Majority of them found the IRC sessions effective and useful.

It is interesting to note that a large number of our fellow citizens and enlightened persons of society have been participating in IRC organised by IGNOU. For instance, the analysis of data on interactive radio counselling programmes organised by the IGNOU Regional Centre, Hyderabad during April 2004-March 2005 revealed that, on an average, 36 percent and 64 percent calls were received from IGNOU's learners and general public, respectively (IGNOU, 2005b). Analysis of data further revealed that more male (78%) than female learners asked questions in the IRC sessions. It has also been found that more calls (61 percent) were received through STD from long distances. This trend reveals that for learners in rural and far-flung area/places, IRC provides much needed support and is easily accessible to them. It also indicates that learners in the rural areas use radio set in their houses for entertainment as well as information. Some of them listen to IRC at their workplace as well. However, learners in cities listen to radio, usually FM radio, while driving their car to and from their offices.

From personal experiences gathered while participating in IRCs, the author has realised that most of the calls received were of general nature and subject/topic specific calls were only a few. Moreover, the call rate was higher in open/general sessions related to learner support services, examinations, receipt of learning materials than the content specific sessions. It means that there is a need to address such issues of learner support more carefully.

IRC has potential of contributing to increased access to additional source of education and improving the quality of learning. However, it should be implemented by taking into consideration the challenges and problems. In particular, proper designing and planning by the resource person should make it more useful and effective. Similarly, the learners should be prepared to ask questions to clarify their doubts. They can greatly increase the benefit they derive from sessions by spending time afterwards by writing down the main points they picked up. With radio, they can even take notes as they listen.

Discussion

The learners reported that while IRC sessions demanded study of particular topics, face-to-face counselling demanded study of some other topics as well to gain optimally. On the other hand, teleconferencing sessions expect them to study specific topics before participating in the sessions. The examination system and submission of assignment responses demand the learners to follow a different path of preparation. Moreover, their societal commitments take away some of their time. Such a situation, at times, confuses learners and they tend to be strategic learners. They plan their course of study depending on the time available with them to study learning materials, work on assignments and complete term-end examinations. This very significant finding highlights the need to coordinate and unify all these processes.

The experience also reveals that the frequency of face-to-face academic counselling sessions may be reduced to accommodate IRC sessions. This will economize the support services for the institutions in terms of resources and save time and effort spent in travel by learners; through IRC they can participate from their respective places of location.

There is no working model available in India for designing and organizing IRC sessions for a heterogeneous group of distance learners. Different methods and strategies need to be used to bring liveliness and spontaneity in IRC sessions. Besides the presentation-question-answer format (often used method in the IRC sessions), a variety of formats can be tested/tried:

- incidental presentation (teaching)
- only questions-answers (learners and resource persons)

- questions-answers initiated by learners only
- debate
- quiz
- case study
- initiating discussion with answering frequently asked questions (FAQs) as well as intelligently asked questions (IAQs).

Whatever the format(s), the sessions should be organised in a relaxed atmosphere. The sessions should be simple, conversational, interactive and communicative at the frequency of the target group of learners. Humour, if pedagogically valuable, can be added to make learners comfortable in terms of thinking, feeling, laughing, listening and learning. As learning from interactive radio is a new experience and relatively unfamiliar to most of the learners in India, the experts should motivate them to adopt the learning strategies other than print and teacher/tutor/counsellor-based learning.

There is a need for more systematic monitoring and evaluation of the IRC service. All the personnel involved in planning, designing, implementing and evaluating should get constructive feedback on regular basis and carry out tracer studies. The findings should be fed into the system for further improvement. Research needs to be made integral part of the system providing two-way communication to stakeholders/beneficiaries.

This model views all the stakeholders in IRC communicating with each other in a continuous loop. The learner forms the pivot of all activities, which is involved in the topic selection to make it need-based. One IRC session may be mutually exclusive; nonetheless, it is inter-linked with the next session (by informing the learner about the topic, date, etc. of the next session). Setting proper learning environment in which trained resource persons with clear measurable goals interact with learners and strengthen the built-in interactivity.

The IRC, as a method of delivery and supporting education at a distance, is distinguished by its ability to support immediate two-way communication among a group of learners and teachers. Thus, IRC closely resembles the conventional classroom transaction at a distance. Major advantage is its interactive capabilities and the facilitation of immediate, simultaneous and sustained communication among learners. However, it demands considerable attention to create conducive learning environment. The experience gained so far from the interactive radio counselling sessions revealed that increased and more creative use of the potential of the audio medium shall enhance its utility. Moreover, in addition to what has been given in the course material, IRC sessions should provide more and in-depth information.

It has been observed that, besides IGNOU, the learners of other universities and general public also listened to and participated in the interactive radio counselling sessions being organised by IGNOU. There seems a steady growth in the number of non-traditional adult learners who recognise the increasing value of lifelong learning as a means to upgrading or changing careers and shaping the quality of their lives. And most of these learners opt for distance learning, including interactive radio, because of its convenience and flexibility (Moskowitz, 1988). IRC is another tool to meet the needs of these adult learners and enlightened persons. This issue needs to be kept in mind while planning use of IRC for distance teaching and learning.

To popularize the IRC sessions, the learners and general public should be informed well in advance through various means of communication such as, television, newspapers, bulletins, etc.

As revealed from the feedback and research studies, the IRC sessions were particularly useful for female learners, who faced a lot of difficulties in attending counselling sessions at their study centres. However, they need to be motivated to ask questions and gain optimally from the sessions. IRC programmes could be repeated in evening slot for wider utilisation.

The IRC can be made effective by:

- setting right environment at both the teaching and learning ends. This can be created by catering to the specific learning needs, and
- involving talented teachers, trained and with positive attitude, in developing and delivering the IRC sessions with focus on course objectives.

To sum up, interactive radio counselling can act as an effective tool for open and distance learning only if the sessions are planned, designed, implemented and monitored systematically. With advance information to learners, IRC can help them control their learning (Chaudhary and Bansal, 2000). In the age of rapidly evolving technologies, institutional success may be determined, in part, on its ability to exploit IRC effectively to further its goals.

References

Agrawal, B.M. and Ganesan, S. (2003). *A Study on IRC Phone Callers' Feedback*. IGNOU Regional Centre, Bhopal, mimeo.

All India Radio (2005). http://www.allindiaradio.org

Bansal, Kiron and Chaudhary, S.V.S. (1999). Interactive radio for supporting distance education: an evaluative study, *Indian Journal of Open Learning*, 8(1), 61-71

Chaudhary, S.V.S. and Bansal, Kiron (2000). Interactive radio counselling in IGNOU: a study. *Journal of Distance Education*, 15(2), 37-51.

Edirisingha, P. (1995). *A Study of How Computer-based Media could Improve the Distance Learning of UK Farmers*. Paper presented at IXth Annual Conference of AAOU, Taiwan ROC, December 3-5.

IGNOU (2005a). *Annual Report.* New Delhi: Indira Gandhi National Open University.

IGNOU (2005b). *Interactive Phone-in Radio Counselling Programme*. IGNOU Regional Centre, Hyderabad, mimeo.

Karnik, K. (2000). Roundtable Conference on Gyan Vani, IGNOU, August 17-19, 2000.

Moskowitz, Hilda (1988). *The Annenberg/CPB Project: A Midcourse Perspective.* Paper presented at Changing Roles in Education and Training Proceedings of the Fourth Annual Conference on Teaching at a Distance, Madison, Wisconsin August 2-4, 1988.

Pal, R. (2001). Audio conferencing for primary school teachers: an experiment with off-timing of AIR. *Perspectives in Education*, CASE, M.S. University, Vadodara.

Sukumar, B. (2001). IGNOU interactive radio counselling: a study. *Indian Journal of Open Learning,* 10(1), 81-92.

Venkaiah, V. (2005). Educational media in Dr. B.R. Ambedkar Open University with special reference to teleconferencing. In Reddi, U.V and Mishra, S (eds.), *Educational Media in Asia.* Vancouver: Commonwealth of Learning.

Professor Sohanvir Chaudhary is former Director, School of Education; currently Director, DEP-SSA (MHRD), Indira Gandhi National Open University, New Delhi.
Email: chaudhary38@hotmail.com

18

Globalisation, e-Learning and Development

Ram Takwale

Introduction

In an event organised by the Commonwealth of Learning (COL) in May 2005, COL's President and CEO, Sir John Daniel posed a question about the relevance and need of COL in the present context. The COL is an intergovernmental organisation established by the Commonwealth Heads of Government in 1989 to encourage development and sharing of open learning/distance education knowledge resources and technologies (www.col.org). During the last 15 years, the Open and Distance Learning (ODL) has been accepted by many Governments and education institutions as a credible mode of education. It has grown very rapidly with the adoption of Information Communication Technologies (ICT). Since then it is felt that the COL has fulfilled its purpose of promotion of ODL, and hence the issue of its relevance for continuation is almost settled for future.

Every educational institution and organisation should also pose the question: Are they relevant and should they continue to exist with the same structure and functions in the context of emerging knowledge society. The strategy adopted by the COL is to shift the focus in ODL from 'learning' to 'development' and make it directly and explicitly relevant by adopting the goal of 'Learning for Development'. In this change of focus, the COL is guided by the global discussions and directions of development evolved and adopted by the UNESCO through its Millennium Development Goals, which were adopted by all countries of the world in 2000; and the programme of the United Nations Decade of Education for Sustainable Development (2005-2014) adopted by the UN General Assembly in December 2002 (www.unesco.org).

The universities are established for creation, preservation and dissemination of knowledge. The recent global changes have contributed a major addition of development to their functions.

In the context of the 21st century, the goal of a university is to offer education for development of not only individuals but also of institutions, organisations, communities and societies. The traditional three functions of creation, preservation and dissemination of knowledge by a university are usually carried out through seven core processes (Takwale, 2003) of teaching, learning, evaluation, creating knowledge resources, developing infrastructure facilities, creating educational environment and managing education. Educational systems followed by institutions are undergoing a radical change due to extensive applications of ICT. Information Technology (IT) is a driving force that is responsible for creating globalisation, a process not only for connecting people for their communication, but also for linking their work and collaborations. This unique nature of new technologies for linking people and their activities separated in space and time enables the system and institutions to carry out their operations from any place located anywhere. Today it is possible in corporate sector to have planning and managing office in New York, Research & Development (R&D) in Bangalore, production centre in China and distribution and sale services management in Singapore. With all these, an industry is becoming a distributed industry; and various units of industry, though separated geographically, work as if they are located on one campus. This is the process of virtualisation, and has been made possible by the IT revolution currently sweeping the world.

The broadband Internet and digitisation of information have made virtualisation possible. (Digitisation is a process in which information is converted and stored in the binary code that helps users to manipulate and change the information as required.) The technology-mediated processes are now creating new directions and ways of development; these are helping to create new ways of living, working, learning, developing, marketing, organising and managing. Technology mediation has evolved basically the processes of virtualisation, digitisation, and customization. The result is a distributed system of working, learning and developing; it is imparting us a central position. The industrial revolution had created a faceless society; the information society is restoring human face and human identity.

This chapter concentrates on articulation of globalisation, education and learning as an instrument of sustainable development of people and their communities. It should be noted that most of the development described in this chapter refers to the last decade i.e. since Internet became global in 1995. The technology and its mediation for socio-economic processes are fast changing due to profound discoveries in fields such as Information Technology, Biotechnology and Nano-Technology; and new sweeping inventions and creations will continue till technologies mature. Some experts are of the view that the maturation period for inventions and changes in IT is likely to continue for two to three decades and during this time processes of mediation would be constantly changing. This is therefore a period of rapid change and transformation; and new technologies developed for customer-friendly uses would always be better and superior. This, of course, would contradict the saying ‘old is gold’. The technology dependent goals and models of institutions established during industrial age, and the processes evolved to carry out institutional functions, are likely to become irrelevant in the information or knowledge age. The constants and conservables are those that are related to human beings and their social nature. Much of the knowledge, experience and expertise created earlier are likely to be not usable and relevant.

Information Technology mediated processes are at the initial stages of creation and development. Under this transient situation, while writing this chapter, we have relied on generalizations and projections of the results of experiments that are going on in India. These projects and programmes, like technology and its mediation, are in the stage of evolving; and hence, while remaining objective and universal, the author's perspective and approaches have certainly influenced selection and treatment of topics, which is unavoidable in any writing.

Globalisation and its Stages

Globalisation is a process in which people, articles, goods, services, ideas and knowledge flow from one place to another, usually separated by long distance or continents. This process of transfer, migration and resettlement is going on since ages and has helped civilizations to grow and spread. Globalisation acquired importance and impact in the second millennium. Land and coastal routes were used earlier to travel between Europe, Africa and Asia. However, since Columbus discovered America in 1498, a new era of intercontinental flow started. The then nation-states used new ways of transportation, initially for trade, and later on to conquer territories often motivated by religion and / or imperialism. The power of the nations then was brawn and muscles, horses and animals, and was used and still continues to be used for exploitation and gaining riches. The impact of this globalisation is that it has helped create colonies and migrate people, develop science and technology and reduce the world to a smaller accessible size. The auto machine led technology revolution, started with steam engine, electric machine, factories and mass production systems, has helped to link different regions through their markets. The market and business are existing since the beginning of human civilisation. They were earlier in the form of barter trade and commerce in a small locality and regions, and later on expanded internationally to fulfil people's needs and requirements. Markets have fulfilled basic and higher needs of people and societies, and simultaneously, in unequal situations, have been used for exploitation by the powerful to become richer, stronger and more developed.

In the book '*The World is Flat*', Thomas Friedman has given a brief history of the globalised world in the 21st century by describing modern development through three stages. The first stage of globalisation was brought about by the nation-states (1490-1800); the second stage of globalisation was created by companies for profits through markets (1800-2000); and the third stage of globalisation is being developed by individuals and their collaborations since 2000 (Friedman, 2005). The march from the nation-state to individuals via companies and multi-nationals has been achieved due to revolutionary changes in technologies, particularly in communication and transportation. The impact of globalisation and expanding markets is the falling costs, increasing access to wide-variety and participation of larger masses in the development. The first two stages of globalisation continued till the middle of 20th century and were dominated by the North, especially Europe, America and Japan, who account for about 2 billion people. However, from the second half of the 20th century, and especially during the last ten years, the Russians, Chinese and Indians have started participating and have added nearly 2.5 billion people.

Technology Mediation

Technology – soft or hard – has played very important role in development and progress of societies. Access to knowledge spread widely with the invention of printing technology in the 15th century. And auto-machines enabled us to create factories, which have added wide variety of application and helped speeded production, created products and services for utilities, extended outreach and coverage, and create Industrial Society. The major success of Industrial Revolution was mass-production and mass-circulation that enabled people to live better, know more, participate widely in development and lead healthier and richer life. The Information Communication Technologies (ICT) have helped to bring people and places together, to reduce and eliminate their barriers and offered innovative and entrepreneurial opportunities to individuals and groups to develop and prosper. ICT is changing nature of society essentially due to Micro-electronic and Digital Revolutions. ICT is offering:

- One to one communication (telephone, cell-phone)
- One to many communication (TV, Radio Broadcasting)
- Many to many communication (Internet and broadband communication)

IT offers storage and search (CD ROM, A/V tapes, Servers), networking through wires (optical and copper wires) and wireless (WiFi, mobile telephony and mobile Internet), and recording, replicating and copying facilities. Storage and processing powers are increasing continuously – processing power doubles every 18 months; and cost reduction, increased bandwidth for communication; extension of outreach and coverage, and increased access and participation are becoming regular news features of fast development of communication technologies. The broadcasting, telecommunicating and computing technologies are now converging; and convergence is going to be offered at home on TV screen, and outside on mobile cell-phone or PDA (personal digital assistant) screen. The convergence is influencing not only industrial world, but also having profound impact on social, economic and political sectors. The whole society, all living and working places and people, is getting connected, and a scenario is created where communication is possible from anywhere by anyone at anytime.

The information network consists of three layers: hardware, software and content-ware. New paradigms are made possible due to newly generated processes of virtualisation, digitisation and customisation or personalisation. The process of customization is a unique feature of the information society and a creation of IT. It aims at knowing personal or group needs and requirements, and organising supply of product and services that fulfil them.

By employing Internet, mobile technologies and networking, an infrastructure is getting created, which allows many collaborative processes such as open-sourcing, out-sourcing, off-shoring and in-sourcing (Friedman, 2005). In the coming ten years it is expected that most of the people in India would be connected. The driving force for this transformation is in fact the market expansion, changing nature of work and participation, and new opportunities of development and prosperity. The networks all over the world are changing the very nature and concept of markets. The market is expanding and extending to all places of work and all walks of life. This is bringing in a sort of convergence or confluence of interests of producers and customers. The producer's object is to sell a product and service the customer at an affordable cost while maintaining internationally prescribed quality, now provided by so many international agencies for the safety of customers and markets. For achieving lower costs, some provider companies have started reducing their production or service operation costs by enabling customers to share work. One such example is of the US based Southwest Airline, which eliminated travel agents and front-desk service of giving e-tickets and down-loadable boarding passes online. Cost reduction is passed on to the customer. In fact, providers have also to worry about purchasing power of the customer. Higher the customer purchasing power, bigger is the market. Hence many companies have started creating wider base, by widening multinational nature and by enabling participation of local and home based expertise. In fact the next generation paradigm is of enabling a customer to participate in production and distribution/deployment processes, whenever possible, for enhancing his/her purchasing power and spreading provider market. The distinction between producer and customer in such a development would slowly get reduced; when customised products and services become highly satisfactory to fulfil distinctive personal needs, a situation gets created where distinction between producer and consumer reduces, and a new information society worker, the prosumer (producer + consumer), gets created. The provider company has to maintain and enlarge its market share and customer base for its own survival and growth; and has to adopt a process of fulfilling not only immediate customer needs but also their future needs. The provider, therefore, catches, retains and follows the customer for fulfilling his/her life-long needs.

The convergence or development of prosumers requires:

1. Creation of 'level playing field' (Flat World) by creating networks and just-in-time services. This needs infrastructure with broadband Internet network and personal devices for accessing.
2. Development of new processes, habits and values essential for horizontal collaboration and partnership.
3. Enable larger number of people separated in time, space, communities and cultures to share their needs, and requirements as well as their expertise, experiences and capabilities to participate in all types of discoveries, innovations and entrepreneurial activities (Friedman, 2005)

The rapid development of newer and versatile technologies in IT is expected to change nature of communication further. The technologies such as development of high fidelity Internet that can deliver 'immersive' technologies, and nano technologies are going to change communication and help in raising overall quality of life. The major direction of development visualized by 2020 is of personalization of mass technologies and linking these with local, contextual and need-based aspects of developmental processes. IT can help recreate humanization lost in the industrial society and, if used properly, can become a great equaliser (Venkateshan, 2005).

All these would need moving away from segregated and top-down control and command systems towards horizontal, participative and collaborative alliances and partnerships with a view to create a new world social order; the next goal of third millennium. The global need of governance system is being felt more intensely since the Second World War, and the development of global institutions such as UN, UNESCO etc., was the first step towards international governance. The need is of evolving global governance for global society, created by developing universal man with universal value system, which we believe, has to be based on policies based on inclusion and participation, justice and equity.

Education: System for Providing Learning

Development of civilization is closely related to learning and education system obtained in communities and societies. Learning takes place everywhere at all times. Learning is a process in which individual, group and communities internalise and reconstruct their own knowledge. It is described by the UNESCO's Four Pillars of Education: *learning to know, learning to do, learning to live together* and *learning to be*. Learning is knowing: creating knowledge base. Learning is doing: developing skills, competencies and capabilities. Learning is living together: developing attitudes, values and approaches essential for living, working, creating, organising, managing, caring and sharing. Learning is being: continuously evolving, liberating, elevating individuals to higher levels of achievements.

The systems of education have been evolved and classified into formal education (face-to-face and highly structured instruction), non-formal education (open and distance but structured instruction) and informal education (incidental and unstructured instruction). Education has always been a sub-system of the existing social order. It is a great instrument for liberation and equalisation. Education helps acquisition of knowledge, and consequent empowerment and creativity. Technologies, soft and hard, are the instruments and tools for socio-economic change and progress. The driving force is provided by the aspirations for better and richer life, social and national prosperity, peace, security and happiness. Technology, like education, has been an empowering tool; and technology mediation and knowledge intensive education and learning have now become powerful instruments for socio-economic and cultural transformation of people, communities and nations.

In India, the education in 'Agrarian Age' was limited to a few (class education), essentially belonging to the ruling and powerful classes. It was associated with religion and learning from Guru, the teacher, was the practice. The ancient Gurukul system promoted oral learning tradition that emphasised memorisation; the Guru was given highest regard and respect. The Gurukul system was highly personalised, need-based, decentralised, learner-paced but teacher-centric and socially supported. It was relevant to the social needs. Unfortunately lower castes and women were given no right to education during medieval period. The 'Industrial Age' changed the scenario. Machines and industries created working and developing opportunities for many. Industries were concentrated in big towns and cities; and the very nature of industry promoted centralisation and urbanisation. Mass-education emerged to fulfil the growing need of trained work force and professionals needed by the industry. Like a factory, education acquired rigid form essential to tackle large numbers. The open universities designed and established were modelled on 'Industrial Form' of education, based on a definition of distance education by Otto Peters. The education concentrated on 'content', industrial values with greater 'market' orientation and used principles of division of labour, 'same fit for all' and 'more of the same'. The Industrial Age education is highly hierarchical with top-down control. However, since education deals with individual learning and performance, and has to nurture mind and intelligence to create and preserve knowledge, the educational institutions, wherein R&D dominated, saw the development of liberal and divergent thoughts, which influenced social, economic and cultural changes. The industrial society has followed inclusive policies that allowed education to spread from classes to masses.

The emergence of highly networked society, created due to revolutionary changes in IT, is now developing new paradigms of education. Initially the technology has been used to support the existing processes of formal or open distance education for speedy and efficient services, for expansion to cover large numbers and for maximising fee incomes (Farrel, 1999). Virtualisation and digitisation are used to support industrial model of education, the teacher-centric model of formal education. This education is content oriented, campus and classroom bound, often not linked with individual and societal needs. The open distance education has also more or less retained the same form with some added flexibility to learners in choosing pace, place and time of learning. The ODL has partially helped resolve the Sir John Daniel triangle of quality-access-cost through quality instructional materials made available to large numbers at lower fees. However it is far away from solving the quantity-quality-equity triangle — reflecting the goal of 'Quality Education for All'.

e-Education

By using the processes of virtualisation, digitisation and customisation-personalisation, it is possible to establish virtual, educational institution (s) with distributed campus having infrastructure and facilities such as distributed classrooms, learning and teaching resources and learner support systems. At present, the e-education system is getting evolved along two major directions or streams:

1. *Teacher-Centric e-Education* with 20th century models with increasing learner flexibility.
2. *Learner-Centric e-Education* with 21st Century models of need based and demand driven e-Learning services.

Both the streams of e-educational transformation may ultimately integrate into one resulting into *e-Education/e-Learning for sustainable development.* This may happen due to technology convergence and its application to developmental processes; or starting originally with group learning and creating e-education for individual and group development processes. Incidentally e-Education also evolves through a triple convergence of formal, non-formal and informal modes of education.

The teacher-centric and learner-centric models are essentially the top-down or bottom-up models of education; the former facilitates the knowledge created globally to be brought to the learners; and the latter one is bottom-up model catering to the needs and requirements of students — the global as well as local needs of development. Both the directions would slowly merge into the e-education with increasing horizontal interactivities and communication.

We give here the efforts going on in Maharashtra for developing e-education. (www.mkcl.org). The infrastructure of networks and access centres has been created all over Maharashtra with 2,500 access centres equipped with licensed MS-office software, connecting nearly 15,000 computers linked with total e-governance with e-learning software giving all academic and administrative support facilities. It also contains two-way audio-graphic conferring facility at all places and video-conferencing facility at a few places. The software for virtual organisation and management and for digitisation of information with Shareable Content Object Reference Model (SCORM) compliance is available. During the last three years since establishment, Maharashtra Knowledge Corporation Limited (MKCL) has enrolled and supported 2 million learners, with 250 thousand students in one batch of April 2005. Similarly, IGNOU began to offer e-learning from 1999 in areas of IT, Management, Library automation and resettlement and rehabilitation. MPBOU, YCMOU and a few other open universities are also in the process of offering e-learning programmes.

The e-Education System essentially consists of (Takwale, 2003):

1. *Planning and development system for designing courses and education system.*
2. *Network development and delivery system:* The e-Education system is designed with VPN (Virtual Private Network) to support learners, experts and support service. It also uses the Knowledge Grid framework.
3. *Content development and integration system:* It allows experts and teachers to work together virtually. Instructional designers, content experts, media experts and Quality Assurance experts can jointly develop instructional material, which could be assessed through preview by selected students. The final content can then be replicated and web-casted or replicated on CD ROMs and mass-circulated.
4. *Delivery management system:* It consists of
   a. *Administrative and Management Support System* to support applications, selection, registration, fee-collection, delivery, learner and teacher activity management, examination and instant certification.
   b. *Learning Management System* to manage learner-teacher and learner-resource interactions and interactivities, which could be recorded and analyzed for personalization. (Mass-personalisation)
   c. *Assignment Management System* in which assignments are given to each learner on personal basis, and learner submissions are evaluated by tutors anywhere in the system, and feedback is given to students. Not only print, but voice is also used in interactions. Learners can have chat/discussions with tutors and peers; and learner portfolio gets developed.

d. *On-line Evaluation and Examination System* with instant e-certification.

e. *Classroom Participation System enables* learners to participate in any lecture, seminar, tutorial or workshop, synchronously or asynchronously, and uses both print and voice communication.

5. *Total management system.*

New systems are being designed for teacher-centric resource based learning and certification. It is suitable for top-down dissemination of knowledge and skills development.

e-Education for Development and Sustainability

Development of new paradigm in using ICT is to develop demand driven need-based education and learning system that helps learners to link learning with working and developing through life-long learning. Development is a process in which knowledge, skills and capabilities are applied to solve the problems faced by an individual or group or community for producing value added products and services or for creating values through innovative and creative processes. The process should lead to prosperity, which in turn could be measured in terms of productivity, quality, profitability and sustainability, the four criteria proposed by Dr. M.S. Swaminathan (Swaminathan, 2005). The words such as value, profit, prosperity should not be taken in terms of money alone; these ought to be related to richer and higher quality life of an individual, family or community/village.

As pointed out earlier, the process of globalisation and exploitation of international markets is required to observe International Organisations for Standardisation (ISO) norms and standards, maintain prescribed quality and environmental norms for which certification by recognized international agency is becoming essential. The norms and standards are dependent on how process is observed by following prescribed procedures. Continuous supervision by the ISO agency and periodic certification is becoming essential.

The whole shift is to the process management with appropriate inputs, throughputs and outputs and outcomes. In earlier systems, the processes and systems were managed manually, and were dominantly dependent of input norms, and results were judged by the outputs at the end of the process. This made process control and standardisation very difficult. Now that ICT is available and most of the communication is electronic, the process control is convenient, as in industry, as any process could be well standardised and customised to have desired outcomes.

The first stage of a new system development or transformation of the old to new is to create required infrastructure, resources, processes and systems. All these have to go through seven processes of institution building before starting operations. Change over to process management for desired performance achievement is the major transition in the system. The system follows institutional capability and maturation & personnel maturation models (CM & PMM). The core values and concepts that are embodied in the seven categories of the Baldridge National Quality Programme (BNQP, 2005) are:

- Leadership
- Strategic planning
- Student, stakeholders and market focus
- Faculty and staff focus
- Process management
- Organisational performance results
- Measurement, analysis and knowle dge management

The education and learning system can be judged continuously by assessing *approaches* adopted to develop strategies to fulfil needs and requirements of target groups, *deployment* of processes and operations with appropriate systematic alignment to achieve the results, *learning* of lessons out of the cycle of operations, and *integration* of learning into the system. The system becomes quite dynamic and is suitable where processes are changing to suit the requirements of the customers. This is therefore most suitable for educating, learning and developing. (TCS, 2004)

One of the major paradigms for development is the bottom-up system (*Antyodaya*) with people participation and action (MKCL & NETRA, www.parivartan.net). In India and generally in South Asia, the most successful mechanism of development involving people is the Specific Interest Groups (SIGs), working and developing together. *Prayog Pariwar, Swadyaya Pariwar* and Self-Help Groups (SHGs) have shown very successful results. The groups and their community have organisational empowerment. The creation of bottom-up system would need software to promote application and work-flow management that enables knowing the individuals and groups, finding out their needs and aspirations-expectations, customization of curriculum for specific need based training and education of a group— the process of customization of education, deployment of knowledge and skills, assessment of learning achieved and lessons learnt and internalised. The cycle of learning and developing would repeat, with addition of knowledge and technology each time to build up capability and achieve better performance. This is, in fact, a capability-maturation and capability-building model and is non-competitive or self-competitive in nature. Promotion of such a model is no doubt a great social and developmental task. The learning and developing, besides being life-long, is also generative of local expertise, experience and knowledge, making the whole knowledge generation distributive, socially creative and locally innovative.

The National Assessment and Accreditation Council (NAAC) of India has adopted Quality Assessment and Accreditation model based on Seven Institutional Functions depending mostly on input and output measures. The process gives institutional assessment and accreditation. In order to make the institution dynamically changing and reforming, it is proposed to adopt Baldridge Model referred above for improving educational performance for making education relevant to the changing needs and global contexts. The NAAC has prescribed five core values, namely (Takwale, 2004):

- Contribution to national development
- Fostering global competencies among students
- Inculcating value system in students

- Promoting the use of technology
- Quest for excellence

It is hoped that application of the model to educational institutions would lead to a model of excellence in developmental education. It should also lead to continually learning and developing institutions. However, due to the vast diversity and large number of colleges and universities in face-to-face system, the task of assessing all institutions is undoubtedly Herculean but it has gained momentum in the past few years and may take sometime before all institutions are assessed. As far as ODL system is concerned, Distance Education Council has been mandated under Statute 5(2) of IGNOU to promote, coordinate and regulate the standard of education. In formative years, it collaborated with NAAC and developed tools and benchmarks for assessment of print, delivery and support. DEC has now created a database on the nature of courses, student profile, faculty, etc. and is in the process of developing comprehensive reports in respect of each Open University and Distance Education Institute. With the availability of EduSat, immense possibilities present us to take quality tele-education to the last mile by creating knowledge repositories of quality materials and opportunity for virtual teacher-learner interaction for use by each ODL institution.

Earlier, we considered technological and educational triple convergence. The third triple convergence is emerging out of bottom-up model of learning for development; the convergence of 'work': working, learning and developing. A system of e-education or e-learning with all the three convergences together or 3x3 Convergence or Grand Convergence could be what would be ideal for developing and developed societies, for their progress and change. The Grand Convergence in e-education would develop a platform on which integrated way of living-working-developing-learning could lead to L3 (life-long-learning) people and their L (learning)-Groups and L-Communities.

One of the major issues is the sustainability of development of individuals, groups and communities. In the networked world, even though cooperative efforts would create level playing fields, those who are learned, competent and competitive may have better and higher achievements, creating disparities. Even though all disparities cannot be eliminated, the process of equalization can be initiated. And it requires everyone to work together for shared goals of human development. The very nature of existing markets that are harnessed with competitiveness for earning profits and riches, need a fundamental change; a change of attitude and approaches for sharing technological and knowledge resources and caring for the weak and disadvantaged. The Grand Convergence should be used to solve the value triangle of quality-quantity-equity for all learning groups and learning communities in terms of their own models of development and progress without exploitation. It would need creation and inculcation of universal human values for living and working together peacefully. The developmental models so created would be infinite; they would depend on localities, socio-cultural and economic contexts and local environments. One has to identify unity out of diversity for creating sustainability. The sustainability has to be sought in the contexts of both localisation and globalisation. It therefore moves towards creation and inculcation of universal human values; and gives higher goals and purposes for education and learning. Creating commonwealth for learning and learning commons for development and progress for all may be a goal of learning and educating and a way for peaceful coexistence and happy communities.

Present Status and Directions of Development

India has already accepted ODL as a national policy for increasing access and outreach. It is developing ICT as a national policy for creating knowledge economy and is supporting ODL through broadcasting, broadband Internet, mobile technologies and EduSat. The Union Government has supported many training and educational programs of IGNOU; the prominent being empowerment of women through self-help groups, teacher education under SSA, Intellectual Property Rights, Panchayati Raj, Value Added Products from Fruits and Vegetables, Dairy Farming, Rural Artisans, Small Scale entrepreneurs, etc. Many new initiatives to develop application of ICT in ODL have also come up, and in some, the COL is playing catalytic role for evolving new paradigms of Technology Mediated Open and Distance Education (Tech-MODE).

Following are a few selective examples of the initiatives that may have long-term impact on developing new paradigms:

1. Educational Satellite of India (EduSat) launched by Indian Space Research Organisation (ISRO) would help in creating distributed classrooms and network of schools and higher education institutions for offering quality education to all. IGNOU is leading the utilisation of EduSat and creation of National and Regional Networks with missionary zeal. Education should soon reach each TV home in the country.
2. Virtual Academy for Semi-Arid Tropics (VASAT) (www.vasat.org) promoted by International Crops Research Institute for the Semi-Arid Tropics (ICRISAT) and supported by Consultative Group on International Agricultural Research (CGIAR) has been established for disseminating knowledge to farmers particularly in draught prone areas by disseminating research and technology outputs to farmers.
3. Establishment of private-public-community partnership with win-win approach, now being promoted by the Central and State Governments through contract farming and direct entry of farmers into markets. This would help in creating linkage between industry, markets and farming. A successful enterprise supported by COL for farmers was created for additional employment and earnings with bank credit and link with milk processing plant in Tamilnadu. IGNOU has initiated work in collaboration with Hero Honda to produce trained motor mechanics.
4. Development of consortium for L3 (Life-long-learning) farmers and teachers in India for bringing about systemic transformation in farming and school education for development.
5. Establishment of a private company for profit by the State Government and Universities in Maharashtra for developing new paradigms and fast changes in education and for avoiding digital divide (MKCL: www.mkcl.org)

6. Group learning and developing: Indian experience of SHGs, *Prayog Pariwar* (Experimenting Groups) or *Swadhyaya Pariwar* (Self-study Groups) have shown remarkable achievements, in individuals as well as group learning, developing and creating local specific knowledge and services. They are empowered in mobilizing themselves into organisations that participate and influence socio-economic processes of development. *Prayog Pariwar* has contributed significantly in establishing the agriculture programmes of YCMOU.

Searching and developing dimensions of partnerships that lead to sharing and caring, to universal value systems for supporting knowing, doing, living together and developing continuously is a task to be accomplished through learning for development. Essentially this is a quest for exploring various dimensions of freedom and fraternity for universal man /woman and global society.

Concluding Remarks

India has shown remarkable progress in IT and is experimenting and developing technologies that could transform existing working and living ways within a decade or two. Global competitiveness has helped, in spite of initial hardships, to gear up industries and become globally competitive. However, the same cannot be said about education. India has a big but still inadequate system of education with top comparing well with the best in the world. The newly found Indian identity in industrial development has been well supported by intelligent and capable Indian graduates produced by Indian education and trained in industry. Still the Indian system of education as a whole is far away from being of high quality and competitive in global context. It is heavily constrained by conservative and rigid structures and old mind-sets. Moreover, the system is heavily guarded by various Councils at the national level under the pretext of quality maintenance but with little gains. It is also a fact that innovations and new paradigm development in evolving e-education is extremely difficult. New paradigms in e-Education for development would need freedom and support that is difficult in a conservative setup. What is, therefore, needed is a free space for new paradigm development; opportunities for relating programs with institutions, industries and communities, development of technology mediation with mass-personalisation and strong linkages with R&D in India for making education knowledge-intensive and development-centric.

References

Baldridge National Quality Program (2005). *Education Criteria for Performance Excellence, MBNQ Award Program.* www.baldridge.nist.gov

Daniel, John (2005) Learning for Development: What kind of development? What kind of learning? Speech at the Institute on Open and Distance Learning for Development: The role of ODL in delivering MDGs held at Vancouver, 5-7, May.

Farrell, G. (1999). *The Development of Virtual Education: A global perspective.* Vancouver: The Commonwealth of Learning.

Friedman, Thomas (2005). *The World is Flat: A Brief History of the Globalised World in the 21st Century*. Allen Lane – an imprint of Penguin Books.

Peters, Otto (1967) Distance education and industrial production: a comparative interpretation in outline. Available http://www.fernuni-hagen.de/ZIFF/PETERS.HTM

Swaminathan, M.S. (2005). *Serving Farmers and Saving Farming: J P Naik Memorial Lecture (2004-05)*. Pune: IIE.

Takwale, Ram (2003). Challenges and opportunities of globalisation for higher education in India - alternatives though e-Education. In *UGC Golden Jubilee Lecture Series*. New Delhi: UGC.

Takwale, Ram (2004). Leveraging quality assurance and accreditation in higher education for developmental education. In *Quality Higher Education and Sustainable Development*. Bangalore: NAAC.

Tata Consultancy Services (2004). *TCS Education Excellence Model* (based on Educational Criteria for Performance Excellence) TCS.

Venkateshan, Ravi (2005). NASSCOM (www.nasscom.org) Newsletter, February 2005.

Professor Ram Takwale is Emeritus Professor; Chairman of the National Assessment and Accreditation Council; Chairman of Education Sub-Committee of the Maharashtra Chamber of Commerce, Industries and Agriculture; former Vice Chancellor of University of Poona and Indira Gandhi National Open University; founding Vice Chancellor of Yashwantrao Maharashtra Open University; and former Chairman, Distance Education Council.

19

Knowledge Revolution Through Satellite Based Education

H.P. Dikshit

Introduction

On the eve of independence of our country, the founding fathers of Indian Republic were confronted with a defining transition of history of our country. They had to urgently deal with some very serious challenges which threatened to tear our social fabric apart. Obviously, people were required to participate in building confidence and capabilities, creating awareness to be informed citizens and empowering them to contribute in the process of national development and reconstruction. The complexities of the problem and magnitude of difficulties in achieving our cherished goal of total transformation of our society is reflected in the fact that at that stage the literacy rate was just 20% and only 2% of them were females.

Education liberates, empowers, enlightens and enables successful reconstruction of free civil societies. In view of such considerations, the leading personalities of those times highlighted the requirement for educating our people. The vast multitude of human resource had to be properly channelised and trained with some priority. Pt. Jawaharlal Nehru, the first Prime Minister of India declared that the most important task for the country was to focus on educating every Indian. In order to fulfil our mission to educate the nation, we have now realized that our efforts were not commensurate with the task that was to be accomplished. In spite of several major initiatives, we are still far from the target of achieving total literacy. Without bothering too much about what did not happen in the past, we have to look to the future and develop capabilities to handle education and training of large target groups of learners under tight time-frames.Nehruji expressed this very effectively in the following words:

> In India, we face many difficult problems. Don't be worried. Don't be frustrated by the immensity of the problems. The problems are immense, no doubt, but so is our will and our determination and so is the will of the innumerable people of India.

In the contemporary scenario of rapidly growing global competition and development, we are compelled to move fast with greater priority and urgency to develop knowledge base around us. His Excellency Dr. A.P.J. Abdul Kalam, a distinguished scientist and President of India, in his inspiring book: *Wings of Fire*, has highlighted that *"If you want to leave your foot prints on the sands of time, do not drag your feet."*

We realised, though late, that we had to develop new strategies to supplement and extend the traditional systems of education with innovative and flexible systems, capable of providing quality education to large target group of learners in reasonable neighbourhood of their dwellings to suit their requirements and expectations. The following observations made by Swami Vivekanand are as relevant and significant in the present day context as when they were made:

> The chief cause of India's ruin has been the monopolizing of its education and grabbing of the land by a handful of men. If we are to rise again, we shall have to do it by spreading education among the masses.

Sustainability of the new systems in terms of low costs and maintaining quality are other important parameters, which have to be assured. It is in this scenario that the potential and capability of Open and Distance Learning (ODL) system was uniquely realised and it emerged in our country.

It is now well understood that the ODL system is capable of handling a variety of large target groups of learners with different levels of understanding to meet their multidimensional requirements and expectations. Starting with education for awareness, school education to higher education and research are being covered by several ODL institutions successfully and efficiently. Unfortunately, in the process of a very rapid growth, some weaker systems have also emerged. In order to transform such systems, Distance Education Council has aggressively carried out a massive campaign to transform them by extending financial and professional support. Our goal is to encourage development and sharing of quality content and to improve the quality of student support to learning.

Local Revolutions with Global Impact

Instead of revolutions which emerge from conflicts between communities and nations, a meaningful revolution in the contemporary global scenario has an entirely different shape and form. It is based on acquiring knowledge and its useful applications for the general well being of the people. We have focussed on agriculture revolution, information technology revolution, and space technology revolution. Some choose to name these as green revolution, grey revolution and knowledge revolution for economic reasons. These have led to interesting and useful global competition in developing knowledge societies and generating new capacities and capabilities, which have direct relevance to the national needs and requirements. In this context it has been realised that there is some urgency in redefining and repositioning education, which needs to be revolutionised and to evolve new systems capable of meeting the foregoing challenges. This is perhaps the time for us to act fast as indicated in the following quote by Pt. Jawaharlal Nehru: "A moment comes, which comes but rarely in history, when we step out from the old to the new".

In the past few decades, we have witnessed three very visible and vibrant revolutions in our country with global impact. One is, of course, in the area of Information Technology that has placed our country as the most favoured destination for Information Technology Applications in the World. It is indeed very satisfying to observe that in achieving this success and placing India among the few most advanced nations in Information Technology, the Distance Education has played a very crucial role. As we advanced in Information Technology, we needed the support of a large number of human power trained in Information Technology, and it is very satisfying to mention that the open university system very well fulfilled this national requirement. Indeed, the National Open University alone has provided education to nearly 150 thousand students in Master's Level programmes in Information Technology to meet this crucial and massive requirement.

Knowledge revolution and the ODL

Our country is credited with a revolution in the sector of Space Technology and its Applications. We are thrilled to observe that the Indian Space Research Organization (ISRO) has successfully achieved indigenous capabilities to design, develop and launch satellites. We are now rated among the top six countries in the world with such capabilities. We have really excelled in this area. The vision of the founder of Space Technology in our country has been guiding our pursuits:

> We are to play a meaningful role nationally, and in the community of nations, we must be second to none in the application of advanced technologies to the real problems of man and society.
>
> **Dr. Vikram Sarabhai**

ISRO has always focused its strides to provide support to initiatives aimed at development of our society. Thus, the research and exploration of the outcome of research for applications in ISRO was oriented towards space technology for rural development and education from the very beginning. As far back as 1975-76, Satellite Instructional Television was conducted using USA Application Technology Satellite (ATS6). This pioneering effort was the first successful experiment in development, testing and management of satellite based instructional television system especially covering the rural areas. 2400 locations in six states were networked through satellite communication to receive instructional television programme in the field of education from August 1, 1975. The duration for telecast of the programmes consisted of 4 hours. ISRO took the responsibility of overall system management and also had specific responsibility for the hardware elements. ISRO also produced 160 science education programmes for children of 10-12 minutes duration each. Major responsibility for programme production was with the National Television Broadcast Organisation supported by the Govt. of India, Ministry of

Information and Broadcasting. The Ministry of Education, Govt. of India, in collaboration with concerned State Governments and other organizations, handled the Teacher training programme. Nearly 24,000 primary school teachers were trained in October 1975 through multimedia package specially developed for science. In the following year, the teacher training programme was further extended to include more teachers. The programmes were first produced in Hindi and then dubbed into other languages like Telugu, Kannad and Oriya. The success of this initiative led to further interventions made by ISRO in providing satellite communication for education and community development programmes of different Ministries and Organisations. Starting from 1970s, within a period of nearly 30 years, ISRO has emerged as one of the international giants in satellite capability for various applications with direct impact on the quality of life of our people – a mission that the founder had envisaged.

As IGNOU approached twentieth year of IGNOU's glorious presence and contributions in the field of education through ODL system, we decided to extensively review and revisit the system and set our vision and mission for the institution through interaction with academics and other functionaries working within the system and some experts from outside the system. Thus after deliberations in the Planning Board, Academic Council and the Board of Management of the University, we formulated the Vision and Mission statements for IGNOU:

Vision

Indira Gandhi National Open University, the national resource centre for open and distance learning with international recognition and presence, shall provide seamless access to sustainable quality education, skill up-gradation and training to all by using innovative technologies and methodologies and ensuring convergence of existing systems for massive human resource required for promoting integrated national development and global understanding.

Mission statement

To advance frontiers of knowledge and promote its dissemination through sustainable open and distance learning systems seamlessly accessible to all, from among whom the leaders and innovators of tomorrow will emerge, the University shall:

- Strengthen the development of national resource centre to set a proactive role model for high quality open and distance learning system.
- Share professional capabilities and resources to maintain and coordinate standards of distance education in the country.
- Continuously assess and accredit institutions of open and distance learning to promote centres of excellence in the country.
- Develop networks using emerging technologies and methods with global reach for effective programme delivery.
- Provide an intelligent flexible system of education to meet the challenges of access and equity and facilitate development of knowledge society.

- Forge convergence of all systems and work for seamless education across national boundaries to develop global collaborations and partnerships.
- Provide education and training for skill up-gradation and lifelong learning for all.
- Promote national integration and integrated development of our people.

The vision and mission statements have been greatly influenced by an important mandate given to the university by an act passed by the Indian Parliament in 1985 which mandated us *inter alia* to focus on education for the well being of our people. From the quote of Dr. Vikram Sarabhai, we note a great commonality between ISRO and IGNOU working for the common cause of improving the quality of life of our people. This is very unique and different from mission of any other institution of higher learning in the country.

ISRO and IGNOU have been collaborating in using satellite communication to enrich learning processes and increase access to education through distance mode. Distance Education, which is dynamic and innovative, successfully absorbed the technology to provide more effective learning support. Thus capability for four TV-channels and two interactive networks dedicated for education had been developed under ISRO-IGNOU collaboration by 2003.

EduSat and Education

In order to fulfil the requirements of education for all, the Government of India took a major decision through the Indian Parliament in the year 2001 making education compulsory for every Indian in the age group of 6 to 14. This task is to be accomplished by the year 2015 under a major initiative known as *Sarva Shiksha Abhiyan*. We were also conscious of considerable pressures for increased access to higher education that would emerge from the decision for compulsory school education in the near future. The massive educational setup and systems required to handle such large numbers lead us to plan *inter-alia* for development of effective satellite communication systems with extensive point to point reach covering the whole country. Thus, some successful joint interventions between ISRO and IGNOU and some other educational institutions and organizations propelled the idea of designing and developing a dedicated satellite for education by ISRO. It is fascinating to observe that within a short period of less than 2 years, ISRO successfully designed, developed and launched a dedicated geo-stationary satellite for Education known as the EDUSAT on September 20, 2004. We are unique in the world in this respect and we feel that this capability will immensely support our mission to provide seamless education and to accomplish the target of education for all. The following observation of His Excellency Dr. A.P.J. Abdul Kalam, the President of India about the potential use of EDUSAT for education is very encouraging and illuminating:

> Democratization of knowledge indicates knowledge for anyone, any time, any place. EduSat will be extremely helpful in making this shift possible and decreasing the digital divide.

Coordination, Promotion and Utilisation of EduSat Networks

Soon after the successful launch of the EduSat, two parallel coordinating and monitoring agencies were put in place; one each by the Ministry of Human Resource Development (MHRD), Government of India and another by ISRO. In view of our long experience in using the capabilities of Space technology in education, the Vice-Chancellor, IGNOU was nominated to Chair a National Core Group on EduSat utilisation and coordination with members from different national organisations in education and some senior official from the MHRD, Ministry of Agriculture, Government of India and ISRO. We have been working on this massive task of developing 5 National and 28 state level interactive networks based on VSAT technology. The Core Group has made presentations and interventions in several meetings with all the state functionaries and policy makers. In the first phase, IGNOU has created 131 interactive VSAT terminals across the country, which has greatly enhanced effectiveness of our applications of ICT for education. National networks with 100 similar terminals, one each for All India Council for Technical Education, National Council of Educational Research and Training and University Grants Commission, are in different stages of development.

State networks for the North-East Region with one hub at each of the state Headquarters and fifty interactive terminals to be funded by ISRO are being set up. In the state of Jammu and Kashmir we are putting up two Hubs one each at Srinagar and Jammu supporting two networks with fifty interactive terminals each to be funded by ISRO. For other states, we are setting up one hub and ten interactive terminals funded by ISRO, and the State Government will fund a minimum of 40 additional terminals. Just like the National Core Group, similarly structured state level Core Groups for development and effective utilization of the EDUSAT have been functional in most of the states. The requirement of expansion of these networks is also being processed through a new Centrally Sponsored National Scheme under the Ministry of Human Resource Development. This scheme is likely to include not only EDUSAT supported networks but also other technologies based on fiber optics.

EduSat has six transponders each for Ku and Extended C Band networks. The transponders for Ku Band provide one national beam and 5 regional beams. The national beam would support 5-6 Ku Band national networks with a footprint covering almost the whole country (except the Andaman and Nicobar islands), but including our neighbouring countries like Bangladesh, Bhutan, Nepal, Sri Lanka and Maldives. The eastern part of Pakistan is also reachable by this network. We view this capability as an important tool for creation of regional networks for sharing our resources and capacities for the cause of educational development and advancement of our region for better understanding and friendship. We are already processing a request from Sri Lanka for the national EduSat network. Each regional beam will support 4-5 state level networks, which fall in their respective footprints. Thus all the national networks and majority of state networks will be on Ku band. However it is not feasible to provide Ku band networks for the states of Madhya Pradesh, Maharashtra, Rajashtan, Uttar Pradesh, which are only partly covered by any individual regional beam.

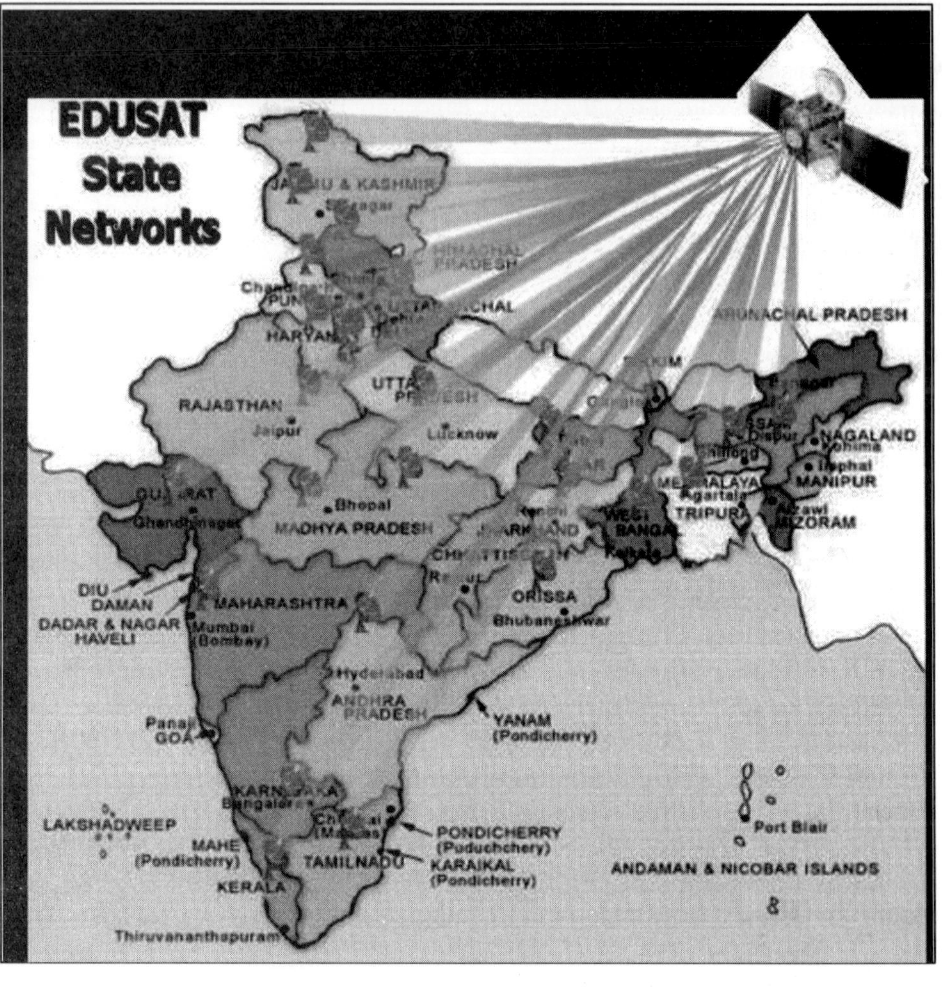

The Extended C band network has footprint larger than even the national Ku band; it covers the whole country including Andaman and Nicobar Islands. Thus states beyond Ku band reach are being provided with Extended C band connectivity. The cost of a hub at the teaching-end and ground equipment at virtual classroom end for this category of network is slightly costlier than the corresponding components for Ku band network. The greatest advantage of these satellite supported networks is that we can ensure point to point two way audio and video communication from the teaching-end to the learning-end located anywhere under the footprint of the satellite beam.

The main Hub for EduSat has been located in Space Application Centre of ISRO at Ahmedabad. But this causes 50% loss of bandwidth for connecting the main Hub with sub-Hubs of the national beam, which are mostly located in Delhi. It would therefore, be advisable to shift the main hub from Ahmedabad to Delhi, which will double the bandwidth capacity of the national networks supported by EduSat.

EduSat networks have capabilities to support:

- Satellite communication enabled education
- Virtual classrooms
- Video on demand
- Database access
- National and State level repositories
- On-line operations
- Linking FM radio stations of IGNOU for simultaneous broadcast of programmes.

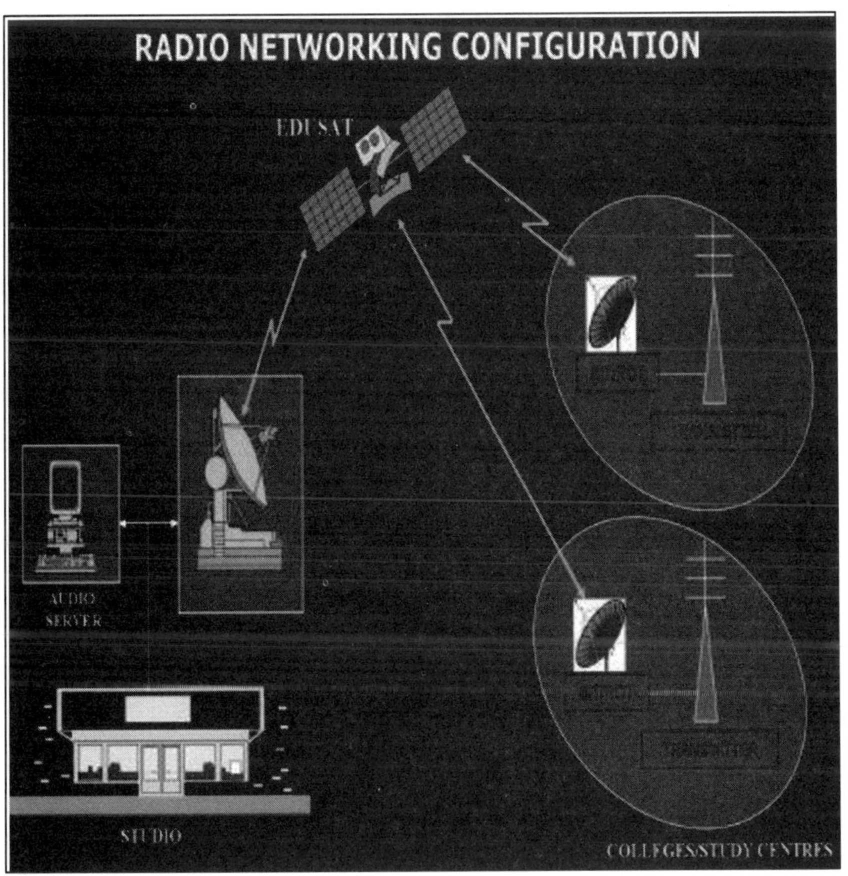

We realised the importance of these capabilities for the ODL system for extending its reach and improving quality of student support to meet the requirement of large number of learners spread all over the country and beyond. IGNOU has the unique distinction of planning for effective usage of the EduSat capability even before the satellite was launched. Thus, the final 10th Plan project proposal of the University included specific plans for EduSat utilisation which were discussed for financial support from the Government of India. Our pre-launch preparations were very well timed because we received the approvals from the Ministry of Human Resource Development, Government of India in October 2004, which coincided with the period when the EduSat satellite was launched and made functional.

ODL contributes to EduSat network

The setting up of Sub-Hub and Satellite Interactive Terminals at 131 learner-end locations for IGNOU was taken up from January 2005. These locations are well spread covering the whole country. However, in April 2005, when the terminals and the Sub-Hub had been installed in several locations, we encountered a major problem of integrating the terminals with the ground equipment at virtual classroom-ends. At this critical moment of the development of our EduSat supported national network, the technical staff of IGNOU developed in-house technical capabilities for integration and perfected it at 5 locations near Delhi. The usual approach to complete the work of integration at all locations would have been to send our technicians to all the 131 locations to make our national network functional. This would have meant enormous costs on travel and considerable delays in activation of the terminals. At this moment of crisis, we made an unique contribution.

We decided to use our existing one-way video and two-way audio C Band network to explain technical operations involved to locally identified persons trained in basic computing. In most of the cases, we identified our own students staff and trained them in the process of integration from the studio in Delhi. This worked extremely well and we could get all our virtual classroom-ends activated within a very short period of time. More than this, we created local capabilities for maintenance of network, which is so crucial for its uninterrupted functioning. The Chairman and other senior officials of ISRO appreciated this very useful, cost-effective and dynamic approach and we decided to develop a joint ODL programme on the basic technical issues related to EduSat network. This programme has since been developed jointly by Technical and ODL experts from IGNOU and ISRO.

IGNOU Leads Revolution in Education

The third major revolution, has been greatly influenced and even complimented by the other two revolutions in the sectors of Information and Space Technologies. This is in the form of emergence of Open and Distance Learning system with global impact, which has revolutionized the education system of our country. This revolution has emerged silently but very rapidly, successfully and effectively during the last two decades. This is confirmed by the fact that as of today, nearly 25% of the total number of students in higher education are receiving education through the ODL mode. The National Open University alone provides education to nearly 12 % of students in higher education. Similarly, several State Open Universities are providing massive education in the country primarily focused on the region of their location. The system is dynamic with modular approach, which provides multilevel entry and exit to suit the convenience of learners. It is cost-effective and has developed excellent synergy with the conventional system in terms of sharing of facility and faculty to optimally utilise the existing infrastructure and human capital. The enrolment on an average, in OUs has grown at the rate of about 24% per year. Due to success achieved and credibility gained by the ODL System, especially the OUs, the Ministry of Human Resource Development, Government of India has given special focus to development and expansion of the system during the 10th Plan Period.

IGNOU is currently providing education to nearly 1.3 million students with presence in 30 countries. We have been extensively using one-way video and two-way audio and radio broadcast systems for providing learner support to the students for more than a decade now. But it is fascinating to interact and see our students through two-way video and two-way audio EduSat supported network, which we have started using recently.

As a provider and facilitator of education, we draw immense satisfaction and joy in seeing the young men and women produced by our systems to achieve highest levels of success in different sectors of their choices. We witness this happen year after year, which makes us visualize the greatness, uniqueness and nobility of our responsibilities and encourages us to move forward with greater enthusiasm. We equip and enable a large number of committed and motivated students with beaming faces. We tend to arouse confidence, new ambitions and dreams in the minds of our students and also remind them about their responsibilities and abilities to significantly contribute for the cause of national development. The very thought of the process is striking and exciting. We can thus look back with some satisfaction to observe that the number of students in IGNOU almost got doubled during the last four years. We are encountering greater challenges in sustaining quality education with increased numbers but with our strong commitment and determination, we have been evolving new strategies and new initiatives with continuous increase in number of students year after year. Education for more students from our system means greater contribution of the institution for development of the nation and societies around us. The fact that every tenth student seeking higher education in the country, is studying with us is a source of great inspiration, admiration and satisfaction.

In terms of international impact of our system, it may be mentioned that we are present in thirty countries and this is expanding. The success of the system was appreciated in a meeting of the Heads of Countries in the SAARC region held in January 2004 in Islamabad. It decided to form SAARC Consortium for Open and Distance Learning (SACODiL) with its first secretariat at Indira Gandhi National Open University with Vice Chancellor of the University as the Chairman of the Board of Governors. We recently hosted Second Summit of Presidents and Vice Chancellors of nearly 20 Mega University of the world in September 2005, where the constitution and functions of Global Mega University Network (GMUNET) were finalised. During this Summit, it was decided to set up the first secretariat of GMUNET at IGNOU for the period

2005-2008 with Vice-Chancellor, IGNOU as the Chairperson and Vice-Chancellor, The Open University of UK as the Vice-Chairperson.

It is now clear that the ODL system is in the process of redefining education and repositioning the objectives of educational institutions. It has great potential for transforming large human workforce into skilled capital under tight time frames. Such a transformation will completely change the view of large population being a serious problem to an extremely useful human resource, which can make significant and visible contributions for the cause of national development. There cannot be any dispute about the importance and the national priority that it deserves. We encounter this requirement in almost all areas of human development. As a first step, in any process of implementation of projects and plans, we require, as an essential prerequisite, of trained master trainers in large numbers who in their turn carry out the process to educate, motivate and create necessary awareness for further target groups of people. Several Institutions in the ODL system have already made a visible and successful intervention in this direction. This is what I refer to redefining education for a very purposeful and directed education. The tailor-made, prescription based education, which is often quite independent of the learners' varying capacity, capability, aspirations and expectations is being transformed to education for people as per their expectations, needs and requirements, at their convenience, pace and place.

A New Initiative to Reach the Grassroots

We are aware of the fact that 70% of our post-matric students do not have any reasonable access to any institution of higher learning in a reasonable neighbourhood. With the availability of new technology enriched capabilities, we are uniquely placed to effectively utilise these to extend ODL system of education to provide access right upto the grassroots locations of the country. During the last few years, IGNOU has given special focus to extend its reach to remote and less-developed areas of our country. A few Regional Centres and Sub-Regional Centres have been set up especially for this purpose and we have received extremely encouraging response from our learners in these most un-reached regions. In order to extend the existing reach, IGNOU submitted a proposal to the Ministry of Human Resource Development and ISRO for value addition to school education through satellite communication network and make it accessible to all the schools in one of the identified remotely located district and one block each of a few other neighbouring districts in distant and least developed areas of our country. This pilot project was approved with appropriate funding both from MHRD and ISRO. IGNOU shall provide additional support from its own resources.

We are acting fast to implement this innovative pilot project in a very strict time schedule. Teachers are being trained in content generation for basic education in Mathematics and Communication Skills through Hindi medium. The target date for beginning of the pilot project is December 2005. The project implementation is being carried out under an Apex Core Group consisting of experts and academics from Indian Institute of Technology, Kanpur, Pt. Dwarka Prasad Mishra Indian Institute of Information Technology, Jabalpur Inter University Consortium for ICT enabled education of IGNOU and some Senior Officials of the Central and State Governments. We intend to develop content through a joint effort of IT and ODL experts in institutes of national importance and the teachers from the remote and less developed areas. Starting from Arunachal Pradesh and Assam in the East to Rajasthan in the West, we will be able to develop a network, which will be used for education with the capability of making further successful interventions in other areas focused on community development and welfare.

As the implementation of this project proceeds forward, I am sure, the connectivity will be utilized for a variety of applications leading to upliftment and raising of standards of our people living in distance places. Some internationally recognised medical professionals are also taking very keen interest in this pilot project and we are in the process of using this connectivity for tele-medicine also. We are sure that we will fully implement the pilot phase and will be in a position to extend it to cover all the districts of some of the most backward regions to really make a dent in improving quality of life of our people dwelling in some of the lest developed regions. We have the experience of using IT capabilities for empowering students in a few thousand primary schools located in remote and less developed areas under the Headstart project (Sharma et al; 2001 and Dikshit; 2002) and nearly 400 schools under the CLASS project. In order to ensure uninterrupted functioning of the network, we have decided to use solar panels to support the learner end locations due to unreliable power supply in those distant places. We also have a few mobile interactive terminals, which could be taken to the most distant places by using automobile vans.

Pan-African Network and IGNOU

In many developing countries, one of the greatest barriers in the process of equitable development is non-availability of even reasonable infrastructure facilities. In this context, ICT is getting greater preference and priority in many developing countries over the development of basic infrastructure like building of roads etc., which require substantial financial support and take much longer time. In this background, several countries have greatly benefited by putting ICT networks, which are being used extensively for education, community health and many other such aspects. His Excellency, Dr. A.P.J. Abdul Kalam, the President of India in his address during the inaugural session of the Pan African Parliament held at Johannesburg on 16 September 2004, suggested development of a Satellite and Fiber Optic network to provide communication and connectivity for all the 53 member countries of Pan African Parliament with India. The members of the Pan African Parliament greatly appreciated and supported the idea. As a follow up to the above commitment made by the President of India, the Prime Minister's Office decided to identify the Ministry of External Affairs, as the nodal agency for project implementation. Thus the officials of Rashtrapati Bhavan, Prime Minister's Office and External Affairs Ministry along with experts from ISRO, Telecommunication Consultants India Ltd. (TCIL) and an expert from Indian Institute of Science, Bangalore worked together to finalise a proposal for establishment of a Pan African network through a combination of Satellite and Fiber Optic connectivity with primary goal to use it for tele-education and tele-medicine (Bhaskarnarayan et al, 2005).

In June 2005, the President of India convened a meeting of the Heads of Missions or their representatives in Delhi of all the 53 member countries of African Parliament and discussed the proposal with them. IGNOU was also invited to participate in this meeting for a possible role in providing education through Pan African network. It was decided that IGNOU should use the Pan African network for delivery of programmes first in English and then subsequently translate and transform its courses and programmes for delivery in other languages like French, Portuguese, Spanish, etc. for African countries using other languages. This programmes could be provided as such or transformed to suit local requirements and context.

Pan-African network will finally connect two institutions from India and three Universities from Africa to 53 learning centres – one each in every member country of African Parliament Union. We are the first University in India, to be assigned the responsibility of providing education to these countries of Africa through the Pan-African Network. We are expected to initiate programme delivery and also have a hand holding arrangement with the host institutions in African to develop capacity locally so that within a period of first three years, programme design and development and delivery system could be handled locally. Beyond three years, the collaboration could continue on one-to-one partnership between India and Pan-African countries on win-win basis. Thus, five teaching ends and 53 virtual classrooms will be available on the network for teaching-learning process. Further expansion of the network to other locations by adding more VSAT terminals as well as broadband and wireless connectivity will be possible by adding additional elements and bandwidth. The Pan-African network is also scalable to support other services with minor upgradation at the Hub and bandwidth. For the network, a Pan-African Hub will be set up in some suitable location in Africa and a Tele-education Hub of ISRO located at Ahmedabad or Bangalore in India will be connected with IGNOU. Thus, the lessons originating from IGNOU will reach the Pan-African Hub through under sea cable and get it uplinked through it to reach the learning centres – one each in the 53 countries. The network will have the capability of running four parallel channels at a time.

Emerging Applications of Technology

The concern in ODL system for the convenience and requirements of learners has propelled the system to be more dynamic with greater contemporary relevance. Some of the best systems in the ODL system have therefore kept pace with new dimensions of technology and are able to successfully absorb them in expanding access and improving quality of programme delivery. Satellite Communication, which we have been using extensively, requires a very heavy initial expenditure in developing infrastructure and it also requires optimal utilization of the capability, which is available round the clock for economic viability. Our experience in IGNOU shows that it takes quite sometime before Satellite networks are fully utilized for various reasons. It takes time to acquaint the learners in usage and benefits arising from the new technology. Further some minimal local expertise has to be developed and put in place for ensuring uninterrupted usage of the network. It is from this point of view that the fiber optic connections, if available, are preferable because one is required to pay for the precise usage of the connectivity as per one's requirement. Thus, starting with connectivity for a shorter period we can expand its usage as the learners get accustomed to it and feel convenient with the system. However, the viability

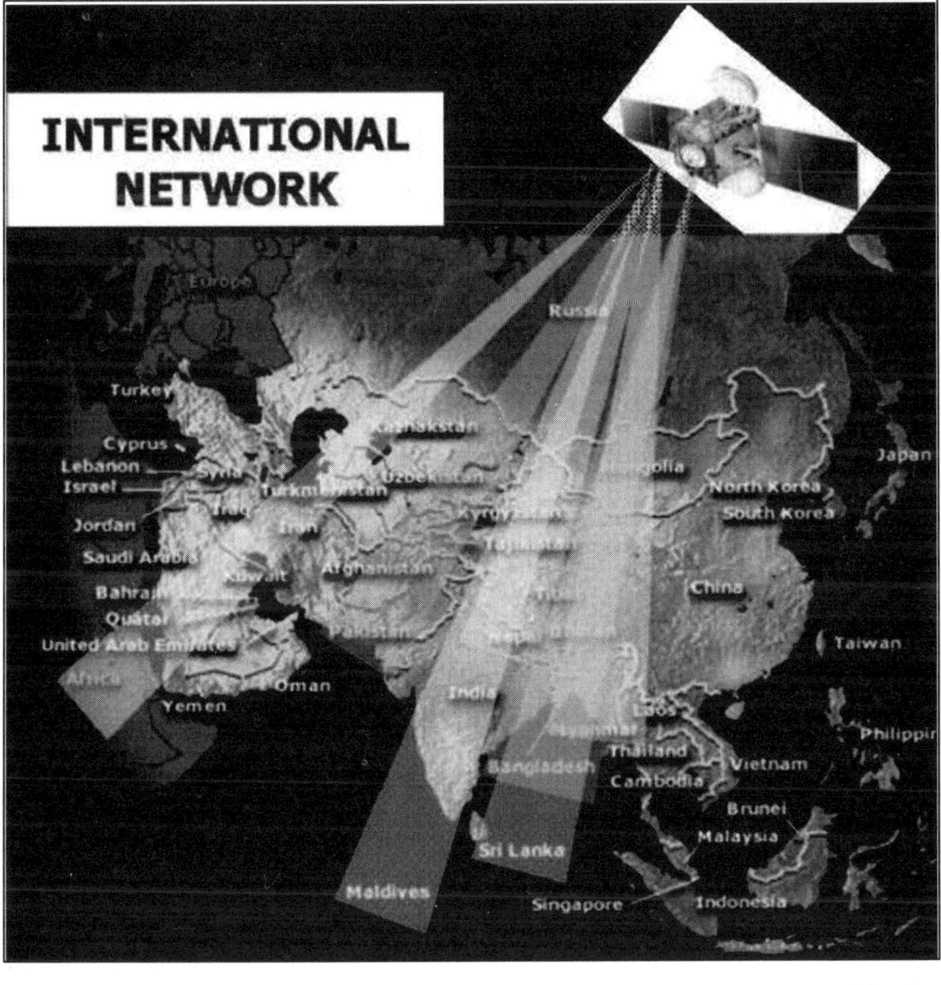

of the fiber connectivity to some of the most remote places is an issue and provides Satellite Communication, which is point to point, its significant advantages. It is, therefore, advisable to use convergence of all technologies available to suit our requirement and learners' convenience. Thus, IGNOU is using Fiber Connectivity, Extensive Satellite Connectivity and also Radio Network of 40 FM Radio Stations that are being developed across the country. A very useful combination of EduSat capability and FM Radio Broadcast Network is being developed under IGNOU-ISRO Collaboration where we would be able to simultaneously broadcast programmes of common interest through two or more FM Radio Stations located at different places.

A very significant and relatively newer technology available to us is the mobile cell phones. Besides their easy access and convenient handling, the new mobile phones are empowered with enormous technological capabilities such as pocket radio, pocket PC, internet connectivity, remote television, SMS, e-mails etc. The cost of both the mobile phone and charges for their usage has been declining very fast, in spite of increase in their technical capabilities. Nearly 760 million people across the world are buying mobile phones per year. The number of mobile phone users has been increasing in India at a very fast rate. Nearly 24 million people buy mobile phones in India per year, which means that five mobile phones are being bought in India every minute. The profile of buyers also represents all sectors of our society. It is estimated that by the end of the current year, about 70 million Indians will have mobile phone facility. Besides the convenience in using mobile phones, in many areas, the reliability of mobile phone over Landline Phones is comparable, if not better.

It in this context that in IGNOU we have started planning for programme delivery to our learners using Mobile Phone technology. The Satellite Networks that IGNOU has been using over the years have been mostly dependant on location of Receive/Interactive Terminals, which have of course been placed at any location of our choice accessible to our learners. However, dissemination of programmes beyond the location of satellite terminals is only possible through networks available with thousands of cable operators spread all over the country. We approached some of the major cable network providers but the expected cost by such operators was very expensive. Thus, in spite of the fact that transmission of our programmes through cable-operated networks would increase access to our learners considerably, we are not able to use these networks to ensure reasonable costs to students. However, Direct to Home (DTH) platform, which has been introduced in India, only a year ago has provided a viable alternative for increasing access of our network. One of our networks has been included in the DTH bouquet of channels. This provides a very cost-effective system to expand our reach beyond the existing locations, which consists of nearly 800 on C-band Network and 131 on EduSat interactive network. Besides these, 950 terminals shall be available on the new network, which is likely to become functional from December 2005.

Satellite Communication Technology is also undergoing very dynamic changes and efforts are being made by different organizations to launch heavy satellites with greater capabilities, which lead to cost effective usage of band width reducing prices on customers. Thus, ISRO is planning to send a new series of Satellites under INSAT 4A. The first INSAT 4A Satellite has already been designed and developed and is expected to be launched in December 2005. This has been specially designed to meet the requirement of DTH, which is in considerable demand. The Satellite will have 12 Ku Band transponders to support DTH. This Satellite is perhaps the heaviest of all launched by ISRO so far. ISRO has been very generously sharing resources with IGNOU for the cause of education under our common mission and concern to improve the quality of life of our people and we expect to receive continued support from ISRO for DTH facility.

Several private providers who are also launching Satellites for world wide coverage and it is expected that these providers will further bring down the cost to attract more customers. One such initiative is being undertaken by London based INMARSAT, which has launched INMARSAT 4 F1 Satellite, a few months ago covering the Indian continent and is in the process of launching another satellite INMARSAT 4 F2, which will cover one third of the earth surface, including North and South America. It is expected that the availability of this Satellite will greatly accelerate transfer of files through mobile phones at low costs. With such facilities, perhaps we can think of providing education across cotinents in countries like Brazil, where the Government has showed some interest for cooperation with IGNOU.

Development of National Centres: New Dimensions in Innovations

Continuing the tradition, we consolidated and diversified our system in several directions. As of today, the ODL system has become highly technical and professional with enormous researches being carried out the world over. We have identified some major interventions for development of a strong ambience for research in IGNOU. We are also in the process of identifying some of the best quality learning materials, which could form part of a National Pool of quality content, and shared with other institutions. Through EduSat supported networks, we are now developing National Repositories for Library, Learning and Research materials, videos on demand etc. for easy and seamless access by different target groups of learners in the ODL system.

By 1996, IGNOU had developed nine Schools of Studies offering programmes in fairly diverse areas. In 2002, we visualized an important role of IGNOU in providing education and training in two new areas: Agriculture and Law. As a prelude to formal existence of the two new Schools, we had initiated activities under these Schools by inviting or associating some experienced academics.

Development of programmes in agriculture, food processing, animal husbandry and other allied areas are being undertaken, with financial support from the concerned Ministries of the Government of India. A project for designing, developing and delivering an online certificate programme in food safety sponsored by the Ministry of Health and Family Welfare is also being developed by IGNOU. The School of Agriculture is also working on a Ministry of Food Processing Industries sponsored project to develop competent and productive Human Resource in the area of food processing and value addition. An awareness package in Hindi on Dairy Farming for Swaranjayanti Gram Swarozgar Scheme is being developed on pilot basis under a project sponsored by the Ministry of Rural Development. The package will be implemented in the states of Bihar, MP, Chhattisgarh, Jharkhand, UP and Rajasthan. The Central Silk Board and IGNOU are collaborating to develop educational and training programmes in sericulture for unskilled or semi-skilled youth. Under this scheme, the Certificate programme in Sericulture, Diploma programme in Silkworm Rearing and Diploma Programme in Silkworm Seed Technology are to be developed.

The School of Law would cater to continuous professional development of personnel engaged in legal education, including specialised areas such as human rights, intellectual property rights, corporate laws, laws on environment and such other emerging areas. A Postgraduate Diploma Programme on Intellectual Property Rights developed jointly with WIPO, Geneva has already been on offer. We have also started working on setting up of the following new centre.

Inter-University Consortium for Technology Enabled Flexible Education and Development (IUC-TEFED)

IGNOU has played a very crucial and central role at national and international levels to pioneer and promote technology-enabled education. In the emerging scenario of the three successful revolutions described above it is very important to motivate a massive movement for developing content at a very large scale with different objectives for a variety of teaching-learning applications. Several institutions and organizations have been making efforts in this direction but that does not seem enough to meet the massive requirement of education and training for different target groups of learners. We believe that shifting the paradigm from *'ICT-based systems and strategies'* to *'ICT-enabled systems and strategies'* is desirable. There is an urgent need to develop capabilities in a very large number of institutions across the country for use of new methodologies for education and training through virtual learning processes. We have to encourage capacity building for development of constructivist models of online learning, and for asynchronous and technology-mediated teaching-learning. The existing and emerging technologies would be primarily used as carriers of information and for interactive delivery of learning material for optimal utilization of the resources. The main focus would be on development of capabilities, enlargement of capacity for effective replication of innovative and interactive software/courseware, keeping pace with changes in mechanism of educational delivery and linking education with integrated development. Particular emphasis shall be given to interactive multimedia, R&D in ICT-enabled education, online repositories, and development of converged LMS for online education within a framework of blended learning. This Consortium has been being set up to promote collaborative research and develop resource base by sharing experiences on a common platform for optimum utilisation of IT in the ODL system.

National Network for Open and Distance Education (N-NODE)

N-NODE is a dedicated hybrid communication network, using combination of technologies such as Satellite communication, WILL and fiber optic suited to the specific purpose and location. It will provide connectivity to the University at headquarters, Regional Centres (RCs) and Study Centres (SCs). IGNOU will also be connected with all the State Open Universities (SOUs), which in turn may have further connectivity with their RCs, SCs and other distance education institutes within the state. It will facilitate tele-counselling, teleconferencing, increased interactivity, online admissions and evaluation, etc.

National Centre for Innovations in Distance Education

The Centre has been created to provide intellectual, financial and technological support for application-based research so as to plan for standardisation of the system and development of resource materials. The major areas of activities would be identification of innovative practices and development of guidelines, mechanism and modalities for convergence of different systems of education for seamless access, system analysis for improving efficiency and effectiveness, development of national programmes and study materials which could be adapted by other institutions as per their requirements, improvement of evaluation strategies, development of training and vocational programmes, skill development and demand driven programmes, and Total Quality Management (TQM) of various facets of the system.

National Centre for Differently Abled (NACDA)

It is unfortunate that nearly 10% of our people in India suffer from disabilities and there is a pressing need to put in place some massive training and education systems to meet the requirements of this special target group of people. IGNOU has been working in collaboration with Rehabilitation Council of India for developing training and educational programmes for the empowerment of people with disabilities. The use of appropriate technologies (multimedia, interactive teleconference, TV/radio broadcast) for specific learner groups helps in reaching out to such groups at their chosen place and pace. We have just completed a joint project with National Human Rights Commission of India and Canadian Human Rights Commission. The goal of this project was to increase respect for human rights of the persons with disabilities and to create conditions for the effective use of international and domestic human rights instruments for the protection and promotion of the rights of persons with disabilities. Apart from developing a variety of new programmes for imparting education for people with disability, the centre will also facilitate i) collaboration and networking with national and international agencies working in this area; ii) development of innovative approaches and practices for training and rehabilitation of people with disabilities; and iii) sharing expertise and extending support to other such programmes in the country.

References

Bhaskarnarayan, A. et. al. (2005). *PAN-African Network through Satellite and Fiber-Optics for Tele-Medicine and Tele-Education.* A project proposal jointly developed by officials of the Rashtrapati Bhawan, Indian Space Research Organisation, Ministry of External Affairs, Government of India and TCIL and an expert from Indian Institute of Science, Bangalore.

Bhatia B.S. and Dikshit H.P. (2004). *A Dedicated Satellite for Education.* A paper presented at State Ministers of School Education chaired by the Union Ministers for Human Resource Development, Govt. of India, October.

Dikshit, H.P. (2002). Multidimensional strategy and capability of ICT to reach the most distant and deprived. *Proceedings of UNESCO-LEARNTEC 2002 Conference*, Karlsruher, published by Karlsruher Messe – und Kongress-GmbH, February.

Dikshit, H.P. (2005) *Vice-Chancellor's Convocation Reports presented in 14th to 16th Convocations of IGNOU, February 2003, 2004 and March 2005.* New Delhi: IGNOU.

Dikshit H.P. (2005). *13th Convocation Address of Dr. B.R. Ambedkar Open University.* Hyderabad, January.

Dikshit H.P. (2005). *Prof. G.R. Damodaran Endowment Lecture organized by GR Damodaran College of Science.* Coimbatore, July.

Sharma, Amita et. al. (2001). Headstart: Computer Enabled Education and Development. *Collection of Workshop Papers on Information and Communication Technology for Professional Development of Primary Education Personnel of DEP-DPEP.* Edited by Sitansu Jena et. al., February.

Dikshit H.P. (2004). *Building capacities of education through cross boarder provision.* UNESCO–OECD Australia Forum on Trade in Educational Services, Sydney, October.

Dikshit H.P. (2004). Key Note Address at *Tele Learning Conference*, organized by Department of Space, Government of India. Thiruvananthapuram, October.

Dikshit H.P. (2003). Quality Education: Challenges and Tasks Ahead. *90th Annual Conference of ISCA*. Lucknow, January.

Dikshit H.P. (2005). Using Space Technology For Societal Needs - Space Based Education. *92nd Annual Conference of ISCA*. Ahmedabad, January.

Dikshit H.P. (2005) *Technology Enabled Learning in the Context of Small Island States*. Public Lecture, Mauritius, August.

Dikshit H.P. (2003). Mission and Prospects of Distance Education in India, Action for the Future of Distance Education – Innovation and Collaboration. Address at *World Summit of GMUNET*, Shanghai, China, November.

Dikshit H.P. (2005). Dedicated ICT Networks for Education. Address at *GMUNET-Second World Summit*, New Delhi, September.

Professor H.P. Dikshit is Vice Chancellor, Indira Gandhi National Open University and Chairman, Distance Education Council. He has the rare distinction of being the Vice Chancellor of four Universities: two conventional and two open. He also served in the past as President, Association of Indian Universities as the senior-most Vice Chancellor in the country. Currently, he is Chairman of the National Core Group on EduSat Utilisation, Government of India.
Email: hp_math@ignou.ac.in

20

Tamil Virtual University: Some Experiences

V.C. Kulandaiswamy and M. Ponnavaikko

Introduction

Virtual education is a form of distance education. It was the emerging technologies, like the web, multicast network infrastructure and multimedia technology which have the potential to make it possible to create distributed environments, providing complete location-independent access to learning resources. Virtual education incorporates all activities of a real university including registration, enrolment, payment of fees, delivery of lessons, on-line lecturers, interactive sessions, assignments, evaluation including intermediate tests and final examination and award of grades and certificates.

There are many virtual models and virtual campuses in the globe. Tamil Virtual University (TVU) is one such model, promoted by the Government of Tamil Nadu to cater to the language and cultural needs of Tamil diaspora. Established in July 2000, the TVU has grown with a wide range of virtual repositories of resources relating to the history, art, literature and culture of the Tamils.

This chapter presents a brief account of the establishment and development of Tamil Virtual University.

History

Indians are one of the five races in the world who have a world wide presence, the other four being, the English, the Chinese, the Japanese and the Jews. Among the Indians, the Tamils constitute an important component and they live in over 60 countries, in considerable numbers in some and in small numbers in some others. Tamil is a national official language in two countries, namely Sri Lanka and Singapore, a State language in India and a recognised language in many countries. The Tamils living abroad need to be familiar with Tamil language and be in touch with their heritage, in order to preserve their culture, tradition and values.

There is awareness among the Tamils living abroad that they must not lose their cultural roots. There is evidence of growing interest in learning Tamil language, Carnatic music and Bharathanatyam. In this effort, they need help. It is with a view to meeting the requests often made by the overseas Tamils that the Government of Tamil Nadu decided to set up the TVU. During the Valedictory function of Tamil Net'99 on February 8, 1999, the then Chief Minister, Government of Tamil Nadu announced that a 'Tamil Virtual University' would be set up to meet the cultural needs of the Tamils around the world.

On the recommendation of an Advisory Committee under the Chairmanship of Dr. M. Anandakrishnan, the Government set up a High Level Committee in May 1999 under the Chairmanship of Dr. V.C. Kulandaiswamy, former Vice-Chancellor, Indira Gandhi National Open University, to prepare the development programme for the proposed University. The Committee submitted in 1999 a detailed report covering all aspects of establishing a Virtual University for Tamil.

The TVU aims at providing Internet based resources and opportunities for Tamil communities living in different parts of the globe as well as others interested in learning Tamil and acquiring knowledge of the history, art and culture of the Tamils.

In January 2000, the Government of Tamil Nadu passed orders to set up a Tamil Virtual University as a Society, defining the organizational mechanism. The proposal included a Board of Directors comprising 7 to 9 members, including the Chairman and the Director of TVU. The Government entrusted the responsibility of initiating the steps for establishing the University with Dr. Kulandaiswamy. The TVU was registered as a Society on 12th May 2000. The TVU started functioning in a small room at the ELNET Software City, Taramani on October 16, 2000, with the appointment of the Director, two Deputy Directors, one Senior Tamil Professor as a Senior Consultant, two Assistant Directors, one lexographer and a few more secretarial and computer system administrators and programmers. The web content development began in November, 2001 and the University was formally inaugurated on February 17, 2001 and dedicated to the world community.

Development of TVU

The Government of Tamil Nadu allotted a space of 1400 sq.ft. in ELNET Software City, Taramani. The construction activity for building the office was started; computers and accessories, communication systems and the other office equipments were procured and a 64 kbps ISDN Internet connection was obtained.

In order to make use of the services of an Internet Service Provider (ISP) in the U.S., Messrs Surf India was identified and the web server of TVU was placed in their Internet servic e centre in New Jersey sharing their 45 Mbps Internet connectivity. Then TVU website was registered with an address www.tamilvu.org through Network Solutions, U.S. For secured transactions of credit cards and transmitting private documents via the Internet, a protocol called SSL (Secure Sockets Layer) certification was installed in the server. To enable the prospective beneficiaries to register for access to the TVU web contents on payment, a payment Gateway was installed through ICICI. Thus, the TVU was set ready for its academic growth.

Target groups and their needs

The target groups for TVU include:

- Tamils in countries like Mauritius, Reunion, Fiji, South Africa, Sri Lanka, Malaysia and advanced countries like U.S., Canada, Australia, U.K. and Singapore.
- Students who may be opting for Tamil as one of the subjects in a University Programme.
- Scholars engaged in Tamil research.
- Others interested in learning Tamil.

The Tamils in South Africa, Mauritius, Reunion and Fiji settled there from the middle of the 19th century and are losing touch with their language and culture, generation after generation. They want the younger generation to learn Tamil and the level of learning Tamil in these countries is that of the beginners, starting from the alphabet.

In Malaysia and Singapore, Tamil is taught in schools; in Sri Lanka, Tamil studies are available up to University level. Tamils in these countries need opportunities for gaining knowledge in Tamil language, literature, art and culture and to pursue higher studies in Tamil.

Tamils in advanced countries like U.S., Canada, Australia, and U.K. organise week-end classes for their children to train them to understand and speak functional Tamil and to some extent read and write. Some have prepared CD ROM contents for learning basic Tamil. Further, some Universities in these countries offer programmes in which Tamil may be taken as a subject for credit. To meet the requirements of the Tamils in these parts of the world, the courses offered by TVU shall be such as to supplement the knowledge that these students gain through private arrangements.

As for those Tamil students who may be engaged in research, the requirement may be in the form of literature for reference or dictionary material.

Development of academic programmes

To meet the global requirements cited above, the Academic Programme of TVU includes curricula at two levels of education, namely Beginners' level and Higher level.

The Beginners' programme includes a Certificate Course offering Tamil language equivalent to the 6th Standard in Tamil Nadu Schools, and a series of Advanced Certificate Courses, Level-1, Level-2 and Level-3 to cover the Tamil skill sets offered in 7th & 8th, 9th& 10th and 11th & 12th standards, respectively. The Higher level programme at present offers a modular programme equivalent to B.A. (Tamil), consisting of Diploma and an Advanced Diploma programmes leading finally to a Bachelor's degree.

Beginners' programme

The Certificate course of the Beginners' programme comprises three levels, namely (i) Basic, (ii) Intermediate, and (iii) Advanced. The structure of the courses and the skill sets were developed by three sub-committees. The course materials were designed with multimedia contents, including audio, video, animation, pictures, text, etc. in a self-learning format, with the help of web content designers. The Programme includes an education primer at the kindergarten level.

Basic Level Lessons

At the basic level, the lessons are offered to enable the child to learn, to read and write Tamil alphabets with the help of animated contents. Tests have been added for self-evaluation. The alphabets are taught starting with the letters having simple shapes. To help the learners practise in Tamil sounds, 16 rhymes are appended to these lessons. A table of Tamil alphabets is given with audio files to hear the pronunciation of each letter when clicked on the letter. A glossary of about 900 words, taught at this level is given with audio files to hear the correct pronunciation of a word and to spell the letters while reading the word.

The skills imparted at this level are equal to the first standard and a part in the second standard of school education in Tamil Nadu. The lessons offered at this level are delivered through explanations in English.

Intermediate level lessons

The skill sets offered in the second to fourth standards of school education in Tamil Nadu are covered in the Intermediate level certificate course. Twenty lessons are included to be learnt through listening, reading, writing and conversation. Exercises in grammar are given in each lesson. In these lessons, the students are familiarised with commonly used words like the names of animals, birds, vegetables, flowers and fruits and the words used at functional levels at home, restaurants, functions and festivals. Each lesson is provided with an exercise in spoken Tamil through audio and animation techniques. After going through these lessons, a candidate is able to read a given text, to write a spoken text and to freely converse in Tamil. They also learn the basic Tamil grammar.

The students enrolling for this level of lessons are expected to know about 1000 words. The lessons are delivered in Tamil with instructions in English and all icons are in bi-lingual mode for easy understanding.

Advanced level

Advanced level certificate course includes the skill sets offered in the 5th and 6th Standards of school education in Tamil Nadu. At this level, higher-level skills are given through 18 lessons using Multimedia and information communication technologies (ICT).

After going through these lessons, a candidate is able to acquire skills to understand simple Tamil poems, to narrate an instance, to understand literary articles, to write letters of different types, to write and understand simple articles, and to understand stories.

Primer education (Kindergarten level)

The basic level of lessons as stated earlier do not introduce Tamil alphabets in the conventional order. Through the feedback received from the Tamils settled abroad, it was understood that this system may suit the children living in Tamil speaking environment but the children in non-Tamil speaking environment should be first taught through oral tradition and than made to speak and understand spoken Tamil. For this purpose, primer education level of lessons were developed as a prelude to the basic level lessons. The primer education includes seven sections, comprising rhymes, stories, conversation, common words, events, numbers and letters. The lessons with exercises are delivered through voice and verbal mode with the help of animation. After going through these lessons, the learner is able to learn the lessons offered under basic level of the certificate course.

Higher level programmes

Diploma, Higher Diploma and Bachelor Degree programmes are offered as an integrated unit. As in the case of the degree programmes offered in Tamil Nadu, this programme consists of three parts. Part 1 consists of the mother tongue or the regional language, Part 2: study of a foreign language and Part 3 Tamil language, literature, history, culture and art as major subjects of study. Parts 1 and 2 are exempted if a student has already acquired a degree from any recognised university in the world. However, students not possessing a degree are exempted from both or either of the Parts 1 and 2. Those who are not covered under either of these cases, have an option to undergo the papers under Parts 1 and 2 offered by TVU. Part 1, offered by TVU has four papers in Tamilology with a total of 8 credits and Part 2 offered as an option has four papers in the areas of translation, manuscriptology, information technology and news media with a total of 8 credits.

Part 3 has 21 papers on Tamil language, culture, literature, history, art, etc. offered as C-level, D-level and A-level courses. C-level contains 4 papers, D-level contains 8 papers and A-level contains 9 papers. Each paper carries four credits.

- One who completes the four C-level courses and obtains 16 credits is awarded a Diploma in Tamil.
- A Higher Diploma in Tamil is awarded when C and D-level courses worth 48 credits are completed successfully.
- To qualify in Part-3 of the degree programme, one has to complete 21 papers worth 84 credits.

The lessons have been designed in an interactive format. Each paper is provided with an introduction covering the gist of the topics covered in audio and text modes, both in Tamil and

English. Similarly, at the opening of a lesson, a general briefing on the content is provided. The poems quoted in the lessons are supported with audio clippings. To review and for self-evaluation, self-assessment questions are provided. For each lesson, a two minute lecture by an expert is given as a video clipping at the end. (In IGNOU terminology, the terms course, papers, and lessons used by TVU are synonymous to programme, subject/course and units, respectively.)

Development of a digital library

The TVU has developed a very rich and modern digital library. It consists of three sections: i) literature section, ii) dictionaries section, and iii) cultural and other resources section. The literature section has a collection of works of Sangam, post-Sangam, medieval and modern periods. Selected books are also given in Roman script. Further, the dictionary section has a rich collection of dictionaries including six volumes of the Tamil Lexicon. Thesaurus and small dictionaries are also in the digital library. The cultural and other resources section includes the following:

- Video clippings on Tamil cultural events like Kavadi Attam, Poykkal Kudirai Attam, Mayilattam, Karakattam, Theru Koothu, Pavai Koothu (Puppet show), Nadaswaram, Jallikattu, Bharathanatyam, etc.
- Video clippings with commentary on 125 Siva and Vaishnava Temples in Tamil Nadu.
- Photogallery consisting of 125 Siva and Vaishnava Temples in Tamil Nadu.
- Tamil Technical Glossaries, including more than 200 thousand Tamil technical terms with search facilities in disciplines like Arts, Science, Engineering, Medicine, Law, Agriculture, Information Technology.
- Links to other Tamil websites.

Delivery Systems

To visit the TVU website, one has to register as a visitor, auditor, student, or library member. For registration, no fee is charged. Provisions are available for individual as well as group registration. A student can enrol for a programme when he/she fulfils the prescribed requirements and pre-requisites.

Tutoring and counselling

The period of study for lessons enrolled is six months. A teacher is assigned for every block of six lessons in the case of Diploma/Degree programmes or for all the lessons in each level of study in the case of certificate courses. All the students enrolled for a block/level of lessons are put under an e-group. The teacher allots time slots for studying and completing the lessons in a block or in a level of study in stages. If a student wants to discuss on any topic related to the subject of study, he/she can fix a convenient time with the teacher through e-mail or a chat through chat server facilities. The teacher monitors the progress and paces learning of the students; gives assignments and evaluates them.

Evaluation and award

Every student is evaluated through on-line as well as off-line tests and examinations. There are two components of evaluation for each paper: internal continuous assessment and end-semester examination. Continuous assessment is made through on-line assignments and objective type on-line tests with the help of question banks stored in the web server. The end semester examinations involve long-answer questions. A question bank for the end semester examination is placed in the web server. Whenever a student wants to take the end-semester examination after fulfilling the requirement, he/she goes to the study centre and the authorised person in the study centre generates a question paper from the question bank in the web server. The candidate writes the examination in the study centre. The answer book is evaluated by the adjunct faculty of TVU. If the adjunct faculty is not available, the answer book is sent to the TVU headquarters for evaluation.

The students can get to know their marks from the website directly. The grade sheets and the certificates are awarded to the students through the allotted study centre.

Role of study centres

Study centres play an extremely important role in transaction of virtual education. A student registers through Internet. Evaluation is also carried out through Internet. There is a possibility that someone enrols and someone else takes tests as a proxy. The study centres help to avoid such an undesirable event from happening. When a student registers for a course to study, he/she is advised to report to a study centre. The study centre then issues an Identity Card with his/her photograph and signature, duly countersigned by the study centre administrator. The students are clearly advised that they should take their on-line as well as off-line examinations only at the designated study centres. Study centres are set up through an MoU with TVU. Each study centre has facilities such as a computer centre with Internet facilities and an administrative office to attend to the registration of students and library members, issue of identity cards, management of TVU study materials, furnishing necessary information on the TVU programmes, conduct of on-line and off-line tests and examinations, and for the co-ordination of the adjunct faculties of TVU residing in the concerned regions for evaluating the answer books and arranging for counselling.

The TVU has so far set up nine study centres the world over. Of these, five are in different parts of US and one each in Canada, Malaysia, Mauritius and Sri Lanka.

Acceptance and Appreciation

Soon after the inauguration of TVU website, thousands of Tamils from different parts of the world started visiting the website. Within 15 days of inauguration, 493 of them from 30 countries registered as visitors, students and library members. Till July 2005, about 15000 persons from 94 countries have become the users of the TVU website as registered visitors, students, auditors and library members (Table 1). As on 7th July 2005, the total number of enrolments was 6989 from 65 countries out of which 1896 students have enrolled for the certificate course, 2303 for the Diploma-cum-Degree course, 26 for auditing and 2764 as library members. Good number of enrolments are from countries like Sri Lanka (2856), India (2378), USA (848), Mauritius (148), Singapore (134), Malaysia (80), Australia (75), UK (75), UAE (63) and Canada (48). In the other 55 countries, the number of enrolments vary from 1 to 45. The demand for the Degree programme is more in countries like Sri Lanka, India, Singapore and Malaysia.

Table 1: Details of registration and enrolments at TVU

Date	Cumulative usersincluding course enrolments and library		Enrolments in courses	
	No. of Candidates	No. of Countries	No. of Candidates	No. of Countries
01/03/2001	493	30	138	17
15/06/2001	2120	54	310	24
06/11/2002	4669	90	582	33
31/03/2003	7091	94	2491	40
04/05/2004	9540	94	2575	47
08/08/2004	10517	94	3312	51
06/12/2004	11789	94	4149	57
07/03/2005	12942	94	4965	58
07/07/2005	14969	94	6989	65

Feedback

In any non-formal education system, feedback from users, promoters, peers and other stake-holders provides useful inputs to review and improve the system. Many Tamil associations running week-end Tamil Schools started enrolling their students into the certificate programme of TVU. California Tamil Academy, New Jersey Tamil Arts and Cultural Society Tamil School, Fermont Chinmaya Mission Balavihar Tamil Classes, The Tamil School of Tamil Association of Greater Delaware Valley, Philadelphia and Sishya School of India Tamil Schools in New York and Canada signed an MoU with TVU offering their schools as the study centres of TVU. The students of California Tamil Academy were the first to receive the TVU Certificates. Fifty eight students out of 140 students enrolled for the basic level of the certificate course, took the final examination and fifty five of them qualified to receive the certificate for the basic level of the certificate programme.

The opening of TVU was considered as a big boon for the Tamils in South Africa, Mauritius and Reunion. In February 2002 the Mauritius Tamil Cultural Centre signed an MoU with TVU for establishing a study centre and about 150 students enrolled for the certificate programme of TVU.

In South Africa, the South African Tamil Federation (SATF) and over 40 other Saiva temple organisations have shown keen interest to promote TVU programmes. The SATF is trying to establish study centres with Internet facilities in different parts of the country through the financial assistance from the government. In the meantime, the interested Tamils have procured a few copies of the CD ROMs having basic level lessons of TVU, made multiple copies and distributed to the interested children and institutions.

In Sri Lanka, a recruit-cum-service agency, namely 'Dana International Educational Services (Pvt) Ltd. (DIES), Colombo took the initiative for promoting TVU programmes in Sri Lanka and signed an MoU with TVU for setting up study centres of TVU in Sri Lanka. Subsequently DIES established 3 centres, one in Colombo, second in Ratnapuri and the third in Oluvil. Till July 2005, about 2900 students have enrolled, of which 1100 are in the certificate courses and 1800 are in the degree courses.

Support from IGNOU

The Vice-Chancellor, IGNOU visited TVU, had an appraisal of TVU programmes and agreed to support Tamil Virtual University with overwhelming interest and appreciation. To this effect an MoU was signed between IGNOU and TVU to allow the students of TVU to use IGNOU lessons to complete Part-I or Part-II under languages.

Appreciation from Commonwealth of Learning (COL)

The web-based programmes of TVU impress all who visit it. COL sanctioned a pilot project worth CD$ 75000 towards the tuition and content development support for training 40 teachers in Malaysia drawn from the schools adopted by TMI-Nusantara Consultants through the web based degree programme of TVU.

Problems and Constraints

One innovates in adversity and necessity. The TVU was established at a time when the technology for developing virtual campus was in its early stages. Moreover, there were no models of virtual universities to follow in its design and development. Hence, at every stage of the development, the University had to innovate to overcome problems from unknown domains; it was really a pioneering effort.

Constraints in development and delivery of contents

The development of web contents for the planned curriculum is tripartite: course writers, web content designers, and TVU. The lesson developers were pooled from the conventional system. They had no experience in writing interactive course material for distance learning. Hence, workshops were held to train the lesson writers to prepare material for effective learning with question banks for on-line and off-line tests and examinations. In spite of the training, the resource persons had to re-write the lessons several times to reach the desired level of acceptance.

The next issue was to locate vendors for web-enabling the study material and library contents. In 2000, when TVU started functioning, there were only a few vendors in and around Chennai with some experience in developing multimedia based web contents. Through a strict selection process, 12 vendors with varied experience were identified. Barring a few, they had no experience in developing web contents in Tamil using the TAB encoding standard for Tamil, standardised by the Tamil Nadu Government. The identified vendors were involved in web enabling the contents of TVU through on-the-job training and with strict quality control. The vendors had to re-do the jobs many times till an acceptable standard was reached.

Learners' problems

The main problem of TVU Learners is that of access to the Internet. The Internet penetration as of now varies from 1.8% in Africa to 68.0% in North America and 14.6% in the world as a whole. The penetration in Asia, the largest and most populated region, is about 8.9% (www.internet world stats.com, 2005). In many countries, the Internet browsing is very costly. Accessibility and the cost pose problems to the students of TVU. To overcome these and facilitate anytime, anywhere learning, TVU chose to provide the study material in the CD mode also. Text mode course material is under preparation. For the purpose of on-line registration and evaluation, TVU insisted that all the study centres should have Internet facility for the use of TVU students.

Conclusion

The TVU has been set up to provide Internet based resources and opportunities for the Tamil communities living in different parts of the globe as well as those interested in learning Tamil and acquiring knowledge of the history, art, literature and culture of the Tamils. TVU website is rich in content, elegant in presentation and effective in delivery. The digital divide however remains the main concern. But this problem is likely to be over in coming years because of fast and cost-effective access to the Internet. In fact, Internet penetration into the world population as on July

2000 was only 6.84%; (Table 3). In five years, due to concentrated efforts from all concerned, the level of Internet has doubled; 14.6% by July 2005 from 6.84% in July 2000. (Tables 2 and 3).

Table 2: Internet usage as on July 2000

World regions	% penetration into population	% of users
Africa	0.40	0.76
Asia / Pacific	3.04	25.76
Europe	15.54	27.79
Middle East	1.29	0.59
North America	55.16	41.05
Latin America	3.21	4.04
World	6.84	100.00

Source: www.nua.ie/surveys

Table 3: World Internet users and population statistics as on July 2005

World regions	Population (2005 Est.)	Internet usage	Usage growth 2000-2005 (%)	% Population (penetration)	World users (%)
Africa	896,721,874	16,174,600	258.3	1.8	1.7
Asia	3,622,994,130	323,756,956	183.2	8.9	34.5
Europe	731,018,523	269,036,096	161.0	36.8	28.7
Middle East	260,814,179	21,770,700	311.9	.3	2.3
North America	328,387,059	223,392,807	106.7	68.0	23.8
Latin America/ Caribbean	546,723,509	68,130,804	277.1	12.5	7.3
Oceania / Australia	33,443,448	16,448,966	115.9	49.2	1.8
WORLD TOTAL	6,420,102,722	938,710,929	160.0	14.6	100.0

Source: www.InternetWorldStats.com

Even with this limited availability of Internet facilities, Tamils from 94 countries are making use of the TVU website and nearly 7000 students from 65 countries are studying in the different academic programmes. With improvements in Internet infrastructure, it is bound to be more easily accessible at low cost. Then the usage of the web based resources of Tamil Virtual University should increase exponentially.

TVU has ambitious plans to introduce new packaged programmes for the tourists to learn functional Tamil, on performing arts, general studies in Tamilology, Tamil computing, etc. TVU has also been contributing to the development of Tamil software and tools for enabling Tamil language to handle in Tamil technological advancements. It is hoped that TVU will ultimately emerge as an international university serving the Tamil diaspora and all those who may be interested in Tamil language and culture.

References

www.nua.ie/surveys, Accessed on July, 25,2005

www.internetworldstats.com, Accessed on July 25, 2005.

Prof. V.C. Kulandaiswamy has been the Vice Chancellor of three universities, including IGNOU. He has been awarded by the GoI with Padam Shri and Padam Bhushan for his scholarly contributions to Tamil literature, enriching Civil Engineering discipline and administrative capabilities par excellence. He is a prolific writer and very effective communicator. As a former President of Association of Indian Universities and Chairman, Distance Education Council, he has made very significant impact in the area of management of higher education.
Email: vckpp@hotmail.com

Prof. M. Ponnavaikko is former Director, TVU. Before joining TVU, he was Head, Department of Computer Science and Engineering, Crescent Engineering College.
Email: ponnav@gmail.com

SECTION IV

INSTRUCTIONAL DELIVERY AND QUALITY ASSURANCE

21

Networked and Decentralised Learner Support

S.R. Jha, C.K. Ghosh and P.K. Mehta

Introduction

The Open and Distance Learning (ODL) system is almost universally acknowledged as learner-centric because all thoughts, plans and activities focus on the learner (Panda, 2005; Garg, 2004). ODL is aggregate of the expressions—'Open Learning' and 'Distance Education'. 'Open Learning' is a philosophy, that is, a way of life which manifests itself through several facets of openness, whereas 'Distance Education' is a mode which has evolved through different stages. While a very high quality of the instructional content can be ensured through rigorous adherence to the principles of instructional methodology, it is likely that the learner nurtures a sense of isolation. Since learners are away from the institution and virtually loner, it becomes necessary for the ODL institutions to develop mechanisms for two-way communication and observe effective teaching-learning. It has been our experience as insiders that a learner in ODL system has the hangover of the conventional classroom teaching and feels more comfortable with face-to-face interaction with teachers. Such interactions are primarily content based. The learner support services are characterised by a 'continuity of concern'. From this viewpoint, the entire gamut of the ODL system turns out to be an exercise in learner support services (Koul, 1989).

In ODL System, a learner may require multilevel support because of their diverse backgrounds, learning habits, and mediums of instruction. The variation is across the regions and even within a region it may be influenced by the economic gap and digital divide between the rural and urban population. Therefore, efficient management of learner support services is crucial; more so the system is attracting growing public attention and the enrollment is increasing rapidly. For this we should continuously reflect on the practices, review decisions and re-engineer and restructure mechanisms. In this Chapter, we have discussed how decentralised learner support in networked learning environment can help address the challenges adequately by combining the domain expertise of conventional peers and technology expertise of distance educators. Since the ODL system relies heavily on trust of and owes its success significantly to collaborations with conventional peers and institutions as partners, a constant dialogue is necessary so that they begin to own it. This would help retain reputed institutions and discourage sub-standard operators in the network.

Learner Support

Learner support is a mechanism to help the learner learn. In conventional system, classroom transactions, peer-interactions and library are essential ingredients of learning. In ODL system, multiple media—print, audio, video, radio, TV, teleconferencing and videoconferencing—instructional package, face-to-face counselling, continuous assessment and hands-on-experience constitute learner support.

It is now universally accepted practice to involve acknowledged experts in the curriculum design and content development. Moreover, adherence to principles of education technology enables us to produce very high quality self-instructional materials where teacher has been built into the text. IGNOU and UKOU presents extremely good examples; their materials are sought after by students and institutions alike within their own countries and outside. However, to facilitate learner for self-actualisation, it is necessary to bridge the gap between instructional materials and actual learning. The early recognition of this fact by the policy makers brought learner support at the forefront of its planning, development and delivery activities. The broad *objectives* of learner support services are to:

- help learners gainfully utilise the learning package by augmenting it with academic support;
- develop effective two-way communication for breaking isolation, pacing learning and develop identity;
- help learners make their choices and decisions in respect of their progress in a programme;
- arrange access to resources and opportunities for technology mediated and/or face-to-face interaction depending on the spread of learners; and
- provide feedback to course material developers.

To meet these objectives effectively, the learner support services are conceived in view of:

- academic and administrative needs of learners;
- socio-economic, cultural and technological context; and
- financial, administrative and academic resources of the institution.

Institutions which do not take such factors seriously into consideration at the planning stage, lend themselves to criticism for standards. Though it is often tempting and convenient to offer minimum support and adopt models already developed by others, the former approach affects quality adversely and the latter option may not prove effective and/or efficient for the simple reason that two institutions may not be alike in all respects. It is for this reason that assessing and accreditating agencies have derecognised several institutions in 2005.

The most important factor in deciding the nature of learner support services is obviously the academic needs of the learners. The simple way to do so is to know their *problems*, arising due to organisations, personal and locational contexts. Our analysis brings forth the following:

- inadequate interaction with teachers, who can facilitate learning;
- lack of personal rapport as well as opportunity for comparison and competition with fellow learners and isolation due to geographical remoteness;
- non-familiarity with skills of self-study, i.e. with the learning package delivered through print and e-media, reading and comprehension, writing and note-taking, scheduling and time management;
- late receipt of study material due to non-adherence of affiliating institution to operational schedules;
- limited access to information and services;
- systemic non-responsiveness and inefficient management services;
- problems arising out of time-constraint due to social, family or work obligations; and
- financial constraints, physical disability, lack of appropriate environment for study.

The above list is by no means exhaustive and we can categorise the *needs* of learners according to stages of interaction/progression:

- pre-admission counselling to develop familiarity with the institution and its practices, understand implications of being a distance learner, and make right choice of course in an academic programme;
- induction to apprise how to learn at a distance; and
- regular personal or technology mediated interaction with teachers/counsellors/tutors/peers.

In addition, specific-groups such as physically handicapped, females and homemakers; people living in the remote areas and prison inmates, have special needs because of peculiar situations.

Since educational activity in general and distance education in particular is planned, organised, delivered and received by people living in varied socio-cultural and economic profile and working in a particular environment, it is definitely influenced by the latter. The learners are attracted to ODL system for reasons such as missed opportunity, flexibility of time and space, and need for on-the-job upgradation of knowledge and skills (Holmberg, 1981). Institutions operating in developing countries like India have to address challenges of tremendous geographical diversity, socio-cultural groups with varying practices, and perceptions of and approaches to education, mindsets conditioned by the conventional teaching-learning methods, and access to technology. Seven open universities in India have three-tier system: Headquarters, Regional Centres and Study Centres. Regional Centres are engaged in academic administration and act as intermediary between HQ and Study Centres, most of which are located in institutions of higher learning, act as centres of activity for academic transaction. Five open universities with comparatively low enrollment and DEIs, but for a few exceptions, operate in two tier mode: Headquarters and

Study Centres. The national university has recently experimented with the concept of sub-RC which have been located in regions predominantly inhabited by SC/ST and low literacy populations.

Since most of the learner support centres are located far away from an ODL institution, availability of qualified teachers/tutors at these places, an important determinant in providing learner support, is ensured. ICTs provide many other options to overcome this limitation. In respect of financial resources, two options are available to any institution: to plan only such learner support services as may be operationalised within the limits of the financial resources of the institution or to make collaborative arrangement with other institutions/organisations with a view to share the cost of support services. This makes it imperative for an ODL institution to carefully consider the issues of availability of academic resources, costs, and long-term financial sustainability.

A typical ODL institution is required to address aspects such as pre-admission and post-registration counselling support, information on material receipt, returning evaluated assignments, library, term-end examinations etc. While counselling provides personal touch, assignments are tool for pacing learning and establishing two-way didactic communication. An efficient and proactive administration is a pre-requisite for high quality learner support services. Institutions having administrative systems in tune with the philosophy of learner support only can provide support services of desired quality. It is, therefore, important to introduce periodic review mechanism.

Programme delivery through learner support centres invariably leads to a rather huge and spread-out organisational structure. Therefore, it would be prudent to decentralise some of the activities for efficient time management and efficient learner support. The important point is to identify the activities to be decentralised and the extent to which it ought to be done.

Which Support Services are to be Decentralised?

It is normal practice that an organisation with national/state-wide presence, having potential to grow and which cares for customers, normally begins its operations centrally and in course of time, depending on the demands and complexities of the operations, goes for decentralisation in a phased manner. This is true of ODL institutions as well. Therefore, to identify support services which should be decentralised, we need to examine the issue of decentralisation in the context of their organisational structure. The operations in ODL system can be better understood in terms of the structural elements, concepts and principles of industrial production (Peters, 1989). It is, however, important to note that such a comparison does not necessarily imply that the teaching and learning in ODL institution per se can be equated with industrial processes.

The delivery model in ODL system universally is of distributed functional nodes within organisational structure with centralised control. For example, in IGNOU and six other State Open Universities (BAOU, BRAOU, KSOU, MPBOU, VMOU, YCMOU) all functions/operations related to learner support services are coordinated by the Regional Services Division (RSD) at the respective headquarters. The Regional Centres, which facilitate, operationalise and supervise support services in the field, are the outposts of the RSD. (The national university has located most of its RCs in state capitals, whereas RCs of SOUs are in district headquarters.) Such a set up encourages development of expertise in an area of activity. However, with the growth of an institution in terms of geographical expansion, learner enrolment, number of academic programmes, and the number of regional and learner support centres, limitations such as slower response time, bottlenecks due to sequential implementation of decisions and narrow perspective among the field level functionaries, are likely to arise.

Decentralisation essentially refers to delegation of authority to execute assigned tasks and responsibilities well by the functionaries lower in the organisational hierarchy. It can help

- improve institutional response time;
- higher level officials to devote more time to plan growth strategies by off-loading routine activities;
- decision making in the context of the user; and
- encourage innovation (by field functionaries) and create a sense of belonging.

Despite such obvious advantages, decentralisation without efficient coordination and supervision may not produce desirable results; in fact prove counter-productive. The most important factors that should figure in decision making before decentralising operations are availability of appropriate human resources at the field level, work culture, etc. Against this backdrop, we analyse the issue of decentralisation in the Indian context in general and in the context of IGNOU in particular.

The *services* that can be decentralised are:

- student registration
- counselling (pre-enrolment as well as academic) including assignment evaluation
- material despatch
- examinations
- evaluation
- finance.

We now discuss these with specific reference to practices highlighting difficulties encountered in real situations.

Student registration

A general practice of ODL system is to centralise admission in formative years of an institution or when a new programme is launched. This involves

- release of advertisement;
- receipt of application forms and their processing;
- conducting entrance tests, if stipulated, and declare merit list
- issue enrolment numbers i.e. RC/SC code to students as well as RCs;

- sorting out inconsistencies and despatching regret letters;
- creating and maintaining digital database; and
- receipt and reconciliation of fee records.

As such, centralised model helps in establishing norms and speedy disposal of teething problems. However, as numbers grow, it becomes necessary to decentralise operations to RC/SCs. IGNOU decentralised student registration to RCs in 1991 with a view to develop a more learner-friendly system. RCs now perform most of the above stated functions; conduct of entrance examinations and declaration of merit list in such cases, however, continues to be centralised activity. MPBOU authorised its SCs to register students according to the approved guidelines since the beginning. But for a few, DEIs continue to follow centralised model. Unfortunately, a few single and dual mode recognised as well as private institutions have created national presence and entered into franchising arrangement with private entrepreneurs. Though there is nothing wrong with the concept and is in fact needed to meet the required educational needs of ever growing student population, its practice has serious adverse implications for quality of education. In fact, there is an immediate need to act and curb sub-standard institutions.

Counselling

Pre-enrolment counselling plays a very important role in learner support and most institutions take it rather seriously. This service is provided at the SC as well as the RCs/HQ. In addition to F2F interaction, the prospective learners are provided literature which contains information on the university, the academic programmes and learner support services. IGNOU has put in place a combination of centralised and decentralised operations. For academic counselling, invariably services of such experts are used as are identified by the SCs on the basis of prescribed qualifications and experience. These academic counsellors provide a backup support to the learners and help them in clarifying their difficulties in comprehension of the subject matter and pace their learning. For engaging academic counsellors, the bio-data are generated at the SC, sent to the RC, which, in turn, forwards the same to the respective Schools of Studies, with their recommendations, for decision. This activity is invariably time consuming, and continues to be largely centralised, in spite of arguments for and against. Some associated issues are as under.

- It has been recommended by leading distance educators that RCs should be developed as *academic-cum-administrative outposts* of the University wherein each RC could have, at least, one academic representing a School of Study at the headquarters with the specific provision of exchange posting so as to integrate field experiences in planning and development of academic programmes.
- At learner support centres located in rural and remote places, non-availability of academic resource persons as per prescribed eligibility norms comes as a major handicap for requisite quality of academic counselling. This creates a paradoxical situation where efforts to "reach the unreached" remain without primary support services. It may be worthwhile to record responses to FAQs, and a series of lectures, which could be televised and also played at such SCs particularly.

- The cost per learner of organising counselling sessions is bound to be more for low enrollment programmes or study centres located in far-flung areas. Therefore, it would be more appropriate to introduce *intensive counselling sessions*. However, its academic utility remains to be assessed particularly in the context of remote learners.
- As per the philosophy of ODL-system, counselling sessions are supposed to be problem-solving session (IGNOU, 2001a). Learners are expected to study the course material of their own, note down their doubts/difficulties and then only come to the counselling sessions to discuss their doubts/difficulties with the academic counsellors. However, learners coming with conventional mindset expect that the counsellor should lecture. This gap between the perceptions of distance educators and distance learners about expectations from the counselling session is a cause of concern and needs to be addressed.

Material despatch

IGNOU's first experience with decentralisation of an operation with direct influence on learner support services was in the year 1990 when the despatch of study materials began for a few high enrollment programmes. The decision was prompted by the fact that learners experienced difficulties in receipt of study materials in time. The decision was supposed to minimise the complaints of non-receipt or inordinate delay in the receipt of study materials and help in providing timely academic support services to learners at the study centres. Truck-loads of study materials were sent to RCs, which subsequently segregated and sent the study materials of all the study centres in the region. Learners were informed to collect study materials from their respective study centres. This operation indeed helped in timely receipt of study materials by students and timely organisation of support services at the study centres. However, after two-three cycles of decentralised distribution of study materials, the process had to be centralised for following reasons:

- increased costs in decentralised operations;
- difficulty in identifying a reliable national level agency to carry study materials from head-quarters to RCs;
- logistics problems faced by RCs to send materials to SCs;
- problem of storage of materials at the RCs/SCs;
- inconvenience to students to receive study materials at SCs.

It seems the University could not foresee operational problems before deciding on decentralising operations.

Assignment evaluation

The provision of assignment in the ODL-system has been made to serve as a teaching tool and an instrument of continuous assessment of the learners (IGNOU, 2001b). These carry substantial weightage (25 to 30 per cent) in the final grade. The preparation of the assignment, the key and the marking scheme is a centralised activity as responsibility of teachers in Schools of Studies. The evaluation of tutor marked assignments is normally decentralised to the academic counsellors attached to the SCs. For monitoring purposes, about 2% evaluated assignments are sent to the Programme/Course Coordinator(s).

In view of its function as a teaching-learning tool, evaluation of assignments is expected to be accompanied by detailed *tutor comments* so that learners know of their deficiencies and benefit from comments. In spite of orientation and re-orientation, counsellors, do not feel keen to write tutor comments with the result that assignments are reduced to testing tools. In fact, there is a vast gap between the practices and values—moral and ethical—of the learners, as evaluators, and private operations notwithstanding, systemic inadequacies, which cause unwanted delays.

In view of the above academic and operational reasons, the design, evaluation and even retention of assignments has been a subject of continuous debate in ODL institutions (Deshmukh, 2005).

Library

The library at RC or SC is provided as resource centre for distance learners. The selection of books for the libraries at SCs is done centrally by the Schools of Studies as per the requirements of the academic programmes offered. However, utilisation of this facility by learners is not very encouraging.

Electronic media

The multiple instructional package envisages e-media as an important component of learner support system. In India, exhaustive media networks have been created in view of their potential to reach the last mile, but it remains highly under utilised. Most of the DEIs continue to be first generation providers and OUs have a mix from second to fifty generation (Taylor, 1998).

Finance

For about eleven years since its inception, the operations related to finance and administration in IGNOU remained largely centralised. During these years, the University realised that these operations have direct or indirect bearing on the learner support services. As a result, with effect from 1st April, 1996 these operations were largely decentralised to the regional centres. Some features of the centralised and decentralised operations related to finance and administration which have a bearing on learner support services are shown below at Table 1.

Table 1: Decentralised operations and learner support services

Serial Number	Centralised Operations (Before 1st April, 1996)	Decentralised Operations (w.e.f 1st April, 1996)	Implications and Remarks
1.	Salaries of all members of staff of every SC were released from the headquarters	Salaries are getting released rom each RC in respect of the staff of the said RC	All related Accounts Registers are being maintained at the respective RCs.
2.	Grants for organising learner support services were released to the Study Centres from the headquarters. The bills pertaining to all learner support activities at the Study Centres were being processed at the headquarters.	Grants are received at the RCs from the Hqrs. RCs release the grant to the SCs. The bills of the SCs are processed at the RCs.	Delays in payments for various support services have got minimised; since payments are activity based and thus, through this mechanism monitoring becomes more meaningful.
3.	The appointments of all the part-time staff at the Study Centres were handled at the headquarters.	The appointment of the Coordinator of a Study Centre and the Programme -In-Charge of a Programme Study Centre are being done from the headquarters on the basis of recommendations made by the Regional Director, but the appointment of all other part-time staff at the learner support centres is being handled at the RC. of an RC over the learner	The headquarters is not in touch with the part-time staff at the learner support centres, whereas the RCs are. In case of any requirement for a exigent change or otherwise, the intervention from the direct. So it helps in RC is quicker and exercising the control support centres.

So far we have discussed different operational feature of the learner support services and we have highlighted the relative merits and demerits of decentralisation. We are living in the information age and so it would be worthwhile to discuss the role of information and communication technologies (ICT) in enhancing the quality of learner support services.

Potential of ICT and Networking to Improve Learner Support Services

Over the last decade, there has been a phenomenal increase in the number of learners in ODL system. Prior to 1985, about 9% students were studying at a distance. This number has now increased to about 24% and is poised for further growth. In absolute terms, it is about 2.5 millions which poses a big challenge to the system particularly in a scenario of increasing expectations and waning level of tolerance. To cater to such larger numbers, there is a growing realisation within the institution that efficient management of such a spread-out organisational structure calls for taking recourse to emerging technologies and innovative methods for sharing information and delivery of programmes, skills and competencies.

ICT possibilities adopted so far

The role of radio and TV for education and empowerment has been discussed elsewhere in this book and we do not intend to go into details again, except to state that availability of *Gyan Darshan* I on DTH platform has extended the reach of IGNOU to four million TV homes.

Development of media networks and institutional networking under MHRD, GoI supported N-NODE initiative of IGNOU have also been described in detail in different chapters. Suffice it to mention here that most OUs and a select few DEIs are resorting to use of World Wide Web and Internet to disseminate latest information on all aspects of learner support services, eliminating unnecessary wait. IGNOU is using its website for following services:

- checking the postal address of the learner;
- declaration of result;
- status of course material despatch;
- online submission of examination form;
- assignments of different programmes/courses and access question papers of previous term-end examinations; and
- share information on establishment of new and closure/shifting of existing Study Centres.

The answer perhaps lies in technology. Ever since, the launch of the Training and Development Communication Channel (TDCC) of IGNOU and ISRO, IGNOU has been utilising the satellite based technology to a great extent. It uses the teleconference mode through one way video and two way audio for conducting administrative as well as academic sessions. The experts deliberate from the Studio of EMPC which is uplinked to the satellite which in turn beams the signals down to all the locations which have the receiving terminals. The satellite is not choosy about the location for its downlinking and so such programmes can be viewed anywhere provided it has the reception system and a Television. The viewers can even interact with the experts sitting at the studio. IGNOU is further going to enhance satellite based teaching-learning with the launch of EduSat, the first ever satellite launched in the world solely for the purpose of education and development. We shall discuss later in this section how EduSat can help improve the quality of counselling.

Possibilities through EduSat

EduSat provides the facility of video conferencing i.e. two-way audio and two-way video. The linkage to the earth station can be established through one national beam on Ku Band, one national beam on extended C-Band and 5 regional beams on Ku Band. The regional beams have opened the possibilities of having teaching ends in any part of the country. The satellite interactive terminals can be the receiving as well as teaching ends. Leading expert and gifted teachers can now be made to interact with learners through lectures or discuss from any one of the teaching ends. All OUs have been provided access to EduSat supported network.

EduSat also provides the possibility of the use of a variety of academic resources by a teacher. The teaching as well as the receiving ends can be suitably integrated with a computer network. The facilities of multimedia like touch-screen, animation, power point, etc., can be built in into the process of teaching. In other words, teaching can be made much more enriching, enjoyable and interesting by bringing in elements other than chalk and talk.

EduSat is being utilised by different organisations for their teaching-learning transactions. For example, the IITs for Engineering Education, UGC for higher education, NCERT for school education and so on. However, for optimal use of EduSat facilities, proper planning needs to be done by bringing in the SOUs into the fold of the tele-counselling network. With the shift of focus of the ODL-based institutions towards technology mediated instructions, we can consider taking measures for networked learner support using EduSat as a vehicle.

Where to Go from Here?

The main objective of ODL system is democratisation of higher education. This has thrown open opportunities to learners of diverse academic background and locations. However, access and quality are said to be inversely proportional. Based on our IGNOU experience, we recommend the Operationalise Learner Support Services (Fig. 1).

In spite of its phenomenal growth, dynamism to adopt latest technologies for programme delivery mechanisms, we need to address the challenges of Enrollment, Retention and Acceptability (ERA).

We have outlined the possibilities of technology mediated instructions backed up by suitable networking. The tools at our disposal are indeed modern and updated. However, we have to remember that the efficacy of the tools depend on the persons who handle them. Thus we need to have continuous training and orientation of the personnel who manage the system and more than training and orientation towards the tenets of the system, we need value orientation (Bhajanananda, 1996). We exist for the learners and so we should be able to understand the value of our learner. Then only we would be able to improve the learner support services.

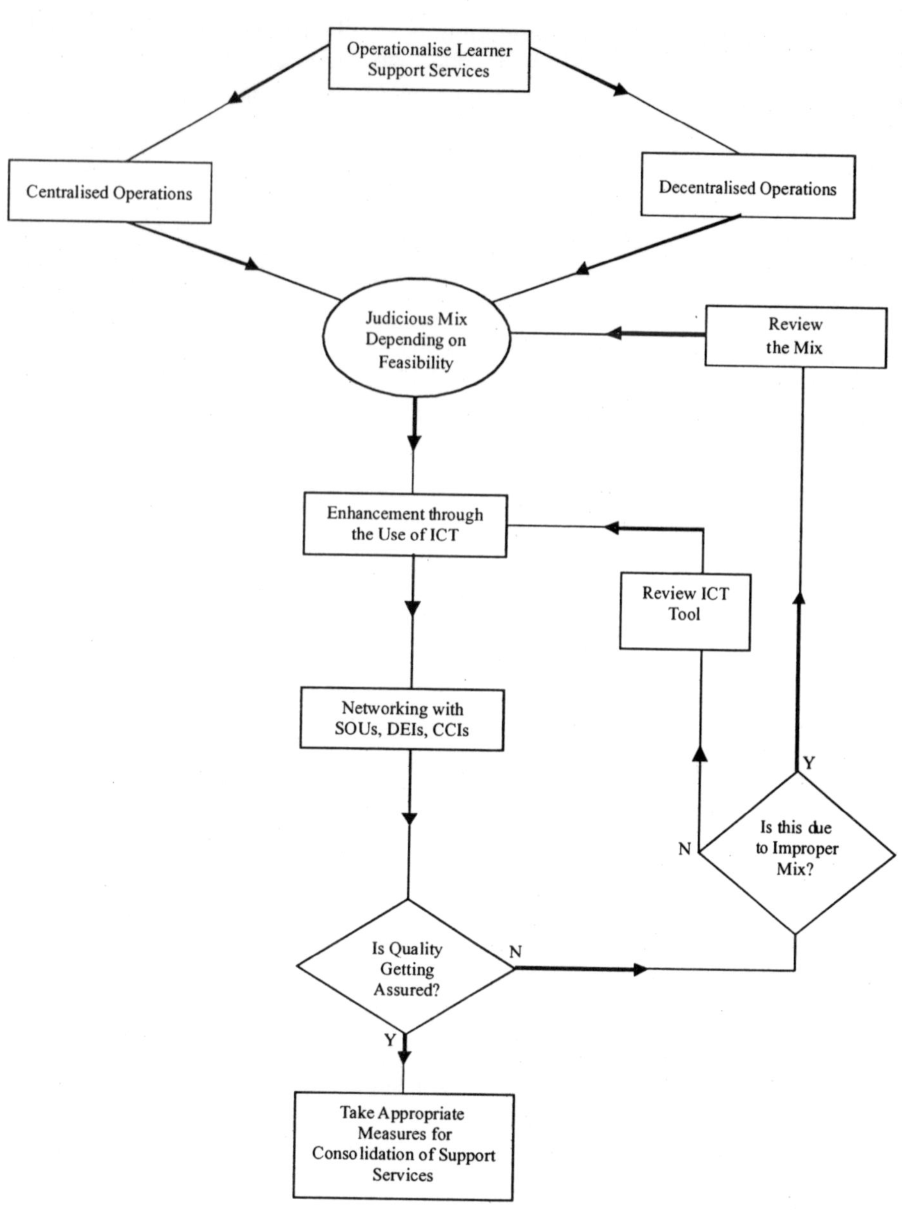

Figure 1 : Operationalise learner support services

Last but not the least, it is true that the prime concern about networking of learner support services is technology. But more than technology, networking is a concept—i.e., a philosophy of inculcation of proper spirit of teamwork between the several institutions spread across the length and breadth of our country and even beyond international boundaries. An institution may be great in one respect or the other, but when it comes to bringing them together, the synergy must work. We conclude this article by remembering Sir Arthur Eddington who said, "We often think that when we have completed our study of `one', we know all about 'two' because 'two' is 'one' and 'one'. We forget that we still have to make a study of 'and'."

Let our efforts and endeavour in establishing efficient networked learner support be a journey of the study of and so vividly portrayed by Sir Arthur Eddington.

References

Bhajanananda, S. (1996). *Values: The Key to a Meaningful Life.* Chennai: Sri Ramakrishna Math.

Deshmukh, A. (2005). Continuous assessment in open education. In Garg, S. et al., (eds.), *Four Decades of Distance Education in India: Reflection on Policy and Practice.* New Delhi: Viva Books (this book).

Garg, S. (2004). Role of distance education in widening access: the experience of IGNOU, *Staff and Educational Development International.* 8 (2-3); 85-93.

Holmberg, B. (1981). *Status and Trends of Distance Education.* London: Kogan Page.

IGNOU (2001, a). Counselling and Tutoring Services. *In Learner Support Services,* Staff Training and Research Institute of Distance Education, Indira Gandhi National Open University, New Delhi.

IGNOU (2001, b). Interaction through assignments. *In Learner Support Services.* New Delhi: IGNOU.

IGNOU (2004). *Information Base on Open Universities: Distance Education Institutions and Correspondence Course Institutions.* DEC, IGNOU.

IGNOU (2005 March). *Sixteenth Convocation: Vice Chancellor's Report.* Indira Gandhi National Open University, New Delhi.

Koul, B.N. (1989). Beyond Interaction and Independence: IGNOU Experience. Paper presented at ICDE, 1989, UKOU.

Panda, S. (2005). Higher education at a distance and national development: reflection on the Indian experience. *Distance Education* (Australia), 26 (2), 205-225.

Peters, Otto (1989). The Iceberg has not yet melted: Further Reflections on the Concept of Industrialisation and Distance Teaching. In Keegan, D (ed), *Otto Peters on Distance Education: The Industrialization of Teaching and Learning.* London: Routledge (pp. 195-209).

Taylor, J. (1998). Flexible delivery: the globalisation of lifelong learning. *Indian Journal of Open Learning*, 7(1), 55-65.

Dr. S.R. Jha is Reader in Physics, Indira Gandhi National Open University, New Delhi.
Email: srjha@ignou.ac.in

Dr. C.K. Ghosh is Director, Regional Services Division, IGNOU, New Delhi.
Email: ckghosh@ignou.ac.in

Dr. P.K. Mehta is a former Pro-Vice Chancellor, IGNOU. He also served as Director, Regional Services Division and Student Registration and Evaluation Division, IGNOU.
Email: mehta_pk@yahoo.com

22

Monitoring Learner Support Services

Sanjeev Pandey and Masood Parveez

Introduction

Development and maintenance of support services is one of the major considerations in the open and distance learning system, particularly to create, among the learners, a sense of belongingness to the institution. With the advancement in information and communication technologies, heterogeneous and diverse learner groups who are geographically scattered and having increasing expectations from all concerned, necessitate effective management of support services to ensure proper teaching and learning conditions. Satisfying the varied and at times unique needs has become a complex challenge, especially when we are functioning at the cutting edge of educational delivery. In the distance education system, as adopted by the conventional institutions, providing support services could be a limited exercise through print material, to facilitate the learners in the process of their studies. However, with the introduction of electronic media to support the learners such as audio, video tapes/discs, broadcasting, computer mediated and online learning, virtual classroom, the nature of the support service has also undergone tremendous change. Coupled with this, the continuous need of education and training, particularly in the newer areas of skill development, training and employment, emergence of newer non-conventional providers of education and training, (who are competing with the existing providers in terms of quality, standards and relevance) call for regular monitoring and adequate strengthening of the support services to ensure quality and efficiency.

Need for Student Support Services

The provisions of student support services reflect the institution's commitment to distance learners who are virtually invisible and are rarely able to speak for themselves when decisions are taken. Various factors contribute to the development of the support system of any institutional setup. Each support system, represented in any distance teaching institutions, is unique and what is provided in it depends on the target learners, the package which is employed, the delivery form, the status of the organization and the socio-economic and educational culture in which it operates (Sewart and Grugeon, 1994). Whatever support services are put in place by an institutional setup, it should

i) enable learners to effectively utilize the learning packages provided by the institution and also facilitate process of study;
ii) enable learners to make their choices and decisions by providing them proper guidance and counselling and help them through academic, administrative and information support; and
iii) provide opportunities for human interaction to reduce the learner's sense of isolation, caused mainly by deficient personal contact.

The emerging information and communication technologies have brought about significant changes in the kinds of learners served by the distance education institutions, in the delivery of programmes of study and the configuration of support services. In such a scenario, the success of student services would depend on various factors and more importantly on the success and satisfaction of the students. This requires laying down such systems wherein the learners are able to relate themselves to the institution – the system which will admit and register students, ensure delivery of the teaching materials, provide online information through web, allocation of appropriate tutors for counselling, timely receipt of the evaluated assignment responses, accurately and speedily recording the grades, change of address, timely communications about the examinations, manage assessment scores and so on (Tait, 2005).

For effective functioning of such a system, proper coordination and follow up at every level is a must, which could be achieved through regular monitoring of the support services.

The learner support system of any distance education institution encompasses a broad array of services offered to the students, which varies from institution to institution. Whatever be the level and area of operation, the services should broadly address the following needs of the learners:

i) *Information support:* Learners should be provided all necessary information prior and during the course of their studies so that they can make appropriate decisions about their studies and also have access to all necessary resources and support services. This includes information about various programmes, admission requirements, fee structure, study material, system of assessment and other support services offered by the institution.
ii) *Institutional support:* Information about the academic support: who are the academic counsellors, where the counselling sessions would be held, provisions of assignments, provision

of practicals for practical based programmes, use of electronic media such as audio, video, teleconferencing, interactive radio counselling, facilities, etc.

iii) *Learning centres:* where the students will have the access to the counsellors, library facilities, access and use of electronic equipments to supplement the learning material, submissions and evaluation of assignments, term end examinations and other general support.

iv) *Feedback:* to the students on assignment responses and other study tasks to facilitate process of study and also to reduce sense of academic isolation.

Network of Support Services

Over a period of time, different forms of distance education have emerged with different type of support systems. Sewart (IGNOU, 2000) has classified three different models of support systems. The first two models mainly rely on the print media wherein the learners are sent the printed materials which are used by them. They send back the assignment responses to the study centres for assessment and comments. In the second model, an additional input in terms of compulsory seminars have also been included. The third category is based on the UK Open University model wherein different forms of communication and support are offered to the learners who choose them as per their requirement. These include mediated or face-to-face means or combination of both through study centres, regional centres or communication networks. The Indira Gandhi National Open University (IGNOU) has adopted this model to provide highly integrated learner support services through a network of study centres, regional centres and the headquarters. One of the main objectives of IGNOU has been to provide opportunities of higher education to a large segment of population and to develop new programmes to enrol adult learners for whom access to the formal system was difficult or impossible. Over the years, IGNOU has been able to develop and offer large number of programmes of study, to a large body of learners located in different parts of the country and outside India, and has in the process emerged as the largest (open) university in the world.

The student support services at IGNOU are managed through the Regional Services Division (RSD) with the support of Regional Centres (RCs) and Study Centres (SCs). The RCs and SCs provide facilities in terms of general and programme specific information, student enrolment, academic support relating to counselling, assignment evaluation, conduct of examinations etc. Various administrative and financial parameters which have been laid down, though not directly linked with the support services, play an important role as supplementary operational linkages in strengthening the support services. Since its inception in 1985, the network of the support services of IGNOU has grown manifold from 4 RCs and 40 SCs in 1987 when it had started its operations to 57 RCs, 4 Sub RCs, 1300 SCs and 38 Partner Institutions operating in 30 countries overseas.

Regional centres act as the resource centres of the university in respective regions. It performs multifarious academic, promotional and administrative activities and are manned by full time academic, administrative and other support staff. Broadly, the functions performed relate:

- to pre-entry guidance and include general information about various programmes of the university;

- providing counselling and tutoring support; audio, video and teleconferencing support; assignment evaluation and handling, processing of grades;
- conduct of term end examinations including evaluation of project reports, particularly for the computer programmes etc.

Various academic activities undertaken relate to:

- student admission and maintenance of their records;
- orientation of the coordinators, counsellors and other functionaries in the distance education system;
- identification of institutions for setting up of SCs;
- selection of counsellors;
- development of region specific academic programmes;
- monitoring of learner support centres particularly with regard to counselling, assignment evaluation and other learner support matters;
- conduct of term end examinations; and
- organising seminars and workshops, maintenance of support services etc.

Besides, it also performs various administrative and promotional functions such as appointment of staff at the RCs and SCs, financial management, preparation of annual accounts, budgetary estimates; developing and disseminating publicity material; liaisoning with state authorities and other institutions, interactions with media etc.

SCs are the main providers of support services in the open university system which are housed in existing educational institutions of higher learning such as universities and colleges; non-governmental organizations etc. All along the endeavour of IGNOU has been to set up study centres in at least every district of the country. As specified earlier, currently their number is 1300. The SCs are the first points of contact at the local level for the prospective and enrolled students and act as a nodal institution for dissemination of information between the university and the learner. To suit the requirements of the learners as also to match the infrastructural support, various types of SCs have been evolved and set up by IGNOU, such as Regular Study Centres, Programme Study Centres, Special Study Centres, Recognised Study Centres, Work Centres and Partner Institutions. All these centres are characterised by:

a) Shared/reserved space in the host institution;
b) Minimum equipments and facilities provided by the university;
c) Local part time staff mainly drawn from the host institution; and
d) Limited working hours (for IGNOU students).

The SCs are headed by a Coordinator who is assisted by a few Assistant Coordinators (depending upon the student enrolment) and other support staff who work on part time basis. These are mainly drawn from the host institution. The major activities performed at the SCs include student guidance and counselling (both theory and practicals); appropriate usage of the audio, video and teleconferencing facilities to supplement the face to face counselling sessions; extending library services; assignment evaluation and handling; identification of counsellors and recommending their names as per requirement; undertaking promotional activities; liaisoning with regional centres and headquarters; administration and management of various activities; conduct of term end examination and entrance examination. Over the years, these activities have been decentralized, particularly to include financial management.

Monitoring of Support Services

In a comparatively short span of two decades, IGNOU has been able to establish itself with a vast network of SCs and their variants which are managed and coordinated through the regional centres and headquarters. It is evident from the fact that today IGNOU has become the largest open university in the world by providing cost effective quality education to a large section of the population including those living in far flung and remote areas. It has been recognized as a Centre of Excellence by the Commonwealth of Learning. Its total registered student enrolment is more than 1.3 millions pursuing a variety of academic programmes ranging from purely academic to predominantly vocational/professional development programmes to more general awareness programmes. To cater to such a large body of learners residing in different parts of the country and outside, with provision and active usage of multimedia including electronic media, it becomes imperative to provide effective support services to the learners to enable them to complete their programme of study. Such effectiveness could be ensured through regular monitoring, particularly in view of the learner centric approach adopted by the university, its national jurisdiction, openness and flexibility in terms of relaxed entry qualifications, duration, place and large number of widely scattered academic counsellors and functionaries who work on part time basis.

As mentioned elsewhere, the success of the university is directly linked to high quality academic programmes and more importantly to the programme delivery and support services offered to the students. This requires that the communication network between the headquarters, regional centres and study centres should enable all concerned to provide the necessary information and also the feedback for bringing about desired action and improvement. Besides, the various components of the support services, particularly at the study centres, are to be regularly reviewed to ensure its effectiveness so as to meet the objectives for which they have been provided.

What to Monitor

Among the multifarious activities that constitute the essentials of support services to be monitored, the major ones can broadly be categorized as follows:

- Academic Counselling and Student Guidance
- Dispatch of Self learning materials
- Assignment Handling and evaluation

- Support of Electronic media
- Examination and Evaluation
- Student Administration and Financial Management

Academic counselling and student guidance

Academic counselling is one of the crucial components of the student support services provided by any distance education system. Its importance lies in the fact that the problems arising out of self-instructional material and support of other non-print media are solved through human contact during the counselling session which facilitates the process of study of the learners. The human element introduced through the counselling sessions enable the learners to overcome the barriers related to study skills, orient the learners to the system of distance education, familiarize them with the subject matter and resolve even the non academic problems that act as an obstacle in the process of study. As stated earlier, counselling is not restricted to the subject matter, but it has to be related to the general guidance and advice to the students about the choice of the courses, follow up activities to be undertaken for successful completion of the programme. The main activities that need to be monitored relate to:

- Whether the counselling sessions are planned and held as per the prescribed norms, guidelines and schedules of the university;
- Whether the counsellors engaged are approved by the university or not;
- How well the counsellors are acquainted to the system of distance education, his/her knowledge of course material, assignment contents, use of audio/video to supplement counselling;
- Other qualitative skills, including communication, type and level of interaction with the learners etc.;
- Continuity, commitment and willingness of the counsellors.

Dispatch of self learning materials (SLM)

Despite the advancements in the information and communication technologies and their impact on the institutional systems as adopted by the distance education system, print medium continues to occupy a central position. Accordingly, these learning materials are to be planned, designed and developed in such a way so as to facilitate the process of individualized learning, specially keeping in view the profile of the learners and practice of the institutions. In particular, a decision is required on the type of modules, printed blocks(s) in each course, programme guide, A/V cassettes/CD ROMs etc. to be sent to the individual learners and/or to be used at SCs/RCs (Bates, 1993).

Dispatch of the learning material to the learners, as per the academic schedule of the institutions is of great importance. Even well designed, high quality self learning materials with exhaustive content coverage will loose its significance if it does not reach the learners in time. To ensure this, there has to be an effective planning and its implementation for production, distribution and inventory management, to minimize the possibility of delayed/non receipt of material by the learners. An equally important factor is availability of the study material and other support material (like programme guide, manuals, project guide etc.) at the SC for use of the counsellors and students.

Needless to mention that with the changes/modifications in the procedures, schedule, norms and other conditions, these are to be incorporated in the support material to facilitate the procedural requirement both to the study centre functionaries, counsellors and the students. Accordingly the important activities to be monitored are:

- Dispatch of study material and the assignments to the enrolled students, newly activated study centres and replenishment of the material to the RCs;
- Proper inventory management to be linked with the current enrolment and future enrolment of students to ensure timely availability of study material;
- Timely transmission of the admission data to the Material Production and Distribution Division.
- Printing and availability of study material from the concerned School of study.

Assignment handling and evaluation

Assignments in the open university system constitute an integral component of the overall programme package, as they form a considerable proportion of final grades, varying from 25% to 30% of the total weightage. It is an important tool which enables the teacher to measure the level of the understanding of the course content by the learners. Assignments provide the learners an opportunity to converse with the tutor, to receive advice on their problems and to confirm their understanding of the problem (Lewis and Spencer, 1986). In fact, assignment submission has been regarded as a critical mechanism for prompting and pacing individual's study and acts as a vehicle for feedback and dialogue with the tutor. Assignment turnaround time and reflection of its grades are two important aspects that need to be regularly monitored, to gauge the effectiveness of the support services. One of the deficiencies faced by the distance education system is the delay in feedback, owing to slowness in the communication process as also the usage of appropriate comments on the written work of the learner to highlight the strengths and weaknesses of the response. Since assignments are an important part of the overall evaluation process of the open university system, it must be ensured that these are sent as per the prescribed procedure as also the time schedule specified. The general assessment of the assignments also help in developing, modifying and reviewing the system to find out whether the educational objectives match the learning experiences of the students. Accordingly, it acts as an important mechanism for collecting information and making appropriate decisions that could influence future institutional policies and decisions. Some of the important issues to be followed up relate to:

- Timely receipt of assignments by the students and the SCs;
- Submission of completed assignments by the students at the SCs as per the prescribed schedule;
- Evaluation of assignments and its dispatch to the students as per the laid down norms including the time frame;
- Appropriateness of the grades with justifications duly elaborated in terms of tutor comments to effect improvement in the learning process;
- Data entry of the assignments at the study centre, its dispatch to the RCs for onward transmission to the headquarters as per the pre-determined schedule of the university;
- Correct reflection of the grades so received in the grade cards of the students.

Support of electronic media

Media selection and its use is yet another important decision to be made by the open university, particularly in view of the teaching functions it performs, as also its role in supporting the self learning material and the face to face counselling sessions. Advancing and disseminating learning and knowledge by a diversity of means including the use of communication technology is one of the main objectives of IGNOU.

Keeping this in view, the multimedia packages provisioned by the University for the learners include audio/video tapes/discs, interactive radio counselling, one way video two way teleconferencing, online content delivery and the recently launched two way audio and two way video connectivity at RCs and SCs through EduSat. Each of these are provided individually or in combination or complementary to one another.

The delivery of the course content through these media has to be such that it complements the learning through the study material and contact sessions to enable the learners understand the subject matter properly. Some of the areas that deserve coordination and follow up are as follows:

- Availability and use of audio/video tapes at the SCs as per the courses activated and also the University guidelines.
- Advance information to the students about the forthcoming interactive radio programmes/ teleconferencing sessions with courses/areas to be discussed.
- Availability of the infrastructural support along with staff to support the EduSat terminals and the teleconferencing sessions.
- Upkeep and maintenance of the audio/video, teleconferencing, equipments use of audio/ video.
- Encouragement to students for use of audio/video and for participation in the teleconferencing under the guidance of the concerned counsellor.

Examination and evaluation

Evaluation of the learners is an integral part of any educational system to ascertain the level of understanding and also assessment of their performance. Examinations are essential instrument for measuring and improving the quality and quantity of learning. IGNOU has been able to design, develop and implement an examination system, which distinguishes it in terms of scale and scope, adopted by similar other institutions. It follows a three pronged strategy of evaluation:

- Self assessment by the learners through self check exercises provided in the study material;
- Continuous assessment through the assignments, project reports, practicals, log books, workshops and seminars etc. as per the requirement of the programme of study.
- Term end examinations, held twice a year in June and December, taken by the students at the end of the academic session and within the maximum stipulated time frame for completion of the programme.

Proportionate weightage is allocated for final assessment of the student. On successful completion, the student is awarded a certificate/diploma/degree. As per the inbuilt flexibility provided in the system, the students have the freedom to appear in the examination at any of the activated examination centres.

The major activities to be monitored relate to:

- Timely dispatch of the hall tickets to the learners with correct examination centre, courses opted for. Adequate arrangement to be made at the regional centres for issue of the admit cards.
- Conduct of examination at various examination centres as per the prescribed procedures, guidelines and norms.
- Recruiting support staff for effective conduct of examination.
- Ensuring timely dispatch of the answer sheets and reports to the Student Registration and Evaluation (SR&E) Division.
- Undertaking surprise visits to the examination centres to ensure regularity, order and adherence to the university rules and norms.
- Maintaining effective coordination and communication with examination centre and SR&E Division.
- Turnaround time of the evaluation of assignments and project reports received at the SCs/RCs with correct grading and appropriate tutor comments.
- Processing of grades of evaluated assignments projects etc and their transmission to regional centre/ SR&E Division for its timely reflection in the final grade card.

Student administration and financial management

It includes various important activities other than those specified above which are performed at the RCs and SCs and which have direct implication on the support services offered to the students. These mainly pertain to the following:

Admission and re-registration of student

These are performed at the RC and is one of the most important activities which calls for adequate arrangements, meticulous planning and effective implementation, and:

- Ensuring that admission and re-registration activities are done as per the schedule, eligibility criteria, guidelines and procedures of the university.
- Scrutiny of the admission forms, finalizing of admission after removing the errors, transmitting the data to the headquarter, SCs and the students on confirmation of their admission.
- Maintaining student record, effecting changes in the addresses, SC and RC and maintaining proper follow up.
- Arranging induction programmes for the newly admitted students and orientation programme(s) for the counsellors, functionaries of the RC/SC to acquaint them with the system of distance education.

Staff development

Training and staff development is an integral part of the overall objective of the IGNOU. Accordingly, training programmes should be developed particularly to acquaint the functionaries in the distance education skills and techniques by:

- Organising regular training and orientation of the counsellors, coordinators and other functionaries working in IGNOU for enabling them to render effective services.
- Determining training needs, identifying participants, developing suitable training material, planning and organizing the training and orientation programme.

General administration

- Ensuring availability of the manpower both at the RC and SC for providing adequate services.
- Maintenance of equipments including audio, video, teleconferencing which effectively contributes towards the academic support to the students.
- Ensure proper library facilities and its use at the SC.
- Ensuring availability of relevant study material, information leaflets, programme details.
- Regular stock verification.

Financial management

- Adherence of procedural formalities and schedule for the maintenance of accounts as per laid down financial/accounting code of the University.
- Various sources of receipt of funds such as fee realisation, sale of forms, grants, special advances etc. to be remitted/utilized as per the laid down norms.

- Processing of recoupment bills received from the SCs, as per the rules, particularly in relation to the number of students enrolled, norms of payment to the counsellors, assignment evaluation and handling and other practical components.
- Incurring expenditure as per the delegated authority and also the well-defined heads of accounts/expenditure.
- As far as possible, various payments to be made through cheque only.

Monitoring Mechanism

To ensure effectiveness of the operational efficiency of the University, various mechanisms have been developed. These have been gradually modified and improved over the years to ensure effective outreach system and student support service, with a view to make the RCs and SCs more responsive to the changing needs and requirements of the diverse learners.

The monitoring of the support services in the university is mainly undertaken at the headquarters level and at the RC level. At the headquarters, a task force has been constituted which regularly reviews the working of the support system of the university. Besides, there is a mechanism of monthly monitoring report through which information on various aspects of the support system are obtained from the RCs. The details of the different mechanisms are given below.

Monitoring at headquarter level

Task force

The major objective of the working of the task force is framing appropriate operational guidelines to ensure availability of the requisite facilities in terms of infrastructural and human support so as to ascertain optimal efficiency of the support system with broad monitoring mechanism. The task force mainly reviews the operations of the student support services and suggests ways and means for improving the delivery system and also to achieve the desired objectives as per the prescribed procedure and time schedule. It also suggests measures to be taken for streamlining various operations across academic schools and functional divisions, to achieve greater efficiency and speed of the different activities, which influence the support services. Effective utilization of the electronic media particularly tele-conferencing, EduSat, Gyan Vani programmes etc. are also suggested for making the system more receptive to the requirements of the learners.

The major activities reviewed by the Task Force, mainly relate to admission and re-registration of the students, production and dispatch of study material, incorporation of the assignment grades received from the study centres, result declaration of the term end examination. Besides it also suggests measures to be initiated including operational strategies for resolving the bottlenecks which affect the support services and to make it more responsive to the needs of the students.

Monthly monitoring report

To review the functioning of the support services at the RCs and SCs, a mechanism of monthly monitoring report has been developed, incorporating various parameters of the learner support. These reports are regularly sent by the RCs by 10th of every month, which are assessed in terms of support services and various other factors. Assessment is also done of the different issues, vis-à-vis their requirement from concerned school/division. These monthly monitoring reports enable the headquarters to get necessary feedback from the regional centres and study centres and also the clarification and support required from the schools/divisions in resolving different issues to facilitate functioning and also to strengthen the learner support activities.

The report provide inputs on different academic, administrative and financial matters which has bearing on the working of RCs and SCs, as also its effectiveness in terms of the learner support system. Different pre-defined/determined parameters that have been incorporated in the report mainly relate to enrolment of the students in the current and previous cycle, activation of new SCs/programmes in the existing centres, a detailed status of the counselling proposed and held including practical sessions, audio/video sessions, number of assignments received and evaluated, interactive radio counselling sessions, working status of the teleconferencing centres, availability of the manpower at the RCs, number of queries received about the programmes and schedule of the university etc. It also includes information about select administrative mattes including coordination and management of SCs; expenditure incurred on the counselling and assignment evaluation and various administrative heads such as daily wages, tele-communication, travelling allowance, conveyance, medical reimbursement, etc., which has implications on support services. Besides, it reflects grants received, the amount of expenditure incurred, the amount of fee received and remitted to the headquarters etc. There is a separate column wherein various measures that have been initiated by the RCs for improving the support system and the issues that are pending at the headquarters. This report is processed on the basis of the information received and the action desired at the headquarters. Various pending issues pertaining to different schools/divisions are sent to them with a request to expedite the pending matters and also to specify and clarify measures for bringing about necessary changes in the support services. Based on the feedback received, necessary information/communication is sent to the concerned regional centres for taking corrective actions and also to initiate activities as proposed.

The information received particularly on matters such as enrolment pattern, expenditure pattern, various pending issues etc. are used to assess the performance of the RCs and its learner support centres in terms of the support services. The University has been able to work out per student cost of the programme delivery and also the expenditure incurred. Over a period of time, with more of decentralisaiton of the activities at the RC level, these monitoring reports have enabled the university to obtain information about the various aspects of learner support including constraints which it faced in providing the requisite services at the field level, and the corrective actions required for effecting necessary improvement. This calls for the RC to streamline its functions and also to become more responsive to the needs and requirements of the learners vis-à-vis their role in providing effective support services. Notwithstanding the measures taken by the University to strengthen the support system, the issues relating to the non-receipt of the study material, non-reflection of the assignment grades, non-declaration of the result, non/delayed transfer of the student records pertaining to inter-regional transfer etc. are the ones which assume more importance in terms of their direct bearing on the effective support system as such these are resolved on priority basis.

Zonal meeting

These interactive meetings of the Vice-Chancellor, head(s) of the schools/divisions and the Regional Directors constitute a critical component of the monitoring of delivery mechanism and services provided by the university. These act as an important platform for assessing the working of the support systems of the university and also for bringing about desired changes and the initiatives to be taken at the field level. All the RCs of the university are divided into 5 distinct zones, which participate in zonal meetings and present their status reports. Various issues are discussed in detail and many pending matters are resolved on the spot. Such meetings give an opportunity to each of the participants, to adopt better practices initiated by other RCs and also for effecting necessary improvement in the support systems.

Monitoring at regional centre level

Monthly report

Just like the RCs send monthly reports to the Headquarters, the SCs are also required to submit a report. A major portion of the inputs which are provided in the monthly monitoring report prepared by RCs, are received from the SCs in the specified format, on matters relating to academic counselling, assignment evaluation and expenditure incurred under different academic and administrative heads. These information also provide inputs for initiating various corrective measures, particularly with regard to counselling scheduled and held, assignments received and evaluated, use of audio/video etc. to improve support services in the region.

Visit to the learner support centres

Regular inspection and surprise visits of the academic staff working at the RC is one of the major monitoring exercises undertaken by the RCs to ensure proper working of SCs and also effective utilisation of the support systems for the learners. These visits give first hand information, through the interaction with the students, the academic counsellors and also the SC functionaries, about the prescribed schedules and standards, as also its implementation. Inspection of the various records, particularly about counselling, assignments, cash book etc. enables the RC functionary to verify the support services extended to the students as per the prescribed norms of the university. Based on the feedback, these visits facilitate on the spot corrective actions particularly on various matters. As have been specified earlier, these visits, act as a strengthening force for the support to the learners and gives an opportunity to understand whether the aims and objectives of the support system are being realized or not through efficient and effective usage of the available resources including ICT based facilities.

Constraints and Implications of Monitoring

Given the integrated linkages which the academic functions of the University have with other related activities, developing a system to regularly monitor the support services becomes imperative. Various mechanisms including the feedback reports that have been developed and put in use for monitoring purposes, mainly measure the pre-defined/determined activities that have been achieved or the shortfall in their achievements. These do not reflect the possible causes of the delays/ factors that have been responsible for the inefficiencies in the support system.

Considering the nature of the open and distance education system wherein various academic, administrative including production and distribution related activities are interlinked and integrated, basic understanding of inefficiencies in the support system arise from the procedural requirements, which at times act as constraints in effective support services. This mainly stems from the fact that IGNOU utilizes team approach for planning, designing and development of the course material and various supplementary learning (aids, audio/video etc.) using various mechanisms for quality control. Hence, the emphasis is mainly on the counselling, evaluation and other support systems which directly influence the effectiveness, efficiency and quality of student support services. Various factors such as non-availability of desired material both hard copy and audio/ video, lack of timely communication about the changes effected in the schedule, particularly at the SCs, lack of appropriately trained manpower having sensitivity to the requirement of the learners etc. acts as an impediment in effective support services to the learners. As specified earlier, the support service at the study centres is mainly provided by the teachers working in the conventional system, that too on part time basis. Even though such teachers are motivated and have also been oriented to the system of open and distance education however, it has been experienced that problems related to their commitment in terms of quality and reliability, particularly in regard to assignment evaluation does affect the smooth services. At times, lack of infrastructural facilities particularly with increased enrolment also causes the problems in providing appropriate support services.

Over the years, with the expansion in the operations of the University in terms of student enrolment, number of programmes on offer, number of leaner support centres, the monitoring of the support services have become more critical, so as to make it quick efficient and effective in responding to the needs of the learner.

As mentioned elsewhere, learner support service includes not only availability of high quality academic programmes, but also ensuring that the students receive study materials in time, are assessed and evaluated with in the stipulated time frame, and are provided academic guidance and tutoring support through range of media, including face to face. It should also facilitate resolution of non-academic problems which might affect the study of the individuals.

On the other hand use of ICT based techniques in providing support services have assumed greater importance, over the years, particularly tele-conferencing programmes that have been effectively supplementing the face to face sessions. Further, with the launch of EduSat, its extensive reach and connectivity, can further improve quality of education. It has the advantage to reach out to a large segments of learners, simultaneously satisfying their needs with more focused approach. This has proved to be a very effective strategy in providing support to the students. Its capabilities to enrich the existing curriculum and pedagogy at different levels by employing the available technologies, including virtual classrooms, video on demand etc. add new dimensions in strengthening the support system of the University.

To achieve more efficiency and effectiveness, the work procedures as also the work ethics need to be changed, to make the support system more receptive to the ever-changing requirement of the learners. Enough provisions should be made for incorporating various administrative and financial considerations for facilitating the support service to the students.

It should also be understood that the problems of the distance learners are unique and require to be handled differently, particularly in view of the environmental factors and external system on which IGNOU depends. Efficacy of the delivery system will greatly depend on not only on efficient modes of providing services but also on the individuals who in majority of the cases are not full time staff of the University.

Conclusion

Student support services are the most vital component of any open and distance education system. It includes wide range of academic and other related activities. The support services should not only be responsive to the needs of the distance learners but should also be accessible and usable. Fulfilling the learner support services needs of diverse distance learners has indeed become a challenging task faced by the distance education systems, particularly when the institutions are increasingly trying to provide increased access to the educational opportunities particularly to those living in far flung and remote areas through extensive use of technology based/mediated strategies. In view of these facts, monitoring of the support services has to be a continuous and ongoing exercise on the part of the institution, which could bring about constant improvement through innovations in the support services.

References

Bates, T. (1993). Theory and practice in the use of technology in distance education. In D. Keegan (Ed.), *Theoretical Principles of Distance Education*. London and New York: Routledge.

IGNOU (2000). *Support Services: Need and Mechanisms,* ES-313: *Learner Support Services*, Block -1. Staff Training and Research Institute of Distance Education, Indira Gandhi National Open University.

Lewis, R. & Spencer, D. (1986). *What is Open Learning*. London: CET.

Sewart, D. & Grugeon, D. (eds.) (1994). *Developing Distance Education*. Oslo: ICDE.

Tait, Alan (2005). Management and services to students. In S. Panda (Ed.), *Planning & Management in Distance Education*. London and New York: Routledge Falmer.

Dr. Sanjeev Pandey is Deputy Director (Vice Chancellor's Office), Indira Gandhi National Open University, New Delhi.

Dr. Masood Parveez is Regional Director, Delhi Regional Centre I, Indira Gandhi National Open University, New Delhi.

23

Online Learning Support

V.S.P. Srivastava, Shashi Bhushan and Bhupesh Khatri

Introduction

Technological developments such as internet have revolutionized new and innovative approaches to learning. This has resulted in providing online learning opportunities which have had phenomenal growth in popularity within a very short period of time. When the widely known TCP/IP protocols were invented, such a huge user community of internet was not even imagined. Today almost each and every computer in the world has access to internet for one or the other application access. Every year, more and more institutions are offering online programmes at certificate, diploma, graduate and postgraduate levels. Much of this increase is due to the demands of new sets of skills, more job opportunities, availability of huge bandwidth, availability of PCs at low cost and emergence of a large online learning community.

In the context of online learning, all teaching and learning frameworks must address several issues: skills to be imparted, instructional design, quality of support service, learner' access capability (with internet bandwidth, PC), and finally the cost. But the most critical component of an online programme is a learner support system based on good technologies and infrastructure. Some research studies have come to the conclusion that poor delivery mechanism and support services decrease the motivational level of learners. Acknowledging the fact that these services should be convenient and affordable, easily understood and able to engage students with interactive learning in more ergonomic way, it has become apparent that online learning support is an essential component in the educational experience of distance learning. We describe our proposed framework of online learning support and its components; followed by presentation of some case studies, and a summary.

Online Learning Support Framework

The framework for online learning support may be broadly put into three main modules of the integrated delivery system. These modules may be: online delivery and services, course design, and technology to implement the entire system. The integrated delivery system should be able to support the course delivery, administration and learner support as shown in Fig. 1.

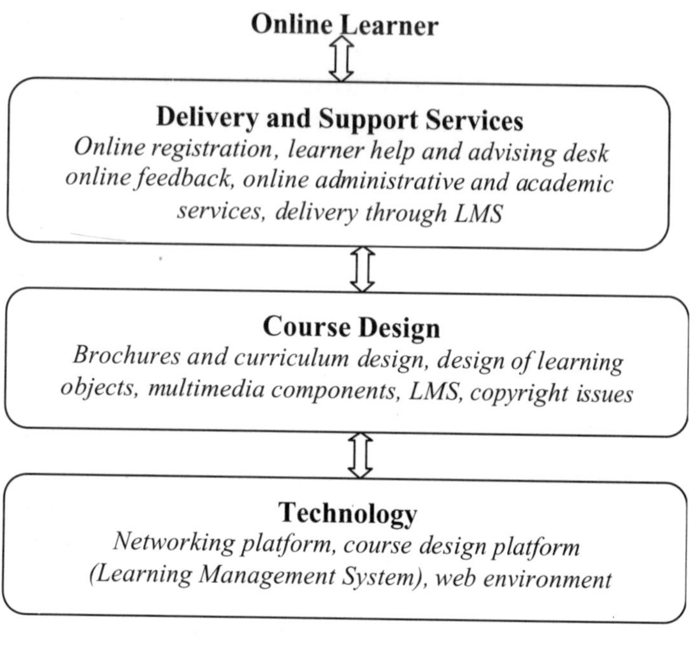

Figure 1: Online learning support framework

Technology

Online learning is gradually becoming bandwidth-intensive. A robust connection to the internet and any of web services will be required to assure prompt response and reliable service. The infrastructure for successful online education involves three major components: reliability, fast connectivity and backup support. First, the institution hosting the coursework must have adequate and reliable servers. Second, the internet connectivity from the host servers must have adequate speed and capacity for the usage it will receive. Connections for students and teachers must also be adequate for the delivery of the content. High speed modem connections are essential for courses that include streaming media or large files to be downloaded. Unreliable internet connections are inadequate for any content. Finally, the desktop computers for participants and teachers must be adequate to display the content, perform "plug-ins" for multimedia, and operate reliably. The system must support backup facility to minimize down-time and eliminate loss of data.

If a server was to crash in the middle or end of a semester and all data were to be lost, it would amount to a disaster for the students, the faculty and the institution. It would be the equivalent of the classroom building and the faculty offices burning down, incinerating all of the grades and records of the term. Back-up systems are just as necessary as fire alarms and sprinkler systems.

Another option is to outsource the servers and their support. The advantages of outsourcing are many for smaller online programmes. With 50 or fewer classes in online mode, this option may be the most cost effective and reliable. A few personnel must be however hired, less bandwidth to the internet will be required, and round-the-clock service should be ensured. Larger online programmes are likely to find that they can be provided with a more efficient and responsive way when organized and monitored internally.

Web developers are needed to create the online classrooms and website designs to support the online classes. Even when faculty use "turnkey" online classroom packages, web developers are needed to customize some of the materials that are to be placed in the virtual classroom. The web developer can build the linkages from the online classroom to the campus, web pages and other ancillary online support sites.

All such support services require a good network set up covering all locations and spreads of the institution offering online programmes. Today when giga bit connectivity is readily available, campus LANs and further links to extranets must have good backbone supported with high end switches for effective and quality on line learner support.

Course design

Online education is widely considered as learner-centric education and the classroom education is generally regarded as instructor-centric education. Due to shift in the learning paradigm from classroom education to online education, the role of the instructor has become more of a facilitator and moderator. The online courseware, as such, should offer a wide variety of learning opportunities for discussion (i.e. asynchronous and synchronous), collaboration, motivation and self engagement. It must include diversified learning methods: deep learning, critical learning, higher order learning and possible learning.

The courseware that holds the elements of content, assessment tools, and interactivity tools together is a critical element of a successful online course. For example, the ability to archive chat and threaded discussion is needed so that instructors can evaluate student work and students can reflect and process the discussion. Opening some content in new browser windows should be thoughtfully considered as part of the design process. Assessment tools that provide feedback, allow for single or multiple attempts, and control over whether assessments are timed or untimed are all important features. Multimedia should be used to address various learning styles. Also, audio narration of on-screen demonstrators go quite far beyond mere text explanations of some process or phenomenon. The software used to host the site must be capable of working with these various media.

Using Learning Management System (LMS) is the current trend for design, planning, management and administration of online courseware. There are several basic options available when deciding upon implementing LMS. These are:

- Purchasing an off-the-shelf LMS and using it as it is.
- Purchasing an off-the-shelf LMS and modifying it to suit the requirements.
- Having an LMS custom-developed for your needs.
- Developing your own LMS based on the architecture of the 'open knowledge' initiative.

Of course, the best option will depend upon the budget, project timing, how closely an off-the-shelf LMS programme supports unique needs of overall e-learning plan. Copyright issues also have to be addressed while planning for the online project.

Online delivery and support services

The success of online learning model depends on reliable, secure and good support services. We broadly categorize into two types of support services:

i) Essential support services
ii) Additional support services

Essential support services

It starts even before enrolment of students into an online programme. Support required during admission, evaluation, and even after completion of the degree. The very first contact a prospective student will have with an institution will be through the institution's website. It is essential that this website should invite to the prospective students and that it provides them with all of the information that they need to enrol into a programme.

The university catalogue and the application brochures for different programmes must be kept on-line which will work as an informal contact between the university and the prospective students. Email facilities must be there for these students too. Secured, consistent, and environment with full integrity should be created to support the online delivery of grades and transcripts to students. In the on-campus education system, students can merely drop in the registrar's office to obtain a transcript of their coursework. It should be just as easy, or easier, for online students to get the same service.

Many students want to see the university campus virtually before they make a final choice for admission. The campus website, if supported with a link to slide show for the campus, will help in gathering further information by the interested and making them feel ease about taking admission to the institution. After admission is finalised, the online class schedule (chat session etc.) for relevant materials (courseware, powerpoint slides, audio/video lectures) must be posted in advance. The facilities for online submission of assignment and all results in respect of term end, practicals, viva-voce etc. should also be made possible through the site.

Additional support services

Online students at many universities pay more tuition fee than on campus students. But in terms of facilities, the campus students get much more. Of course, some of these facilities such as, swimming pool, gymnasium, healthcare etc. cannot be translated into online services. Also, as it is observed these days, some university sites have started offering services such as online placement assistance, career advice, and online libraries. The on-campus system that provides a wide range of student services is likely to be at competitive advantage. In sum, all of the interactions between the students and the university should be supported through online.

Case Study – Indira Gandhi National Open University (IGNOU)

In open and distance learning (ODL), efforts are generally made to provide easy access to the learners at their access points. Their queries pertaining to programmes on offer, delivery methods, admission procedure, pre and post examination activities are the main concerns. The delivery mechanisms as such must be able to address these issues generally. Our experience in providing such facilities through information technology at the Indira Gandhi National Open University – the single largest open university of the world – is of concern in this section. It is widely accepted that IT has been playing a significant role in making open and distance learning a success. IT clubbed together with communication technology has a great potential in providing opportunity to one and all living even in the most remote area world wide. Internet applications have further brought laurels to the system giving ample opportunities in bridging the gap of distance. As such, it is observed that information and communication technology (ICT) has overcome the limitations of the existing models of teaching including ODL.

An open and distance delivery system has a number of activities required to be performed for the learners in terms of:

- Admission
- Performance evaluation
- pre/post examination
- Academic courseware preparation and distribution
- Multimedia production and communication facilities

Prior to admitting learners it is required to provide answers to relevant questions pertaining to 'what and how' about 'programmes on offer' by the ODL institution. In order to have an effective and efficient system for information flow, better management control and quality student service, a combination of local and wide area networks is essential. The Indira Gandhi National Open University (IGNOU) is the single largest open university in the world today, having more than 1.3 million students on its roll including newly admitted and re-registered students. Its regional centres, study centres, and regional computing centres all over India and in other countries come together through internet-based applications and through IGNOU web site which is extensively rich in providing both static and dynamic information. Large databases with enriched metadata are maintained in-house centrally at the computer division for providing student support services.

Challenges in the ODL system

The very first challenge is that of bridging the gap between the education seeker and the education provider. Once students take admission, despatch of material to the right address at the right time, i.e., well before conducting counselling sessions, is the next challenge. The mode for delivery of material and other information to the students must be efficient enough. Bringing out regular updated reading material in terms of booklets, multimedia CDs, web contents etc. are another challenge which needs to be addressed time and again in the system as students are scattered over various corners of the country, including remote areas. They may not have access to any library system - whether online or offline - in their neighbourhood. Hence, the reading material has to be self-explanatory and it has to be presented and made available in concise and precise manner. To meet such a requirement, the institution needs to have a dynamic system material generation/ development and delivery.

Performance evaluation in terms of quizzes, assignments and semester-wise examination are required to be carried out in each semester for meeting quality standards. Evaluation activities, as such, are a further challenge in the ODL system. Maintaining huge and large data base of students for their admission, re-registration, pre- and post-examination activities, evaluation etc. are aspects which require equal attention for maintaining, monitoring and managing quality education. Maintenance of meta data has to be sufficient enough for meeting all the requirements - starting from day-wise operational information to MIS and then for meeting the requirements of the apex decision-making body at the top management level.

Communicating with learners is another aspect to be looked into through a combination of conventional postal system, e-mailing/messaging, and the institutional web site. With e-mailing becoming popular it is yet another challenge to address queries, feed back etc. on-time using the state-of-the-art technology. Setting up the virtual campus, its maintenance and management has to be efficient enough to dynamic, interact with the learners time and again for online education, discussion, chat, and feedback. Technological support should pay, at the same time, enough attention towards their upgrading and maintenance.

Meeting the challenges

At IGNOU, steps have been taken to have quality delivery mechanism for all the processes governing various activities. After the students are admitted at about 50 regional centres country-wide, they are allotted to a study centre in their neighbourhood at the nearest location. For the IT stream, there are regional computing centres to take care of online courses in terms of course delivery and for practical sessions including for other courses.

IGNOU students are from various background – some may be working on transferable job, some with parents transferable job, some may be married female students while pursuing the course. Hence there is the requirement of "address changes" around the year. Similarly when Term End Examination (TEE), at the end of each semester, is held in June and December every year, results are required to be put on the IGNOU website *www.ignou.ac.in* so that students could know about their performance from any where they have access to the internet. Prior to conduct of the TEE, Hall Ticket for appearing in the examination is required to be made available (also) online. Input to the Hall Ticket comes from the prior submitted Examination Form provision for which has also been provided through the IGNOU website apart from the facility of off-line form submission. Student Grade Card which reflects all the courses in terms of marks/grade obtained is also available to students through the site. Similarly when Entrance Tests are conducted as a pre-requisite to taking admission in programmes like Management, Bachelor in Education etc. test results are required to be put on website too.

Having seen the enormous requirement towards student support services, the university's Computer Division took up the task of developing web-based solutions. The very first attempt in meeting such requirements was towards grade card declaration and address checking. Because of popularity of the IGNOU website, requests started pouring in for further coverage in terms of wider applications for student support services. The next application was for declaring the term end examination result which had also higher website hits. Apart from the above applications, such online support services at present cover material despatch to the students, hall tickets, entrance tests, convocation list, online examination form submission, assignment results, practical/ project results and notices to students for various meetings/seminars/counsellings/practical examinations/schedules/chats etc.

Metadata is maintained separately for student support services in the Microsoft environment. Integrated modules talk to each other for data sharing. In case of student record about nine million of data records are available in database tables. Programme-wise data base is maintained by the SR&ED which is responsible for admission and re-registration. Once data is compiled it is used for further processing to meet various requirements and for further uploading to the IGNOU website.

It has been in the past observed that hits relating to online 'examination form submission' and 'term end examination result' are of the tune of about 60 to 70 thousands per day in peak periods i.e. around March and September each year. It is found through analysis that online form submission for TEE contribute to the tune of about one-third of the total applications (forms) for the examination hall tickets. The most popular application for online support, found on the basis of the website hits, was the one for TEE results which had about 76% of students appearing at TEE. This was, however, only 30% for the online submission of examination forms. Students who check their grade card constitute about 63% of the total students appearing for the TEE. Data pertaining to material dispatch/return/re-sent suggests that about 40% of the students registered through fresh admission in various new programme and re-registered for the ongoing programmes had visited the site. In December 2004 TEE a total of 2,11,472 students had appeared of which 1,59,998 (76%) checked their term end results through the website and 1,28,184 (63%) checked their grade card. A total of 84% online filing of term-end examination form was towards four programs of studies only: Master in Computer Applications (39%), Bachelor in Computer Applications (20%), Management Programme (13%), and Bachelor Degree Programme (12%). As such, the remaining programmes being offered by IGNOU had only 16% contribution towards usage of this particular online support.

Figures 1-4 provide visual idea about web services usage. These services are being provided online through various dynamic pages which connect to IGNOU virtual database.

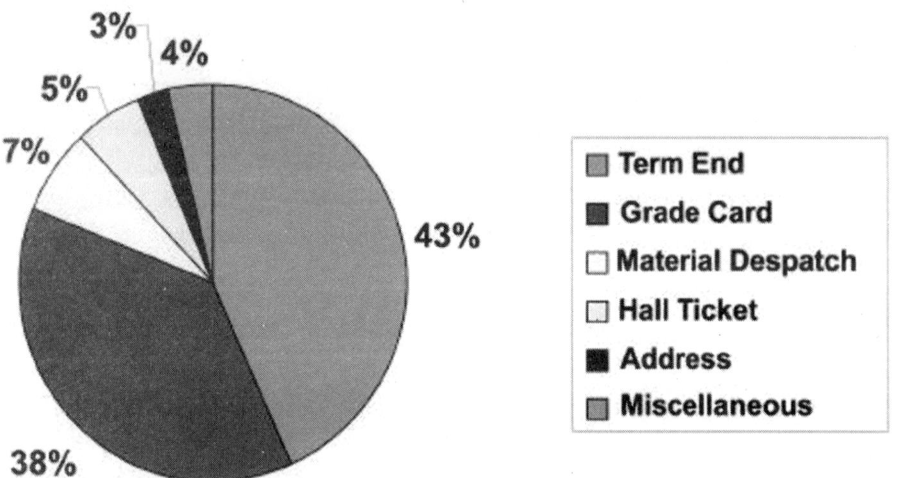

Figure 1: Web hits for student support (January – July) 2005

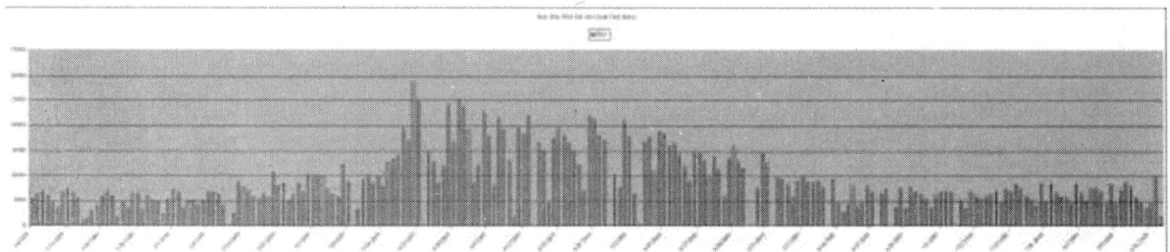

Figure 2: Date-wise web hits for grade card status

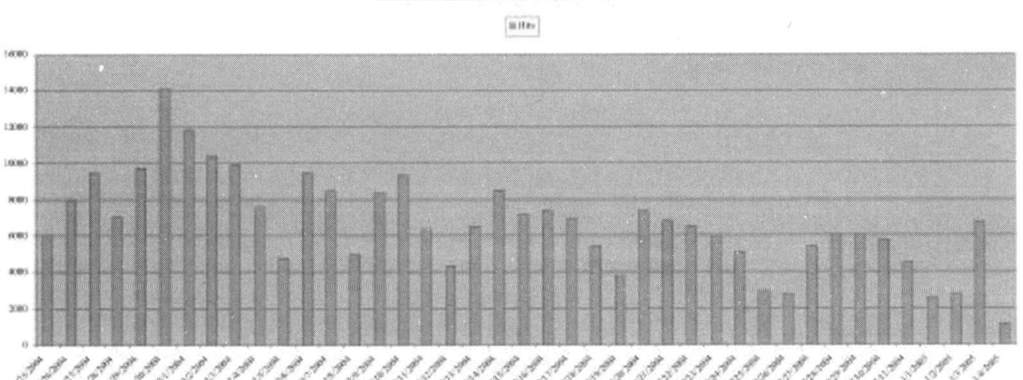

Figure 3: Date-wise web hits for hall ticket download (Dec 2004 TEE)

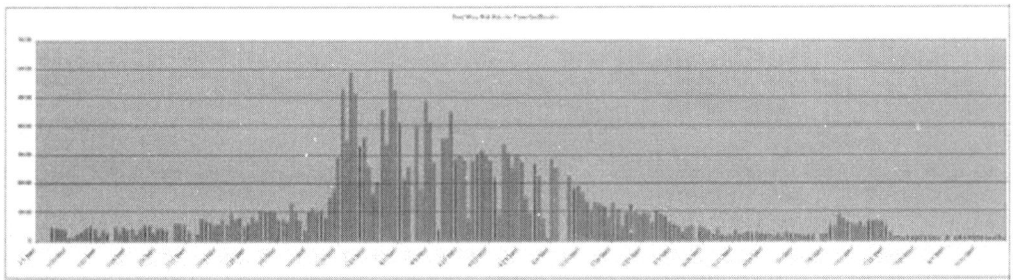

Figure 4: Date-wise web hits for term-end results

Conclusion

Online education is required to have a well planned scheme and well designed technology to support various services which go towards meeting the needs of learners in respect of pre-admission enquiries, and the entire process of admission, course delivery, and evaluation related activities. Course delivery should have sufficient time devoted to making efforts to bring out user friendly and cost-effective course materials. ODL institutions, as such, need to plan and work for bringing the advantages of the new technology to their students and making the delivery system friendly, in-time, and demanding. Websites and other course materials hence must be congruent with the course, and the course goals and objectives must be made very clear. Support services must be prompt enough in responding to all the queries, whether online on through phones, emails, chats and so on. System design, as such, must be exhaustive to accommodate the prime requirements of metadata. The system should be flexible enough to meet the demand-based requirements of students regarding delivery and responding to queries.

Dr. V.S.P. Srivastava is Joint Director, Computer Division, Indira Gandhi National Open University, New Delhi.
Email: vijaysrivastav@ignou.ac.in

Shashi Bhushan is Reader, School of Computer and Information Science, Indira Gandhi National Open University, New Delhi.
Email: shashibhushan@ignou.ac.in

Bhupesh Khatri is Software Engineer, Computer Division, Indira Gandhi National Open University, New Delhi.
Email: bkhatri@ignou.ac.in

24

Continuous Assessment in Open Education

Anuradha Deshmukh

Introduction

Among the three inter-related processes in education, viz. teaching, learning and evaluation, the process that has resisted reforms and change, even in well established conventional universities, is 'evaluation'. Learner evaluation helps in understanding the outcome of learning - both quantitative and qualitative. Unfortunately, evaluation remains the least developed, though paradoxically, in the Indian socio-cultural context, in spite of the fact that it is the most important link in the educational process.

'Learner evaluation' has often been discussed from two points of view: *Formative* and *Summative*. Formative evaluation is used to collect information about the learner's achievements during the learning process or during the formative stage of learning. The instruction at this stage is fluid and flexible and quick remediation can take place if undesirable outcomes are apparent (Verduin & Clark, 1991). Summative evaluation, on the other hand, is done at the end of the learning period.

Even today, however, experts use a variety of dichotomies like *prospective vs. retrospective, naturalistic vs. experimental, holistic vs. analytic* and *process vs. outcome*. As such, each of these expressions focuses on a specific aspect of the evaluation process. However, *process vs. outcome* comes closest to the terminology more in vogue in the Indian distance education, i.e. Continuous Assessment (CA) and Term End Examination (TEE).

Apart from providing a more reliable measure of the student's progress as compared to a single-point, one-time end-examination, as stated in the *Guidelines for Continuous Internal Evaluation* (UGC, 1982), as well as the Monograph on Internal Assessment for Universities (AIU, 1984): "Continuous Assessment has many advantages both for the teacher as well as for the learners. It serves to update the teachers' judgements about their students and provides an idea of the progress of their achievement. It enables students to understand their strengths and weaknesses", thereby contributing to effective learning. Moreover, it 'encourages students to apply themselves assiduously to their studies throughout the year instead of concentrating their efforts towards the end of the term or session', a practice, which research findings have shown, results in better long-term retention of knowledge.

Continuous assessment (CA) which serves such useful functions is especially important in the open distance teaching-learning system. The distance learners are typically self-instructional learners. As Rowntree (1989) puts it, "It is important to remember that self-instructional learners are working on their own. They may be anxious about what assessment will require of them, but may be unable to question in this regard. They may not even know other learners with whom they might discuss this. One may not know until it is too late how one's learning is being affected by assessment demands. Hence, with self-instruction, assessment needs to be thought out more carefully and spelled out more explicitly than is usually the case with face-to-face teaching."

The *isolated learning situation* of the distance learner that is implicit in Rowntree's remarks, has also been discussed in the research literature. The personal support system of the distance student is highly impoverished. The on-campus student, on the other hand, has people who may support him, reassure him, teach him and tell him things. The very fact that distance learners are isolated from fellow students and instructors deprives them of environmental stimuli which can contribute to and guide their learning (Deshmukh, 1997). In the absence of a technology-supported infrastructure, they are then unable to obtain feedback, exchange information and ideas and reinforce their interest in the subject matter through such exchanges (Howard, 1985). Due to lack of opportunity for comparison with others, individual students cannot estimate their achievement sufficiently reliably (Sageder, 1988). In order to break this 'isolation', as the adult learners engage in their learning tasks, they need to be provided with opportunities for feedback. Such 'Feedback' may come directly from the instructor or tutor or from the learning materials provided to the students. Continuous Assessment components serve as an important source of feedback to the distance learners. Whatever their form, the initial non-contiguous two-way communication channel, is usually activated by the submission of the written assignment by the distance learners to their tutors/counsellors. The tutor's comments on these assignments (feedback) serve to build the didactic dialogue (Rathore, 1993) and quality (Holmberg, 1995). An assignment, as Thorpe (1987) states, is the single most important mechanism for prompting and for pacing the individual's study and offers the only vehicle available to all students for feedback and dialogue with a tutor about their individual progress.

Why is 'Feedback' important in the first place? To collate from what theorists have stated as well as from our own experience as distance educators, feedback helps learners to pace their learning through study material and allows them to gain from mistakes. It encourages those learners who have got an assignment question right, comforts learners who have made mistakes, reassuring them that the mistakes were 'reasonable' and that it was 'useful' to have discovered them and directs how to get them right next time (Race, 1990). *Error correction and reinforcement* are the two major reasons usually cited for including feedback in instructional systems, although it has been reported that error correction is a more important justification for providing feedback than its reinforcement function (Kulhavy, 1977; Bernard & Naidu, 1992). However, it must also be noted that merely providing for feedback through a Continuous Assessment component is not sufficient. The 'quality' of feedback given to students studying at a distance is of critical importance to their experience as learners (Deshmukh, 2003). According to available literature, some dimensions of feedback considered to be important are: (a) content of feedback; (b) the degree to which it is personalised, (c) the timing or immediacy of feedback and (d) its 'regularity'.

Good feedback, it has been argued, is explanatory rather than judgemental, pedagogic rather than classificatory. Feedback in the form of a mark or a grade is not very useful to the distance learner (Store & Armstrong, 1981). As Rowntree (1989) comments, 'Feedback from assessment only begins to be useful when it includes verbal comments'. Feedback should inform the learner about what was correct or incorrect in the application of a certain procedure and should apprise the learner about the adequacy of prerequisite knowledge (Howard, 1987). Feedback in the form of written comments, it has been argued (Koul, 1987), must not hamper the motivation of the distance learner. The comments must be well-thought out, deliberate, palatable, precise and pedagogically purposeful. They should not be in the form of global evaluations like good, poor etc. but rather, they should enable students to discern between approach, way of solution and final results. They should promote students' understanding of probable causes of failure, in particular and possibly provide hints at additional learning materials so as to help the students' self-recovery from errors (Sageder, 1988). After all, whether there is a grade or not, the learner is looking for feedback on general progress with the course and specific help with areas of difficulty (Thorpe, 1993). Although good feedback provides verbal comments, it should also be concise and pertinent (Store & Armstrong, 1981).

The importance of immediacy of feedback to students at a distance is one of the best understood concepts in distance teaching and one of the most difficult to achieve because of inevitable communication delays (Store & Armstrong, 1981). A review of the studies conducted independently by several researchers - Biswal (1979), Sahoo (1985), Mouley (1986) and Kumar et al (1986) - indicates that submission of assignments is appreciated by students only when they are received back, properly commented on and in time (Rathore, 1993). The timing of assignments, research shows, is generally an important issue for students and the need for a rapid return of assignments is one of the cardinal requirements in distance education (Thorpe, 1987). Many researchers refer to this as the *'turn-around time'* of assignments and it has been recommended that the turn-around time for the corrected assignments should in no case exceed 3 weeks (Singh, 1995). Summarising from what has been stated thus far, it is obvious that provision of 'Continuous Assessment' in the overall assessment of learning is of paramount importance in the distance education setting, especially in terms of the opportunity it provides for obtaining feedback. However, with the emergence of mega open universities, which enrol millions of learners, it is important to use technology for effective and speedy evaluation using on-line/web-based and computer-based assessment packages.

Historical Development

Learner evaluation has been the subject of academic deliberations for rather long, particularly in the conventional university setting, especially in view of the role played in this regard by the various Commissions appointed from time to time and the UGC. The 'Examination Reforms Plan of Action' of the UGC that was being implemented since 1974 for instance, clearly stated that Continuous internal evaluation should supplement the final examinations. Furthermore, it was also mentioned that "to avoid deliberate tendencies towards high or low marking, all internal assessment should be 'Open' i.e. marks or grades should be immediately known to the students and that the assessed answer-paper should be returned to the students so that they can complain/ seek a clarification regarding their grades". Prior to this, the Mudaliar Commission (1952-53), meant primarily for Secondary Education and the Kothari Commission (1964-66), had also placed special emphasis on Continuous Assessment. As a consequence of these recommendations, pioneering work with respect to Examination Reforms was undertaken by the Gauhati and Calicut universities. Many other universities also responded enthusiastically in the initial stages. However, practice did not conform to and kept pace with plans and recommendations. Therefore, although Examination Reform along the recommended lines was undertaken seriously by a few universities in the country, by and large, the initial enthusiasm at trying out something different and pedagogically useful, gave way to reluctance and desire to continue in the same manner largely because of the administrative problems involved in running the system and inertia to change. However, it is now agreed generally that evaluation should be multilevel and induce continuous improvement of methodology. It should support acquisition of knowledge and skills and help bring about changes in attitude and behaviour. But in ODL system, characterised by heterogeneity in learner backgrounds, learning-styles, experiences and socio-cultural origins, the usefulness of a single instrument to measure individual progress can be even more doubtful. There is therefore need to evolve a system which is free from subjectivity and arbitrariness so as to enhance the learning process (Travis, 1996).

The question whether or not performance in Continuous Assessment (CA) should be combined with that of the final or Term End Examination (TEE) has been debated and discussed considerably. Even now it remains inconclusive and controversial. Some educationists have emphasised that the two (CA and TEE) measure different abilities and that their results should therefore, not be combined. Taylor, Morgan and Gibbs (1982) recommended that the two assessments should not be combined before verifying their accuracies. Without this, it is probable that the total of the two assessments may be more erroneous than a single assessment. He recommended that only more accurate component should be considered for giving credit in university examinations. The other school of thought holds that combination of CA and TEE assessment marks does not significantly improve the prediction of student performance. However, there is also a line of thinking suggesting that the total of Internal Examination, i.e. IE and External Examination (EE) marks is more reliable than the external examination marks taken separately. The UGC has adopted a rather pragmatic approach. It has stipulated that while marks / grades of internal evaluation and external examination must be shown separately, an overall grade / composite result of these two forms of assessment should also be shown in the marksheet / grade card as this is needed for admission to higher courses and also by the employing agencies for recruitment purposes. A related issue that has also surfaced repeatedly is the proportion of weightage to be given to the internal and external components when combining the two. Here too, variations are seen across institutions.

As in the conventional universities, developing a credible system of learner evaluation has been the subject of much discussion in the open-distance learning system. Though concerted initiatives have been taken in this regard by a few Open Universities and Distance Education Institutes in terms of creating structural units in their organisational set-ups to address the issues involved, it is yet to be addressed in a comprehensive manner. Apart from a variety of internal meetings and workshops held by each institution to discuss the issue in detail and work out strategies for the future, an important event was the Roundtable-cum-Workshop on '*Assignments in Distance Education*' organised at Dr. B.R. Ambedkar Open University by Indira Gandhi National Open University (IGNOU) in August, 1999 wherein the academic as well as administrative/operational issues involved in incorporating Assignments as modes of Continuous Assessment were discussed threadbare. During this Roundtable, a sharing of how each Open University in the country handled the Continuous Assessment component also took place (Panda, Garg & Srivastava, 1999).

Present Status

There is today clear consensus among all the functionaries in the distance education system that inclusion of Continuous Assessment component in all the curricular offerings, however diverse they may be, should be an integral part of the student evaluation system on account of its inherent pedagogical usefulness. If one does a comparative analysis of the approaches adopted by each institution, one finds considerable inter-institutional similarities with respect to using Continuous Assessment in the student evaluation systems, although considerable programme-wise variations do appear. Typically, inter-institutional and programme-wise variations revolve around the following parameters:

- Types of CA modes
- 'Weightage' in overall assessment
- Number / frequency and optional vs. compulsory nature
- Conduct, assessment and turn-around time
- Reporting of performance and feedback to the learners.

Types of CA modes

The kind of assessment modes and evaluation strategy planned for a course can often determine how and what the learners will learn. Hence, it is important to use the right strategy of assessment for the particular kind of learning one wants to encourage.

a) *Self Assessment:* It is the most common CA mode based on the exercises and self-test, in-text questions that are an integral part of their instructional material. This mode of CA, if taken seriously by the learners, becomes a very valuable formative evaluation tool. It does not carry any weightage in the final evaluation of the student. The 'online self-testing' facility offered in recent times by some open universities to their students for certain academic programmes, provides them greater opportunities to assess their own learning and readiness to undertake tests and examinations in a particular course.

b) *Class Tests (CT):* In India, this mode is a unique feature of student evaluation system of the Yashwantrao Chavan Maharashtra Open University (YCMOU), though it is also used by other universities abroad. Their major objective is to provide the learner with a testing situation that is similar to what he/she is going to face later through TEE. The nature of questions asked (both objective and subjective-type), their answering format, the per question answering-time and other aspects of the testing situation are also similar to the TEE. Students, therefore, get exposure to and practice in facing a structured, exam-like situation with fixed time constraints (Deshmukh, 1999).

c) *Assignments:* Unlike the structured situation of 'class tests', assignments are typically answered by a student at his own place of convenience, within a reasonably long time-span and with full liberty to go through his instructional and reference learning material. The assignments are of two types: Tutor Marked Assignments (TMA) and Computer Marked Assignments (CMA). The nature of questions asked in TMAs varies considerably across academic programmes in terms of number, length of expected answer, and depth of content coverage. Such Assignments are generally assessed by the tutors/counsellors, a term that originated in the UK Open University. Variations are also noted in terms of the educational objectives tested through these assignments, some of these requiring the student 'to apply' theoretical concepts to a new situation or 'to analyse' the components of a given problem and some merely testing his basic understanding/comprehension of a concept/principle/theory and the like. These assignments take an 'in-depth' form and are also followed by oral presentations in seminars. Most open universities in the country have adopted the use of TMAs as tools for teaching-learning and developing empathy with learners. Considerable programme-wise variations are noted, however, within the same institution with respect to the nature of assignments given to students.

The computer marked assignments, which are generally multiple choice questions (MCQs), are more suitable for measuring factual knowledge. Objective type tests can also have other formats like fill in the blanks, word/number entry, etc. With the availability of high speed computers and their applications in evaluation, it is possible to offer a huge variety of question formats. Several packages are available for electronic delivery of objective tests. These packages can generate feedback and administer marks. Computers can generate different tests automatically from a question bank. Computerised delivery supported by automated working and feedback is a flexible and efficient method of providing formative assessment. The use of electronic methods is aided by the emergence of Optical Mark Reader (OMR) and Intelligent Character Reader (ICR) connected to a computer. The National Informatics Centre has developed Computer Aided Paperless Examination System (Mehta and Sexena,

2004). IGNOU also developed an on-line and on-demand model, called IGNOU online examination system, for MBA. Every student registering for an exam is given a password for logging on the site. The question bank is characterized by item difficulty, course coverage, etc. An examinee is awarded marks as soon as the work is submitted and these get recorded in the server for entry into respective student grade card.

d) *Workbooks:* These may be considered as an extension of the concept of 'assignment' as a mode of continuous assessment. Typically, workbooks (occasionally referred to as 'Activity Books') consist of a set of several assignments, with space provided for the instructor's or counsellor's ratings or marking. They are more commonly used for practical courses requiring specific psychomotor skills as for instance, in the field of computer science, medicine, and electronics engineering. In such cases, workbooks also provide a useful form of recording regular work done in the laboratory and experiments or practical tasks performed. Workbooks have been used for courses involving a field work component as well as in certain professional programmes like MBA and PGDHHM. Although workbooks serve as a useful form of continuous assessment, they are also often used as components of summative evaluation and workbook-based assessment scores are therefore combined with the Term End Examination in several academic programmes in different universities/institutions.

e) *Projects:* A few universities also use projects to assess the progress of learner in a course. In IGNOU, projects are used as integrated component in several courses in BCA/MCA programmes. It enables the learner to correlate his learning with the immediate environment around him/her.

Weightage in overall assessment

By and large, the weightage for continuous assessment in the overall performance of the learners among almost all the distance education providers range between 25% to 30%, with a few variations for certain programmes. In IGNOU, continuous assessment component is treated as a separate passing head in programmes like B.Ed, MCA etc. and the marks therein are also clubbed with the Term End Examination component. However, several studies reveal that learner performance in continuous assessment component does not conform to his/her TEE component; it is in fact much higher (Khare et al., 2004). In rare cases, like for example, the 'Diploma in School Management' offered by YCMOU, the entire learner evaluation system is based on continuous assessment, i.e. on the basis of performance throughout the duration of the programme, without holding a separate Term End Examination. There are also certain programmes for which the weightage of the Continuous Assessment component in the total performance is to the extent of 40%. Such cases are, however, rather few and majority of programmes in most of the distance education universities in India more or less conform to the 30% weightage level.

Number / frequency, and optional vs. compulsory

Differences are noted among institutions in terms of the number of Continuous Assessment modes used and the extent to which completion of the same becomes a necessary pre-condition for appearance at the End Examination. By and large, the number of assignments varies from 1 to 3 per course, depending mostly on the credit points allotted to the course. Besides, the policy adopted across many institutions is that appearance for the End Examination of any course should not be dependent on completion of the CA component. Some institutions do not give opportunity to reappear for the same later. Non-completion of CA in such cases therefore results in proportionate loss in the overall assessment of the student. In certain technical skill-oriented programmes like those in the field of computers, electronics and the like, however, or those of a professional nature like Library Science, Journalism and Teacher Education, continuous assessment components generally constitute a separate head of passing and a student cannot qualify for a degree or diploma in such programmes without satisfactory completion of the same.

Conduct, assessment and turn-around time

The conduct and assessment of continuous assessment components is an important challenge faced by distance educators across the country, a challenge that becomes more pronounced because of the huge geographical area to be covered and the fact that the distance learners being pre-occupied with a number of commitments often find it difficult to adhere to the time schedules pre-determined for completion of CA components.

Apart from administrative considerations like time-tabling, arranging for adequate space and supervision, the development of evaluation tools (tests, assignments, etc.) and the identification of appropriately qualified and experienced persons for timely assessment of student responses to these CA components, also remain important concerns. The turn-around time varies according to the programmes with technical programmes in the area of computer science and the like having higher turn-around times because of difficulties in procuring the required experts. By and large, however, these turn-around times vary from approximately 1 to 3 months and in some cases, the students know about their CA performance only at the time they receive their Statement of marks for the End Examination!

Reporting of performance and feedback to the learners

Reporting of performance of learners has also been a much discussed issue in the open and distance learning setting. While some open universities have gone ahead with an elaborately developed grading system, particularly for professional programmes like management, engineering, computers, IT, and health, a simple marking system is more commonly used for general education programmes. Even in cases where grading has been adopted, there are rather few instances of direct grading. Rather, the tendency is to first mark the tests / assignments / seminar presentations / workbook activities and then report the totals in the form of grades. Attempts have been made by some universities particularly in the context of their Post Graduate and Research programmes to include tutor comments along with the grades/marks by way of feedback to the learner.

However, in most cases and especially in connection with large-registration programmes, the feedback communicated is purely in terms of marks/grades.

Summarising the broad approach presently adopted by most open universities, it may be stated that Test/Assignment designing and development' is done centrally by every open university,''test administration' of the continuous assessment components is decentralised and handled mostly at the study centre level with some control from the university headquarters, 'performance assessment' is done partly by counsellors at study centres and partly managed at headquarters depending on the assessment tool used and 'collation of data, result-processing and result declaration' are activities handled centrally. Even though attempts have been made to provide prompt formative feedback to the learners so as to guide them in their future study, it must be accepted that there is yet much to be achieved in this respect.

Limitations

The limitations experienced with Continuous Assessment stem essentially from the difficulties in operating a mass-scale system through the distance education mode. Some of the ones mentioned during the 'round-table on assignments' (1999) are valid even today. These and certain others are as listed below (Panda et.al, 1999).

- Late receipt/non-receipt of assignments by learners/study centres/regional centres.
- Difficulties in procuring the desired level of committed academics for preparing and assessing the CA components and frequent non-availability of marking schemes for ensuring objectivity in assessment.
- Weak infrastructure and facilities as well as inadequately trained manpower at the study centres for the organisation of tests / assignments. A consequence of this is that proper maintenance of records, though vital, faulters, causing a lot of inconvenience to learners.
- Poor payment structures among open universities for all categories of work associated with the design, organisation and assessment of assignments.
- Occasional unfair practices adopted by the students (plagiarism/copying) and lack of the required supervisory control at the study centres.
- Inordinately long turn-around time from the time the learner submits his Continuous Assignment components until the time he receives his grades / marks based on performance in them.
- Occasional non-inclusion of grades or marks in mark-sheets due to delayed transmission of performance details from the respective study centres to the university Headquarters.
- Lack of a proper monitoring system, especially with respect to the assessment of CA components.
- Inadequate formative feedback to learners apart from communication of marks or grades.

While undoubtedly, there are many difficulties experienced in making the CA system work, most of the distance education providers (Open Universities as well as CCIs) have tried out their own strategies for dealing with these limitations. Focused attempts at training of personnel involved in implementing the CA components at the study centres have been made by certain universities in addition to making some periodic upward revisions in remuneration levels to these persons. The organisation of Class tests is given due importance through deployment of persons for smooth conduct. The monitoring of assessment of assignments, even though on a sample basis, is undertaken by a few State Open Universities apart from IGNOU, with the help of the core faculty at the Headquarters of the University concerned. The system of monitoring has not, however, been as refined as that in the UKOU (Satyanarayana and Sesharatnam, 1992), wherein the system as it is implemented "provides opportunity for rendering an academic's teaching visible to another, thus enabling staff to learn from each other's work and advice". There has also been an emphasis on the part of the university administration to enforce submission of assignments by students within a stipulated date, failing which the assignments may not be assessed at all. Non-inclusion of marks or grades in the student mark-sheets have been looked into on a case-to-case basis and appropriate modifications have been made in the same in the event of direct evidence in support of the student's claim. The important pedagogical issue of giving feedback to the learners apart from marks/grades has been handled by universities mostly in the case of academic programmes having comparatively low enrolment or in programmes at the Post-graduate and Research level. In certain universities initiatives have been taken wherein the evaluator apart from assigning marks/grades, writes out margin notes indicating all the improvements necessary or suggests that the learner consults some reference books for improving the quality of his assignment responses.

IGNOU has done away with the assignments for all its certificate programmes of six month duration in view of inordinately long turn-around time and non-reflection of assignment grades. In fact, two very contradictory views on the utility of assignments for other programmes have emerged in IGNOU. While the purists insist on continuation of their pedagogic value, pragmatics advocate abolishing these as they have failed to serve the required purpose. The former insist on improving the internal mechanisms, the latter cite volume of work generated and lack of support from Study Centres as serious impediments.

Innovations

Innovative initiatives in the area of Continuous Assessment have tried to synthesise pedagogy and technology. At times, however, technology has been the more important of the two while in certain other situations, pedagogy has been at the forefront. Some of these initiatives are as indicated below:

- Training regarding communicating feedback through tutor comments has been imparted in certain universities even though its impact in terms of discernible changes among evaluators of assignments has yet to be demonstrated. This, however, still remains an important application of pedagogy.
- Computerised paper-setting through well-characterised 'question banks' for tests and assignments (sometimes referred to as an 'assignment bank') has also been successfully experimented with respect to some select academic programmes by some Open

Universities.However, this initiative has not yet been generalised to a large number of academic programmes.

- A refined version of computerised paper-setting is 'Online Self-Testing', a technology-based innovation that is gradually gaining ground in the Indian distance education setting.
- The development of Open Question Bank (OQB) software for faster preparation of assignments and Term End Question papers is also being attempted by certain universities. Tangible results in this regard are as yet awaited.

Conclusion

The history of examination reforms in India down the years shows ample instances of how administrative considerations have hampered the progress of academic reform in this area. With the tremendous advances in computer science and Information and Communication Technologies, we are today much better equipped and certainly much more capable of addressing administrative constraints effectively. As has already been mentioned, a systematic methodology for giving prompt and effective feedback to the learners, especially through relevant tutor comments has yet to be developed and is certainly a matter that should concern policy-makers and practitioners of the DE system. Technically, it appears that it should not be very difficult for us today to work out a system wherein each learner is able to receive prompt, accurate, frequent and personalised feedback regarding his performance in any kind of assessment situation. The feedback that is presently predominantly in the form of marks/grades, may then regularly be given in a way that provides a definite direction and motivation for further learning. Only then can we claim to have dealt with the distance learner's anxiety and feelings of 'isolation' effectively. To remind ourselves of the advice given by the noted distance educator, Rowntree, the following may be borne in mind:

"Do all you can to make each assessment a learning experience - and not just a formal check-up on what has been learned already".

References

AIU (1984). *Monograph on Internal Assessment for Universities*. New Delhi: Association of Indian Universities.

Bernard, R.M. & Naidu, S. (1992). Post-questioning, concept mapping and feedback:a distance education field experiment. *British Journal of Educational Technology*, 23 (1), 48-60.

Biswal, B.N. (1979). *A Study of Correspondence Education in Indian Universities*. Unpublished Ph.D. Education Thesis, M.S. University of Baroda.

Deshmukh, A. (1997). *A Study of the Importance and Effectiveness of Formative Evaluation in the Academic Performance of Distance Learners*. Unpublished doctoral thesis submitted to the University of Mumbai.

Deshmukh, A. (1999). *The Role of Assignments in YCMOU: A Status Paper*. Paper presented at the Round Table–cum–Workshop on Assignments in Distance Education, B. R. Ambedkar Open University, Hyderabad, August, 26-27.

Deshmukh, A. (2003). *Internal Assessment and Feedback in Distance Education*. Paper presented at the UGC-sponsored Refresher Course in Distance Education, Yashwantrao Chavan Maharashtra Open University, March 10-30.

Holmberg, B. (1995). Communication and study access-quality in distance education. In Bakhshish Singh (ed.), *New Horizons in Distance Education*. New Delhi: Uppal.

Howard, D.C. (1985). Reading and study skills and the distance learner. *Distance Education*, 6(2), 169-188.

Howard, D.C. (1987). Designing learner feedback in distance education. *The American Journal of Distance Education*, 1 (3), 24-40.

Khare, P., Saxena, A. and Garg, S. (2004). Performance analysis of IGNOU science students in theory courses through data mining. *Indian Journal of Open Learning,* 13(1), 29-49.

Koul, B.N. (1987). Tutor comments: A distance teaching technique. In B.N. Koul, Bakhshish Singh & M.M. Ansari (eds.), *Studies in Distance Education*. New Delhi: AIU, 39-52.

Kulhavy, R.W. (1977). Feedback in written instruction. *Review of Educational Research,* 47, 211-232.

Kumar et al. (1986). In H.C.S. Rathore, Treatment given to assignment responses at the correspondence institutes: A study of students' reactions. *Indian Journal of Open Learning*, 1993, 2(1), 23-27.

Mehta, P.K. and Saxena, A. (2004). Emerging trends in student assessment in ODLs. *Indian Journal of Open Learning*, 13(2), 167-179.

Mouley, V. (1986). *Correspondence Education in Indian Universities: A Review*. A report submitted to the U.G.C., New Delhi.

Panda, Santosh. Garg, Suresh and Srivastava, Manjulika (1999) *Roundtable cum Workshop Report: Assignments in Distance Education*. New Delhi: IGNOU.

Race, P. (1990). *The Open Learning Handbook: Selecting, Designing and Supporting Open Learning Materials*. London: Kogan Page.

Rathore, H.C.S. (1993). Treatment given to assignment responses at the correspondence institutes: A study of students' reactions. *Indian Journal of Open Learning*, 2(1) 23-27.

Rowntree, D. (1989). *Assessing Students: How Shall We Know Them?* London: Kogan Page/ New York: Nichols Publishing Company.

Sageder, J. (1988). Tests as means for promotion of learning from distance teaching. *Distance Education*, 9 (2), 234-249.

Sahoo, P.K. (1985). Distance education in Indian universities: Some concerns for further development. *The Education Quarterly*.

Satyanarayana, P. and Sesharatnam, C. (1992). Student assignments for submission in distance education. *Kakatiya Journal of Distance Education*, 1 (2), 17-45.

Singh, B. (1995). IGNOU research project on correspondence/distance education in India: some findings & recommendations. *Journal of Higher Education,* 18(1), 181-193.

Store, R.E. and Armstrong, R.J. (1981). Personalising feedback between teacher and student in the context of a particular model of distance teaching. *British Journal of Educational Technology*, 12(2), 140-157.

Taylor, L., Morgan, A. and Gibbs, G. (1982). The orientation of open university foundation students to their studies. *Teaching at a Distance*, 20, 3-12.

Thorpe, M. (1987). Student assignments. In M.Thorpe and D.Grugeon (Eds.), *Open Learning for Adults*. UK: Longman Group Ltd.

Thorpe, M. (1993). *Evaluating Open and Distance Learning*. Sussex: Orient Longman.

Travis, J. (1996). Meaningful assessment. *Clearing House*, 69, 308-312.

UGC, (1982).*Guidelines for Continuous Internal Evaluation*. New Delhi: University Grants Commission.

Verduin, J.R. (Jr.) and Clark, T.A. (1991). *Distance Education: The Foundations of Effective Practice*. San Francisco: Jossey-Bass Publishers.

Dr. Anuradha Deshmukh is Head of evaluation, Yashwantrao Chavan Maharashtra Open University, Nashik.
Email: anuradhadeshmukh@hotmail.com

25

Computers Hands-on and Lab Practicals in Distance Education

Akshay Kumar and Jyotsna Dikshit

Introduction

One of the most challenging aspects of the Computer Science and Information Technology courses run in distance education mode is to provide students with computer hands-on and lab practical experience in places other than the main campus that are equivalent to the other existing conventional educational system which have fully functional and well equipped computer labs on campus. Computer hands-on and lab practical are very crucial for the students enrolled to achieve the desired learning goals. The lab components are essential for any computer science programme and are delivered along with the theoretical sessions at the centres. The hands-on practical are very important for the computer science course as it provides the basic application knowledge to the users without which the professionals may be found wanting in the industry. However, the objectives of delivering the practical at different levels are different. For example, packages such as, word processor, spreadsheet, DBMS, and programming language including C, C++, JAVA are delivered at Bachelors/Masters level. Some of the latest tools are also included as practical components for the students at Master Degree level. For basic computer awareness programmes hands-on practical mainly evolved around office related skills of computers, which include handling of computers, dealing with the word processor, spreadsheets, presentation software and dealing with the other application packages. For a successful computer program the practical components have to be suitably supported by detailed discussions on related theoretical aspects of these practical. The high level skills are required at the graduate, PG diploma. The skills required at the masters' level involve in-depth logic, which includes implementation of program during application development. This chapter focuses on the existing scenario of computers hands-on and lab practical experiences of the Open and Distance Learning (ODL) systems in India with two case studies, and suggests alternative activities to lab experiences, which will help in overcoming the limitations of computer hands-on and lab practicals.

IGNOU: A Case Study

Indira Gandhi National Open University (IGNOU) started its Computer Science programmes in 1991 with a course named "Diploma in Computer and Office Management" (DCO) and since then IGNOU has advanced to a great extent as far as Computer Science courses delivery is concerned. Experiences obtained from DCO programme, lab practical were used for the certificate, Bachelor degree, and Masters Degree programme in computer applications of IGNOU. The School of Computer & Information Sciences of IGNOU, since 1991, have been offering the following programmes having hands-on and lab practical sessions:

- Diploma in Computer Office Management (DCO) (not on offer now)
- Master of Computer Application (MCA) (Revised curriculum is on offer)
- Bachelor of Computer Application (BCA) (Revised curriculum is on offer)
- Certificate in Computing (CIC)
- Certificate in Networking Oriented Computing (CNOC)/Certificate in Website Design Management. (not on offer now)
- Bachelor of Information Technology (BIT) (not on offer now)
- Advanced Diploma in Information Technology (ADIT) (not on offer now)

Diploma in Computer & Office Management (DCO)

DCO was the first computer programme offered by IGNOU. The objectives were not only to impart knowledge of office and computers but also impart information on usages of latest technologies at that time including computers to office goers through Distance Education mode. It involved 80 hours practical time spread over 27 sessions over the year. The detailed scheme of theory and practical sessions along with the necessary video was prepared for this programme. The schedule was prepared for the reason that hands-on practical required some basic theoretical knowledge by the users in order to use the computer meaningfully and gainfully. The scheme meticulously presented the delivery of theory and practical sessions and was created as a schedule of operation for the programme. The practical sessions were of 3 hours duration with one counsellor handling 20 students during practical sessions. In the scheme there was no detailed elaborations of practical components. The practical components involved in DCO include word processor, (Word Star at that time), spreadsheet (Lotus at that time), simple programming language (BASIC at that time) DBMS (dbase at that time) in addition applications were developed using dbase and Excel. The students were given hand on time on these applications. These applications included Financial Management, Inventory Management, Text based management system, etc. The practical examination was given the weightage of 15% of the overall 100%. The practical examination duration was one hour for each course. For better organisation DCO practical of two sessions were combined as one practical examination with separate marking for both the examinations. DCO was successfully run for about four years with increasing enrolment trends. Thus become popular among the students every year.

Masters of Computer Application (MCA)

The success of DCO made us to launch one of our most ambitious but successful programs called Master of Computer Application (MCA). The MCA is of 3 years duration launched in 1994. The MCA had 180 hours of practical time every year at that time. The practical component of MCA are given in Table 1.

Table 1: Practical components in MCA (old)

Year	Practical on	No. of practical sessions (3 hour duration)
1st	Data Structures through 'C' and 'PASCAL'	22
	UNIX commands and Shell programming	14
	Assembly Language Programming	10
	Cobol Programming	10
	DBMS	4
2nd	Fortran Language, Statistical & Numerical Techniques	17
	Novell Netware, Network	21
	Assignment Project	08
	Assignment, Project	08
	CASE Tools	06
3rd	C++ Language, Project	20
	UNIX Operating System Administration, Project	14
	Lisp/Prolog Programming Language, Project	14
	ORACLE / Ingres	12

MCA had practical components involving strong practical skills, which included Programming in C, and C++, DBMS, Networking Implementation, Data Structure implementation, Fortran, Unix Operating System, etc. MCA had practical examinations only in the first year in three subjects. The students had accepted the hands-on practical in MCA and it received huge enrolment. MCA had also a project course, which a student used to undertake at an industry/company. The project was provided in the $5^{th}/6^{th}$ semesters. The MCA programme has been revised from January 2005. With the experience of old BCA/MCA and VCI - the School has created the following model of practical delivery for revised MCA programme:

- There should be separate courses for the theory and practical.
- Practical course should be grouped together to form a lab components / lab course.

- Each credit of lab should have a maximum of 30 hours of practical time.
- A lab manual must be prepared, detailing some basic way of functioning during the lab and activities that are to be undertaken in each of the session. Lists of problems are given, which the students need to solve during the session. These problems although need to change after two to three years. These problems provide the student a backbone for practical sessions.
- The students are evaluated on their performance in these labs sessions.
- 40% assignment marks are based on the lab session/lab records the students should undertake compulsorily. However, 40% marks are awarded for the problems given in the assignments, which are revised every year. An important component of all these practical activities included 20% marks for viva-voce to ensure that the authenticity of student work.
- These lab components and theory courses are scheduled in a such a fashion that the lab components of these courses falls only after the theory counselling of the related lab material has been conducted. Thus providing, the theory and practical mix for the students learning.

The practical component of present MCA programme are given in Table 2.

Table 2: Practical components of MCA programme (New)

Year	Course Code	No. of practical sessions (3 hours duration)
1st	Internet Concepts and Web Design	20
	C and Assembly Language Programming Lab	20
	Lab (based on MCS-021, 022, 023 & 024)Data & File structure, Operating Systems concepts and Networking Management, Introduction to DBMS, Object Oriented Technologies, and JAVA programming	40
2nd	Lab (based on MCS-032, 034 & 035)Object Oriented Analysis and Design, Software Engineering, Accountancy and Financial Management	30
	Lab (UNIX & Oracle)	20
3rd	Lab (based on MCS-051, & 053)Advanced Internet Technologies, Computer Graphics and Multimedia	20

Bachelor of Computer Application (BCA)

BCA was launched in 1996. BCA requires a practical component of 270 hours. The initial BCA involved some of the courses of Bachelor Degree Programme (BDP) of IGNOU and the first year courses of MCA. Some of the additional practical courses like Internet, C++, VB were also part of this BCA. However BCA was revised in July 1998 and it has 120 practical hours in the first year and 120 hours in the second year and 180 hours in the third year (Table 3).

Table 3: Practical component in BCA programme (revised 1998)

Year	Course title	No. of practical session (3 hours of duration)
1st	Computer Fundamentals & PC Software	10
	PC Software Application Skills	6
	'C' programming and Data structure	24
2nd	Introduction to system	13
	Window Programming	10
	Multimedia	5
	RDBMS Lab	12
3rd	Computer Networks	6
	TCP/IP programming	10
	Introduction to Software Engineering	4
	C++ and Object Oriented Programming	12
	Introduction to Internet Programming (Java, Active X) 10	
	Intranet Administration	6
	Project	12

Certificate in Computing (CIC)

Certificate in Computing was launched in 1996. CIC is a six months program. CIC had practical component of 40 hours. The sessions of CIC were distributed over 2 ½ hours and mainly covered aspects of windows, word processing, presentation and spreadsheet.

Certificate in Network Oriented Computing (CNOC), and Certificate in Website Design Management (CWDM)

The school also experimented and launched short term capsule providing intensive practical at multimedia learning centres (these centres were created all over Delhi with required hardware/ software infrastructure). Two courses namely, Certificate in Network Oriented Computing (CNOC), and Certificate in Website Design Management (CWDM) were launched in this category. Later these courses were offered through more advanced model of delivery: that is through internet. However, this Internet based delivery scheme, on request from the students, was converted into integrated mode in which the Internet as well as formal distance education mode of delivery were combined into one. Practical in internet mode were primarily at the discretion of the student and chat was the supportive tool for helping the students. The students were also given some Internet access time for these courses to conduct the theory and practical.

Advanced Diploma in Information Technology (ADIT) and Bachelor of Information Technology (BIT)

In 1999, the experience of these Internet modes gave birth to Virtual Campus Initiative (VCI) through which skill oriented courses were delivered. The two main courses of this category were BIT and ADIT programmes, and required very high hands-on sessions that include time of on-line material access as well as practical.

The practical component of BIT and ADIT programmes are given in Tables 4 and 5, respectively. These courses were delivered through tele-learning centres.

Table 4: Practical components of BIT

Year	Semester	Course Title	No. of hands sessions (2 hrs. duration)
I	1	Win 98, Network Operating System, How to use Internet, MS-Access, MX-Excel, JAVA, MS-PPT, Windows NT/2000 Assignments	77
	2	Advanced MS-Access, Project, MS-Project, Network Analysis Tool, HTML, JavaScript, JDBC, Web Administration, Visual Interdev, ASP Programming, MS-Word, Pagemaker, Corel / Illustrator, Photoshop/Fireworks, Assignments	120
II	3	VB, SQL Server, C++, DHTML, Dream weaver, Director, Flash, Java, DHTML, Dreamweaver, Assignment	90 (Computing) and 63 (Multimedia)
	4	Project Coding, Management, Tools, Prolog, LISP, Assignment	47
III	5	Unix Shell Script, C++ Programming, Data Structure through C++, Oracle, SQL, MS-Project, Assignment,	68
	6	Visual Basic Programming, VC++ programming, Advance JAVA, Assignments.	67

Table 5: Practical components of ADIT

Year	Semester	Course Title	No. of hands session (2 hrs. duration)
1	1	Unix Shell Script, C++ Programming, Data Structure through C++, Oracle, SQL, MS-Project, Assignments	68
	2	Visual Basic Programming, VC++ programming, Advance JAVA, Assignments.	67

Delivery of Practical Components at IGNOU

The practicals were conducted at the study centres of IGNOU which have all the facilities including Hardware and Software required for completion of the courses. The responsibility of the Hardware and Software licenses lie remain the study centre. IGNOU does not provide any hardware and software licenses to the study centres. Two students share a machine and the duration of each session is 3 hours. These sessions are conducted during the weekends (Saturday and Sunday). The monthly schedule is drawn by the study centres and displayed for the students who are divided into number of batches. Depending on the requirements, the students need to undertake one session (three hours) or two sessions (6 hours) over the weekends. In fact, hands-on practical provide the average hands-on requirement for the students. A student can practice more on own by hiring suitable services in the market. IGNOU does not have the provision of these additional sessions.

The coordinated mixture of theory and practical schedule is created so that the students get the maximum benefit. As a general policy all the practical courses have a practical examination. In practical examination students' performance is evaluated over the semester. At study centres assignments are also given to the students, which they do on their own. The project/practical assignment is always the part of the course. During these assignments a student need to implement a problem in the required software and demonstrates the adequacy of skills. In addition, the term-end examination is also conducted to ensure the students performance. 75% attendance in these sessions is compulsory for the students, otherwise the students is not permitted to appear in the examination.

In the VCI, the student had to do almost all the activities at the Tele-Learning Centres where the electronic course material is made available. Therefore, two to 2½hours of hands-on practical time is allowed to students. Out of which the students can do lab practical, Internet access, download study material, chat with the counsellors etc. In addition, teleconferencing sessions were made available to the students. VCI programmes (BIT & ADIT) were also supported by the lab manual concept where a large number of problems have been designed for the students which they undertake during the lab sessions.

Limitations and innovations

The prime limitations of these sessions were:

- Non-availability of practical counsellors
- Non-availability of infrastructure
- Need of additional material

Some of the innovations adopted by IGNOU in offering practical in computer programmes are:

- Guided mix of theory and practical sessions in Distance Education mode.
- Use of Internet technology and related communication technology for delivery of guided theory and practical

- Use of multimedia CD for delivering skill based educational contents.
- Implementation through students' project and assignment activities which are guided to mix students learning.
- Use of latest technology. Technology proposes to impart to control stimulated practical environment giving flexibility.

MPBOU: A Case Study

Madhya Pradesh Bhoj (Open) University (MPBOU) in 1997 started Computer Science programmes (Master in Computer Application (MCA) and Certificate in Computing (CIC). In the beginning the university offered its computer science programmes in its seven regional centres in the State of Madhya Pradesh (including present Chhattisgarh). During the first few years, the university offered computer hands-on and lab practical with the help of hired computer labs in reputed regional engineering colleges/universities and other colleges of the state. Expert faculty of the respective Regional Engineering Colleges/Universities and other colleges were hired for providing practical counselling and hands-on training to the learners.

The following computer programmes having practical and hands-on components are on offer since 1998 at the Institute of Information Technology, MPBOU:

1. Master of Computer Application (MCA) (Revised curriculum is on offer)
2. Certificate in Computing (CIC) (not on offer now)
3. Bachelor of Computer Application (BCA) (Revised curriculum is on offer)
4. Certificate in Computer Operation (CCO) (not on offer now)
5. Certificate in Computer Application (CCA) (Revised curriculum is on offer)
6. Diploma in Computer Application (DCA) (Revised curriculum is on offer)
7. Bachelor of Information Technology (BIT)
8. Master of Science (Computer Science) (M.Sc. CS)
9. Master of Science Information Technology (M.Sc. IT)
10. Diploma in Web & Multimedia Technology (DWMT)
11. Diploma in Linux Essentials (DLE)
12. Diploma in Education Technology (DET)

Some of the highlights of laboratory course at MPBOU are:

- All the programmes right from Certificate programmes to Postgraduate programmes have practical components.
- MPBOU has well established multimedia labs at its Regional Centres with internet connection for the students to experience and perform computer practical anytime even after the practical counselling sessions are over.
- Before and after the counselling sessions students actively participate in the discussion forums and virtual chats to solve their problems.
- Except the few certificate and diploma programmes almost all the other programmes have project work, which a student undertake, at an industry/company/the university itself.

- The project work is discussed at length with the counsellor and faculty through online expert help systems, discussion forum and web-based two-way videoconferencing. This starts from the beginning of the 2nd year of a 3-year programme. For other diploma and postgraduate courses in which the duration is 1 or 2 years, the students start interacting from the beginning.
- The students take advice on the type, nature and scope of the project they wish to undertake depending on their area of interest and future trends.
- In a few programmes where some centres have less than 20 students enrolled, the university experimented the virtual lab initiative using the net-meeting software.

Community-based programmes

MPBOU since its establishment has been heavily involved in massive computer literacy programmes of the state government. It also provided hands-on experience, lab manuals and interactive computer lessons to train the teachers and students of the well-known Computer Literacy Awareness in Secondary Schools (CLASS) project and HEADSTART project.

CLASS project

We started with a survey of the status of the project through actual visits to the centres and discovered that almost negligible percentage of centres under the CLASS project were functional. We transformed the whole process by introducing centre and community oriented and focused approach by developing capabilities locally. Instead of arranging teachers from outside we trained the teachers who were locally available. For maintenance we trained about 100 fresh science graduates and trained them in use of a troubleshooting kit.These students were excited to visit the centres and also got jobs elsewhere within a few months of their actual field experience. By 1997, this produced visible success and as against a target of training 15,000 students per year, we could achieve the training of 30,000 students. In 2002 the government made some enhancements in the scheme of CLASS project and it identified 44 school of excellence as the resource centres to run the project. The University with the help of government fund established a well equipped lab of 10 P4 computers and launched Certificate in Computer Application and Diploma in Computer Application Programmes. Local teachers with minimum computer qualification (degree or a diploma holders) were provided hands-on computer training at the multimedia labs of MPBOU. These teachers then trained the students to achieve their learning goals of these programmes, which also promoted building confidence in them to handle practical components efficiently.

HEADSTART project

The state of Madhya Pradesh in collaboration with MPBOU designed and developed a unique programme on improving the quality of education at the grassroot level using emerging Information and Communication Technologies. The two embarked upon an idea of developing state-wide network for providing computer enabled education even in those schools, which were situated in the remotest corners of the state with heavy rural and tribal population. As a pilot project 1000 schools were meant to be activated from July/August 1998 session. 2000 teachers, two from each school, were trained on computer operations, use of innovative and interactive software and build confidence in them to use computers. Trainings of teachers were conducted at six different Regional Centres of the Open University by very efficient faculty. This resulted in achieving the target of 2000 well trained teachers who were sufficiently motivated to accept the challenge of providing computer enabled education in the 1000 selected schools deep in the interior of the State.

Virtual campus

The university launched its virtual campus in 1999 with the following three basic courses for the well being of the community:

- Certificate in Computer Operation
- Communicative Skills in English
- Reproductive Child Health

At that time the course was mostly text based and less interactive. In 2004, the University launched a free online course on Computer fundamentals and MS-Office packages. This programme was launched keeping the need of the community in mind. The programme is purely online and has computer simulations for hands-on experience. The programme has a virtual environment for students where they can log on anytime, anywhere to not only study online but also to practice the practical components using computer simulations. The student can also download video based demos to revise the practical components of the programme.

Computer programmes at MPBOU

MPBOU is running a wide range of computer programmes right from computer awareness programmes to computer professional programmes like MCA, M.Sc (IT) and M.Sc (CS). A list of these programmes including their practical delivery mechanism and innovations involved are given in Table 6.

Table 6: Outline of CS and IT programmes at MPBOU

Programme name	**Duration**	**Lab component**	**Practical delivery mechanism**	**innovation**	**futuristic approach**
Master of Computer Application (MCA)	3	Programming in C, Programming in Visual Basic, C++, DBMS, Networking	180 hrs of practical session; face-to-face practical sessions with expert counsellors	Online guidance to students before and after practical sessions using expert sessions and	A network setup and implementation multi-media CD

		Implementation, Data Structure implementation, Programming in JAVA, VC++, Internet Programming, etc.		discussion forums	is under development to provide practical insight to the networking fundamentals and concepts.
Master of Computer Science (Computer Science) (M. Sc. CS)	2	C++ , Networking Implementation, Programming in Java, .Net, Oracle, Linux System Administration, Advance networking	180 hrs of practical session; face-to-face practical sessions with expert counsellors	Industry interactions for project development.	-
Master of Computer Science (Information Technology) (M. Sc. IT)	2	Programming in C, PC Software, Programming in C++, Oracle, Visual C++, RDBMS, Data Structure implementation, Advanced Java	160 hrs of practical session; face-to-face practical sessions with expert counsellors	Final year project discussion forums.	-
Bachelor of Computer Application (BCA)	3	Programming in C, PC Software, Programming in Visual Basic, DBMS, Networking Implementation, Data Structure implementation, Programming in JAVA, ORACLE, Internet Programming	180 hrs of practical session; face-to-face practical sessions with expert counsellors	-	-
Bachelor of Information Technology (BIT)	3	Programming in C, PC Software, Programming in Visual Basic, DBMS, Networking Implementation, Data Structure implementation, Programming in JAVA, E-commerce, XML, Multimedia,	180 hrs of practical session; face-to-face practical sessions with expert counsellors	-	-

		.NET, WAP and WML ORACLE, Internet Programming			
Diploma in Web & Multimedia Technology (DWMT)	1	Macromedia Flash, Dreamweaver, HTML, ASP, JSP etc.	96 hrs of practical session face-to-face practical sessions with expert counsellors	Virtual lab using net meeting	To provide pure online education and online assignments for this course
Diploma in Linux Essentials (DLE)	1	Shell Scripting, Linux installation, basic Linux commands, system administration, networking etc.	96 hrs of practical session face-to-face practical sessions with expert counsellors	A CD on Linux basic command simulation for students to practice anywhere on a computer system	To develop online and offline (interactive multimedia kit) for learners to perform hands-on lab anytime anywhere
Diploma in Education Technology (DET)	1	Ms-Office packages, Image editor like Photoshop, basic flash	96 hrs of practical session face-to-face practical sessions with expert counsellors	-	-
Diploma in Computer Application (DCA) (Revised curriculum is on offer	1	Programming in C, Visual Basic, PC-Packages, FoxPro	96 hrs of practical session face-to-face practical sessions with expert counsellors	-	-
Certificate in Computer Application (CCA)	6 months	PC-Packages, FoxPro	32 hrs of practical session face-to-face practical sessions with expert counsellors	-	-

Delivery of Practical Components at MPBOU

The practical session are conducted at the study centres of MPBOU where all the facilities including Hardware and Software are made available to the students. The responsibility of the Hardware and Software licenses lie with the study centre. MPBOU does not provide any hardware and software licenses to the study centres. 1:1 student computer ratio is provided and the duration of each session is 2½ hours. These sessions are conducted during or after the face-to-face contact sessions in the evening between 5.30 to 8.00 pm. The schedule is given to students at the respective study centres during their induction programmes. The schedules are again reconfirmed to the students via e-mail, their virtual learning environment and e-notice boards. In fact, hands-on practical provide the average hands-on requirement for the students. A student can practice more at the university study centres later depending on availability of computer time.

A coordinated mixture of theory and practical schedule is created so that the students get the maximum benefit. All the practical courses have a practical examination. In practical examination students' performance is evaluated over the semester. At study centres assignments are also given to the students, which they do on their own. The practical assignment is always the part of a course. During these assignments a student need to implement a problem in the required software, and demonstrates the adequacy of skills. Thus, MPBOU has a blended approach for delivering computer hands-on and lab practical to its students as shown in Fig. 1.

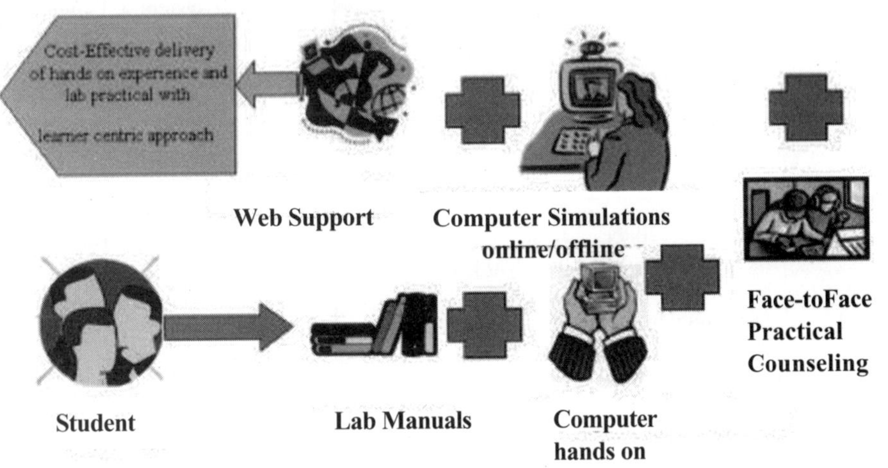

Figure 1: A blended approach for delivering computer hands-on and lab practical

Conclusion

The hands-on practical have been successful in computer science courses for all the programmes which have been important to the Distance Education mode students. The IGNOU students are found to be having reasonably good skills as far as practicals are concerned. The practical sessions, which have been given by IGNOU, include all aspects of computer science including programming and application. The project component of the IGNOU has strengthened the course delivery and enhanced the student's skill for quick absorption in the industry. Viva-Voce component in all project/practical is an excellent way of checking the authenticity of student work. Both these case studies presented here showcase the heavy importance given to hands-on practice and lab components in teaching computer application and information technology courses and programmes, as the employability of the passouts is a major concern to establish credibility of these programmes. Success of the graduates of these two universities in the employment market is an indicator of the acceptability and quality of the programmes in terms of theory and the practical components.

Sh. Akshay Kumar is Reader in SOCIS, Indira Gandhi National Open University, New Delhi.
Email: akshay@ignou.ac.in

Dr. Jyotsna Dikshit is Reader in M.P. Bhoj (Open) University, Bhopal, India.
Email: jdikshit@hotmail.com

26

Quality Assurance of Distance Education

V.S. Prasad

Introduction

John Ruskin once said, 'Quality is never an accident; it is always the result of intelligent effort.' Distance Education, variously known as open learning, distance learning, flexible learning, distributed learning, online learning, e-learning, resource-based learning, technology-mediated learning and such other nomenclature, with different shades of meaning and also used interchangeably, has come to stay as an important philosophy and form of education in the 21st century. In India, around 25 percent of tertiary learners are getting their education through distance mode. In the coming years, the educational planners are hopeful of increasing this number to 40 percent. This is an indication of the important place distance education has come to occupy in India's education and human resource development efforts. At the same time, there is insufficient public understanding of distance education functions and awareness about concerns regarding its quality assurance. Even though distance education systems and practices greatly vary and are context-specific, the experts in the field consider quality assurance as the common priority (Daniel et al., 2005).

Every age has its defining elements, which describe the purpose and nature of social processes of that age. It is generally assumed that tradition is the defining element of ancient society; religion is the defining element of the middle ages; reason is the defining element of modern society; and quality is the defining element of the knowledge society. Quality, in terms of fitness for purpose, excellence, perfection, standards, value for money, consistency, transformation and relevance, defines in different ways all the activities of the knowledge society. Quality makes the knowledge relevant to social and individual needs. Quality also enables the persons, societies and nations to acquire the competencies required for living meaningfully in a competitive globalised world. That is, quality is a requirement across the board. Distance Education, which is considered an important solution to meet the demand for mass education in developing countries, without quality may instead become a big problem. In this chapter, we reflect on this important problem. The approach is more of an insider's experience and concerns, than a scholarly analysis of the problem. The author, with his more than two decades of experience in various capacities in open universities and agencies engaged in institutional assessment and accreditation in India, has presented the operational picture of quality assurance contexts, practices and lessons with a hope that it will generate further discussion and action. The term, 'Distance Education' (DE), is used in this paper as a generic description of activities of open universities and distance education/ correspondence course institutes of conventional universities.

Education as Quality

Education, a process of creation, preservation and dissemination of knowledge, and development of skills and attitudes is an important element and basis of a knowledge society. The quality of the knowledge society depends on the quality of education. The Chinese philosopher Confucius considered that the goal of education was to produce men of quality who combined competence with virtue. From this perspective, we may consider education as quality. Quality as fitness of purpose defines the goals of education and provides answers to the 'what' of education; quality as excellence and standards in performance defines the processes of education; quality as value for money provides benchmarks for the output of education and quality as a transformation gives us the indicators to judge the outputs of education. In this sense, we may say that education is quality (Prasad, 2003). This is equally applicable to distance education.

As such, open learning has its genesis in mainstream face-to-face classroom based conventional education. But, the experience of about four decades of practice of distance education in India has brought forth two distinguishing features which deserve particular mention in the context of this discussion on quality. Firstly, the beginnings and early growth of DE systems in India were mainly motivated by access concerns. In the 1960s and 1970s, many students who could not get admissions in conventional institutions opted for distance learning. Policy makers also opted for encouraging distance education as a less costly option. As a result, large enrolment was considered a goal and an achievement of DE institutions. Quality did not get the attention it deserved and this attitude made it weaker option; recognition alluded DE. Secondly, in the context of structural readjustment in the 1990s where higher education was treated more as a private than public good, DE institutions began focussing more on surplus generation or profit-making practices in their operations. During the last decade, many more international players have begun operating in the DE field in India. Most of them are guided by the profit motive. As a result, quality has been a casualty and many unhealthy practices by DE institutions have been observed. There is another paradoxical development. Some of the prestigious institutions, known for their provision of high quality conventional education, are also being accused of providing low quality DE. The paradox is that the profits generated by providing low quality DE are used for the provision of high quality conventional programmes! It is alleged that some of the dual mode universities are using the distance mode programmes more to generate resources to subsidise and strengthen their conventional education programmes.

Some of these trends and developments have resulted in a strong expression of public concern about the quality of DE in India. As a response, many initiatives have been taken at the national and institutional levels to regulate the DE provision to ensure quality.

Quality Assurance Initiatives

The Distance Education Council (DEC), a statutory body of the Indira Gandhi National Open University, is entrusted with the responsibility of co-ordination and maintenance of standards in DE in India. The DEC has taken many initiatives for quality assurance in collaboration with national agencies like National Assessment and Accreditation Council (NAAC), National Board of Assessment (NBA), Indian Nursing Council (INC), National Council for Teacher Education (NCTE), All India Council for Technical Education (AICTE). Some of these are: (a) development of norms and guidelines for development and delivery of programmes in DE; (b) development of norms and guidelines for assessment and accreditation of DE institutions; (c) development support for promotion of quality; (d) development of database on the system operations; (e) publication of quality promotion materials; (f) encouragement for resource sharing through a common pool of best materials; (g) training support for development of human resources and transformation of materials into self-instructional format; and (h) support for research on quality assurance.

The University Grants Commission (UGC), the apex body of higher education in India, also has initiated many measures for the maintenance of standards in DE systems. Considering that there is a kind of mass proliferation of off-campus study centres with sub-standard facilities and inadequate attention to the quality of education imparted, the UGC, in consultation with the DEC, has formulated regulations for "Franchising of Higher Education Through Off-campus Study Centres: UGC Norms". The UGC norms spell out in detail the regulations for the delivery mode, the use of Information and Communication Technologies (ICT), and the organization and governance systems of off-campus study centres. The other national professional bodies like the AICTE and the NCTE have formulated detailed norms and regulations for offering professional programmes in engineering, management, pharmacy, architecture, teacher education, etc. through the distance mode in collaboration with DEC. Under these initiatives, expert committees of collaborative institutions visit the DE centres for on-the-spot assessment. The NAAC, under an MoU with the DEC, developed the instrument for assessment and accreditation of distance education institutions. The NAAC has brought out a number of publications on quality higher education which are equally relevant to distance education. The Ministry of Human Resource Development (MHRD) has formulated guidelines for the operations of off-shore educational institutions in India.

The brief account given above shows that there are attempts to put in place the framework of quality assurance in India for distance education. Many agencies like the MHRD, DEC, UGC,

AICTE, NAAC, NCTE and other professional agencies are involved in this process. Here, four concerns deserve special mention. One, there is lack of clarity about the role of the multiple agencies involved in this process. There are even overlapping areas of influence with the result that co-ordination among them is a cause of some concern. Secondly, many institutions feel that they are burdened with regulations by too many bodies and some try to play one against the other to escape responsibility. Thirdly, the enabling systems, structures and processes are too weak to implement the norms and regulations of quality assurance formulated by regulatory and professional bodies. The guidelines and regulations seem to be mere expressions of good intentions but formulated without paying sufficient attention to the operational framework required for the realisation of the intentions. Fourthly, the regulatory framework is considered rigid and unrealistic, lacking the flexibility to adapt to the diversity of local contexts and emerging concerns. As Philip Crosby put it: "Quality has to be caused, not controlled". It is understood that the MHRD is apprised of some of these concerns and is contemplating to establish Distance Education Council as an independent authority (presently it is with Indira Gandhi National Open University) to act as a national all-encompassing coordinating and quality assurance agency vested with authority to regulate all institutions engaged in delivery of distance education in all its varied forms and formats, including satellite supported interaction and online offer.

Some Lessons

The Indian distance education system can be described as 'one system, many models'. There is a great variation in the quality assurance policies, systems and practices of these institutions. At one end of the spectrum, we have Indira Gandhi National Open University with commendable quality systems and practices. Some state open universities have also developed quality learning materials and put in place practices of quality assurance. At the other end of the spectrum, many conventional institutions are offering sub-standard distance education programmes with large enrolments by franchising delivery. Many foreign and Indian institutions are also offering on-line education and training programmes. Mechanisms to ensure the quality of these programmes are yet to be developed. In this varied situation, drawing any lessons of experience will always have exceptions. In this section, some conclusions, based on author's feel of the situation, are presented to focus on broad trends which require close attention and action to ensure the quality of distance education in India (Prasad and Venkaiah, 2005). Some of these are:

- The Indian higher education setting shows that the DE is a response to the challenges of access and equity to quality education. The availability of the huge human resources and physical infrastructure in the conventional system, through partnerships for resource-sharing has contributed significantly to rapid strides of DE. Many Open Universities and DE Centres of conventional universities are able to provide higher education to millions with the optimum use of human resources and the infrastructure of the higher education system in the country. The Indira Gandhi National Open University serves its more than 1.3 million cumulative student population, with 350 thousand annual intake, by 300 full-time and 35,000 part-time academic staff from conventional system through 1300 study centres in institutions of higher learning.

Dr. B.R. Ambedkar Open University, with small full-time faculty of 75, is admitting more than 100 thousand students annually in different programmes. This is true of many other state open universities and correspondence course institutions. It has implications for quality concerns. The quality of distance education is partly determined by the quality of conventional higher education in the country due to the reliance on counsellors, lesson writers and examiners who come from the conventional system. Further, the DE system depends on the learning resource facilities that are offered and managed by the conventional system, of course along the guidelines of the DE system. This is more relevant when the convergence mode of delivery of education through joint offerings is becoming more common. So the quality of distance education operations is partly a reflection of the quality of higher education system in the country as well.

- Large enrolments in distance education programmes are not matched by requisite efforts for quality. In spite of Daniel's convincing argument of iron triangle, consisting of the vectors of access, costs and quality, as the success formula for open and distance learning, Indian DE institutions are not able to come out of the trap of inverse relationship of numbers and quality. In the academic community, there is a strong feeling that large numbers are affecting quality maintenance adversely. This is partly a result of their prejudices and partly because of their experiences. Daniel (2004) has explained in many of his works, how educational technology can help in ensuring the quality of distance education systems. In India, due to financial constraints, the use of educational technology, across the board, has been very limited to make a positive difference to quality. The extensive use of educational technology in teaching-learning, support services and system management will facilitate more interactivity, better connectivity and greater efficiency, resulting in higher quality of distance education. We are adopting alternative modes of education without effectively integrating alternative technologies required for that. We need to re-engineer learning environment for quality education.
- The sustainability of quality operations requires institutionalisation of quality. The institutionalisation of quality processes in DE institutions is very weak. The quality concerns are flowing more from above and are not uniformly spread. The quality of operations is a reflection of individual initiatives and efforts, than an institutional response. In such situations, sustainability becomes difficult. The open universities like Indira Gandhi National Open University, and a few other state universities, have well-defined systems and procedures for different activities of distance education operations like design and development of learning materials; student support services; student-evaluation and management operations etc. But the same cannot be said of operations of all state open universities and distance education centres of dual mode universities. To enhance sustainability, the institutionalisation of quality operations needs to be strengthened comprehensively. Every DE institution has to be encouraged and supported to create its own internal quality assurance structures and processes to ensure the quality of operations. Management of any large system requires an

efficient governance system. Leadership plays a very important role in institutionalising a flexible, open and responsive governance system which is *sine quo non* of quality.

- The drive for quality is not strong enough among a large number of staff of DE institutions. There is a passive response to quality initiatives. As Aristotle said, "The sustainability of quality is possible only when quality become a habit." Quality is an attitude of mind. How to internalise quality as a value among all the staff of the DE institutions is a major concern. Incentives for quality and disincentives for lack of quality may have to be thought of. More attention has to be paid to strengthening staff development programmes. IGNOU and a few other state open universities have taken many initiatives in staff development activities. More concerted efforts by all DE institutions is needed to build the institutional capabilities in quality assurance.
- The assessment and accreditation activities of the DEC, NAAC and other agencies are in the initial stages of development and their initiatives are yet to create the desired level of impact. There is a need to seriously consider the role these bodies could play in ensuring acceptable levels of quality in DE programmes, especially in ensuring comparability of quality and standards of programmes offered by dual mode universities and many private and international providers. The assessment and accreditation processes should help in bringing more transparency into the operations of DE institutions. In the context of the profit-making operations of DE institutions, the transparency of operationsmay result in more public pressure to maintain standards. More dissemination of information on the activities of DE institutions to all stakeholders will play a positive role in sustaining quality.
- Most of the stakeholders (learners, parents administrators and practitioners) are more interested in the timely conduct of examinations and the award of degrees on time. The concern of a large number of students is to get the degree/certificate, without much pressure for quality of the system. The nature and orientation of students is a critical factor in the quality of education. The DE institutions, in their desire to admit large numbers for various reasons, appear to overlook the desire to provide quality education, and are at times not able to ensure minimum competency levels of admitted students. This leads to low success rate and high drop out rate, reflecting on the quality of the system.
- In India, the research studies on quality assurance in distance education have not been of a high enough standard, in spite of commendable research studies from STRIDE (IGNOU), GRADE (BRAOU) and a few other institutions. Research studies can provide useful inputs to quality assurance. There is need for more action-research studies into different aspects of quality assurance which can be used as inputs for quality improvement of operations.

Conclusion

Quality of education is mainly the function of motivated students, committed staff, good infrastructure and efficient governance systems. This is true of all modes and all levels of education. The distance education context in India is a complex phenomenon of co-existence of different operational systems in terms of ownership systems, management practices, teaching-learning practices, delivery systems and programme focus, all functioning under the generic description of distance education. In such a context, any set of general observations will have a few exceptions. The best example of quality assurance of IGNOU and a few other DE institutions deserves wider dissemination and adoption. There are enough guidelines/benchmarks for quality assurance of distance education developed by international and national agencies. The challenge is in implementation. How do we make quality a 'habit of mind' and 'habit of action' is the critical concern of all those engaged in distance education. Capacity building in quality assurance across the board of distance education institutions is the only answer to these concerns.

References

Daniel, John, Kanwar, Asha & Uvalic-Trumbic, Stamenka (2005). *Mega Universities = Mega Quality?* Address of the President of Commonwealth of Learning at the 2nd World Summit of Mega Universities (September 25). New Delhi. http://www.col.org/speeches/ JD_0509MegaUsDelhi.htm.

Daniel, John (2004). *From the Triangle to the Pentagon: Open Universities in the 21st Century.* Address of the President of Commonwealth of Learning at the Asian Association of Open Universities 2004 Conference (November 28-30). http://www.col.org/speeches/JD_0411AAOUTx.htm

Prasad, V.S. (2003). Quality higher education. *Educomm Asia,* 8(4). Available at http://www.cemca.org/newsletter/june2003/junehtm2003.htm

Prasad, V.S. & Venkaiah, V. (2005). *India's first Open University: Experience of Two Decades.* Hyderabad: Dr. B.R. Ambedkar Open University.

Professor V.S. Prasad, a former Vice Chancellor of Dr. B.R. Ambedkar Open University, is Director, National Assessment & Accreditation Council, Bangalore.
Email: prasadvs99@hotmail.com

27

Promotion and Coordination of Distance Education: Role of National Open University

C.L. Anand and Suresh Garg

Introduction

Education is a liberating force and pre-requisite for regeneration of society, empowerment of people, national integration and international understanding and peace. Monopolising education is fret with dangers of inequities and disparities, as amply demonstrated in pre-independent India. The noble mission of the founding fathers of the Republic to create Educated India led to the demand of creating institution of higher education at the rate of about 10%. However, due to limited resources and lack of appropriate expertise, the higher education system comprising face-to-face (F2F) classroom-based teacher-centric system could grow approximately at the rate of 5%. This deficit over the years and concerns about the relevance, access and equity, lifelong learning, training and retraining began to create serious concern.

In 1961, Kothari Committee recommended creation of educational provisions through correspondence courses on pilot basis at Bachelors degree level in liberal arts with study materials developed by gifted teachers and use of communication technologies so as to optimally utilise intellectual and infrastructural resources. The experiment met with success and the Education Commission (1964-66) recommended it as a viable option for offer of quality education as widely as possible, including professional education. This led to rapid spread of correspondence education. However, the system inherited rigidities of the conventional system — run of the mill courses, same duration of programmes, examination, and entry conditions — and the disadvantage of non-availability of teacher-taught interaction. Unfortunately, not much effort was made to develop quality study materials using rigorous principles of educational technology or understand the need of distance learners. As a result, correspondence courses soon began to lose parity of esteem and by 1980 were relegated as weaker option; it was a mode for the rejects though it was catering to about 8% learners in higher education. Some of these issues have been raised by V.S. Prasad in his chapter in this volume.

This forced a serious reconsideration and although the first open university had come into existence in 1982, the national open university was created in 1985 by an Act of Parliament in search of more resilient and responsive educational system for all with a unique mandate which combined the roles of a university and national apex agency:

- widen equitable access to high quality education at affordable costs to all by offering innovative and need-based programmes of study at different levels using contemporary tools and techniques; and
- promote, coordinate and regulate the standards of education offered through distance mode.

These aspirations find reflection in the Vision statement of IGNOU:

> Indira Gandhi National Open University, the National Resource Centre for Open and Distance Learning with international recognition and presence, shall provide seamless access to sustainable and learner-centric quality education, skill upgradation and training to all by using innovative technologies and methodologies and ensuring convergence of existing systems for massive human resource required for promoting integrated national development and global understanding.

The University received full support from various national and international agencies in its formative years. We were fortunate to pool support of conventional peers from across the length and breadth of the country, though at times there was scepticism, probably due to ignorance. However, as years progressed, the University began to 'register' its presence, progressed fast in a complex environment and grew in all directions and dimensions — horizontally as well as vertically. As the second largest mega university in the world, now it leads a movement in higher education in the country. This is well illustrated in the statement of Dr. K. Kasturirangan, Former Chairman, Indian Space Research Organisation (ISRO) 'IGNOU is a trailblazer in India's quest for establishing a knowledge-based society in 21st century. It is more than an institution, it is a movement for the cause of education and knowledge. Whether in reaching out to the vast magnitudes of people, who are unable to access formal educational systems or in the integration of the best knowledge and skills through national and global networking using the most advanced techniques, the University's future role will be that of a front man' (Kasturirangan, 2003).

Expansion of the Open Distance Learning (ODL) System in the country, after the success of IGNOU, has been tremendous. Now, we have one of the largest distance education provisions in the world comprising 13 OUs and 106 CCIs. Moreover, it has now gained national character and acceptance as it enrols every fourth student in higher education. It is increasingly being felt that problems arising out regional imbalances, and lack of vocational education, as also equalisation of opportunities, can find answers in the flexibility and innovativeness of the IGNOU-led ODL system.

IGNOU as an Agency for Change

In the world of open and distance learning, IGNOU has come to acquire a prominent place. In the country, it is unique among universities and experts believe that its success can catalyse change. It has been contemplated to promote, coordinate and regulate ODL System at the national level. In fact, the IGNOU Act 1985 envisages that the 'objects of the University shall be to advance and disseminate learning and knowledge by a diversity of means, including the use of any communication technology, to provide opportunities for higher education to a larger segment of the population and to promote the educational well-being of the community generally, to encourage the Open University and distance education systems in the educational pattern of the country and to coordinate and determine the standards in such systems, and the University shall, in organising its activities, have due regard to the objects specified in the First Schedule' (IGNOU, 1998). IGNOU has, in fact, a dual role to play. For its programme offerings, it develops and produces courses for delivery of open learning through distance mode. It has the jurisdiction over the entire country to offer programmes at different levels — awareness, certification, diploma and degree; and in different fields — liberal education, physical and natural sciences, and professional education (engineering, information technology, medical, law, teacher education) for indigenous capacity building and meet the requirements of world markets. The number of academic programmes has risen from just 2 in 1987 to 108 in 2005 and caters to the educational needs of over 1.3 million learners.

Following a variety of reformative course design and development models, IGNOU has, with the help of conventional peers, created a repository of high quality self-instructional materials — print, A/V, audio-vision — strongly grounded in curriculum and instructional design principles. Special emphasis is on socially relevant and emerging areas such as human rights, women empowerment, intellectual property rights, environment and sustainable development, tourism and services management, HIV/AIDS, medical waste management, community cardiology, teacher training, training parents and care givers of physically challenged, nautical science, social work, food management and dietetics, and distance education. The basket of awareness programmes of life skills include training of rural artisans, masons, auto-mechanics, tannery and footware industry workers, computer literacy for school dropouts and so on. Similarly, in India, female literacy, particularly among muslim community, is very low. To take education to all has been accorded high priority in recent years. IGNOU is using its ICT capabilities to reach the hitherto unreached. Moreover, special Regional Centres/sub-Regional centres/Study Centres have been started to bring such people in the mainstream of education. The ODL system has grown at the rate of 27% and we account for 24% students in higher education, we need to do more to achieve the Tenth Plan target of 40% by including deprived groups such as child labour, street children, migratory and nomatic population. The teacher-learner process of the University is based on:

- open and flexible multi-channel learning;
- modular and credit-based courses;
- self-learning and self-pacing;
- credit accumulation and credit transfer; and
- strong curriculum and instructional design.

While creating a niche for itself as academic leader, IGNOU has ushered in a silent change in the world of open distance learning by emphasising on:

- sharing study materials and physical resources, a national pool of best materials is being created in DEC;
- forging alliances and convergence by developing/offering joint programmes in collaboration with conventional institutions such as Maulana Azad National Urdu University, Harish Chandra Research Institute, World Intellectual Property Organisation, among others;
- use of multiple media for educational delivery to respond to heterogeneity and diversity;
- attracting and nurturing talent and build in-house capacity through training programmes for teaching, non-teaching and professional staff;
- awareness on shelf-life of a course and need of revision/academic audit to determine continued relevance;
- march towards self-sustainability by generating funds received in fee, grant-in-aid, sponsored projects and managing them well; IGNOU and YCMOU are now able to meet the recurring expenditure and do not depend on the State for such finances;
- exporting education and competing with the best; IGNOU has its presence in 30 countries offering 22 programmes;
- assessment and accreditation by Distance Education Council; a number of programmes offered by CCIs have been approved now and are available on DEC website;
- expansion of ODL system by advising State Governments to establish open universities and managers of conventional universities to create Directorates of Distance Education;
- promotion of research and innovation with emphasis on systemic aspects in respect of improving subject communication and learner support, conducting tracer studies and participate/organise conferences/seminars to share experiences and evolve best practices;
- creation centres of excellence by promoting particular strengths of an institution; and
- developing databases of distance education.

IGNOU has led from the front and is providing leadership in the use of technology in education. It has recently created an Inter-University Consortium for Technology Enabled Flexible Education and Development (IUC-TEFED) and a National Centre for Innovations in Distance Education to provide a forum for sharing experience with national and international experts, who visit the University for a specific period of time and deliver seminar/lectures or conduct training courses. In 2004-05, IUC hosted the visit of four international experts and conducted three-week training programmes, one in collaboration with Commonwealth Educational Media Centre for Asia

(CEMCA), Commonwealth of Learning (COL), one in collaboration with SAARC Consortium for Open and Distance Learning (SACODiL) and one on its own, on initiating the distance educators in the use of interactive multimedia for enriching self-instructional materials and for online learning. The international participants were sponsored from African and Asian countries such as Ghana, Tanjania, Bangladesh, Bhutan, Maldives, Nepal, Pakistan and Sri Lanka.

A spin-off effect of sharing study material is to improve quality of education and provide authentic materials even to conventional students at affordable costs. IGNOU is therefore meeting this long felt need of Indian higher education system. Probably for the first time in the history of Indian higher education system, a university, IGNOU, has promised to contribute 25% in 10th Plan for ODL system from out of its revenue for creation of an edifice — National Network for Open and Distance Education (N-NODE) — meant for use of many.

Apex Body for Distance Education

The IGNOU has been contemplated as an apex body to promote, coordinate and determine the standard of education offered by ODL systems by any means, forms and formats, including online, web-based, satellite supported interactive videoconferencing, etc. The role of IGNOU in the coordination and maintenance of standards in distance education may well be described in terms of its operations at three levels: (i) maintenance of standards in respect of the university's own programmes; (ii) coordination of standards in the State Open Universities (SOUs); and (iii) monitoring the upgradation and conversion of study material of the Correspondence Courses Institutes (CCIs) and DEIs into SIMs. Section 5(2) of IGNOU Act states as follows:

> 5(2) Notwithstanding anything contained in any other law for the time being in force, but without prejudice to the provisions of sub-section (1), it shall be the duty of the University to take all such steps as it may deem fit for the promotion of the Open University and distance education systems and for the determination of standards of teaching, evaluation and research in such systems, and for the purpose of performing this function, the University shall have such powers including the power to allocate and disburse grants to Colleges, whether admitted to its privileges or not, or to any other university or institution of higher learning, as may be specified by the Statutes.

In order to fulfil the mandate stipulated in section 5(2), IGNOU, by a resolution of the Board of Management, set up a body under the designation Distance Education Council (DEC).

The power and functions of DEC are defined under Clause 4(a)(xviii) of Statute 28 of the IGNOU Act:

> to take such measures as are necessary, consistent with the objects of the University to provide an innovative, flexible and open system of University education for the promotion, including introduction and continuation, of courses and programmes which conform to the standards prescribed by the DEC to maintain such standards in the institutions offering distance education programmes and to prevent through such

> measures as are considered appropriate, institutions from offering courses and programmes which do not conform to the standards laid down by the Council.

The mandate of Council is vast and requires strategic planning and concerted efforts to realise it by encouraging innovation in diversity. It has the potential of blossoming into a National Institution for Assessment & Accreditation of ODL system. With this in view, BOM of IGNOU identified a few thrust areas and worked out strategies to achieve the goal of high quality open distance learning. These are reflected in the vision statement of DEC:

> Distance Education Council, shall provide academic guidelines to promote excellence, encourage use of innovative technologies and approaches, enable convergence of all systems and sharing of resources through collaborative networking for access to sustainable education, skill upgradation and training to all.

Technology as Tool for Quality Improvement

It is common experience that no single technology can be used by any institution for all purposes; there should be media-mix depending on availability of technology and accessibility of the target groups. The use of information and communication technology (ICT) is an important feature of the ODL System. IGNOU has successfully demonstrated its effectiveness for blended learning as well as in other operations such as the production and delivery of learning materials, strengthening the student support services, managing the evaluation system, etc. Its state-of the-art Electronic Media Production Centre (EMPC) serves as a model resource centre in production, dissemination and transmission of audio-video programmes, conducting teleconferencing and interactive radio counselling. The Tenth Plan document emphasised the need for establishing N-NODE under the umbrella of IGNOU's capabilities to connect all OUs and CCIs.

The University has succeeded in his endeavour to a great extent; all SOUs and 700 other sites have been connected through Extended C-band supported teleconferencing and 131 EduSat supported videoconferencing centres. While delivering the 16th Convocation address in IGNOU (2005), His Excellency, Dr. A.P.J. Abdul Kalam said,

> IGNOU has a major role to play in this transformation process of our society into a knowledge society through value added distance education system. There has been considerable effort to apply technology for improving the delivery of distance education system over the years. With the availability of an exclusive education satellite (EduSat), the time is ripe for making intense use of ICT to create an interactive virtual classrooms in all our remote areas (Abdul Kalam, 2005).

He further said,

> I understand IGNOU has taken number of steps to apply ICT for providing value added services to distance education students. Your effort in launching the Gyan Darshan, Gyan Vani, Teleconferencing, Interactive radio counselling …are indeed a

progressive step towards the distance and wider outreach of the educational programmes (Abdul Kalam, 2005).

IGNOU is now using online education to train Indian diplomats the world over and is about to plunge into tele-education project of GoI for 53 countries of African Union. Within the country we are:

- sharing channels of *Gyan Darshan* and 40 FM stations of *Gyan Vani* with SOUs and other institutes for inter-regional cooperation as well as local development;
- extending financial support to improve inter-institutional networking and computerisation of all activities for better learner support; and
- contributing for creation of N-NODE and encourage teleconferencing, telecounselling, online admission and examination for increased efficiency and productivity.

Under N-NODE, IGNOU has established connectivity with all SOUs through teleconferencing and EduSat supported 131 Satellite Interactive Terminals (SIT). This facilitates quick interaction and academic exchange. Moreover, the location of SITs in conventional institutions acting as our Study Centres also provides useful inputs to conventional students and peers. Other components of N-NODE include *Gyan Darshan* TV Channel, *Gyan Vani* radio cooperative and radio-counselling. The transmission of *Gyan Darshan* channels is automated through the installation of a video server at IGNOU providing downlink facilities to more than 500 centres of IGNOU and around the same number of other institutions in the country, including the State Open Universities, is benefiting the learners in particular and society in general. IGNOU plans to utilise the network of radio stations under the *Gyan Vani* FM initiative to offer a mix of primary, secondary, technical and higher education and continuing and distance education in areas such as environment, science and technology, health, social justice, women's empowerment, career counselling, etc. This radio cooperative is being operated in collaboration with SOUs and other conventional universities and is expected to meet the long-felt need of imparting instruction in regional language. IGNOU proposes to pool best programmes produced by different stations so that the most enriching experiences and best practices could be shared and operations economised.

IGNOU signed an MoU with Prasar Bharti to use 186 radio stations of the All India Radio for interactive radio-counselling. This is presently limited to weekly one hour 'live' phone-in counselling programme conducted on Sundays. Under this programme, experts respond to students' queries from their home via telephone. We are using it extensively in the State of Jharkhand for teacher education under 'Mukt Samvad' initiative from Ranchi and Bhagalpur Radio Stations of AIR, for one hour every day. These facilities are shared with the State Open Universities, which, in the process, have developed requisite expertise. Moreover, radio-counselling has also facilitated promotion of the regional languages as medium of instruction.

Quality in Distance Education: DEC

Quality is an issue of serious concern for credibility and acceptability of the ODL System.

Though the University has put in place very rigorous quality assurance measures for development and delivery of education, it has, through DEC, strived hard to address the issue raised by Prasad in his chapter in this volume. For this, it entered into MoU with other national apex agencies like All India Council of Technical Education (AICTE), National Council for Teacher Education (NCTE), National Assessment and Accreditation Council (NAAC), among others. Norms and guidelines have been finalised for recognition of ODL institutions, and programmes including professional education (management and IT) in collaboration with AICTE. A partnership has been forged with NCTE for recognising teacher education institutions and M.Ed programme is being developed in DEC-NCTE collaboration.

In pursuance of its mandate, the University has been striving, ever since its inception, to promote and strengthen the open and distance learning systems in the country by providing possible necessary guidance and support. In particular, it has provided technical and financial assistance to facilitate the development of new programmes and courses, expansion of study centre facilities, establishment and expansion of VSAT system, teleconferencing and broadcasting. It has also undertaken various activities and launched schemes for promotion of the distance education systems. A brief account of some of these measures follows.

Promotion of ODL system

IGNOU through DEC, provides development grants to the State Open Universities and Directorates of Distance Education in the Conventional Universities. There are at present 11 SOUs and another three are likely to be established soon. Likewise, there are 106 CCIs functioning in the conventional universities. The quantum of grant sanctioned to the SOUs has risen to Rs. 15.65 crore in financial year 2005-06. Likewise, the amount sanctioned to the CCIs has increased to Rs. 4.85 crore in financial year 2004-05. This has enabled the ODL institutions to strengthen the infrastructure, augment student support services, and conduct staff development and training programmes. The grants have also helped in the networking of institutions leading to overall improvement in the quality of distance education. A break-up of the DEC grants to SOUs and CCIs during the 9th Plan are given in Tables 1 and 2, respectively. Similarly, for the 10th Plan, the corresponding figures are given in Tables 3 and 4.

Table 1: Grants to open universities during 9th Plan

(Rs. in Lakhs)

Sl. No.	**Heads/ Subject**	**1997-98**	**1998-99**	**1999-2000**	**2000-01**	**2001-02**	**Total**
1.	Development of course material	9.75	65.0	172.0	455.0	144.0	845.75
2.	Student support services	21.75	145.0	240.0	207.0	80.0	693.75
3.	Staff training development	33.00	25.0	65.0	115.0	26.0	264.00
4.	Staff on contractual basis	0.00	25.0	50.0	47.0	72.2	194.2
5.	Un-assigned grant	18.5	18.5	18.5	18.5	35.0	109.00
6.	A/V production	28.00	Nil	46.5	25.0	0.0	99.5

7.	Quality improvement measures	25.00	0.0	0.0	40.5	5.0	70.5
8.	Information technological support	0.00	0.0	64.0	20.0	219.0	303.00
9.	Strengthening of regional services	0.00	0.0	85.0	0.0	25.0	110.00
10.	Research and development	10.00	0.0	50.0	25.0	15.0	100.00
11.	Computerisation	66.00	0.0	23.0	25.0	83.0	197.00
12.	Development of multimedia facilities	58.00	0.0	0.0	0.0	36.0	94.00
13.	Library/books	0.00	0.0	37.0	65.0	44.0	146.00
14.	Infrastructural	22.00	0.0	75.0	51.0	0.0	148.00
15.	Project fund assistance	0.00	4.0	0.0	0.0	0.0	4.00
16.	Virtual learning	0.00	0.0	0.0	100.0	0.0	100.00
	Total	292.00	282.5	926.0	1194.0	784.2	3478.70

Table 2: Grants to CCIs during 9th Plan

(Rs. in Lakhs)

Sl. No.	Heads	1998 -99	1999-2000	2000-01	2001-02	Total
1.	Development of course material	57.5	218.5	192.0	119.0	587.0
2.	Staff training and development	14.5	42.0	24.0	6.0	86.5
3.	Multimedia facilities	0.0	9.0	63.0	46.0	118.0
4.	Quality improvement measures	0.0	0.0	44.0	1.0	45.0
5.	Computerisation	0.0	26.9	34.0	54.0	114.9
6.	Library facilities	0.0	4.0	26.0	26.0	56.0
7.	Student support services	0.0	75.5	61.0	54.0	190.5
8.	Staff on contractual basis	0.0	0.0	0.0	7.2	7.2
9.	Development of A/V programme	0.0	26.6	23.0	9.0	58.6
10.	Technology support	25.0	41.5	23.0	7.0	96.5
	Total	97.0	444.0	490.0	329.2	1360.2

Table 3: Grants for SOUs in 10th Plan (till financial year 2005-06)

(Rs. in Lakhs)

Sl. No.	Heads/ Subject	2003-04	2004-05	2005-06	Total
1.	Development of course material	100.0	110.0	350.0	560.0
2.	Student support services	39.0	70.0	195.0	304.0
3.	Staff training development	20.0	22.0	105.0	147.0
4.	Staff on contractual basis	-	45.0	105.0	150.0

5.	Un-assigned grant	26.0	30.5	45.0	101.5
6.	A/V production	5.0	-	30.0	35.0
7.	Quality improvement measures	4.0	35.0	75.0	114.0
8.	Information technological support	77.0	81.0	280.0	438.0
9.	Strengthening of regional services	5.0	-	-	5.0
10.	Research and development	-	-	30.0	30.0
11.	Computerisation	42.0	65.0	250.0	357.0
12.	Development of multimedia facilities	-	-	-	-
13.	Library/books	5.0	37.0	100.0	142.0
14.	Infrastructural	33.0	-	-	33.0
15.	Project fund assistance	-	-	-	-
16.	Virtual learning	-	-	-	-
	Total	356.0	495.0	1565.0	2416.5

Table 4: Grants for CCIs in 10th Plan (till financial year 2005-06)

(Rs. in Lakhs)

Sl.. No.	**Heads**	**2003-04**	**2004-05**	**2005-06**	**Total**
1.	Development of course material	190.0	109.5	220.0	519.5
2.	Staff training and development	-	1.0	72.0	73.0
3.	Quality improvement measures	-	0.5	-	0.5
4.	Computerisation	-	35.5	15.0	50.
5.	Library facilities	-	26.0	-	26.0
6.	Student support services	57.0	42.5	87.0	186.5
7.	Technology support	128.0	55.0	91.0	274.0
	Total	375.0	270.0	485.0	1130.0

It may be mentioned that BRAOU and YCMOU have derived maximum benefit to create their own structures.

The utilisation of annual grants released to the ODL institutions is closely monitored. In the year 2004-05, more than twenty special committees were sent to monitor the utilisation of grants and on the spot assessment of the functioning of structures created for programme delivery by respective institutions.

As important programme of the DEC, IGNOU is to identify, from time to time, priority areas in which distance education programmes need to be developed and supported. It has recently identified professional programmes in areas such as management, computer, education, library science, etc. and has come out with norms and standards for the development and launch of these programmes through distance mode in a way that would ensure quality of education. The development of norms and standards in other areas are also being contemplated. These norms include guidance on aspects such as curriculum design, eligibility criteria, selection procedures, duration, student intake, learning resources, delivery mechanism, student evaluation, library services etc. in respective areas of professional education. In addition, the guidelines give concrete suggestions on monitoring and performance review stressing the importance of evolving mechanism of quality assurance in various phases of a given programme.

Evaluating programme materials in DE

The DEC, IGNOU has vigorously launched a programme of evaluation of materials in distance education prepared by various institutions. It has initiated approval of ODL programmes in order to maintain optimal standards in the system of delivery. The coursewares submitted by the distance education institutions are evaluated by expert committees in terms of content and overall quality of materials in the context of open and distance learning. A scheme has been prepared involving a large number of experts who are periodically engaged in the evaluation of materials received by way of giving comments and suggestions for improvement. The DEC has also taken up the impact assessment of distance education institutions of conventional universities.

Establishing an accrediting mechanism

At present there exist three types of accreditation agencies in the country: NAAC, which does institutional accreditation of the conventional universities and the affiliated colleges; the National Board of Accreditation (NBA) which accredits programmes of the AICTE affiliated courses in Engineering and related areas; and the Accreditation Board (AB) which entertains only the ICAR related programmes in Agriculture. These agencies are concerned with the institutional/ programme accreditation in the face-to-face mode. The DEC, IGNOU is responsible for accrediting ODL institutions. It has in collaboration with NAAC evolved separate criteria for the Open Universities and CCIs. Accreditation is done based on self-appraisal reports of the institutions followed by visits of peer experts. This forms the basis for recognition and accreditation of distance education institutions. These reports are also used by DEC to determine the quantum of financial support to the respective institutions. The guidelines for seeking approval, together with necessary proformas for furnishing requisite information, are issued by the DEC.

Being a statutory body, the DEC 'prescribes standards to determine the minimum level of infrastructure and academic staff for the ODL institutions which offer or intend to offer education through distance mode' (DEC, 2004). This is applicable to SOUs; CCIs/DEIs in conventional universities/ Deemed Universities/IITs/IIMs; the ODL institutions registered as societies/trusts aided or privately managed; all levels (certificate/diploma/degree) and types of programmes (professional, vocational/general education/awareness). The guidelines for foreign universities running DE programmes in India (independently or collaboratively) with Indian higher education institutions are to be finalised in the light of the policy of GoI. It is 'mandatory for all institutions to seek prior approval of the DEC for existing and new programmes and accreditation by the Board for on-going programmes offered through DE mode' (DEC, 2005). Recently, programmes of three Deemed to be Universities have been derecognised. Though such a decision may be harsh on ignorant students, it is perhaps necessary and desirable also for quality of education.

Creating database on ODL institutions

Authentic data is always desirable but hard to compile. Recently, the DEC, IGNOU decided to create an elaborate database on ODL institutions in the country as an annual publication. Its latest publication 'Information Base on Distance Higher Education in India - 2004' gives a comprehensive picture as regards the OUs/CCIs/DEIs. It provides up to date information on aspects such as growth of enrollment, programme offerings, study centres, delivery mechanism, availability of infrastructure, etc. in the distance education institutions. It also deals with enrolment patterns, learner profiles, financial position, student support services, qualification patterns of staff, the use of communication technologies etc. and thus serves as reference point and benchmark on Indian distance education, so vital for policy planners, distance educators, researchers and others interested in and concerned with the development of ODL System in India.

Extending research support

The DEC, IGNOU has a scheme of research projects to encourage system-based research. A grant amounting to over Rs. 15 lakh was released in the year 2002 in addition to a sum of Rs. 78 lakh provided to researchers as travel grant. The scheme is intended to promote investigation of specific problems about the concepts and practices in the distance mode of learning, in-depth studies on evaluation of distance education programmes, new technologies and their application, tracer studies on growth, success and retentivity rates as well as their acceptability. Projects under this scheme are categorised as major and minor research projects with the level of financial assistance of up to Rs. 20 lakh and Rs. 30,000/- respectively. This is meant for minor equipment, books and journals, field work, contingency, etc. required for the projects. In addition, the scheme provides for mini research projects with the financial assistance of Rs. 10,000/- enabling teaching and other academics in the SOUs and CCIs to process/finalise their on-going research work.

Future Directions

In view of the fact that the distance mode is increasingly becoming the mainstay of education in India, the dual role of IGNOU may have to be redefined. Experts are of the view that IGNOU should act as a research-intensive national resource centre, act as role model for SOUs/CCIs in instructional methodology, applications of new technologies etc. for value added distance education and facilitate convergence of all systems for seamless access and withdraw from programme offerings. Similarly, to be more effective, DEC should be an independent authority created under an Act of Parliament with all the powers and functions envisaged as of now for all forms of education — online, satellite-based, blended DE with multiple instructional package — imparted by any institution in the country.

References

Abdul Kalam, A.P.J. (2005) *16th Convocation Address.* New Delhi: IGNOU.

DEC (2004). *Handbook on Recognition Process for Distance Education Institutions.* New Delhi: DEC, IGNOU.

DEC (2005). *Information Base on Distance Higher Education in India.* New Delhi: DEC, IGNOU.

IGNOU (1998). *The Indira Gandhi National Open University Act 1985 (No. 50 of 1985).* New Delhi: IGNOU.

Kasturirangan, K. (2003). *Convocation Address.* New Delhi: IGNOU.

Professor C.L. Anand is former Vice Chancellor, Arunachal Pradesh University, Itanagar and former Pro-Vice Chancellor of IGNOU.

Professor Suresh Garg is Pro-Vice Chancellor, Indira Gandhi National Open University, New Delhi.
Email: scgarg@ignou.ac.in

28

Best Practices in Open and Distance Learning

Ranjan Welukar

Introduction

In India, due to historical reasons, the majority of society was denied access to education; the downtrodden and women were not entitled to education due to social and religious restrictions. Therefore, when the country achieved independence, universal education arrived as a new concept for the people. When the British left India in 1947, there were 20 universities and 590 colleges to cater to a country of 350 million people. More than 70% people lived in villages, who mostly were non-literate. The country faced several challenges, but lack of education appeared to be the greatest hurdle. Although the Indian Constitution had set for itself very noble goals like equality, fraternity and liberty, poor literacy rate seemed to be a great deterrent in achieving them. A lot has been done since then and today we have one of the biggest educational apparatus; it has fallen woefully short of societal expectations and aspirations at all levels - primary, secondary and tertiary. The dropout rate from 1st to 12th standard is about 75% and we are yet to achieve universalisation of primary education. The decision of Indian Parliament to make education compulsory for children in the 6-14 years age group is bound to generate additional pressure on the system as well as exchequer. In spite of 344 universities, 18000 colleges and a lot of expenditure in absolute terms, we have not touched the double digit as far as access to higher education is concerned. The post-globalisation and liberalisation world order has generated additional challenges with far reaching implications.

Open and distance learning (ODL) evolved in different ways, forms and formats in different countries across the world. The roots of this non-formal mode of education can be traced back to the middle of the 19th century. It has been known by various terms like Correspondence

Study/Education, Home Study, Independent Study, Private Study, External Studies, Distance Teaching, and Distance Education etc. The establishment of the first Open University in Milton Keynes in 1969 was a major breakthrough in the field. As a result of the success of UKOU, a model became available to many developed and developing countries and led to a new wave, a paradigm shift in the way education and training can be imparted notwithstanding the fact that different institutions adopted different practices of open learning. Though minor variations were inevitable in specific contexts, rapid growth of information and communication technologies (ICT) and their application for delivery of education enabled such institutions to provide greater access with highly cost-effective solutions.

It has been witnessed since long, particularly in education, that new ideas emerge and some take shape over years, compelling us to redefine our initial classifications. ODL, which itself, came into being as an innovation and one of the best practices in education, has now grown into a system in which we can identify certain best practices of its own. As such, use of the term best practices has generated considerable debate and in our view the best is always elusive; one has to search for it continually. But experts are of the view that identification of the certain core principles for quality assurance and standardisation and their integration into various processes constitute best practices in ODL. Essentially a practice ought to be viewed in context and relative terms, depending on the perspective and preparedness of the stakeholders, as also availability of ingredients. For learners, the best practices help them get highest grades and excellent placements, while academics may take knowledge and peer recognition perspective. For employers, accomplishments and suitability may be the indicators, whereas for the State, addressing the challenges of access and equity cost-effectively may constitute the best practice. For a developed nation, availability of the latest and most sophisticated technologies may be the best, whereas for a developing society ridden with malnutrition and poverty, mere provision of education may be viewed as the best practice. For a system, quality of products, processes, and services, development of innovative programmes in emerging areas at affordable costs and generating human capital capable of accelerating pace of new knowledge constitute best practices.

ODL and Globalisation

Presently three most discussed words in the world of education are access, equity and cost. Governance and quality have been added to suit the Indian context; the Daniel triangle was modified to Nigvekar pentagon (Daniel, 2004). Now it seems we must add the sixth vector - innovation - to support and address other five concerns.

Although globalisation has created new avenues and opportunities and some believe for the 'haves' and rich nations, it has definitely exposed the world to trends like the digital divide, the quality divide and the consequent socio-economic divide. Now the world stands fragmented on these issues; those having access to computers and those without, live in two different worlds! To bridge this rapidly growing gap caused by socio-economic divide, an aggressive use of ODL is inevitable. The 7-C approach, recommended by the UNDP (1999), will succeed only if the best practices in ODL are followed on a universal basis.

Connectivity: Establishing telecommunication and computer networks is inherent to the efficiency and efficacy of distance education practices; in so doing it is able to use infrastructure of reputed colleges and universities for face-to-face transaction. We have to devise mechanism for aggressively implementing connectivity as a tool and utilising the same for universalisation of education in the best possible way.

Community: Since ODL, by focussing on facile and universal access to knowledge and skills, is creating a learning community all over the world so that community rather than individual approach would prevail. The dedicated educational satellite EduSat launched by Indian Space Research Organisation, ISRO, for education is a unique example of group access and community development through use of ultra modern technology for education. The OUs such as Indira Gandhi National Open University, Madhya Pradesh Bhoj (Open) University, B.R. Ambedkar Open University, Yashwantrao Chavan Maharashtra Open University have established satellite interactive terminals with multiple teaching ends for using this tool very aggressively through well established networks in their respective areas of jurisdiction.

Capacity building: For a country endowed with 42% population living below poverty line, the only way to empower its people and raise the quality of their life is through development of skills and competencies. Creation of a critical mass of authentic researchers and resource persons for generation and dissemination of knowledge is another major challenge. Moreover, in the emerging knowledge society, constant updating is also one of the most important and crucial aspects to remain relevant as established theories are being often challenged. The same is also true of technology. We are now using it for sharing the findings with contemporary researchers instantaneously through e-connectivity.

With aggressive use of technology, ODL can take up the huge responsibility of knowledge and skills upgradation of a large number of people spread over vast geographical area and engaged in multiple activities, besides education.

Content: The Internet has made everything ultimately democratic and easily accessible. This has led to a situation in which a person living in the equatorial area of Africa can learn about the latest atmospheric trends in Norway or a student in an atoll in the South Pacific can learn about the latest trends in information technology in MIT, or IIT-Kanpur, India, without moving an inch from his/her location. The technology has led to globalisation of the content with the facility of maintaining its locality as well. ODL has absorbed the boons of technology and passed them on to the learner. Through online or satellite based education, even cross-border delivery of education has become a distinct reality. Only recently, GoI has taken an initiative to impart tele-education and tele-medicine in 53 countries of African Union.

Creativity: Since ODL is essentially an initiative to free the learner from the captive classroom conditions; it allows complete freedom to innovate and nurture creativity. For developing countries with poor resources and huge populations, ODL provides probably the easiest path for development. With the availability of Internet, mobile phones and other recent learner support systems, the concepts of mobile vans, television and radio seem to be days of distant past. These have brought about quantitative and qualitative changes in the teaching-learning processes and provide greater opportunities for self-actualisation to learners.

Collaboration: The facile and liberal nature of the ODL system has made collaborations easy. Ever since the UK Open University developed tailor-made courses for industries, who have skill-oriented specific requirement of the content, collaboration of educational institution with industries, social organisations and even individuals has become a special feature of the ODL system. The national open university of India has been collaborating with a wide range of educational, developmental and funding national as well as international institutions/organisations for design and delivery of customised education. This has been carried forward by the State Open Universities in good measure.

Cash: ODL system has practised best practices by devising innovative ways to fund the knowledge society. Unlike any conventional university, the YCMOU has even tilled its land and sold its farm produce such as mangoes, drumsticks, grapes and nursery saplings on the campus. Funds have also been generated through collaborations forged with public/private institutions for computer, management, tourism and other such programmes in India. Revenue generation has also helped the ODL system to get over the public sector mindset of state financing. Now IGNOU and YCMOU do not depend on state grants for salary and other recurring expenditure. This is due to the fact that these cater to the higher education needs of about 15% of the sum total of the annual enrolment in higher education.

The system is new and challenging as compared to the conventional system of higher learning. Therefore it becomes imperative for the system to work differently and innovatively to realise its full potential. However, professional approach is pre-requisite for growth. Keeping this in mind, the open universities are continuously striving toward professional management of various services for need-based educational and training programme design, development and production using principles of educational technology. For delivery of programmes, technology - print, A/V, radio, TV, teleconferencing and now videoconferencing - is being harnessed extensively.

Management of Services

ODL supposes that students need counselling at every stage of their progression and the system has developed an in-built mechanism for support services and helping them to succeed in learning.

Student registration

Aggressive use of information and communication technologies has led to quick processing of information with precision of details. It is now possible for a student to register from home in an online programme. This saves effort, time and money for the student community making registration an easy and convenient activity. Effective responsive units of the registration process make it a further pleasant and an inexpensive experience for the students. Unlike the conventional universities, an ODL organisation has to create a large-scale demand for its products to ensure cost-effectiveness. Extensive pre-enrolment publicity in different forms and formats is a necessity to the extent of almost becoming a mandatory requirement by the very nature of the system.

Invariably an ODL organisation uses several media of mass communication. The pre-registration counselling, seldom available in the conventional universities, offers personal touch in ODL. Recently, the YCMOU ran some 12 help-lines throughout the day in Maharashtra in its 35 districts of operation for pre-registration counselling that resulted in a rise of 7000 students in its current admission session. IGNOU has created student support centres in each of its 32 Regional Centres and at the Headquarters. Experience shows that this activity not only minimises many of the initial problems of transition but is also useful in planning studies and consequent retentivity and success rates (Garg, 1999).

Production and distribution of learning material

The system of review of the study material, its editing, vetting by a team of experts ensures quality at every ODL institution. The print material is distributed by post from the Headquarter or through a network of study centres entailing co-ordination between several agencies within and outside the organisation. Audio and visual materials are used mainly for TV and Radio programmes. In the case of YCMOU, the collaboration with ISRO has led to production of special audio visual study material for its virtual classroom spread over 100 study centres in Maharashtra. IGNOU and BRAOU have accumulated a large repository for use at Study Centres. As such, these are used as add-on supplementary support, unlike in UKOU, where these have been integrated into the print. This variation has been thought of due to localised condition. Recently Takwale (2003) and Dhanrajan (2003), while reflecting on the best practices have suggested enhanced use of e-medium, networking and collaboration as other strategies to enhance quality of learning environment.

Academic support

After distribution of specially designed study material that helps independent study, every student is provided administrative and academic support through Regional Centres and Study Centres. Best practices demand easy access to information they need. Printing FAQs and updating information on student record (assignment grades, term-end examination (TEE) scores, change of Study Centres, status of material despatch) on Web should ease life for those enrolled. As far as academic support is concerned, we need to provide access to excellent library, laboratory (wherever hands-on experience is an integral component) and counsellors/tutors. Counselling is arranged at the convenience of learners in order to encourage interaction. Besides this, counselling could be made available through radio, television and the Internet on a regular basis. However, technology can facilitate not teach. We need to ensure that learners have easy access to counsellors to clear their doubts and difficulties with regard to the self learning materials or grades obtained in TMAs etc.

Assessment and evaluation

An ODL learner may have been cut off from educational atmosphere for a long time. He/she, therefore, is apprehensive of his/her abilities of learning and performance in the evaluation process. To adequately respond to this situation, YCMOU introduced the concept of class-tests as a substitute for continuous assessment so as to prepare its learners for appearing in the term-end examination. It is unique to YCMOU in India, though it is practised widely elsewhere.

As the ODL learner may be enrolled in some other programme as well at a conventional university, examination dates sometimes overlap. To meet this challenge, YCMOU devised a unique remedy. The papers that are likely to overlap with the examinations of other universities are offered twice in the same schedule but with altogether different questions. This allows an ODL learner to earn dual degrees. In technology-oriented courses, online examination offers an efficient and prompt mode of evaluation.

Management of Processes

To match rapidly changing needs of content and continuous updating thereof, ODL organisations often depend on outsourcing. Invariably, the best expertise available in the country/state is used to design curriculum that addresses most recent developments and trends. This helps them in creating quality assets without creating a permanent unprofessional liability. Not many permanent professors are appointed for development of study material but services of experts in the conventional system/ industry/corporate sector field are borrowed on case to case basis. This not only helps in cutting costs but also ensures better quality and accountability. The team approach affords to pool quality content and transform it so that it is easily comprehensible, authentic and has relation to the context at the level of the target group. The ODL study material preparation team also consists of a content editor and an audio-visual editor. This ensures that the content is made palatable to a student obtaining knowledge through multiple media. The team approach of ODL ensures timely decision-making on development, adoption, transformation and translation of content with periodic revision.

Development of learning material

Unlike the tell and test, chalk and talk approach of the conventional system, in an ODL institution the design of the study material plays a major role in the process of learning. For this reason alone, the process has been made extremely rigorous. And, an invisible teacher is built in to the study material. In certain advanced stages, 'reflective action guide approach' is also adopted in a few ODL institutions.

To ensure quality, objectives of learning are first decided and then a design is developed with the help of experts in different domains of the learning process. The audio-visual component is also considered simultaneously to suit the needs of technology used in disseminating the content. The script editors enjoy full liberty and access to the content writer in a team atmosphere, thereby making things easy and palatable to the learner in the end. After development of material a mandatory preview is carried out. After appropriate revisions, if any, the material is made available to a batch of students and feedback is obtained from them along with that from the counsellors and experts. The consequent second revision makes the product flawless.

Modularity in curriculum, need-based and vocationally-orientated courses, openness to change/ revision/updating, a unique ability to cater to the needs of a heterogeneous group of learners are some of the special features of an ODL institution. Besides these, a learner-centred approach both in development and delivery of instructional material, facile learner mobility - vertical as well as lateral - through credit accumulation and transfer, responsiveness to the needs of specific learner groups (e.g. physically challenged) also constitute a major hallmark of the ODL system. Its easier integration of technology with pedagogy, its ability to access expertise from wherever possible, and the aggressive usage of the Internet make ODL a fountainhead of the best practices in the field of education as a whole.

In addition to the above, the open universities have succeeded in developing a consortium approach to content development and their leadership in collaborative projects with government, NGOs, universities and international agencies are also setting examples for the world of education as a whole.

Assessment and Accreditation

In view of its industrial nature of operations, ODL system lends itself naturally to corporate concepts such as quality, accountability and strategic planning, completely alien in education parlance before the emergence of ODL system. Recognising their importance and the competitive scenario of the post-GATS world order, Distance Education Council has, in collaboration with NAAC, AICTE, NCTE and other apex agencies, devised benchmarks and quality indicators to assess quality of services provided by ODL institutions. Since the requirements of distance learners and methodologies of open learning are vastly different from those of conventional learners and conventional universities, the mechanism of quality assurance and control have greatly helped the system to receive national acceptability and character. Evaluation of learning materials and on the spot assessment of infrastructure has helped in improving the quality of support services.

Conclusion

In the last decade of the 20th century, several innovations have taken place in operations' management such as open-sourcing, outsourcing, off-shoring, in-sourcing, supply chaining, in-forming, etc. All sectors are gradually absorbing the sweeping changes of the 21st century innovations in their own pace and fashion. ODL, however, has been faster in adopting these innovations compared to other systems of higher education. The adaptability of ODL to innovations has shown impressive results. The system has emerged as a great facilitator to large sections of society for enhancing access to higher, vocational and technical education to all at different levels with special attention on disadvantaged groups; women, physically challenged, SC/ST populations and those living in the remotest and educationally backward regions. It has also succeeded in relating the developmental needs of the nation as a whole while designing various programmes for individualised study and growth. Due to the application of modern communication technology it has become possible for ODL to innovate and enjoy the benefits of a flexible approach.

Change is inevitable. The number of inventions and innovations that have taken place in the last century is several times larger and faster than all the previous years of recorded history. This has led to a dire need of continuous acquisition of new set of skills. ODL has enabled society to cope up with this huge challenge. The greatest accomplishment of the ODL system is in its unique ability to absorb all innovations and a sustained endeavour to remove the gap between the haves and have-nots of the world of knowledge which in fact, constitute the foundation of all other disparities in other areas of human development. The challenge lies in continuing to remain relevant by offering cost-effective innovative programmes which support development of individuals, society and the nation.

References

Daniel, John (2004). Inaugural lecture: 'Initiatives on Online Learning and Educational Multimedia'. International Workshop on Interactive Multimedia for Distance and Online Learning, IUC-DEC-COL, New Delhi.

Dhanrajan, G. (2003). Best practices: then and now. In V.S. Prasad, (ed.), *Best Practices in Open and Distance Education*. Hyderabad: BRAOU

Garg, S. (1999). Convergence of conventional and distance modes - development and delivery in the university of the South Pacific. *Indian Journal of Open Learning*, 8, 131-138.

UNDP (1999). *Human Development Report*. New Delhi: OUP.

Takwale, R.G. (2003). 'Managing paradigm shift in parameters and benchmarks for best practices in open and distance education'. In V.S. Prasad, (ed.), *Best Practices in Open and Distance Education*. Hyderabad: BRAOU.

Prof. Ranjan Welukar is Vice Chancellor of Yashwantrao Chavan Maharashtra Open University, Nashik, Maharashtra. Before joining YCMOU, Prof. Welukar was HRD lead officer, CYP Asia Region.

Email: ranjanwelukar@yahoo.com

29

Quality Assurance in Distance Education: DEC Initiatives

Suresh Garg and Madhulika Kaushik

Introduction

In India tertiary education infrastructure comprises about 300 universities and 18,000 colleges. These cater to nearly 12 million learners, who constitute only 7.5% of the eligible age group of 17-23 years. This percentage is of an order of magnitude less than that of developed countries and resulted in a deficit because of unmet demand for higher education; the annual requirement grew at the rate of 10% whereas the provisions increased at the rate of 5%. Moreover, 70% of our population does not have access to higher education within 50 km of their habitat. This is not an adequate response to national needs for higher education in a fast growing economy, where aspirations for higher education are set to rise as an outcome of both policy initiatives (i.e. Sarva Shiksha Abhiyan) and the escalation in proportion of the young population aspiring to be part of the success saga of an India under transition.

The open learning system has its genesis in this gap between demand and supply for higher education, the removal of which has remained unfulfilled by the conventional mainstream system of education, a gap that is bound to be further compounded by the fast rate of obsolescence of knowledge in information era and consequent need for continuous training and re-training. In this background of life long learning (L3), open learning has now come to be accepted universally as a viable philosophy of education and distance mode as a flexible, dynamic, credible, learner-centric and cost-effective mode of education based on industrial processes. Since the system lends itself to technology, it is geared to be more efficient, innovative, futuristic and endowed with immense capacity and capability to respond to the issues and challenges emerging from L3 as well as issues of enhancing access and providing equity in educational opportunities at different levels to our people. It is particularly suited to cater to large numbers and geographically inaccessible and the remotest areas inhabited by economically poor, socially excluded and educationally backward.

The higher education system in the country has witnessed definite preferences of students, parents and employers for certain institutions. Cambridge, Oxford, Princeton, MIT, Stanford, London Business School are some of the examples. In India, IIT and IIM graduates are preferred and much in demand. Similarly, even within a university, a few departments or colleges are preferred over others. This is essentially because of the desire for quality and perception of quality assurance measures applied by teachers and researchers as well as institutional support mechanisms. Quality, experience shows, may be affected, if expansion is uncontrolled. But if organisational focus is on making quality inherent to all its processes, the organisation can sustain pressures generated by the diversity and multiplication of learner population and their individualized needs, as well as multi-level requirements. We would, however, have to be proactive in search of intent and purpose, identify priorities and practice ethos of sharing and partnership (Hope, 2004). Under the impact of the twin phenomena of globalisation and liberalisation, education has become a marketable commodity for cross border delivery. It has to respond to emerging needs, trends, practices and competition. This has put the issue of quality assurance in education, an elusive element in educational parlance before the emergence of open distance learning, at the centre stage. There is now general concern for ensuring quality in education and supporting best practices (Despande and Murgridge, 1994; Gupta, 2005) and our focus here is on open education at tertiary level. In India, 12 open universities and 106 conventional universities are, as of now, offering education through the distance mode which now falls under the quality assurance ambit of the Distance Education Council (DEC), created under the Statutes of Indira Gandhi National Open University to promote, strengthen and regulate the standard of open-distance learning in the country. It is within the authority of DEC to lay down policies and procedures concerning norms and standards in distance education and promote their compliance. In this chapter, after discussing the broad parameters of quality assurance framework in the context of open and distance learning, we share the steps taken by DEC to discourage sub-standard institutions and support quality programmes in recent years.

What is Implied by Quality Assurance?

Quality, accountability, strategic planning etc. have been corporate concepts. The Bureau of Indian Standards defines quality as the totality of features and characteristics of a product/service that bear on its ability to satisfy stated and implied needs (BIS, 1988). Quality perceptions in the context of distance education vary considerably across institutions, so also its definition. Quality has been viewed in terms of fitness for purpose, perfection, and conformance to standards, value for money, consistency, and relevance (Green, 1994). Warren et al. (1994) have identified two broad areas of quality assurance: the processes involved in both production of materials and delivery of education. We also need to add criteria such as access, flexibility and innovation to the quality requirements. A good quality open learning system brings higher education within the reach of target population using innovative strategies, flexible enough to provide for their occupational, personal and professional exigencies of time, place and pace. In addition, quality in open and distance learning systems has to be responsive to the requirements of L3 to keep the human resource pool of the country at the cutting edge of competitive excellence.

Powar and Panda (1995) observed that 'an institution of high quality is one that effectively meets its stated purpose(s) or mission(s), which should have taken into account the client's stated as well as implicit needs'. Since education and learning are transformative processes, the assessment of quality includes both the outcome quality and the process quality. Prasad (2003) argues that 'quality as fitness of purpose provides answers to education for what; quality as excellence and standards in performance defines the processes of education; quality as value for money provides benchmarks for the output of education and quality as a transformation gives us the indicators to judge the output of education'. The prevalent view amongst educationists and scholars is that quality can be ensured only through convergence of theory and practice so that our product (graduands) can relate to the 'world of work' well. Seen from this angle, quality may be regarded as a developmental goal and therefore a never ending process.

Holmberg (1995) has suggested that high quality DE should seek to encourage students for deep learning through empathy approach in real and simulated communication. He writes, "in agreement with common sense and everyday observation, I assume that feelings of personal relations between student and teacher promote motivation, study pleasure and effectiveness of learning. Such relations can be fostered not only by personal interaction, i.e., real communication but also by a kind of simulated communication which can be brought about by a personal style of presentation that attempts to involve the student emotionally in the study and a conversational manner of writing which consistently addresses the individual student and asks for his/her reaction, views and experiences."

Any quality assurance system in the context of ODL, therefore, needs to incorporate elements of TQM in design, development and delivery processes as well as the evaluation and certification processes used (Garg and Sharma, 1997).

Process Quality Assurance

The ODL system is learner-centric and we have to offer what learners need in changing scenario rather than offering more of the same with no value addition. Also, to meet the challenges of global competitiveness, let us first examine the measures required under various process heads vis-à-vis DEC initiatives.

Design of ODL programmes

At the design stage of ODL programmes, key parameters of relevance in local, national, regional and international context, access and equity in contemporary realities have to be clearly ensured. Relevance of the programme content to the fast changing societal needs and employer requirements as well as responsiveness to the competencies profile most highly sought by the employer need to be incorporated. At the same time, programmes need to be seen as comparable to the best put on offer by the conventional systems for parity of esteem and acceptability by the society in general and employers in particular. These could be achieved by the following:

- Standardisation of a well understood and clearly defined system of credits to be assigned to different components of course work and consequently the credit worth of each course, module and programme in terms of learner workload. This would enable establishing equivalence and credit transfer across institutions and across open and conventional systems.
- Making programme expert committees fairly broad based, and pooling the best available expertise in the country.
- Ensure industry-institution interaction by involving stakeholders in the expert committees to incorporate a realistic picture of employer needs in terms of required competencies.
- Conducting a need survey prior to the proposal of the programme to ensure that the programme is reflective of learner and societal needs in that domain.
- Leveraging available expertise from other institutions/outside experts, to ensure that the best resource pool is available to conceptualise and design the programme.
- Identifying possible areas of technological intervention and accessing expertise across institutions, and build collaborative dynamic networks.
- Collaborating with educational institutions both national and transnational, and/or industry and professional organisation where knowledge or experience pool exists, to conceptualise and design innovative, contemporary programmes.
- Institutionalising open and transparent mechanisms to review and approve the programme design by academic bodies to ensure the impossibility of a less than excellent programme being put on offer.
- Reviewing the programme content, through a system of peer review, internal and/or external, every three to five years to ensure continued relevance.

DEC has been providing financial support to establish technological infrastructure, including computerisation of various activities, and creation of multimedia centres since the beginning of Ninth Plan.To standardise curriculum for national acceptability, DEC has taken initiative to design teacher education programme in collaboration with National Council for Teacher Education (NCTE). Moreover, DEC has advised SOUs and DEIs to refrain from 'reinventing the wheel' and design programmes which (a) are financially viable and based on market trends and empirical evidence, (b) cater to the unreached and special groups, and (c) are not cost-intensive.

Development of content

ODL systems, in quality assurance context, have a distinct edge over other systems in that the teaching-learning tools in use, whether by way of print material, audio-video programmes, tele/ videoconferencing, or CD-ROMs, etc. are in the nature of public presentations, which, being tangible outcomes of work produced and open to public scrutiny, necessitate a certain quality consciousness among the institutions developing them. For this reason, ODL institutions follow rigorous curriculum development processes based on benchmarks and quality indicators which can meet expectations of parity and monitoring mechanism. We need to keep futuristic demands and emerging trends in view. Some of the practices which could be leveraged include:

- Identification of learning outcomes for each module, programme course and unit for clarity of vision about what should form part of the content and how should it be presented.
- Building the teacher into the text by ensuring interactive content with possibilities of formative self-evaluation and testing; bringing live examples from the immediate environment and context makes the material more comprehensible and alive. To ensure that the material is comparable with the best in the world in terms of level of academic excellence, we need to pool the best possible subject experts from across the country and put the produced effort through rigorous consultations and discussions. Moreover, ensuring that learning habits, attitude and context are not obscured is an important requirement. These should be self-motivating, promote deep learning and self-learning for exploring the unknown and develop problem solving skills.
- Participation of stakeholder in the development of content generation to ensure relevance and 'fitness for purpose' aspects of quality in ODL materials.
- Orientation of course content developers and experts available in the conventional institutions as well as professional spheres in the principles and best practices in self-instructional material development helps in ensuring uniform and acceptable standards.
- Institutional mechanisms for language and content editing by acknowledged experts should be a necessary component of the course development process. This helps to bring authenticity, clarity and comprehensibility.
- Developmental testing among intended target segments needs to be done to elicit feedback on relevance of content, difficulty levels, achievement of learning outcomes and effectiveness of self-evaluation components.
- Deciding upon the shelf life of a given course, say three or five years, beyond which the course will have to compulsorily be put into the revision cycle enables constant relevance of the material.

As such, developing learning materials by integrating print, A/V and other media solutions is now an advanced science and requires extensive effort and expertise. DEC has provided financial as well as technical support to all DEIs and SOUs to transform study materials into self-instructional format. Moreover, to encourage in-house capability building for material development, workshops have been organised with the support of IGNOU experts. For increasing acceptability and credibility of the system, DEC initiated the process of assessment of materials and accreditation of institutions. Quality indicators to suit the requirements of ODL system have been evolved in collaboration with NAAC and other leading experts. The materials found deficient in quality are sent back with suggestions to improve. Keeping the interests of learners in focus, institutions have been advised to desist from offering sub-standard programmes.

Requests have been received from DEIs for allowing offering of professional, money spinning programmes such as B.Ed, MBA, and MCA. When it was observed that most of them were ill prepared in terms of intellectual capital and resource materials, DEC evolved the concept of national pool of best materials. The collection is expected to increase access, help develop ethos of sharing, promote excellence and innovation through collective wisdom, forging strategies, and alliances. Another consideration is to concentrate on identified strengths of different institutions and encourage these to emerge as centres of excellence.

It is expected that, as we grow, more ODL institutions shall contribute to the common pool. However, to promote the system, institutions have been advised, if they so like, to use DEC approved materials through adoption, translation and adaptation. This has shown positive results and a growing number of institutions are coming forward to avail the benefits of this provision. The sharing of materials has helped avoid duplication of efforts, save costs and maintain quality without any compromise on innovation in diversity. Encouraged by this trend, DEC has initiated development of joint teacher education programmes in collaboration with NCTE.

Delivery of ODL Programmes

Quality assurance in the delivery of education includes relationship between the institution and its students, reliability of schedules and effective student support services. For these, ODL systems utilise a variety of options and media, the key objective being to create as responsive and as effective a network of learner support systems as possible. An entire spectrum of possibilities — from a brick and mortar network of study centres, facilitating face to face interaction and serving as the focal point of all academic services, to web and wire based learner support services — is available to choose from, depending on the requirements of the programmes and the respective learner segments. Similarly, a variety of media options, blended into the optimum media-mix can add value to the teaching-learning transaction. Academic services like counselling, mentoring and assignment evaluation are performed by counsellors or mentors available at the centres or at the serving ends of the web based service networks. Maintaining parity in standards of quality across nationwide learner support networks is often an issue that defines the differentiation between an excellent ODL service provider and an average one. Measures to assure quality in the delivery of ODL programmes include but are not limited to:

- Ensuring easy access to routine information on counselling schedule, conduct of examination, assignment evaluation.
- Developing benchmarks for all key aspects of service delivery viz. material despatch, counselling sessions, examination schedules, assignment delivery and evaluation, declaration of results, responsiveness to learner queries and complaints, timing and conduct of interactive teleconferencing and radio counselling sessions, broadcast of A/V programmes, etc. and

ensuring implementation of these desirable performance standards across the board for all programmes.

- Maintaining responsive relationship between an institution and its learners by institutionalizing systems of receiving formal and informal feedback about all aspects of programme content and delivery.
- Aiming at zero error student support services and complete reliability of all schedules.
- Taking complete responsibility of investing in the quality of part-time academic resources, like counsellors and mentors through sustained programmes of counsellor orientation, training and re-training so that they can develop an empathy with their learners and pace their study through didactic interaction in the form of tutor comments within stipulated turn around time.
- Institutionalizing mechanisms of monitoring the quality and adequacy of learner support services regularly.
- Putting in place an efficient complaint redressal mechanism to minimize possibility of grievances.
- Investing in research to constantly search for higher levels of effectiveness and efficiency in service delivery.

The poor and sub-standard programmes offered by correspondence course institutes in initial years and franchise to non-educational organisations by some of our universities earned us poor credibility and relegated the system to the second option category and that too for rejects. This was in spite of the great promise and expectations of this alternative mode of education advocated by the Education Commission (GoI, 1966). In the past few years, however, DEC has taken several corrective measures pro-actively to meet the challenges of credibility arising from such practices. Basic norms and guidelines specifying minimum infrastructure (physical as well as human capital) with focus on self-evaluation have been issued, for creation of new and recognition of existing centres of open learning as well as regulating the delivery mechanism. These were preceded by extensive consultations with highly reputed national leaders in DE, past and present. The Chairpersons of UGC, AICTE and DEC issued a joint letter, on the initiative of DEC, to the Vice Chancellors/Heads of Institutions of Higher Education in the country highlighting the Gazette Notification No. 44, F. No. 18-15/93-TD, V/TS.IV dated April 8, 1995 issued by MHRD, GoI, which made it mandatory for every ODL institution, created by an Act of the Indian Parliament or a State Legislature, to seek recognition of their programmes offered through distance mode for validity of certificates awarded for Government employment. The process of assessment of learner support capabilities through on the spot visits has now been established and accepted. On the basis of such reports, DEC has advised SOUs to avoid 'controlled franchising' in offer of professional programmes in collaboration with private providers. Instructions have also been issued that failure in compliance will attract provisions of penalty including withdrawal of financial support and derecognition of their programmes.

In this phase of significant changes, perhaps DEC has to play a much greater role because ODL system is quite different from other systems in terms of distinctive, unique features, practices and complexities, levels and forms of interventions, and variability/diversity of its learners, who range from non-literate and neo-literates field workers to professional degree (MBA, MCA, MBBS, LLB, BTech) holders. DEC has also advocated the concept of continuous self-assessment and academic audit with internal and external experts/peers. The initial response, particularly from SOUs, has been very encouraging.

Technology as an enabler of quality assurance

Application of IT as universal enabler of widening access and reach has extended the horizons of ODL systems. It is now possible for ODL teachers to provide very rich and interactive teaching experiences to their learners across distances, both synchronously and asynchronously with the help of ICT solutions. In addition, technology in the open universities has been effectively utilised to contribute to the quality assurance initiatives by:

- putting relevant and frequently asked information about counselling schedules, assignment grades, examination schedule on the Web;
- providing updated and continuously relevant course materials using electronic master copies, online editing, etc.;
- incorporating high levels of interactivity in programme delivery;
- obtaining high levels of stakeholder feedback;
- improving responsiveness of the entire system and reduce turn-around time in various operations;
- maintaining real time information flows across nationwide offices and across national borders; and
- putting updated institutional profiles in the public domain.

DEC has extensively supported institutions to create networked environment, by computerising all activities for fast processing of information and enhanced responsiveness. To make use of *Gyan Darshan* initiative, special grants have been sanctioned to create Direct Reception Stations, which facilitate live interaction. Similarly, FM radio stations have been commissioned and are being operated in conventional universities with full financial support.

Developing competitive consciousness

A sensitisation of the competitiveness imperatives arising in the wake of gloabalisation and the impending developments in the GATS negotiation is a needed, proactive initiative that ODL institutions must take. Cross border supply of education through the ODL system is among the most potentially rapid developments that could follow once India's commitments on offers and requests have been negotiated. Institutions on a systemic basis therefore have to look at their competitive positioning and the value chain they create in the consumer's eyes. In the global competitiveness scenario, the systemic and institutional mechanism that will be needed include:

- A transparent and well communicated system of accreditation and quality assessment to aspire to and achieve levels of quality gradation for institutional positioning and capacity to attract diverse learner populations. The system of accreditation put in place by DEC for quality assurance will have to be enlarged to include possibilities of cross border offerings and in course of time incorporate a National Qualifications Framework for various disciplines and qualifications being offered through ODL mode in the country.
- Sustained investment in research, both academic and systemic should be an avowed policy for relatively new and evolving institutions and systems. DEC has extensively supported systemic research through major and minor project funding, sponsored tracer studies, participation in international as well as national conferences. With ODL institutions, however, research needs to be keenly supported through top management support, sustained recognition and application of innovation in the ongoing systems.
- Sustained investment in human resource development in the ODL systems as a long term strategy for ensuring competitiveness should be nurtured. Academic as well as supporting services expertise and experience in an institution are the non-replicable competitive advantages that need to be sustained. Provisions for visiting Professors, emeritus professors, adjunct faculty, faculty exchange, secondments and research collaborations with the best ODL and conventional institutions could be some of the strategies for faculty development, sustained commitment to quality and long term faculty retention.

Collaboration, Convergence and Partnership

One of the less obvious dimensions of quality is related to the most efficient use of resources, especially when these are limited. The ODL system in the country has been charged with the responsibility of taking the benefits of higher education to vast sections of its population and contributing to the task of life long education of its professional workforce in all spheres. As a developing economy, the nation has experienced resource crunch for higher education. It is therefore imperative that financial discipline is promoted and observed for optimal utilisation of available resources. Networking of ODL institutions, creating sharable resource pools, convergence with conventional institutions, use of open media and open source software, sharing of available software and partnership in creation of new sharable content as well as collaborative use of available satellite and ICT resources and enabling seamless mobility of learners through credit transfers is likely to contribute positively to the quality of higher education in the country.

With the high levels of competitiveness pressures likely to be unleashed in the rapidly globalising world order, investment in the quality of education is no longer an issue of choice; it is now a survival and growth imperative. To meet transnational competition and address the issue of incorporating quality assurance, DEC has successfully intervened in all facets of operations and processes. However, some educationists and educational administrators are of the view that much more can be achieved if DEC is created as an autonomous apex authority through an Act of Parliament like UGC, AICTE, NCTE and like other councils vested with authority to promote, and regulate open learning in all forms and formats.

References

BIS (1988). *Quality Standards.* New Delhi: BIS.

GoI (1966). *Education and National Development*. New Delhi: GoI.

Deshpande, P. and Mugridge, I. (1994) (ed). *Quality Assurance in Higher Education*. Vancouver: COL.

Garg, S. and Sharma, S.C. (1997). Teaching science through distance mode in the USP region: Practices, concerns and search for quality. *Staff and Educational Development International*, 1, 59-67.

Green, D. (1994). *What is Quality in Higher Education*? Buckingham: SRHE and OU Press.

Gupta, S.P. (2005). *Quality Assurance in Distance Education*. Allahabad: UPRTOU.

Holmberg, B. (1995). Communication and study access - quality in distance education. In Singh, B. (ed.), *New Horizons in Distance Education*. New Delhi: Uppal Publishing House.

Hope, A. (2004). Towards developing an effective quality assurance system for open and distance learning programmes: Global and translational approaches. In Sharma, R. (ed.), *Assessment and Accreditation in Higher Education*. New Delhi: AIU.

Powar, K.B. and Panda, S.K. (1995). *Higher Education in India - In search of Quality*. New Delhi: AIU.

Prasad, V.S. (2003). *Best Practices in Open and Distance Education*. Hyderabad: BRAOU.

Warren, J, McManus, K. and Nazar, R. (1994). Quality assurance and distance education: A review of the literature, in Deshpande, P.M. and Mugridge, I. (Eds), *Quality Assurance in Higher Education*. Vancouver: COL.

Professor Suresh Garg is Pro-Vice Chancellor, Indira Gandhi National Open University, New Delhi.
Email: scgarg@ignou.ac.in

Professor Madhulika Kaushik is Professor, School of Management Studies, Indira Gandhi National Open University, New Delhi.
Email: mkaushik@ignou.ac.in

30

Cost of Dual Mode and Single Mode Distance Education

Ruddar Datt and Ashok Gaba

Introduction

The open and distance education system in India has expanded both horizontally and vertically. The University of Delhi was entrusted the responsibility of introducing correspondence courses in 1962 on pilot basis. Encouraged by the success, it was followed by Punjabi University, Patiala, in 1969 and other subsequently. Till the first open university, now known as Dr. B.R. Ambedkar Open University, BRAOU, was established in Hyderabad by the state government of Andhra Pradesh in 1982, the correspondence course institutes enrolled about 9% learners. The establishment of Indira Gandhi National Open University (IGNOU) in 1985 by the Central Government led to the acceptance of open learning as viable philosophy of education. At present, we have twelve open universities and 106 Correspondence Courses Institutions (CCIs)/ Directorates of Distance Education located in conventional universities. In addition to this, private providers like All India Management Association, Symbiosis Institute of Management, Narsee Monjee Institute of Management, etc. are also providing tertiary education through distance mode. The open-distance learning system now enrols about 400,000 students at tertiary level is said to be cost-effective, even for science and technology programmes (Pillai and Naidu, 1998). In this chapter, we report comparative per student costs of dual mode and single mode distance education. The analysis is based on cost data available from only 4 dual mode (public) and 4 open universities.

Cost Analysis of ODL

There is a general feeling, that open learning is inexpensive. This may not be necessarily true. The costs depend largely on the media used and learners enrolled in a programme/institution. Experience shows that planning an ODL system, we must ensure that the variable cost per student is less than that in conventional system through economies of scale help bring down the average costs per student. These considerations have very significant implications for the choice of media, infrastructure and quality of student support services. Invariably, the ODL system is initial cost-intensive and may not necessarily involve inexpensive learning.

It is now well known that in face-to-face mode, about 90% expenditure is on payment of salaries. Moreover, this variable has tendency to rise over time. The choice of media also influences cost of education in ODL system. Since open education aims to maximise accessibility to educational opportunities, a variety of media, like the print material, radio, TV/CDs/Internet/ telephone, fax, tele/video-conferencing are used for imparting instruction. The costs of the teaching through different media vary mainly because fixed and variable costs vary significantly from media to media. For instance, fixed costs for TV are much higher than those for radio. It can be lowered if mechanisms for using existing broadcasting installations are put in place. In addition, the organisational structure is also an important factor.

For small audience size, media like slide projector and tape-recorder provide greater cost advantages over the bigger media like TV, computer-based instruction or Internet. In ODL, teaching-learning choice of media mix is very crucial. For choosing an appropriate media, socio-cultural aspects are also taken into account. So, we can say that the cost of education in ODL system depends on the extent of the utilisation of resources, the types of technology, the size of enrolment and the nature as well as number of courses offered. It is also influenced by the quality of paraphernalia like paper used for printing the learning materials, the quality of equipment for electronic media or the extent of multimedia use in computer-based instruction. Therefore, costs in ODL can be expressed symbolically as

$$C = f\,(E_n, C_n, S_n, M_c, E_{nq}, F_p) \qquad (1)$$

Where C, E_n, C_n, S_n, M_c, E_{nq}, and F_p respectively signify costs, number of learners enrolled, number of courses/programmes offered, number of staff (teaching and non-teaching), choice of media, quantity and quality of media, and faculty (counsellors/coordinators).

Generally, in face-to-face classroom teaching, teaching cost is treated as variable cost and is directly related to the output of learners. Therefore, fixed costs in F2F teaching are less than those in ODL. In ODL, the expenses incurred on printing of learning material; audio/video/ television/radio/ telephone/fax etc and other media constitute variable cost are incurred irrespective of the number of learners enrolled in the system. The cost function of ODL for N learners can also be expressed as:

$$TC = FC + V/N \qquad (2)$$

where TC, FC and V denote total cost, fixed costs, and variable cost per unit of output, respectively. The average cost is derived by dividing the total cost by the number of units.

Review of Literature

Studies reported by Indian scholars mostly pertain to the analysis of sources of income and expenditure of the system and unit cost analysis in comparison to F2F stream. The studies of Biswal (1979), Sahoo (1985), Datt (1988, 1994), and Gaba (1997, 2004), have shown that tuition fee was the major source of revenue of ODL institutions.

Pandey (1980), Ram (1984), Gupta (1985) and Gaba (1997) have reported that the unit costs of correspondence courses are much lower than those of the regular courses. Datt (1988) further pointed out that unit costs as well as state subsidy was higher in conventional system. Ansari (1987) analysed cost-efficiency and cost-effectiveness of the ODL system. His calculation shows that per student cost of distance education is only 15 to 20 per cent of the cost in formal system. He also pointed out in spite of this the ODL system may not be as cost-efficient as the formal education. Datt (1994) calculated the break-up of costs into academic costs, non-academic costs and other costs and found that academic costs varied from one correspondence institutions to another. Pillai and Naidu (1997) analysed the unit costs of IGNOU. They found that the faculty's salary consumed the major chunk of funds while developing of print material for an eight credits course. They further found that economies of scale could be maintained up to an enrolment of 300,000 students. Naidu (2001) analysed the per student costs (including private cost) for the entire duration of the MCA programme of IGNOU. He found that, on an average, MCA students spend the most, followed by B.Sc., B.A. and PGDHE students. Kulandaiswamy (2002) has analysed capital and operating costs of IGNOU and found that whereas capital expenditure on buildings and campus development reduced over the years, that on equipment, furniture and library increased steadily. On the other hand, the analysis of operating costs of IGNOU show that expenditure on development and production of course material has remained almost constant, at the level of 28 percent, but the percentage expenditure on student support services has almost doubled; from 29.8 percent to 57.48 percent.

Wagner (1972) has reported an average (recurring) cost of undergraduate programme at UKOU, with a student enrolment of 36,500 as £251. This was about one fourth of the cost of the conventional universities in the country. Harwood and Kim (1985) have noted that the South Korean state spent an equivalent of US$ 10.29 millions on the Korea Air Correspondence University during 1972-81, to produce 33,838 graduates at a cost of just over US$300 per graduate. On the other hand, 124 conventional colleges graduated 28,000 students at an average cost of $ 675. Lockheed et al. (1991) in a World Bank study found that the Sukhothai Thammathirat Open University (STOU), Thailand, produced graduates more economically than conventional universities. Nielsen et al. (1991) studied the cost-effectiveness of distance education for teacher training in Indonesia and Sri Lanka and found that the distance education programmes in both Sri Lanka and Indonesia cost significantly less than the F2F teaching. The total annual costs per capita were 17 to 60 percent of campus-based programmes. Cumming and Olaloku (1993) have also reported that the unit cost per graduate of the distance education B.Sc. programme was less than that of the regular programme. Rumble (1998) analysed the cost-effectiveness of distance education at secondary level and concluded that the number of students enrolled play most significant role in determining the cost-effectiveness. Some ODL system such as the Correspondence Course Unit, Kenya (with 340 to 2,900 students each year) could be more expensive than the traditional system. At the tertiary level, the cost per graduate at the British Open University (which has an annual enrolment of 20000-25000) is about half of the cost of a graduate at conventional university, while the cost per student per year is about one third of a student in a conventional university.

Quite a few studies have been conducted on costing of electronic and print media in education (Wells, 1976; Jamison et al., 1978; Perraton, 1982; Fwu et al., 1992; and Bates, 1995). On the basis of these studies, we can draw some broad conclusions:

- production costs are higher for film and lower for radio;
- fixed costs for transmission are much higher for television than for radio;
- audio cassettes are likely to be cheaper than the radio where viewership is restricted;
- the costs of taxonomy of open and distance learning differs from F2F teaching.

Charbonneau and Cunningham (1993) found that at Athabasca University, video-conferencing resulted in savings on travel reduction in instructional time and costs (50%), and an increase in faculty productivity. Stahmer (1995) analysed the cost of computer-based training in comparison to classroom-based training through examples. He examined the case of the low development costs and found that the cost per student of computer-based training was roughly half that of face-to-face training.

The development of online courses has raised many questions concerning their costs. Hulsmann (2000) found that costs of producing material in CD-ROM was forty times more than in print. According to him, assignment evaluation had the highest unit cost in the case of one-to-one communication. Where there was an opportunity for group study, cost per student was very sensitive to the size of the group, and technology. For example, tutoring through video-conferencing is costlier than face-to-face tutoring. But it saves travel costs and the opportunity costs, i.e. the time spent by students in travelling.

The analysis of research findings reveals that open and learning system is cost effective and has the advantage of economies of scale. However, studies on costing in single mode and dual mode open and distance education in India, especially, the costing of audio/video/information technology, are still in its infancy.

Funding: Indian Scenario

The Government of India has been meeting the entire cost of development of all and maintenance of most of the central universities established under various Acts of Parliament. The pattern of funding is on net deficit basis i.e., the deficit in expenditure after adjusting the income received from other sources against the gross operating costs is met through government grants. However,

IGNOU, established by an Act of Parliament, has been mandated with the dual responsibility of offering distance education programmes, and coordinating and maintaining standards of distance higher education institutions in the country. The University worked hard towards self-sufficiency and is now contributes about 25% of the total Tenth Plan Expenditure for ODL system from its own resources. It shows that it is possible to impart quality education even without state funding if the faculty and management devise strategies for generating revenues beyond programme fee and manage these efficiently.

The funding to State Open Universities and DEI/CCIs has been regulated w.e.f. the IXth Plan. DEC assistance is provided as development grants; un-assigned grants; and research and development grants.

Table 1 shows that the three of the four CCIs are generating about 100% income through students' fees and other sources: University of Mumbai (100%), Annamalai University(100%) & Andhra University (99%). However, other institutions generate three fourth of their income through students' fee and other sources: YCMOU (90%), BRAOU (82%), University of Delhi (73%), UPRTOU (71%) and IGNOU (71%). These findings are in conformity with the analysis of Datt (1994) and Kulandaiswamy (2002) that the major source of finance of DTIs were student fee and very rarely were funds raised through other sources.

Table 1: Sources of income of selected OUs and CCIs, 2003-04 (estimates)

(Rs. in million)

Institutions	Government	DEC	Fees & others	Total
OUs				
IGNOU@	853*	0	2120	2973
	(28.69)	(0.00)	(71.31)	(100.00)
BRAOU	59	0	273	332
	(17.77)	(0.00)	(82.23)	(100.00)
YCMOU	20	7	246	273
	(7.33)	(2.56)	(90.11)	(100.00)
UPRTOU	8	2	25	35
	(22.86)	(5.71)	(71.43)	(100.00)
CCIs				
Andhra University	0	1	153	154
	(0.00)	(0.65)	(99.35)	(100.00)
University of Delhi	50	0	134	184
	(27.17)	(0.00)	(72.83)	(100.00)
University of Mumbai	0	0	132	132
	(0.00)	(0.00)	(100.00)	(132.00)
Annamali University	0	0	366	366
	(0.00)	(0.00)	(100.00)	(100.00)

Sources: DEC (2004) Information base on distance higher education in India, New Delhi: IGNOU, and IGNOU (2005-06) *Financial Estimates*, New Delhi: IGNOU

Note: *Figures in the brackets are percentage to total.*

@ = *Data of IGNOU is related to year 2004-05 (Budget estimates)*

* = *Includes Rs. 813 million plan grant.*

Table 2 gives costs per student for OUs and CCIs in India. The data reveals that CCIs are more cost effective than OUs. This apparent cost advantage is reflective of first generation of open-distance learning dominated by print. Both mode of distance teaching institutions with an enrolment of more than 10,000 are able to keep the cost per student less. However, correlation between enrolment and unit cost is strong i.e. 0.82 for OUs and 0.31 for CCIs. As these are cross sectional data for both types of institutions, the variety of factor determining costs show that variables like staff-student ratio, number of courses run by CCIs and extent of media utilisation, student services etc. affecting costs. Since the data are at current prices, the effect of increase in cost as a consequence of inflation is also reflected. This implies that if the cost per student is measured at constant prices, the effect of rise in enrolment is reducing the unit cost would be certainly much greater.

Table 2: Enrolment and cost per student of selected OUs and CCIs, (2003-04)

OUs			CCIs		
Institutions	**Enrolment**	**Cost per student (in Rs.)**	**Institutions**	**Enrolment**	**Cost per student (in Rs.)**
IGNOU	366161	8118	Andhra University	73923	2080
BRAOU	190230	1745	University of Delhi	141649	1641
YCMOU	102642	2323	University of Mumbai	55558	512
UPRTOU	8025	2527	Annamalai University	98963	3824
Coefficient of correlation	0.82			0.31	

Source: As Table 1 & Annual Report of IGNOU, 2004-05.

The Tables 3 show that OUs like UPRTOU, YCMOU and CCI of University of Mumbai were surplus generating largely due to less number of academic/non-academic staff, efficient use of technology. In all the CCIs, the core staff is linked with respective universities and they draw their salaries from the main university budget head. Most institutions spend little on student support services, library facilities, audio-video and multimedia utilisation. Similarly, expenditure on design, development and production of print course lessons is also very low particularly in the case of CCIs as presented in Table 4. Institutions, which incur deficit, are subsidized either by the Centeral Government through IGNOU-DEC or the concerned State Government. In addition to DEC supported and concerned state government, both types of institutions generated resources from student fees as presented in Table 1.

Table 3: Cost and fee of education per student in OUs and CCIs, (2003-04)

Institutions	Enrolment	Cost per student (in Rs.)	Fee per student (in Rs.)	(Surplus/ deficit)	Student/ staff ratio	Programmes on offer
OUs						
IGNOU	366161	8118	5790	-2328	276	101
BRAOU	190230	1745	1435	-310	337	26
YCMOU	102642	2323	2397	74	371	78
UPRTOU	8025	2527	3115	588	113	38
CCIs						
Andhra University	73923	2080	2070	-10	443	29
University of Delhi	141649	1641	946	-695	305	10
University of Mumbai	55558	512	2376	1864	722	7
Annamalai University	98963	3824	3698	-125	113	184

Source: As Table 1 & 2.

Trend of Expenditure of Open and Distance Teaching Institutions

It has been observed from the above analysis that some institutions had spent little on other components of ODL system like students support services, library multimedia etc. On the other hand more than 20% expenditure was incurred on student support services by OUs like, IGNOU (43%), BRAOU and UPROU (26%) in compression to CCIs (less than 10%). The data available of selected institutions indicates the trend of expenditure is in 'others' category for which most of the institutions did not specify the details in this heads as presented in Table 4.

Table 4: Trend of expenditure of selected OUs and CCIs, 2003-04 (estimated)

(Rs. in Million)

Institu-tions	Salary		Total salary	Infrastruc-ture	Programme development	SSS	Total	Other
	Teaching	Non-teaching						
OUs								
IGNOU*	82	151	233	n.a.	260	650	370	1513
	(5)	(10)	(15)		(17)	(43)	(25)	(100)
BRAOU	27	46	73	21	32	86	119	331
	(8)	(14)	(22)	(6)	(10)	(26)	(36)	(100)
YCMOU	37	n.a.	37	9	15	8	170	239
	(15)		(15)	(4)	(6)	(3)	(71)	(100)

UPROU	1 (0)	36 (23)	37 (23)	1 (0)	n.a.	42 (26)	79 (50)	159 (100)
CCIs								
Andhra University	26 (17)	n.a.	26 (17)	19 (12)	22 (14)	12 (8)	75 (49)	154 (100)
Delhi University	37 (16)	68 (29)	105 (45)	n.a.	n.a.	20 (9)	108 (46)	233 (100)
Mumbai University	4 (13)	14 (47)	18 (60)	5 (17)	5 (17)	1 (3)	1 (3)	30 (100)
Annamalai University	116 (31)	n.a.	116 (31)	108 (29)	108 (29)	3 (1)	42 (11)	377 (100)

Source: As Table 1 and data provided by Finance & Accounts Division, IGNOU.

A mixed picture emerges from the above case analysis. Most of the CCIs incurred expenditure on salary heads only rather than other components of ODL. On the other hand, OUs incurred expenditure on almost all the components of ODLs like salary, infrastructure development and students support services. IGNOU had incurred recurring expenditure on other head like regional service division (35%), electronic media production centre (17%), different schools of studies which include salary of faculty (14%), material production and distribution (12%), student registration and evaluation (11%), administration (9%), self learning, and construction and maintenance of campus (2%) during 2004-05 (projected) as shown in Figure 1. It is understandable that IGNOU had already been established and it's expenditure share is proportionally distributed among all the major complement of ODL system.

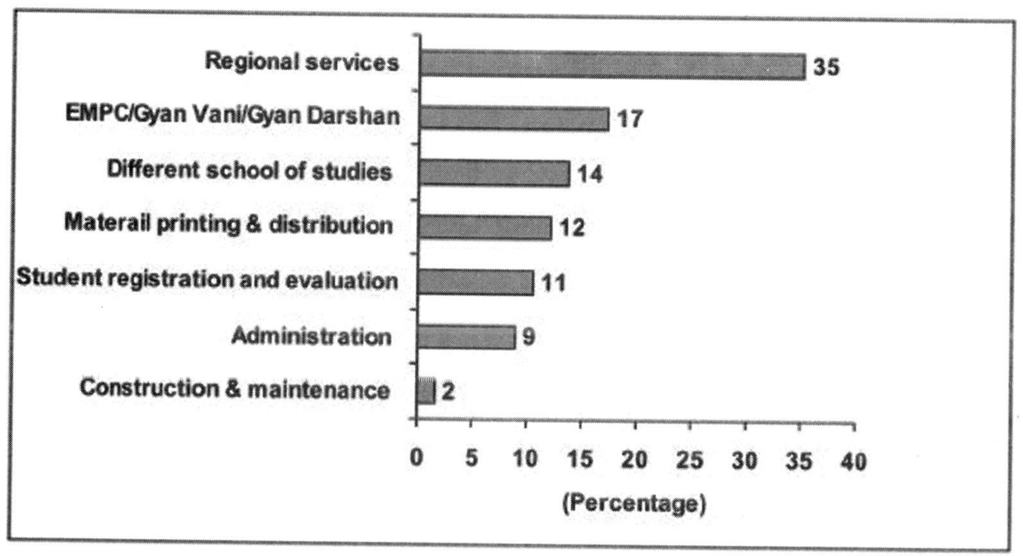

Figure 1: The major areas of IGNOU's revenue expenditure (Plan+Non-Plan) during 2004-05 (projected)

Discussion

It has emerged from the above analysis that the per student cost of CCIs is less in comparison to OUs. It is understandable because they are unable to develop study material in self-instructional style and do not even use media or ICT. In most cases, the programme offered by CCIs are the same and do not have the students support system. It may be noted that there is a limit to lowering the unit cost of distance education if quality is to be maintained. In some DTIs the learners are on the job and some cases, a large percentage of students are younger and unemployed. Therefore, there is a possibility for on the job learner to get higher subsidy and it may not reach those learners who are unemployed and belong to economically weaker sections of the society. This would require a strong base line data and comprehensive studies on these issues by each DTIs. This may help the funding authority in releasing the grant. It has been established that most of the CCIs generated sources of income through students fees spending on them little.

On the other hand, CCIs have been able to provide educational opportunities to many, but they are still lagging behind in qualitative improvement. These institutes still suffer from several limitations. They are treated as departments of the conventional universities to which they are attached. Their curriculum and course are similar to the ones offered by conventional universities. Most correspondence courses were the same degree programmes that their mainstream universities and colleges offered. Koul (1997) reviewed research studies on ODL system conducted by Indian scholars and analysed that while developing the self-instructional materials, the course team approach had not been adopted by most of the academics of CCIs. No effort has been made to revise the reading materials. Not much attention had been paid to assignments, most of which were not evaluated, corrected or returned to the students on time. He further stated that in the absence of 'study centres', or contact points for students, personal contact programmes were not regularly organised.

The utilisation of information technology (Internet & Web based education) is nil in almost all the CCIs in the country. Laboratory and library facilities were not available in these institutions, and where they existed, they were not readily accessible to students. Above all, most of these institutes were considered as income generating centres. Of the income earned, only small proportion of it was spent on those learners who pay; the balance is utilized as income for the parent university, which has been spent on other heads of the conventional system particularly in the cases of CCIs. These institutions function within and under the control of the mainstream university in which they are located; and, therefore, have little autonomy in financial decision-making.

It is a matter of concern that mass education may dilute the quality of education. Amartya Sen rightly observed, "University education in India is in a state of crisis. It is not a crisis of lack of resources. It is deterioration in quality. The quality would vary from one university to another. However, the minimum level of quality should be ensured". This statement is equally applicable to ODL system. It must be emphasized that quality is related not only to development of good print materials but also the learners support services at delivery centres. There is a need to develop institutional mechanisms for maintenance of quality in the system particularly in the areas of learner support services.

Qualitative upgradation and not quantitative expansion is the need of the hour, as far as the existing higher educational institutions are concerned. A proper system of subsidization needs to be developed based on certain norms of expenditure per student. It is good to have an Open University in every state, but the availability of CCIs and Regional Centre of IGNOU at respective states needs to be kept in mind.

It requires additional financial resources for meeting the target groups that are outside the existing higher education system in the country. In recent years, much of the debate as to the future of higher educational system has revolved around mainly the financial resources needed to match the increase in enrolment and escalating expenditure. There is a need for collaborative programmes and other activities within the different DTIs so that the expenditure of these institutions could be reduced and learners could take advantage of this. There is a need for restructuring of ODL system in the country. Policy makers should re-think about distance education policy. Presently, flexible learning model based on on-line delivery via the Internet is gaining momentum all over the world and in India as well. There is already emerging the fifth generation of distance education based on the further exploitation of new technologies. There is a need for proper networking of these institutions so that duplication of courses could be avoided. Focus should be on learners support, which should be equipped with all modern technologies i.e. delivered through online.

Conclusion

We may conclude our discussion by reasserting that distance education has a vast potential for growth in a developing country like India. It is much more cost-effective than the formal system. There is a need for raising the efficiency of the present organizational system for the improvement of the ODL programme. In this context, major emphasis is to be given on appointment of regular staff (academic and non academic) at CCIs. The priority of expenditure should be on all components of ODL system i.e. student support service, quality of the print material, ICT and multimedia. DTIs should also strengthen their financial position by raising the revenue through sources other than the students. Certainly, it would require a change in the central and state governments policy on distance education system in the country.

References

Ansari, M.M. (1987). Determinants of costs in distance education. In B.N. Koul et al. (eds.), *Studies in Distance Education*. New Delhi: AIU and IGNOU.

Bates, A.W. (1995). *Technology, Open Learning and Distance Education*. London: Routledge.

Biswal, B.N. (1979). A study of correspondence education in India. Ph.D. Dissertation, The M.S. University of Baroda, Baroda

Charbonneau, J. and Cunningham, C. (1993). *Videoconferencing in distance education: economic and pedagogical consideration*. Paper presented at VII Asian Association of Open University's Annual Conference, Hong Kong.

Datt, R. (1994). *Cost of Distance Education in India: A Study of Cost of Distance Education Institutions with Different Size Classes*. New Delhi: NIEPA.

Datt, R. (1988). Distance education versus traditional higher education: A cost comparison. In B.N. Koul et al. (Eds.), *Studies in Distance Education,* New Delhi: AIU and IGNOU.

DEC (2001). *Open Universities in India: Brief Information*. New Delhi: DEC, IGNOU.

Fwu et al. (1992). The national technological university. In Rumble, G. et al. (eds.), *Vocational Education at a Distance: International Perspective*. London: Kogan Page.

Gaba, Ashok (1997). Is open schooling in India really cost effective? In Mukhopadhyay, M. and Parhar, M. (Eds.), *Open and Distance Learning.* New Delhi: Jawhar Publication.

Gaba, A. (2004). Funding of open and distance higher education in India: Quality and policy issues. *University News,* 42(8), 23-29.

Gupta, M.L. (1985). *Indian Economy and Higher Education with reference to Correspondence Education.* Jaipur: Institute of Correspondence Studies, University of Rajasthan.

Harwood, R.F. and Kim, S.H. (1985). Seoul super school. *ICDE Bulletin*, 8.

Hulsmann, T. (2000). *The Costs of Open Learning: A Handbook*. Oldenburg, Bibliotheks-und information system der Universitat Oldenburg, Carl von Ossletzky Universitat.

IGNOU (2005). *Financial Estimates (Plan and Non-Plan), 2005-06*. New Delhi: IGNOU.

Jamison, D.T., Kales, S.J. and Well, S.J. (1978). *The Costs of Educational Media: Guidelines for Planning and Evaluation.* Beverly Hills: Sage Publication.

Koul, L.C. (1997). Open and distance education: trend report. In NCERT (ed.), *Fifth Survey of Educational Research.* New Delhi: NCERT.

Kulandaiswamy, V.C. (2002). *Education for Knowledge Era Open and Flexible Learning.* New Delhi: Kogan Page.

Lockheed, M, Middleton, E J and Nettleton, G. (1991). *Educational Technology: Sustainability and Effective Use*. World Bank, Population and Human Resources Department, Education and Employment Division, Background Paper Series PHREE/91/32, Washington D.C.

Naidu, C.G. (2001). *Student Costs in Distance Education, A Research Report.* New Delhi: IGNOU.

Neilson, D.H., Tatto, T., Djabil, A. and Kularatne, N. (1991). *The Cost-effectiveness of Distance Education for Teacher Training*. http://wbweb4.worldbank.org/DistEd/Management/Benefits/dev-03.html.

Pandey, S.K. (1980). Economics of Correspondence Education in Indian Universities. Ph.D. Dissertation, Meerut: Meerut University.

Perraton, H. (1982). *The Costs of Distance Education.* Cambridge: IEC.

Pillai, C.R. and Naidu, C.G. (1997). *Cost Analysis of Distance Education.* New Delhi: IGNOU.

Pillai, C.R. and Naidu, C.G. (1998). Cost-effectiveness of science education at a distance. In Suresh Garg et al., (eds.), *Science & Technology through Open & Distance Education*. New Delhi: Aravali Books International.

Ram, S. (1984). An Evaluation of Correspondence Education in terms of Cost and Academic Performance. Ph. D. Dissertation, Meerut University, Meerut.

Rumble, G. (1998). The Costs and Costing of Distance/open Education. *http://wbweb4.worldbank.org/DistEd/Management/Benefits/Cost-ol.html*

Sahoo, P.K. (1985). A Study of Correspondence Education in Indian University. Ph.D. Dissertation, M.S. University of Baroda, Baroda.

Stahmer, Anna (1995). Assessing costs, benefits and return to investment for technology-based training: tools for decision-makers. Paper presented at online educa conference, Berlin, November 24-25.

Wagner, L. (1972). The economics of open university. *Higher Education*, 1.

Wells, S. (1976). Evaluation criteria and effectiveness of instructional technology in higher education. *Higher Education,* 5(3).

Professor Ruddar Datt, Ex-Principal, School of Correspondence and Continuing Education, University of Delhi, Delhi.

Dr. Ashok Gaba is Deputy Director, Staff Training and Research Institute, Indira Gandhi National Open University, New Delhi.
Email: akgaba@ignou.ac.in

31

Cost and Quality of Distance Education

C.G. Naidu

Introduction

Like many other countries around the world, in India also the education sector is funded largely by the State. The proliferation of social demand for higher education, revolutionary developments in information and communication technologies (ICTs) and resource crunch to meet the financial requirements of the conventional system led to the emergence of distance education. From this perspective, some of the significant objectives of distance education are to: (a) enhance access with equality, (b) keep low unit costs, and (c) maintain the quality of programmes and outputs.

The use of technology involves higher fixed costs and reasonably lower marginal costs. Therefore, when large number of students are enrolled, the fixed costs are spread contributing to lower unit costs. However, the proliferation of technology, the economic limitations of disadvantaged groups in having end nodes for receiving the programmes, the exclusive demands for student support for women, differently-abled and other disadvantaged groups, and the requirement of hands-on experience for some professional programmes raise doubts about the cost-efficiency of the distance education programmes. For example, a problem may arise when a distance education institution extends its operations to more regions and communities and the average number of students associated with a centre may decrease. On the other hand, any compromise on the effective use of technology and student support services may lower the quality of programmes and outputs and raise scepticism about the system.

In this chapter we have analysed the following questions:

- How have the costs and quality considerations influenced the evolution of distance education in India in the last four decades?
- To what extent are the changes in the costs related to the changes in the quality of distance education?
- How are the distance education outputs affected by the changes in the costs?
- How can we improve the quality at reduced costs?
- How important is it for policy makers to understand inter-relationships between the costs and quality to facilitate decision making?

Historical Developments

Soon after independence, demand for higher education increased significantly to meet the social aspirations for improvement in the quality of their life. The number of education sectors grew at the rate of 10%. However, the Central and State governments were able to create infrastructure which grew by 5%. As a result, backlog began to pile up and generated pressure for allocation of financial resources in their budgets. Many experts in higher education and education committees appointed by the Government of India also referred to the decline in the quality of higher education in the conventional system. Among others, this was reflected in terms of an increase in teacher-student ratio and a decline in per student unit costs at constant prices. Due to inherent mechanisms of the conventional system, the per student unit costs cannot be reduced without diluting the student-teacher ratio and not meeting the other basic infrastructure. This is likely to lead to compromise in the quality of higher education.

Correspondence Course Institutes

An Expert Committee under the Chairmanship of Prof. D.S. Kothari recommended the introduction of correspondence courses in the country to absorb the additional demand for higher education involve gifted teachers to add to quality of education in the conventional system and utilisation of scarce resources. In 1962, the University of Delhi created a School of Correspondence Courses and offered undergraduate programmes with an enrolment of 1112 in that year. By 1981-82, the share of correspondence education to total higher education increased to 6.16% (Naidu, 1995). Experience shows that the system has offered lower per student unit costs but the quality concerns of these programmes soon became a major concern. In 1990, a working group on Promotion of Distance Education observed that, "The quality of correspondence education is invariably viewed either indifferently or inferior to that of the formal education. Besides, the correspondence education had hardly used the technology of distance mode either by developing self-learning print material or by introducing video and audio material... The provision of counselling and guidance were also non-existent." (UGC, 1990, p.55). Besides, the group was of the view that very few educational institutes in the country make proper resource allocation to correspondence education.

The observations of the working group could be some of the indicators of the poor quality of correspondence education. Although, the system was able to offer the programmes at a lower per student unit costs. The economies of scale were not in operation. Datt (1991) studied the relationship between enrolment and cost per student over a period of time after depleting the inflation factor using consumer price index. The estimates of the slope coefficients of the linear regression equations computed for various correspondence institutes show that there was a negative slope for most of the institutes and yet the economies of the scale was very weak. This is due to the fact that in the absence of technology (where high fixed and low marginal costs prevail), most part of the per student unit costs accounted for variable costs. The fixed costs were very minimum leading to low quality of programmes. Also, 50% of institutes generated surplus income through fee from students. Datt further argued that the surpluses are generated by keeping skeleton staff and spending very little on production of audio/video programmes and production of reading materials. This again shows that these programmes are offered at lower costs by compromising the quality of the process of programme development, production, and delivery.

Open Universities

In order to overcome the drawbacks of correspondence course institutes, the policy makers in India established open universities as single mode systems. In 1982, the State of Andhra Pradesh created an open university at Hyderabad with its state jurisdiction. At the national level, the Indira Gandhi National Open University was established in 1985. Substantial investments have been made in developing multi-media instructional materials. These multi-media include printed material, audio/video programmes, counselling, radio/TV, and teleconferencing. A number of regional centres, study centres, programme specific centres have been established to strengthen the student support services and provide laboratory/computing facilities for hands-on experiences.

The range of delivery technologies available to the distance education institutes can be classified into high cost media and low cost media (Pillai and Naidu, 1997). The low cost technology includes print, counselling (face-to-face), and audio/video programmes. The high cost delivery technology includes TV, radio, teleconferencing, and online programmes using computer networks. All the open education institutes in India invariably use the low cost technologies. According to Pillai and Naidu (1997), "Not because they are relatively cheap, but because the technologies involved make it easy to produce and distribute learning packages and they are more easily accessible to students." On the other hand, the high cost technologies involve not only higher costs but also difficulties in accessing these technologies by the students because of their socio-economic and geographical disadvantages, and weak delivery networks. For example, the computer networks are limited to only urban areas.

Naidu (1994) used sensitivity analysis to examine whether the economies of scale operate in the case of IGNOU. He separated the fixed costs and variable costs (in relation to the students) based on the actual costs and then worked out the average cost per student for different hypothetical number of students. The following cost functions were plotted on a graph for a range of hypothetical students.

$$TC = F + V \times N,$$

$$AC = \frac{TC}{N},$$

and

$$MC = V$$

where TC, F, V, MC and N respectively denote total cost, fixed cost, variable cost per student, marginal cost per student, and number of students.

Naidu found that as the enrolment increases, the cost per student declines implying the operation of economies of scale. The economy of scale was very significant for increases in enrolment up to certain level of enrolment (140,000). Even beyond that level of enrolment, since the marginal cost is less than average cost, it was concluded that IGNOU programmes are cost-effective for higher levels of enrolment (200,000 or more). This means that distance education provides greater economies of scale at early stages of increase in enrolment as fixed costs are spread across more and more students. Thereafter, economy of scope operates. IGNOU employs intensive application of technology as a medium of instruction. A number of study centres/ programme centres and regional centres were established for providing student support services and provision for hands-on experience. The behaviour of costs on these activities are fixed or semi-variable in nature. An empirical study of Naidu (1994) establishes the potential of the distance education in meeting large social demands without compromising the quality of programmes.

The cost-effectiveness of distance education programmes was also measured by comparing the unit costs with conventional programmes. Naidu (1994) compared the per student costs of three distance education institutions (IGNOU, YCMOU and BRAOU) with a sample of conventional colleges in India for a period of three years (1989-90 to 1991-92). The empirical analysis showed that for all the three years, per student unit costs of distance education programmes were less than the unit costs of conventional programmes. When compared with conventional colleges, the per student cost of IGNOU, YCMOU, and BRAOU was 36.5%, 40.4%, 14.2% respectively.

Present Status

Presently there are 12 open universities in single mode and 106 correspondence course institutes (CCIs) in the dual mode in India. The share of distance education to the total enrolment in the higher education was about 9% in the year 1995. This increased to 25% in the year 2004. The 10th Five Year Plan envisages that this will increase to 40% by the end of 2006-07. The growth of open universities and CCIs in terms of number of programmes/courses, students registered, range of programmes, regional and study centres, etc. are very significant (Tables 1 to 3).

Table 1: The size of IGNOU

Year	No. of Programmes	No. of Courses	Students Registered	Regional Centres	Study Centres	Range of Programmes
2004-05	101	900	3,66,161	48	1255	C,D,UG,PG,Ph.D

Note: *C=Certificate, D=Diploma, UG=Undergraduate, PG=Postgraduate*

Table 2: The size of different SOUs in 2002-03

SOU	Year of Establishment	No. of Programmes	Range of Programmes	Students Registered	Regional Centres	Study Centres
BRAOU	1982	23	C,D,UG, PG, Ph.D	125225	23	144
VMOU	1987	25	C,D,UG, PG, Ph.D	12036	6	48
NOU	1987	20	C,D,UG, PG	4395	-	6
YCMOU	1989	78	C,D,UG, PG, Ph.D	110683	8	1450
MPBOU	1995	77	C,D,UG, PG, Ph.D	137326	11	1013
BAOU	1994	11	C,D,UG	1260	2	70
KSOU	1996	56	C,D,UG, PG, Ph.D	32150	6	65
NSOU	1997	5	C,D,UG	2712	-	47
UPRTOU	1998	41	C,D,UG, PG	2999	-	34
TNOU*	2002	-	-	-	-	-

Source: Information base on open universities, distance education institutes and correspondence courses institutions, IGNOU, New Delhi, 2003

Note: *BAOU=Dr. Babasaheb Ambedkar Open University, Ahmedabad, BRAOU=Dr. B.R. Ambedkar Open University, Hyderabad, KSOU=Karnataka State Open University, Mysore, MPBOU=Madhya Pradesh Bhoj Open University, Bhopal, NOU=Nalandha Open University, Patna, NSOU=Netaji Subhas Open University, Kolkata, TNOU=Tamilnadu State Open University, Chennai, UPRTOU=U.P. Rajashri Tandon Open University, Allahabad, VMOU=Vardhaman Mahaveer Open University, Kota, YCMOU=Yashwanrao Chavan Maharashtra Open University, Nashik.*

Table 3: Students Enrolled in IGNOU, SOUs, and CCIs/DEIs

Year	Unit	IGNOU	SOUs	CCIs/DEIs	Total
1997-98	Number	163394	272189	626471	1062054
	(%)	(15.38)	(25.63)	(58.99)	(100.00)
1998-99	Number	172548	302114	725781	1200443
	(%)	(14.37)	(25.17)	(60.46)	(100.00)

1999-2000	Number	196650	367655	815630	1379935
	(%)	(14.25)	(26.64)	(59.11)	(100.00)
2000-01	Number	304681	498382	880200	1683263
	(%)	(18.10)	(29.61)	(52.29)	(100.00)
2001-02	Number	301724	618295	963980	1883999
	(%)	(16.02)	(32.82)	(51.17)	(100.00)
2002-03	Number	316547	724102	1185898*	2226547
	(%)	(14.22)	(32.52)	(53.26)	(100.00)

* Provisional

Source: *Tenth Five Year Plan: Open & Distance Education and IGNOU*, Ministry of Human Resource Development, New Delhi, 2003.

IGNOU and some SOUs have sufficient financial and human resources to maintain the quality of large number of programmes and provide effective student support services. This is not the case with other state open universities and CCIs. In the CCIs, the academic staff is virtually non- existent. In the SOUs like MPBOU, NOU, NSOU, BAOU and VMOU the number of academic and support staff seems to be minimal in relation to the number of programmes and students. For example, in MPBOU, in 2002-03, there were only 27 academic staff and 174 support staff whereas the number of programmes and students was 77 and 137,326, respectively. These trends once again raise the quality issues even among the single mode open universities. In such a scenario, it is difficult to produce and deliver quality programmes with minimal funding through distance education. Even attracting quality students and producing quality graduates is almost incomprehensible.

In 2002-03 out of the total enrolment in distance education in India, 14.22% were from IGNOU, 32.52% from SOUs and 53.26% from CCIs. This shows that CCIs still dominate the enrolment. However, the CCIs are still considered as revenue generating institutes for their parent universities, which make up their budget deficit by the money generated through distance education programmes. Consequently, no money is left for the CCIs to spend for offering quality programmes and providing effective student support services. The respective state governments who fund the parent universities do not have separate budgets for CCIs. This is one reason why the distance education programmes offered by premier institutes are still not recognised even by those conventional universities that have distance education programmes. For example, Prasad (2004) states that "the Birla Institute of Technology and Science, Rajasthan and the Jawaharlal Nehru Technological University, Andhra Pradesh are two prestigious engineering education providers in India. Even though their conventional programmes are of world-class standards, the distance education programmes of one are not recognised by the other."

The Distance Education Council (DEC), a statutory body of IGNOU, provides financial support to SOUs and CCIs in the form of developmental funds for infrastructure, institutional reforms, academic improvement, staff development and training, student support services, computerisation and networking of institutions and improvement of quality education. Recently, it has initiated steps to create a pool of best study materials. With provision for adoption/adaptation and allowance for innovation and diversity. Sharing these materials with SOUs and CCIs would definitely help to overcome quality concerns and add to cost-efficiency as the wheel will not be reinvented again and again. However, a lot more still remains to be done for improvement in the quality of their programmes development and delivery.

Spending more money to achieve the same result does not mean that the programmes are of high quality. The internal cost-efficiency of distance education is very important. In other words, the productivity of an institution should be of an acceptable level. The retention rates, dropout/graduation ratios, and the minimum norms for faculty productivity, are widely used to measure the performance of distance education institutes. The productivity indicators are not only useful for measuring the quality of distance education programmes but also for measuring their cost-effectiveness. For example, unit costs per student are seemingly low for a distance education institution when sufficient number of students are enrolled. If the dropout rates are very high, the cost advantage may not work. Therefore, in order to retain the cost-effectiveness advantage of distance education, the institutes concerned should try to improve their productivity levels.

The recent technological advances have made it possible for distance education to have a variety of media options for teaching-learning. However, the printed material in the self-learning format still dominates all other media. Audio/video programmes, counselling, Radio/TV, teleconferencing, computer networks are considered as supplementary to the printed material. Each of these media have their own cost structure. For example, the cost of delivering a radio/TV/teleconferencing programme is independent of the number of students who have access to it. That means, from the institution point of view, all the costs are fixed in nature and there are no variable costs in relation to the students. However, it may also cost to the students to buy the receiving gadgets (Radio/TV etc.). For video and audio programmes, there is an immediate variable cost for duplication and distribution.

There is no preset norm for mix of these media. Different institutes and different programmes within the same institution apply the proportion of media-mix differently. If these supplementary media are not used or found inaccessible by the students, all the costs incurred go waste, except to say that their programmes use multimedia and are therefore effective. For example, IGNOU uses most of the educational media. Naidu (1998) analysed different media used by IGNOU and its emphasis (Table 4). However, from the student's point of view, most media other than print found to be not effective for a variety of reasons.

Table 4: Media emphasis

Media	Who bears the cost	Emphasis
Printed material	IGNOU	Highest
Video programmes	IGNOU	Limited
Audio programmes	IGNOU	Limited

Teaching (Counselling)	IGNOU	Limited
Radio	All India Radio - IGNOU	Limited
TV	Doordarshan - IGNOU	Limited but likely to be intensified
Teleconferencing	Indian Space Research OrganisationIGNOU	Limited but likely to be intensified

Source: Naidu, C.G. (1998).

If the mix of the media is not in right proportion and if there are problems with their effectiveness, then these programmes prove to be failing their advantage of cost-effectiveness. In such cases, the institutes should focus on their cost-efficiency.

One of the greatest benefits of distance education programmes in India is their unlimited quantitative access to the socio-economic and geographically disadvantaged prospective students. This advantage provides an opportunity to the institutions and funding agencies to maintain the equity. The distance education system also promises cost-efficiency. Therefore, the social equity and cost-efficiency put together help the education policy makers in taking decisions in favour of distance education.

Limitations

One of the significant limitations of distance education is low retention and low success rates. Many of the students either drop out from the programmes they have enrolled or fail to complete the programme successfully. These trends may raise quality concerns of the programmes. The reasons could be either internal to the institution or pertain to the students' personal problems.

The potential of cost-effectiveness of distance education programmes may not apply if the dropout rates are very high when compared with the conventional programmes. Naidu (1994) applied sensitivity analysis and compared the costs of IGNOU undergraduate programmes with those offered by conventional colleges for various dropout rates. He found that when the difference between the two systems is very high (more than 70% dropout in distance education and below 20% dropout in conventional system), the advantage of cost-effectiveness may not apply. On the other hand, if one assumes that there is a 0% dropout rate in the conventional system, then IGNOU should not lose more than 60% of its students in order to retain its cost-effective advantage. Similarly, employability of learners may also have implications for quality and cost-efficiency.

For a distance education institution, simply having larger number of students does not necessarily mean that its programmes are cost-efficient. A number of factors decide the cost-efficiency of distance education programmes. Multiplication of media, number of study centres per programme, number of students per programme, number of optional courses per programme, etc. either individually or in combination contribute substantially to the increases in fixed and/or semi variable costs. Unless sufficient number of students are enrolled for each stratum of these parameters, the individual programmes may not be cost-efficient. The quality of students enrolling for distance education programmes in India is throwing a challenge to prove its worth in terms of retention rates or pass out rates. This is particularly true for programmes and geographical regions where the students choose distance education as an alternative. When the institutions keep certain standards to decide the worth of students for their certificates/degrees, many of the students who could not meet the standards either withdraw before taking examination or fail to clear it.

Normally, different cost studies assume a particular mix of media, technologies, and support services. The right mix of these may result in improving the quality of the programmes. At the same time, the cost structures, also vary accordingly. Most of the cost studies assume that the process and/or output quality is constant. What is compared is only the unit costs. As there are usually differences in the quality of process and output, it is important to first measure cost-effectiveness and then relate it to cost.

As explained earlier, proliferation of programmes, courses, study centres, may raise new issues and concerns in terms of quality and costs. For example, offering too many similar programmes may lower the number of students enrolling for each programme. Some times there may be seemingly larger number of students for a programme when looked at the total number of students enrolled. If we look further, the distribution of students among different study centres and per course per study centre may give a different picture. Because of this, there will be a dilution of certain student support services in order to regulate the expenditure.

Unfortunately, another perceived limitation of the open system is in attracting and retaining talent, as many still consider it a weaker option. This is unfortunate!

Innovations

The development of self-instructional materials and other educational technologies has made it possible to maintain the quality of the programmes and offer them to large student populations at lower cost. In addition, large number of skilled, semi-skilled, and part-time staff are associated in providing student support services. In order to enhance the quality of programmes, the staff needs to be trained. The student feedback is another activity that helps to take corrective measures. All these may cost something to the institution. If the gain resulting from undertaking such training programmes and feedback research is more than the costs involved, then one should go for such innovative quality improvement strategies. For example, in IGNOU, the Staff Training and Research Institute of Distance Education (STRIDE) is involved in conducting training programmes for improving quality of materials provided by various distance education institutes in India and other developing countries.

In India, each open university has its own funding sources and regulations. All the distance education institutes are under a dual mode system. Very few institutes have the financial and human resources to develop the programmes that involve high fixed costs. For this reason, through Memorandum of Understanding (MoU) IGNOU is sharing its programmes with other State Open Universities and Distance Education Institutes in the dual mode system. This way the institutes can minimize the costs and at the same time maintain the quality of the programmes.

Collaborations with different agencies for developing programmes and participation of industries and user organizations for delivery of programmes not only act as cost cutting measures to the distance education institutes but also enhance their quality. For example, for many of the programmes offered by IGNOU, the funds come from respective sponsoring agencies for the development and production of materials. This ensures maintenance of quality at this stage. Similarly, the participation of public and private institutions in delivery of IGNOU programmes helps IGNOU avoid long term investments in creating infrastructure. The creation of its own infrastructure may involve huge investments and the main threat from this strategy is the sustenance of programmes in the long run. Instead, the delivery of programmes to the student with the participation of public and private institutions who have quality infrastructure not only minimises the costs but also helps in right policy decisions.

Conclusion

Design, development, and delivery of programmes are some of the functions of a distance education institute that generally reflect their quality assurance initiatives. The cost structure on these functions also shows the cost-effectiveness. Evaluation standards of students, the student progress rates, and the data on students and the feedback to a great extent reflects the quality. DEC has taken several initiatives for quality assurance. Development of norms for assessment and accreditation of open and distance education institutes is one of them. It is time for many open universities and CCIs to get evaluated and graded accordingly. One of the problems that is ailing distance education institutes in India is poor quality students at their enrolment stage itself. It is not that the process quality of these institutes is inferior to the conventional colleges. Then the assessment and accreditation of distance education institutes by DEC or by some other national level accreditation institutes like National Assessment and Accreditation Council (NAAC) will help in measuring the process quality. In the event that the process quality of these institutes are rated better than many conventional colleges then the tag of inferiority may automatically get removed. In this context the example of UK Open University (UKOU) can be a great encouragement to others. Daniel (1977) explains that the UKOU was rated 10th in rank among 101 universities in Britain.

The Internet has a great potential of emerging as a dominant ICT among all media including the print. Yet, the success of Internet remains to be seen particularly in developing countries for a variety of reasons. In addition to the design, development, production, and delivery costs associated with the print, the Internet has some additional costs and resource factors, which influence its successful take-off. The additional costs include hardware, software, courseware, dedicated expert manpower, and access. Also, the costs can be both at the institutional level and student level. Consequently, unless the institutions and students are ready to meet these costs, the success of Internet in ODL remains limited.

References

Daniel, John (1997). Mega-Universities, Virtual Universities and Knowledge Media: Can We Have Quantity with Quality. Keynote Paper presented at AAOU Conference on Quality Assurance in Distance and Open Learning, Kuala Lumpur, November 11-14.

Datt, Ruddar (1991). *Study of Cost of Distance Education Institutes with Different Size Classes in India*. Research Project Report, School of Correspondence Courses and Continuing Education, University of Delhi.

Naidu, C.G. (1994). Some economic aspects of conventional and distance education systems in India. In Dhanarajan, G. et al. (eds.), *Economics of Distance Education: Recent Experience*. Hong Kong: Open Learning Institute.

Naidu, C.G. (1998). The economics of quality in distance education: An Indian perspective. *Indian Journal of Open Learning*, 7(3), 245-254.

Naidu, C.G. 1995). Social demand and educational planning in India. In Murali Manohar, K. (ed.), *Perspectives in Distance Education*, Warangal: Indian Distance Education Association.

Pillai, C.R. and Naidu, C.G. (1997). *Economics of Distance Education: The IGNOU Experience*. New Delhi: Indira Gandhi National Open University.

Prasad, V.S. (2004). Quality Assurance in Open and Distance Learning in the Indian Context: A Case Study. Paper presented to the Institute: Strategies for Sustainable ODL, Commonwealth of Learning, Canada.

UGC (1990). *Proceedings of Conference of Vice-Chancellors*. New Delhi: University Grants Commission.

Dr. C.G. Naidu is Deputy Director in Planning Division of Indira Gandhi National Open University, New Delhi.
Email: gajendraC1@rediffmail.com

SECTION V

STAFF DEVELOPMENT AND RESEARCH

32

Human Resource Development for Distance Education

Santosh Panda, Sanjaya Mishra and C.R.K. Murthy

Context

Unlike the conventional system of higher education which in the late eighties gave impetus to professional development of teachers through the academic staff colleges established in the conventional universities, the distance education system in India has stressed on the need for training different functionaries within distance education, including teachers, from the very beginning. Training, a sub-set of professional development, has received considerable attention, because the system of distance education operates in a different framework, and that most of the staff working in open universities and distance education institutions come from conventional background, generally with an inherent inclination towards face-to-face teaching. Without training, it would be difficult to expect improved performance and adaptability of the methods and techniques of distance education (this though has to be seen in conjunction with continuing professional development as an individual reflective habit). Distance education started in India in 1962, but training on distance education received its due place only after the establishment of the Indira Gandhi National Open University in 1985. A Division of Distance Education (DDE) was established in 1986 to develop appropriate human resources to take up required functions in academic, administrative and technical tasks in distance education.

In this chapter, we discuss the developments relating to only academic staff development in distance education. We believe that staff development is a systematic process to improve the efficiency of the academic and professional staff towards achievement of organisational goals and contribute to their articulation, refinement and sustainability. The process of staff development covers activities over and above training within its fold: it must be seen within the framework of continuing professional development (CPD).

The first staff development programme at IGNOU was conducted in October 1986 by the DDE with assistance from the UNESCO regional office, Bangkok (Koul & Murugan, 1989). The 10-days national programme on production of self-learning material was intended to enable course writers to produce quality learning materials. In January 1987, IGNOU launched the Diploma in Distance Education programme as a long term staff and professional development programme; and since then, based on considerable experiences, our understanding and capabilities have grown in respect of staff development in distance education, and related developments within the system including state open universities and dual mode distance education institutions.

In the following sections, while delineating an historical account, we reflect on what we have gained and how we are planning to proceed in future. The milestones on staff development given in Table 1 is a quick reference to the developments in this area.

Table 1: Milestones on staff development

Milestones
1986 • Establishment of a Division of Distance Education (DDE) at IGNOU.
1987 • Launch of a Diploma in Distance Education programme by IGNOU.
1989 • A national level workshop was organised in collaboration with UNESCO in January 1989 for development of training packages in DE. • 217 students of DDE were awarded diplomas at the first Convocation of IGNOU held in February.
1993 • The Masters of Arts in Distance Education (MADE) programme was launched by IGNOU. • A Centre for Training was established at Yashwantrao Chavan Maharashtra Open University (YCMOU), Nashik. • IGNOU was designated as Centre of Excellence for Training in DE by COL.
1994 • The Diploma in Distance Education programme was restructured and upgraded to a postgraduate diploma. • At the Commonwealth Heads of Governments meeting (CHOGM) held at Cyprus, the COL announced The Rajiv Gandhi Fellowship (RGF) Scheme for foreign students to take up IGNOU programmes (particularly PGDDE and MADE). • A Centre for Staff Training and Development (CSTD) was established at Dr. B.R. Ambedkar Open University, Hyderabad.
1995 • The first revision of the PGDDE and MADE courses was completed. • A national workshop on development of question banks and test items was organised.

- The first offer of IGNOU-RGF-COL scheme for PGDDE and MADE programmes was made in 19 countries.

1997-98

- STRIDE provided consultancy services to NIE, Bhutan in 1997-98; the Indian Army in 1997-98 and Department of Personnel and Training, Government of India in 1998-2000.
- Attachment programmes were introduced in 1998, with faculty members from the Open University of Sri Lanka being attached to STRIDE for training in DE methodologies.
- A perspective paper on staff development was developed which guided such future activities in a coherent and comprehensive manner.

1999

- Faculty members from Bangladesh Open University and from Seychelles were attached to STRIDE for research and training.
- Meeting of heads of staff development and training of open universities was held in March in collaboration with COL.
- The first round table on assignments (as part of a series of round tables on various themes of DE) was organised at BRAOU, and subsequently on media at YCMOU and on course development at NSOU.
- STRIDE provided consultancy to International Institute for Capacity Building in Africa (IICBA) in September.
- 'Report of Administrative Reforms Committee: Training of Non-Academic Staff' was passed in the BOM of IGNOU, which guided such future activities for non-teaching and professional staff.

2000

- The first series of academic counselling workshops for IGNOU PGDDE students of Ethiopia and Liberia organised.
- Second revision of the PGDDE and MADE courses was completed in October, under a project partly funded by COL, in order to internationalize the courseware for the students of the Commonwealth countries.
- The second offer of IGNOU-RGF-COL scheme of PGDDE and MADE was made in another 10 countries.

2001

- A national workshop on Research in DE was organised in March for training DE researchers.
- A workshop on E-Learning, the first of its kind, for in-house faculty of IGNOU was organised in July.
- The G. Ram Reddy Research Academy of Distance Education (GRADE) was established at BRAOU, Hyderabad.
- The first 'Refresher Programme' (on Distance Science Teaching) was organised by IGNOU (STRIDE-SOS-DEC) which subsequently led to conduct of such programmes in future.

2002

- RGF-COL workshop for academic counsellors of the PGDDE programme was held at New Delhi in March.
- The first workshop 'interactive multimedia for distance and online learning' as a part of the series of subsequent such workshops, was organised for the teachers of IGNOU. This was subsequently taken up as a series by the Inter-University Consortium in 2004-05 for SAARC, Commonwealth countries, and Indian OUs and DEIs.

2003

- IGNOU PGDDE programme was offered through IICBA in Ghana.
- A national workshop on Web-CT and E-learning was held in October.
- RGF-COL workshop for counsellors of MADE programme was held at New Delhi in November.
- Refresher programmes in 'Distance Teacher Education' and 'Distance History Education' were conducted in December.
- The first course revision workshop was organised at IGNOU which led to policy formulation in the university on revision of courses and budgetary provisions therein.

2004

- Attachment programme for faculty and administrative heads of NOUN, Nigeria was organised at STRIDE in June.
- National training workshop on research methodologies for DE, sponsored by COL, was organised at GRADE, BRAOU.

2005

- The Master of Arts in Distance Education programme, sponsored by the COL, was offered in Nigeria with 50 students (administered by the National Open University of Nigeria).
- Non-academic staff development programmes, in a series, were revived; and workshops for Assistant Registrars, SOs, SPAs and PAs, and Senior Assistants and Assistants were organised.
- A new series of research studies on dropout, costing, employability, differently-abled, programme evaluation, alternative unit structure, disadvantaged learners, learner support, virtual research, and eLearning services initiated. These studies shall further contribute to staff development for research in distance education.
- Four roundtables on learner support services are being organised at four state open universities representing distance teaching institutions in four regions in the country.

Training Needs of Academic Staff

Identification of specific training needs of academic staff in distance education has been a topic of many national, regional and international gatherings, as 'distance education systems are complex and require a multitude and multiplicity of competencies and abilities across professional categories. The requisite combination of skills is often dependent upon a number of changeable and evolving factors and must be carefully assessed to ensure appropriateness and relevance in the local content' (COL, 1994, p.1). The national workshop on 'The Development of Training Packages in Distance Education' organised by IGNOU and the UNESCO Regional Office, Bangkok during January 1989 listed the training needs of administrators, academics, technicians and supporting staff in substantial detail. Within the academics, the workshop listed the training needs of course writers, evaluators, editors, distance tutors, counsellors, curriculum designers, researchers, programme evaluators, and educational technologists. The workshop participants also developed outlines for four training packages in the following areas after due evaluation of the existing resources:

- Course design and course preparation
- Audio and video preparation
- Academic counselling, assessment of assignment, and management of support services
- Management/administration (Koul & Panda, 1989).

Following this national workshop, IGNOU conducted a Training of Trainer (TOT) workshop from in January-February, 1989 especially for the senior academic staff of IGNOU who would play the role of trainers for other staff members. Organized with the assistance of the erstwhile Overseas Development Administration (ODA), UK the programme identified the training needs of full-time academic faculty, course writers, editors, script writers, and academic counsellors, apart from honing the training skills of the select group of trainers (Koul & Murugan, 1989). The Commonwealth of Learning (COL) organized a Round Table on 'Training Distance Educators' in April , 1990 at Vancouver. This round table identified six major areas for training:

- General orientation to distance education
- Policy, planning and management of distance education
- Instructional design and course development
- Technology in course developments
- Student support services
- Research and evaluation (COL, 1990).

Later, in 1994, the COL organized an 'Asian Regional Workshop on Training' in July, 1994 at New Delhi in which experts from India, Bangladesh, Maldives, Pakistan and Sri Lanka presented their training needs (COL, 1994). A review of the reports on the training needs shows clearly lack of research on the training needs of academic staff in distance education, and therefore, the concomitant professional development strategies in-context. However, these reports had so far been quite successful in shaping the direction of training in the Indian sub-continent. The perceived needs of training by senior academics and administrators in distance education and the deliberations therein, help us in developing training curriculum for different categories of personnel. The exercise on identification of training needs, contents and strategies for both teaching and non-teaching staff vis-à-vis IGNOU's Administrative Reforms Committee in 1999 was handy in visualising and implementing subsequent training programmes described in the next section. These reports are however quite dated, and much has changed subsequently (especially on the ICT applications) since the last report of 1994. It is now high time to refine the training needs at both the organisational level and the individual academic level, and design training programmes accordingly.

Academic Staff Training at IGNOU

As mentioned earlier, IGNOU has attached great importance to academic staff training since its establishment. Creation of the DDE as early as in 1986 was an indication towards this commitment. Initially, training programmes at IGNOU started with the assistance of ODA and UNESCO. But, in order to develop the local capacity, the DDE developed and launched a long term professional distance training programme, i.e. Diploma in Distance Education in 1987 and a Master's Programme in Distance Education in 1993. The diploma programme was also upgraded to a postgraduate diploma in 1994. The Postgraduate Diploma in Distance Education (PGDDE) and Master of Arts in Distance Education (MADE) programmes were helpful in developing the much needed human resources for running the huge network of open universities and distance education institutions (DEIs) in India. These programmes were also used by countries in the African and Caribbean region for their national development and developing competencies of teachers in distance education. In 1993, The Commonwealth of Learning 'after careful scrutiny of the training work done by Indira Gandhi National Open University (IGNOU) declared it as a COL Centre of Excellence for Training in the South Asian region for five years and took upon itself responsibility to help widen the impact of training activities of IGNOU in the Asian region' (COL, 1994, p. 2). Following this, the DDE was upgraded to the Staff Training and Research Institute of Distance Education (STRIDE) in 1993. The STRIDE (including the erstwhile DDE) has so far conducted approximately 338 training programmes (excluding the programmes for counsellors) and has trained above 7200 personnel working in the distance education system. Table 2 gives an overview of the training programmes conducted at STRIDE. Table 3 shows the number of successful PGDDE and MADE graduates since 1990 who are trained human resources for the system of distance education in India.

Table 2: Range of training programmes conducted by STRIDE

Sl. No.	**Types of Programmes**	**No. of programmes organised at**					**No. of participants attended**
		Delhi	**DEIs**	**OUs**	**Abroad**	**Total**	
1.	Models of course design and development	1	-	-	-	1	50
2.	Development of self-learning materials	16	38	15	-	69	1786
3.	Editing	2	1	-	-	3	73
4.	Revision of self-learning materials	1	-	-	-	1	45

5.	Student assessment and evaluation	2	-	-	-	2	62
6.	E-Learning and interactive multimedia	4	-	-	-	4	95
7.	Academic counselling	5	2	1	-	8	236
8.	Quality assurance	-	1	-	-	1	42
9.	Programme evaluation	2	-	-	-	2	47
10.	Research methods	2	-	1	-	3	91
11.	Distance education: Overview	3	-	-	-	-	21
12.	Refresher programme	3	-	-	-	-	18
13.	Round table conferences	-	-	4	1	5	175
14.	Training of trainers programmes	8	-	-	-	8	101
15.	Attachment programmes	8	-	-	-	8	26
16.	PGDDE and MADE counselling workshops	-	-	-	17	17	350
17.	Orientation to course writers in various disciplines	200 (approx.)	-	-	-	200	4000 (approx.)
18.	Orientation programmes for counsellors of different academic programmes at Regional Centres	-	-	-	-	**	**
	Total	257	42	21	18	338	7202

** These programmes are organised by the Regional Centres in collaboration with the Schools of Studies with inputs from STRIDE. A large number of such programmes covering about 15,000 counsellors were conducted in which STRIDE faculty have given direct and indirect inputs.

Table 3: PGDDE and MADE graduates

Year	DDE/PGDDE	MADE
2004	142	20
2003	118	31
2002	119	10
2001	86	24
2000	69	30
1999	139	66
1998	101	22
1997	28	14
1996	82	43
1995	82	43
1994	94	67

1993	102	–
1992	141	–
1991	270	–
1990	217	–
Total	1790	370

At IGNOU academic staff development has been visualized as a continuous activity in the lifecycle of the teachers, thus enabling them to be knowledge seekers and enabling them to reflect on what they do and how they do. This is highly essential for distance education where all learning materials are open to public scrutiny and peer review for ensuring quality and credibility. In light of this, the general objectives of training academics and teachers at IGNOU are to:

- Enhance professional knowledge and understanding in a discipline and the system
- Enable them to cope with the latest technologies, systems and innovations
- Bring out right attitudinal orientation
- Support teachers in their career advancement.

Types of Training

Within the framework of continuous professional development of academics and based on the past experiences within and outside IGNOU, the training programmes at the University were revisualised and reorganised towards the late 90s, and, for quite some time are being conducted at four levels: induction, orientation, refresher, and specialized. This institutional reorientation was an outcome of deliberate efforts and under the aegis of constant interaction with the COL and other distance teaching institutions in the country; the requirement of the past Administrative Reforms Committee of IGNOU; and the requirements of the emerging ICTs (Panda, 1999).

Induction programme

Every teacher and academic joining IGNOU undergoes a 5-day induction training, with the objectives of familiarizing him/her on the methods of distance education, the operational mechanisms of IGNOU, roles of teachers and academics, and importance of project and time management in distance education. The participants are usually supplied with a compendium of select readings, and the internal faculty members and other officials serve as resource person to facilitate the sessions.

Orientation programme

The orientation training is equivalent to the orientation programme conducted by the Academic Staff Colleges (ASCs), and carries a workload of 144 hours for the participants; usually organized at a national level for a period of 10 days face-to-face, combined with self-learning packages. Teachers are also encouraged to attend orientation programmes organized at other academic staff colleges.

Refresher programme

For promotion to the cadre of Lecturer (senior scale), a teacher, besides the above orientation programme, needs to undergo subject specific refresher courses from any Academic Staff College of conventional universities. One may also go through the PGDDE of IGNOU which is recognized by the University Grants Commission (UGC) as equivalent to two refresher courses for teachers of distance education. The STRIDE has been conducting discipline based refresher programmes in the line of the ASCs from time to time. Such programmes cover 50 percent weight each on the discipline and distance education areas. Refresher programmes for science distance teaching, education distance teaching, and history distance teaching have been organised in the past.

Specialized training

Specialized training programmes of 1-5 days duration are organized by STRIDE on specialized areas such as learner assessment, media, student support, information technology, programme evaluation, course revision, interactive multimedia, online learning, and others either by STRIDE or IUC or in collaboration with other divisions of IGNOU. These programmes are basically need based and are pitched at an advanced level.

Approaches to Training

Besides the continuing professional development model of induction-orientation-refresher-specialized training, IGNOU organizes training in other modes as well. With its responsibility to maintain the standards of distance education in the country, STRIDE is actively involved in organizing training programmes at national, regional, and institutional level. The national level programmes are mostly organized at the headquarters; and since July 1995, participants pay certain fees to attend this programme (Mullick, 1997). Training programmes are also organized at DEIs and SOUs on their request. As more and more institutions receive grants from the Distance Education Council, this type of training programme has been on the increase. The Karnataka State Open University (KSOU) under this programme transformed its learning materials for the masters programmes/courses successfully. Other organisations adopting such a model are UP Rajarshi Tandon Open University, Allahabad and Tamil Nadu Open University, Chennai. Such an exercise is collaboratively undertaken by STRIDE/IUC, Schools of Studies, and DEC.

Another model of staff and professional development, adopted by STRIDE, is the thematic round tables conducted at SOUs at the regional level. So far four thematic round tables have been completed as a collaborative exercise of STRIDE and DEC:

1. Round Table on 'Assignments' at Dr. B.R. Ambedkar Open University, Hyderabad (August, 26- 27, 1999).
2. Round Table on 'Academic Counselling' at Karnataka State Open University, Mysore (August, 25-26, 2000).
3. Round Table on 'Self-Learning Print Material Development' at Nataji Subhash Open University, Calcutta (September, 9-10, 2000).
4. Round Table on 'Media Delivery System' at Yashwantrao Chavan Maharashtra Open University (February, 22-24, 2001).

Another series of such collaborative four regional round tables on learner support services are being organised in the next few months.

Training Methods and Strategies

Except for the long term professional development programmes (PGDDE and MADE), 'face-to-face' is the predominant method of training with occasional use of teleconferencing. This is a critical issue, as we preach distance education through the face-to-face mode. Only one training programme on self-learning material development was organized through an innovative multi-modal strategy covering distance learning (one month), face-to-face training (5 days) and workplace based learning (3 months) in 2002. However, this programme could not be considered a successful model due to less number of participants. Nevertheless, the innovation confirmed the feasibility of distance training. While discussing the competencies of academic counsellors at IGNOU, and emphasizing their need for training, Mishra (2005) recommends a staff development strategy based on competence framework and use of evidence based certification and mentoring. There is a need to experiment with new methods and strategies for training. Use of audio-visual medium, PowerPoint and, of late multimedia in the face-to-face sessions to enhance the discussion and facilitate training/learning is a common practice by the trainers. Another critical issue is the availability of qualified and effective trainers in distance education. Realizing this, in 1997 STRIDE organized a Training of Trainers (TOT) programme for Directors of DEIs, who were expected to be trainers and facilitators at regional level, allowing the STRIDE faculty to focus on new and emerging areas. However, this exercise too could not be sustained, since those trained in the TOT were either not utilized or were not available due to their own organizational and personal compulsions. There is enough scope for experimenting with the TOT strategy by developing trainer support materials to increase the effectiveness of training.

Training Materials

Development of training materials has been a matter of top priority to facilitate development of trainer capability and also to have sufficient reading materials for the workshop. With the fast developments in all the fields of distance education, and taking cue from the workshop on training packages organised in 1989, STRIDE has developed the following training materials for use in training and staff development.

- Handbook-1: *Open and Distance Education*
- Handbook-2: *Effective Learning*
- Handbook-3: *Academic-Counselling in Open and Distance Learning*
- Handbook-4: *Assessment and Evaluation in Distance Learning*
- Handbook-5: *Development and Revision of Self-Learning Materials (under publication)*
- Handbook-6: *Editing in Distance Education*
- Handbook-7: *Media and Technology in Distance Education (under publication)*
- Handbook-8: *E-Learning (in progress)*
- Handbook-9: *Support Services in Distance Education (in progress)*
- Handbook-10: *Planning and Management of Distance Education*
- Handbook-11: *Cost Analysis in Open and Distance Learning*
- Handbook-12: *Programme Evaluation in Open and Distance Education (in progress)*
- Handbook-14: *Psychological Skills for Open and Distance Learning*
- *Training Manual for Non-Academic Staff in Distance Education*
- *Self-Learning Material Development: Developer's Handbook*
- *Learning Activities in IGNOU Study Materials*

These materials are available free of cost to all the SOUs, DEIs (and some international/overseas DTIs on request) for use in their training programme and for faculty library to consult from time to time. A series of video programmes on various aspects of distance learning are available under the aegis of EduSat since 2005.

Critique on Training

The value of training can be measured at four different levels – reaction, learning, performance and results. All the training programmes concluded with the customary reaction level evaluation leading to preparation of a workshop report. It is really not known how best these reports are utilized. We are yet to attempt evaluation at other levels in a systematic manner. But, at the performance level, we can say emphatically that these training programmes have led to satisfactory improvement in the performance of the teachers. The growing number of academic courses and programmes are testimony to it. Moreover, with training, almost all teachers at IGNOU have some kind of understanding of curriculum design and instructional development, thereby reducing their dependence on professional instructional designers at STRIDE and, this has resulted in the overall reduction in material production time. A results-level analysis may quantify the value (in terms of cost-saving) of such changes in the performance of teachers. However, training is also often criticised by internal faculty on many accounts. In the context of counsellor training, Murugan (1994) says:

> Some of them do not fully recognize the need for training. Even if some do perceive the need, they are reluctant to devote the amount of time required for it. And, a few of them discount some of the training because they believe what they receive from the personnel of the University is a manifestation of their own little obsessions (p.12).

This is also true to other training as well. Another important issue is the 'in-service' training approach in contrast to 'pre-service' training before recruited to distance education/distance teaching. One of the authors (Mishra, 2004) of this chapter while criticizing the 'in-service training' had to say the following:

> ... people join the Distance Education System without having the inclination and attitudes appropriate to it. In such a situation any amount of 'in-service' training makes no difference in their approaches. These groups of teachers are actually more concerned about their subject knowledge and erosion of their academic powers and authority through the approaches of Distance Education. It has been observed that such notion are due to a false perception of accepting a specific format of self-learning material supplied by IGNOU as the only way to design instructions. Many teachers feel suffocated to fall within this narrow lane to knowledge dissemination (p.12).

Such teachers fail to see the value of learning design and thus are more vociferous against training (in-service). Criticisms notwithstanding, there are some evaluation studies (Murthy & Ramanujam, 1997; COL, 1998; Ramanujam, 1999; Murthy, 2004) that report positive impact of these training programmes. It is generally felt that a 'pre-service' training model might be more appropriate along with the continuing professional development model of staff development. Koul (1990) also supports the 'pre-service' training in distance education. Besides, one of the authors of this chapter (Panda, 2004) points out that training must be seen in the form of continuing professional development, and that CPD must contribute to continuing critical reflection, and to individual development, besides institutional growth and development.

Distance Education Training in State Open Universities

Realizing the importance of regular staff training, SOUs had also in the past started establishing training centres. Dr. B.R. Ambedkar Open University (BRAOU) established a Centre for Staff Training and Development (CSTD) in April 1994. This unit continuously organized training for teachers, media staff, study centre heads, and academic counsellors. With the establishment of the G. Ram Reddy Academy of Distance Education (GRADE) at BRAOU recently, the training and research activities have been further intensified. In 2004, it organized a national workshop on 'Research Methodology Training' sponsored by the COL. In this programme, the Practitioners Research and Evaluation Skill Training (PREST) in Open and Distance Learning materials developed by COL and International Research Foundation for Open Learning (IRFOL) were tested for wider use. The Yashwantrao Chavan Maharastra Open University (YCMOU) also established a Centre for Training way back in 1993 and conducts induction programmes for the academic staff and orientation programmes for academic counsellors regularly. The Vardhman Mahavir Open University (VMOU) has also established a Staff Training and Research Institute of Distance Education (STRIDE) that organizes training programmes collaboratively with the institutions like IGNOU.

Prospects

With tremendous expansion and increasing diversification of the distance education system, and intensified community orientation as well as international offer of distance education programmes, the importance of human resource development (HRD) is being increasingly recognised as never before. The unprecedented developments in information and communication technology in the past couple of years both necessitate HRD in newer areas and skills, as well as facilitate newer strategies of professional development. While professional development activities had so far focussed on development of print and audio-video based learning materials and the allied delivery mechanisms, technological and pedagogic developments in the contemporary time are necessitating diversification and reforms in professional development areas and strategies so as to address the global changes as well as contemporary research on human learning. Therefore, while the ongoing professional development activities shall continue to be intensified and to focus on R&D-based reforms in areas of course design and development, instructional delivery and learner support, and mechanisms of collaboration and networking for these, new professional development initiatives need to be recognised, prioritised and supported. STRIDE (IGNOU) and GRADE (BRAOU) have already initiated independent and collaborative activities to address the issues of professional development based on conduct of contextual research and understanding of global innovative/best practices.

A recent study on multiple media preferences and strategies (Dikshit et al, 2003), which has led to significant policy changes in instructional design and deployment at both the national open university and other distance education institutions in India, suggested that all the distance learners did not have the same preference for the existing media of distance teaching-learning and the way those had so far been designed to communicate content and address interaction and engagement. The online learners strongly preferred alternative strategies involving interactive multimedia content in CD-ROM (besides the self-learning materials in print) and online learner support. The study also indicated wider preferences for the way interactive multimedia and online support are to be designed. Today, therefore, the option of instructional basket includes content delivery through print, audio, video and interactive CD, and learner support through study centre, two-way teleconferencing and the web. This is also being designed to be supplemented by online learning resource repositories. These developments have led to, in the recent past, initiation of preliminary activities for the DE system (Garg and Panda, 2005) as well as newer initiatives and R&D projects (Bhushan, 2004; Kanjilal et al, 2004; Panda and Bala, 2004; Garg and Panda, 2005; Panda et al., 2005; Panda, Reif and Garg, 2005; Thomas et al, 2004; Vijayshri, 2004). An overarching facilitating media as well as challenge to newer professional development is EduSat (satellite for education) launched in India in 2004, as well as the concomitant R&D requirements in converging the wireless EduSat Intranet and the wired Internet. A convergence of conventional distance learning and modern distance education is underway towards "blended learning" and associated human resource development and newer instructional design. This requires a re-orientation of the mindset towards the blended approach; the associated skills should obviously follow.

References

Bhushan, S. (2004). Online learning of diplomacy. *Indian Journal of Open Learning*, 13(1), 113-117.

COL (1990). *Report on a Round Table on Training Distance Educators*. Vancouver: Commonwealth of Learning.

COL (1994). *Asian Regional Workshop on Training, July 25-28, 1994, Delhi*. Vancouver: Commonwealth of Learning.

COL (1998). *External Evaluation Report of STRIDE Programme*. Vancouver: Commonwealth of Learning (unpublished).

Dikshit, J.; Gaba, A.; Bhushan, S.; Garg, S. and Panda, S. (2003). Learning attitude, motivation, and preferences of online learners. *Indian Journal of Open Learning*, 12(3), 149-167.

Garg, S. and Panda, S. (2005). Interactive multimedia on distance and online learning. *Indian Journal of Open Learning*, 14(1), 97-98.

Kanjilal, U.; Ghosh, S.B. and Kumar, A. (2004). Web enhanced training programme on WINISIS: IGNOU-DSIR initiative. *Indian Journal of Open Learning*, 13(1), 110-113.

Koul, B.N. (1990). Instructional design and course development: A training perspective'. In *Report on a Round Table on Training Distance Educators*. Vancouver: Commonwealth of Learning.

Koul, B.N. and Murugan, K. (1989). *Workshop: Training the Trainers*. New Delhi: DDE, IGNOU.

Koul, B.N. and Panda, S.K. (1989). *Report of the National Workshop on the Development of Training Packages in Distance Education, 9-19 January, 1989*. Bangkok: UNESCO and New Delhi: IGNOU (unpublished).

Mishra, S. (2004). Human resource planning and development for distance education in India. *University News*, 41(46), 8-13.

Mishra, S. (2005). Roles and competencies of academic counsellors in distance education. *Open Learning*, 20(2), 147-159.

Mullick, S.P. (1997). Staff development at national open university. In Panda, S. (ed.), *Staff Development in Higher and Distance Education*. New Delhi: Aravali Books International, 199-204.

Murthy, C.R.K. & Ramanujam, P.R. (1997). *Rajiv Gandhi Fellowship Scheme: Report of the Internal Evaluator*. STRIDE Research Report, New Delhi: IGNOU (unpublished).

Murthy, C.R.K. (2004). Programmes for professional development in distance education: Perception and views of international students. *Indian Journal of Open Learning*, 13(3), 283-291.

Murugan, K. (1994). The status and prospectus of counsellors training: The IGNOU experience. *Indian Journal of Open Learning*, 3(1), 11-15.

Panda, S. (1999). *Policy Paper on Academic Staff Development*. New Delhi: IGNOU (mimeo).

Panda, S. (2004). People: staffing, development and management. In Perraton, H. and Lentell, H (eds.), *Policy for Open and Distance Learning*. London: RoutledgeFalmer.

Panda, S. and Bala, M. (2004). Online research resources for teachers and trainers. *Indian Journal of Open Learning*, 13(1), 119-122.

Panda, S.; Librero, F. and Batpurev (2005). *A Platform for Virtual Research and Virtual Research Training in Asia*. IDRC, Canada Research Project for Asia, Indira Gandhi National Open University, New Delhi.

Panda, S.; Reif, L. and Garg, S. (2005). *Status Appraisal and Policy Formulation for eLearning in India: Developing a Roadmap with Indicators and Benchmarks for Quality Assurance, Standardisation and Service Excellence*. GTZ/Crystal Research Project, German Agency for Technical Cooperation and Indira Gandhi National Open University, New Delhi.

Ramanujam, P.R. (1999). *STRIDE Training Programmes: Their Impact on the DOL System in South Asia*. STRIDE Research Report, IGNOU: New Delhi (unpublished).

Thomas, A.; Kapur, D. and Kumar, A. (2004). Capacity building and training in the area of food safety through an online certificate programme. *Indian Journal of Open Learning*, 13(1), 107-109.

Vijayshri (2004). ICT-enabled educational training through interactive multimedia CDs. *Indian Journal of Open Learning*, 13(1), 118-119.

Professor Santosh Panda is Director, Staff Training and Research Institute of Distance Education, & Head of Inter-University Consortium, Indira Gandhi National Open University, New Delhi.
Email: spanda@ignou.ac.in

Dr. Sanjaya Mishra is Reader, Staff Training and Research Institute of Distance Education, Indira Gandhi National Open University, New Delhi.
Email: s-mishra@ignou.ac.in

Dr. C.R.K. Murthy is Reader, Staff Training and Research Institute of Distance Education, Indira Gandhi National Open University, New Delhi.
Email: murthycrk@hotmail.com

33

Non-Teaching and Professional Staff Development

C.R.K. Murthy and R. Satyanarayana

Introduction

Human resource formation through professional development programmes in every sector of the society is gaining momentum due to the fast changing societal conditions in this era of globalisation. There is a growing feeling that human resource development through informal sources and formal education and training alone may not be adequate to cope with current challenges faced by them. Moreover, there is emphasis on continuous and lifelong education/training in every area of human activity. The education sector is no exception; rather it is more crucial for education and training as every society produces human resources through it for other sectors of the economy. The open and Distance Education (DE) system is a major innovation within the education system, and has been contributing to the change process. Obviously, DE personnel also require continuous and lifelong education/training on the job as well as through formal professional staff development programmes/activities. Another important consideration for staff development in the Open and Distance Learning (ODL) system is its complexity and diverse functions and activities to be carried out by various categories of personnel: teaching, non-teaching (support and services), media, computer and other professionals at headquarters and regional centres. In addition to these full-time staff, part-time staff such as coordinators, assistant coordinators, counsellors and other functionaries at study centres also need training on continuous basis.

An attempt is made in this chapter to focus on the non-teaching and professional staff development activities in single mode and dual mode institutions in India. The chapter is divided into three parts: the first part presents the historical development/evolution of staff development activities for non-teaching staff; the second part deals with the present status and challenges; and the third part highlights the future scenario in this area of activity.

Evolution of Staff Development

Though non-teaching staff provides support to the teacher in discharging his/her responsibilities effectively and efficiently, their role in various activities such as delivery mechanisms, media, support services, computerisation and networking, registration and evaluation, finance and general administration is very crucial for the overall growth of the system and the institution. And there is a great need for professional staff development programmes for the non-teaching staff working in ODL institutions. In fact, it is an essential component of system development. In conventional institutions also, all these years, staff development was not given much significance; may be the nature of their activities did not demand such professional training. The National Education Policy (NEP 1986), stressed on training and professional development in institutions of higher learning (GoI, 1986). Consequent to that, Academic Staff Colleges were established in the higher education sector for teachers; and for non-academic training, professional agencies like Institute of Secretariat Training & Management (ISTM) took up the responsibility for such training, though on a limited scale. With the increasing competitiveness and the globalisation process, many conventional institutions are seriously stressing on staff development for teaching and non-teaching staff.

However, in the ODL institutions such training has become inevitable due to a variety of tasks to be performed by both the teaching and the non-teaching staff. Hence, ODL institutions all over the world, and starting with the UKOU, felt the need for professional development for both teaching and non-teaching staff. The only difference was in strategy—some institutions planned activities since the beginning of the establishment of the institution, while some others started a few years later emphasising on learning the activity on-the-job.

For the first time training was given attention, particularly to academic staff members, at AP Open University, Hyderabad (now known as Dr. B.R. Ambedkar Open University). Experts were invited from other ODL institutions and some senior staff were deputed to other ODL institutions for detailed study. However, this was not on a larger scale or in a planned manner. In case of non-teaching staff development, no activity of any kind was visualised initially. The Indira Gandhi National Open University (IGNOU), in order to strengthen its own institution and to lead the DE system in the country paid attention to staff development activities since its inception. To organise these activities for both teaching and non-teaching staff, IGNOU established a Division of Distance Education (DDE) in 1986. The strategies followed by the DDE in the staff development area were:

- Inviting ODL experts as consultants under the IGNOU-ODA, UK collaborative project, in key areas such as course development, media, support services, computerization and warehouse management.

- Deputing senior academics and non-academic staff (largely individually, on few occasions in groups) to UK for a brief visit to study UKOU and other institutions under the IGNOU-ODA project.
- Developing a long-term professional development programme i.e. Diploma in Distance Education (DDE) of one year duration and offering to both in-house staff and those from other ODL institutions, i.e. those who wanted to develop human resources in the area of Distance Education.
- Offering short term training programmes to newly joined faculty/academics by inviting external experts and also through the faculty of DDE.

In addition to the above training programmes, the academics were exposed to audio and video script writing by overseas experts. The staff of the Communication Division were deputed to short visits/training abroad under IGNOU-ODA and Japanese International Collaboration Agency (JICA) projects. Professionals and staff of CCIs and SOUs also participated in some of these programmes. The Computer Division also organised training of teacher as well as non-teaching staff in computer proficiency, networking and implementation of Oracle.

These strategies were followed mainly to train the academic/teaching staff. However, the non-teaching staff also benefited to some extent. Since inception, the Division of Distance Education attended to the training needs of non-teaching staff. The short term training programmes conducted for them are:

- Induction programmes for the newly appointed staff
- Refresher programmes for section officers and other categories
- DTP familiarization programme
- Specialised workshops on student registration and evaluation
- Training programmes on administrative and financial rules
- Computer training for staff of regional centres
- Orientation-cum-training programmes for RC staff (organized at various RCs)

The erstwhile Communication Division (now Electronic Media Production Centre: EMPC) also organised various programmes for the faculty:

- Workshops organised with the help of faculty from IGNOU and outside institutions
- Production methodology and script writing
- Audio recording and music appreciation (for staff of the Communication Division)
- Type writing in Hindi on videotapes (for CD staff)
- Script writing (for CD staff)

Training programmes were also organised by the erstwhile Communication Division (present EMPC) for IGNOU staff with overseas expertise support. Some of these are:

- Basic production methodology
- Presentation techniques

- Video editing and video equipment maintenance
- TV lighting techniques
- TV sound recording
- Studio production on multi-camera set up
- Technical operations

Functionaries of study centres and regional centres comprise significant human resource base of any distance education system. Especially the part time functionaries like coordinators, assistant coordinators, academic counsellors, who are new to the system, need induction and training at regular intervals. Other managerial and support staff working at these centres do need training on various aspects of the system and operations. Considering the significance, training in the following areas are conducted by STRIDE and respective Schools of Studies in collaboration with the Regional Services Division:

- Periodical orientation programmes for coordinators and assistant coordinators of study centres on various operations
- Monitoring activities of study centres
- Orientation programmes for discipline-wise academic counsellors.

Table 1 records the type of training programmes/workshops organised by the erstwhile Division of Distance Education (DDE) and the STRIDE since 1987 to October, 2005 for the non-teaching staff of IGNOU.

Table 1: Short duration training programmes organised by DDE/STRIDE for non-teaching staff

Sl. No.	Type of training programmes organised	Number of programmes organised	No. of participants attended
1.	Induction for Secretarial Staff	4	74
2.	Induction of JATs	3	70
3.	Skill development and office procedure for secretarial staff	3	62
4.	Training on Attitude Development for Secretarial cum Administrative Staff	3	60
5.	Training on Attitude Development for JATs	3	60
6.	Orientation-cum-Workshop for DRs/ARs/SOs	1	23
7.	Workshop on Improvement of Efficiency for DRs/ARs/SOs	1	21
8.	Induction Programme for newly joined SOs & Sr. Assistants	2	34
9.	Induction for newly joined Assistants/ Sr. Assistants	4	112

10.	Orientation-cum-Workshop for recently promoted SOs/SPAs/Sr. Assistants/ PA-II/Assistants	5	65
11.	Orientation-cum-Training for Assorted groups of Sr. Asstt./Assistants	2	20
12.	Refresher Programme for Non-Academic Staff	2	40
13.	DTP Familiarization and Computer Training Prgramme for RC Staff	2	36
14.	Workshop on Admission and Evaluation	3	68
15.	Training Programme on Administrative and Financial Rules	3	82
16.	Orientation-cum-Workshop for ARs	1	26
17.	Orientation-cum-Workshop for SOs	1	21
18.	Orientation-cum-Workshop for SPAs/PAs	1	27
19.	Orientation-cum-Workshop for Sr. Asstts/Asstts.	1	33
	Total	45	934

Analysis of Table 1 indicates that 20 different types of programmes ranging from induction into respective cadres to specialised areas like computer applications, administrative and financial procedures, admission and evaluation systems. This shows that the training programmes have evolved over the years keeping in view the evolving functional needs of the institution during the last two decades. So far 45 programmes have been organised covering 934 members of non-teaching staff at various levels. These efforts indicate the seriousness and importance attached to staff development activity at IGNOU.

The non-teaching staff is also deputed to training programmes conducted by reputed training institutes in India, in administrative reforms, financial management, sensitivity towards learners and downtrodden, and related areas.

In addition to the short term training programmes listed in Table 1, STRIDE had developed two long term professional development programmes i.e. PG Diploma in Distance Education (PGDDE) and M.A. in Distance Education (MADE). Many academics and non-teaching staff of IGNOU have already enrolled and successfully completed these programmes. As a policy of encouragement and reward, IGNOU gives one increment to any staff who completes the PGDDE programme successfully. Many non-teaching staff have in the past enrolled themselves in MADE, so that they complete and obtain a Postgraduate degree, which many of them did not posses when joined the institution.

If we analyse the scenario at the national level, not much attention was paid to non-teaching staff development by institutions except IGNOU and BRAOU, Hyderabad; the latter organised training programmes in the area of administration. BRAOU has established a training unit to cater to the needs of teaching and non-teaching staff development.

The comprehensive study conducted by Singh (1993) on correspondence and distance education in India also emphasised the need for staff development for both teaching and administrative staff. This was because coming from conventional institutions they were new to the DE system. The study further revealed that staff development had been completely neglected by the CCIs. The study clearly brought out that very little had been done on administrative staff training.

In the following section, the present status of staff development activities for non-teaching staff, and the issues and challenges faced in this regard, are analysed.

Present Status - Issues and Challenges

Apart from IGNOU, training units have been established in BRAOU, Hyderabad, YCMOU, Nashik, and VMOU, Kota. At BRAOU, the training unit was upgraded to a full fledged G.Ram Reddy Academy of Distance Education (GRADE) with functions of research and training. GRADE is organising programmes for non-teaching staff, particularly in the area of computer applications. The training unit at YCMOU, known as Academic Services Division, is responsible for training both academics and non-teaching staff. Sengupta (1997) has reported that senior administrative staff is more receptive to new inputs in the five training programmes organised at YCMOU. The VMOU has established a training unit titled as 'STRIDE' which has been organising training for both academics and non-teaching staff. As such, non-teaching staff training has not been given as much attention as the academic staff development. The feedback received from participants of training programmes conducted up to 1995 revealed that every participant had taken the programmes seriously and with interest, and provided good suggestions for improvement of the future programmes (Sengupta, 1997).

Unfortunately, in the CCIS/DEIs, training is not a issue of priority at all, particularly for the non-teaching staff. The situation of DEIs in India can be compared with a few other institutions including UKOU where training was not paid attention in the beginning of its establishment, on the assumption that the staff learn on-the-job. These institutions though realised the significance of staff development and established training institutes/centres after a few years of their establishment. IGNOU is an exception as it established a training unit in the beginning and has reviewed its policy from time to time.

In the Indian scenario, the perceptions, factors and reasons that affect the staff development activities in DEIs are many and varied:

- The significance of training in general and in complex DE system in particular is not felt by many DEIs, particularly the CCIs.
- Some DEIs are convinced of the need of staff development but due to lack of adequate resources, both human and financial, they fail to establish a unit or undertake the activities on a planned and larger scale.
- A majority of CCIs/DEIs do not have enough core faculty to carry out main academic activity, in such cases visualizing staff development for non-teaching staff sounds a hollow exercise.
- The attitude of both management and employees in general that staff development means a wastage of time and resources.

- Orienting staff to new challenges faced by ODL institutions in terms of large numbers to cater, diverse target groups to cover, multiple roles to play, quality support services to provide with individual attention and extensive use of newer technologies is not a simple task.

Based on the comprehensive report of the Administrative Reforms Committee (ARC) (IGNOU, 1999) (developed on the basis of a study and university wide consultations across various sections of staff), the BOM of IGNOU in its 65th meeting has identified the following objectives, areas of training and target groups:

Objectives

i) To prepare the staff for active participation in the system at the point of entry - a sort of familiarisation.
ii) To upgrade knowledge and skills and consequently enhance efficiency in performing the assigned functions through continuous training.
iii) To equip the staff to cope with varying responsibilities, which may have to be shouldered due to transfer of personnel from one functional area to another and also due to promotion from one cadre to another.
iv) To cope with the new technologies and systems and innovations therein.
v) To develop a positive attitude towards work, colleagues and students.
vi) To inculcate a sense of belongingness to the institution.

Areas of training

- General training initiatives
- Specialized training initiatives

Target groups

- Section Officers
- Assistant Registrars
- SPAs and PAs
- Assistants and Senior Assistants
- Junior Assistants cum Semi-professional Assistants and
- Messengers/Attendants.

It took some time to implement the new policy on training for reasons other than academic. However, under a dynamic initiative of the management, a series of training programmes have been organised in 2005:

- Orientation-cum-workshop for Assistant Registrars
- Orientation-cum-workshop for Section Officers

- Orientation-cum-workshop for SPAs and PAs
- Orientation-cum-workshop for Senior Assistants and Assistants.

New programmes are planned in the coming year in collaboration with SOUs and CCIs. The themes to be covered in these programmes are:

- DE scenario at national and international levels.
- Brainstorming on existing practices of administration and search for new management techniques relevant to ODL systems.
- Expectations and problems of DE learners: sensitivity of institution and role of an employee.
- Coordination, supervision and monitoring.
- Student evaluation; issues at SCs, RCs and Headquarters.
- Financial reforms and Management of finances in ODL systems.
- EduSat, IMM, Online technologies enabled management: Needs and requirements of learners.
- Computer applications in workplace.
- Inter-personal relations in office management.

The above themes/topics indicate the efforts to meet the needs of various functional areas/ operations. The major thrust of these training programmes is to bring attitudinal change in the staff so that they can be more sensitive to the needs of distance learners and pay individual attention and nurture talent to take on new/additional responsibilities due to transfer and promotion, which make them move from one functional area/cadre to the other. This warrants that training programmes should have a few common themes/topics across categories of staff, to enable them to face the new situations and challenges, and to have comprehensive understanding on the system dynamics. It is worth mentioning in this context the comparative study of various training institutions including IGNOU by Panda and Prakash (1997). They have observed that: "in IGNOU programmes, it is believed that no knowledge and skill can become effective unless the trainees have a proper perception of or attitude towards work, people and environment."

Analysis of the feedback of the participants (about 100 in number) revealed the following issues:

- Majority of them expressed that themes/topics covered are very useful to their nature of work and this would help to improve their performance.
- Most of the participants mentioned that - first time they got an opportunity to attend the training of this kind; which is motivating and enabling them to be more sensitive towards distance learners.
- The participants felt the duration (3 days) of the programmes was too short, which did not allow enough time for discussion on all important issues. Almost all the participants suggested that the future programmes of this type should be at least of five days duration.
- Some participants were of the view that they should also be consulted in the design of the programme.

Professional Development and Future Scenario

The effectiveness and efficiency of ODL institutions is highly related to the efficiency and effectiveness of the personnel in the competitive global scene. Indian ODL institutions can ignore this fact at their own peril. The future of Indian ODL institutions is bound to be further challenged by the invasion of reputed institutions from abroad. On the other hand, declining government funding for Indian ODL institutions make them to think of various alternatives for their survival and existence. Various operations of ODL institutions are highly interrelated, and efficiency of these operations determine the success or otherwise of any academic programme. Prasad (1996) rightly pointed out "the grand designs may crash to ground if not properly implemented. The administrative efficiency of the institution is a critical variable in providing the services". If that is the case, the personnel involved in these operations and their professional and continuous development need to be addressed in a professional way. A few strategies/ approaches suggested for this purpose include the following:

- Smaller CCIs/DEIs can join in networks and offer short term training programmes to their non-teaching staff.
- SOUs can have its own training unit/centre and plan the activities for non-teaching staff training.
- IGNOU with established training unit i.e. STRIDE has to offer programmes not only to its staff but to other ODL institutions. STRIDE has to use both face-to-face and modern technology (EduSat and other) in providing training to their own widespread network of RCs and SCs and other ODL institutions;
- The collaborative programmes should be organised to share best practices which can be adopted by other.
- Training cannot be a one time affair, it has to be seen as continuous and life long process.
- Because of complex nature of operations and competitiveness, DE systems are thinking seriously about continuous and lifelong learning through staff development activity.

Staff training is an instrument to enhance the capabilities of the staff, and development is a process of advancement or progression in an organisation by acquiring necessary knowledge, skills and attitudes (Prasad, 1994). There is a need for networking of the training units/centres with incentives to the participants of the training programmes, while linking them to career development schemes.

References

IGNOU (1999). *Report of Administrative Reforms Committee (1999): Training of Non-Academic Staff.* New Delhi: IGNOU.

GoI (1986). *National Education Policy.* New Delhi: Ministry of HRD.

Panda, Santosh and Prakash, Shital (1997). Professional Development of University Administrative Staff. In Panda, Santosh (ed.), *Staff Development in Higher and Distance Education*. New Delhi: Aravali Books International.

Prasad, V.S. (1994). *Staff training and development in distance education: An interface*. Hyderabad: Dr. B.R. Ambedkar Open University.

Prasad, V.S. (1996). Developing improved strategies towards better student support services. *Kakatiya Journal of Open Learning,* 2(2), 1-18.

Sengupta, Souri (1997). Staff development for Non-Academics of Open Universities. In Panda, Santosh (ed.), *Staff Development in Higher and Distance Education*. New Delhi: Aravali Book International.

Singh, Bakshish (1993). Indira Gandhi National Open University (IGNOU) Research Project on-Correspondence/Distance Education in India: Some Findings and Recommendations. *Kakatiya Journal of Open Learning*, 2(2), 71-88.

Dr. C.R.K. Murthy is Reader, Staff Training and Research Institute of Distance Education, Indira Gandhi National Open University, New Delhi.
Email: murthycrk@hotmail.com

Dr. R. Satyanarayana is Reader, Staff Training and Research Institute of Distance Education, Indira Gandhi National Open University, New Delhi.
Email: Dr_RSN@hotmail.com

34

'Education for All' and Professional Development of Education Functionaries

Sohanvir S. Chaudhary, Kiran Mathur and Santosh Panda

Education for All: International Efforts

At the beginning of the new millennium, above 880 million adults in the world were illiterate; about 110 million children were attending school; discrimination against women and girls was common; and the quality of learning for millions of children and adults was not satisfactory. The existing data alarmed the international bodies and organizations to do something about basic education of out-of-school children, dropout children and illiterate adults. Delegates from 155 countries, as well as representatives from some 150 organizations, agreed in the world conference on 'Education for All' (EFA) in 1990 (March 5-9) at Jomtien, Thailand to universalize primary education and reduce illiteracy significantly before the end of the decade. The vision that all children, young people and adults have the fundamental right to a basic education for developing their talents, improving their lives and transforming their vision was adopted by the conference. The participating countries committed themselves to act cooperatively through their own spheres of responsibility, taking all necessary steps to achieve the goals of 'education for all'. They called on governments, concerned organizations and individuals to join hands in this urgent undertaking for achieving the goals of EFA.

In April, 2000 the World Education Forum adopted the *2000 World Dakar Framework for Education for All*. This *Framework* reaffirmed the goal of EFA laid out by the Jomtien World Conference on EFA. It committed governments to achieving quality basic education for all by 2015 or earlier, with particular emphasis on girls' education.

The third High Level Group (HLG) meeting held at New Delhi in November, 2003 focused on education of girls, and was "encouraged by the evident progress in gender parity particularly at primary level where the proportion of girls to boys enrolled rose from 88 per cent in 1990 to

94 per cent in 2000" (www.unesco.org). However, the HLG expressed concern that 57 per cent of the world's out-of-school children were girls and that almost two thirds of the 860 million non-literate people were women. The girls continue "to face sharp discrimination in access to education at all levels" (www.unesco.org). Participants proposed a series of immediate measures to be taken by governments, agencies, NGOs and civil society to boost efforts to achieve gender parity in education by 2005 and gender equality to 2015, the deadlines set by 164 countries at the World Education Forum held in Dakar, Senegal.

Education for All: National Efforts

Since independence in 1947, the central and state governments in India have been expanding the provision of primary formal and non-formal education to realize the goal of Universalisation of Elementary Education (UEE). The challenge now is to sustain and deepen the current reforms in education and encourage the system of local planning and management for expanding and improving primary education. Many initiatives by central and state governments including operation blackboard, decentralized planning and management of elementary education (with the involvement of *Panchayati Raj* institutions), National Programme of Nutritional Support to Primary Education (Mid-day Meal Programme), District Primary Education Programme (DPEP), Bihar Education Programme, Uttar Pradesh Basic Education Programme, Andhra Pradesh Primary Education Programme, Lok Jumbish Project, Shiksha Karmi Project in Rajasthan, and others had been undertaken to improve access to quality primary education.

Sarva Shiksha Abhiyan (SSA, i.e. EFA)—a mission started in 2002 as an extension of District Primary Education Programme (DPEP), intended to universalize elementary education by community-ownership of the school system. It was a response to the demand for quality basic education all over the country. SSA is also an attempt to provide an opportunity for improving capabilities of all children in the age group of 6-14 years by 2010. The other objective included bridging the social, regional and gender gaps, with the active participation of the community in the management of schools. The basic features of SSA are as follows:

- Clear time frame for universal elementary education.
- Demand for quality basic education all over the country.
- Opportunity for promoting social justice through basic education.
- Effective involvement of and partnership with *Panchayati Raj* institutions, school management committees, village and urban slum level education committees, parents/mother-teacher associations, tribal autonomous councils and other grassroots level structures in the management of elementary school education.
- Political will for universal elementary education across the country.
- Opportunity for states to develop their own vision of elementary education.

With the above features, the SSA is geared to achieve the following objectives:

- All children to be in schools, education guarantee centres, alternate schools, 'back-to-school' camp by 2003 (now revised to December 2005).

- All children to complete five years of primary schooling by 2007.
- All children to complete eight years of elementary schooling by 2010.
- Focus on elementary education of satisfactory quality with emphasis on education for life.
- Bridge all gender and social category gaps at the primary stage by 2007 and at elementary education level by 2010.
- Universal retention by 2010.

Education for All and Parameters of Quality

Quality education stands at the heart of EFA, although focus on access in EFA has overshadowed the issues of quality. The six goals adopted at the World Education Forum in Dakar, implicitly or explicitly integrated a quality dimension. The EFA Global Monitoring Report (UNESCO, 2005) clearly states that quality must be seen in the light of how the purpose of education is defined. Two principal objectives are emphasized: i) to ensure the cognitive development of learners; and ii) to emphasize the role of education in nurturing the creative and emotional growth of learners and in helping them to acquire values and attitudes of responsible citizenship.

The Report highlights the needs for more and better trained teachers, improved textbooks available to all learners, pedagogical renewal and conducive learning environments. The Report adopts a framework that takes into account the following five major factors affecting quality:

- Learners, whose diversity must be recognized
- National economic and social context
- Material and human resources
- Teaching and learning process and the outcomes
- Benefits of education

By focusing on these factors and the way they interact, it could be possible to draw up a comprehensive map for understanding, monitoring and improving quality. Evidence from data on national and international assessments suggests that in many countries, children are not mastering basic skills. Low achievement is widespread and most seriously affects countries where a school system is weak in terms of enrollment and school resources.

Quality issues in elementary education revolve around the quality of infrastructure and support services, quality time, teacher characteristics and teacher motivation, pre-service and in-service education of teachers, curriculum and teaching-learning materials, classroom processes, evaluation, monitoring and supervision.

The following are the parameters against which quality education is judged:

Access and equity

The goal of achieving universal primary education (UPE) has been on the international agenda since the Universal Declaration of Human Rights affirmed, in 1948, that elementary education was to be made free and compulsory for all children. It is the basic concern of all United Nations conferences/declarations that irrespective of caste, creed, location or sex, all children must be given access to education of comparable standards. As per the SSA norms a school or alternative schooling facility must be available within 1 km of every habitation and unserved habitations have provision for opening a new school/setting up of EGS as per state norms.

Teaching learning process/material

Effective teaching-learning process is imperative to improve the quality of education. How well children are taught and how much they learn is likely to have a crucial impact upon the length and value of their schooling experience. SSA advocates structured teaching—a combination of direct instruction, guided practice and independent learning. Pedagogically sound language policy, allowing children to learn in their mother tongue for at least their first few school years, has a positive impact on learning. Learning materials strongly affect what teachers can do. SSA has made provision for teacher grant of Rs. 500 per year to be used for developing teaching learning material to make effective transaction of curriculum.

Minimum levels of learning (MLLs)

SSA has emphasized the MLLs, laid down by National Policy on Education (NPE), 1986 (revised in 1992) across the elementary schools in the country. The strategy of MLLs for improving the quality of elementary education has been seen as an attempt to combine quality with equity. The main indicator of the quality of elementary education can be visualized in terms of its product – the learners' achievement both in scholastic and co-scholastic areas i.e. the performance in various subjects of study and habits, attitudes, values and life skills necessary for becoming a good citizen.

To achieve MLLs the teacher has to re-organize curriculum to imbibe local needs; develop competency-based and contextual teaching-learning material; improve teaching-learning processes to make them child-centered; activity-based and mastery learning oriented and provide remedial teaching and enrichment programmes at due occasions in all classrooms; introduce formative evaluation and grading system to make it stress free for children and reduce curriculum load.

Evaluation techniques

Comprehensive and continuous assessment, advocated under SSA, is a tool to improve both teaching and learning. Performance of children has to be constantly monitored in consultation with parents but shall not be restricted only to cognitive areas. SSA advocates for innovative assessment techniques that take child's performance in a holistic way, i.e. cognitive, psychomotor/ skills and affective (values, creativity, emotion, etc.) development. All these domains are given due weightage in SSA.

Professional Development of Education Functionaries

Functionaries associated with SSA include teachers, teacher educators and educational administrators at the state level (i.e. SCERT faculty), district level (i.e. faculty of DIETs, CTE, IASE and DRGs/DEOs), block level (i.e. Block/Cluster Resource Centre Coordinators), village level (i.e. community leaders and VEC, MTA and PTA members), and the school level (i.e. headmasters).

Professional development of headmasters/administrators

Schools need help to find their own solutions to improving quality, within well-defined accountability frameworks. The head teachers are critically important to this endeavour. Greater autonomy can make a difference provided that schools are well supported and have established capacity and strong leadership. Investment in services, networks and structures to develop and share educational knowledge can enable schools to make much better use of their resources, to learn from each other and to better inform policy. To ensure quality in the inputs and processes necessary of quality achievement on the part of administration/management is aimed at the following:

- Primary assessment of the existing levels of learning achievement.
- Modification of the minimum levels of learning (MLLs) to suit local situation if needed.
- Initial and recurrent orientation of teachers to competency-based teaching.
- Preparation of teacher training handbooks for MLLs-based teaching.
- Introduction of continuous and comprehensive evaluation of students and using evaluation results for remedial action.
- Preparation of unit test and other evaluation materials and putting them in an item pool for using as and when required.
- Using MLLs norms as and when textbooks are revised.
- Provision of competency-based teaching learning materials to make the educational process activity-based and joyful.

Professional development of teachers

There is a need to strengthen recurrent training of teachers. Therefore, time and money invested on initial training and ongoing professional development of elementary teachers need to be balanced. Their mastery over curriculum, their competencies/skills and their expectations of students all contribute to quality education. The quality of teaching-learning process depends upon the professional knowledge and skills of the teacher who should be well qualified, committed, motivated and responsible for bringing desired changes in the society. This needs to be reflected through his/her behaviour and action in and out of school. If she/he wants that children should come to school regularly and learn, she/he has to evolve effective strategies to bring qualitative changes in their behaviour.

The teacher has to facilitate child-centred and activity-based learning. S/he has to integrate learning process with learning by doing, learning by observation, work experience, art, music, sports and value education. Teachers' role in preparation of textbooks and secondary learning materials need to be enhanced. Thus, teachers play a crucial role in achieving SSA goals of quality education including 100 per cent enrolment in age group 6-14 years. Their capacity building is a big challenge in front of state governments.

Types/categories of teachers

There are two major types of teachers working in the elementary schools.

i) Regular teachers: There are again two types of regular teachers:
   a) First, the fully qualified primary teachers as per the norms laid down by National Council for Teacher Education (NCTE) are expected to have twelve years of school education followed by two years of primary teacher training. However, the practice differs from state to state. There are teachers with ten years of general education and one year of primary teacher training. A large number of teachers recruited before 1986 had ten years of general education. There are teachers who have eight years or less of general education. It is estimated that there are about 0.24 million under-qualified teachers in the country (GoI, 2004).
   b) Second, there are a large number of untrained teachers working in primary schools. As per the latest data available about 14 per cent teachers at the lower primary level and 13 per cent at the upper primary level are untrained (DEP-DPEP, 2003).The fast changing knowledge in all spheres of life requires continuous updating of knowledge among teachers. Therefore, the primary/elementary teachers have to enrich their knowledge and skills continuously so that they can use innovative teaching learningmethods and media. Thus, SSA has made provision for 20 days in-service training of all elementary teachers every year by each state.

ii) Para teachers: Engagement of para teachers or volunteers was started to appoint educated unemployed youth living within a radius of 5 km of the single teacher primary schools having educational qualifications ranging from primary to graduation. They are known by various names such as Shiksha Karmi, Shiksha Mitra, EGS volunteers, etc. They have been engaged to maintain national teacher-pupil ratio and provide access of primary education to every child as per the norms of SSA. Usually these teachers are posted in the schools located in remote and difficult terrains. Under the EGS and AIE schemes, the state governments have employed 0.177 million para teachers. The academic and professional qualifications of these para teachers are considerably lower than those required for regular appointment. These para teachers also need continuous updating of their knowledge (GoI, 2004).

Teacher training institutions

As envisaged in the NPE (1986, 1992) the state, district and sub-district level teacher education institutions have to take active part in training of elementary teachers. Therefore, the following infrastructure has been provided.

i) Strengthening of State Councils of Educational Research and Training (SCERTs) is an important initiative under SSA to perform multifarious roles and responsibilities relating to research, development, training, extension, documentation and consultancy. Though majority of the states have established SCERTs, most of them require upgrading in terms of better infrastructure and faculty to enable them to come up to the level of vibrant state level organizations, capable of playing an effective role as lead institutions. Efforts are on to make the state level institutions autonomous and independent with overall responsibilities to supervise and guide functioning of DIETs, CTEs and other teacher education institutions in the state.
ii) Establishment and strengthening of DIETs is a major intervention under SSA for organizing pre-service and in-service teacher education at the district level. It has been envisaged that DIETs would provide training and resource support, extension/guidance, training materials, teaching aids, evaluation tools and others to elementary school teachers in the district. It is also expected that DIETs would undertake action research to make education more conceptualized and solve problems faced by the teachers.
iii) The State Project Office (SPO) in each state organises training programmes at block/cluster resource centres. SSA has made provision for training of each teacher.

Training areas

The elementary school teachers need training in three main areas:

i) Curricular areas: These include hard spots (difficult concepts) in teaching of content in Mathematics, Science, Languages, and Social Sciences. Hard spots are concepts, which teachers find difficult to teach and the learners find difficult to understand.
ii) Pedagogical areas: Besides teaching the content, the teachers also require capacity building in issues related to the teaching-learning process, which include minimum levels of learning (MLLs), child-centred approach, classroom transaction, evaluation techniques, development of teaching-learning materials (TLMs), innovative teaching learning methods, and others.
iii) Contextual areas: There are certain issues that require special attention of the teachers to improve educational status of all groups of children. These relate to girls' education, gender sensitisation, special education bridge courses for out of school children, quality management, education of disadvantaged groups of society, and community mobilisation, among others.

Modes of Training

Broadly there are two modes used for training of teachers under SSA: face-to-face cascade mode and open distance learning mode.

Face-to-face cascade mode

The cascade mode is used in the conventional face-to-face in-service training of teachers. This mode requires training of teacher educators at various levels, starting from 'master trainers' to grassroots level teachers. In-service training of teachers and other functionaries through the face-to-face mode requires more efforts, time and money. There is a transmission loss in the training programmes being organised at the various levels. Besides, the teachers have to be withdrawn from the school during the training programmes which hamper the teaching work in the schools. As a result, many states are not able to conduct 20 days in-service training of all elementary teachers regularly. Conducting such programmes every year for each teacher through face-to-face mode with available infrastructure is a big challenge for the states.

Open distance learning (ODL) mode

The open distance learning mode is also being used in education and training of in-service teachers. Distance education technologies such as teleconferencing, video conferencing, innovative self-learning modules, phone-in facility, audio-video broadcast/cassettes have made it possible for teachers and other functionaries to upgrade their knowledge and competencies without leaving their work place. Thus, the open and distance learning mode is effective to supplement the face-to-face mode due to the following merits:

- Providing training to a large number of teachers within stipulated time period.
- Imparting training without dislocating teachers from their work place.
- Providing hands-on practice during classroom transaction.
- Providing standardized training to all teachers throughout the state in curricular, contextual and pedagogical issues.
- Imparting training using multimedia packages.

Intervention of Distance Education Programme (DEP) in Professional Development of Teachers and Other Functionaries

The Distance Education Programme (DEP) is a national project initiated by the Ministry of Human Resource Development (MHRD), Government of India on July 1, 2003 for distance education activities under SSA. IGNOU was entrusted the responsibility to implement distance education activities of the project all over the country. Before DEP-SSA, DEP-DPEP (1996-June 2003) was functional in 18 DPEP states namely, Assam, Andhra Pradesh, Bihar, Chhattisgarh, Gujarat, Haryana, Himachal Pradesh, Jharkhand, Kerala, Karnataka, Maharasthra, Madhya Pradesh, Orissa, Rajasthan, Tamil Nadu, Uttar Pradesh, Uttaranchal and West Bengal. The target group was primary education (classes I to V). As SSA was launched in all the 28 states and 7 UTs, the project was extended up to upper primary stage (classes VI to VIII). DEP-SSA is one of the major interventions in SSA focusing on strengthening training through the open distance learning system. SSA involves training of a large number of teachers and other functionaries to improve quality of elementary education and hence help the states achieve the objectives of SSA. To professionally carry out this enormous task of training using only face-to-face model would not be possible. Hence, DEP-SSA was created as a national centre by MHRD, GOI to provide distance education inputs and materials for professional development of teachers and other functionaries associated with SSA.

Objectives of DEP-SSA

The main objectives of DEP-SSA include:

- Providing technical support in designing, developing, producing and delivering distance learning (DL) inputs and materials for training the elementary education personnel.
- Building capacity among institutions and people at national, state, district and sub-district levels in designing, developing, producing and delivering DL inputs and materials.
- Reducing transmission loss by suitable DL interventions, thereby increasing consistency and quality of training effort.
- Developing materials as well as organizing inputs for district level personnel.

Main focus

The main focus of DEP is to strengthen institutions at the state (SCERTs), district (DIETs), and sub-district levels (BRCs and CRCs), by building capacity of personnel associated with SSA, such as teachers, teacher educators and other functionaries including VEC members in content, pedagogy and contextual issues. The process of capacity building in development of materials and inputs involves need assessment, training inputs, content briefs, script writing, production, duplication of learning/training materials, and implementation of training inputs in the field.

Major contributions of DEP-SSA

The learning-training materials for in-service training of elementary teachers are being developed using three media viz. print, audio and video. DEP has assisted many states in planning and developing following DL materials for professional development of teachers and other functionaries through organizing capacity building workshops.

Print medium

Print material is developed in the form of self-learning materials, posters, brochures, leaflets, manuals, workbooks, etc.

i) Self-learning material: Self-learning materials (SLMs) have been developed on hard spots identified by the teachers in curricular and pedagogical issues. These SLMs have been used during training of teachers as well as during classroom transaction as these facilitate teachers to teach in a more effective manner. Besides, training/practical manuals, workbooks and guidebooks have been developed in self learning mode to use other electronic media. These SLMs have been developed through a number of training-cum-development workshops organized by DEP in collaboration with respective states. During these workshops subject experts and teacher educators have been given training to develop SLMs on identified areas. Sometimes competent teachers were also engaged as they know how to teach a concept effectively. During DEP-DPEP (1996-2003) 11 out of the 18 DPEP states had organised preparatory workshops for development of DL materials. In all, 314 participants identified and developed 350 content briefs on Mathematics, EVS, languages and other general topics. These content briefs dealt with hard spots and other pedagogical issues e.g. school readiness programme, teacher motivation, multi-grade teaching, activity-based teaching, education of children with special needs, girls' education, issues in primary education, school management, teaching learning process, etc. Table 1 summarizes major tasks completed during 1996-2005 in respect of development of self learning material.

Table 1: Capacity building of teachers and teacher educators in developing self-learning materials

States	Areas of Modules	No. of beneficiaries trained
Andhra Pradesh	Subject areas and pedagogy	85
Assam	Multigrade, activity-based teaching, awareness package for education personnel and IED	68
Bihar	Multigrade teaching, language, maths, EVS, teaching and evaluation of non-cognitive areas in multigrade teaching	112
Chhattisgarh	Languages, maths, science and social sciences	32
Chandigarh	AS volunteers	26
Gujarat	Activity based teaching-learning, classroom management; role of teacher in community mobilization	06
Haryana	Subject areas, pedagogy and multigrade teaching	27
Jharkhand	IED on various disabilities, languages, maths, science, social studies	60
Karnataka	English, maths and science, IED, girls education	104

Kerala	English, maths and science	53
Maharashtra	Mathematics, marathi and EVS	66
Madhya Pradesh	Hindi, mathematics, EVS, English and instructional methodology	52
Nagaland	Content areas	25
Orissa	Language, maths, & EVS, MTA, girls education	101
Punjab	Language and girls education, bridge course for out-of-school children	50
Rajasthan	Maths, language, science and EVS	40
Tamil Nadu	Language, maths, and EVS	46
Tripura	Content areas	39
Uttar Pradesh	Vision of an ideal school; child psychology; learning process; communication; school resources and their use, use of TLM, continuous and comprehensive evaluation	40
Uttaranchal	Teaching aids, IED, DEP	53
West Bengal	Pedagogy, IED, girls education, community mobilization	49
	Total	1119

Different states developed material based on: content (Andhra Pradesh and Assam - Abhigyan, Himachal Pradesh - Samridhi, Madhya Pradesh, Maharashtra and Orissa – Eklavya); pedagogy (Uttar Pradesh - SOPAN and Tamil Nadu for AS Instructors); support material (West Bengal - handbook, workbook and activity books for teachers); IED (West Bengal, Gujarat, Orissa, and Assam); multi-grade teaching (Bihar and Assam); girls education (Haryana, Himachal Pradesh – Maa Beti Mela); action research (Karnataka, Haryana – capacity building); EGS (Madhya Pradesh and Orissa); alternative schooling (Assam and Tamil Nadu); newsletter (Uttar Pradesh - Shikshak Preshak, West Bengal – Yogsutra, Bihar – Pahel, Gujarat – Prathmik Shiksha Sarwani and Andhra Pradesh – Velugu); posters (Gujarat – 74), brochure (Karnataka and Rajasthan).

Capacity building workshops on development of SLMs were conducted in Bihar, Tripura, Himachal Pradesh, West Bengal, Punjab, Tripura and Madhya Pradesh during 2003-04. About 150 teachers, teacher educators and subject experts were oriented in developing SLMs on hard spots.

Similarly, in 2004-05, 18 states (Andhra Pradesh, Assam, Chhattisgarh, Gujarat, Jharkhand, Karnataka, Kerala, Maharashtra, Meghalaya, Mizoram, Nagaland, Orissa, Punjab, Rajasthan, Tamil Nadu, Tripura, Uttaranchal and NE region) organized planning workshops in which about 400 SSA functionaries suggested DL activities. Training-cum-development workshops for print material were organized for capacity building of educational functionaries in 18 states (Andhra Pradesh, Assam, Bihar, Chandigarh, Chhattisgarh, Haryana, Himachal Pradesh, Jharkhand, Karnataka, Kerala, Maharashtra, Nagaland, Orissa, Punjab, Rajasthan, Tripura, Uttaranachal and West Bengal).

ii) Other print material: Besides SLMs on content and pedagogy issues, capacity building workshops were also conducted to develop newsletters, brochures, posters and calendars for community mobilization purposes. These materials included: newsletters (Andhra Pradesh, Bihar, Gujarat, Uttar Pradesh and West Bengal); guidelines to use media (Chhattisgarh, Gujarat, Kerala, Karnataka, Maharashtra and Orissa); telematerial (Andhra Pradesh, Gujarat, Haryana, Himachal Pradesh, Maharashtra, Madhya Pradesh, Orissa; Tamil Nadu and Chhatisgarh); supplementary reading material (Haryana, Orissa, Rajasthan and West Bengal); folders and brochures (Gujarat, Haryana, West Bengal and Rajasthan).

Non-print media

Considering the potential of non-print media a number of audio and video programmes were developed through capacity building workshops by DEP-DPEP-SSA in collaboration with states. Audio-video programmes were developed on hard spots, effective classroom processes, community mobilization, IED, girls education, among others.

i) Audio programmes: Audio programmes include broadcast as well as non-broadcast modes.
   a) Radio broadcast: Radio as a medium of mass communication has extensive reach all over the country. Majority of teachers, parents and children have easy and affordable access to radio. In India many educational institutions and organisations, both at the central and state levels, use radio for information, motivation and teaching purposes. Radio programmes are very useful for teaching of languages, e.g. story telling, poem recitation, pronunciation, and grammar.

      Radio programmes are developed in the form of live and recorded. Live radio programmes include radio conferencing/phone-in-programmes, interactive radio counselling. Content-based interactive radio programmes facilitate interaction between the teachers and children/listeners and therefore, are effective in dealing with curricular as well as contextual issues.

      DEP-DPEP promoted radio programmes in different states during the project period. The states of Andhra Pradesh, Himachal Pradesh, Karnataka, Maharashtra were the lead states under radio broadcast and phone-in-programme. Other states viz. Assam, Kerala, Orissa and Uttar Pradesh also used it on moderate scale. Some states used radio broadcast mainly for curricular areas related to primary school curricular viz. language, Mathematics and Environmental Studies (part I and II) and other for contextual issues. Andhra Pradesh named these radio broadcasts as *Vindam Nerchukundam* (Listen and Learn); Himachal Pradesh *Gyankalash*, and *Hello Ankur,* Jharkhand *Nava Vihan* and Karnataka *Keli-Kali* (Listen and Learn). All these states prepared audio scripts and produced these for radio broadcast. A large number of teachers and children have got the benefits of these educational radio broadcast. A summary of such radio programmes is mentioned in Table 2. Besides radio programmes, interactive phone-in programmes were also conducted by Himachal Pradesh (*Hello Ankur*), Andhra Pradesh, Orissa, Jharkhand, Maharashtra and Madhya Pradesh

Table 2: Capacity building in radio broadcast

States	Title of the programme	No. of radio programmes	Area	Beneficiaries
Andhra Pradesh	Vindam Nerchukundam	190	Content	Students, teachers
Assam	Prathimik Starart Chatra – Chatrik	25	Content, pedagogy, context	Students, teachers, BRCCs, VECs
Chhattisgarh	Gyandeep	24	Content, context pedagogy	Students, parents, teacher and community
Gujarat	Radio campaign	Need based	context	Students, parents, community
Himachal Pradesh	Gyan kalash	120(70)	Content, pedagogy, context	Teachers, parents ICDS members, community, BRCCs, CRCCs, teacher educators
Jammu & Kashmir	Jingles	Need based	Context	Parents and community
Jharkhand	Nava Vihan	5	Context	community
Karnataka	Keli-kali	60	Content, and pedagogy,	Students and teachers
Kerala	NA	15	Content	Students and teachers
Maharashtra	NA	18	Content	Students and teachers
Orissa	Ankur I & II	29	Pedagogy and context	Teachers and community
Rajasthan	Radio campaign	Need based	Context	Parents and community
Tripura	NA	26	Content, pedagogy	Students, teachers
Uttar Pradesh	Sadhan	45	Content, pedagogy, context	Students and teachers

The states of Orissa, Kerala and Tripura developed audio scripts during 2003-04. The state of Andhra Pradesh had broadcast 85 radio programmes on Telugu, English, Mathematics and EVS for the students of classes III and V. More than 17000 teachers and about 7,00,000 students were benefited by these programmes. In the year 2004-05 states like Assam, Chhattisgarh (24 programmes in Gyandeep), Gujarat (jingles and radio spots for enrollment drive), Jammu and Kashmir (jingles in local languages), Orissa (Ankur I and Ankur II),

Rajasthan (Sab padhen sab badhen) and Tripura had organized radio broadcast through AIR. Three phone-in programmes by Andhra Pradesh (2) and Orissa (1) had also been organized.

b) Audio cassettes/CDs: Audio cassettes /CDs provide considerable freedom to learners to choose to listen at a time and place convenient to them. Audio cassettes/CDs are very useful for teaching languages and children with special needs (visually disabled).

The audio programmes were used in two ways: i) for training through audio-cassettes as in the case of Haryana (Prerna Geet, Hanste Gaate, Tarang, etc.); and ii) for radio broadcast as in case of Himachal Pradesh, Maharashtra, Karnataka, Andhra Pradesh, and Orissa. In all, 317 audio programmes were produced (1996- 2003) in different states for radio broadcast; of these 208 audio programmes were used in Karnataka, 91 in Andhra Pradesh and 18 in Maharashtra mainly in content areas of Mathematics, EVS and languages.

Similarly in 2003-04, 6 capacity building workshops were held to develop audio / radio scripts in the states of Assam, Tripura, Haryana, Andhra Pradesh and Jharkhand. More than 120 teachers developed about 50 audio scripts on need-based curricular, contextual and pedagogical issues.

Table 3: Capacity building in audio script writing

States	No. of beneficiaries	No. of draft scripts developed
Andhra Pradesh	86	70
Assam	20	26
Bihar	24	12
Chhattisgarh	34	32
Gujarat	52	25
Haryana	15	4
Himachal Pradesh	32	6
Jammu & Kashmir	20	30
Jharkhand	34	26
Karnataka	121	92
Kerala	36	24
Maharashtra	27	18
Madhya Pradesh	63	57
Orissa	95	58
Tamil Nadu	59	27
Tripura	24	13
Uttaranchal	18	15
West Bengal	55	20
Total	878	555

In the year 2004-05, 14 states (Andhra Pradesh, Bihar, Chhattisgarh, Gujarat, Haryana, Jammu & Kashmir, Jharkhand, Karnataka, Kerala, Meghalaya, Orissa, Punjab, Tamil Nadu and West Bengal, organized workshops to develop audio/radio scripts. About 375 teachers and experts developed more than 150 draft scripts. As depicted in Table 3 a total of 878 participants developed 555 draft scripts of audio programmes.

ii) Video programmes: Like audio programmes the video programmes can be classified into three categories a) television programmes (broadcast), b) cable television, and c) video cassettes/CDs. Television has greater appeal than the audio and print-media. The video cassettes/CDs being more flexible and convenient to use are more suitable to individualized learning as compared to television broadcast.

Table 4: Capacity building in video script writing

States	No. of video scripts	Participants
Andhra Pradesh	21	63
Assam	05	43
Bihar	23	67
Chhattisgarh	20	24
Himachal Pradesh	13	55
Jharkhand	—	20
Kerala	27	50
Maharashtra	10	26
Mizoram	—	24
Orissa	16	23
Rajasthan	13	50
Tamil Nadu	13	35
Tripura	—	40
Uttaranchal	17	17
	178	537

As video programmes are expensive programmes, it is necessary to identify relevant content/ context for it. DEP organized workshops to help states/UTs to identify contents for video production and to develop user guide covering objectives, content briefs and pre-and post viewing activities. Training programmes are also organized to help teacher educators to use video programmes during teacher training programmes. Such training programmes were organized by the states of Andhra Pradesh, Bihar, Gujarat, Madhya Pradesh, Maharashtra, Orissa and Rajasthan to facilitate educational functionaries for using video programmes during teacher training.

Kerala and Orissa have developed video scripts on scholastic and contextual issues for teachers. Chhattisgarh, Gujarat, Orissa, Tripura and Maharashtra have initiated video production on teaching of different subject areas and contextual issues (Table 4).

Also, a training-cum-development workshop was organized by Kerala for IMM-CDs in content area.

Teleconferencing

Teleconferencing is an effective medium to provide learning experiences to a large number of participants positioned at different locations without withdrawing them from the workplaces/ schools. High quality and consistency in training can be possible in teleconferencing as exposure to multiple perspectives from the primary sources is provided, and therefore, there is a little loss of quality in transaction. Teleconferencing makes possible uniform, interactive training and it also reduces the sense of isolation, encourages sharing of comments and ideas, and helps to solve the problems of the field functionaries in remote rural areas.

In DEP teleconferencing as an effective tool has been used by many states. Capacity building programmes for the education functionaries and teacher educators from state project offices, SCERTs, DIETs, BRCs/CRCs as facilitators, panelists and anchor persons have been conducted to facilitate them in conducting successful teleconferences. During capacity building programmes hands-on experiences were also organized by utilising satellite communication facilities available at Delhi (EMPC), Gujarat (BISAG), Madhya Pradesh (SATCOM), Karnataka (ANSSIRD), Orissa (BPFTI), and Hyderabad (APNET).

Teleconferences relating to curriculum issues were activity-based teaching in sciences and basic concepts in mathematics at the primary and upper primary stages, teacher training in languages, development and use of teaching learning materials; project work, developing writing skills in children and pedagogical improvement in the classroom.

Contextual issues covered under teleconferencing were related to integrated education for the disabled, education of the girl child, action research, roles of DIETs, BRCs, CRCs, and VECs in facilitating training programmes for various target groups, roles of parents in helping the child in academic activities of the scheme, micro planning, tribal education, community mobilization, universalisation of elementary education and alternative schooling.

During the period of DEP-DPEP, 115 teleconferences were organized mainly by 16 states namely Andhra Pradesh, Assam, Chhattisgarh, Gujarat, Haryana, Himachal Pradesh, Jharkhand, Karnataka, Kerala, Madhya Pradesh, Maharashtra, Orissa, Rajasthan, Tamil Nadu, Uttaranchal and Uttarpradesh. A very large number of beneficiaries (about 150,000) participated in these teleconferences (Table 5).

More than 56,000 participants participated in 27 teleconferences organized during 2003-04 by the states of Chhattishgarh, Gujarat, Maharashtra, Madhya Pradesh and Orissa on curricular issues, civil works, orientation of BRC/CRC coordinators, teaching of various subjects, NPEGEL, girls education, financial norms, etc. in the state itself. The states of Madhya Pradesh, Gujarat, Orissa, Karnataka and Andhra Pradesh regularly organize teleconferences due to availability of satellite communication.

In all 30 teleconferences were organized during 2004-05 by Andhra Pradesh, Assam, Chhattisgarh, Gujarat, Himachal Pradesh, Maharashtra, Madhya Pradesh, Orissa and Rajasthan. In total 250 RPs/ panelists and 42,000 participants at various centers participated in the teleconferences.

Table 5: Teleconferences organized by states

States	No. of teleconferences	Beneficiaries
Andhra Pradesh	8	Teacher educators, MRPs, DRPs, Faculty of DIETs
Assam	4	BRC/ CRC coordinators and teachers
Chhattisgarh	4	CACs and teachers
Gujarat	24	Teachers, BRC/CRC coordinators, DIET faculty
Haryana	11	Teacher educators, BRC/CRC coordinators and DIET faculty
Himachal Pradesh	6	BRC/CRC coordinators and DIET faculty, teachers, MTA members
Jharkhand	2	VEC members, teachers and EGS instructors
Karnataka	17	BRC/CRC coordinators and DIET faculty, DRPs, teachers
Kerala	5	BRPs, DIET faculty, parents of children with disability DPEP officials,
Madhya Pradesh	19	EGS instructors and primary teachers
Maharashtra	11	Teacher, DIET faculty, CRCCs, VEC members,
Orissa	30	BRCCs, DIET faculty, Tribal/ gender coordinators, MTA/ PTA members, teachers
Rajasthan	5	Teachers, BRC/CRC coordinators and DIET faculty, VEC members
Tamil Nadu	5	Teachers, VEC members, BRPs, and CRCs
Tripura		
Uttaranchal	1	DIET faculty, BRCCs and NPRCs, DIET faculty
Uttar Pradesh	5	Teacher educators, teachers, VEC members and DPEP officials
Total	157	

Conclusion

As noted earlier, the DEP-SSA project was launched on July 1, 2003 as an upgraded version of the erstwhile DEP-DPEP which was operational only in 18 states. The present project is an integral component of SSA and aims at providing need-based, local specific in-service training for teachers and other functionaries directly involved in elementary education programme. The Ministry of HRD, Department of Elementary Education and Literacy has sponsored the DEP-SSA project which is located at IGNOU, New Delhi. The project has been extended to all the 28 states and 7 union territories of the country to achieve universalisation of elementary education.

While designing and developing the framework for implementation of SSA, the MHRD considered the significant role of the role of the open and distance learning and envisaged the distance education mode as an important input for the in-service education of teachers and other personnel in the area of elementary education.

The implementation of SSA necessitates training of large number of teachers, para-teachers and other functionaries to bring out qualitative improvement in elementary education. In view of the enormous task of training teachers and other functionaries, face-to-face approach has to be supplemented or complemented by distance mode. Therefore, the Distance Education Programme (DEP) has become a relevant and practical alternative to facilitate the training of teachers and other functionaries involved in the implementation of SSA in the country by providing distance learning inputs and materials to them.

One of the major activities of the distance education project was that in order to sustain the system of in-service education of elementary teachers as capacity building of institutions and people at State, District and Sub-districts levels in terms of designing, developing, producing and delivering distance learning materials.

For development of self learning materials, or a number of training-cum-development workshops had been organized for teacher educators in curricular, contextual and pedagogical issues. The main issues dealt during these workshops include hardspots in languages, mathematics, sciences and social sciences at elementary stage. These SLMs were then edited and finalized with the help of national level subject experts. Other pedagogical and contextual issues on which SLMs were developed included activity based teaching-learning process and materials, continuous and comprehensive evaluation, multigrade teaching girls' education, education of children with special needs, etc. Besides SLMs other forms of print material such as newsletter, brochures, folders, calendars, posters, manuals for audio/video materials, telematerial and guidelines were developed by many states mainly for community mobilization.

References

DEP-DPEP (2003). *Distance Education Initiatives in DPEP*. IGNOU-NCERT Collaborative Project sponsored by MHRD, New Delhi: IGNOU.

UNESCO (2005). *Global Monitoring Report Education for All: The Quality Imperative*. Available from *http://portal.unesco.org/education*.

GOI (2004). *Manual for Planning and Appraisal*, New Delhi: Department of Elementary Education & Literacy.

Professor Sohanvir Chaudhary is Director, DEP-SSA, Indira Gandhi National Open University, New Delhi.
Email: chaudhary38@hotmail.com

Dr. Kiran Mathur is Programme Officer, DEP-SSA, Indira Gandhi National Open University, New Delhi.
Email: kirandepssa2004@yahoo.com

Professor Santosh Panda is Director, Staff Training & Research Institute of Distance Education; and Head, Inter-University Consortium, Indira Gandhi National Open University, New Delhi.
Email: spanda@ignou.ac.in

35

Research on Indian Distance Education

Lokesh Koul

Introduction

Distance education refers to that mode of education where the interacting learner and teacher are separated by space or space and time. It occurs in different contexts and countries with different meanings such as 'open education', 'correspondence education', 'external study', 'off-campus study', 'distance education and open learning'. These terms have been applied and used interchangeably by different researchers to a great variety of programmes, providers, audiences and media. The hallmarks of these terms are the separation of teacher and learner in space and/or time (Perraton, 1988), the volitional control of learning by the student rather than the distant instructor (Jonassen, 1992), and non-contiguous communication between student and teacher, mediated by print or some form of technology (Keegan, 1986; Garrison and Shale, 1987). The separation of teacher and learner, found in many definitions, is central to the whole concept of distance education (Rumble, 1989). Separation of teacher and student and absence of classroom instruction have led to the conclusion that distance education is "time free" and "space free". The use of various technologies like print based media and postal communications, electronic networking, teleconferencing, Internet, E-mail etc. has reduced the degree of physical separation of a teacher and the distance learner. It has ensured a high degree of interactivity between teacher and distance learner living in far flung and isolated areas thousands of kilometers away.

Initially, a number of researches on distance education in the advanced and developing countries were undertaken for developing concepts, theories and planning need based programmes for various types of groups in different countries (Holmberg, 1967; Wedemeyer, 1971; Garrison, and Shale, 1987; Shale, 1988; Rumble, 1989; Moore, 1989; Garrison and Baynton, 1989; and Saba, 1989).

In his article on the contributions to the theory of distance education, Moore, (1989) points out that two articles published in 1972 were among the first attempts to define 'distance education' and its constituent elements. These were said to be learner independence, which Moore called 'learner autonomy', interaction between learner and instructor which he called 'dialogue', and certain characteristics of course design named as 'structure'. 'Distance' was defined as a function of two variables called 'dialogue' and 'structure' (Wedemeyer, 1971).

A common concern of thinkers about the theory of distance education has been the interrelationship of dialogue, structure and autonomy. Apart from early contributions made by other early researchers, including Wedemeyer (1971), Holmberg (1967, 1983) and Keegan (1986), there have been hundreds of references to and uses of theory in recent years in many countries with special emphasis on the interrelationships of the instructional possibilities opened up by the new interactive telecommunications. The work of Keegan (1986) in Australia; Garrison and Shale (1989), Garrison and Baynton (1989) in Canada and Saba (1989) in the United States have provided valuable insights into the autonomy dimension of distance education.

In eighties, most of the researches on distance education' have focused on the 'effects of specific methods'. Wyllie (1981), Brown, Nathenson, and Kirkup (1982), Kelly, P. et al. (1983), Rosing (1985), and Laaser (1986) studied the effects of audio tape; Bates (1982); Ema (1984), Arias-Godinez (1984), Barrett (1984), McCormick (1985), Sakamoto (1986), and Halliwell (1987) of radio; Harper and Kember (1986) of correspondence instruction; Millard (1985) of auxiliary tutor-counselling; Pythian and Clements (1980) and Murgatroyd (1980) of tutorials; Robinson (1981), Davis (1984), Winders (1985), and Persons and Catchpole (1987) of audio conferencing; Koch (1981), Robertson (1981), Sutterfield (1981), Tate (1983), Corbett (1985), Nelson (1985), Mackerron (1985), Brown. (1986), and Wiesner (1986) of video conferencing; and Smith (1987) that of interactive video. Sometimes two or more were compared to ascertain their relative merits in obtaining desired learning outcomes. For the most part, the focus was on specific outcomes of participation rather than on the learning process. In fact, few studies actually dealt with the dynamics of students acquisition of new knowledge, skills, or sensitivity (Cookson, 1989).

The researches on 'student outcomes' in the context of distance education can be classified under: (i) students' reasons for dropout; (ii) student profiles; and (iii) institutional factors. Woodley and Parlett (1983) have recognized student dropout as "a systematic problem, relating to the institution's working. Rather, imaginative and carefully selected interventions are needed at various points throughout the system.

Studies by Holmberg (1983), Scales (1984), Siqucira and Lynch (1986), Taylor et al. (1986), and Persons and Catchpole (1987) have confirmed that contacts with students via print, multi-media, face-to-face tutorials, interactive computer conferencing and counselling significantly raises the persistence and achievement outcomes of distance students and promote their study, pleasure, motivation, and feelings of personal relation.

The researches on distance education in the global context have dealt with a number of issues and problems like redefining the role of partners in distance education and open learning teams, philosophy and theory of distance education, technology selection and adoption, design issues, methods and strategies to increase interactivity and active learning, learner characteristics, learner support, operational issues, policy and management issues, equity and accessibility, and cost benefit analysis (Sherry, 1996). The results of the studies have made a significant impact on the growth and development of distance education in India in terms of dual mode, single mode and consortia. They have helped to understand the evolution of distance education system as a viable alternative mode and its implementation in a variety of forms and models which have been adapted by a host of systems in the developing world.

Studies on Distance Education in India: A Historical Review

In India, the trend of researches on distance education conducted during the last four decades in terms of its quality and depth is not encouraging. Except for a couple of studies, the researches have been mostly conducted by the individuals drawn from the conventional university system. It is argued that academics of open universities as well as the correspondence/distance education institutes of the conventional universities occupy themselves in designing and preparing instructional materials and evaluation of assignments of distance learners, thus they hardly get time for undertaking research projects. The absence of M.Phil and Ph.D. programmes through distance mode has also contributed to this scenario.

A brief review of the studies with reference to: (i) growth and relevance of distance education system; (ii) needs, characteristics and profile of distance learners; (iii) development and production of course materials; (iv) instructional strategies and methodology; (v) economics of distance education; and (vi) management and comparative studies, is briefly presented is the following sections. This review is not restricted to data-based empirical field studies only but also to some relevant theory based papers so as to reflect trends in research on distance education in India.

Studies on growth and relevance of distance education

The studies pertaining to the growth of distance education and its relevance in India would not only help to view the current developments of the system in the right perspective but also aid in effective planning of future action. In this category we may include the studies conducted by Anand (1979), Biswal (1979), Khan (1982), Datt (1984), Balasubramaniam (1986), Jayagopal (1987),

Prasad (1987), Bhattacharya (1991), Pandit (1994), Srivastava (1995), and Pandey (1996). These studies highlight the gradual growth of distance education in the Indian perspective. The findings indicate that since the programme was merely an extension of the system of the regular courses offered by the formal universities, it has limitations in meeting the academic and socio-economic needs of target groups of distance learners. However, the studies have pointed out that the distance education programmes proved their efficacy as suitable modes in providing educational opportunities to various disadvantaged groups like women, scheduled castes, scheduled tribes, slum dwellers and ruralities, and also to general masses.

The enrolment statistics in respect of Institutes of Correspondence/Distance Education (CCIs) within conventional universities and institutions exclusively termed as open universities (OUs) indicated significant rise in percentage of enrolment during 1999-2000 as compared to 1990-1991 and 1995-1996 (Table 1).

Table 1: Growth of distance education and open learning

Period	Enrolment in Higher Education(in millions)			
	Conventional university system	**CCI**	**Open universities**	**Total (in millions)**
1990-1991	4.90 (89.74%)	0.56 (10.26%)		5.50
1995-1996	6.42 (87.05%)	0.75 (10.12%)	0.21 (2.83%)	7.38
1999-2000	7.73 (83.02%)	0.96 (10.35%)	0.47 (6.64%)	9.16

Source: 1) UGC: Annual Report 1998-99
2) UGC: Correspondence and Distance Education, Enrolment Statistics, 1995-96
3) DEC: Open Universities in India, 2001
4) AIU: Handbook on Distance Education 2000

Based on the UGC publication, correspondence and distance education enrolment statistics 1995-96, the number of universities offering correspondence education programmes was 53 in 1995-96. There was wide regional disparity with South accounting for 56.7 per cent; the North 32.7 per cent; the West 8.4 per cent and the East 2.2 per cent. Women account for 44.85 per cent in the enrolment in correspondence education programmes.

The professional areas accounted for about 27.5 per cent at the undergraduate level and 16.0 per cent at post-graduate level.

Presently there are 11 open universities and 106 dual-mode university distance education institutes/ centres in the country, offering more than 2.8 million students, 429 academic programmes and 3,817 courses through a network of 105 regional centres, 4229 study centres and 62,270 counsellors/tutors (DEC, 2004).

The information in respect of eleven open universities pertaining to their year of establishment, number of courses offered, students (registered and on rolls), number of regional and learner support centres, faculty strength etc., as in 2005, is presented in brief in Table 2.

Table 2: Status of Open universities in brief (2003-04)

Sl. No.	Details of Information	Universities											
		IGNOU	BRAOU	VMOU	NOU	YCMOU	MPBOU	BAOU	KSOU	NSOU	UPRTOU	TNOU	Total
1.	Year of Establishment	1985	1982	1987	1987	1989	1991	1994	1996	1997	1998	2002	
2.	Programmes on offer	101	25	33	22	78	77	17	19	8	38	23	441
3.	Courses of offer	900	332	255	148	355	611	140	244	29	562	231	3807
4.	Students Registered (000s)	366.1	190.2	5.9	1.8	102	192.2	13.8	19.5	14.7	8	9.39	23.7
5.	Students on Rolls (000s)	1,311	190.2	5.9	8.4	800	199.2	68.8	33.1	225.2	22.1	9.3	2873
6.	Regional Centres/ P.G. Centres/Recog-nised Regional Centres	54	23	6	-	8	10	3	6	1	-	-	111
7.	Learner Support Centres (Study Centres /Work Centres etc.)	1257	149	52	7	1425	1070	78	186	76	65	23	4388
8.	Academic Counsellors	33366	5344	2465	452	8949	8000	979	1050	2473	885	87	64,838
9.	Students awarded degrees (up to 2001)	53298	3030	-	404	60673	68343	1403	5065	-	-	-	-
10.	Audio Programmes	1293	127	-	-	345	19	9	77	207	227	-	2304
11.	Video Programmes	1792	121	-	-	333	6	16	7	13	-	-	2288
12.	Staff	1369	565	525	46	277	240	84	419	16	71	65	3577

IGNOU: Indira Gandhi National Open University; BRAOU: Dr. B.R. Ambedkar Open University; VMOU: Vardhman Mahavir Open University; NOU: Nalanda Open University; YCMOU: Yashwantrao Chavan Maharashtra Open University; MPBOU: M.P. Bhoj (Open) University; BAOU: Babasaheb Ambedkar Open University; KSOU: Karnataka State Open University; NSOU: Netaji Subash Open University; UPRTOU: U.P. Rajarshi Tandon Open University; TNOU: Tamil Nadu Open University.
Source: DEC (2001), DEC (2004), IGNOU (2005).

Table 2 indicates that IGNOU offers 101 programmes with a total number of 900 courses, which is maximum in comparison to other state open universities in 2005. The university has the largest number of (54) regional centres and (1257) learner support centres (study centres). The delivery system adopted by IGNOU for the courses include printed material, audio cassettes, video cassettes, radio broadcasting and phone-in counselling – Gyan Vani, TV broadcasting – Gyan Darshan, lab. based practical, including face-to-face training, contact and counselling sessions, on line education and tele-conferencing. Thus, the University is adopting a multi-media/multiple media approach in teaching-learning. Most of the technology has been adopted by other state open universities too.

The contribution of distance education at the school stage also has been significant. Making a humble beginning in 1979, National Institute of Open Schooling (formerly National Open School) presently has a cumulative active enrolment of over two lac students drawn from each state and UT of India. These students include prioritised groups, namely, rural people; urban poor; girls and women; scheduled castes, scheduled tribes and backward classes; physically and mentally challenged; war widows and ex-servicemen; the unemployed or part employed; groups in need of a second chance education for employed, better employment or self employment; and school drop outs after the primary or middle stage (NOS, 1991; NIOS, 2005).

The region-wise profile of the students enrolled with NIOS indicate that highest enrolment is from Northern Region, followed by the Eastern Region. The lowest enrolment is from the Southern Region. The enrolment in vocational courses from different states and union territories indicate that highest number of students enrolled is from Delhi, followed by Andhra Pradesh, Kerala and Uttar Pradesh. The prevailing imbalances in terms of rural-urban, gender, priority groups, regional language vs. national language, different zones and states have been reported in the studies by Sujatha (1989); Chakraborty (1996, 1994); Srivastava (1995); and Sharma (1996).

Studies on needs, characteristics and profile of distance learners

In the studies of Anand (1979), Khan (1982), Gomathi (1982), Pilliai and Mohan (1984) and Sahoo (1985), improvement of qualifications and the desire to continue with higher education were identified as major motivating factors for joining the correspondence course. Non-availability of time, mental maturity, non-existence of colleges in the locality, heavy expenses in formal colleges, age, marital status, regional background, parents' education, employment, paucity of time, poor financial condition and poor performance in the last qualifying examinations were found to be some other additional reasons. A sizable number of distance learners was identified as first generation learners.

Distance learners enrolled with IGNOU were found to possess average academic self-concept, good study habits and favourable attitude towards distance education by Kumar (1998, 1999). The studies conducted by Upreti (1988), Gautam (1990) and Pugazhenthi (1991), in addition to other factors, also explored those distance learners' characteristics and aspirations who had joined teacher education programmes through the distance education mode. The results indicate that majority of students joining B.Ed and M.Ed. courses were from rural background and had graduated in humanities and social sciences with low marks percentage at high school and college level.

Studies on development and production of course materials

A number of studies on the development and production of course materials, both at the macro and micro-levels have been conducted by Biswal (1979), Gupta (1985), Mulay et al. (1986),

Pillai (1988), and Rathore (1991). The findings have pointed out that the instructional materials supplied to the distance learners are not designed scientifically. The course materials are mostly written in essay-type format lacking the pedagogy of self-learning. Moreover, the materials are sketchy and the contents are not fully elaborated and explained with sufficient examples/illustrations. The self-tests/exercises at the end of the course units are stereotyped and hardly develop interest among the students. However, in some studies it was found that the students, mostly at the university level, depend solely on print-based course materials/lesson scripts for completing their studies. A large majority of students, reported difficulties in the comprehension and language of the course materials in the studies conducted by Sahoo (1985) and Koul (1987). It has been pointed out by Biswal (1979), Datt (1984), Mulay et al. (1986) and Pugazhenthi (1991) that the revision and evaluation of the course materials is hardly carried out by the, institutions and in view of this, the internal faculty members of various correspondence institutes had expressed a desire to undergo training in writing scripts for course materials and in the pedagogy of distance education.

In order to improve the quality of the course materials it is advocated that we must adopt the idea of 'course writing teams' instead of leaving it to an individual teacher to write lesson/scripts. Only one study by Venkataiah (1989) on the feasibility of course materials for distance learners by a course team has been reported. The major findings of the study are: (i) the Course Team Approach of the British Open University, though expensive, is feasible, economically viable and justified if the course material is used for a large number of students; and (ii) the Course Team Approach will ensure good-quality instructional material.

It has been pointed out by Weingartz (1981) that 'course writing team' approach is expensive, and it may lead to depersonalised style of presentation contrary to the style of didactic communication and may tend to support the presentation of learning material as ready-made system rather than as guide to problem-solving. Hence, the efficacy of the team approach in course writing and its economic viability needs to be studied in the Indian context.

Studies on instructional strategies and methodology

This section is confined to a discussion of the studies pertaining to: (i) instructional processes and the role of information technology; (ii) submission of assignments; (iii) role of the personal contact programmes; and (iv) study-centre support services.

The instructional process and the role of information technology

The success of open and distance education programmes depends largely on effective and flexible guided instruction. Koul et al. (1987), and Amritavalli (1987) have pointed out that the absence of prolonged human interaction with the distance learner gives the open learning system a propensity for greater dependence upon information technology. In order to improve the open learning system, effective and meaningful use of various aspects of information technology like electronic publishing of course materials, computers and telecommunications has been suggested. But these should not be introduced with a view to replacement of the essentials of the traditional teaching-learning strategies like chalk-and-talk, book-and-examination, etc. The experiences of a few open learning institutions in the developed countries have demonstrated that a 'lecture controlled' approach was found to be more effective in expanding the reach of distance education. Under such a system, while the media personnel would play the supportive role of extending the reach of education, the lecturer would deliver lectures as he would do in a traditional classroom. The TV programmes of IGNOU and UGC (country-wide classroom) are worth mentioning in this context. Though the utility of these telecasts as a supplement to distance learning programmes is somewhat doubtful. Studies conducted by Biswal (1979), Khan (1982), Sahoo (1985),

Balasubramaniam (1986), and Rathore (1991) revealed that none of the institutes of correspondence courses telecast educational TV programmes. However, an account of the education television programmes telecast by Madras Doordarshan for students of formal education, adult and non-formal education has been presented by Ananthasayanam and Rajamani (1988). Nagaraju (1982) found radio programmes useful in the in-service teacher training programmes in Kerala State, though all the teacher-trainees did not regularly listen to all the radio broadcasts related to the training course.

Shah and Mandal (1993) found the use of instructional strategies (video film and booklet) effective in teaching home science and in improving English language competence. The effectiveness of IGNOU ETV programmes in direct, talkback and interactive modes was explored by Goel, D.R. and Sarangi (1995). Using a purposive sample of 7 IGNOU ETVs as the context of the tele teach, a significant gain in six out of seven IGNOU ETV programmes through direct and talk back modes was observed. There was also significant gain through all the 7 programmes in the interactive mode. A study by Venkaiah (2005) revealed that teleconferencing is widely used by Dr. B.R. Ambedkar Open University to supplement the learning process.

In the distance education system it is strongly advocated that various media need to be integrated for making the instructional process effective. The main problem is not how many media should be used but how we integrate the media with the course structure. In this context, Pathak (1987) has also emphasised that instead of aiming at the 'Multimedia Approach', we need to aim at the 'Integrated Media Approach'. He opined that an 'Integrated Approach' takes into account the possible value and suitability of each medium and links each new medium with the existing media.

At the school level also, the role of media has been considered important in distance education in the studies by Sahoo et al. (1997), Dass and Dass (2001), and Sahoo and Mucchal (2001). The strategy involving printed lesson, video and discussion was found to be effective.

Submission of assignment

Students' Response Sheets generally attached with the course material supplied to the distance learners are considered as one of the effective means for providing feedback to learners to support their learning outcomes. The studies by Biswal (1979), Mulay et al. (1986) and Rathore (1991) revealed that most of the students, who received the evaluated response sheets well in time, appreciated compulsory submission of assignments and found them useful to some extent in pursuing their courses. But the study by Pillai and Mohan (1984) reported that students do not appreciate the compulsory submission of assignments.

The didactic comments of the tutors/teachers on assignments provide a meaningful feedback to distance learners. Some studies were conducted to assess the didactic quality of the tutor's comments. Mulay et al. (1986) found that the comments varied from institution to institution. Biswal (1979), Nagaraju (1982) and Sahoo (1985) pointed out that the tutors/teachers of distance education institutions did not make serious attempts to clarify students' efforts. The students wanted detailed comments on their assignments and appropriate evaluation of their performances. In view of the importance of the comments of the tutors, Koul (1987) suggested that if teachers in distance/open learning systems are made aware of what teaching-type comments are like, and what they can do in terms of teaching, and how they might be written and used purposefully, the system of distance teaching will function more effectively than they do otherwise.

Role of personal contact programmes

Personal Contact Programmes (PCPs) provide face-to-face support to instructional programmes in the distance education system. Anand (1979), Biswal (1979), Sahoo (1985),

Balasubramaniam (1986), Mulay et al. (1986), and Rathore (1991) reported that almost all the distance education institutes had the provision of PCPs though there is a significant variation among the institutions in the organisation of the PCPs with regard to the duration, participation of staff and students, and mode of conducting the programmes. The findings indicated that lack of facilities for boarding and lodging at the venue of PCP, nature of employment, lack of prior information about the timings of PCPs, financial constraints etc. influence attendance of distance learners.

The methods used for teaching in PCPs were lectures followed by questions-answers. Because of paucity of time, most of the teachers covered the selected topics through lectures. Anand (1979), Biswal (1979), Khan (1982), Pillai and Mohan (1983), Sahoo (1985), Balasubramaniam (1986) and Rathore (1991) found that most of the students who attended PCPs expressed a positive opinion about their usefulness in terms of clarification of doubts, getting inspiration for further studies, better preparation for examination, solving academic problems, and effective teacher-student interaction. Success in distance learning system was found to be intimately associated with PCPs in a study by Gautam (1990).

The drop-out rate in the distance education system was reported to be high in the studies by Khan (1982), Sahoo (1985), and Balasubramaniam (1986). Mostly, the drop-outs belonged to the upper age-groups with larger gap of time between their last qualifying examination and admission in the present courses; they belonged to the poorer academic and family background, rural areas, the female group, and the employed class of people. Non-attendance in PCPs, lack of library study facilities, lack of proper teacher-student contacts, non-availability of reference materials, non-payment of semester fees, non-submission of the required number of assignments, family problems, less contact with teachers, and difficulties in studying the course materials/ lesson scripts were reported to be the major problems of the drop-outs. Quite a large number of drop-outs aspired for continuing with their studies further provided certain improvements are brought about in the PCPs.

At school stage the factors, viz., lack of supervision at the head quarters and study centres, little time allocated for PCPs, lack of interest shown by tutors and their negative attitude to wards distance learners, lack of seriousness among the learners and location of study centres, were found to be responsible for low attendance in PCPs organised by NIOS in the studies by Sachchidananda (2002) and Sharma (2002).

Study centre support services

Singh (1987) Mani (1987), and Rathore (1991) in their studies have pointed out that a network of study centres is of vital importance to distance education institutes for providing useful support to students in their learning pursuits. Each study centre should have a counsellor who is competent enough to give general counselling, advice and guidance to students on the methodology of learning through the distance education system and general aspects of the various courses. In some cases, the students among other aspects of the support system reported that the 'study centres' are very few and ill-equipped. They expected that the study centres should have a full-fledged library equipped with standard texts and reference books, radio, audio-tapes, TV, video-cassettes and a full time instructor for academic and administrative counselling.

Management and comparative studies on distance education

The studies in the organisation and management of different aspects of distance education in comparative perspective have been conducted by various researchers.

Anand (1979), Pandey (1980), and Nanda (1997) studies found the achievement of distance education students better in comparison to regular students; whereas the achievement of latter was found to higher than that of the former by Sahoo (1985), Mulay et al. (1986), and Bahuguna (1988).

Khan (1991), reported a year-wise increase in the enrolment from 1977-78 to 1988-89 of B.Ed. students in distance education in Kashmir University when compared to the formal system. The per capita cost in the distance education system was reported to be less when compared to formal mode. The pass percentage in both the streams was almost equal.

The study on approaches to learning and academic performance of students in conventional and open universities in a comparative perspective by Das (1992) revealed that the students in the open university significantly differed from students in the conventional university in terms of the learner; content and context approaches to learning.

Kanchan (1996) undertook a study to investigate to what extent distance education programmes introduced by the Institute of Correspondence Education, University of Jammu and IGNOU were feasible in Jammu region in respect of their relevance to the needs of the students, problems faced by these organisations in the implementation of distance education programmes, and realisation of objectives set out by the two universities. The findings revealed: (i) instruction to distance learners enrolled with both the institutions is mostly imparted by the teachers drawn from formal system and hence most of them are not specifically acquainted with the instructional technology of distance education and open learning; (ii) both the institutions enrolled students from rural and urban areas; (iii) teachers engaged by IGNOU are provided orientation through seminars, workshops, and refresher courses. The teachers are also trained in the use of latest technologies so as to equip them with innovative techniques which they may use in the development of self-instructional materials and other software; (iv) IGNOU also provides help to distance learners through TV and teleconferencing; (v) pattern followed by the Jammu University in the preparation of instructional material is more or less like a textbook. But in case of IGNOU, the modular approach is specifically followed, with adequate number of examples, illustrations, learning exercises, activities, self tests and references. The materials are developed and edited meticulously by the experts and (vi) the submission of assignments in both the institution is compulsory. Similar results, with respect to preparation of instructional material availability and use of student support services, and evaluation procedures, were reported by Sharma (1999) in the comparative study of the distance education programmes of IGNOU, H.P. University (ICDEOL) and also by Patil (1997) in the study comparing the management of distance education offered by university of Mysore (ICCEM) and IGNOU.

The organisation and management of distance education programmes under the control of BRAOU was studied by Naidu (2000). The findings indicated that there is a need: (i) to evolve strategies by the university to develop better relations with students, meeting the problems of dropouts, meeting the needs of the students through well organised programmes of counselling and guidance and augmenting new infrastructure facilities for future courses and programmes; (ii) for establishment of more number of study centres to provide opportunities in remote and backward areas where higher education facilities either do not exist or are meagre; and (iii) for policy making and better student support services including delivery system.

At the school level, Chakraborty (2004) in the comparative study on spatial distribution of study centres of National Institute of Open Schooling (NIOS) and Rabindra Muktya Vidyalaya (RMV) found a significant difference between NIOS and RMV in base planning and objectives underlying the distribution of study centres in different districts of West Bengal. NIOS has a clear dominance in hill areas, whereas RMV does not have such features. Remote hill areas like Darjeeling and Purulia have remained beyond the attention of both the organizations.

Studies on economics of distance education

Studies on economics of distance education mostly pertain to the analysis of sources of income of the system and expenditure, unit cost, and cost benefit analysis, especially in comparison to those of the conventional mode. Biswal (1979), Khan (1982), and Sahoo (1985) in their studies have revealed that the major sources of finance of distance education were students 'fees, and rarely were funds raised through grants from other sources'.

The studies by Pandey (1980) and Ram (1984) have pointed out that the unit costs of correspondence courses were much lower than those of regular courses. With regard to recurring income, it was found that correspondence courses supported themselves without government subsidy and mostly depended on students' fees. However, in the case of nonrecurring income no difference was found between the two streams. Gupta (1985) found that the development of correspondence education in Rajasthan had not taken into account the economic needs of the State.

A comparative study of unit costs in the School of Correspondence Courses and Colleges of Delhi University by Datt (1987, 1988) revealed that in the latter, not only the unit costs but also state subsidy was substantially higher than in the former. He suggested that keeping the norm of one-third of the cost of distance education system as against the formal university system, it would be desirable to realise 25% of the student expenditure from student fees while the remaining 75% should be state subsidy. Ansari (1987) attempted to isolate the factors which may be responsible for making the system of distance education cost-efficient and cost-effective. He identified choice of educational media, number of students and number of courses as the major determinants of the distance learning system and argued that while the fixed cost of the preparation of course material may be cheaper under the correspondence method, the same may be relatively higher under the audio-visual method because of the involvement of costlier transmission and reception equipment and a relatively high level of salaries of technical and media personnel. The variable costs in both the cases would, however, depend upon the number of students and the number of courses offered. Azad (1987) has suggested that the expansion programmes of distance education in India should be based on a well thought out. Integrated plan of development, taking into consideration the manpower needs of the country on a long-term basis. Further, the investment, particularly in the electronic equipment utilised by the distance education systems, should be planned on the basis of their academic effectiveness. In the comparative study by Agrawal (1987) unit costs of distance and conventional system in the context of the Entrepreneurial Development Training Programme conducted by the Small Industries Service Institute (SISI), Karnal through regular mode and the All India Manufacturers Organization (AIMO). New Delhi, through correspondence, it was revealed that the unit cost at AIMO is higher by 39% than that at SISI, which is mainly due to the lower level of utilisation of the teaching and administrative staff at AIMO. As the major portion of the expenditure is incurred on staff salaries which influence the fixed costs, there is need to make optimum and efficient utilisation of the existing staff. Because of inadequate data, it was difficult to draw conclusions about the extent of unit cost variations in the professional education provided through regular and distance education, in a comparative perspective.

In the studies at the school level Gaba (1999, 1997), and Sujatha (1989), it has been pointed that open schooling is cost effective.

Overview of Research Studies on Distance Education

In the proceeding section, the history of the quantitative growth and trend of research during the last four decades in the distance education system have been traced. The analysis of research studies reveals the following significant features of the system along with the scope and quality of research conducted in this emerging area:

- Research in distance education system did not make much headway during the seventies. It gained momentum in the quantitative terms during eighties when more and more institutes/universities started course through distance mode. Barring a couple of studies, the researches did not show any qualitative trend with respect to the theory and practice of distance education.

  Most of the research studies are descriptive surveys confined to comparison of enrolment figures of students in distance education courses offered by various institutions. The specific causes of high enrolment or dropout in different courses/institutions among various categories of distance learners have not been studied in any of the researches. Taking education to the doorsteps of the 'needy' is the prime mission of distance and open education programmes, there is hardly any study to trace specifically the enrolment and drop out phenomena of learners from the far flung hill areas, tribal habitations, coastal and dissert areas, slums, and areas which remain snow bound during most part of year. No in-depth studies using case studies have been undertaken to identify the specific causes of drop-out phenomena among distance learners in the context of girls and other disadvantaged groups like scheduled castes, scheduled tribes, OBC, and ruralites.

  The issues related to the needs and characteristics of distance learners; status of study centres; students support services in terms of counselling, production and delivery of instructional materials, organisation of personal contact programmes; and finances have been studied as isolated events lacking diagnostic, follow-up and remedial research.
- Major chunk of studies have been undertaken on distance education programmes at tertiary level offered by institutes of correspondence education of conventional universities and open universities. Studies on the role of open schools (NOIS and SOSs) on various important issues of school education in the context of universal elementary education (UEE) and education for all (EFA); vocationalisation of education; and equity, relevance and excellence have been mostly neglected.
- Research studies have mostly adopted descriptive survey approach and quantitative analysis techniques. The experimentation for testing the efficacy of various approaches, interventions and models; case study approach; use of interviews and observations; qualitative data analysis techniques have been mostly neglected in the conduct of studies. Impact and intervention studies for programme development and evaluation of distance education system have also been ignored.
- Studies are based on arbitrary combinations of variables relating psychology, economics, sociology, pedagogy, media (print and electronic), management, etc. without taking into

consideration their implications for the clientele and catchment area, thus lacking long-range perspective and relevance to future planning of distance education programmes.

- The findings of the studies in comparative perspective indicated that the instructional material prepared and developed by IGNOU is greatly appreciated by the teachers associated with distance education programmes and distance learners because the quality and standard of the course content is maintained by involving professionals and experts from the field and adequate time is devoted in preparing the materials. However, course materials prepared by most of the correspondence/ distance education institutions of conventional universities are poor in quality and prints because these institutions hardly involve professionals of quality due to lack of finances. The materials in most of the cases are prepared in a hurry.
- In the management and organisation of contact programmes, a number of problems pertaining to infrastructure, use of technologies, accommodation for resource persons and distance learners have been highlighted by the studies. Such problems are more prevalent in case of distance education programmes of institutes of correspondence courses of conventional universities.
- The distance education programmes offered by conventional universities use print-based instructional materials. However, some state open universities use multi-media based instructional technology. IGNOU, in addition to multi-media, use latest communication and information technologies including teleconferencing in providing instruction and counselling to distance learners.
- There is no provision of 'Regional Study Centres' in most of the conventional universities in their catchment areas for providing 'support services' to distance learners; whereas, IGNOU has established an extensive and effective network of Regional Study Centres all over the country for providing services to its clientele in registration, enrolment, contact programmes, counselling, library facilities, and other academic support.
- The teachers associated with the distance education courses in conventional universities are hardly provided any orientation in the theory and practice of distance education programmes; whereas, IGNOU is providing orientation to course writers through seminar and workshops. Distance Education Council (DEC) of IGNOU is also taking meaningful steps in assisting other state open universities and conventional universities offering distance education to share the expertise and resources of IGNOU for faculty improvement, and development and use of instructional materials.
- While analysing various issues and problems of distance education, it has been found that the researchers have used the research processes and techniques as practised in conventional system. This may be because of their orientation and training in the conventional education institutions as well as their attachment with these institutions. They might be looking upon conventional universities as standards for acceptable norms, credibility and the role models. This may also be because most of them have started their career in the formal system as well as they got all their qualifications, academic or professional, from formal system (Mishra, 2004). Distance education research has unique problems which are quite different from the

research of conventional system. IGNOU has instituted a scheme of research projects in distance education to:

(i) encourage system based research; (ii) take up in-depth studies for evaluation of the programmes, their impact and effectiveness with a view to bring about correctives; (iii) investigate specific problems about the concepts and practices in vogue in the distance education system and to find solutions to them; and (iv) undertake research studies on new technologies, their potential and application for deciding the quality of their operational procedure (DEC, 2000).

Future Research Priorities in Distance Education

India is a vast and the most diverse country in the world. It is continental in size, extending over an area of 32,87,268 sq.km. from snow-covered Himalayan heights to tropical rain forests of South. Its physical framework is very striking because of the vast diversities in climatic conditions which influence the socio-economic condition, cultural characteristics educational opportunities of its people. In 1947, when it attained freedom from the British rule, most of its diversity was latent within the passive underclass at the bottom of the socio-economic pyramid. Over the years the population has tripled to the tune of over 100 crores and side by side there has been an increasing manifestation of social and economic diversities in terms of caste and community, dialect, manners and customs, ways of life and entertainment, education, health, levels of development and so forth. It is expected that by 2025 India's diversities will stand fully revealed when its population will have given rise to about 130-140 crores. These diversities are up thrusting from below, each newly empowered group would try to tangle with and push against those above and below it in a bid to establish its identify and to access and participate in the system. "The next two decades are", as Verghese (2002) puts, "therefore, likely to be conflict prone and will need careful political and social management through a widening and deepening of access and participation. The established order must yield to change on the basis of liberty (empowerment), equality (social justice), and fraternity (togetherness as citizens, in place of zealotry)". Education can play a significant role in accelerating the pace of change. But in its efforts the county is faced with the challenge of planning *Education for All* at primary stage and ensuring equality of educational opportunities at all levels, when the very base, because of the increase in population and widening diversities, is expanding at a fast pace. No doubt, in the last five decades, the efforts in expanding and equalizing educational opportunities to all at the school and higher stages have been encouraging. The results are visible even in the rural and backwards regions of the country. But the progress in terms of providing equal opportunity in education to all is not evenly distributed. The degree and level of education varies from place to place, depending on the nearness or accessibility of a village to urban centres; the rate of literacy; the quality of local leadership; the traditional roots and attitude towards modernisation; communication network and exposure to the outside world; basic economic problems as a result of poverty; and the interaction at the socio-economic levels. In this context, the education system requires to handle large numbers and be accessible to people at large especially at the bottom of the 'socio-economic pyramid' so as to meet the goals of social justice. The formal classroom system alone is unable to cope up with the situation. Presently at the higher education level, the distance and open education encompasses over 25 percent of the total student enrolment. In the Tenth Plan period (2002-2007), the 29 states in the country are expected to have one Open University each, and the distance education system is expected to cater for the educational needs of at least 50 percent of the additional student enrolment. The Tenth Plan proposal of increasing student enrolment in higher education from the present 6 percent to 10 percent implies an additional student enrolment of over seven million of the relevant 18=23 year age group (Panda, 2005). Since the distance education system also may not be able to cope with this load, proper data and research base are needed for strengthening the links between policy, planning and practice in distance education. The research in this emerging area must be able to: (i) generate knowledge on various components of distance education: theory and its relevance with respect to different dimensions of Indian society, process and product, and cost effectiveness; (ii) help practitioners in the distance education system to encapsulate their experiences for the benefit of the system and future researchers; (iii) identify the underlying issues of learner characteristics and needs; (iv) study the influence of media upon the instructional system; (v) focus on the issue of equity of access to interactive delivery systems;

(vi) identify the roles of teacher, counsellor/facilitator, and student in the distance education process; (vii) contribute to the emergence of distance education as a discipline; (viii) strengthen the morale of the distance education community in the country and help to attract talent to this emerging area; and (ix) provide results of empirical researches with regard to the potential of distance education to ensure high quality and relevant education to a large number of needy learners at a reasonable cost. To achieve these objectives, it is suggested that IGNOU and UGC at the tertiary level, NIOS and NCERT at the school level may undertake the responsibility of commissioning and assisting research projects jointly so that the two systems – formal/ conventional and the distance/open – could come together. This will help the students in the open system to enjoy the benefits of the more flexible system together with the credibility which the conventional system offers.

The research in distance education and open learning needs to relate itself effectively to the formulation of the theory and practices of the system. Some priority areas are identified which may be of immense help to researchers in selecting the problems.

- There are diverse groups in India with specific needs. The identification of the academic, professional and vocational courses keeping in view their needs of diverse groups with the help of comprehensive survey studies is needed.
- In most distance learning situations, a culture specific/ localised theory has a greater prospect of success than a general instructional theory intended to function satisfactorily in diverse settings with a variety of practitioners. Studies for developing localised/culture specific teaching-learning modes need encouragement.
- Interest in distance education is especially high in the areas where the student population is widely distributed and scattered. Research may be undertaken to help each area to plan and

design its own form of distance education in accordance with the local needs and resources, target groups, and background of organisations which provide instruction.

- The success of any distance education programme mostly rests with the planning and development of curriculum, and production of course materials keeping in view the background and needs of distance learners. In this exercise there may be radical departure from many of the concepts, approaches and methods of the formal system. In designing effective curriculum programme and developing course materials, one must consider not only the goals, needs and characteristics of teachers and distance learners, but also content requirements and technical constraints. The curriculum and course materials along with their technological requirements, especially at the higher levels, need to be developed using experimental and follow up studies for testing their adequacy and efficacy in the development of knowledge, critical thinking, and higher cognitive and affective abilities.
- The efficacy of the course team approach' in course writing and its economic viability, as practised by British Open University and IGNOU, needs to be studied in the context of various state open universities and state open schools.
- Orientation and training of teachers, administrators, and other supporting staff associated with distance education and open learning system should be based on various models developed through experimental and longitudinal studies. The models may be restricted to script writing, editing, organisation of contact programmes, evaluation of assignments, computer applications, office management, production of audio-video programmes, choice media and communication technology.
- Studies on augmentation and strengthening of student support services, improvements in the delivery system, decentralisation of administration and extensive use of communication technology may be undertaken using experimental and case study approaches.
- The evaluation of learning outcomes of distance learners need not be done using a system of formal/conventional mode. It should keep in view the needs and requirements of distance learners. Thus well designed experimental studies for developing comprehensive formative and summative models for evaluating the performance of distance learners may be undertaken.
- Studies for evolving model guidelines/parameters for assessing and monitoring the quality of the educational provision available in the distance education institutes in conventional universities, open universities, and open schools using longitudinal and experimental designs may be conducted.
- Distance education has special connotation and framework within which the total set up of curriculum design, instruction, learning and evaluation operates. The research in this area, therefore, has unique problems, quite different from research of formal/conventional system. As such the tools and techniques drawn from other disciplines can not be adopted as such. It should create its own standards for deciding the quality of its operational procedure. The

studies in this area also calls for devising appropriate set of research designs, tools and techniques, keeping in view the specific features of the system.

- Cost-effectiveness of the on-going programmes of distance/ open education in relation to institutional costs and private costs need to be studied.
- Impact studies pertaining to organisation, methods, procedures, and results in terms of the learning outcomes of distance learners, and the impact of distance education on the different aspects of development of various target groups be encouraged for policy planning.

The Indira Gandhi National Open University (IGNOU) at the higher education level and the National Institute of Open Schooling (NIOS) at the school stage, as the apex autonomous institutions, need to take effective steps based on sound theoretical background and research rationale, to promote the cause of open education for the benefit of needy and unreached groups of Indian society.

Besides providing education to out of school children through distance mode, NIOS has introduced 'Examination-on-Demand Scheme' to reduce the burden of examination among the distance learners. It claims that this innovation at the school level will give a big boost to the open learning system in the country. The NIOS proposes to have content free and competency-based examinations, which means that no particular book will be used to formulate questions, but the questions would be set from general reference (NIOS, 2002). It also plans to develop local specific study materials and models for effective transaction of curriculum at various levels of school education keeping in view the needs of distance learners belonging to various regions of the country. All these steps require a sound research base which can be provided by initiating action research, experimentation and case studies on various themes of open education at the school stage.

IGNOU is mandated to function as more than a university because of the responsibility entrusted to it to co-ordinate, promote and determine standards of distance education systems in the country. Through Distance Education Council (DEC), it has taken various initiatives for promoting quality research in distance education and open learning at the fundamental and applied levels in order to constantly enrich the theory and practice of distance education. A list of thrust areas for research in distance education has also been provided by DEC (2000). It includes: curriculum design, problem of distance learners, constraints of development of learning materials (print and non-print), student support services, student evaluation, economics of distance education, media in distance education, management of open and distance education system, application of new technologies, quality assurance, effectiveness of research methodologies in distance education, open education network, technology communication system, effective learning strategies in individual/independent study network (web-based) learning, on demand examination on intranet and internet, audio graphical contribution in preparation of self learning materials, and fusion of text, sound images on CD for in-depth study in professional courses. IGNOU has introduced Ph.D. programmes in some disciplines and proposes to start M.Phil courses. This would be helpful in promoting on-campus and off-campus research activities, which must aim at improving the effectiveness and efficiency of the system itself. The financial support for research fellowships and projects by IGNOU through DEC is also a major initiative to encourage researchers for undertaking quality research in distance and open education.

References

Agrawal, P.D. (1987). Unit cost in conventional and distance education system: A case study. In B.N.Koul, et al. (eds), *Studies in Distance Education*. New Delhi: AIU and IGNOU.

AIU (2000) *Handbook on Distance Education*. New Delhi: AIU.

Amritavalli, R. (1987). Role of audio-visual aids in distance education. In, B.N. Koul et al. (eds.), *Studies in Distance Education*. New Delhi: AIU and IGNOU.

Anand, S. (1979). *University Without Walls*. New Delhi: Vikas Publishing House Pvt. Ltd.

Ananthasayanam, R. and Rajamani, N.C. (1988). Role of television in distance education: An experience from education television (ETV) programme of Madras Doordarshan. *Journal of Educational Planning and Administration,* 1, (2 & 3).

Ansari, M.M. (1987). determinants of costs in distance education. In. B.N. Koul et al. (eds.), *Studies in Distance Education*. New Delhi: AIU and IGNOU.

Arias-Godinez (1984). Non-Formal Education through Radio and the Social Reproduction/ Transformation of a Rural Community in Veraçruz, Mexico. *Ed.D. Dissertation,* University of Houston.

Azad, J.L. (1987). Financing of distance education: some basic issues. In. B.N. Koul et al. (Eds.), *Studies in Distance Education*. New Delhi: AIU and IGNOU.

Bahuguna, R.C. (1988). A comparative study of correspondence and formal education. *Journal of Educational Planning and Administration*. Vol. 2, No. 3 & 4.

Balasubramaniam, S. (1986). The status of correspondence courses in India. *University News* 24 (42).

Barrett, J. (1984). Student-tutor communication in radio tutorials. *Programmed Learning and Educational Technology*, 21 (4), 333-335.

Bates, A.W. (1982). The impact of educational radio. *Media in Education and Development,* 15(3), 144-149.

Bhattacharya, Sudip (1991). Open University - It's Scope and Possibilities: An Analysis of Tagore's Educational Thoughts in Evolving a Conceptual Framework of Open University in India. *Ph.D. Education,* Viswa-Bharati University.

Biswal, B.N. (1979). A Study of Correspondence Education in India. *Ph.D. Education*, The Maharaja Sayajirao University of Baroda.

Brown, B.J. (1986). An Exploratory Study of Motivational Characteristics of Adult Distance Telecourse Learners. *Ed.D. Dissertation*, University of South Dakota.

Brown, S., M. Nathenson, and G. Kirkup (1982). Learning from evaluation at the open university. ii. helping students to learn from audio-visual media. *British Journal of Educational Technology*, 13(3), 217-236.

Chakraborty, K.N. (1994). A critical study of 1990-94 enrolment in the national open school. *Indian Journal of Open Learning*, 3(2), 40-45.

Chakraborty, K.N. (1996). Language bias in self learning and its impact on enrolment in the national open school. *Indian Journal of Open Learning*, 5(1), 28-33.

Chakraborty, K.N. (2004) Comparative study on spatial distribution of study centres of NIOS and RMV in West Bengal. *OSAC Journal of Open Schooling*, 4(2), July-Dec.

Cookson, P.S. (1989). Research on learners and learning in distance education: A review. *The American Journal of Distance Education*, 3(2).

Corbett, J.W. (1985). Adult Learning and Instructional Television: The Effects of Cognitive Ability and Television Viewing Habits on Achievement Following Mediated Instruction. *Ph.D. Dissertation*, Wayne State University.

Das, Mamata (1992). Approaches to Learning and Academic Performances of Students in Traditional and Open Universities: A Comparative Study. *Ph.D. Education*, Jawaharlal Nehru University.

Dass, B.C. and Dass, S. (2001). Viewing doordarshan (TV) programmes, preferences of high school students. *Indian Journal of Open Learning*, 10(1), 100-109.

Datt, R. (1984). Planning and development of distance education. *Journal of Higher Education*, 9(8).

Datt, R. (1987). Distance Education Versus Traditional Higher Education: A Cost Comparison. In B.N. Koul et al. (eds.) *Studies in Distance Education*. New Delhi: AIU and IGNOU.

Datt, R. (1987). *Status of School of Correspondence Courses and Continuing Education*. University of Delhi, School of Correspondence Courses Project.

Datt, R. (1988). Distance education in A.D. 2000. *Journal Educational Planning and Administration*, 2(3 and 4).

Davis, D.J. (1984). Evaluation and comparison of teleconference training with face-to-face training. *American Journal of Distance Education*, 3(2).

DEC (2000). *Research Projects Scheme in Distance Education*. New Delhi: IGNOU.

DEC (2001). *Open Universities in India: Brief Information*. New Delhi: DEC, Indira Gandhi National Open University.

DEC (2004). *Information Base on Distance Higher Education in India*. New Delhi: DEC, Indira Gandhi National Open University.

Ema, E.A.J.U. (1984). Educational Radio and Rural Development. *Ph.D. Dissertation*. University of Michigan.

Gaba, A.K. (1997). Is open schooling in India cost-effective? In Mukhopadhyaya, M. and Parhar, M. (eds.), *Open and Distance Education*. New Delhi: Jawahar Publishers.

Gaba, A.K. (1999). Cost Analysis of Open schooling. In Panda, Santosh (ed.), *Open and Distance Education – Policies, Practices and Quality Concerns*. New Delhi: Aravali International.

Garg, S. (2004). Role of distance education in widening access: The experience of IGNOU. *Staff and Educational Development International*, 8(2-3), 1-9.

Garrison, D.R. and Baynton, M. (1989). Beyond independence in Distance Education: The Concept of Control. In Moore, M.G. and Smith, G.C. (eds.), *Readings in Principles of Distance Education*.

Garrison, D.R., and Shale, D. (1987). Mapping the boundaries of distance education: Problems in defining the field. *The American Journal of Distance Education*, 1(1), 7-13.

Gautam, R. (1990). A Study of Success in Distance Learning System in Relation to Some Key Learned and Institutional Variables. *Ph.D., Education*. Kurukshetra University.

Goel, D.R. and Sarangi, D. (1995). The IGNOU ETV: Different telemodes. *The Progress of Education,* LXIX(8), 148-152.

Gomathi, M. (1982). A Critical Study of the Participants' Evaluation of Selected Postgraduate Courses of the Correspondence Education Programme of Madurai Kamraj University. *Ph.D. Education,* University of Madras.

Gupta, M.L. (1985). *Indian Economy and Higher Education with Reference to Correspondence Education.* Institute of Correspondence Studies, University of Rajasthan.

Halliwel, J. (1987). Is distance education by radio outdated? *British Journal of Educational Technology,* 17(3), 212-222.

Harper, G. and Kember, D. (1986). Approaches to study of distance education students. *British Journal of Educational Technology,* 17(3), 212-22.

Holmberg, B. (1967). *Correspondence Education.* Malmo, Sweden: Hermods.

Holmberg, B. (1983). Guided Didactic Conversation. In D. Sewart, D. Keegan and B. Holmberg (eds.), *Distance Education: International Perspectives,* London: Croom Helm.

IGNOU (2005). *IGNOU Profile 2005*. New Delhi: Indira Gandhi National Open University.

Jayagopal, R. (1987). Open university system and weaker sections: A prototype programme for marginal farmers. In B.N. Koul et al. (eds.), *Studies in Distance Education.* New Delhi: AIU and IGNOU.

Jonassen, D.H. (1992). Applications and Limitations of Hypertext Technology for Distance Learning. Paper Presented at the *Distance Learning Workshop*, Armstrong Laboratory, San Antonio.

Kanchan, Bala (1996). Distance Education Programmes at College and University Levels in Jammu Region: An Evaluative study. *Ph.D. Education*, Himachal Pradesh University.

Keegan, D. (1986). *The Foundations of Distance Education*. London: Croom Helm.

Kelly, P. et al. (1983). Tutor tapes for tutorial service. *Teaching at a Distance*, 23, 60-62.

Khan, I. (1982). Suitability of Teaching English Through Correspondence Courses as Offered by Some Indian Universities at the First Degree Level. *Ph.D. Eduation,* Utkal University.

Khan, N. (1991). Effectivity of Distance Education Programme with Reference to the Teachers' Training Course, Kashmir University. *Ph.D., Education,* University of Kashmir.

Koch, L.D. (1981). Factors Influencing the Selection of Non-Traditional Study at the Open University of Maryland. *D.Ed. Dissertation,* Pennsylvania State University.

Koul, B.N. (1987). Tutor-comments: A distance teaching technique. In B.N. Koul et al. (eds.), *Studies in Distance Education*. New Delhi: AIU and IGNOU.

Koul, B.N.; Singh, Bakhshish and Ansari, M.M. (eds.). (1987). *Studies in Distance Education*. New Delhi: AIU and IGNOU.

Kumar, Anil (1998). An Investigation into the Distance Learners' Academic Self-Concept, Study Habits and Attitude Towards Distance Education in Relation to Academic Performance at First Degree Level. *Ph.D. Education,* Ch. Charan Singh University, Meerut.

Kumar, Anil (1999). Open university distance learners' attitude towards distance education. *Perspectives in Education*, 15(3), 165-173.

Laaser, W. (1986). Some didactic aspects of audio-cassettes in distance education. *Distance Education*, 7(1), 143-152.

Mackerron, J.L. (1985). Conditions that Affect Participation in Distance Education at Selected Institutions Producing and Using Television-Assisted Instruction in the United States. *Ed.D. Dissertation,* Syracuse University.

Mani, G. (1987). Evaluation of distance education. In B.N. Koul et al. (eds.). *Studies in Distance Education.* New Delhi: AIU and IGNOU.

McCormick, R. (1985). Students' views on study at the radio and television universities in china: An investigation in one local centre. *British Journal of Educational Technology,* 16(2), 84-101.

Millard, J. (1985). Local tutor-student contact in the open university. *Teaching at a Distance*, 26, 11-22.

Mishra, S. (2004). Process-issues for organising research in distance education. *Indian Educational Review*, 40(1), 22-42.

Moore, M. (1989). Recent contributions to the theory of distance education. *Open Learning*, November.

Mulay, V.; Phutela, R.L. and Nadir, R. (1986). *Correspondence Education in Indian Universities.* (UGC Project), Central Institute of Educational Technology, New Delhi: National Council of Educational Research and Training.

Murgatroyd, S. (1980). What actually happens in tutorials? *Teaching at a Distance*, 18 (Winter), 44-53.

Nagaraju, C.S. (1982). *Evaluation of Correspondence-cum-Contact In-service Teacher-training Programme in Kerala.* Institute for Social and Economic Change, Bangalore. (Ministry of Education. Government of India Financed Project).

Naidu, G.V. (2000). Organisation and Management of Distance Education Programmes Under

Nanda, Renu (1997). A Study of Non-Formal Education Programme in the Jammu Division. *Ph.D. Education*, University of Jammu.

National Institute of Open Schooling (2002). *On-Demand Examination Scheme*. Report of the Conference, May 10-11.

National Institute of Open Schooling (2005). *Handbook for Academic Facilitators of NIOS.* New Delhi, NIOS.

National Open School (1991). *A Decade of Open Learning*. New Delhi: NOS.

Nelson, P.A. (1985). The Effects of Field Independent-Dependent Cognitive Style on Achievement in a Telecourse. *Ed.D. Dissertation,* Brigham Young University.

Panda, Santosh (1995). Review of research on Indian distance education. *Journal of Higher Education,* 18(3), 469-484.

Panda, Santosh (2005). Higher education at a distance and national development: Reflections on Indian experience. *Distance Education*, 26(2), 205-225.

Pandey, S.K. (1980). Economics of Correspondence Education in Indian Universities. *Ph.D., Economics*, Meerut University.

Pandey, Saroj (1996). Distance learners' profile: A case study of IGNOU. *Education in Asia,* 16(3&4), 131-134.

Pandit, P.V. (1994). Role of Distance Education in Empowerment of Women – A Case Study of Dr. B.R. Ambedkar Open University. *Ph.D. Education*, Osmania University.

Pathak, A. (1987). Media in Distance Education: Need for an Integrated Approach. In B.N. Koul et al. (eds.), *Studies in Distance Education*. New Delhi: AIU and IGNOU.

Patil, S.S. (1997). Management of Different Forms for Distance Education at Higher Education Stage in Karnataka and its Futures Towards 2005 A.D. *Ph.D. Education,* Devi Ahilya Vishwavidyalaya, Indore.

Perraton, H. (1988). A theory for distance education. In D. Sewart, D. Keegan, and B. Holmberg (eds.), *Distance Education: international Perspectives (*pp. 34-35). New York: Routledge.

Persons, H. and M. Catchpole (1987). The addition of audio-teleconferencing to interactive telecourses: An experimental analysis of dropout rates. *Distance Education*, 8(2), 251-258.

Pythian, T. and M. Clements (1980). Post-foundation tutorial planning. *Teaching at a Distance* 18 (Winter), 38-43.

Pillai, J.K. and Mohan, S. (1983). *Impact of Correspondence Education on Society*. Madurai Kamraj Univ. (Financed Project).

Pillai, J.K. and Mohan, S. (1984). Impact and Performance of Correspondence Education Programme of Madurai Kamraj University. *Ph.D., Education,* Madurai Kamraj University.

Pillai, S.S. (1988). Preparing a Database for Designing and Developing a Postgraduate Diploma in Teaching of English for Specific Purposes, Distance Learning Programme for Teachers of English in Professional Institutions in India. *Independent Study*. Madras: Technical Teachers Training Institute.

Prasad, V.S. (1987). APOU learner profile: A case study. In B.N. Koul et al. (eds.). *Studies in Distance Education*. New Delhi: AIU and IGNOU.

Pugazhenthi, G. (1991). A Study of Teacher Education Programme Through the Correspondence System in Madurai Kamaraj University. *Ph.D. Education,* The Maharaja Sayajirao University of Baroda.

Ram, S. (1984). An Evaluation of Correspondence Education in Terms of Cost and Academic Performance. *Ph.D. Education,* Meerut University.

Rathore, H.C.S. (1991). A Critical Evaluation of the Systems Adopted for Management of Teaching and Learning in the Existing Correspondence Institutes in India. *Independent Study*. New Delhi: National Institute of Educational Planning and Administration.

Reddy, Venugopal V. and Manjulika, S. (2002). *The World of Open and Distance Learning.* New Delhi: Viva Books Pvt. Ltd.

Robertson, C.C. (1981). A Comparison of Attitudes Toward and Achievement in Biology and Descriptive Characteristics Between Community College Students Enrolled in Alternative Instructional Modes. *Ph.D. Dissertation,* North Texas State University.

Robinson, B. (1981). Telephone tutoring in the open university: A review. *Teaching at a Distance*, 20 (Winter), 57-65.

Rosing, H. (1985). A Determination of the Effectiveness of an Audio-Tutorial Method of Learning in Teaching Mathematics to Academically Disadvantaged College Students. *Ph.D. Dissertation,* Loyola University of Chicago.

Rumble, G. (1989). On defining distance education. *The American Journal of Distance Education,* 3(2), 8-21.

Saba, F. (1989). Integrated telecommunications systems and instructional transaction. In Moore, M.G. and Smith, G.C. (eds.), *Readings in Principles of Distance Education*.

Sachchidananda (2002). Role of Academic Facilitation at Study Centres of NIOS in Bihar and Jharkhand. *Project Report*, New Delhi: NIOS.

Sahoo, P.K. (1985). A Study of Correspondence Education in an Indian University. *Ph.D. Education,* The Maharaja Sayajirao University of Baroda.

Sahoo, P.K. and Mucchal, M.K. (2001). Effectiveness of video instruction strategies in general science and social science at secondary stage of national open school. *OSAC Journal of Open Schooling*, 2(1), 58-73.

Sahoo, P.K. et al. (1997). Effectiveness of NOS video instructional materials with and without talk-back mode at secondary stage. *Educational Herald*, April-Dec.

Sakamoto, T. (1986). Take-off of the Japanese university of the air. *The American Journal of Distance Education*, 3(2).

Scales, K. (1984). A study of the relationship between telephone contact and persistence. *Distance Education*, 5(2), 268-276.

Shah, A. and Mandal, S. (1993). Use of modern and conventional media for distance education: An experiment. *Journal of Indian Education*, 19(1), 34-41.

Shale, D. (1988). Towards a reconceptualization of distance education. *The American Journal of Distance Education*, 2(3), 25-35.

Sharma, A.P. (2002). A Study of Organisation and Implementation of Personal Contact Programme run by the NIOS in Rajasthan. *Project Report*, New Delhi: NIOS.

Sharma, O.P. (1996). Attendance in personal contact programmes and performance of open learners – A correlational study. *Indian Journal of Open Learning*, 6(1 & 2), 71-75.

Sharma, P.N. (1999). Distance Education Programmes at Tertiary Level in Himachal Pradesh: An Evaluative Study. *Ph.D. Education,* Himachal Pradesh University, Shimla.

Sherry, L. (1996). Issues in Distance Education. *International Journal of Educational Telecommunications*, 1(4), 337-365.

Singh, B. (1987). Student Support Services. In B.N. Koul et al. (eds.), *Studies in Distance Education.* New Delhi: AIU and IGNOU.

Siqueira de Freitas, K. and P. Lynch (1986). Factors Affecting Student Success at the National Open University, Venezuela. *Distance Education*, 7(2), 191-200.

Smith, Eric E. (1987). Interactive Video: An Examination of Use and Effectiveness. *Journal of Instructional Development,* 20(2), 2-10.

Srivastava, M. (1995). Effectiveness of Distance Education: A Case Study of Karnataka State. *Ph.D. Education*, Jamia Millia Islamia.

Srivastava, R. (1995). Open Learning: Socio-Economic Analysis of NOS Learners. New Delhi: NOS, Mimeo.

Sujatha, K. (1989). Distance education at school level in India. *New Frontiers in Education*, 19(2).

Sutterfield, W.F. (1981). An Analysis of the Perceptions of Telecourse Students, Faculty, and Administrators at Tulsa Junior College. *Ed.D. Dissertation,* Oklahoma State University.

Tate, F.R.S. (1983). The Effect of Community College Students' Cognitive Style on Achievement in a Telecourse. *Ph.D. Dissertation,* Georgia State University, College of Education.

Taylor, J.C. et al. (1986). Student Persistence in Distance Education: A Cross Cultural, Multi-Institutional Perspective. *Distance Education,* 7(1), 68-91.

UGC and DEC (1993). Guidelines for Correspondence Education Programmes, IGNOU, New Delhi.

UGC, (2000). Correspondence and Distance Education Courses: Enrolment Statistics, 1995-96, New Delhi.

Upretti, D.C. (1988). Impact of Teacher Training Through Correspondence Course (B.Ed. SSCCC) on Upward Occupational Mobility of the Elementary Teacher in the Western Region. *Independent Study*. Bhopal: Regional College of Education.

Venkaiah, V. (2005) Educational Media in Dr. B.R.Ambedkar Open University with special reference to Teleconference, in Usha V.Reddi and Sanjaya Mishra (eds). Educational Media in Asia, Commonwealth of Learning.

Venkataiah, N. (1989). Preparation of course materials for distance education: Course team approach. *Indian Educational Review,* 24(4), 39-46.

Verghese, B.G. (2002). The Indian Idea: Towards Fraternity-III Emerging Diversity and The Imperative of Social Reform. *The Tribune*, August 14.

Wedemeyer, C.A. (1971). Independent Study. In *The Encyclopedia of Education*, L. Deighton (ed.), 548-557.

Weingartz, M. (1981). Ziff Research on Distance Education. *Distance Education*, 2(2).

Wiesner, P.K. (1986). Communication in Distance Learning: An Exploratory Field Study of Adults Enrolled in Telecourses Offered by New Jersey Community Colleges. *Ed.D. Dissertation,* Rutgers University.

Winders, R. (1985). Teleconferencing: Student interaction by telephone - The PACNET experience. *Programmed Learning and Educational Technology*, 22(4), 327-333.

Woodley, A. and M. Parlett (1983). Student drop-out. *Teaching at a Distance* 24 (Autumn), 2-23.

Wyllie Wydra, E.J. (1981). The Influence of Redundacy, Analogies, and Field Dependency Upon Learning of Scientific Materials from Audio-Tapes. *Ph.D. Dissertation,* Louisiana State University and Agricultural and Mechanical College.

Professor Lokesh Koul recently retired from Himachal Pradesh University, Shimla, India. He had been Head and Dean, Faculty of Education in the University.

SECTION VI

COLLABORATION, NETWORKING AND INTERNATIONALISATION

36

Institutional Networking and Resource Sharing

M.M. Pant and D.C. Pant

Introduction

Distance learning, its recent manifestation as e-learning, and its future incarnation as m-learning had initially been driven by the desire to reach out to learners who could not access the formal and mainstream educational system. In due course, it realised the potential of delivering learner-centred education. Today it is seen not so much as an education only for the 'have-nots' but as a form of education that can respond better to the specific needs of learners. It is seen as the most likely system to implement inclusive education, resulting in the universalisation of education at all levels. The overwhelming challenge to the system is one of maintaining a high quality learning experience, while catering to an ever growing student population, with increasingly reducing government funding. Moreover, because of knowledge explosion witnessed in the last decade, it is being increasingly realised that all the desired learner experience may not adequately be generated or supplied by a single institution. To respond to this paradigm shift more adequately and fulfil learner needs and institutional goals, many attempts in a variety of different ways have been made to enter into institutional collaborations, networking and resource sharing. In India, Distance Education Council has initiated steps to promote creation of a national pool of resources and national network of distance education institutions (IGNOU, 2004).

In this chapter, we have discussed the issue of institutional networking and resource sharing drawing upon the experience of computing technology, which has evolved from the very powerful mainframe computers of once upon a time, to PCs, the networked computers with distributed computing to now an all pervasive web-based platform, where the network is seen as the computer, and a failure of the network is intimately linked to the breakdown of computing environment. In the same model, the educational enterprises would also evolve as networked organisations, and may be in the future as educational grids, similar to the power grids, so that a learner would not even know all the sources from where the resources have originated in a given learning session.

Review of Earlier Work

A fairly comprehensive review of the state of networking has been done by Gupta et al (2004). They have cited some successful experiments spanning the variety of collaborative initiatives and it is hoped that fostering a paradigm shift to networked partnership would enable the gainful harnessing of the benefits offered by the latest technologies through useful synergies. They have also identified a few problems. We quote:

Networking and collaboration, in spite of their multifarious advantages, are not automatically designed to result into a positive sum game unless all stakeholders are prepared to invest effort in the smooth running of the collaborative effort. While Memorandum of Understanding or collaboration provide the legal and regulatory framework for collaboration and institutional networks, an attitudinal framework towards shared objectives and an institutional commitment towards the proliferation of these goals is what really makes a collaborative network hum with life and rise to desired productivity levels. Most conventional universities and quite a few ODL institutions have been found to be so engrossed in their own institutional operations and priorities, that collaborations are often reduced to be the subject matter of announcements from the podium, useful inclusions in the annual reports and indeed good boardroom discussion. According to Welukar and Deshpande (2002), individual institution accountability, evaluation of continuous performance, fostering a culture of open dissent, having flexible rather than rigid approach, willingness to invest the necessary time and talent of the participating institutions, dedication and commitment at all levels, and effective communication and focussed approach are key success factor, in an institutional collaborative activity. From our own experience, we have realised that the clarity of initial documentation of the agreement, complete procedural sanction and institutional commitment from concerned parties are the most important determinants of success of collaboration. Supportive top management, and continued support encompassing changes in leadership are the other vital requirements.

The solution, in their eyes is a better co-ordination and coherence amongst the UGC, AICTE and the DEC. Here we wish to place an educational and technology perspective on these, and suggest ways and means of progressing further.

Possibilities of Networking

What we are presenting here is an exploration of the core issues, which is in a way moving from the art of teaching to the Science of Learning, a thought initiated by Skinner when he developed the ideas of a teaching machine. From those initial path breaking ideas about half a century ago, when computers were not really around, to the recent exponentially progressing technologies and their convergence is leading to the possibility of reaching the ideal that we have been striving for in the creation of a Networked Learning Environment. Gupta et al (2004) have categorised collaborative and networking efforts as either national or international. This distinction is true for administrative and legal purposes, but from a technology perspective, these barriers have been overcome. But we may have possibly another dividing line, the digital divide in terms of the access routes of digital resources. We now have one set that is being digitally pampered in digital homes with ipods, blogs and podcasting at a level of their becoming personal broadcasters, and the other digitally starved, waiting their turn for a 100kbps stream to download the essential information and pursue the future learning in an off-line mode.

The possibilities of networking and resource sharing arise and would yield significant tangible benefits in the following areas:

- Learning resources
- Expertise in distance learning
- Subject matter experts
- Instructional design
- Academic credits
- Technological Infra-structure
- Evaluation techniques
- Mastery Learning
- Personalisation
- Access interfaces
- Quality Standards
- Professional developmental networks

While we will refer to several past experiences in forging such relationships, the thrust of our argument is to identify some fundamental issues that need to be resolved if the goals are to be achieved. We will not, in the interests of readability, cover each of the above items in detail, but rather focus on the two broad areas of 'content' and 'learning transactions', which between them cover the entire issues. In our view, content may be priceless or seem worthless depending on the quality of learning transactions. Many universities use the same books and the same curriculum, but still the quality of learning imparted has wide variations. Even within a university, there could be as many standards as individuals. There are many good expositions on quality and standards, and we will not repeat them here.

One of the simpler manifestations of networking and resource sharing is the use of course materials prepared by one institution as instructional resources by another institute. IGNOU encouraged other institutions to adopt or adapt materials developed by it to service their learners under policy guidelines and licensing agreements. However, in its relationship and lead role with other State Open Universities and Distance Education Institutes in conventional universities, it propelled the concept of a 'common pool of courses' that could be adopted/adapted/translated by others. This not only had implication of lower costs and high quality, it helped cut down lead time for the preparation of materials and offer of programmes, thereby contributing to achieve the Tenth Plan targets of 30-35% enrolments. Moreover, this concept helped share best practices, and innovation in their widest diversity. The teacher education programmes of Padmavati Mahila Vishvidyalaya, Tirupati is being adopted by S.V. University, Tirupati, whereas IGNOU materials have been translated by Maulana Azad National University in Urdu, Babasaheb Ambedkar Open University in Gujarati, by BRAOU in Telugu and so on. UPRTOU, VMOU and other open/conventional universities have adopted computer, management, tourism, and several others programmes of IGNOU and supplemented them with additional information.

The Commonwealth of Learning did a similar project of cooperatively developing materials for the management programme by national open universities in the SAARC region and then making it available for others to use. South Asia Foundation has adopted this approach for development of Environment and Sustainable Development Programme. IGNOU developed a programme on Intellectual Property Rights (IPR) in collaboration with WIPO and so on. Some distance learning institutions, typically Athabasca University and the University of South Pacific among others, adopted well known text books published by reputed publishers and then created 'wrap-around materials' and instructional guides for the course. The UKOU had also developed several courses around well accepted books. The IGNOU, in the early stages of offering of its computer programmes, also relied on such an approach.

Limitations

It comes as a surprise to many implementers of a flexible learning environment, how quickly many constraints start appearing in the ideal of anytime, anyplace any learning, which is the utopian goal of distance learning. In the early days of the IGNOU, many of its vision statements referred to the possibility of it being the only system where a student could study Physics and Philosophy concurrently. But the fact that this may not be really possible dawned upon us very quickly. Say to begin with, conceptually we begin with the general guideline that the undergraduate degree program is a three year program in which a student would take a load of 32 credits per year. If we have say 60 courses of 8 credits each, a student could choose typically 4 courses per year. Thus if all students would be free to choose any combination of the courses, the number of possible combinations would be 60´59´58´57/(4´3´2), which comes to 5´59´29´57 =1,95,054.

Handling the logistics of such a wide variety of possible combinations is almost unmanageable. For example, while making packets for dispatch, this would lead to deciding between course-wise dispatch or student-wise dispatch, and this is why the timely dispatch of course materials is itself a very major issue for distance learning institutions, particularly with large enrolment. The same multiplicity and complication will arise in assignment evaluation, Term-End Examination, entering grades and so on. Therefore, we can choose to restrict (i) enrolment and/or (ii) course offerings. While the former will have adverse implications for cost, the latter will reflect on quality. Therefore, a judicious combination will be one possible way out of this complexity. Alternatively, we digitise the course material, and create repositories. Every student can be given a password as practised in BIT and ADIT. With the emergence of portable data formats and the possibility of push technologies that the large scale distribution of personalized course materials has become a practical possibility.

Chunking of Course Materials

As said earlier, one of the basic reasons for not enough exchange of learning resources has been the large monolithic nature of university courses. The use of a credit system facilitates some level of learner mobility, but we need to get a little lower down in terms of giving legitimacy to fractional credits, almost to the last minute of didactic interaction. In a way, we are suggesting some kind of a nano-technology for multimedia learning materials (Table 1).

Table 1: Chunking of a multimedia course (fractional credits)

Sl. No.	Descriptor	Credit value	Duration of didactic interaction
1.	Course Module	3 to 6	45 to 90 hours
2.	Unit	1	15 hours
3.	Capsule	0.1	1.5 hours
4.	Session	0.05	45 minutes
5.	Nugget	0.025	22.5 minutes
6.	Sachet	0.02	18 minutes
7.	RLO/ crystal	0.01	9 minutes
8.	Granule	0.005	4.5 minutes
9.	Short learning object	0.001	54 seconds

There is a thumb-rule that for most courses, the additional amount of student effort put by a student is almost equal to that of the didactic component. In specific contexts, this could vary quite widely. While this may be a good thumb rule, it is possible to have detailed monitoring systems, that can now actually measure in great detail the student efforts, by measuring the reading rates, the activity patterns, the clickographic profiles etc. It is also possible to design an adaptive learning system, that can significantly reduce testing times as well as learning times.

Searching the Required Resource

From 1989, when Tim Berners Lee at CERN, created the web browser for rapid sharing of the results of their research by physicists, the Internet and the browser have totally transformed the ways to access electronic resources. By 1994, Amazon had created a system of sharing automated personalized recommendations; a model of peer to peer automated communication. By 1998, Google mesmerized the world by the highly successful search technology created by two Stanford University programmers. In 2002, Google created Google news, which was edited entirely by computer software and not by human editors. The year 2002 was also the year of the blog, which gave almost everyone a right and opportunity to publish on the net. Coupled with Friendster, the possibilities of social networks were being established. By 2004, Google had launched Gmail, a free e-mail service with 1 GB of storage, more than enough for any learner to store his 'content' and 'transactions' online. And when that would be exhausted, there were very light, handy USB drives, pen-drives, which could almost be classified as a fashion accessory. In brief, by 2005, anyone with access to a basic computer and Internet connection, has huge resources that could be accessed for free, even from profit making corporate entities. Add to that the opportunities from the Open Source Software Community, including free courses from institutions such as the MIT, and we have the kind of resources never seen before. By 2006, we would see the emergence of 'Grids' which would allow users to store and share media of all kinds, always on, always online.

Projecting these historical facts into the future and with cooperation and competition between the major players such as Microsoft, Yahoo, and Google, the dream of 'information on tap' fit for use by the learner or teacher would have been realised. Ironically though by the same time any possibility of 'potable drinking water on tap' would possibly have been forgotten. This would happen in the next 5 to 10 years by which time, the world's information would have been organized and made universally accessible and useful. Some people have referred to this as EPIC, an Evolved Personalised Information Construct, to which everyone contributes, and from which everyone draws upon, with tools for filtering, ordering, prioritising, delivering deeper understanding, a broader coverage and nuanced in the way the user wants.

In the past decade, several educational organisations have, instead of focusing on the core issue of an improved teaching learning process, got diverted with creating technologies, and while some of them have been able to create packaged products for use by others, many have lost their direction as well as their money, having found themselves marginalized by better technologies that became mainstream.

What we are trying to suggest is that the basic technologies should be the pervasive and ubiquitous. Educators need to collaborate to deliver learning and research.

Reconciling Quantity with Quality

It has been almost axiomatic that with increasing numbers, the quality of the learner experience would decline, and many of our regulating bodies have created policies to have a large number of institutions each of which cater to a small number of students. However, this has only ensured rapid decline in the quality of instruction in the lower 50% of the institutions. The right implementation of distance learning deploying current and emerging technologies allows the possibilities of creating mega-trans-national universities with consistent deliveries. The recent initiative of GoI to establish a VSAT based infrastructure for connecting all 53 African Union countries is an excellent initiative in international cooperation and use of technology (2005) for empowerment and raising the quality of life of fellow human beings. Under this initiative, a network of satellite and fibre optics based centres is being created to provide electronic and knowledge connectivity for tele-education, tele-medicine, Internet, videoconferencing and support e-governance, e-commerce, infotainment, resource mapping and meteorological services connectivity. It is envisaged to connect five universities, 53 learning centres, 10 super speciality hospitals and 53 patient-end locations. The content shall be provided by IGNOU and AIIMs, New Delhi. Recent collaborative initiatives of SACODiL and GMUNET on cross-border delivery of education also have genesis in the realisation that, if managed well, we can increase our pool of learning resources for the well-being of our societies.

It is clear now that successfully networked institutions, both conventional and modern, will be able to bring together synergies that would result in creating a learning experience that may be significantly superior to the limited experience in a single Institution classroom. To illustrate, let us just consider one aspect. In a traditional institution, all learners are given an opportunity to hear the same set of lectures (often in groups of about 50 students), access to the same notes and library resources, but at the examination time there is the standard Bell type distribution of grades suggestive of the normal distribution curve. The major paradigm shift that can be brought about is that the bell curve could be transformed to a flat curve, with almost no failures, somewhat along the goals of six sigma in manufacturing. By having access to a variety of learning resources, which a learner can transact according to his/her needs, he/she can achieve the goals of mastery learning. Just imagine a system with millions of enrolled students, each of them being able to produce full evidence of all the competencies and skills that were the goals of learning agreed to at the outset. The paths that they traverse would differ, but they would all arrive at the same destination, and no waste of human resources. It means that search for self-actualisation is more important in the context of quality of output; contemporary ICT in fact can accommodate large numbers and expanded logistic operations at high quality and that too efficiently.

The Road Ahead

From one point of view, which is what we are developing, the role of institutions of higher learning is the transition from primarily an information dissemination institution to a knowledge creation organization. If we extrapolate the effect of the convergence between different technologies and the rapid innovations in them, it is clear that in a decade from now, access to information would have been facilitated to a level, where almost everyone can get the bare information needed or prescribed. The recent rapid strides in wireless technologies from infra-red, to blue-tooth to Wi-fi and on the horizon Wi-max will further boost the wireless access to the networks through a range of portable and hand-held devices; the ideas of science fiction are now a reality! But the challenge would be to handle the information overload, have assurance that the information provided is valid and authentic, and that the learner has acquired the skills to be able to deploy the available information in meaningful contexts and for informed decision making.

This would mean the need for specialists in various areas to work together with educationists and researchers in cognitive sciences. The implication for the teacher in the classroom would change completely; from storehouse of knowledge to a facilitator and motivator. Moreover, he will be required to be constantly upgrading himself to be able to respond to learners and command respect.

Some concrete action points that need to be worked upon are as follows:

- Creating an enabling framework for collaboration and sharing of resources. It is unfortunate that as of now, the regulating bodies neither promote nor accept any sharing of resources, human or otherwise.
- The management of the Intellectual Property of the contributing institutions as well as the individuals would be a critical factor. This can be either by implementing the TRIPS principles or the alternative of 'creative commons' or both.
- A separation of the functions of teaching, evaluation and certification and of curriculum and qualification framework, and standards driven quality mechanisms, rather than ad-hoc arbitrary inspector oriented approach, much like the separation of the executive, legislature and the judiciary in governance.
- Sponsoring a repository of re-usable learning objects, of various denominations, as mentioned in Table 1.
- An agreed set of meta-data standards to allow a rapid and useful exchange of such learning resources. They would have to be related to SCORM in some way, but in detail our own.
- Given the individual and competitive nature of institutional identities, an external voluntary set-up such as the Internet standard may help a form a better glue, and allow the academics join the group in their individual capacities as well. We need a fraternity of independent researchers and educators to get this really going. Sometime in the future, they could get up and say 'Yes, we did start the FIRE".
- An important issue that must be adequately addressed is the training and orientation of all 'dramatis persona' into the principles and methods of the new model. Assuming that the migration is easy has led to many disappointments. A short course on 'learning to e-learn' is important for all participants
- The emergence of mobile technologies and hand-held devices such as smartphones, PDA's, ipods etc. must be acknowledged as the most effective way to connect to learners. Hence the importance to chunking referred earlier and the possibilities of creating media that can be delivered to such devices as MP3 audio files and short video clips. We must remember that the latest ipod that has been recently launched can hold 150 hours of video, about 1000 hours of audio and a large amount of text and images. More than enough for a semester worth of learning resources for a learner.

The tasks listed above are challenging, but not impossible. Distance learning has already travelled a long and arduous path from being just acceptable, to some parity of esteem, to showing promise, to being seen as the possible solution to universal education, and now may actually emerge as the superior learning experience riding upon universally available technology. It is indeed reminiscent of the story of the 'ugly duckling who turned into a swan'.

References

Gupta, S., Kaushik, M. and Garg, S. (2004). Networking and collaboration in open distance education. *Indian Journal of Open Learning,* 13 (3), 293-302.

IGNOU (2004). *Annual Report: 2003-04*. New Delhi: IGNOU.

Welukar, R.M. and Deshpande, S. (2002). Growing together through consortium. *University News*, 40, 51.

Prof. M.M. Pant and Shri D.C. Pant are former Pro-Vice Chancellors of IGNOU.
Email: Professor@MMPant.org; dineshpant@hotmail.com

37

National, Regional and Global Collaborations

S.R. Jha, Sanjay Gupta and Suresh Garg

Introduction

The phenomenal growth of Open and Distance Learning (ODL) system in India in the last two decades is a testimony to the increasing demand for education, in general, and higher education in particular. The system has attracted learners due to some of its unique features such as relaxed entry criteria and flexibility of space and time. This has resulted into enrolment of astronomical number of learners. Further, recent developments in the field of education such as Dakar Declaration on basic education for all by 2015 and policy initiatives such as *Sarva Siksha Abhiyan* are bound to increase demands on the ODL system in the coming years. It is projected that by the end of year 2007, about 40 percent students with multidimensional diversity are likely to enrol in the ODL institutions for higher education.

We have to innovate and try different strategies to address the issues likely to emerge in the field of higher education because of large numbers, lack of funds, increasing demand for on-job training, entry of for-profit organisations in education, growing emphasis of the Governments and policy makers to link education with holistic – social, political and economical – development of people, growing demand for online learning, shift from teacher-centredness to learner-centredness, global competition and the resulting demands on quality and cost-effectiveness, commodification of education, etc. Bilateral and multilateral collaboration with a variety of institutions/organisations is a useful tool to tackle these multifaceted challenges facing higher education.

It is perhaps a fortunate coincidence that evolution of the ODL system and its ethos was accompanied by local as well as global developments in the field of education, which made it imperative for ODL institutions to enter into collaboration with sister and peer conventional institutions. Since its inception, the ODL system has been conscious of not to reinvent the wheel. It has been a policy driven endeavour to pool the best available academic expertise for the design and development of quality learning materials and collaborate with the local institutions to use their academic and physical infrastructure for effective delivery of educational programmes. These practices are so pervasive among the ODL institutions, particularly in Indira Gandhi National Open University (IGNOU), that team work, collaboration and partnership have evolved as the ethos of open and distance education in India. Such systemic ethos resonate well with the need for collaboration to address contemporary issues.

In recent years, we have witnessed the creation of inter-university consortia, enhancement in the scale of operation of the institutions of higher education and tendency to pool resources to reduce costs and raise the quality of education. An impetus to all these developments has been provided by the revolutionary transformation and rapid growth of Information and Communication Technologies (ICT). Their application in the delivery of education has thrown open a world of opportunities and challenges to the institutions of higher education. However, owing to its ethos and ability to adapt to the needs of the times, the ODL system is in an advantageous position and has been able to evolve positive responses to these developments (IGNOU, 2005). In this chapter, we have discussed some of the important national, regional (within South Asia) and global collaborations forged by open education institutions to keep pace with changing demands of learners. We begin by outlining the areas of collaboration.

Areas of Collaboration

Collaboration may be defined as a well laid down relationship between two or more institutions for achieving common goal(s), which otherwise may be difficult for any single institution, conventional or open. An added dimension of collaboration amongst ODL institutions is learning from each other by sharing experiences and the best practices. Since development and delivery of educational programmes by an ODL institution involves a variety of activities, collaboration can be in one or more than one areas. Some of the important areas of collaboration include:

- curriculum design and development;
- development of learner-friendly study materials;
- devising appropriate teaching-learning strategies;
- certification;
- funding and sharing of financial responsibilities;
- learner support services;
- research and innovation; and
- application and development of ICTs to enrich learning experiences.

The above list is by no means exhaustive. With the success of various collaborative ventures, ODL institutions are entering into collaboration with institutions/organisations of diverse background with the ultimate objective to serve the learners better. The reasons for collaboration could be financial, technological, pooling of expertise or catering to specialised needs.

Financial: Bringing down the cost of programme production and delivery is one of the major incentives for collaboration. Since development of learning material involves considerable expenditure and is one of the major activities of ODL institutions, pooling of expertise and resources helps reduce the cost of programme production and delivery with lower per unit cost. Many a times, depending upon the similarity of curriculum, it is more cost-effective for institutions to adopt/adapt/translate high quality and widely accepted learning materials from another institution rather than develop it from scratch. Distance Education Council (DEC), IGNOU is facilitating this through creation of a national pool of the best print materials and digital repositories. Such economy measures have helped ODL institutions to be self-sustaining with negligible dependence on state finances. IGNOU, in fact, has committed, out of its own resources, about 25% funds of the total 10th Plan (2002-03 to 2006-07) budget for ODL system in the country.

Technological: Providing opportunities to its learners for interaction with peers and teachers is an important ingredient of the learner support services in the ODL system to overcome one of the serious systemic limitations, namely, the sense of isolation felt by the learners. The availability of EduSat exclusively for education has opened fertile vistas for videoconferencing and Internet based interaction channels. In fact, it is now possible to deliver tele-education and educate people all over the country simultaneously. IGNOU is leading a movement for establishing collaborations between ICT rich and ICT poor institutions. We now have virtual universities and consortia to offer online education and tele-education. Soon IGNOU shall provide education to the people in 53 African Union countries.

Niche and specialised learner needs: Demand for on-job training, upgradation of knowledge and skills and customised training/educational programmes for a relatively small group of learners is increasing with time. It is neither desirable nor feasible for any institution to possess human resources and other infrastructure in-house to cater to all such demands. More and more institutions are collaborating with industry and/or national and international professional bodies/ specialised institutions/corporate houses for development and delivery of such programmes. For instance, IGNOU is offering the programme on Nautical Sciences in collaboration with Directorate General of Shipping, Govt. of India (GoI) and for motor mechanics in collaboration with Hero Honda, a corporate house. Similarly, State Open Universities (SOUs) are offering computer education programmes in collaboration with private providers such as IBM, NIIT, etc.

We now describe the major collaborative ventures initiated by IGNOU at the national, regional and global levels.

National Collaborations

In the past few years, IGNOU has entered into collaboration with a variety of academic institutions and professional organisations – conventional universities, SOUs, national institutes of repute, corporate world and industries and the Ministries of Central Government and State Governments. These collaborations are for one or more of the following purposes:

- joint programme offerings;
- developing customised educational/training programmes;

- sharing programme delivery networks;
- capacity building;
- institutional networking;
- sharing learning materials; and
- quality assurance.

With universities

- IGNOU offers its programmes in English and Hindi languages. In order to enhance access to Urdu speaking population and overcome the language of transaction as a barrier for learning, it entered into collaboration with the Maulana Azad National Urdu University (MANUU), Hyderabad to offer Bachelor of Education, Post Graduate Diploma in Journalism and Mass Communication and programmes in area of Food and Nutrition in Urdu language. Under the arrangement, IGNOU's learning materials have been translated into Urdu language by the MANUU and the programme is delivered by MANUU. The final degree (B.Ed) will be awarded jointly. The admission criteria for various programmes and their assessment have been adopted from IGNOU to maintain uniformity and standards. This collaboration was prompted by the needs of the people of educationally disadvantaged sections of the society, who had had their secondary and higher education in Urdu language. Similarly, Baba Saheb Ambedkar Open University, Dr. B.R. Ambedkar Open University, and Tamil Nadu Open University have translated IGNOU study materials into Gujarati, Telugu and Tamil languages, respectively.
- Lalit Narayan Mithila University (LNMU), Darbhanga is a conventional university and has started its distance education operations recently. Apart from the Bachelors Degree Programme, LNMU wishes to offer a variety of programmes in the field of food and nutrition, computer literacy, etc. through distance mode. It has, therefore, entered into collaboration with IGNOU to use its learning materials for programmes in these areas. Since LNMU caters to a large geographic area in north Bihar through its affiliated colleges, it is hoped that this collaborative arrangement will take quality academic programmes to hitherto unreached areas and LNMU will be saved from duplication of efforts in developing the learning package. IGNOU has entered into similar agreements with Jadavpur University, Tamil Virtual University, among others.
- IGNOU has been collaborating in the areas of sharing of resources and capacity building with the State Open Universities and Correspondence Courses Institutes of conventional universities through DEC. One of the major initiatives undertaken by IGNOU through DEC in recent years is the creation of national repository of learning materials, training initiatives in multimedia supported course design and development. This collaborative initiative among ODL institutions in the country provides single window service to all the new institutions. The advantages of creation of such a repository would be to minimise the lead time in offering new programmes, ensure cost-effectiveness, maintain quality and provide uniform education. All open and a large number of conventional universities are availing the facility.

With national institutions of repute

- IGNOU has been collaborating with Indian Space Research Organisation (ISRO) since 1992 with the objective of creating ICT resources. We established Extended C-Band supported vast teleconferencing network and Ku-Band supported satellite interactive terminals. With IGNOU being designated as the nodal institution for the utilisation of EduSat, this collaboration has acquired added dimensions: capacity building, creation and transmission of courseware, evolving strategies to enhance interactivity between learners and teachers. The successful operationalisation of EduSat is a testimony of effective working of the collaboration between these two organisations.
- The collaboration of IGNOU and Harishchandra Research Institute (HRI), Allahabad, a premier research institution under the Department of Atomic Energy, GoI, has facilitated introduction of high quality Integrated Ph.D. Programmes in Physics andMathematics. The candidates are selected through a rigorous process of testing and interviews. This is in consonance with the mandate of IGNOU to further the cause of higher education in India by promoting quality research.
- IGNOU is collaborating with Narayana Hrudayalaya, Bangalore to develop an academic programme in the field of Community Cardiology for medical graduates. This is an outcome of the shared vision of the two collaborating institutions that there is a growing need of training and updating the knowledge of medical practitioners in the village and remote areas about basic skills and recent developments in cardiac care.
- IGNOU entered into collaboration with the National Institute of Fashion Technology (NIFT) for offering dual degree programme. Under this arrangement, learners pursuing full-time educational programme at NIFT were allowed to simultaneously enrol in IGNOU's Bachelor in Computer Applications (BCA) programme. The objective was to provide an opportunity to learners to simultaneously earn two degrees so that they have wider career options.
- To improve the quality of life of persons with autism, cerebral plasy, mental retardation and multiple disabilities, the University is collaborating with the Rehabilitation Council, the National Trust and the National Association of Blind for design, development and implementation of capacity building and leadership training programmes for such persons. Recognising the need to sensitise people, in general, and administrators and local level functionaries, in particular, towards disability issues, the collaborating institutions are also organising joint teleconference programmes to reach out to them.
- Recently, IGNOU signed an Memorandum of Understanding (MoU) with Lal Bahadur Shastri National Academy of Administration for offer of Master's Level Programme in Public Policy to the probationers of Indian Administrative Service (IAS).

With the ministries of the government of India and state governments

- IGNOU has collaborated with the Ministry of Human Resource Development (MHRD), GoI to develop a variety of specialised educational and training programmes. Under this collaboration, a certificate level programme on empowering women's self-help groups has been developed and anyone above the age of 18 and having functional literacy can join the programme. To enhance the interaction between the women's self-help groups spread across the country and teachers and professional experts in the area, 150 direct satellite receive terminals have been established for regular teleconferencing. For the *Navodaya Vidyalaya Samiti* under the MHRD, IGNOU has developed the Postgraduate Certificate Programme for professional development of the PG teachers of *Navodaya Vidyalayas*. The programme aims at acquainting teachers with innovative teaching-learning methods, content upgradation and personality enrichment. Also, the collaboration between IGNOU and MHRD has resulted in the development of the Postgraduate Diploma in Intellectual Property Rights to cater to the emerging need, in globalised society, to safeguard indigenous as well as new knowledge created by human minds.

- In collaboration with the Ministry of Rural Development, GoI, IGNOU has developed a training and education programme for the elected members of the village *Panchayats* to enhance awareness about their roles and responsibilities in management of developmental activities at the grassroots. The programme has been received well all over the country and various state governments have shown keen interest in adapting it at the local level.
- IGNOU, in collaboration with the Ministry of Agriculture, GoI has developed customised awareness level educational/training packages to sensitise and motivate people engaged in the agriculture sector for adoption and application of scientific principles and practices. It is hoped that such an educational intervention will lead to enhancement in productivity and ensure the quality of product of this vital sector of the national economy.
- In collaboration with the Ministry of Food Processing, GoI, IGNOU is developing customised vocational and entrepreneurial education and training programmes for the workforce engaged in the food processing industry like fruits and vegetables, dairy, poultry and meat, fish and aquaculture and grains, pulses and oil seeds. The collaboration is aimed at training people in modern techniques in these areas so as to ensure value addition.
- State Govts. of Jammu and Kashmir (J&K), Jharkhand and Chhattisgarh have shown keen interest in the educational programme developed by IGNOU for training their primary school teachers. The programme was originally developed for the untrained, in-service primary/elementary school teachers of the North-Eastern States and Sikkim. As a result of collaboration between these State Govts. and IGNOU, 7000 teachers from J&K, 18000 teachers from Jharkhand and 5000 teachers from Chhattisgarh have been sponsored for the Diploma in Primary Education (DPE) programme of the University. Such collaborations have been prompted to meet the demand for trained teachers at the primary level in view of the national commitment towards universalisation of elementary education.
- IGNOU has collaborated with different wings namely Army, Navy, Air Force, Assam Rifles and Central Reserve Police Force (CRPF), Ministry of Defence, GoI to provide single window service to the personnel of these organisations desirous of enrolling in the academic programmes of IGNOU.

- The collaboration between IGNOU and the Directorate General of Shipping (DGS), Ministry of Shipping, GoI has resulted in development and launch of a full-fledged Bachelors Degree Programme in Nautical Sciences. Since India is a major provider of workforce for the shipping industry world wide, the demand for highly skilled and trained cadets and the job potential for them is very high. The development and delivery of this high quality programme in mixed-mode is the outcome of the synergy of the academic expertise available at IGNOU and the skill training expertise of DGS recognised institutions. 50% training is provided in face-to-face (F2F) mode and the other half through distance mode.

With corporate world/industry/small and medium enterprises

- Recognising the need of on-job training and skill upgradation of persons, mostly from the marginalised sections of the society, IGNOU has forged many collaborative ventures. For example, user-friendly training materials have been developed for persons working or aspiring to work in the footwear industry, in collaboration with the Footwear Design and Development Institute (FDDI), Noida (UP). This is expected to enhance the quality of their product and make it globally acceptable at competitive prices. Similarly, a training programme in pottery design and production has been launched in collaboration with Khadi and Village Industries Commission (KVIC) for rural artisans with Construction Industry Development Council (CIDC) for construction workers to and technical staff in our defence services help uplift their quality of life. Educational programmes are being developed for generating skilled workforce in agriculture, food processing, sericulture, bamboo and rattan in collaboration with various ministries and government agencies. These systematic efforts are expected to empower the excluded and marginalised significantly.
- IGNOU has entered into collaboration with Hero Honda Motors Limited (HHML) to jointly develop a training programme for the development of trade level skilled manpower across the country for motorcycle servicing and repair.

Regional Collaborations

The countries in the South Asian region, namely, India, Pakistan, Bangladesh, Sri Lanka, Nepal, Bhutan and Maldives are characterised by common features; they face similar problems in the areas of health, environment, human rights and development. The recognition of the role of education to improve the state of affairs in all these areas led the chief executives of ODL institution in these countries to put in place collaborative mechanisms so as to learn from each other's experiences and explore the possibilities of joint development and delivery of educational programme to meet common objectives. IGNOU, being the national ODL institution in the Region, has been at the forefront of this endeavour, coordinating various activities and programmes with sister institutions in the countries of the region. IGNOU has been closely associated with the following two significant regional collaborative arrangements.

SAARC Consortium of Open and Distance Learning (SACODiL)

SACODiL is a collaborative arrangement among the ODL institutions in the South Asian Association for Regional Cooperation (SAARC) countries. It came into existence due to the initiatives taken at the Summit meeting of the Heads of State or Governments of the SAARC countries in 1998. The realisation that South Asia has one-fifth of the world's population and nearly half of the world's illiterate people led them to forge this joint venture, as the conventional education system in the member countries would not be able to meet the goals of E-9 initiative.

The broad objectives of the consortium are:

- sharing resources, including courses, and personnel currently available at collaborating institutions;
- joint development of programmes/courses;
- evolving mechanisms for credit transfer, accumulation and accreditation; and
- using ICT infrastructure to reach out to remote and under-privileged sections of the society.

The responsibility for determining the principles, policies and priorities that will guide the activities of SACODiL, to function as a regional platform for cooperation and collaboration are vested in the Board of Governors, which comprise the Vice Chancellors of the National Open Universities and the Heads of major open and distance learning institutions in member countries. The first meeting of the Board of Governors of the SACODiL was held at IGNOU, New Delhi in January 2005 with Vice Chancellor, IGNOU as the first Chair of Board of Governors for three years w.e.f. January 1, 2005. The action plan for activities to be taken up on a priority basis was formulated and the following areas were identified for immediate action (SACODiL, 2005):

- collaboration with UNESCO, COL, DFID(UK) and other international agencies for the implementation of regional programmes to further enhance the scale of operation;
- mutual recognition of Bachelors degrees awarded to students coming out of formal pattern of schooling, that is 12+3 years, to facilitate learner mobility from one member country to another without jeopardising his/her education. Further, norms are being developed to facilitate credit transfer;
- ensure compatibility of software used by participating institutions to harness the potential of ICT in the collaborative venture in the best possible manner;
- use EduSat for interaction;
- work towards attainment of Millennium Development Goals (MDGs) identified by UNESCO;
- create a database of best practices in the ODL institutions in the region; and
- develop SACODiL repository for research and digital library.

The SACODiL secretariat, located at IGNOU organised training workshops at IGNOU and Open University of Sri Lanka (OUSL) in interactive multimedia and reviewed the progress towards attainment of MDGs.

South Asia Foundation (SAF)

The leading open universities (IGNOU, AIOU, BOU, BRAC, BRAOU, OUSL) in the SAARC nations came together and jointly developed PG Diploma Programme in Environment and Sustainable Development. This collaboration was supported by the South Asia Foundation (SAF), a non-profit, philanthropic organisation, with its headquarters in Switzerland and regional offices in each of the SAARC countries. SAF seeks to promote cooperation, peace, understanding and progress through education and sustainable development among the people of South Asia in areas such as environment and sustainable development, women's empowerment, human rights, preservation of heritage and culture, peace and cooperation.

The collaborative venture took shape in a meeting of the Vice-Chancellors of the leading open universities of SAARC nations in the year 2002 in France, where the need for collaboration among these institutions was articulated. It was agreed that the expertise available in the region could be fruitfully harnessed for the development and delivery of educational programmes in the areas of common interest. Some salient features of the multilateral collaborative initiative are:

- Collaboration among the institutions is coordinated and facilitated (by way of funding the developmental cost of learning materials) by SAF and at the same time, each participating institution collaborates with SAF in an autonomous manner.
- The educational programmes are designed and developed jointly in which each participating institution provides the expertise available with it and shares experiences with each other.
- Though the educational programmes are developed in a collaborative mode, each participating institution has the freedom to adapt the courses as per the local needs and conditions before launching it in their respective countries.

The Post-Graduate Diploma in Environment and Sustainable Development (PGD-ESD) was developed jointly by six open universities from India, Pakistan, Sri Lanka and Bangladesh, each country contributing at least two courses. In all, nine courses were developed. There was a clear distribution of responsibilities of each participating institution in respect of joint design and development of the programme and the related administrative requirements of the participating institutions to launch this programme in their countries.

The curriculum design of the programme was finalised on the basis of draft curriculum received from each country and subsequently, participating institutions were given the responsibility to develop one or more courses. The courses so developed were made available to each institution with the freedom to adapt the same as per local requirements. In this manner, the lead-time for the development of course material was reduced drastically and at the same time, learners in each country benefited from the experiences (presented in the form of case studies in the course materials) pertaining to environment and sustainable development in the neighbouring countries.

As per the implementation strategy agreed upon, ODL institutions from each country entered into a separate collaboration with SAF for launching the programme.

Global Collaborations

At present, IGNOU has about thirty five joint collaborations with institutions in thirty countries around the world, which have resulted in the offer of 22 programmes in areas such as Management, Computer and Information Sciences, Teacher Training, Tourism, Nursing, Commerce, Liberal Arts, Intellectual Property Rights, etc. This has benefited Indian diaspora, particularly in the Middle-East and Africa. We mention here some significant milestones in these collaborative ventures (IGNOU, 2004 and 2005).

Commonwealth of Learning (COL)

IGNOU developed Commonwealth Executive Master of Business Administration (CEMBA) Programme in collaboration with AIOU, OUSL and BOU under the umbrella of COL. The broad objective of the CEMBA programme was to offer new/complement the existing MBA programmes currently on offer in the Commonwealth countries to meet the social and professional demands for management education at the post-graduate level and contribute to national development. A similar programme in the area of Public Administration, namely the Commonwealth Executive Master of Public Administration (CEMPA) has also been developed by IGNOU in collaboration with COL. COL has also collaborated with SOUs, UGC, NCERT, NAAC and other such institutions in as diverse areas as agriculture, teacher education, media studies, distance education, street children, among others.

Commonwealth Secretariat

The Commonwealth Youth Programme (CYP) is the outcome of a long-term partnership between Commonwealth Secretariat, IGNOU and a few other universities in the commonwealth. This programme is intended to train youth for development work through the distance mode. The programme has unique modules that are being offered as stand alone packages, which lead to Certificate/Diploma level certification. A few regional modules have also been added on family life education and personality development.

IGNOU – WIPO collaboration

A Postgraduate Diploma Programme in Intellectual Property Rights has been developed by IGNOU in collaboration with World Intellectual Property Organisation (WIPO) to create awareness about intellectual property rights, sensitise people about the need to safeguard indigenous knowledge as well as new knowledge. It has been received well by the professionals as also scientists all over the country.

IGNOU – CHRC – NHRC collaboration

A tripartite collaboration between IGNOU, the Canadian Human Rights Commission (CHRC) and the National Human Rights Commission (NHRC) of India has resulted in a series of ongoing workshops and internship programmes for the protection and promotion of human rights, particularly, those of people with disabilities.

UNESCO initiatives

IGNOU, in collaboration with UNESCO and MPBOU, Bhopal has developed training modules and resource kits for training of in-service primary teachers in the area of ICT-enabled basic education. The objective of this collaborative venture is to enable teachers to use various educational softwares in teaching and learning of mathematics, English language and environment education. Another collaborative venture between IGNOU and UNESCO led to implementation of training programmes for university science teachers from South Asian countries and professionals working in the field of ICT-enabled education. These training programmes were particularly focussed to benefit people living in remote and less developed areas, village level developmental functionaries, local self-government functionaries, etc.

Collaboration with CGIAR

Facilitated by the International Food Policy Research Institute (IFPRI), IGNOU is collaborating with the Consultative Group on International Agricultural Research (CGIAR) to work with the Global Open Food and Agriculture University (GO-FAU) to develop and deliver distance learning programmes for improvement of knowledge and skills of the students of agriculture science and professionals working in the agriculture sector.

Global Mega-Universities Network (GMUNET)

GMUNET came into being in the year 2003 in Shanghai, China in response to UNESCO's call for international cooperation in distance and open learning for achieving the goal of Education for All. Four mega universities from India (IGNOU, BRAOU, YCMOU and MPBOU) joined the network. It underlined the role of open and distance education in building a globalised, interdependent and learning society, bridging the digital divide and the knowledge gap between and within nations.

In the first world Summit of Mega-Universities, participants from 15 mega-universities deliberated on the challenges and opportunities facing the ODL system globally and discussed strategies based on innovation and collaboration for the same. GMUNET took a concrete shape in the Second World Summit of Mega Universities held in New Delhi in 2005 under the auspices of IGNOU. The broad objectives of GMUNET included in the joint declaration were to (GMUNET, 2005):

- promote collaboration among mega-universities for curriculum design, development and delivery, research, exchange of experts, assessment and analysis of market demands, cost effectiveness, etc.;
- promote joint offering of programmes at all levels;
- act as a forum for advocating the cause of ODL in development agencies; and
- promote the use of ICT and ICT-enabled technologies in all operations of the ODL system and sharing of resources and expertise for the same.

A very compact organisational structure has been put in place for the GMUNETcomprising the Chairperson, Vice Chairperson and the Secretary for planning, organising, coordinating and evaluating activities in the following areas:

- Quality assurance in distance education
- Research and development
- Innovative application of ICT for delivery of education
- Education for community development.

The world level Summit of the Network will be held every three years to monitor the progress and chart the future course of action.

The success of the experiences narrated here has established the fact that collaboration is the need of the hour at national, regional and global levels. However, the path to success has been strewn with manifold challenges and has thrown up several issues that need to be addressed to make the most out of the collaborative ventures. We highlight some major issues.

Collaboration: Issues and Challenges

Though it seems obvious for institutions to collaborate for the ensuing benefits, working out and implementing a collaborative arrangement is a daunting task for a variety of reasons: funding, ownership, possible mismatch in the visions of the collaborating institutions, organisational structure, work ethics, lack of perfect understanding amongst collaborating institutions, etc. It requires a very high level of maturity, persuasive power and participation on the part of leaders of such collaborative ventures. Before entering into any collaborative arrangement with other institutions/ organisations, an ODL institution must analyse their needs, strengths and weaknesses, context of collaborative venture, objectives to be achieved collectively, and the work culture, motivation and track record of other institutions/organisations.

The growing emphasis on universalisation of primary education and consequent demand on the higher education in the next few years, the gradual shift towards vocationalisation of secondary and higher education, democratisation of higher education due to conscious policy decisions in the developing countries are bound to increase pressure on the ODL system both in terms of numbers and availability of funds. The educational programmes have to be diversified in view of the contemporary socio-economic needs of the people. An increasing demand for accountability also keeps ODL institutions on their toes. The rapidly growing demand for education has been accompanied by the rise of market forces in this sector spurred by globalisation and liberalisation.

All these factors place a demand on the collaborating institutions to considerably shorten their transit response time to develop up-to-date tailor made programmes for various segments of the population. This requires quick decision making and rapid adaptability of the system to the demands placed on them. The conventional methods of discussions, parleys and deliberations in face-to-face meetings may soon have to give way to quickly organised video/audio conferencing facilitated by the ICT for reducing the time lags between designing developing and implementing programmes and for ironing out problems.

The World Trade Organisation's (WTO) General Agreement on Trade in Services (GATS) has influenced the higher education scenario globally. GATS is a multilateral agreement under which WTO members commit voluntary liberalisation of trade in services, including education. Under GATS, education has been recognised as a tradable service, which has *inter-alia* brought in commodification of education. The most significant impact of this development has been the growing role of market forces, the entry of for-profit organisations and emergence of trans-national education providers. The market forces guided by the logic of demand and supply have begun to control the affairs of education as a business enterprise with little concern for the broader objectives of education for human development. These developments have tended to increase operational costs, marginalise philosophical and literary pursuits, stifle the advancement of knowledge and render both theoretical and liberal education irrelevant. If national governments do not evolve suitable guidelines, the consequences may be more serious particularly for the ODL system than envisaged, since, for technological reasons, the multinational educational enterprises find it easier to enter the field of distance education through online/joint offerings. The publicly funded, non-profit ODL institutions are facing stiff competition from private, for-profit educational institutions. This calls for ever increasing collaboration and formation of consortia among non-profit educational institutions in order to collectively compete with the market forces by cutting costs, improving quality, enhancing access to diverse educational and training demands.

An analysis of the experience so far brings to the fore the failure of conventional higher education institutions in producing appropriately trained workforce as per the socio-economic requirements of the country. For example, India has one of the largest systems of higher education with 336 Universities and about 18,000 colleges which together produce millions of 'trained' human capital every year. Yet the country is faced with the dilemma of an unemployable workforce and shortage of appropriately trained human capital in traditional sectors of the national economy such as agriculture, civil infrastructure, cottage industry, etc. as well as the rapidly expanding modern sectors of economy such as IT, telecommunication, etc. There seems to be a yawning gap between the demands of the economy and the 'supply' of skilled and employable workforce from educational institutions. This is also due to the fast pace of technological developments in the manufacturing and service sector and equally fast rate of obsolence of technology. Thus, on-job training and upgradation of knowledge and skills should figure higher in the priorities of higher education. However, due to their inherent structural rigidities, conventional institutions of higher education are unable to meet these demands. This mismatch can however be actively addressed by the ODL system by practising ethos of sharing and collaboration. The challenge lies in a rapid assessment of the real socio-economic needs and demands and offering capacity building programmes attuned to those needs in the least possible timeframe.

There is a growing realisation among policy makers at the national and international levels that institutions of higher education must engage purposefully with the present and felt needs of the society such as universalisation of elementary education, health and nutrition, human rights, consumer protections, environment and sustainable development, resource management, participatory planning and development, and the market demand for skilled workforce. This has signalled a clear shift in the perceived role of higher education institutions: the traditional perspective on creation and dissemination of knowledge has given way to that of capacity building and training in skills needed for human and economic development of the nation as a whole. Thus, continuing education and lifelong learning have become important concerns of the higher education institutions. The ODL institutions have risen to this challenge and have been on the forefront in the efforts for addressing these demands on higher education by forging collaboration with institutions of high repute in different areas. However, there is still a long way to go to attain the stage, where these expectations of the society from the institutions of higher education are met satisfactorily. These can be summarised well in the words of Robert Frost, the renowned American poet:

The woods are lovely, dark and deep
But I have miles to go, before I sleep.

Conclusion

In recent years, the ODL institutions have discovered the benefits of collaboration with sister institutions and professional organisations for addressing a variety of educational needs of all sections of developing societies. Among the many benefits resulting from collaborative efforts are: the capacity to cater to larger numbers, reduction in costs and lead time to meet the demands of the learners and adoption of good practices in the collaborating institutions. Such efforts also help educational institutions to prepare for a future in which the non-profit educational institutions would be competing with for-profit institutions in the market place, and acquire a competitive edge so that every individual is able to access, in an equitable manner, the desired educational opportunities for his/her own and societal betterment.

The ODL System in India has acquired vast experience of working in collaboration with a variety of institutions and organisations at the national, regional and international levels. The lessons learnt in this process will hopefully equip it to prepare well for many more meaningful collaborative ventures in the future.

References

GMUNET (2005). *Declaration of the Second World Summit of Mega Universities.* IGNOU, New Delhi, September 23-25 (mimeo).

IGNOU (2004, 2005). *IGNOU Profile 2004 and IGNOU Profile 2005.* New Delhi: IGNOU.

SACODiL (2005). Report: First Meeting of the Board of Governors of SACODiL. IGNOU, New Delhi, January 19-21 (mimeo).

Dr. S.R. Jha is Reader in Physics, Indira Gandhi National Open University, New Delhi.
Email: srjha@ignou.ac.in

Dr. Sanjay Gupta is Lecturer in Physics, Indira Gandhi National Open University, New Delhi.
Email: drsgupta@ignou.ac.in

Professor Suresh Garg is Pro-Vice Chancellor, Indira Gandhi National Open University, New Delhi.
Email: scgarg@ignou.ac.in

38

Globalisation, Internationalisation, GATS and Cross-Border Distance Education

K. B. Powar

Introduction

Globalisation, as commonly understood, is the convergence of economies and the liberalisation of trade and markets. Internationalisation refers to the integration of an international dimension in any activity and is generally accepted to be a response to globalisation. The for-profit aspect of internationalisation of education has been brought into focus by the General Agreement on Trade in Services (GATS). Trade in education services, across national borders, is generally referred to as Cross-border Education (CBE). This chapter briefly reviews the important characteristics of Globalisation and internationalisation, outlines the more important provisions of GATS and discusses the possible implications of the agreement on cross-border education through the distance mode.

Globalisation and Internationalisation

The term globalisation has caught the imagination of people belonging to all sectors of society including the policy makers, entrepreneurs, businessmen, professionals and educators. In many ways it has become a cliché term. Knight and de Wit (1997) define it to be "the flow of technology, economy, knowledge, people, values, ideas...across borders. Globalisation affects each country in a different way due to a nation's individual history, traditions, culture and priorities. Globalisation increases and reflects the growing connectivity and inter-dependence amongst nations". This definition acknowledges that globalisation is a multi-faceted process and can have different impact on different countries. Knight (2005) points out that a number of factors are seen to be fundamental to globalisation. These include the knowledge society, information and communication technologies, the market economy, trade liberalisation and changes in governance structures. It is debatable as to whether they are catalysts for globalisation or consequences of globalisation. Either way, they have a tremendous impact on the education sector.

The definition of internationalisation has evolved over the last decade and a half. Arum and Van de Water (1992) proposed that internationalisation refers to "the multiple activities, programs and activities that fall within international studies, international educational exchange and technical cooperation". Later Knight and de Wit (1995) replacing the institutional activity approach by a process or organisational approach, defined internationalisation of higher education as "the process of integrating an international/intercultural dimension into the teaching, research and service functions of the institution". Kalvermark and Van der Wande (1997), taking a broader view, described internationalisation to be "a systematic, sustained effort aimed at making higher education (more) responsive to the requirements and challenges related to the globalisation of societies, economy and labour markets". Fava-De-Moraes and Simon (2000) see the ultimate goal of higher education to be that of enabling graduates of all countries to perform optimally in national and international global markets. Effectively, internationalisation of higher education is a response to globalisation that incorporates global, national and local events.

Globalisation and internationalisation are sometimes used as synonymous and interchangeable terms. Hence, it is necessary to understand the differences between their meanings and, therefore, the implications of their use. Van der Wande (2001) explains that while "globalisation relates to the process of increasing convergence and interdependence of economies, and to the liberalisation of trade and markets… internationalisation refers more to the process of promoting cooperation between states, or to activities across state borders". From the national and trade perspectives there are two important differences. First, that while in the process of globalisation the power of the nation-state is diminished, in internationalisation there will always be a central role for the nation-state (Scott, 1998). And second, while globalisation is regarded as a macro-socio-economic process that cannot be influenced at institutional level, internationalisation is perceived to be an internal response to globalisation which can be shaped and influenced at the institutional level. The roles of these two processes are also perceived to be different. As Neave (2001) puts it: "There is a view which distinguishes between globalisation and internationalisation on the grounds that the former is taken up with the tentacular spread of economic hegemonism, while the latter is concerned more with spreading the principle of equity between nations and peoples". It is obvious that educators are concerned more about internationalisation than upon its impact on globalisation.

Van Damme (2001) describes internationalisation in terms of objectives and activities. According to him the objectives include "diversification and growth of financial input by the recruitment of fee-paying foreign students, the broadening of curricula and educational experiences for domestic students in foreign-partner institutions, regional networking in order to allow a more effective/cross effective use of resources, to provoke a process of collective institutional learning and development, or the enhancement of quality of education and research by bringing students and staff in the realm of international competition". The activities that contribute to achieving these objectives include "joint research projects, student exchange programs, staff mobility projects, specially designed programs aimed at foreign students, joint curriculum development initiatives, specific initiatives in the context of university development aid-policies, etc.".

The rationales for internationalisation are varied – academic, socio-cultural, political and economic. For centuries, the academic rationale was the most important. In the twentieth century, the socio-cultural dimension became significant. After World War II, the political rationale gained ascendancy (at least for a short period) with aid being the operating process. Today, the driving motivation for the internationalisation of higher education is economic. What is noteworthy is that the transition from aid to trade has been smooth. The changes in the dominant rationale reflect new developments in society as also variations in international perspectives.

General Agreement on Trade in Services

The General Agreement on Trade in Services (GATS), which came into force in 1996, is a multilateral agreement that is based on the premise that progressive liberalisation of trade in commercial services will promote economic growth in WTO member countries. It provides legal rights to trade in all services, except those (like defence) that are provided entirely by the government. GATS has three parts. The first part is the Framework Agreement containing 29 Articles. The second part consists of national schedules that list a country's specific commitments on access to the domestic market. The third part consists of a number of Annexes, Ministerial Decisions, Schedules of Commitment etc. Presently, GATS covers 161 activities falling within 12 services; education is one of them.

Under GATS, member nations have obligations of two types – General and Conditional. General Obligations are those that apply automatically to all member countries regardless of existence of commitments made for any sector. These relate to Most Favoured Nation (MFN) treatment, transparency, and establishment of administrative reviews, procedures and disciplines. Under conditional obligations each country has to identify, if it so wishes, sectors/sub-sectors, and modes of supply, under which it is willing to make commitments (with limitations if it so desires) relating to market access and national treatment.

The basic principles of GATS are:

- There has to be progressive liberalisation with the process being irreversible because of binding commitments on negotiated levels of market access.
- Countries are free to decide which service sectors they wish to subject to market access and national treatment disciplines. In theory, if a country is unwilling or not prepared to open up a particular service sector, it can say so.
- Under Most Favoured Nation (MFN) treatment no discrimination can be made amongst members in terms of treatment accorded to the service suppliers. The guiding principle is 'favour one favour all'.

- Under the principle of 'National Treatment' nationals and foreigners need to be treated equally. There can be no discrimination between national/local and foreign service-providers. However, under certain conditions there can be limitations on National Treatment.
- There has to be transparency with all policies related to barriers to market access, and discriminatory restrictions by the members have to be notified.

Education Services presently has five sub-sectors, namely, Primary Education Services, Secondary Education Services, Higher Education Services, Adult and Continuing Education Services and Other Education Services. There is a proposal from the United States to add two other services, Training Services and Educational Testing Services, under Other Services. Higher Education services include:

- Post-secondary, sub-degree technical and vocational education services that cover a great variety of subject-matter programmes and emphasise teaching of practical skills, but also involve theoretical background instructions.
- Education leading to a university degree or equivalent that is usually provided by universities or specialised institutions. These not only emphasise theoretical instructions, with practicals, but also research.

GATS recognises four Modes of Trade in Services, namely Cross Border Supply, Consumption Abroad, Commercial Presence and Presence of Natural Persons.

- Cross Border Supply is the provision of service across national borders without the physical movement of the provider or consumer. Example is provision of distance education.
- Consumption Abroad is the provision of service through the movement of the consumer to the country of the provider. Example is a student proceeding to another country to study.
- Commercial Presence is the provision of services by establishing commercial facilities in another country. Example is the setting up of local campus in another country or partnerships through twinning or franchise arrangements
- Presence of Natural Presence is the provision of service through travel of a person to another country for rendering of service. Example is the movement of faculty.

Cross-Border Education

Cross-border Education is defined by UNESCO and OECD, in their 'Guidelines for Quality Provision in Cross-Border Higher Education' (UNESCO-OECD, 2004) as "higher education that takes place in situations where the teacher, student, programme, institution/provider or course materials cross national jurisdictional borders. Cross-border education may include higher education by public/private and not-for-profit/ for-profit providers. It encompasses a wide range of modalities in continuum from face-to-face (taking various forms from students travelling abroad and campuses abroad) to distance learning (using a range of technologies and including e-learning)".

Cross-border education has been in existence since ancient times when it was manifested in the movement of scholars across national borders to gain knowledge, spread ideas and propagate thoughts. Centres of education, in the early civilisations of China, India and the Mediterranean region, attracted students from different countries. Examples are the universities of Takshashila, Nalanda, Vikramshila and Vallabhi on the Indian sub-continent that, during the first to eighth century A.D., attracted students from far-off China and Mongolia. The first of the modern European universities at Bologna, Oxford and Paris (eleventh and twelfth century A.D.) were founded as centres for travelling students, teachers and monks. Cross-border education acquired a formal dimension in the early nineteenth century, grew steadily during the twentieth century, incorporating along the way, the concepts of academic collaboration and institutional partnerships. Following the advent of globalisation, in the last decade of the last millennium, the growth has been almost exponential and today cross-border education is an integral part of higher education.

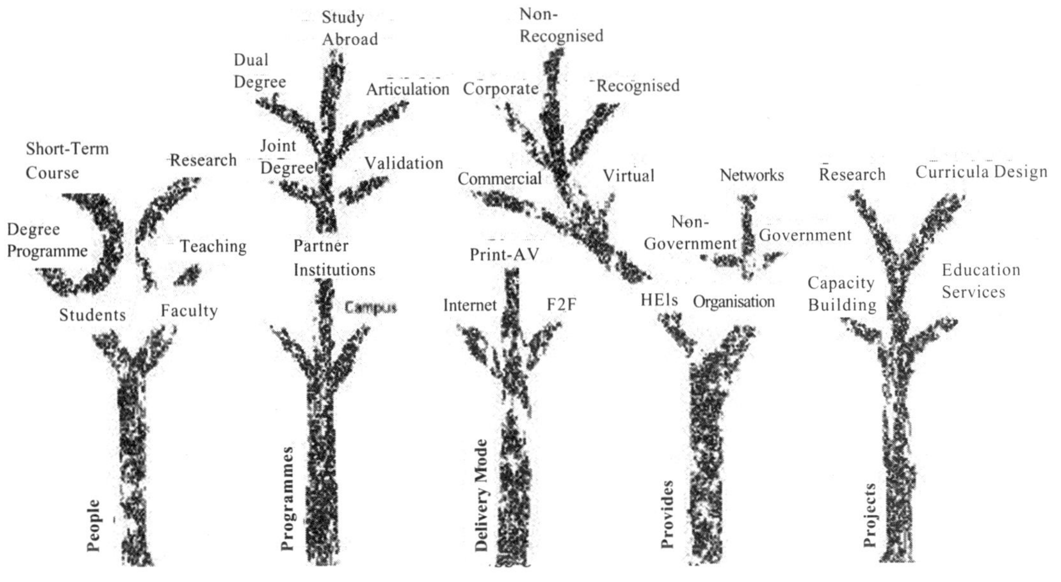

Cross-border education has a number of facets that combine to give myriad possibilities. These different facets are illustrated in Fig. 1. (The forest of cross-border education)

Cross-border Education through the Cross Border Supply Mode is manifested in distance education, which takes basically two forms – conventional distance education using print and audio-visual material as the delivery mode, and e-learning using predominantly Internet technology.

Conventional distance education is well established in both the developed and developing countries. In the western world, reputed universities like the U.K. Open University, Fern-Universitat in Germany and Universidad Nacional de Educacion a Distancia in Spain have off-shore centres. However, the number of foreign students is relatively limited. The developing countries, especially those of Asia, have a number of universities that offer quality distance education programs at low cost i.e. 15 to 40 percent of the cost of formal education (Yoshida, 2001). These include mega universities like Indira Gandhi National Open University in India, the Shanghai T.V. University in China, the Monterrey Institute of Technology and Higher Education, Mexico and the University of South Africa in South Africa. They offer off-shore programs to neighbouring countries.

India has twelve open universities and 106 centres of distance education in dual mode universities. They provide education at about 40 per cent of the cost of education through the formal mode. The possibilities of India (or the other Asian countries) importing education from the developed world, through this mode, are therefore low. On the other hand, some Indian universities have recently started offering degree programmes, through the distance mode, in countries having a large Indian diaspora. The Indira Gandhi National Open University is the prime example.

Cross border supply through the Internet has immense potential as innovations in information and communication technologies are providing alternate and virtual ways to deliver higher education. The established open universities are not the sole, or even the principal, providers. New types of providers such as international companies, for-profit IT and media institutions, and corporate universities, have entered the scene. With prospects of large profits, public and private institutions now vie to offer services across national borders to meet the demand, especially in disciplines like management and trade that have strong international components. International providers may target lucrative markets in the developing countries where there is great demand for professional education and relatively few opportunities. India is perhaps an exception, at least as far as computer education in concerned. Some well-known training institutes based in India offer, globally, further education programmes in professional areas like computer application (software development). NIIT offers programmes in 44 countries where it also has study centres. And very recently the Indira Gandhi National Open University has been assigned the role of content provider for the tele-education component of a Pan-African network which plans to reach out to 53 countries of the African Union. These are pointers to the role that India can play in providing cross-border distance education.

Notwithstanding the above, as the developed nations have far superior infrastructure and financial resources, there is a lurking fear that the indigenous higher education systems of developing countries may be inundated by the flow of superior quality programmes from the developed countries. Hence, India and other Asian countries may have to regulate cross-border supply of education, using electronic transmission, by framing appropriate legislation or through other measures, including the non-recognition of degrees awarded through the e-mode, and denial of permission for joint ventures and upper limit on fee as well as backflow of funds.

Epilogue

In India, GATS is often seen as a challenge to our existing education system and even a threat to the social fabric of the nation (Powar, 2005). However, a pragmatic appraisal of available information suggests that cross-border education does not, at present, constitute a major problem.

This is because first, for the average student, cross-border education is neither accessible, nor available or affordable. Second, the foreign providers from the developed countries concentrate on the countries that rank high in the Human Development Index. Most of their students come from such countries and there are a very small number from countries like India that rank low in the HDI ranking (Daniel et. al., 2005). In order to make a significant incursion into India, the foreign providers will have to cut costs dramatically, increase efficiency and offer programmes that are more relevant. Till then, the foreign providers can only reach the minuscule minority comprising the 'creamy layer'. On the other hand, GATS may be seen as a wake up call for re-organizing our education system and making it more flexible and quality-oriented. So far as distance education is concerned, GATS offers great opportunities for India, for the simple reasons that the Indian open education is well developed and cost-effective. Moreover, we have the capacity to innovate and the advantage of home-turf. India needs to take advantage of the favourable situation and establish itself as a provider of distance higher education, especially e-learning in the areas of computer science and information technology, teacher training, management, nursing, health care and medicine.

References

Arum, S. and Van de Water, J. (1992). The need for a definition of international education in U.S. universities, In C. Klasek (ed.), *Bridges to the Future: Strdtegies for Internationalising Higher Education,* Carbondale, Illinois: Association of International Education Administrators.

Daniel, J., Kanwar, A. and Uvallic-Trumbic, S. (2005). Who's Afraid of Cross-Border Education?: A Developing World Perspective. *INQAAHE Annual Conference, Final Plenary Session: Quality Assurance in Transnational Issues,* Wellington, New Zealand.

Fava-De-Moraes, F. and Simon, I. (2000). Computer networks and the internationalisation of higher education. *Higher Education Policy*, 13(3), 310-324

Knight, J. (2005). *Cross-border Education: An Analytical Framework for Program and Provider Mobility.* Manuscript, CIDEC-OISE, University of Toronto.

Knight, J. and de Wit, H. (1995). Strategies for the internationalisation of higher education: historical and conceptual perspectives. In De Wit, H. (ed.), *Strategies for the Internationalisation of Higher Education.* Amsterdam: EAIE.

Knight, J. and De Wit, H. (eds.), (1997). *Internationalisation of Higher Education in the Asia-Pacific Countries.* Amsterdam: EAIE.

Kalvermark, T. and Van der Wande, M.C. (eds.) (1997). *National Policies for Internationalisation of Higher Education.* Stockholm: National Agency For Higher Education.

Neave, G., (2001). Policy making perspectives for eastern Europe. *Higher Education Policy*, 14(3), 194-197.

Powar, K.B. (2005). Implications of WTO/GATS on Higher Education in India. Preprint, UNESCO Regional Seminar on the *Implications of WTO/GATS on Higher Education in Asia and the Pacific,* Seoul, 26-39 April.

Scott, P. (1998). Massification, internationalisation and globalisation. In Scott, P. (ed.), *The Globalisation of Higher Education.*Milton Keynes: SRHE/Open University Press.

UNESCO-OECD (2004). Guidelines for quality provision in cross-border higher education (Draft-Revised after Public Consultation).

Van Damme, D. (2001). Quality issues in the internationalisation of higher education. *Higher Education,* 41(4), 415-441.

Van der Wande, M.C. (2001). Internationalisation of higher education: about new trends and contrasting paradigms. *Higher Education Policy*, 14(3), 249-259.

Yoshida, A. (2001). Distance higher education and a new trend of virtual universities in Asia. In Tschang, F.T. and Della Senta, T. (eds.), *Access to Knowledge: New Information Technologies and the Emergence of the Virtual University*. Amsterdam: Pergamon-Elseiver Science.

Professor K.B. Powar, President, Edupro Foundation, is a former Secretary General of the Association of Indian Universities, New Delhi and former Vice Chancellor of Shivaji University, Kolhapur. He has written extensively on Indian Higher Education. His recent books include *Performance Indicators in Distance Higher Education* (Co-authored, 2000), *Indian Higher Education: A Conglomerate of Concepts, Facts and Practices* (2002), *Internationalisation of Higher Education: Focus on India* (2003) and *Quality in Higher Education* (2005). In addition, he has published about 60 articles and edited 16 volumes on higher education.
Email: edupro5@yahoo.co.in

39

International Offer of Distance Education Programmes

Ved Goel

Introduction

In the middle of 1980s there were concerns about the mobility of students among the Commonwealth countries as the number of students going overseas for higher education had considerably decreased. There were two main factors which led to the decrease: i) there was a view that higher education is as much a private good as it is a public good, and ii) the universities in the UK had considerably increased the fee for foreign students thereby making access to UK's higher education institutions difficult for students from developing Commonwealth countries. During late 1980s Australia also followed the model of the UK and raised the fee for foreign students, which also constrained students from the developing countries from accessing higher education in the Australian universities. During one of the conferences of Commonwealth Education Ministers the issue of student mobility in the Commonwealth was discussed. At this conference the Ministers constituted a Standing Committee on Student Mobility. It was during the meeting of this committee it was concluded that if students cannot be moved to the programmes, as is the case in formal mode of learning, then the programmes should be moved to the students, as is the practice of distance education. This gave birth to of the concept of 'programme mobility' (Daniel, 2004). The underlying theme of this paper is international programme mobility.

The international delivery of higher education has given rise to a number of new terms including 'borderless', 'transnational', 'trans-border' and 'cross border' education. Borderless education refers to the blurring of conceptual, disciplinary and geographic borders traditionally inherent to higher education. While the term borderless recognises the disappearance of borders, other terms infact emphasize their existence. However, considering the massive growth of distance education and online education, the existence if geographic borders appear to be of little significance. Therefore, while borderless education is important, the notion of education moving across countries has been termed as cross-border education. No distinction has however been made between the terms cross border and trans-border education.

According to McBurnie (2000) Monash University draws distinction between "internationalization" and "becoming global" as follows:

'Internationalization' is taken to mean a way of thinking and acting which is not constrained by national boundaries or traditions and which actively seeks inspiration, understanding, and input from outside Australia. "Becoming global" refers to the process of locating operations, either physically or virtually, around the world (Monash University, 1999)

Peter Scott, the Vice-Chancellor of the University of Kingston, addresses the distinction between 'globalization' and 'internationalization' in the following way: "… not all universities are (particularly) international, but all universities are subject to the same processes of globalization—partly as objects, victims even, of these processes, but partly as subjects, or key agents, of globalization" (Scott, 1998).

If we try to explore the factors responsible for the internationalization and globalization of higher education we can clearly see that globalization of the economy and developments in technology are responsible for producing a global knowledge economy. This growth in knowledge economy is leading to globalization of higher education institutions and the programmes they offer. Besides internationalization and globalization of higher education institutions is also taking place due to social, political, economical and academic reasons (de Wit and Knight 1999). Globalization of higher education institutions is leading to cross border delivery of their programmes. The institutions, which have made cross border operation as an important corporate agenda, are incorporating the international dimension into their courses and have made it as a criteria for all course approval systems. Such institutions before launching a programme in a foreign country study the accreditation requirements of the country and adjust the content and delivery of its programmes accordingly. This not only improves the acceptability of the programme in the foreign country but also enhances the academic legitimacy of the institution offering the programme.

Appropriate adaptation of curriculum is an important issue in places in which higher education institutions offer its programmes overseas. According to Global Alliance for Transnational Education (GATE):

> Materials and learning resources used should normally be adjusted to be culturally appropriate to the range of students to whom the courses are being offered. Where such adjustments can be justified, as inappropriate, prospective students must be specifically advised (GATE, 1997, Appendix E).

GATE has established quality assurance principles for transnational education especially for programme mobility, which covers the following topics (GATE, 1977):

- Goals and objectives
- Standards

- Legal and ethical matters
- Student enrolment and admission
- Human resources
- Physical and financial resources
- Teaching and learning
- Student support
- Evaluation procedures
- Third party agreements

Models of Programme Mobility

A number of models are being use to deliver trans-border education. These include distance and e-learning; licensing, validation and franchising arrangements and twinning. It is estimated that the demand for trans-border higher education will expand even faster than that for students attending foreign universities in face-to-face mode. The demand for international higher education will arise as a result of demands in the labour market both in the home country as well as internationally, national research requirements, economic and social developments including developments in trade at the national level and perception of domestic education.

Internationally a number of public-private and public-public partnerships are evolving to cater to the fast growing demand for international higher education. Across the world, students are looking for benefits from their education, which will boost their personal and professional development. The focus of students seeking higher education from foreign institutions is on the outcomes, in terms of qualifications which are internationally recognised and which represent a good return on their investment of time, money and effort. Distance education offers a realistic financial option for many international students to obtain foreign qualification without leaving the home since it allows them to study within their own culture, in the comfort of their home and at their own time. Already a number of public sector institutions from different countries are offering their programmes through distance mode in other countries as private sector institutions. It is interesting to realise that while an institution may be a public or private sector institution in its own country, it becomes a private university, in terms of legislation, in the foreign country as soon as it crosses its jurisdiction. It is for this reason that in most countries trans-border providers of education are referred to as private providers.

A number of universities have set up private companies as part of their operation to manage their transnational business since cross border education is now recognized as an enterprise and a profession. These companies offer programmes of the university under the banner of the parent university. This has been done with the objective of fostering performance-based entrepreneurial approach.

Thus programme mobility can take a variety of forms encompassing several aspects of educational cooperation. It may range from exchange of ideas and collaborative research, sharing of resources including courseware, transfer and or creation of new technologies, credit exemption and credit transfer, twining and franchising arrangements, adaptation and adoption of course materials and sharing of student support services. The South Asian Consortium of Open and Distance Learning (SACODiL) an organization created by the Heads of governments of South Asian Association of Regional Cooperation (SAARC) countries is considering policy options for credit transfer and credit exemption including harmonization of technologies so that there could be greater programme mobility in the region. This might lead to creation of global standards in education in the region.

National Regulatory Mechanisms

To safeguard the interest of its learners such that only credible and reputed foreign institutions could offer only accredited distance education programmes in their country, some countries have implemented regulatory mechanisms to authorise and or provide license to foreign institutions to operate on their soil. They have also introduced mechanisms for the accreditation of programmes.

Hong Kong, China introduced Non-local Higher and Professional Education Regulation Ordinance in 1997 (Government of Hong Kong, 1977a, 1977b, 2001). The Government of Hong Kong promulgated the ordinance with a dual aim of (a) protecting its learners from substandard non-local programmes; and (b) enhancing the reputation of Hong Kong as a country which attaches importance to reliable internationally recognised academic and professional standards. The Government has provided the rationale of the ordinance, application forms for programme providers and list of crossborder programmes on its website (www.info.gov.hk/emb/eng/prog_high/nonlocalrules.html). To obtain permission to its programmes a foreign institution has to provide details of programme content, methods of delivery, assessment system and student support services. Foreign providers cannot legally operate outside the framework of the ordinance. According to French (1999) the ordinance fails to address quality of cross border education in Hong Kong for programmes which are being offered from outside Hong Kong through distance mode via mail, fax or the Internet without any physical presence or face-to-face teaching. The reason being that such activities being extra-territorial cannot be regulated by the ordinance of Hong Kong.

In Indonesia for example, programme mobility is a form of twinning. Students can receive qualifications from both the local institution as well as the foreign institution provided they study for at lease one semester abroad in the foreign institution. Before starting a programme in Indonesia a foreign institution has to obtain a license as a "working partner" which requires accreditation of foreign qualification based on the evaluation of its programme by the Directorate of Higher Education of Indonesia. Indonesia believes in equal partnership with local institution which benefits all parties rather than partnership merely for profit.

In Singapore the foreign institution wishing to offer its programme in collaboration with a local partner institution has to apply to the Government and provide (a) details of programme content to be offered; (b) the status of the foreign institution in its home country. In Singapore the local partner can provide infrastructural facilities, administrative and logistic support, marketing of programmes but not teaching (Singapore Ministry of Education, 2000, 2001).

As discussed earlier even though a university is in the public sector in its own country, in most cases, it acquires the label of a private university in the foreign country where it offers its programmes. Amongst several reasons for such a labelling, one of the reasons is that a university in a foreign country operates for profit. This creates difficulty for students of a foreign country since they fail to get a clear message whether the qualification being offered by the foreign institution is equivalent to what is being offered at home and the official status of the university in its home country.

Rationale for Programme Mobility by Indira Gandhi National Open University

The globalization of programme mobility at the Indira Gandhi National Open University is a logical sequence to the globalization of market economy in India. India with its rich cultural heritage in the field of education has a significant portion to contribute to the development of human resource and capacity of developing countries in Asia, Africa, and some Eastern European countries. A discussion paper on 'Internationalization of Education' circulated by the Department of Education, Government of India has summarised the advantages that India posseses in the internationalization of its products and services in education. Language, location, low-cost delivery systems in comparison to developed countries, quality of education, education tradition that combines the pedagogical and technical excellence of the West and value system of the East have been identified as comparative advantages which India enjoys.

Meeting the unmet demand

One of the objectives of offering education through distance by the Indira Gandhi National Open University in a foreign country is to meet the unmet demand for higher education. The programmes being offered in many Gulf countries fall under this category since expatriates and their families have little opportunities of receiving higher education in the State institutions of the Gulf. To launch its programme in the Gulf countries the University had two options: either to open its own branch with its own staff in those countries or to identify a reputable local partner institution in that country who could provide the administrative and academic support necessary for delivery of quality distance education programmes. IGNOU decided to go for the second option. The benefits of the latter option were numerous.

- The local institution understands the market and will be able to tap it.
- The local partner institution could easily identify local tutors and counsellors required for providing academic support and counselling to distance learners.
- The local partner and its counsellors will be able to prove the local context required for the ownership of learning.
- The University will not have to incur infrastructural cost of establishing a branch overseas thereby passing the benefits to learners in terms of cost of the programmes.

The University with the support of the Indian Embassy identifies local Partner Institutions and through an MoU defines obligations and responsibilities of the University as well as of the Partner Institutions (PI). The University provides all the courseware, organizes training of the local tutors and counsellors, certifies the appointment of local counsellors and tutors by the PI, provides all assignments, receives synopsis of the project proposals for the courses where they are applicable and provides feedback to the students. The University receives the final project report for assessment and conducts viva-voce wherever required. The university conducts terminal examinations and receives the answer scripts for marking at the headquarters. The question papers for the terminal assessments are the same as that of Indian students to maintain equivalence in degrees.

The PI on the other hand enrols students on the basis of the entry qualifications prescribed for each programme, collects fee, provides orientation, counselling and space for students to use ICT material, evaluates assignments and provide feedback to the learners, provides space for carrying out any hands-on experience such as using computers for courses in computers. The University is conscious about maintaining the quality and equivalence of degrees being offered overseas, as such it takes all necessary steps to achieve those objectives.

Capacity building in distance education

The Indira Gandhi National Open University also offers its programme overseas with the objective of capacity building of the recipient country. Its programme in many African countries and some Caribbean and the South Pacific countries are being offered with this objective. In this model the University has developed twinning arrangements and partnerships with a state local Institution to facilitate transfer of knowledge.

The University is building the capacities of many African countries in developing open and distance education. In collaboration with the UNESCO's International Institute for Capacity Building in Africa (IICBA), Addis Ababa it is offering the Post Graduate Diploma in Distance Education (PGDDE) and Masters in Distance Education (MADE) in a number of countries in Africa. As different from the previous model where IGNOU took the lead to launch its programme to meet the unmet demand, in this case the initiative for cross border programme mobility came from IICBA. In these countries an institution is identified by IICBA, which enrols learners and provides the necessary counselling and administrative support in collaboration with the faculty of IGNOU. These learners use the courseware including the assignments prepared by the IGNOU faculty. The completed assignments are submitted to IGNOU, which are assessed by its faculty. IGNOU faculty also organizes counselling workshops for the learners in which the faculty of the PI also participates. The projects to be completed as part of the programme are supervised by the faculty of the PI once the IGNOU faculty has approved the synopsis of the project. The learners write the same examination as the learners taking these programmes in India and the IGNOU faculty mark the answer scripts.

In some other countries, the cross border mobility of programmes, with the objective of capacity development in distance education is being carried out in collaboration with the Commonwealth of Learning (COL). Under the scheme of Rajiv Gandhi Fellowship Programme,

COL identifies countries that need support of IGNOU in developing their capacity to take the agenda of distance education forward. The countries concerned identify the institution where the programme is to be based and which needs strengthening. The institution then identifies the learners, which are enrolled at the University and complete the programme as described above. In this model the faculty of the participating institutions is also provided training by IGNOU so that they could offer necessary counselling to learners and as such no counselling workshops are organized directly by IGNOU faculty for learners.

Education for mutual understanding

Recently the IGNOU has also developed twinning arrangement with universities abroad to offer its programmes to the learners in those countries. In this approach academic, political, social and cultural relationships are of prime significance than the narrow economic gain. The focus in such a relationship is not on the financial gain to the exporting institution but on the mutual understanding. In this arrangement, at the degree level, the participating university will offer some of its foundation courses, as requirement of first degree in those countries followed by courses of IGNOU. The partner universities will provide all necessary academic and administrative support and conduct examination of students for which the question papers will be supplied by IGNOU. The papers for the foundation courses will be prepared and assessed by the foreign University whereas those of other papers will be provided and assessed by IGNOU. IGNOU will however issue its certificate/degree on completion of the programme.

Growth of programme mobility

Research indicates that there are a variety of factors which contribute to learners' choice in selecting a particular country or programme for obtaining foreign qualification. These may include:

i) geographical region of the world;
ii) historical connections to particular countries;
iii) language;
iv) education systems;
v) perceived quality and reputation of the country's education provision; and
vi) accessibility, affordability and the employability of the qualification obtained.

There are a number of factors that have been the catalysts for the growth of cross border mobility in higher education. These include: *i*) the emergence of new education providers including multi-national companies and private universities; *ii*) developments in ICT leading to development of new forms of education delivery such as virtual and online learning; *iii*) greater diversification of qualifications and certificates; *iv*) emergence of new areas of learning; *v*) demand for multi-skilling of work force, *vi)* greater emphasis on lifelong learning, and *vi*) the increasing amount of private investment in the provision of higher education.

The literature suggests that cross-border trade in higher education will benefit higher education itself. It is based on the assumptions of the business model that increased market competition provides a strong motivation for institutions to innovate and establish professional networks. There is however no doubt that commercial trade in higher education provides greater opportunities for learners to access higher education. The institutions involved in cross border education recognise that maintaining the quality of higher education, assuring equitable access and empowering/ protecting the learner, provision of demand driven programmes are becoming the key issues in response to the further commercialization and trade of higher education provision.

According to an OECD study (OECD 2004) in 2001 there were more than 70 million students worldwide enrolled in higher education programmes internationally. International students enrolled in Australian institutions alone from their home country through distance education represented 9% of the total enrolment of international students in Australia in 2001. In 2003 they numbered 12386. On the basis of the rough figure students' study online at a distance represented 11% of all international students. The number is expected to rise to 160 million per annum by 2025. It is being estimated that the Asian market for graduate and professional programmes alone is worth US$ 10 million annually.

- It is estimated that the global e-learning market is work around US$ 24 billion.
- The institutions offering distance-learning programmes are being viewed as a threat to the existence of face-to-face institutions.
- Compared to domestic students, foreign students generate a reasonable income to the institutions that are acting in the international education market. The entrepreneurial strategy of the institutions not only creates additional income but also enhances the reputation of the higher education sector of the foreign country.

In 2001 the World Bank and the Australian Government agency AusAid decided to collaborate in a US$ 1000 billion Virtual Colombo Plan to develop cross border distance education for the developing world. The Virtual Colombo Plan faces long-term difficulties since it needs viable local partners and sustainable tailor made technologies. On the top of it needs to provide the content that is relevant and contextual to local circumstances, a formidable task.

Issues in Programme Mobility

Programme mobility and quality assurance and accreditation

There are a variety of higher education institutions across the world and the lack of transparent information about these institutions may lead to poor quality institutions providing cross border programme mobility. How should one ensure the credibility of the institutions and that of the programme being offered? Lack of transparent information about higher education systems may also lead to unscrupulous quality assurance and accreditation agencies to operate and provide accreditation to poor quality programmes. Another related question within the quality assurance is whose quality assurance regime should the learner follow: that of the provider's country or that of the recipient country? The underlying assumptions and operational modalities of quality may be different across borders. This leaves learners in a very vulnerable situation until and unless there are government policies and practices in place to protect learners from sub-standard institutions. Thus policies and practices are required both in the providers' as well as recipient countries, which could ensure that only authentic institutions offer cross border programmes with qualifications, which are valid and comparable internationally. Besides, qualifications being offered must be comparable to the qualifications being offered to its' own learners in the home country of the provider.

To protect learners in countries where governments do not have enough capabilities and effective mechanisms to regulate cross border mobility of programmes, there is a need to develop an international framework for quality assurance and accreditation. There is now a good community of practices in cross border programme mobility both through distance mode as well as virtually which could be used to develop some useful international guidelines on fair and ethical practices in transnational programme mobility. This will protect learners from institutions whose main goal is to maximize profits without any regard to quality of the programme.

Although universities and higher education institutions are not business organizations but cross border education is recognized as an enterprise carried out with economic gain as one of its objectives. Thus higher education institutions involved in cross border education have to carry out a number of business like operations such as costing, marketing, benefit etc. According to Coaldrake and Stedman (1998)

> Universities are not businesses but that they must become more business-like. This remark is easy to make, but what does it mean? It probably means more than signing additional exchange agreements. It probably means to think carefully about product development and market research, about keeping costs down, about good marketing and customer service, and about effective management and quality control. In business, there are winners and losers. It is extremely important that universities do not become losers.

There is no doubt that a university may take pride in offering its programmes internationally. While for the university administrators it may be recognition of their leadership and excellence in education; for the faculty members, who were responsible for the development of the programmes, it is a matter of international recognition of their professional competence. The universities involved with programme mobility however run certain risks, which are an integral part of international operations. As a result of stiff competition, the programmes on offer land under the 'international microscope' as soon as they leave national boundaries. They are thus being informally reviewed for marketing purposes. Poor quality programmes may attract criticism of the university leading to loss of reputation. Also the faculty associated with the development of the programme may loose credibility in the international academic fraternity.

Programme mobility and entry-level requirements

Another practical issue, which relates to programme mobility, is the entry-level requirements in a programme. A number of students in each country may not meet entry-level requirements but the PI (especially in cases where Government is a party to the agreement) may request for admission of such students into a programme on several grounds such as:

- country has limited educational facilities and many students may not achieve required educational qualification;
- student(s) seeking admission has (have) relevant work experience;
- students are not looking for work in the country offering the programme; and
- being an Open University it should have flexible entry-level admission requirements.

Some of these arguments appear to be just and an institution offering its programme internationally will have to take a stand on entry-level requirements keeping in view (a) the requirements of the programme, (b) assumptions made of entry requirements by programme developers (c) chances of success in the programme if entry-level requirements are relaxed and (d) additional student support required on relaxing entry-level admission requirements.

Programme mobility and student support

Programmes being offered through distance mode or virtually require provision of quality student support for its success. There are a number of aspects in students' support starting from pre-admission counselling to the delivery of certificates including delivery of course materials, provision of counselling, feedback on assignments etc. which are crucial for the success of learners. Each aspect of student support is crucial for the satisfaction of student and the PI. Any lapses in quality student support as envisaged in the programme guide may further tarnish the image of the institution.

As discussed above the success of distance education programme depends on the quality of student support. Good quality student support requires availability of associated counsellors in programme areas in the country where students are located. Availability of such counsellors who fully understand and appreciate the objectives of the programme may not necessary be available. The problem further accentuates for programmes, which are in the latest areas of development, and for which very limited manpower may be available in the recipient country.

Another related issue regarding availability of counsellors is the number of counselling sessions and remuneration to counsellors. In countries where PIs are private organizations, market forces determine remuneration. A well-qualified and experienced counsellor may demand a higher remuneration. The PIs however allocate a budget for payment to the counsellor and at times have to compromise either the number of required counselling sessions or the quality of the counsellors to stay within the allocated budget.

Another important aspect of student support is the availability of compatible ICT facilities and connectivity between the recipient and the exporting country. During the programme development, relevant ICT materials and student support facilities are created keeping in view the local infrastructure. When the programme is exported the infrastructure in the recipient country may either be lacking or may not be compatible with that of the exporting country and as such some of the ICT strategies may not be available to the learners in the recipient country. For example, the radio, television and teleconferencing counselling provided to local learners may not become available to learners in foreign countries for obvious reasons. This may put foreign learners to a disadvantageous position.

Language, cultural sensitivity, local context, learning styles, assessment systems and developmental needs are some other important issues which need consideration in programme mobility. Experience of curriculum development and their portability in 60's has shown that 'one size does not fit all'.

Online education

On-line and distance education has been the subject of speculative commercial growth in some countries. For example in the last decade many universities and private providers particularly in UK, USA, Australia and Canada have developed distance programmes solely to be delivered through Internet in foreign countries. One of the advantages of cross-border programme mobility is that it caters to the demands of foreign education with less capital outflow and with less potential brain drain. There is however a question about the extent to which on-line cross-border programmes can replace or complement face-to-face indigenous programmes or replace or complement face-to-face programmes provided by international providers.

Research studies indicate that online education is suitable for certain kind of learners rather than a useful substitute for what exists. Online education seems to be more suitable for postgraduate and continuing education learners especially those who are working full time and are looking for flexibility and non-synchronized communications.

There are however concerns about the cultural-content of the online programmes being offered internationally. Most of the online programmes are in English and often use the assumptions and examples of the country providing the programme. Some learners see no problem with this kind of presentations since this is the experience they would have if they would have been studying in a foreign university but most would prefer programmes that are more cultural and linguistically diverse. Many countries are grappling with this issue since they consider this as infringement on their culture. National governments are constantly asking the question whether the technical and cultural content of online programmes meet the national needs and values. Due to the lack of clarity underlying of principles of online education today, there are very few regulatory mechanisms to the growth of cross border online education.

It remains a challenge to produce online programmes for cross border delivery, which are relevant, and at the same time culturally flexible. The specific cultural requirements for online education will vary across student demographics and from country to country, region to region, and fields of study. Developments of culturally contextual programme for cross border delivery will require partnerships and collaboration of cross border institutions. It is likely that in the longer time, cross border and cross cultural partnerships will emerge to achieve variation and flexibility in content and pedagogy. Despite all challenges facing e-learning it appears that the elearning will be used to a greater extent for cross border education. Over time elearning may get into the mainstream and develop either as a complement to face-to-face cross border education by adding e-learning to the face-to-face education or by supplementing e-learning with contact programmes and other multimedia/print material.

E-learning on a global scale can put into questions certain activities which were a prerogative, if not monopoly, of the state universities and national and sub-regional cultures by a process of destabilization of regulated markets and of engaging in competition, by providing efficient and attractive delivery, just-in-time learning, credibility, quality assurance, relevance, flexibility and portability of qualifications credit, that state universities may have difficulty resisting. (Vlasceanu and Davies, 2001)

In the last decade a large number of Australian universities have developed online programmes either in addition to or more often mirroring face-to-face programmes to be delivered internationally (Gallagher, 2001). The University of Southern Queensland for example has invested in international e-learning as its primary mode. In the second half of 2001, Australian universities had an enrolment of 12,887 foreign students in its distance education programmes. These programmes were being delivered in collaboration with local partner organizations. Learners enrolled in these programmes received learning materials through Internet and or post. They also received some face-to-face guidance provided by a combination of Australian and local partners at the local learning centres (OECD, 2004)

In a UNESCO study (Bates, 2001) suggested that quality online education is not cheaper than face-to-face education, which is more expensive than traditional distance education, which is print based and technologically supported. It is well known that access to and delivery of online programmes depends on availability of efficient and reliable communication systems and the necessary hardware and software, which are compatible with that of the provider. It is also well known that these capabilities are inadequately and unevenly distributed especially in the countries where education is needed most. Most of the developing countries have not invested in improving telecommunication infrastructure bandwidth, cable linkages and satellite receiver distribution technologies as a result of which communication system is relatively poor and does not match the requirements of e-learning programmes.

The UNESCO has launched a project, the Avicenna Virtual Campus to deliver online Science & Technology course modules at low cost. The European Union, UNESCO and several State Governments have funded the project. This programme is being developed by 18 partner institutions and focuses on open and distance learning in France, United Kingdom, Italy, Spain and other Mediterranean countries outside EU. The project will train faculty of partner institutions to develop the materials to be delivered at networked knowledge centres (OECD, 2004).

Challenges of programme mobility

There are a number of challenges, which are facing cross border programme mobility. Some of these are:

- Development of the programmes, which are contextual, socially and culturally relevant, and meets the developmental needs of the recipient country and that of the overseas learners;
- Protection of learners from risks of poor quality programmes through mis-information or lack of information.
- Developing an internationally acceptable community of fair and ethical practices;
- Internationally acceptable quality assurance and accreditation systems of qualifications;
- Improving access to and delivery of online programmes through ICT which uses hardware and software that are compatible with that of the recipient;
- Engaging associated faculty for counselling work that understands the objectives of the programme and distinguishes between counselling and tutoring;
- Provision of demand driven programmes to improve access to higher education;

References

Bates, T. (2001). *National Strategies for E-learning in Post-Secondary Education and Training, Fundamentals in Education Planning No. 70.* Paris: International Institute for Education Planning.

Coaldrake, P. and Stedman, L. (1998) *On the Brink: Australia's Universities Confronting Their Future.* St. Lucia, Queensland: University of Queensland Press.

Daniel, J. (2004). Distance Learning Across Borders: Cultural Imperialism or Intellectual Independence? 18th IDP Australia International Conference: International Education: The Path to Cultural Understanding and Development, Australia 6 October.

French, N.J. (1999). Transnational education-competition or complementarity: The case of Hong Kong. *Higher Education in Europe*, 24(2), 219-223.

Gallagher, M. (2001). *E-Learning in Australia: Universities and the New Distance Education.* 7th OECD/Japan Seminar on E-learning in Post-Secondary Education, Tokyo, 5-6 June.

GATE (1977). *Certification Manual.* Washington DC: Global Alliance for Transnational Education.

Government of Hong Kong (1997a). Non-Local Higher and Professional Education (Regulation) Ordinance. www.justice.gov.hk

Government of Hong Kong (1997b). Implementation of the Non-Local Higher and Professional Education (Regulation) www.info.gov.hk

Government of Hong Kong (2001). Non-Local Higher and Professional Education (Regulation) Ordinance- list of Registered Courses. www.info.gov.hk/emb/eng/prog_high.

Monash University (1999). *Leading the Way: Monash 2020.* Clayton: Monash University. *http://www.monash.edu.au/monashplan*

OECD (2004). *Internationalisation and Trade in Higher Education: Opportunities and Challenges.* Paris: OECD.

Scott, P. (1998). Massification, internationalization, and globalization. In P. Scott (ed.), *The Globalization of Higher Education.* Buckingham: Society for Research in Higher Education and Open University Press.

Singapore, Ministry of Education (2000). *Information Notes: Registration of Distance Learning Programmes*. Private Schools Section, Ministry of Education Singapore.

Singapore, Ministry of Education (2001). *Information Notes: Registration of Distance Learning Programmes*. Private Schools Section, Ministry of Education Singapore.

Vlaesceanu, L.R. and Davies, J.I. (2001). Virtual versus classical universities: Conflict or collaboration? Virtual and classical universities between Complementarity and contrast. *Higher Education in Europe*, 26(4), 475-485.

Wit de, H. and Knight, J. (1999). *Quality and Internationalization in Higher Education*. Paris: OECD/ IMHE.

Professor Ved Goel is from School of Education, Indira Gandhi National Open University, New Delhi.
Email: vgoel@ignou.ac.in

40

International Agencies and Distance Education in India

Usha Vyasulu Reddi

Introduction

Education is today one of the fastest growing sectors in any society. Demand far outstrips supply, whether for formal course related programmes or for non-formal education. Education has been globally recognized as the key to development and as an engine for economic growth in any country and all nations are exploring ways and means of provisioning educational access and opportunities to their citizens at all levels from literacy to post-secondary and to lifelong learning. This is at a time of a reduction in public funding support for education — not as much in the amount as in the manner of its distribution. For instance, with a greater push for universal primary education (enshrined as one of the important Millennium Development Goals), many countries are reallocating financial resources to meet the targets they have committed themselves to globally. Additional allocations for primary education reduce what is available for other sectors. Such a resource crunch at a time of increasing demand has forced post-secondary educational institutions to explore new ways and means of educational delivery. In this perspective, the exponential growth of the new information and communication technologies (ICTs) ▤ from the individualised computer and web assisted learning systems to the more mass directed radio and television ▤ have today offered an unparalleled opportunity to reconsider conventional educational practices. The notion that by using the ICTs, teaching and learning can be taken out of the confines of existing schools and colleges, and teaching can be individualised and insensitive to geo-climatic distances has emerged out of the telecommunications revolution which swept across the world in the 1980s and 1990s.

The emergence of technology mediated or enabled education is what distance education is all about, and Open and Distance Learning (ODL) has arrived both as a discipline and as a mode of educational delivery. In developed countries, ODL has enabled a greater flexibility and choice in education, enabling learning to determine the pace and place of accessing education and at the same time helping educational providers to develop and deliver a variety of qualitatively superior programmes at extremely cost effective rates while increasing enrollments. For the industry, ODL has provided a means by which employees can be trained and upskilled without any disruption of work and in fact, has increased both the skills of their human resources and industrial productivity at the same time. In developing countries, ODL has enabled both public and private sector educational providers to reach out and to provide education to those most in need but least able to access, i.e. to reach the hitherto unreached.

For international development agencies, ODL has opened up new possibilities and opportunities for forging new partnerships to provide meaningful support to implementing agencies engaged at the field level in addressing the global Millennium Development Goals (MDG) agenda. Such partnerships assume importance in an era dominated by a new paradigm in learning which includes on the one hand, the technological capacity to do so, and on the other, liberalisation, privatisation, and globalisation as economic and social realities that are moving the world into a new era of interdependence of systems and protocols. Only partnerships will help both international agencies and national ODL institutions optimise on resources and remain relevant, in a knowledge society, where education has been identified as one of the 12 main services, opened up for free flow of trade between countries, when knowledge will become a marketable commodity, and it will make business sense for people to move into the field of education. In such a situation, the poor and needy may be left out, unless a global partnership is forged to address their needs. Such partnerships could be global, regional, national, or sub-national between different stakeholders, public and private, government and civil society. International agencies form one set of partners. This chapter seeks to explore the nature of such collaborations between international agencies and ODL institutions in developing countries, with a special reference to India.

The Nature of Collaborations

Liberalisation, privatisation, and globalisation constitute the current social, economic, technological and political space. Revolutions in information and communication technologies have reduced national boundaries to lines drawn on maps. Football in Europe affects Kolkata residents; violence in Iraq touches the villagers in Philippines — and the irate Filipino public to force their country to withdraw troops. The Indian Ocean earthquake and Tsunami has shaken global society. The fear psychosis caused by global terrorism and reported in the media makes us wary of our shadow and distrustful of those whom we find different in religion, ethnicity, appearance or apparel. This is the liberalisation process in full swing — a questioning and a shaking loose of cultural values that were long held dear and protected by individual societies as their cultural inheritance.

If liberalisation is a social process, privatisation is an economic process. Such economic realities impact the way in which we have to work and no amount of moralistic preaching can counter the sheer necessity of survival in a highly competitive environment. The forces of liberalisation and privatisation are leading to increased globalisation of products and services — where only the fittest will survive and consumers get access to variety. Technological advances will allow for educational and other products and programmes to be developed in one country, stored and serviced in another, and delivered to learners in a third, as national boundaries become more and more porous. Already the issues over intellectual property rights and patents in the areas of agriculture and pharmaceuticals have been debated and the global divide between the powerful developed countries and the developing countries is widening. There is no reason to believe that it will not be the same in the knowledge industries, including education leading to a widening, rather than narrowing of the digital divide. And with foreign direct investment (FDI) in education being a distinct possibility on the horizon, it seems imminent that globalisation is here to stay for a long time to come.

In such a scenario, the days of the donor-recipient kind of collaborations seem to be over. The potential use of communication technologies to meet the challenges of development started with the pioneering studies in the 1950s and early 1980s. The pioneering study reported by Lerner (1958) showed the link between communication and modernisation of individuals in Turkey. It was followed by a large number of studies in the early 1960s, and an equal number of projects where the role of communication was tested in developmental settings. The Radio Rural Forums of the 1950s and the classic study by Rogers (1969) set the stage for incorporation of communication as a critical element of development programming. At the same time, the UNESCO and Schramm (1964) led initiatives emerged in different parts of the world when countries such as India, Mexico, and China invested heavily in the use of media for educational and developmental purposes.

There is enough global evidence to show that while pilot projects supported by donor funding worked, sustainability of any effort in the long run depended on the institutions and agencies in the field. Very often, results from the field yielded contradictory results — much at odds with planners' expectations. Those that have worked have been large scale implementations in technology delivered education such as Mexico's Telesecundaria (Calderoni, 1998), Brazil's Telecurso 2000 (www.iab.org), and India's Satellite Instructional Television Experiment (SITE) and post SITE educational television. The field evidence has resulted in a rethinking of the ways and means by which international agencies must function to meet their goals.

If the earlier efforts were more paternalistic in nature, recent efforts have been more collaborative among equal partners as it has become increasingly clear that old models cannot work in a world of new realities. ODL is no exception, being more recent. As a consequence, different types of collaborations, consortia and partnerships are emerging. International collaboration in open and distance learning may be classified into two types according to their thrust of activities – multi-purpose networking initiatives and collaborative delivery of ODL programmes (http://asiapacific_odl.oum.edu.my).

Networking could also support or lead to collaborative delivery of international programmes. Multi-purpose networking initiatives facilitate wide-scale promotion of distance education, information and research sharing, and discussion of international and regional issues. It could provide a venue for the formulation of international and national policies and codes of good practices.

The Commonwealth of Learning (COL) (www.col.org), an intergovernmental agency established by Commonwealth governments in 1987 to foster and promote collaboration and partnership in open, distance and technology enabled learning is one of the most successful examples of international collaboration. COL, in turn has fostered partnerships, for networking among various countries and institutions, especially in a South-South context, and has partnered with institutions in various regions and countries of the Commonwealth for the development and delivery of courses. As an international inter-governmental agency, COL has been able to effectively broker partnerships between global donor agencies and regional and national institutions, both Pan-Commonwealth and within specific geographic regions. Its specific work in the South Asian region and specifically in India, is described in their policy and other documents (http://www.col.org/regional/colinAsia.htm).

Other such successful networks are also currently operating. The Global Distance EducationNet (Global DistEdNet) is a knowledge guide to distance education designed to help those individuals and institutions interested in using distance education for human development. The Network consists of a core site and regional sites in all parts of the world (http://www1.worldbank.org/disted and www.col.org/disted).

SACODiL, The South Asian Consortium for Open and Distance Learning is a fledgling organization established under the aegis of the South Asian Association for Regional Cooperation (SAARC) to promote collaboration in open and distance learning among South Asian institutions. It has decided to work towards capacity building using mutual expertise, facilitate learner mobility through recognition of mutual degrees and credit transfer, apart from developing common programmes. Global Mega Universities Network (GMUNET) comprising twenty such institutions from across the world, has decided to work together in collaborative research, applications of ICT for cross-border delivery and development of programmes for community empowerment.

Other kinds of international partnerships are in the nature of institutional collaborations for programme development and delivery. The Commonwealth Youth in Development Programme run across several countries is one such example that shares common curriculum and delivery across several countries. The South Asia Foundation's Diploma in Environment and Sustainable Development, being jointly developed by six South Asian open universities is another example of a working international partnership (http://www.southasiafoundation.org/saf/distancelearning distancelearning.asp). COL's initiated and enabled CEMBA (Commonwealth Executive Master of Business Administration) and the CEMPA (Commonwealth Executive Master of Public Administration) is yet another example of a working international partnership in distance education (www.col.org/clippings/MBA_MPA.htm).

Such partnerships broaden the perspective of partners who need to adapt to each other's working style, methods and viewpoint. Opportunities and avenues for partner institutions to build and upgrade the quality of their services and activities such as course design, materials development, and student support are enhanced in such collaborative efforts. And, from another perspective, one of the strongest motivations for international collaboration is cost-effective market expansion.

Other kinds of inter-institutional partnerships have also been very successful. The scope of collaboration among institutions can range from a few aspects to extensive ones, including the formation of new entities. Forms of international collaboration between institutions can include twinning programmes offering programmes jointly. Such arrangements have distinct advantages of cooperative planning, development, and delivery of programmes. Moreover, the quality of the programmes as also the stature of the institutions involved is enhanced.

Consortia arrangements among several institutions, which provide funding and staff for the joint ventures, can also be undertaken. An advantage of the consortia approach is that it helps institutions address key policy issues in addition to the pooling of resources to achieve educational objectives. Successful consortia are guided by their own mission statements that are reflective of the individual partners' interests. They operate under a governance structure that clearly delineates the roles and responsibilities of partners. They have the firm support of all partners and a funding policy that is agreeable to all.

One could continue to list a large number of such arrangements. Suffice it to say here that no matter what is the kind, successful collaborations in ODL must have some critical ingredients.

The Ingredients of Collaboration

Let us first briefly define collaboration. COL describes institutional collaboration as sharing resources of any type with one or more partner institutions. In Distance Education, collaboration may be between institutions in the same neighbourhood or state, within the same country or region, and anywhere in the world. Institutions do not have to have similar interests or a similar level of expertise to collaborate, but they do need to have resources that other institutions would like to share. In collaboration, institutions share:

- *Knowledge and expertise*: joint research projects, designing and delivering curriculum and course material.
- *Infrastructure*: information and communications technology (ICT) facilities such as video, audio conferencing equipment and computer rooms.
- *Human resources*: formal arrangements for external examination or peer review.
- *Services*: such as libraries, bookstores, student counselling.
- *Costs of starting or maintaining educational programmes* (http://www.col.org/knowledge/ks_instcollaboration.htm).
- *Institutional culture and perspective*: student and/or faculty exchange programmes.

The benefits of such collaborations are many — resource sharing and flexibility; growth of an institutional culture, team work, quality improvement; and cost-efficiencies. But to succeed, collaborative efforts must have:

- *Shared vision and commitment to grow.* Each partner must understand the mission of their joint efforts. Such a shared vision must be internalised among the many units in each partner institution. New entrants to the system need to be oriented; older faculty and administrators need to continuously renew their understanding of the institutional vision and policy.

- *Vision and policies that can be translated into strategic and operational plans* to establish clear priorities, specific benchmarks, time lines, and standards against which they can subsequently be evaluated. Operational plans translate the vision to reality, enable the setting of priorities, determination of specific resources, ways in which such resources will be networked, programmes steered, implemented and monitored, revenues shared, and even include mechanisms where academic freedom and dissent can be handled in a proactive manner. This exercise must take place among all the collaborating partners.
- *Coordinating teams and mechanisms* to take the shared vision to implementation. This may mean new ways of funding and disbursement; facilitative policies, procedures and mechanisms for rationalising work between several disparate academic, production, delivery and learner support units. Intra-institutional mechanisms must be coordinated with and geared to the same processes and those in partnering institutions so that budgets, timeframes, templates, and the many other detailed aspects of programme implementation can take place.
- *Quality control.* Courses offered in collaboration by foreign institutions should be relevant to the needs of the learners and quality standards should be maintained. Quality assurance tools must be jointly developed and equally administered.
- *Mechanism for streamlining procedures.* Differences in key policy areas among institutions must be addressed at the outset so that procedures are streamlined before activities start.
- *Updated programme content.* Course content should be reviewed regularly, revised and updated as needed in the light of changes and developments in the ODL environment.
- *Assumption of main coordinating roles by partners' key decision-makers.* Coordination should be done by people who share the same interests of education and distance learners.
- *Monitoring and evaluation mechanisms* for regular and on-going process evaluation so that the inputs can serve as feedback and feed forward.
- *Leadership.* Like any other venture, the quality of the partnership is only as good as the time and interest that leaders of partnering institutions bring into it.

Forging collaboration and executing it gainfully, as may be seen from the above, is an extremely complex process. While it is easy to list all the ingredients of collaboration, it is much more difficult to make collaboration work on the ground. It requires knowledge, leadership, diplomacy, patience, and in depth knowledge of both domain and processes, along with a great deal of cultural sensitivity, mutual respect and trust. More than anything, collaborations require tolerance as each different aspect unfolds in due course of time.

Earlier, we spoke of the benefits of collaboration. But such benefits come only when we can recognise that in a diverse world, there are different cultural contexts and organisational settings. For this reason alone, for success to be visible in any collaboration, one must look to the long term, and not expect quick results.

Perhaps, this is why it is so difficult to identify and describe specific examples of international collaboration, especially within the South Asian context.

International Agencies and Distance Education in India

Barring sectoral differences, nearly every international donor agency, funding and technical assistance institution has committed itself to the use of distance education as a key strategy to address the MDGs. International funding institutions such as the World Bank and Asian Development Banks include distance education as part of their education desks, while UN agencies such as UNESCO, UNICEF, FAO, WHO, and ITU work within their respective areas of specialization. After Africa, Asia receives maximum attention of funding agencies. Given that South Asia is home to the largest number of poor and deprived, India is one of the major focus countries for support.

India is one of the most important countries of Asia and within South Asia, it is by far the most important and the largest — whether in terms of its size and resources or in terms of its needs. It is both a knowledge society super power and home to the poorest of the world. India can rightfully boast of impressive educational and telecommunications infrastructure as well as of huge open and distance education systems. It is home to the single largest open university in the democratic world with cumulative enrolment of 1.3 million and annual in-take of about 300,000; its experience in distance education dates back to 1962 when the first correspondence course was started at the University of Delhi. Indian and other South Asian open universities have, with some modifications, been patterned on the Open University of United Kingdom. India also has the largest National Institute of Open Schooling with cumulative enrolment of 1.6 million.

For all of this, data on the exact nature, extent and quality of international agency involvement in distance education is difficult to come by. Educational institutions operate as independent and autonomous units — which they are — but rarely do they share information with each other. The Distance Education Council, created as a statutory authority of Indira Gandhi National Open University, is the apex authority for ensuring coordinated growth and delivery of quality education through distance mode. Only recently it has started compiling data on nature of programmes, size of enrolment, modes of educational delivery, area of offering, etc. so as to share information with all concerned (DEC, 2004). However, such information is fairly difficult to obtain from participating institutions and requires a lot of follow up. Therefore, such data and information is likely to have key gaps and may not be most authentic. To that extent, one is constrained at times to gather information in bits and pieces and analyse to find patterns. Existing data point to different genres of international agency involvement in the country. Two international agencies have been key players in educational development—UNESCO and COL. UNESCO has a broader mandate as an organization that supports education, science and culture and communication. COL has been established for and has a more focused mandate to support, foster and promote open and distance learning. It is but natural that the latter agency assumes a far greater importance in the ODL scenario in India.

Grants-In-Aid

Agencies such as UNESCO were involved in early experiments in the use of media for education, beginning with television in 1959. Indian television owes its humble beginnings to grants-in-aid and financial and expert support from UNESCO. Subsequently there has been aid provided by the earstwhile Overseas Development Administration (ODA) and later the World Bank for primary education through the District Primary Education Project-Distance Education Programme.

UNESCO also provided support to India's Indira Gandhi National Open University by funding the UNESCO Chair in Distance Education for a period of five years in the 1990s. The mandate of the chair was to work toward quality assurance in teacher education in open and distance learning.

Other smaller grants from UNESCO to fund small initiatives have enabled the testing of technologies in education. For example, in the period 1998-2001, IGNOU conducted training programmes for science teachers of South Asian Universities and colleges in the use of various media for educational transaction in the classroom or at distance and university science teaching. For primary school teachers, UNESCO sponsored projects on ICT and environmental education have been executed by IGNOU. For secondary teachers, funding has come for training through mobile support and so on. There is some data available but accurate evaluation studies recording the processes and results of such small initiatives are not available in the public domain.

In its early years, the Commonwealth of Learning (COL) supported IGNOU through a grant-in-aid for the establishment and development of the Staff Training and Research Institute for Distance Education (STRIDE). The mandate of STRIDE was to serve as a national and regional resource centre for fostering research, and capacity building in the South Asian region and beyond.

COL's strategy in addressing poverty reduction in South Asia is to facilitate national and international agencies involved in poverty reduction programmes to use ODL for developing entrepreneurial skills for self-employment, continuing professional education, extension and lifelong learning. Partners include agricultural and veterinary science universities, Ministries of Agriculture, open universities and international organisations such as ICRISAT and FAO. Outputs include self-learning materials for agricultural and veterinary science professionals in India and extension officials and rural farmers in Bangladesh, India and Sri Lanka.

Other donor and financial institutions have also supported open and distance education — but more in other South Asian countries than in India. For institutions such as the Asian Development Bank, India has served more as a resource than as a client or recipient country.

Partnerships and Collaborations

COL, as a focused technical assistance agency, has moved away from an era of direct funding support to partnerships with local institutions for indigenous capacity building. Its efforts and contribution to distance education and open learning in India must be seen in this context. The following descriptions of COL activities and partnerships in India are drawn from http://www.col.org/regional/COLinAsia.htm.

Since its inception, COL has had a very close working relationship with Indira Gandhi National Open University (IGNOU) and the National Institute of Open Schooling (NIOS) (formerly the National Open School). Partnering with IGNOU, COL has collaborated in projects ranging from the training of rural youth in commercial agriculture to developing materials for legal literacy among women. One the most successful cases of collaboration has been the Rajiv Gandhi Fellowship Scheme, which is now in the second phase of its presentation. Under this scheme, COL sponsors a cohort of upto fifty teachers from the commonwealth countries to the MA (Distance Education) programme of IGNOU.

COL has worked with other conventional and open education providers and research agencies such as the University of Delhi, National Council for Educational Research and Training (NCERT) and NIOS for South-South cooperation and has facilitated the development of a South Asian Consortium for Teacher Education and Development (SACTED).

There are several such partnerships that COL has facilitated in India — whether in literacy and adult education; lifelong learning for farmers, technology testing using ham and community radio, or a portal to provide informational support for farmers in semi arid tropics. Quality assurance, research in ODL, faculty exchange and attachments, and media education have also been priority areas for support and collaboration by COL.

COL has been the first port of call for support and collaboration in the field of open and distance learning. Such support has been based on the premise that partnerships which enable institutions to build up their own capacities are the best way of ensuring sustainability in the long run and ensure a win-win situation for all partners.

COL's regional agency, the Commonwealth Educational Media Centre for Asia (CEMCA), regularly conducts training workshops in the region on themes as diverse as instructional design and e-learning, publishes a quarterly news journal, *EduComm Asia,* and produces knowledge resources on various applications of ICTs in education.

Finally, in an era of dwindling resources, international agencies have been compelled to partner with each other and with national institutions to ensure relevance, optimise funding, leverage skills and remain faithful to their missions. While agency vision and mission have not changed much, the manner of their working has undergone a paradigm shift.

A Paradigm Shift and its Consequences

Slowly and subtly, but visible over time, there has been a paradigm shift in the way international agencies have engaged with development of distance education in India. Such a shift has been triggered in the first instance, by the global forces of liberalisation, privatisation, and globalisation; which have brought in private sector players and encouraged public-private partnerships. Second, by India's economic growth over the last decade, and its emergence as a global player, with human resources to meet its own and other nations' needs, have transformed the nature of the relationship between India and international agencies. Third, in an era of shrinking resources, donor agencies and technical assistance organisations are also under pressure from their stakeholders to demonstrate success and effectiveness on the ground.

In such a situation, the ingredients of successful partnerships assume importance with an emphasis of equity in both the relationships and in the sharing of resources and systems. Motivations for partnerships are as much based on altruism as on hard realities.

Economic pressures, global competition to survive changing educational demands and paradigms, relevance of content, the need for a "critical mass", increasing educational opportunities, sharing technological resources, improving overall quality are among the motivations for collaboration. But, for partnerships to succeed there has to be a paradigm shift in the way that traditional (whether open or conventional) educational institutions in India conduct their business.

Conclusion

For many years, India was a recipient of international aid. Today, it is a partner and a donor, lending its resources and services to other parts of the world. Its relationship with international agencies has undergone a change since the early years of its independence. It is now seen as an international resource and storehouse of experience in the design, implementation, and evaluation of developmental and educational projects, small and large particularly in IT. Its 'brain drain" has today become its 'brain gain".

Yet today, India and its institutions cannot remain inward looking; nor should they look to international agencies as donors. History has shown that India is a test bed for new educational initiatives and that Indian experience and expertise is valued globally. Indian institutions have much to offer to the world, if they move from being recipients of donor support to collaborators in international educational endeavours. "Sharing" is what collaboration is all about and this is what Indian institutions have to move toward as they partner with international institutions.

References

Calderoni, Jose (1998). Telesecundaria: Using TV to Bring Education to Rural Mexico. *Education and Technology Notes Series,* 3(2) p. 1-10.

DEC (2004). IGNOU Database, New Delhi: IGNOU (Mimeo).

Lerner, Daniel (1958). *The Passing of Traditional Society. Modernizing the Middle East.* New York: The Free Press.

Rogers, Everett M (1969). *Diffusion of Innovations.* New York: Free Press.

Schramm, Wilbur (1964). *Mass Media and National Development.* Paris: UNESCO.

Dr. Usha V. Reddi is Director, Commonwealth Educational Media Centre for Asia, 52 Tughlakabad Institutional Area, New Delhi.
E-mail: ureddi@col.org; Website: www.cemca.org

41

Entry of Foreign Universities in India: Issues and Implications for the ODL Systems

Sunil Kumar

Introduction

Cross border provision of higher education attracts debate for a variety of reasons. The state of Higher Education defines the stage of development of a society, and determines its future. Higher Education, in its form and content, prepares learners in all themes of life that are contextual and relevant to a society. The state of Higher Education also represents the society's present capacity and, future potential for creating knowledge capital, which drives a 'knowledge economy'. Universities are unique not only in possessing the power to produce ideas and knowledge or interpret them, but also because of the academic freedom that they enjoy in most societies. The terms on which societies accept entry of foreign institutions of higher learning, depend on how they perceive the presence of such institutions would impact their national – social, political and economic – interests and, human resource development. No society would adopt policies on cross border provision of higher education because of international pressures. The response has varied – some countries allow foreign universities and institutions to enter their borders only on invitation. Some others insist on State determined approvals of the content of education that would be served, on grounds of protecting national language, culture and other domestic societal sensitivities.

This chapter is intended to, as the title suggests, identify issues and possible implications. It does not contain the official views of the Government of India in regard to the policy on the entry of foreign education providers. A national policy in this regard is presently under wider consultation. Some aspects of it, which are mentioned ahead in the chapter, were put in the public domain in the now withdrawn draft legislative bill on fixation of fee and regulation of admissions in private unaided institutions and, hence it would be premature to predict real outcomes. To begin with, we present a general survey of the variety of ways in which higher education providers move across national borders. It is followed by a description of the general arguments for, and against, the entry of foreign higher education institutions in the particular context of the open and distance learning. Irrespective of adopting policies permitting or disallowing foreign providers, it is imperative to identify and address issues in preparing domestic higher education systems for developments taking place around the world. The present regulatory framework governing the entry of foreign higher education providers have been discussed and areas which need strengthening have been highlighted; particularly in the context of the open distance learning in India. The offer in the GATS regime for education services has been indicated; since there are no agreements, this offer is by no means binding yet.

Cross Border Delivery: Prevailing Scenario and its Implications

Higher Education services are provided across national borders in a variety of ways, which could be broadly categorised as

- programmatic collaboration, which enables sharing of academic responsibility for individual or joint certification with host institutions;
- twinning programmes, whereby students undertake study in the foreign campus of the provider as well as in the host country campus;
- franchises awarded to domestic providers for the use of 'brand' names of foreign providers;
- linking programmes, allowing transfer of credits obtained from domestic providers, for pursuing programmes of study offered by foreign providers in other countries;
- collaboration by a consortium of foreign providers for setting up institutions and offering programmes of study in the host country with management of the institution fully in domestic hands; and
- off-shore campuses of institutions in the exporting countries, offering programmes and certification claiming to be at par with those in the main or originating campus.

In order to understand the implications of the entry of foreign universities and other Higher Education providers on the ODL format, it is important to appreciate the distinguishing features of the ODL system as compared to the traditional classroom-based and campus-based system. Notwithstanding the broad common objective of providing education, the ODL system offers flexibility in terms of:

- age, gender and eligibility related barriers;
- learning habits;
- capacity and capability i.e. the number of learners;
- teacher-learner proximity or the absence of it;

- pedagogical and other mediating processes;
- time and place of study including learner mobility;
- cost-effectiveness; and
- facility and adoption of new technologies which have led to the new paradigms of on-line learning, e-Learning, virtual class-rooms and virtual universities.

The emerging information and communication technologies (ICT) have undoubtedly strengthened and supplemented the traditional system of higher education through campus intranets, online library information systems, campus management information systems, pedagogical aids, dedicated application softwares, and other new fields of knowledge. What the ICT has done to the ODL systems is even more remarkable – it has transformed, and not just supplemented, ODL based higher education – redefining programme material and content creation, cost-effectiveness and pricing through economies of scale and resource sharing and collaboration, multiplying access through satellite, broad-band and wireless connectivity, equity and quality through real time dissemination, interactivity enabled feedback, testing and assessment using audio, video and multimedia. Indeed, every facet of distance education has been impacted positively by the new technologies. The 'correspondence courses' have become archaic. In developing countries with low access rates to higher education in the traditional system, the ODL is not to be viewed in the life-long learning perspective alone. To illustrate, in the Indian context, the access rate to higher education in the eligible age group of 18-23 years is less than nine percent (GoI, 2005), as compared to 20-25% for some other developing countries and up to 50% for developed countries. Even the present access rate would have been impossible without an expanding ODL system spear-headed by the Indira Gandhi National Open University (IGNOU) and other State Open Universities, as well as the distance education offered by the traditional universities and institutions deemed to be universities. The current Indian enrolment in traditional campuses is estimated at 9.4 million, supplemented further by the ODL enrolment, which is reportedly about two million. Evidently, the 10th Plan (2002-07) target enrolment of 12.5 million in Indian higher education is being met substantially through the ODL system, which is the fastest growing sector in tertiary education. Almost 22 per cent of the enrolment in higher education institutions in India is attributed to these Open Universities, which offer doctoral, masters, and bachelor level programmes in subjects as diverse as Tourism Studies, Engineering, Youth Development and Community Cardiology (CABE, 2005). Education planners in India can not, while estimating the demand for Higher Education during the 11th Plan, ignore to factor the snow-balling effect of the Sarva Shiksha Abhiyan (Education for All) – coupled with the potential universalisation of secondary schooling. This may well be true for most developing countries, currently afflicted with the maladies of low school enrolment and high drop out, low access to higher education compounded by low capacity of the traditional campus based system. Inequity in the availability of the traditional higher education institutions across regions, the rural-urban bias within regions and, gender based socio-cultural factors, which inhibit enrolment of women in the traditional campuses, further underline the supplementary role for the ODL system in developing countries.

The argument in favour of the transcending national borders by higher education providers is based on the market-economics premise, that they do so in pursuit of learners, who are the 'consumers'. Going by this argument, declining 'client' population in the relevant age-group in developed countries would necessarily encourage universities to seek enrolment of learners from other countries; and in the long run, cross borders in one or more ways mentioned earlier. According to an estimate, over one hundred thousand Indian students go abroad for higher education. While universities from the US, UK, Australia, Canada vie for foreign students, geo-political considerations of security, which place certain immigration restrictions affecting learner mobility, are bound to compel universities to cross borders in search of learners both, by setting up physical campuses as well as offering education at a distance. While trade in education services has been legitimised under GATS, it is difficult for many to come to terms with the notion that universities can be akin to 'firms' and businesses that can exit the market place, when the going is bad – leaving the learner to fend for himself. In the Indian context, to many, it is outrageous to imagine Indian universities behaving as profit driven corporates – specifically, since the Supreme Court of India, through its various judgements has ruled against commercialisation and profiteering in education, even though successive orders of the apex court in recent times have come around to recognising private effort, justification for generating reasonable surpluses of revenues to be ploughed back for institutional development by private unaided institutions in higher education, as well as the concept of cross-subsidies through differential fee structure as between non resident Indians and others.

Critics fear that cross-border Foreign Education Providers (FEPs) of higher education services may compromise national education systems and, according to this view, the influx of foreign higher education institutions is raising concerns for the integrity of national quality assurance and accreditation systems in developing countries; more than sixty economies world wide have thus recognized that some form of external quality assurance system would be essential to prevent a situation where "rogue providers offering low-quality educational experience and qualifications of limited value" swamp developing nations (OECD, 2004). The introduction of ICTs and internet-based education programs that are beyond the purview of conventional national domestic regulatory mechanisms have only accentuated apprehensions about the inadequacies of national quality assurance and accreditation systems. While the National Assessment and Accreditation Council, an inter-university centre under the University Grants Commission Act and, the National Board of Accreditation under the All India Council for Technical Education Act, along with the various statutory authorities, form a fairly comprehensive framework to ensure quality control for domestic players and, sectoral regulatory guidelines have been prepared, work has started on designing a comprehensive framework, which could address learner anxieties about the quality of foreign education institutions offering programmes across the board.

Regulating Entry of Foreign Providers: Concerns and Implications

The AICTE regulations for entry and operation of foreign universities/institutions imparting technical education in India was notified in 2003. These regulations, which are in respect of technical education, are intended to (i) facilitate collaboration and partnering, (ii) safeguard students' interests, (iii) maintain standards prescribed by the AICTE, (iv) weed out non-accredited FEPs, and (v) regulate FEPs already in India. A procedure has been laid down by the AICTE for registering FEPs seeking to operate through collaboration or on their own. Information is sought on the infrastructure, faculty, fee, curricula, financial resources with the FEP. A Committee of Experts scrutinizes the proposals and, the approvals are valid for a limited period initially. During the validity of the registration, the FEPs are accorded 'National Treatment'. The AICTE Regulations do not permit the 'franchise' route. Accreditation by authorised agency in the home country is a pre-requisite. The FEP is required to furnish the proof of recognition and equivalence of degree, intended to be offered by it in India, in its home country. The FEP is also bound by the advice of the AICTE in regard to admissions, student eligibility and curriculum/courses offered.

Not all regulations intended for the traditional system are equally applicable to the ODL system, even though the broad principles remain the same. The IGNOU Act and Statutes provide for a Distance Education Council (DEC), which is charged with the mandate to maintain standards for education through distance mode. The DEC (Regulations for the Entry into and operation of Foreign Universities/ Educational Institutions imparting Open and Distance Education in India) Regulations, which are to be notified, aim to cater to the ODL system in the same way as the AICTE Regulations do, for the conventional technical education system. The objectives are broadly similar, namely, to (i) "establish a framework for collaboration and partnership" in education, research and training through the open and distance mode, (ii) systematize the operation of existing FEPs operating either individually or in collaboration with Indian institutions, (iii) safeguard the interest of students through a watch on the quality and standards of education, and (iv) ensure accountability for ODL activities. The DEC Regulations are intended to have a wider applicability on all ODL activities carried out in India "in any manner". Indeed, with so many uncertainties and unforeseen modalities in an ever evolving scenario of technological changes, it is not surprising that DEC regulations are broad, all encompassing and, provide for abundant safety as an insurance against the unknown. Both the AICTE and the DEC Regulations mandate that the Missions in India, of the country from where the educational providers hail from, certify the genuineness of the FEPs.

While socio-political issues that affect decisions on the entry of FEPs, as indeed issues in the realm of economics – repatriation of revenues and levying of fee, for example – are important policy inputs; academic issues are, perhaps, even more critical. Foremost among the academic issues of relevance are those relating to the recognition of institutions, programmes and qualifications which protect domestic interests from what are called 'rogue' providers as well as 'rogue' accreditation agencies. In the context of distance education, the problems are accentuated as there is no physical presence of the providers who could be proceeded against, for lapses and sub-standard provisions. An understanding of the evaluation protocols followed in the countries from where the FEPs come, the standards for recognizing the accrediting agencies, transparency and fairness of methodologies are all, important considerations while permitting the entry of FEPs. These need to be expressly spelt out in the DEC Regulations. Regulations in respect of on-line provision of higher education also need to be developed.

There are two approaches to the problem of tackling the technology edge (especially the online and virtual universities) over national jurisdictions: One is to invoke the sovereign power of recognition of qualifications for purposes of employment, professional practice, or higher studies and the other's to frame policy regulations for telecasting – making it mandatory for uplinking from within India – and making it mandatory for those virtual universities to be legal which use '.in' domain names that can be regulated jurisdictionally under the national IT laws. Similar other restrictions are in place in some developing countries. Particular reference can be made to regulation in respect of 'antennae' height in Malaysia and higher internet rates in Jamaica.

Apart from the regulations imposed by authorities such as the Councils, regulations by professional associations has to be factored in determining the programmes, institutions, formats that are to be allowed in the domestic arena. For example, an institution may be accredited for only a few programmes that it offers; its programmes may be accredited or recognised for the traditional mode rather than the ODL mode. It is also possible that not all the accrediting agencies approving various programmes offered by the institution are of the requisite standard or adopting acceptable methodologies. While these propositions may be true for both the traditional as well as the ODL systems, it ought to be understood that entry of a foreign institution in one mode would not necessarily imply that the other mode shall be automatically allowed.

Another critical academic concern is in regard to the nature of programmes that are offered by the FEPs. This is equally true of the ODL as well as traditional system. If private provisioning of higher education in India by universities or deemed to be universities is any example to go by, it is evident that the 'market' considerations of offering programmes which are in 'demand', rather than what may be important from the national development or welfare perspective, are preferred even by the foreign providers. While the foreign providers of the traditional system may prefer to serve in regions with the prospects of better 'demand', leading to skewed regional presence or urban bias, invariably at the cost of students in inaccessible regions; in the ODL mode, virtual provision of course contents being simultaneously available, there is comparatively even access, depending on the status of communication and media. The programmes on offer, however, still show a marked preference for highly saleable professional programmes like business studies and IT, which can attract high fee. However, neglect of research and training in basic sciences, humanities and general education and the emphasis on courses that 'sell' would be common to both types of modes in private provisioning, whether by domestic or foreign providers. As a result, often resource-strapped domestic public institutions are tasked with catering to the economic, social, and cultural development of the country, while foreign institutions engage themselves in 'for-profit' ventures.

It may also be argued, that foreign higher education institutions may threaten the cohesion in society, where the inequality between rich and poor students would be apparent. While students who cannot afford to pay the fees of foreign institutions would be compelled to absorb comparatively inferior education, affluent students (and teachers seeking higher compensation) may be attracted to foreign higher education providers that promise better post-graduation employment opportunities (Breton and Lambert, 2003).

Domestic Regulation: Future Directions

The Government of India is engaged in finalizing a national policy in regard to the entry of FEPs. The issue has been discussed extensively at the national conference of state ministers of higher and technical education in January, 2005 and the policy options are being examined in detail. Rao Committee (GoI, 2005) has recommended a calibrated approach wherein which a trial period, with a built-in review based on experience, has been suggested for abundant caution. According to the Committee, operation of FEPs should be allowed only after putting in place suitable regulatory and monitoring mechanisms at the national level; initially for a limited period on a trial basis. The longer term approval should be considered after a thorough review of performance in the initial short term. One of the options suggested is a provision for a substantial security deposit or corpus fund as a safeguard against 'fly by night' operators. Even initial short-term approvals may be considered only for those FEPs who are accredited in their respective countries of origin. Moreover, there ought to be a level playing field for domestic providers too. There should be a separate treatment for monitoring and regulation for FE Institutions, other than universities. FEPs should not be allowed to repatriate surpluses. India should not make any commitments, which violates this principle.[1]

Preparing domestic higher education institutions for challenges posed by globalization and entry of foreign providers in ODL mode, necessarily demands concerted action in terms of legal reform and a re-evaluation of national education policies. Dynamism in internet-based education would also need to be adequately reflected in the law. In the context of the ODL system, paperless and borderless education requires domestic laws and regulations to provide for technical advancements and develop regulatory frame-works that are capable of maintaining quality in delivery of education at a distance. At the same time, the existing public systems in domestic ODL institutions would have to be strengthened and equipped to meet global challenges. Target-oriented funding of domestic institutions, insistence on quality, infrastructure development, full-time faculty enhancement, and course relevance to national objectives are some aspects that must define India's higher education policy.

Some educationists are of the view that

- the entry of foreign providers would bring about an improvement in the quality of the domestic provisioning of higher education; and
- greater private participation in higher education would lead to the strengthening of the domestic sector, which can then be made more efficient to face the challenges of globalisation.

These need to be considered carefully because it is improbable that merely making such provisions would strengthen Indian higher education – particularly, through the ODL mode. In our view, the caution prescribed by the Rao Committee is important for preventing the threat of crass commercialisation, of indiscriminate spread of study centres and the dishing out of a variety of programmes, some of which are not even amenable to be delivered in the distance mode at present. Public systems in different countries have responded to globalisation in higher education in different ways. Public funded universities in some countries, which are unable to individually compete with the entry of FEPs from the west, have joined hands to form consortia that can jointly vie for students internationally. The University of the Arctic – a consortium of Scandinavian, Russian and Canadian institutions – is one such example of a consortium. In the context of open distance learning, the IGNOU in India has taken the lead in tying up with some of the State Open Universities and conventional institutions of repute to utilise collective strengths under Joint Certification Programmes.

The issue of cross-border provision of Higher Education has to have distinct policy approaches in respect of the two modes. India's strength in open learning gives it certain advantages. Since the ODL systems are not constrained by national borders, most of the mega universities have varying degrees of foreign presence. The IGNOU offers programmes in as many as 30 countries, partnering with local institutions. IGNOU, through its partner institutions, assesses demand for programmes, prescribes eligibility for admissions, arranges for fee collection, distributes course material, collects student assignments and feedback, engages competent counsellors, arranges for evaluation student assessments and examination (Raghvan, 2003). The IGNOU is also collaborating with multilateral organizations like the COL, to develop some of its programmes of studies. For instance, its collaboration with Open Universities in the SAARC region has resulted in common curriculum and Programmes of study under the umbrella of COL. One way to look at the implications of the entry of FEPs in the ODL is to see how such a policy would affect our existing open universities. The IGNOU's leadership role in support of distance education in the SAARC and the African regions – provides favoured nation treatment to countries in the region – would have to be either withdrawn or extended to all member countries of the WTO once India's commitment under GATS are finalised. The funding support and preferential treatment to public providers could also be interpreted as being a "non-tariff barrier", by member nations. Safeguards in this regard have to be worked out. However, there is uncertainty and anxiety over the fate of domestic regulations or safeguards, even if permissible, because in the event of a conflict between such regulations and market access, the latter is expected to prevail under the GATS.

GATS and the Indian position

Although Foreign Direct Investment in education is 100% through the automatic route, as mentioned earlier, the Government of India is presently in the process of evolving a national sectoral policy for higher education. In so far as ODL is concerned, Mode I of GATS (cross-border supply) facilitates foreign universities to enrol students by offering admissions and instructions online. India's offer in the sub-sector of Higher Education under GATS (CPC 923) in respect of Mode I places no limitations on Market Access subject to regulations applicable to domestic providers in the country of origin. There are no limitations on National Treatment.[2] In respect of Mode II (consumption abroad) also, India has offered no limitations on either Market Access or National Treatment. The current offer in respect of Mode III (commercial presence) also has no limitations in respect of Market Access, subject to the condition that fees to be charged can be fixed by an appropriate authority and no capitation fee or profiteering is permitted. The offer in regard to Market Access is also subject to the regulation in place or to be prescribed by the appropriate regulatory authority. There are no limitations on National Treatment under Mode III. India has currently kept its offer unbound in regard to Market Access and National Treatment under Mode IV. The forum of the UNESCO which has shown great sensitivity to social conditions and cultural and human development factors surrounding Higher Education, has also been engaged on the issue of Quality Assurance of cross-border Higher Education. India has concurred with the voluntary and non-binding UNESCO-OECD Guidelines on Cross-border Higher Education, albeit with the observations that i) Foreign institutions should be permitted to operate in the host country only if they are accredited in the home country, ii) Foreign institutions should offer only those programmes in the host country, that they offer in the country of origin, iii) Cross-border education providers may be subject to the same sanctions applicable to domestic providers in the home country, iv) Fixation of fees must be subject to the regulatory framework of the host country, and v) Permission of foreign educational institutions should be guided by principles of mutual recognition and reciprocity.[3]

As mentioned earlier, India is in the process of putting in place a suitable legislative framework for addressing the issue of FEPs in the context of cross-border provision of higher education. A draft legislation had been put in the public domain and is being changed based on the feedback from the state governments, members of the Central Advisory Board of Education (CABE), eminent academia and members of the public. Some of the main provisions of the draft in regard to foreign universities may be mentioned, if only as a pointer to the thinking in this direction. Foreign institutions may have to apply to be notified as a Foreign Education Provider and, for the status of an institution deemed to be a university under the UGC Act. This vital provision would have the impact of bringing FEPs under domestic regulations of quality, standards, recognition most importantly of not being a for-profit body and requiring incorporation under a central or state law as may be applicable. Some other provisions of the draft bill now withdrawn for wider consultations included the provision that no FEP shall admit students without being permitted to do so. A corpus fund would have to be created by way of security, and the fee to be charged would be determined by an appropriate authority. Penalties for contravention of provisions have also been envisaged in the draft. The draft is being reworked at present (http://www.nic.in).

International scenario

Different stake-holders react differently to concerns about globalization of Higher Education – we are one of the largest functioning democracies, where by definition, public opinion refines and distills policy making. The response to the issue of entry of FEPs has to take in to account all view points. It is not a simple question of accepting or rejecting winds of change or competition. We need to debate questions such as: On what terms, and how, do we manage change? Who are the gainers and who loses? Are the fears well founded? Do the seeming positives that the protagonists propound, really beneficial? Calibrating responses to challenges, is often time consuming. There is one set of public opinion in India, which is impatient with our calibrated responses to the issue. There is another set of public opinion, as articulated in various forums, that public policies in a society like ours can not be left to market-theorists alone; that the social justice issues are equally and perhaps more important determinants; that the degree to which we regulate without stifling innovation and efficiency can not be arrived at econometrically alone. It has to take into account cultural specificities. We are aware of what are generally perceived to be the advantages of globalization of higher education, in the literature on the subject. Increased competition, institutional-interconnect, technology over-rides, location-disadvantages, that it supplements and complements domestic education infrastructure; and, so on. However, we are equally aware of several concerns as well: "Commercialisation" or "for profit" ventures in education, militates against certain cultural values. Knowledge, in our value system has always been considered as sharable not tradable; the current world view is different. Yet, as mentioned earlier, judicial pronouncements have, in successive matters before our highest court, come down heavily against any attempts to profiteer from higher education, Demand-Supply mismatch which is one reason for our low access rate, could further be accentuated with unaffordable higher fee. Regulating curricula that may be offered by FEPs, in the social sciences and humanities, that may overlook cultural sensitivities of our people or hurt the sovereignty and integrity of the nation, is also a serious concern. But then, these are not issues peculiar only to us.

India is also reviewing the differing policy stands taken by countries depending on their national interests. For instance, while China requires foreign institutions operating in that country to establish not-for-profit partnerships with Chinese institutions subject to conditions on language and administration, New Zealand and Australia have been committed to full market access and national treatment for private tertiary education providers. Singapore on the other hand relies on external distance education programmes and foreign university branch campuses to supplement domestic demand for higher education, while Malaysia – another developing country – has permitted foreign educational providers on a conditional 'invitation only' basis and its policy is expected to make Malaysia a net exporter of higher education services in the years to come. The Malaysian government, "concerned about the cultural impact" of "foreign and generally instrumental curriculum" has stipulated compulsory subjects in the national language, Malaysian studies, moral and Islamic studies.

Conclusion

The issue of entry of foreign providers in higher education is indeed highly volatile, fraught with academic as well as socio-economic and legal concerns. Pressure of globalisation, escalating demands for higher education and capability constraints in domestic sector of most developing countries favour cross-border supply while concerns of quality, commercialisation and resulting inequity create cautionary pressures against such developments. The desirability of comprehensive domestic regulation to safeguard national interests is now a well understood and convincingly argued fact, one that is being acted upon in various spheres of higher education policy. While with internationalisation of higher education and the trade related imperatives of the GATS era are inescapable realities of our times, timely national response in the form of domestic regulations evolved out of wider consultations with all stakeholders and strengthening of both the domestic ODL and traditional systems will undoubtedly strengthen our position on the global educational scenario.

Notes

1. Report of the Committee on suggesting policy on Foreign Universities in India, MHRD, Government of India, 2005.
2. Website of the Ministry of Commerce, Government of India at nic.in
3. India's stand in respect of Major Programme I - Education at Commission II, UNESCO General Conference, 2005, Paris

References

Breton, Gilles and Lambert, Michel (eds.) (2003). *Universities and Globalisation, Private Linkages and Public Trust*. Paris: UNESCO.

GoI (2005). *Report of the Committee on Suggesting Policy on Foreign Universities in India* (Rao Committee). New Delhi: MHRD, GoI.

GoI (2005). *Selected Statistics (2004-05)*. New Delhi: MHRD, GoI.

IGNOU (2005). *Annual Report 2004-05*. New Delhi: IGNOU.

OECD (2004). *Quality and Recognition in Higher Education: the Cross-Border Challenge*. OECD.

Raghavan, V.V. (2003). Internationalization of Higher Education: The IGNOU Experience. New Delhi: International Division, IGNOU (mimeo).

Report of the Central Advisory Board of Education (CABE) (2005) Committee on Autonomy of Higher Education Institutions, Ministry of Human Resource Development, Govt. of India, June.

Shri Sunil Kumar is Joint Secretary in the Ministry of Human Resource Development, Government of India, New Delhi.
Email: skumar@sansad.nic.in

SECTION VII

OPEN SCHOOLING AND ICT

42

Evolution of the Open School System

Onkar Singh Dewal and Gopa Biswas

Genesis

Educational innovations, as they grow with time, overflow geographical boundaries. When an educational idea, innate or imported, develops and grows into an institutional tree, it needs not only fertile soil but also tender care and thoughtful nurture. This has been true in the case of open learning systems and the Indian open school system is no exception. With the establishment of Open University of U.K. in 1969, seven seas away, and with the setting up of Allama Iqbal Open University in 1974, next door in Islamabad, the zeitgeist in India was ripe and favourable for establishing Open Learning systems.

The Parthasarathy Committee Report, 1975 proposed that a 'National Open University' be established in India. However, the idea at the decision level was deferred and another idea was proposed; to set up an Open School. This shift in focus - from establishing an Open University to setting up an Open School - was guided thoughtfully, by the forces and factors of the Indian education system. The elementary education, a constitutional obligation, was yet to be provided in its full and free form to the school going children. Priority therefore converged on setting up an open school first and then to start an open university. Thus the open school emerged as *"an idea whose time has come"* as said in his inimitable style by Mukhopadhyay (1994, p.1).

Other factors of the emerging national educational scenario also contributed to the decision to first set up an Open School. The UNESCO (1972) Report *"Learning to Be"* advocated a forceful idea of learning society, life long learning and use of alternative schooling structures as key ideas. By 1975 India had adopted non-formal education as an alternative system and also set up Centre for Educational Technology (CET) to promote media based distance education.

India was also operationally getting ready to launch Satellite Instructional TV Experiment (SITE 1975-76) with the help of ATS-6 loaned by the US for a year. The setting up of CET and launching of SITE in 1975-76 provided another basis to start Open School that would harness the potentialities of educational technology and also use TV and radio to support Open Distance Learning (ODL).

As elsewhere in the world, ODL in India evolved out of correspondence education. The seeds of the Open Schooling System in India lie in the correspondence education which began in 1962. The third Five Year Plan (1961-66) included correspondence education and Dr. K.L. Srimali, Union Education Minister and Dr. D.S. Kothari, the then UGC Chairman can be rightfully credited to launch correspondence education in India. In an interview in 1984 with Dr. Srimali in Udaipur, we were told that when he visited the USSR, he was much impressed by the system of correspondence education for working adults. He saw that it helped them both ways; it provided them opportunities to broaden and deepen their vocational competencies and also helped them to improve their educational quality. Dr. Srimali wanted that correspondence education be used for vocational purposes (Dewal, 1992). Consequently the Ministry of Education, Government of India, requested Dr. D.S. Kothari to visit USSR and study the potentials of correspondence education and implement that in India. After Dr. D.S. Kothari's visit, an administrative decision was taken to launch correspondence education. However, the experiment began at the University level first in Delhi University in 1962. Use of correspondence education at the school level came in 1965 when Madhya Pradesh started correspondence education for secondary students at the instance of Council of Boards of School Education (COBSE) to improve academic status of private candidates (Dewal, 1994). The other two Boards that followed suit were Rajasthan Board of Secondary Education and Patrachar Vidyalaya, Delhi in 1968.

Another trend that contributed to the growth of Open Schools in India was that of alternative learning system. The Education Commission (1964-66) made recommendations like undifferentiated curriculum up to class 10; school system to be extended to 12 years; and promotion and strengthening of alternative learning system, part time education, own time education, and Non-formal Education. Satellite based instruction that began in 1975 was an other factor that helped the emergence of Open Schooling in India.

In early 70's, the enrolment of students in primary classes was 86%, elementary classes was 35% and at secondary level 18%. Thus student retention in school system was fairly discouraging. There was heavy drop out. This situation needed alternative approaches to schooling. The policy makers fully realised that more of the same would not work. In 1974, the Report on Universalisation of Elementary Education made a bold recommendation: *"Every child shall continue to learn in the age group 6-14 on a full time basis if possible and on part time basis if necessary"*. This thinking gave a big boost to Non-formal evening schooling, which may seem as the precursor to open school system. Suffice it to say that all pre-requisites required to start an Open Schooling System were already on the ground when the idea of open school caught the attention of the Ministry of Education. The enabling factors related to:

- *Availability of non-formal education* as an alternative structure to formal schooling. It was already on the ground.

- *Availability of media support:* It was to come from the joint efforts of CET (NCERT) and Space Application Centre.
- *Availability of Correspondence Education System*: It started at the University level(1962) as well as at the school level (1965) and was well functioning.

It may be instructive to see how these forces balanced out the forces that resulted into the creation of the UKOU. Lord Perry has observed that three trends influenced Open University education in UK. He says, "The concept of the 'Open University' evolved from the convergence of three major post-war educational trends. The first of these concerns developments in the provision of adult education, the second the growth of educational broadcasting and the third the objective of promoting the spread of egalitarianism in education" (Perry, 1990, p.5). In India, educational broadcasting influenced school and university education effectively. In 1975, the use of satellite in schooling showed a great potential and this trend was effectively used in education. The third trend - egalitarianism in education - gained acceptance as all policy documents stressed universalising elementary education, strengthening secondary education, and popularising vocational education. But with the best of intentions, the first concern 'Universalising Elementary Education' could not be fully achieved even by 2005. In this context, the Open School System is seen as a structural innovation to achieve universalisation of elementary education.

The Pilot Phase

The Open School as a pilot project of Central Board of Secondary Education (CBSE) started in July 1979. But preparation towards it started in 1974. Prof. Rais Ahmed, the then Director, NCERT in consultation with Ministry of Education got prepared a feasibility report on Open School and invited Delhi Administration to launch the project. As Delhi Administration was already running a Patrachar Vidyalaya, they declined the offer. Instead, CBSE got fired by the idea and decided to launch the project. Dr. R.P. Singhal, the then Chairman, CBSE, prepared the project document and got the permission of the Ministry of Education in principle. With hindsight, it can be safely said that without initial support of Ministry of Education, Open School of CBSE would have remained only a glorious name for a Correspondence School.

It is important to note a major shift in thinking while establishing alternative systems of education at secondary and higher education. In higher education the objectives that guided the setting up of alternate systems were to reduce the student number or pressure on conventional institutions and the capital costs and possibly even the recurrent costs (Dewal, 1994). The Open School Project was however set up to accelerate the realization of national objective of Universalisation of Elementary Education. Thus one can see the shift in thinking that led to a search of alternative methods that "reach more people or reach different people or do so cheaply" (Perraton, 1982).

The blueprint of the Open School listed the following objectives (Dewal, 1986)

- To offer opportunities of education to children who complete class VIII but are unable to remain in a regular school;
- To meet the demand for secondary education consequent upon fulfillment of the targets of elementary education;
- To serve the drop outs, left outs, and the push outs in order to bring them back to the main stream;
- To offer an opportunity to girls and women who have no previous qualification but are desirous of receiving education;
- To offer a programme of supervised self-learning for those adults who have entered the world of work but wish to improve their career prospects;
- To equip children and adults of rural areas and to enable them to receive the benefits of latest technologies so that they can contribute to maximization of production and improvement of standard of living;
- To serve those children who belong to the disadvantaged sections of the community; and
- To provide a process of continuing life long education.

One would thus see that preponderance of the sociological objective, rather than economic objective, that guided the establishment of Open School in India.
The logistics and the Plan of Action contained in the blueprint were agreed to in principle by the Ministry of Education and the CBSE was asked to go ahead with the project. On 11th July, 1979, the Director Open School joined on secondment from NCERT. On 28th July, 1979 a high power committee met in Ministry of Education and made the following recommendations:

- The Open School should cater to the needs of school drop-outs. As such, suitable bridge and preparatory courses may be provided.
- The entry requirement to the Open School should not be rigid.
- The examination system should be made more flexible.
- The student may be permitted to sit for all or fewer subjects.

The Open School then galloped on its multiple activities. This included, besides others, finalising scheme of studies and evaluation; constituting subject committees to finalize syllabus; constituting lesson writing teams and orientation to writers and graphic artists; development and production of learning/study material; despatching study materials; organizing personal contact programmes; and conducting the first examination. Some of the important decisions taken during the initial years of Open School (1979-80) proved very beneficial.

Wide Canvas: The catchment area of the Open School was countrywide. Indirectly, it helped to promote and propagate the concept of Open Schooling throughout the country.

Multi-level Courses: In the first phase, the Open School decided to launch bridge level as well as secondary level courses. In the subsequent phases, the Open School planned offering of senior secondary courses, vocational courses and life enrichment courses.

Syllabus: For mainstreaming students to formal system, syllabus in each subject was planned by committees. These committees ensured that offerings in each subject were of the same standard as that in CBSE.

Flexible Scheme of Studies and Examination: The Open School, though a part of CBSE, designed a separate scheme of studies and evaluation. This decision was taken keeping in view the special nature of Open School students. Students were permitted to choose subjects of their liking and interest from a list of several subjects. Flexibilities were also provided to students in the scheme of examination. Students could sit for examination in subjects of their preparedness twice a year extending to five years. Students were given the flexibility to complete their subjects simultaneously or in parts, thus providing flexibility to accumulate credits.

Certification: To provide national recognition and prestige, the certificate was provided by the CBSE under its seal and authority. It built Open School credibility.

Study Material: Open School decided to develop study material through team approach and provide radio and TV inputs to support the contents of the print material.

Student Support System and Personal Contact Programme: Success of OLS depends upon how an institution provides support services to its learners. Provision of student counselling was made available at study centres. The first study centre was set up in Gangtok in Sikkim. In the initial years St. Xaviers of Jaipur provided facilities for student support services. Personal Contact Programmes were held at a few places. Students were also briefed about skills of self-learning and how to study Open School material that included in-text and lesson-end questions.

National Open School

The success of the pilot project, led CBSE to the creation of National Open School in 1989. In 1987-88, the Department of Education, Ministry of Human Resource Development, initiated the preparation of a project report for the establishment of the National Open School, as an autonomous registered society. On acceptance of the report, the Government established the National Open School and the Open School project of the CBSE was amalgamated with National Open School (NOS) on November 23, 1989.

In 1990, NOS was vested with the authority of conducting Secondary and Senior Secondary examinations and certification thereof and a gazette notification in this regard was published. Under this authority, National Open School (NOS) conducted its first Secondary and Senior Secondary examinations all over India in January, 1991 for about 35000 students. National Open School thus became not only a teaching institution but also an examination body, at par with national level and state level examining agencies.

The work of consolidation of previous activities and achievements and introduction of new projects were taken up in a systematic manner during this phase. The various recommendations of the committees like the Jannardan Committee Report, National Policy on Education, 1986, the Programme of Action 1992, and Chitra Naik Committee Report provided a basic policy direction for the National Open School (NOS). The three major roles as envisaged by these committees for NOS are given in the figure below (Mukhopadyay, 1994, p.32).

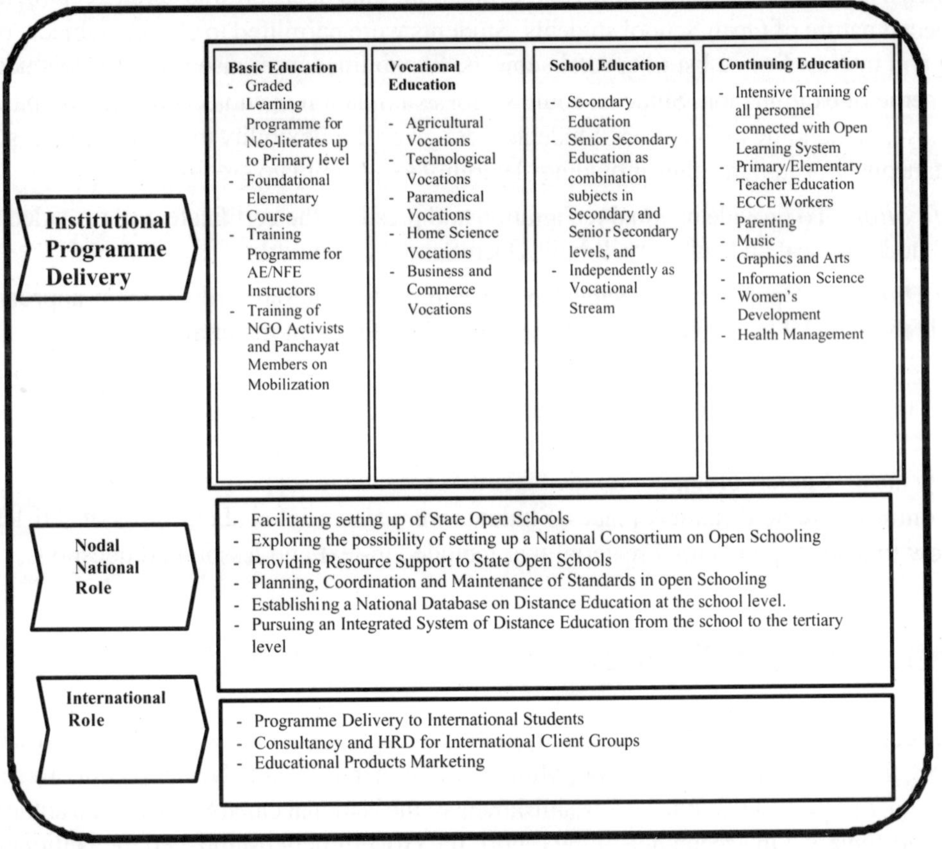

Figure 1 : Systemic view of NOS

In the following paragraphs, some of the important initiatives taken and activities embarked up on by NOS have been highlighted.

Senior Secondary Courses

Till 1985, Open School offered only at bridge course and secondary level courses. In 1986, the decision to start Senior Secondary courses was taken. The scheme of studies was developed and the policy decisions regarding the approach were taken.The task of developing the learning material in Hindi, English, Mathematics, Physics, Chemistry, Biology, History, Geography, Political

Science, Commerce, Accountancy, Economics and Home Science was initiated soon after. Subsequently, more subjects were added to the list and at present the learners have twenty five subjects to choose from.

Vocational Courses

The vocational courses also evolved and multiplied slowly. In 1989 Open School decided to offer Hindi Typing, English Typing, Hindi Stenography, English Stenography and Secretarial Practice in combination with academic subjects. The thinking then was to accredit courses as developed by ITIs, Krishi Vigyan Kendras or other agencies in the field. It was felt that Open School would adopt the courses and offer them to its own learners. However, in the subsequent years, the in-house capabilities of the organisation were further augmented with recruitment of staff in different areas and courses were developed in-house in the fields of agriculture, technology, paramedical and home science. By April, 1992, fourteen new vocational courses were introduced. Today more than 100 vocational courses are offered as single subject courses or package courses for duration of 6 months, one year or two years. Knowledge, skills and qualities of entrepreneurship are essential components in curricula for vocational education with emphasis on practical and on the job training in related industrial units.

In 2002-03, the Vocational Unit, which hitherto was a part of the Academic Department, was upgraded into the Department of Vocational Education.

Regional Language Programme

For universalisation of secondary education, it was decided in 1993 to offer secondary courses in different regional languages. Bengali, Marathi, Telugu and Urdu were taken up in the first phase, and Gujarati, Kannada and Malayalam were taken up in the second phase. This proved to be a bold and far-sighted decision for expansion and acceptance of open schooling as a viable option. The Bengali and Kannada courses are now offered by West Bengal State Open School (Rabindra Mukta Vidyalaya) and Karnataka State Open School, respectively. NIOS still enrols students for other mediums i.e. in Gujrati, Marathi, Telugu and Malayalam at the Secondary level.

Open Basic Education

In June, 1994, the Open Basic Education (OBE) Programme was initiated in response to the imperatives of Joint Initiatives in Distance Education of the E-9 Summit to provide a continuum in primary education up to elementary level. The Open Basic Education courses are offered at three levels – A, B and C - which are equivalent to formal grades III, V and VIII with provision for vocational education at all levels.

The National Open School thus provided a learning continuum from the primary to the pre-degree level with enough courses at all levels. This is illustrated in Fig. 2. However, it is important to note that NIOS developed programmes laterally rather than linearly. The Secondary and Senior Secondary courses were introduced in the first and second phases while open vocational education and Open Basic Education courses came later. Moreover, despite the fact that a cafeteria approach is followed in the secondary and senior secondary levels, not all the courses that are offered today were developed at one go. To date 26 courses are offered at the secondary level and learners can choose from fourteen language courses and twelve content subjects. Similar is the case with Senior Secondary and Open Vocational Education. The flexibility in the choice of subjects takes care of learner interest, need and requirements.

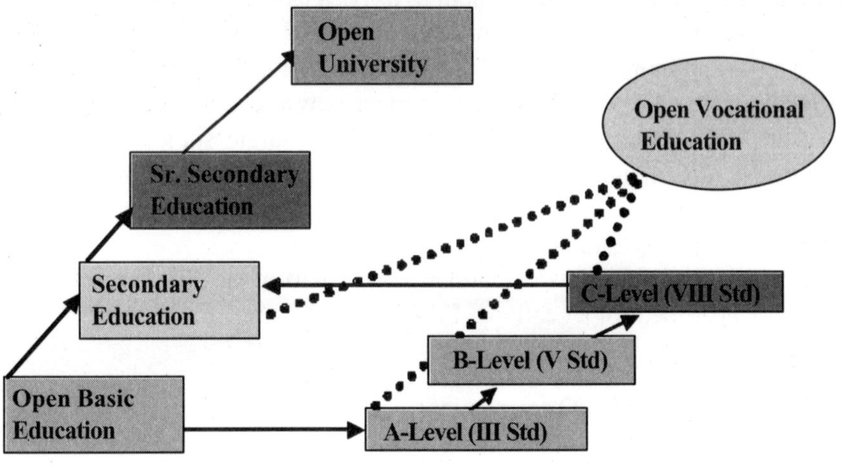

Figure 2 : Learning continuum in ODL at school level

It is widely accepted that a multimedia supported learning environment provides learners with more enriching experiences. Realising this, it was decided in 1992-93 to create a Media Unit to provide audio-video support materials for academic as well as vocational courses. It was visualised that these audio-video programmes would supplement and complement printed self-learning materials and personal contact programmes. The unit started by producing three audio programmes and six video programmes (three each in English and Hindi versions). Today NIOS has 235 audio programmes and 230 video programmes (115 in Hindi and 115 in English versions) and uses a multiple media instructional package: print, A/V, face-to-face counselling, radio and television. A mini studio for in-house production of media programmes has also started functioning since August 14, 2002.

Wider Acceptance

The Open School registered 1072 learners in 1981-82. This provoked a headline in Indian Express "Open School – An Empty School". However, no one then thought that after a little over two decades, the annual enrolment would jump to 253,135 in the year 2004-05. The cumulative enrolment for the last five years is 1,330,427 making NIOS the largest open schooling system in the world. This not only proves the need for open learning system as a parallel channel but also points towards its growing acceptance by the society; learners, parents, employers and peers.

With growing enrolment, NIOS, sought recognition from other Boards and Universities of India to mitigate the difficulties of learners. In 1991, Association of Indian Universities recognised NIOS courses and gradually other universities and Boards of State Education followed suit. Today NIOS is recognised by 23 State Boards of Education and 111 institutions and universities of repute. This recognition has enabled open learners to enrol for higher studies as well as to move to the formal system and vice-versa. It means that open learning as a philosophy of education has been accepted at all levels.

Learner Support

Learner support is the most vital component of open education as it determines the success and retention of learners in the system. Realising this, the founding pioneers of NIOS established a three tier system. According to Mukhopadhyay (2004), "The story of management of Open Schooling would remain incomplete without mentioning the network of accredited institutions or study centres throughout the length and breadth of the country. The organizational mechanism of delivery of open learning is primarily through these study centres". At present there are 2727 study centres catering to learners in India and abroad at different levels. The senior secondary/ secondary recognised/ affiliated schools, which are associated with NIOS as its study centres for academic courses, are referred to as Accredited Institutions. The vocational training centres, which provide theoretical and practical training to learners, are called Accredited Vocational Institutions (AVIs). In order to cater to a different but important target group of children and adults with physical and sensory disabilities as well as the socially and geographically disadvantaged, NIOS has created a network of Special Accredited Institutions for Education of the Disadvantaged (SAIEDs). The Accredited Agencies (AAs) for the Open Basic Education course are usually Non-Governmental Organisations (NGOs) or Zila Saksharta Samitis (ZSSs). These centres provide services to the students from admission to examination. This arrangement, according to Mukhopadhyay (2004) is 'one of the finest innovations in Indian open schooling' as it 'avoids investment of new infrastructure for the open schools and it makes use of the spare time of the existing educational infrastructures'.

Promoting State Open Schools

Although the work of NIOS has been appreciated for promoting school education, a realisation dawned that the cherished goal of universalisation of education cannot be achieved through a restricted choice of media and subjects since India is a Union of 29 states and six Union Territories where different languages and dialects are spoken. Also there are variations reflected in social customs and traditions. It was therefore considered imperative to establish a network of State Open Schools to cater to the needs of learners in different States to study through their mother tongues or regional languages.

In this direction, NIOS has worked consistently and cooperatively with State Governments to help them set up their own Open Schools. In some cases, in addition to technical expertise to develop project reports and study materials, even seed money has also been provided by NIOS. This has facilitated nationwide acceptability of open schooling as an effective and alternative mode of education for socio-economic empowerment.

We now have ten state open schools in Tamil Nadu (1982), Andhra Pradesh (1991), Punjab (1991), Haryana (1994), Madhya Pradesh (1996), Karnataka (1996), West Bengal (1997), Kerala (1999), Jammu & Kashmir (2001) and Rajasthan (2005).

National Institute of Open Schooling

Within a short span of 13 years, the National Open School emerged as the National Institute of Open Schooling (NIOS) because of the many significant innovative initiatives and the great strides made by NOS in the field of school education. Besides performing all the functions that were earlier being executed by the NOS, the NIOS has been mandated to give major emphasis on training of open schooling functionaries and advocacy programmes, both at the national and international level.

As an apex organisation, the NIOS is envisaged to give major thrust to research, development, training and extension activities in open schooling. It has been conducting Instructional Design Training Programmes for Indian participants, with a view to develop appropriately trained humanpower. It is a highly sought after destination of peers from other Commonwealth countries of Asia and Africa. Capacity building workshops for OBE functionaries from different parts of India have also been conducted by NIOS from time to time. A number of on-going Research Projects undertaken by NIOS focus on identified thrust areas of open schooling.

As an apex agency for quality assurance and resource support, the NIOS provides broad learning outcomes, high quality study materials, text-free sample questions and blue prints of examination papers with suggestive marking schemes to Open Basic Education Accredited Agencies all over India.

Use of ICT

In 1989, NIOS made a small beginning in the use of technology with only two personal computers. The Institute has moved a long way since then to be in the forefront of ICT applications. Today, it is equipped with the latest hardware and software and has a full fledged Computer Division which handles all desktop publishing, database management, software development and installation. ICT is optimally used in almost all office activities, result processing and certification. A dedicated DSL (Digital Subscriber Line) has been installed to provide round the clock Internet facility. This not only facilitates networking with regional centres and sharing of information with others, but also allows NIOS faculty to reach learners quickly. The library is fully computerized and the integrated voice response system (IVRS) provides 24 hour automated information throughout the country. All information related to NIOS is available in its websites www.nos.org and www.nios.ac.in.

Innovation (on-demand examination system)

One of the major innovations at NIOS is that of On Demand Examination System (ODES) at the Open Basic Education level. A separate question paper is generated for every learner every time he/she would like to take an examination in each subject offered at this level. For this purpose, a pool of at least one thousand items has been generated for each subject and stored in a computer. The question paper is generated according to the approved design guidelines. This has helped NIOS to make the system of examination independent of fixed time frames and help the learners to take examination as per their convenience.

The experiment proved extremely successful at the OBE ‘C’ level. In 2005, it was further extended to the Secondary level and the learner has the option to appear in ODES and/or public examinations held twice a year. At present, the ODE is conducted on two days of a week and is held only in Delhi. This facility is likely to be extended to other Regional Centres soon.

International collaboration

The Commonwealth of Learning (COL) and UNESCO are the main collaborating partners of NIOS, among others for forging collaborations with other countries. NIOS has set up an International Centre for Open Schooling (ICTOS) for the offer of capacity building programmes to open schooling functionaries. Among many collaborative activities of COL and NIOS, one of the planned activities has been to attach delegates from developing countries to NIOS with the objective to share experiences in various areas of common interest. Organising field visits to different study centres and regional centres of NIOS helps the delegates to learn the intricacies of open schooling. Several delegates from African countries and Asian countries like Bangladesh, Sri Lanka, China, Nepal have visited NIOS under these programmes.

An overview of the evolutionary phases of open schooling in India

The following time-line provides a holistic picture of the evolutionary phases of Open Schooling System in India (Table 1).

Table 1: Time line for Open School/National Open School/National Institute of Open Schooling: evolution of open schooling in India

			State Correspondence/Open School		
			Madhya Pradesh Correspondence School	←	1965
			Cuttack		
			Uttar Pradesh		
			Delhi Patrachar Vidyalaya	←	1968
			Rajasthan Correspondence School	←	1968
1979	→	Pilot Project – CBSE – OPEN SCHOOL Bridge CoursesSecondary Courses			
			Tamil Nadu State Open School	←	1982
1986	→	Decision to Introduce Senior Secondary Courses			
1988	→	Senior Secondary Courses launched			
1989	→	NATIONAL OPEN SCHOOL			
1990	→	NOS vested with authority to examine and certify learners			
1991	→	First Secondary and Senior Secondary Examination conducted by NIOS			
1991	→	Recognition by Association of Indian Universities			
			Andhra Pradesh State Open School	←	1991
			Punjab State Open School	←	1991
1992	→	Admission to vocational courses			
1992	→	Media unit added to Academic Department			
1993	→	First vocational examination conducted			
1993	→	Regional Language Programmes launched			
1994	→	Open Basic Education Project initiated	Haryana State Open School	←	1994

1994	→	Urdu medium programme launched			
1994	→	Academic, technical and financial support to State Open Schools			
			Madhya Pradesh State Open School	←	1996
			Karnataka State Open School	←	1996
1997	→	National Consortium for Open Schooling launched			
			West Bengal State Open School (Rabindra Mukta Vidyalaya)	←	1997
			Kerala State Open School	←	1999
2001	→	OSAC Journal launched	Jammu and Kashmir State Open School	←	2001
2002	→	National Institute of Open Schooling			
2002	→	Creation of Vocational Department and Student Support Services Department			
2005	→	On Demand Examination introduced at secondary level	Rajasthan State Open School	←	2005

Future Vision

NIOS can, with some humility, feel proud of its manifold achievements and innovations, including the large number of students enrolled, and on-demand examination. However, there are a few areas of concern. Immediate steps should be taken to improve the monitoring system. There is a genuine concern for ensuring smooth conduct of science practicals. Moreover, the Institute should establish a placement cell for facilitating recruitment of NIOS learners by industries for on the job training.

National Institute of Open Schooling (NIOS) will be required to play a significant catalytic role in promoting Open Schooling in India and widen its international linkages, specially with institutions in developing countries in the SAARC region and beyond. Though some beginning has been made a more vigorous marketing should enhance its presence considerably in view of economic advantages. With the launch of EduSat, a satellite dedicated to Educational Communication, the NIOS has the opportunity to use the network for its learners and reach out to the unreached spread all over India and promote quality of school education.

References

Dewal, O.S. (1986). *Open School, India: The Preliminary Years : A Case Study*. Deakin Open Education Monograph No. 3, Deakin University, Victoria.

Dewal, O.S. (1992). *Two way Communication: From Correspondence to Distance Education*. In Ortner, G.E., Graff, K. and Wilmersdoerfev, H. (eds.), *Distance Education as Two-way Communication*. Frankfurt: Peter Lang (pp. 246-251).

Dewal, O.S. (1994). Distance open learning : A complementary strategy for basic education for all. In Biswas, Gopa (ed.), *Distance Education in SAARC Countries.* New Delhi: National Open School (pp.54-61).

Dewal, O.S. (1994). Open learning in Indian school education. In Mukhopadhyay, M and Phillips, Susan (eds.), *Open Schooling: Selected Experiences*. Vancouver: The Commonwealth of Learning (pp. 9-16).

Mukhopadhyay, M. (1994). The unfolding of an open learning institution: The national open school in India. In Mukhopadhyay, M and Phillips, Susan (eds.), *Open Schooling: Selected Experiences.* Vancouver: The Commonwealth of Learning, Canada.

Mukhopadhyay, M. (2004). Open schooling. In Rajput, J.S. (ed.), *Indian Educational Encyclopedia.* Vol. II, New Delhi: NCERT.

Perraton, H. (1982). *Alternative Routes to Formal Education.* Washington D.C.: World Bank.

Perry W. (1990). The genesis of the first Open University. In B.N. Koul & J. Jenkins (eds.), *Distance Education: A Review.* New Delhi: IGNOU.

UNESCO (1972). *Learning to Be.* Paris: UNESCO.

Professor Onkar Singh Dewal is former founder director, Open School, Delhi.

Mrs. Gopa Biswas is Deputy Director (Academic), National Institute of Open Schooling, New Delhi.

43

Instructional Development and Delivery

Sushmita Mitra and Anita Priyadarshini

Introduction

Until recently, all of us believed that effective teaching and learning could not occur without face-to-face contact of the teacher and the learner in a classroom.

However, with rapid development in learning theories, and advancement in technology it has become possible to bring in a paradigm shift from institution-led learning to own-time self-learning at a distance i.e., from teaching to self-paced-learning which is more flexible and open. This has led to the rise of alternative delivery systems often known as Open and Distance Learning (ODL) System.

The ODL system benefited a great deal from the innovations in educational technology, bringing in paradigm shift from teaching to self-learning. Traditionally education and learning were restricted by various rigid requirements such as entrance requirements, fixed time and space, fixed curriculum, etc. Such requirements posed geographical, social and cultural barriers including those of gender and also those related to individual characteristics and abilities. The ODL system has overcome these barriers by providing learning opportunities with freedom to learn at a distance. This has been the guiding principle for Open Schooling System also.

The ODL system made its beginning through correspondence programmes. These correspondence programmes, offered by institutions, opened up new opportunities for own-time education—a student could learn on his/her own at a time convenient to him/her without going to an institution. This had been true for school education also. In India, Open School System evolved out of correspondence education at the school level. Correspondence education was initiated at the school level at the secondary stage as early as 1965.

At the secondary level correspondence courses started with the objective of improving the academic standard of private students. The Board of Secondary Education, Madhya Pradesh was the first to start correspondence courses in 1965. The Patrachar Vidyalaya Delhi started in 1968. The Boards of Secondary Education of Rajasthan, Uttar Pradesh and Orissa followed the example and offered correspondence education to students of Class X-XII. All these correspondence institutions at different levels offered the same scheme of studies, syllabus and examination system as the formal system. The only difference was that correspondence students studied at a distance through printed materials whereas the conventional students received face-to-face instructions in the classroom. Often, this resulted in uncertain achievements having an effect on the quality. The system was unable to cope up with very large numbers (quantity) to provide high quality of education and diversity of courses. The use of correspondence as an only medium of communication could not entirely compensate or replace face-to-face instruction, and hence was not able to satisfy the expectation of Distance Learners. Something more was needed. This realisation along with other societal issues prompted the move for starting Open Schools in India with an idea to shift from institution led learning to self-paced learning. Such a shift in the paradigm of learning is depicted in Fig. 1.

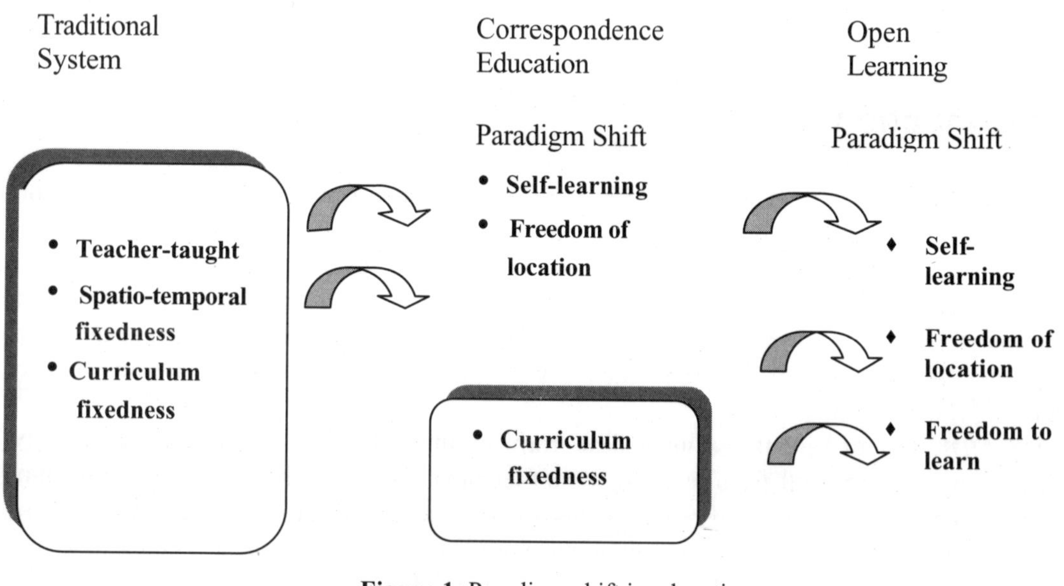

Figure 1: Paradigm shift in education

This paradigm shift has undoubtedly opened up an alternative delivery system of education and training which has a specially designed and developed instructional system.

Revisiting Learning Perspectives and Orientations

Instructional development and delivery is an important aspect as student learning is central to all educational practices. Such student learning is not accidental - it is the direct result of what learning experiences have been designed intentionally or unintentionally by the policy makers, curriculum developers, teachers, subject experts, institutions or even communities. Behind the design of such learning experiences lies the belief about learning. Such beliefs directly influence the learning experiences designed for the students and develop an instructional system, which is effective and efficient.

At this point it would be worthwhile to consider the different perspectives and orientations towards learning in ODL systems. The following views conceptualises how learning is presumed to take place in ODL.

The very basic principle is: Everyone can learn (Burns 1967). In ODL system,

- Learning occurs at a distance when the learner and the instructor/ institution are separated in time and place (Wedemeyer, 1981; Holmberg, 1977; Moore, 1973b; Sewart, 1981; Keegan, 1986)
- Considering learning to be an individual activity attained through a process of internalisation, learners undergo independent study, self-study or autonomous learning (Wedemeyer, 1974; Delling, 1975; Holmberg, 1981; Wiilen, 1981; Moore, 1991).
- Learning is private (Keegan, 1986).
- Learning is mediated by a provider arranging for:
  - guided didactic conversation (Holmberg, 1983), or
    non contiguous communication or
  - two way interpersonal communication to recreate learning link, or
  - educational transaction using technology and communication theory, or
  - virtual contiguity by integrating systems that bring teacher and learner together, optimum dialogue between them and eliminate consequences of being separate in space (Saba, 1990).
- Learning involves collaborated experience between a teacher and a learner, which is totally dependent on a two way communication facilitated by technology (Garrison, 1989).
- Learning considers requirements of both the learning task and learner i.e., principles of pedagogy/andragogy and structure of knowledge has an apparent influence on learning (Verduin and Clark, 1991).
- Learner control is based on the inter-relationship between independence (as in self directed learner), proficiency (as in the ability to learn independently) and support (characterised by the resources available to guide and facilitate the educational transaction, (Garrison, 1989: Amundsen, 1993).

These perspectives about learning facilitated in developing the alternative delivery system for Open Schooling System that provide learners with options for learning that are not limited to traditionally timetabled classroom hours covering a standard course duration and /or options for learning that have time and /or location flexibility.

Undoubtedly such alternative delivery strategies attempt to improve access opportunities for learners and can address a variety of teaching and learning styles. The development of instructional system for Open Schooling evolved over four decades to cater to a very large system thereby establishing a model for other developing countries. It would be worthwhile to examine this development from the point of approach and strategies adopted to have a clear understanding.

Decade One : 1965-1975 - Era of Correspondence Courses offered by Some School Boards

Looking into the purpose of offering secondary education through the correspondence courses by some Boards of school education, it can be considered that the stress at the beginning was undoubtedly to provide coaching to private students through correspondence lessons so that their academic standards improved (Sujatha, 2002). These lessons were developed based on the existing syllabus of the Board without much considerations of the pedagogy of self learning at a distance. In most cases these correspondence lessons were like notes lacking the following:

- Statement of aims and objectives
- Self assessment questions
- Opportunity of engaged active learning.....mostly read passively
- Personal style
- Hints on study skills
- Proper layout of material assisting in reading comprehension.

In some cases list of reference textbooks used by the formal schools were provided at the end of the correspondence lessons and since they were not mandatory, learners may purchase for reference or may not.

These correspondence materials were developed by a single member approach with the member taking responsibility of preparing the material suitable for the students without any corrective suggestions and comments from other experts. In other words, course materials prepared by a subject expert in his or her individual capacity were not a collective product. As a result there was no way to ensure quality of the material. Also the production of the materials was shabby due to poor quality paper and printing.

The correspondence materials were exclusively for the private students which were posted to their residence. There was minimal scope of didactic communication; in some cases a few personal contact programmes were organised by all correspondence institutions except Madhya Pradesh. But the design and structure of such programmes was not a continuous and comprehensive one for the learners during their duration of studies.

The major limitations of the instructional system of such correspondence school education were hence with respect to:

- Ensuring same quality inputs to all learners at a distance as their counterparts in the formal schools following the same curriculum and examination pattern which led to variable attainment of same standard.
- Learner support for self learning was poor leading to unattended learning difficulties for these learners.

Nevertheless correspondence education at school level opened up the possibility from institution-led learning to own-time self-learning at a distance.

By early 1970s it was realised that in spite of increase in number of institutions and enrolment ratio in formal schools there was still an increase in inequality due to lack of access to educational opportunities to many underprivileged communities, and underdeveloped areas. Even if participation was there, retention and school drop outs were also becoming major issues of concern. The school drop out rate was increasingly high. Studies on the reasons of dropping out of the school revealed that the rigidities of the formal schools, the socio-economic conditions of the learners which the formal schools were unable to attend to, the geographical distance and many such learner centric problems were the cause of discontinuing school. With this realisation an attempt was made to look for alternative educational strategies that could consider these real learner based issues.

During this period, developments in learning theories and the move on Skinnerian approach to develop teaching machines, programmed learning (PL) materials for individualised learning and other developments in educational technology strengthened the open learning and distance education system. Taking these developments into consideration, the idea of Open School was recommended by a working group in National Council of Education and Training (NCERT) in 1974 for students 14 years of age and older including adults. It was decided view that the instructional strategies would be based on Open and Distance learning at school level in order to liberate the system from its ingrained orthodoxy and rigidities (Dewal, 1994). The focus was hence on developing an instructional system and delivery mechanism that could withdraw the barriers to access to education.

Decade Two : 1975-1985 - Instructional Development of Open School

This decade was the decade of instructional development. The idea of Open School became concretised in 1978 with the suggestions and advice of experts attending an International Conference on Correspondence Education held in New Delhi. It was decided that Central Board of Secondary Education (CBSE) would consider this concept of Open School and begin it as its project school. Accordingly a Blue Print (Singhal,1979) was developed by CBSE which envisaged the following implications on the instructional development and delivery:

Table 1: Implications of the blue print developed by CBSE

Instructional system envisioned in the Blue Print	Emerging issues for instructional development and delivery
• Providing an opportunity for learning and pursuing further education through a multi-media programme not only on an all India basis but also to cover Indian learners residing abroad and are desirous of receiving Indian Education.	• Coverage has to consider not only the whole country having diversity and variations but also clientele outside the country.
• Instruction to be imparted in English and Hindi.	• The medium of instruction was decided in spite of all India coverage.
• Preparation and production of high quality course materials.	• Development of an approach and process to ensure the quality of the course materials.
• Use of Educational technology and different media including print, audio, radio etc.	• Selection of different media for delivery needed attention.
• Provision of study centres on regional basis to serve as resource centres for help and guidance to the learners.	• Establishment of contact points for the learners to provide support to learning needed to be considered.
• Face-to face programmes as far as feasible.	• Minimising the feeling of isolation of the learners by having human contact for interaction, problem solving and other learner specific requirements.
• A two way communication between the tutor and the learner	• Developing strategies for two way communication.
• Proper counselling of learners before their enrolment and after their enrolment.	• Developing methods and procedures for counselling
• Certification	• Developing a System of examination and certification
• Monitoring, evaluation, and research.	• System needed to be developed in terms of who, where and how this would be done.

The Blue Print also provided guidance and suggestions on the scope and nature of courses, the approach to development of the course materials, the use of educational technology to have multi-media packages comprising print, audio, video materials and on the delivery of instruction. It was a framework for systematically planning, developing and adapting instruction based on identifiable learner needs and content requirements. It strongly emphasised that the Open School will be learner- centred attempting to meet learner needs and capacities as indicated in Fig. 2. In other words the Blue Print provided the necessary conditions for distance education in order to establish a sustainable alternative instructional system for school education without the rigidities of the formal schools.

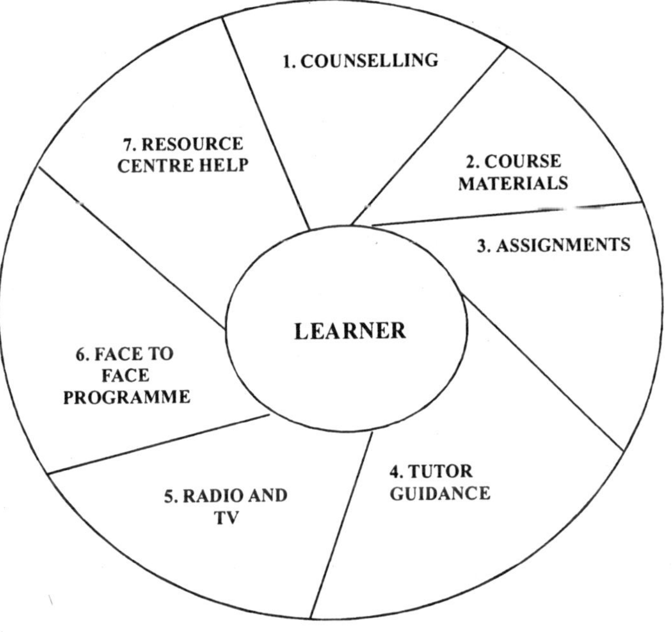

Figure 2: Envisaged learner centred distance education in the Blue Print (1979)

Keeping this Blue Print in mind, CBSE took the bold step to set up Open School (OS) in 1979 which was a considerable advancement over the concept of correspondence education. Thus in this decade the country saw an educational concept becoming a reality with the following developments and outcomes taking place.

Table 2: Developments and outcomes of the open school system

Period (Years)	Stages of development	Outcome
1979-1981	• Setting up various modalities and infrastructure· • Planning and Instructional development for Open School programme.	• Decision on offering bridge courses and Secondary level courses was taken initially. • A separate scheme of studies developed considering the special features of the open system and learner needs i.e. the learners had the option to choose subjects of their choice. • Decision on a flexible scheme of examination with credit accumulation facility providing a

		learner to earn the certificate within a period of five years after registration was taken. • Development of self instructional materials by adopting Subject Team Approach.
1981-1983	• Implementation of the first instructional cycle· • Development of support materials for learners. Conduction of examination	Registration of learners held in May 1981. • Self-Learning materials sent to learners through 5 despatches along with support materials in the form of study guides, glossaries etc.· • Personal Contact Programmes (PCPs) organised for a short duration during vacations. • CBSE conducted examinations from April 1983 twice a year and announced the equivalence of the Open School certificate to other CBSE secondary certificates offered by the formal schools.
1983-1985	• Modification of the strategy of learner support. • Planning for the development of the instruction for Senior Secondary Level.	• Establishment of Resource-cum Study centres for PCP's and other learner related services. • Decisions on the scheme of studies, subjects to offer at the senior secondary level and other related matters

Hence it is evident that a systemic cyclic approach had been adopted by Open School right from its inception:

As evident from Table 2, in the initial two years of establishment of OS, efforts to make the learning process effective was the focus and various steps were followed as given below:

- Developing a meaningful curriculum.
- Developing self-instructional materials primarily in the form of print, and in due course, to be supplemented by non-print media, namely audio/video.
- Developing formative and summative evaluation exercise for the purpose of monitoring learning by the learners themselves as well as by the institution.
- Providing personal contact classes.
- Preparing learners for (public) external examinations.
- Receiving feedback through action-research for improving the system.

For every step the target group was kept in mind and attempts were made to address the issues, which resulted in innovation not only in the processes and approach adopted but also in the structure of the curriculum and instructional materials known as Self Instructional Materials (SIMs).

The curriculum in different subjects was broad-based, intimately linked to life situations of the learners, so that learning was meaningful, lasting and assumed both immediate and long range context. To give an example the curriculum in the subject of Science at secondary level was thematic in nature instead of being discipline based with clear cut demarcation of areas from Physics, Chemistry and Biology. A theme of daily life like Air or Water was selected and the content of the theme followed an inter-disciplinary approach cutting across specialised and related knowledge from physical, chemical, biological and social aspects. This was undoubtedly a departure from the formal school curriculum and yet in favour of general education, which is the primary goal of education up to secondary stage. Similar considerations were made for other subjects also.

Further the openness and flexibility in the scheme of studies also posed a challenge to handle the issue of differentiated subject combinations by learners.

When it came to transaction of these curriculums at a distance, the print medium was considered as the prime instructional method. Accordingly an approach was adopted called the Subject Team Approach (Dewal, 1986). This was an adapted version of the Course Team approach that Open University, UK had developed and was another innovation of cooperative effort in the development of quality printed learning materials. This was again another significant departure from the correspondence education.

In this approach for each subject a Subject Team was constituted which comprised a Team Chairperson and four to six lesson writers. The Team Chairperson was a senior subject expert from the University while the lesson writers were post graduate school teachers, college teachers and other professionals. Each subject team had other members like translators, graphic artists and evaluation experts.

The process followed by the Subject Team (ST) in developing the SIMs was as follows:

- In all subjects an appreciation course for the Team Chairperson was conducted by OS where background papers with respect to the course outline and the functions of the Subject Team members were highlighted.
- The lesson writers were then oriented in 3 day training workshop in which they were briefed about the instructional strategy, clientele group for whom they had to write. Sample materials were also prepared by them in the workshop.
- The training programme was followed by a one day preliminary meeting where the Team Chairperson allocated lesson(s) to different writers through mutual discussion, decided about the approach to be adopted to present the material and plan an operational schedule.
- The writers then went back to their respective places and wrote lessons keeping the following in mind:
  - correct, up-to-date content at the learners' level
  - simple, personal, direct and clear usage of language
  - the presentation in the prescribed format of OS.

The writers got 10 to 15 days to write the first draft.

- The First Review meeting of 2-3 days was then held to discuss the lessons at length with respect to inter-linkages, gaps, overlapping and repetitions and the content clarity.
- The writers then return to their places of work and modify their lessons as agreed upon.
- The Second Review meeting of 2-3 days was held to discuss the modifications/changes carried out and weaknesses if any was further ironed out. Graphic inputs were also listed and given to OS for development.
- Writers then prepared the final draft after validating the material at their own level.
- Try out of the material was done in a limited manner to ensure the effectiveness of the material. Any feedback obtained was incorporated in the lessons before giving it finally to the Subject Team Chairperson for editing.
- Finally the materials were edited by in house academic faculty members who developed the final manuscript to be given for printing.

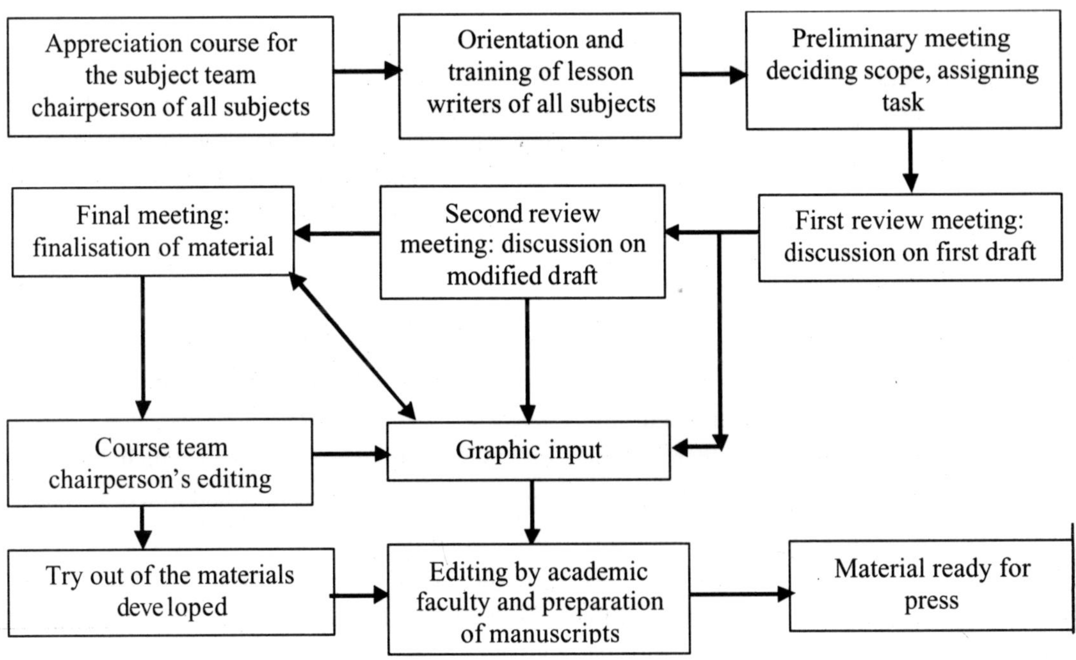

Figure 3: Process of material development

This approach and process had the following advantages:

- Exposition at the development stage provided scope for modifications and changes for better before the product was formed. It provided for deliberation, redrafting and comments, and focused the corrective effort for various interests and sections on the making of the courseware.
- Responsibilities were shared and there was a great potential for cooperative effort. In fact ideas and expressions of many in the subject area got shared very well.
- The material prepared ensured quality to that prepared by an individual.

It had the following disadvantages also:

- It had been a time consuming process. The whole process of development by the lesson writers was planned for not less than 30-40 days. But in practice the time taken was much more.... to keep the potential schedule, many a time steps were skipped and the work was sometimes rushed through having an implications on the quality of the material.
- It was more expensive by giving to large number of persons and undergoing stages of deliberation in work.
- External factors like unavoidable delays on the part of the team members who had prior first and foremost commitments to their parent organisation disturbed the process of collaboration and did not bring forth a perfect output.

However, the efficacy of the print materials developed following this approach depended much on the instructional design of these materials, which in turn was dependent on the nature of subject matter, learner characteristics and previous experiences and the type of learning expected. The design of the text needed to go beyond a simple exposition of subject matter to a design of self-instructional materials so that self-learning at a distance occurred effectively within the learner's context. In the context of open learning and distance education, a SIM is a written elaboration of a set of learning opportunities, organised around a well-defined theme/topic in such a way that, it is a self contained instruction unit to be used in a self learning situation.

Therefore, for a material to be effective in a self-learning situation, the instructional design of the material should guarantee its self-sufficiency. It needed to be structured in such a way that it would help the learner to find their way into the text and to find their way through the text. As such a suggested design for preparing SIMs for Open Schooling learners included the following elements in order of their sequence:

- A clear, relevant and appealing Title
- An Introduction with the important purpose of stimulating interest of the learner in the theme/topic to be unfolded
- A set of objectives with the purpose to make clear to the learner what s/he needs to achieve or be able to do at the end of a particular lesson.

- Main exposition of the content following important pedagogical considerations viz.
  - Selection of content and,
  - Sequencing of content,
  - Meaningful Section wise break up
  - Presentation,
  - Language and style,
  - Illustrations,
  - Strategies of exposing the subject matter,
  - Level of treatment,
  - Evaluation: both formative and summative
- Intext Questions set after every section with a purpose not only to provide feedback to the learners to check their own comprehension of the preceding information input but also to sustain motivation by helping learners to experience success thereby increasing the confidence level of the learners.
- A Summary of the whole lesson serving the purpose of recapitulation, reinforcement, and quick referencing.
- A set of Terminal Questions which covers the whole content area with a purpose to help in consolidating learning through recapitulation, revision of the learning points thereby promoting retention and transfer of learning.
- Key / Answers to the questions at the end of the lesson for immediate knowledge of results as a feedback to the learners.

Undoubtedly this structure had followed the theoretical framework provided by Gagne and Briggs (1974) according to whom, "In making progress from one moment to the next during a lesson, a set of events takes place, which act upon the student and in which he or she becomes involved. This set of events is specifically meant by 'instruction'. The instructional events in a lesson may take a variety of form...these events constitute a set of communications to the student."

In this decade particularly from 1981 to 1983, a considerable time was devoted in developing the instructional cycle which had five phases namely:

- Orientation and despatch of materials
- Correction and return of student assignments
- Setting up regional centres and conducting personal contact programme
- Mailing of sample question papers
- Examination

All these phases were carried out with the first batch of enrolled learners of 1672 in number. In the beginning it was not easy to convince prospective learners about the unique features of Open schooling system for them to take advantage and continue with education. Many strategies were adopted to make a beginning. There were signs of promises after the first examination was taken by CBSE and over the years from 1983-85 the demand to start senior secondary education arose. Hence it can be said that this period was a period of development, applications of theory to practice, concretising concepts to reality and move ahead with new strategies and new programmes to meet the demand from the learning community.

Decade Three: 1985-95 Launching of Senior Secondary Level in the Context of Birth of NOS

The decade 1985 to 1995 marked a watershed in Indian education. The National Policy of Education (1986) was framed and was followed by the Programme of Action (1992). There was a strong move towards finding alternative means for reaching the unreached and to fill the gap that the formal system was not able to tackle. While in 1985 the Indira Gandhi National Open University had been set up by an Act of Parliament, the Open School was given by the Ministry of Human Resource Development (MHRD) the status of an autonomous institution - National Open School (NOS) in 1989.

In terms of academic programmes, the NOS continued with the secondary programme that had already been successfully launched earlier. However, as mentioned now there was a growing demand from the secondary completers for the senior secondary level.

In October 1990 the Government of India, vested the then NOS with the authority to conduct its own secondary and senior secondary examinations and provide certification thereby giving full autonomy to NOS as well as establishing another National Board of Examination

The senior secondary course initiated new paths in openness. In terms of subject choice, till then the formal school system offered courses based upon different streams – Humanities, Science, Commerce, etc. Although the work of senior secondary course was initiated in 1986-87, NOS began offering courses at this level in 1989 without having any *'streaming'*. It offered a cafeteria approach with open choice of subjects and no pre- conditions to those who completed secondary level education. Even if a learner had not studied a particular subject at the secondary level, s/he had the choice to opt for it at the senior secondary level. Another *innovative* feature was the increasing flexibility that allowed a learner to take a vocational subject with an academic subject. The NOS gave certain vocational subjects the same value as academic subjects. From the instructional design point of view this meant that the course content and the materials of these vocational subjects had to be equivalent to say Physics or History. It also brought vocational education into mainstream education—a departure and an innovation in the system.

As regards the instructional design for this level, there were many factors that influenced it. The most important was the nature of the target audience. By that time there was a fair enough idea about those who opted this system of open schooling to pursue their school education. Most of the NOS learners belonged to lower socio-economic strata and were in the 17-19 age groups. The ratio between boys and girls was 64:36 (National Open School, 1992). The group was however, more urban than rural, with family and financial responsibilities. However, as regards attitude, most learners were motivated and mature and keen to complete their course and obtain a certificate at senior secondary level. The educational attainment of the learners at this level was that they were either those who had passed Secondary School Examination under the Open School System or those coming from formal system of education after having passed Secondary School Examination from CBSE or other Boards. Moreover, at this stage there were two categories of students, viz.

- those terminating education after senior secondary stage, and
- those continuing their education for higher learning.

The highlight of this senior secondary programme was that it was improved in design upon the secondary programme. The curriculum was designed by experts from universities, schools and professional institutes. The course team besides the subject experts included content editors, language editors, audio-video support (where possible) as well as graphic artists. Even before the curriculum was designed, the curricula of other Boards were analysed so that all aspects of equivalence were covered. Detailed discussions were held to include new research and new areas. The curriculum document included the subject rationale, modules, and areas of enrichment learning.

A detailed exercise was conducted before the writing of the senior secondary materials. In every subject, modular concept maps were drawn so that the linkages between the topics were clearly delineated. The concept maps were aimed at understanding the structure of the module as well helping the lesson writer and the learner negotiate through the module. A Study Guide was developed to help learners to deal with the materials as well as prepare themselves to be distance learners. The materials were supported with glossaries, Practical/Laboratory manuals and maps. In order to provide learners with examination support, sample question papers were developed. A massive question bank was also developed, having questions of different types and with varying difficulty levels.

The educational attainments and the aspirations of the learners found their reflection in the course design. It was very clear that in a course based upon own pace and own time, only those learning processes and delivery systems could be kept in mind that were based on the learner's real situation. At the outset, it was decided that print, like at the secondary level, would remain the prime medium. Other support materials such as audio – visual materials were to be supplementary to the print medium. The entire course was designed in a modular form and delivered through booklets called *'despatches'*. Each despatch contained 2-3 modules depending upon the course coverage. While in the initial period the despatches used to be posted to the individual addresses of the learners, this practice proved ineffective and also not very economical. Many learners complained of despatches getting lost in the mail or of wrong course materials being delivered. It was then decided at the NOS level that the despatches would be delivered to the learners through the study centres. NOS began transporting the despatches in bulk to the study centres and the learners obtained these from their respective study centres. Such an arrangement also created a stronger relationship between the learner and the study centre.

Academic support was also provided through Personal Contact Programmes at the study centres. While identifying Accredited Institutions to function as study centres for senior secondary programmes, NOS policy required that the teachers be trained Post Graduate Teachers. This was done to ensure that NOS learners received the same level of teaching support as was available for formal school learners. Since at this level the importance of subjects having Practical work as considerable, laboratory facility was provided during the PCPs at the Accredited Institutions (Study Centres). While for most subjects, 30 classes were to be organised at the Study Centre, in case of subjects with Practical work, this number was 35.

Realising that the senior secondary was a terminal examination for the school stage, there was an emphasis on ensuring that the learner received adequate opportunities to assess their own progress before the final public examination. The materials were designed following the same principle as was done for the Secondary level such that they included instructional elements which were meant to help the learners to recapitulate and also reinforce learning. In order to encourage a dialogue between the learners and their tutors, a provision for Tutor Marked Assignments (TMA) was made. These TMAs were given at the end of each despatch and the learner was tested upon the related content. These assignments were assessed by the teachers at the Study Centres from the point of view of highlighting their positive points and thus building up their morale and giving practical suggestions for further improvement in respect of such learning points where the learning had not been adequate. While at one stage 20 per cent weightage in the form of continuous assessment was given to the TMAs, this was later removed. The TMAs presently are only tools for remedial learning. Submission of 2 out of 3 TMAs is however compulsory even though the marks are not counted in the final examination. In the present situation the grades are awarded for TMA which are reflected in the mark sheet.

The objectives of the Open School as given in First Annual Report (1979-80) stated that one of its objectives was to offer Technical, Vocational and Life Enrichment Courses (TVLEC) (Open School, CBSE, 1980). In the decade 1985-95, a number of vocational courses were initiated. NOS began offering vocational courses in 1991-92. There were different types of courses depending upon the technical area and the duration of the course. Short term package courses of 3 to 6 months duration were offered as well as courses that were equivalent to secondary and senior secondary courses and were offered in lieu of an academic course. In these vocational courses the ratio between theoretical learning and hands on training was 30:70. An *innovative feature* of the courses was the inclusion of an entrepreneurship module that focused on how to set up a small business as well as market products.

While the learning process was based upon the learning needs of the learners, there were also some limitations that affected it. From the NOS point of view, the foremost aspect following the launching of the course was to get equivalence from different universities and professional institutions so that NOS graduates would be able to take admissions to these institutions of higher education. While some universities such as IGNOU, after studying the curriculum and course materials, gave the NOS senior secondary course unconditional recognition, others chose to put some conditions. For NOS it was necessary to inform all students about these conditions so that they could plan their higher studies accordingly. In some ways such conditions affected the open subject choice policy of NOS but had to be complied with in the larger interests of the learners. Another disturbing aspect was the domination of the formal school system which affected the material development. In the formal school system the senior secondary stage consisted of two years of schooling viz. Class XI and Class XII. While Class XI examination was an internal school examination, the Class XII examination was a public examination.

However, NOS offering courses at senior secondary level and having no class system had to establish its equivalency and recognition by other School boards/CBSE for its senior secondary examination through its curricular contents and treatment of this content in its learning materials. This meant that the NOS learners had to bear an equivalent study load of two years as against the one year work load of formal school students for the final public examination.

In order to overcome this problem as well as to design a more appropriate learning system, the NOS decided to adopt a modular approach for all its subjects. In this concept the subject was treated as one indivisible unit as far as the credits were concerned. There was no splitting of content into classes XI and XII. Instead, in order to stagger the learning load, the content units were divided into General Foundation and Certification Units (Fig 4). The General Foundation Units formed the base for the learning of the Certification Units. The Certification units aimed at testing critical thinking and contained content of a higher order. The syllabus organised on the basis of these two types of unit maintained proper logical sequence and coherence, using an integrated approach. The NOS public examination was based only upon the Certification Units of the given syllabus.

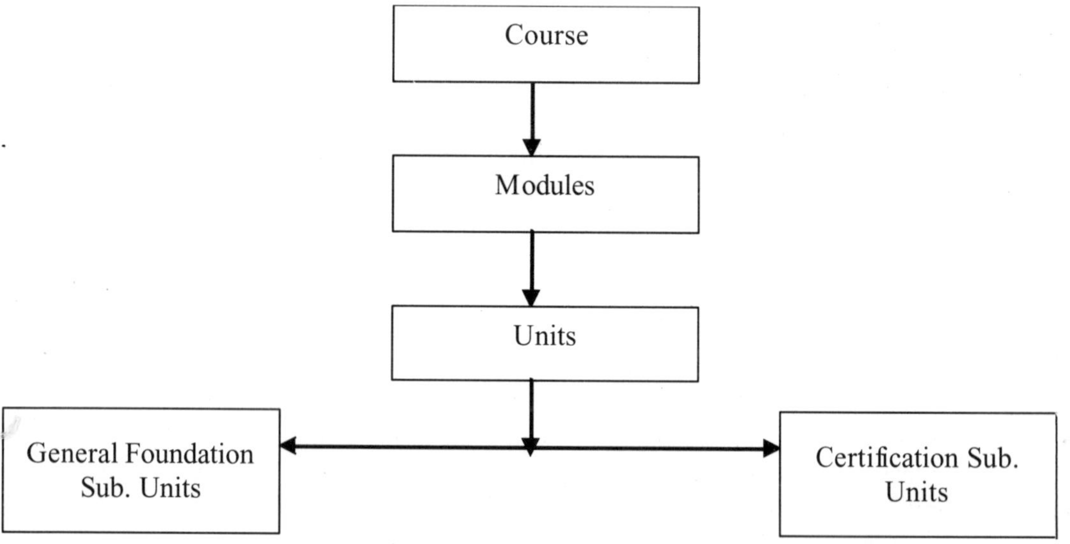

Figure 4: Course structure for senior secondary level

The advantages of this approach were that it allowed the learners to gain knowledge about the entire subject matter and yet they were tested only in areas which were crucial for learning and *retention*. Moreover, it facilitated growth of knowledge in a spiral fashion.

Yet another *innovation* at this stage was the introduction of optional modules in the curriculum. In keeping with the philosophy of openness and with a view to catering to the diversified learning needs of the learners, it was decided that intra modular choice would be made available to the learners. Since the learners were either those who were terminating their studies or those who were pursuing higher education, such a choice helped them to select modules that would be relevant to them in their job / home situation or for higher learning. Thus the curriculum was divided into core and optional modules. On an average the ratio of the weightage between core and optional modules was 70:30. In most subjects there were between two and four optional modules from which the learners had to take any one. For instance the optional modules in English language related to English for Special Purposes (ESP) containing areas like Scientific English, English for Receptionist. The optional modules in Physics were on Photography, Space Physics, Mathematics for Learning Physics, Equipments and Instruments. Learners chose any one module to be examined in the public examination but they could study all modules if they wished to as the learning materials for all were sent to all learners. The first batch registered for Senior Secondary Course in 1989 and the first examination was conducted in January 1991. Out of 13406 learners who appeared for Senior Secondary examination, 3730 i.e., 27.82 %, became certificate worthy fulfilling the laid down criteria (National Open School, 1992). This is the trend even today for all learners who appear in all subjects in the first year of their registration.

Decade Four: 1995-05 towards EFA Initiation of Open Basic Education Programme

By the fourth decade following the initiation of Open Schooling, the Secondary and Senior Secondary Programmes of the NOS had been well established. In 1995-1996 the enrolment figure touched 91,000 (NIOS, 2005 At a Glance) and the all India number of study centres was 522 (ibid, p.6).

During the initial period, the Open Schooling System had focused on the secondary and senior secondary levels. However, the early nineties saw the beginning of a global thrust in the direction of basic education. In 1990, a call for Education for All (EFA) was given at the World Conference at Jomtien. The post Jomtien EFA Summit of Nine High Population Countries adopted the Delhi Declaration wherein a specific resolution was made to work in collaboration on a distance education initiative " ... to better reach neo-literates and marginalised groups..." (UNESCO, 1994). Earlier the National Policy on Education (1986) and the Programme of Action (1992) also called for the strengthening of open learning facilities to meet the challenge of numbers that had to be provided opportunities for basic education. Further there was also a demand created by the large number of adults being made literate through the efforts of the National Literacy Mission (NLM). Both children and adults had to be offered a channel for their upward educational mobility.

In 1994 the NOS initiated the Open Basic Education (OBE) programme whose objective was "to provide primary level education to neo-literates....and to establish a learning continuum through Open Schooling..." (National Open School, 1994). The OBE programme began as a pilot project between NOS and the National Literacy Mission and was offered as an Equivalency Programme under the NLM's Continuing Education Scheme. In 2001 the OBE programme was initiated for out of school children in the 6-14 age groups also. Meanwhile in July 2002,

NOS was renamed by the MHRD as National Institute of Open Schooling (NIOS) not only to institutionalise Open Schooling system in the country but also to extend the role and scope of functioning of the system.

The OBE programme is delivered at three levels A, B and C which are equivalent to standard III, V and VIII of the formal school system. The emphasis of the programme is on the flexibilities of open schooling. There is open choice of medium, no upper age limit, registration up to a period of five years, and examinations twice a year. While certain core subjects such as any one Language, Mathematics, Science and Social Science are offered, yet there is open choice of subjects for vocational courses.

Keeping in mind that the target group is out of school children and adults who are literate and aspire to continue their schooling and that the learning styles and habits of both groups are different, the curricular content for both groups is same but the approach and treatment of transaction is different. While the Accredited Agencies (AAs) offering OBE programme for children can use national or state government prescribed text books, they also have the option of developing their own materials based on the NOS competency based curriculum. This has been done to enable children to move horizontally and vertically to and fro between the formal school system and the OLS.

The learning materials for the adults builds upon the literacy levels acquired following the Post Literacy programme of the National Literacy Mission while adhering to the requirements of equivalency as per the formal school curriculum. The instructional design of OBE course is unique in that the approach for course development is completely de-centralised. The main issue is that the learning materials has to be local-specific and in the mother tongue. In fact wherever possible, common words of local dialect have been used. The learning materials are developed with the help of national, state and district level experts in such a way that while 75% formed a common or core curriculum, the rest is open ended for adaptation to regional needs. The idea is to find place for the reflection of diversity of learning needs of neo-literates belonging to various cultural, linguistic and rural urban settings.

The curriculum developed is competency based and text free. The emphasis is more on practical rather than theoretic aspects. In the case of adult neo-literates, issues of responsible parenthood, reproductive health, and good habits have been included. Another set of competencies included are those related to vocational education. The idea behind this is to prepare adults to undertake economic activities. This issue related to dignity of labour, equal wages for both sexes, entrepreneurship and business ethics are reflected in the curriculum. The curriculum has an option for identification of local specific vocational course. Thus different districts have identified different Vocational Courses. For example preservation of Fruits and Vegetables was developed initially for Ajmer District (Rajasthan), while Cutting and Tailoring was developed for study centres in West Bengal.

The method for instructional development for OBE learning materials varied from state to state. The experimental OBE programme for adults was initiated by NIOS in Rajasthan in collaboration with the State Literacy Mission Authority and State Resource Centre. The learning materials developed used self-instructional methodology. A house style was especially developed for this course. Friendly key words were used. Certain access devices were also developed.

The learning materials were well illustrated in two colours and printed on good quality paper. While in the beginning the idea was to make district based materials for all three levels, this proved extremely difficult both in terms of time and economy. Hence the following three tier model was adopted for development of OBE materials:

- For Level A, every district developed its own learning materials with content based upon local situations and concerns.
- For level B, a common state wise set of materials was developed. However, vocational materials continued to be separate depending upon the local income generating needs.
- At Level C, the course materials prepared by NIOS are to be used.

Hence, the decision to develop learning materials district wise or state wise is taken after intense discussion between NIOS and the state level bodies. For example in West Bengal, one set of materials are being developed in Bengali medium for use across the state.

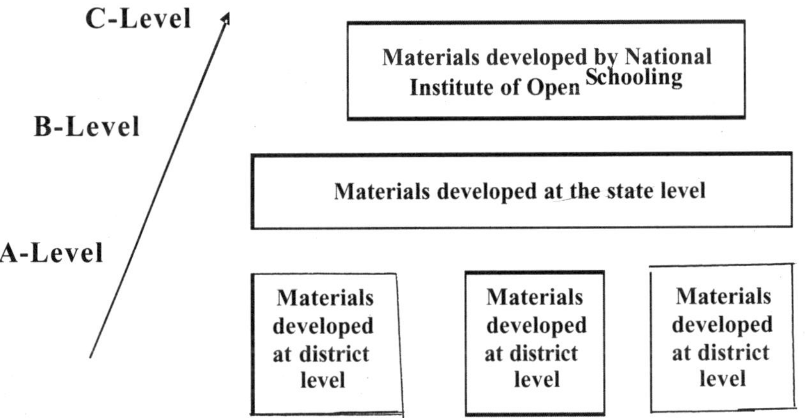

Figure 5: Three tier model for development of OBE materials

In the OBE curriculum the study hours are divided both for self learning and guided learning. The teaching learning process is conducted by non formal education instructors, formal school teachers, educated youth and retired teachers and other community persons. These persons are those who have been involved in literacy and continuing education programmes or primary school teachers. As per a recent research conducted by NIOS, it was found that learners preferred to meet in groups and study in a tutorial method (charcha mandal format) having the opportunity to undergo discussions and interactions amongst each other (UNESCO-NIOS, 2004).

Presently the learning materials are all largely in print media. A small start to introduce non print media has been made with audio- video programmes for Level C. There are also plans to develop radio programmes for neo literates. It is hoped that with the recent launching of the Educational Satellite (EduSat), some content for OBE will also be available through this medium.

Both the material development model as well as the implementation model of the OBE programme has been innovative. Both models are based upon the idea that collaboration and convergence are essential for OLS. The material developed for adult neo literates is based upon the curriculum developed by NIOS in collaboration with the experts in the field. The course team approach is followed with lesson writers comprising local district school teachers, persons working with NGOs and also instructors at the Continuing Education Centres. The experts from the NIOS and state bodies such as State Literacy Mission Authority, State Resource Centres provide resource support. In vocational course professional institutes are involved including (in some cases) Jan Shikshan Sansthans. The learning materials have been printed and distributed by the state level bodies.

As regards the implementation model, here too collaboration has been the key factor. The learners are enrolled at the accredited agency, which may be the local NGOs, madarassas, Government bodies like DIETs, Mahila Samakhya, Zila Saksharta Samitis, (District Literacy Council) Jan Shikshan Sansthans. The onus of teaching learning is on the local agency. The monitoring of the programme is done in collaboration with the state level body. The examination is based upon the design and blue print provided by NIOS. The examination is conducted locally by the state nodal agency and monitored both by NIOS and the state government. The signatories on the joint certificate given for the examination are both NIOS and the accredited agency. This shows that there is a joint responsibility towards the achievement of a common cause. So far more than 75,000 learners have been certified under OBE programme.

Conclusions

In four decades, the open schooling system was able to build and establish a bridge for a learning continuum in ODL system in the country. In fact today the country is ahead of many developing and developed countries to provide another supplementary and complementary system of education from school to university level for its billion people thereby making an attempt to liberate them from the tyranny of rigidities to *freedom to learn*.

Although there have been significant signs of success of the Open schooling system, there are still many miles to go. There is no doubt that collaborations need to be expanded. New partners including the community need to be explored so that programmes are conducted as learning activities. Networking with state governments for recognition of the certificate has to be done. The involvement of the State level bodies as nodal agencies would help to improve the quality of the programme.

As the programmes rest upon the genuine credibility of the local partners, there is therefore, a need to constantly monitor to check the procedures followed for quality transaction of the planned instructional cycle.

Nevertheless over this period it can be claimed that the instructional development and delivery in Open schooling system is a path breaker in many senses. The programmes have created an opportunity for life long learning for anybody and everybody. Panda and Garg (2003), in a recent comprehensive coverage of NOS (now NIOS), had succinctly concluded that the open school has achieved a lot; has miles to go; and that instructional design, training, research, quality assurance and networking of the open schooling system are the priorities for the future. The NIOS has successfully marched in the recent past in these directions.

References

Amundsen, C. (1993). The evolution of theory in distance education. In D. Keegan (ed.), *Theoretical Principles of Distance Education*. London and New York: Routledge, pp. 61-79.

Burns, R.W. (1967). The theory of expressing objectives. *Educational Technology*, 7(20), 1-3.

Delling, R.M. (1975). Distant study as an opportunity for learning. In E. Ljosa, (ed.), *The System of Distance Education*. Malino: Hermods, 55-59.

Dewal, O.S. (1986). *Open School, India: The Preliminary Years, 1979-1983: A Case Study*. Australia: Deakin University, pp. 39-50.

Dewal, O.S. (1994). Open learning in Indian school education. In M. Mukhopadhyay, & S. Phillips, (eds.), *Open Schooling: Selected Experiences*. Vancouver: The Commonwealth of Learning, 9-16.

Gagne, R.M., & Briggs, L.J. (1974). *Principles of Instructional Design*. New York: Holt, Rinehart & Winslon, Inc.

Garrison, D.R. (1989). *Understanding Distance Education: A Framework for the Future*. London and New York: Routledge.

Holmberg, B. (1977). *Distance Education: A Survey and Bibliography*. London: Kogan Page.

Holmberg, B. (1981). Independent study for university degrees: Distance education compared with the Keller Plan. *Distance Education*, 2(1), 40.

Holmberg, B. (1983). Guided didactic conversation in distance education. In D. Sewart, D. Keegan, & B. Holmberg, (eds.), *Distance Education: International Perspectives*. London: Croom Helm.

Keegan, D. (1986). *The Foundations of Distance Education (1st edition)*. London: Croom Helm.

Moore, M. G. (1973b). Towards a theory of independent learning and teaching. *Journal of Higher Education*, 44(12).

Moore, M. G. (1991). Editorial: distance education theory. *The American Journal of Distance Education*, 5(3), 1-6.

National Open School. (1992). *Annual Report: 1990-91*. New Delhi: NOS.

National Open School. (1994). Open Basic Education Programme: Equivalency Programme as part of CE Programme. Approach paper on the Pilot Project of National Open School and National Literacy Mission, New Delhi (unpublished).

NIOS (2005). *NIOS at a Glance*. New Delhi: NIOS.

Open School, Central Board of Secondary Education. (1980). *Annual Report: 1979-80*. New Delhi.

Panda, S. and Garg, S. (2003). Open learning in India with open schools. In J. Bradley (ed.), *The Open Classroom*. London: Routedge Falmer.

Saba, F. (1990). Integrated telecommunications systems and instructional transaction. In M.G. Moore, (ed.), *Contemporary Issues in American Distance Education*. Oxford: Pergamon Press.

Sewart, D. (1981). Distance teaching: a contradiction in terms? *Teaching at a Distance,* 19, 8-18.

Singhal, R.P. (1979). The Open School Project: The Blue Print. New Delhi: Central Board of Secondary Education (unpublished monograph).

Sujatha, K. (2002). *Distance Education at Secondary level in India: the National Open School.* Paris: UNSECO: International Institute for Educational Planning.`

UNESCO (1994). *Education for All Summit of Nine High Population Countries.* Paris.

UNESCO-NIOS (2004). *Models of Equivalency Programmes: Report of the Study of NIOS Open Basic Education Programme*. New Delhi: NIOS.

Verduin, J.R. and Clark, T.A. (1991). *Distance Education: The Foundations of Effective Practice.* San Francisco: Jossey-Bass Publishers.

Wedemeyer, C. (1981). *Learning at the Backdoor: Reflections on Non-traditional Learning in the Lifespan.* Madison, Wis.: University of Wisconsin Press.

Wedemeyer, C.A. (1974). Characteristics of open learning system. In*Open Learning Systems*. Washington: National Association of Educational Broadcasters.

Wiilen, B. (1981). *Distance Education of Swedish Universities: An Evaluation of the Experimental Programme and Follow up Study.* Uppsala: Acta Universitatis Upsaliensis, Stockholm, Sweden, AlmqVist and Wiksell International.

Dr. Sushmita Mitra is Director (Student Support Services), National Institute of Open Schooling, New Delhi.

Ms. Anita Priyadarshini is Deputy Director (Administration) National Institute of Open Schooling, New Delhi.

44

National Consortium for Open Schooling

V.J. Williams and Savita Kaushal

Introduction

India has one of the largest educational systems in the world as it has to cater to educational needs of hundred million children at different stages. Unfortunately, for variety of reasons, the occurrence of dropouts is very high; 40.7% at the primary level and 53.7% at the elementary stage of education (I-VIII). The enormity of the problem caused by out of school children becomes more acute by the pressure generated by passouts from elementary level seeking entry at the secondary level. To cater to such unprecedented demand for education and lack of formal structures to respond to this gigantic task made it inevitable for the Government of India to think about academically sound and economically viable suitable alternatives was only logical to start with flexible schooling system with inbuilt flexibilities about choice of courses of study, place, pace and timings of study and potential for reaching the unreached. Due to these learner-centric characteristics, open schooling was seen as a potential alternative education system to meet the educational needs of out of school children.

In 1989, the Government of India (GOI), Ministry of Human Resource Development (MHRD), established the National Open School (NOS) as an autonomous organisation. In 1990, NOS was vested with the powers to examine and certify its students up to pre-degree level. In July 2002, the National Open School (NOS) was re-christened as the National Institute of Open Schooling (NIOS). The NIOS has taken significant steps for offering various courses and life enrichment programmes, examinations and certification, training and extension programmes through distance mode. For every programme, the self-instructional materials are made available in different mediums of instruction. The programmes are designed keeping the needs, problems, interests and demands of the learners of different regions in view. The enhanced access, relevance, flexibility and openness have promoted efficiency of the open schooling programmes (Panda and Garg, 2003).

The NIOS with current enrolment of about 1.3 million learners is the largest open schooling system in the world (NIOS, 2005). However, along with its role as a national level resource organisation in open schooling, the NIOS should limit enrolment up to a certain limit and support Indian States (29 States and 6 Union Territories), to develop institutions, which can cater to local languages and dialects and variations with regard to social customs and traditions. With the establishment of eleven State Open Schools and one National Open School, a need was felt to establish a forum in the form of National Consortium for Open Schooling (NCOS).

State Open Schools (SOSs) have to assume responsibility for expansion of open schooling programmes, particularly in view of the fact that a large percentage of prospective learners would like to opt for regional languages as medium of study.

The structure of the State Open School may vary according to context and needs of each state. In view of this, the NIOS has made special efforts to support alternative models of SOSs and State Centres for Open Schooling. It is expected that in each state at least one of these would come up. So far twelve states (Andhra Pradesh, Haryana, Himachal Pradesh, Jammu and Kashmir, Karnataka, Kerala, Madhya Pradesh, Punjab, Rajasthan, Tamil Nadu, West Bengal, Delhi) have already set up open schools. Eight more states (Assam, Bihar, Chhattisgarh, Gujarat, Maharashtra, Orissa, Uttar Pradesh and Uttaranchal) are in the process of setting up State Open Schools.

Consortium for Distance Education: the Context of Open Schooling

According to Webster's Dictionary (1985), consortium is "an association or union; a combination of financial institutions and capitalists for the purpose of carrying into effect some financial operation requiring large sources of capital." This definition conceives consortium in a narrow sense. In Oxford Advanced Learner's Dictionary (1989), consortium is defined as "temporary association of a number of countries, companies, banks, etc., for a common purpose."

This definition is relatively broader and extends the association to organisations in a country or more countries. However, neither of these definitions is comprehensive. In UK, in the context of education, this term is used to signify collectiveness of peripatetic teachers with specialist skills. That is, it refers to teachers employed at two or more schools and travelling between them regularly. In US, it refers to a group of schools (usually post-secondary) or libraries that combine selected programmes or resources (Terry Page et. al, 1979, p. 83).

These definitions of consortium provide some basis in the context of open schooling. In the context of open schooling a consortium can be defined as a temporary or permanent association of open schools for the common purpose of i) providing effective education by making it more accessible, relevant, flexible and open to all the needy, deprived and interested people willing to pursue or continue their education through distance mode of learning, and ii) promoting growth and development of open schooling system.

Thus, from the point of view of open schooling, the specific purposes of the consortium are to:

i) Establish effective functional linkage between and among different open schooling institutions;
ii) Promote expansion and development of open schooling systems;
iii) To promote better cooperation, collaboration and coordination between and among member institutions of consortium in respect of development, sharing and maintenance of quality of self-instructional materials; and
iv) Increase the efficiency of delivery of programmes to learners in terms of admission and mobility of learners across the regions and courses/programmes, support services, evaluation, certification and accreditation.

Historical Background

In the Eighth Five Year Plan 1992-97 (GoI, 1992, p.291) it was envisaged that the National Open School (NOS) is expected to provide programme and resource support to state level open schools. In order to maintain quality it was felt that a consortium should be set up in order to facilitate co-operation, collaboration and expansion of activities related to open learning system at state level as well as national level. In order to facilitate better cooperation and interaction among NIOS and State Open Schools and other concerned agencies and the expansion of activities pertaining to the open learning system, a National Consortium for Open Schooling (NCOS) was established in 1997. The NIOS works also as the Secretariat of NCOS. The major objectives of NCOS, which were visualized at the time of its inception, are:

- Sharing of resources, expertise.
- Professional, technical and academic support in setting up of the SOSs/SCOS (state centre for open schooling).
- Designing need specific curriculum, developing/translating self-instructional material in the local medium.
- Human resource development.
- Development of prototype materials and other pedagogical inputs.
- Pace setting and maintenance of database on OLS.
- Organizing national and international conferences/seminars on open schooling.

In this regard the major activities envisaged for NIOS (as NCOS headquarter) are as follows:

1. Persuading the states from time to time to set up/upscale SOSs – advocacy programmes.
2. Providing financial assistance to states for (i) upscaling of open schooling programmes of SOSs, and (ii) setting up of SOSs.

3. Organization of national, regional and state level conferences/workshops/meetings periodically for promotion of open schooling in states.
4. Organization of orientation/training programmes for open schooling functionaries.
5. Coordination and clearing house functions.
6. Research and surveys in the context of open schooling and sharing of outcomes with SOSs.

The NIOS may also provide financial assistance to SOSs for conducting researches in open schooling.

The NCOS as an apex unit of NIOS in the promotion of open schooling (in India as well as abroad) also coordinates the activities of the Open Schooling Association of the Commonwealth (OSAC), international relations (IR), the International Centre for Training in Open Schooling (ICTOS), and Commonwealth of Learning (COL) related programmes.

The NCOS has made provisions to provide technical and professional support in designing, setting up and quality assurance of the State Open Schools.

Goals and Functions of NCOS

The NCOS strives to achieve the following broad goals:

i) To facilitate the apex body role of the NIOS.
ii) To promote better cooperation and collaboration among agencies/ institutions involved in open schooling.

The functions of NCOS are as follows (Fig. 1):

- Providing technical and professional assistance and consultancy to state governments for the establishment of state open schools, and state centres for open schooling.
- Formulating norms and guidelines for maintenance of standards and quality of various programmes/activities to be offered through distance mode and open learning system, including possibility of credit transfer.
- Sharing of resources, expertise, curriculum, instructional materials and teaching-learning strategies of mutual interest and benefit.
- Creating forums such as publications, meetings, workshops and seminars for sharing experiences, increase access and equity and improve quality and standards in the system.
- Developing and maintaining a database on various aspects of open schooling in the country and abroad.

- Facilitating better linkages with international, national and state level agencies in matters concerning open schooling through formal and informal consultation.
- Providing technical support for open schools and such other institutions for developing educational, communication and information technologies in improving the teaching learning process, training and management.
- Initiating other activities and programmes, as may be deemed appropriate, by associating institutions from time to time.

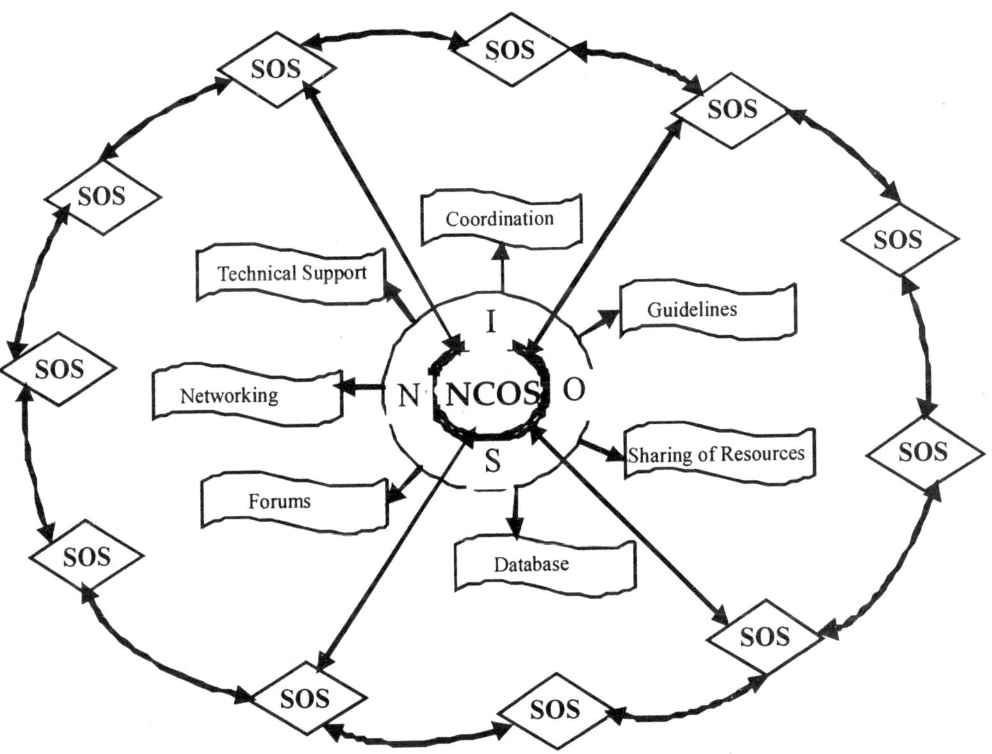

Figure 1: Functions of NCOS

To operationalise its role as open body in open schooling, NCOS has been undertaking many activities to set up and strengthen state open schools and to ensure their cooperation and collaboration with NIOS and other institutions involved in open schooling.

Activities Conducted by NCOS

Setting up state open schools

A scheme of financial assistance to states for setting up of state open schools and for upscaling of the open schooling programme is being operationalised under NCOS. The financial assistance under this scheme is limited to Rs. 20 lakh, which is generally spread over a period of five years.

International role

At the international level, the NIOS has been collaborating with the Commonwealth of Learning (COL), UNESCO, UNDP etc. The NIOS is the headquarter/secretariat of the Open Schooling Association of the Commonwealth (OSAC). The Open Schooling Association of the Commonwealth (OSAC) created with financial assistance from the Commonwealth of Learning (COL), with headquarters at NIOS, New Delhi, functions as liaison agency for information dissemination, coordination and mutual consultation among member countries. The OSAC proposes organizing human resource development programmes for functionaries of open schools, promote research and development activities and take steps to ensure quality of standards. Through periodic meetings, the OSAC will be providing forums for discussion on issues of mutual interest and concerns.

In order to provide a forum across the world for scholarly discussion on concerns and issues in open learning/open schooling and disseminating research, theory and practice, including inter-disciplinary studies, the NIOS, as an apex organization in open schooling, brings out a half yearly publication "*OSAC Journal of Open Schooling*" of international standard. Its inaugural issue was released in November 2001.

Under this forum, NCOS has already organized a few national and international conferences, which provided forums for exchange of ideas and experiences among the Commonwealth countries. NIOS has also organized advocacy meetings and orientation programmes for several developing countries from Africa and Asia in collaboration with COL and UNESCO.

Capacity building of open schooling personnel

A comprehensive plan has been prepared for training of personnel engaged in open schooling programmes. An International Centre for Training in Open Schooling (ICTOS) has been set up at NIOS. This Centre offers certificate and diploma courses in open schooling. The training package for the certificate course has already been developed and printed. The training package for diploma course is being finalised. NIOS is in touch with the Commonwealth of Learning and UNESCO for deputing open schooling functionaries from developing countries for enrolment in training courses of ICTOS. This training centre is also meant for training of in-country open schooling functionaries.

Challenges Ahead

In view of its above-mentioned role and functions, the NIOS has to meet the following challenges:

1) There is a need to identify strategies for sustaining partnership between National Institute of Open Schooling and other institutions working for the promotion of open schooling and distance education.
2) Setting up/upscaling of State Open Schools on priority basis as target groups to take up regional mediums for pursuing various courses of study up to pre-degree level.
3) Sharing of experiences among the states about implementation of open schooling programme.
4) Identification of intervention strategies for quality assurance in the programmes of State Open Schools.
5) Evolving strategies for expediting the process of opening SOS in states that have taken initiative in this regard.
6) Preparation of an action plan at national/state level for expansion/upscaling of open schooling in states.

Future Role

To meet the challenges ahead the NIOS, through the NCOS forum, may adopt the following roles in the near future. Some of the significant recommendations of the National Meet for Promotion of Open Schooling Programme held in Bhopal from 6-7 August, 2004 point to some future activities of NCOS given as follows:

- Keeping in view the EFA goals and to increase access to secondary education, setting up of state open schools may have to be treated on priority basis. NCOS forum may have to interact with States/UTs for early establishment of SOS where such structures have not been established.
- Strategies have to be evolved to up-scale substantially the programme of existing state open schools to meet the huge influx of pass-outs from primary to middle stage and from middle stage to secondary stage. The following initiatives may be taken up:
  (i) NCOS in collaboration with SOS may conduct a quick base line survey for identification of target group in various regions/states.
  (ii) NCOS in collaboration with SOS may conduct a need assessment study to make an estimate about the number of study centres required in different geographical locations according to the ratio of number of learners intending to avail education through open schooling mode.
- Quality assurance in open schooling for establishing credibility of the open schooling system.

NIOS through its NCOS forum may:

- evolve, in collaboration with SOS, indicators of quality in open schooling;
- make periodic curriculum renewal for enhancing relevance and functionality of open schooling curriculum for the divergent categories of target group;
- provide Curriculum Framework in Open Schooling and Guidelines for preparation of ICT enabled print and non-print materials in self-learning mode to SOSs and assist in the adoption/adaptation as well as development of state specific self-learning materials in regional languages reflecting the socio-cultural ethos of the States and learning needs of learners;
- develop strategies for expansion of open schooling programme in the States that have not so far set up the state open schools have to be identified;
- design a systematic and comprehensive programme of training since training seems to be the weakest link in the programme of SOSs. Intervention in the form of development of a systematic and comprehensive programme of training for different levels of functionaries combining the face-to-face mode with distant modes of delivery assumes one of the critical tasks NCOS. Strategies for staff development and professional growth through appropriate exposure visit and short and long term training programme of officials in the partner institutions may be planned meticulously. As noted earlier, the NIOS has set up an International Centre for Training in Open Schooling (ICTOS). This Centre offers certificate and diploma courses in open schooling. The states may take advantage of training of their functionaries by deputing state officials to attend programmes offered by ICTOS.
- Monitor the system of open schooling. A sound and systematically planned intervention with regard to the area of monitoring may be evolved out in near future. A comprehensive framework may be formulated for effective monitoring of open schooling programmes towards building up a sound support system at different stages of programme implementation.

  NIOS in consultation with SOSs and apex national level organizations, viz. Indira Gandhi National Open University (IGNOU), National Council for Educational Research and Training (NCERT), and National Institute for Educational Planning and Administration (NIEPA), and the state open universities may formulate a comprehensive framework for monitoring of open schooling programmes covering all the important aspects. It needs to circulate the 'Monitoring Framework' to SOSs and assist them to plan comprehensive scheme of monitoring. NIOS may also create necessary infrastructure at appropriate levels for regular flow of information through adopting Educational Management Information System (EMIS) at regional centres of open schools, state centres of open schooling, and state open schools.

  NCOS may create and maintain database regularly, plan appropriate action for extending support services to SOS in matters of:

  - Setting up of SOSs.
  - Strengthening existing programmes of the SOSs and their services.
  - Maintaining profiles of study centres – their strength and shortcomings.
  - Learner profile including trend of enrolment and achievement of learners.
  - Status of training of functionaries with special components of the distance mode of education.

  - Training needs of newly opened study centres.
  - Evaluation processes.
  - Upscaling the performance level of study centres.
  - Strengthening student support services with ICT-enabled material and integration of face-to-face mode of learning with distance education delivery process.
  - NCOS to make special efforts for monitoring of research projects sponsored by NIOS/ collaborative research projects to ensure their completion and implementation.
  - NCOS to hold workshops/seminars at regional and state level to discuss developments at SOSs and identify state specific support needed regarding various programme areas.
- To conduct research studies to strengthen the state open schools: One of the thrust areas of SOSs can be to cover the vital issues pertaining to feasibility, the potentiality of the pedagogy of ODL, the modalities for fusion of traditional classroom processes with the emerging techniques of electronic media, development of multimedia packages and their contribution in enhancing learner efficiency with a focus on the autonomy and suitability for the learner. There can be many more areas of research as the system generates new trends and strategies of education.
- Recognition of certificates of SOSs by State Boards of Education and universities is an issue of great concern. NCOS, as an important forum for quality assurance in SOSs, is required to initiate effective dialogue between MHRD, State Boards of School Education, universities and institutions of the higher learning including apex industrial houses for acceptance and recognition of state open school certificates within and outside the state. In addition to this, the NIOS through its NCOS forum may:
  (i) communicate to SOSs concerned regarding the acceptance and recognition of open schooling certificate.
  (ii) work ing collaboration with state open schools, state departments of education to ensure that the standard and guidelines of pupil evaluation are adhered to in holding examinations, processing of results and declaration of results.
- A sound 'forum' may be created for promotion and sharing of research and development (R&D) activities in ODL at national, regional and international level.
  (i) NIOS through NCOS and OSAC forums is required to take special initiatives for promotion and sharing of research and developmental activities in ODL.
  (ii) NIOS in consultation with IGNOU, NCERT, State Open Schools and NGOs may identify priority areas of research in ODL.
  (iii) NIOS to pay special attention for promoting research projects in ODL at:
    - Faculty level (NIOS sponsored)
    - SOS level (NIOS-SOS sponsored)
    - Cross country level (COL, UNESCO sponsored research projects)
    - NIOS may also select apex national/innovative state level agencies based on pre-decided criteria for outsourcing research and development projects.

(iv) NIOS may hold under the aegis of NCOS, national/regional level and international level collaborative seminars/workshops for identification of research priorities in ODL in country specific contexts.

- Alternative strategies may be evolved for fostering networking and linkages for advocacy, promotion of innovations, sharing of resources and sustenance of open schooling programmes at state/national and international level. For this NIOS through NCOS forum may:
  - (i) take initiative through NCOS and in consultation with SOS for evolving effective strategies for networking and sharing of resources at different levels;
  - (ii) develop a comprehensive database about the resources available at national and state level both in print and electronic forms;
  - (iii) work together with SOS under the aegis of NCOS to update the information from time to time;
  - (iv) print the database and upload this on the website;
  - (v) provide an effective platform for sharing of ideas, resources by organizing seminars, conferences, and workshops periodically;
  - (vi) use ICT intensively for promotion and sustaining networking at different levels;
  - (vii) help the SOS to develop their own websites with information regarding admission procedures, admission forms, results, etc. with hyper-linking between the SOS and NIOS;
  - (viii) provide technical and financial support;
  - (ix) help the SOS by linking these through a wide area network covering state open universities, IGNOU and other apex institutions working for open learning;
  - (x) hold periodic meetings/conferences for development of academic and vocational courses;
  - (xi) arrange for short/long term deputation and on-the-job training concerning academic/vocational courses; and
  - (xii) collaborate with apex international organisation like COL, UNESCO etc. to organize conferences in open schooling for sharing and collaboration of ideas.
- More emphasis may be given to the use of ICT for promotion and sustaining the network. Linkages through a Wide Area Network covering state open schools, NIOS, state open universities, IGNOU and other concerned apex institutions working in the area of open learning may be established.
- The nature and type of indicators of quality in open schooling will have to be identified through interactions at different levels.
- Development and use of tools for evaluating the quality of self-learning materials - both print and non-print - and techniques of evaluation are essential for quality assurance. NCOS could take up this task.
- A training package needs to be developed; its design and format may be worked out by NIOS in consultation with SOSs.

- Linking international agencies for academic and financial support to SOSs are essential for programme enrichment.
- Development of resource bank of academic counsellors, editors, writers and evaluators will go a long way in sharing of the existing resources.

Limitations

Since its inception, the NCOS has been endeavouring for promoting, developing and extending open schooling in the country through the state open schools and other agencies in the field of open schooling. But the task ahead is enormous and this is quite difficult to handle with the limited staff strength. The challenge is to invest more energy and resources to improve the system, both in its capacity for outreach and quality. Establishment of NCOS as a national council in the form of a full- fledged department can help NIOS to realize its goals. A lot of rethinking is required in this regard. We have to act on this with a sense of urgency and earnestness.

References

GoI (1992). *Eighth Five Year Plan*. Planning Commission, Govt. of India, New Delhi.

Hornby, A.S. (Ed). (1989). *Oxford Advanced Learner's Dictionary of Current English*. Fourth Edition. Oxford: Oxford University Press.

Longman (1985). *Longman Dictionary of the English Language*. Harlow: Longman Group Limited.

NIOS (2005). *Increasing Access to Education through Open Schooling*. National Meet for Promotion of Open Schooling Programme (6-7 August, 2004).

Panda, S. and Garg, S. (2003). Open learning in India with open schools. In Bradley, J. (ed.), *The Open Classroom*. London: RoutledgeFalmer.

Terry Page, G., Thomas, J.B. and Marshall, A.R. (1979). *International Dictionary of Education*. London: The English Language Book Society and Kogan Page.

Webster, N. (1985). *New Webster's Dictionary of the English Language*. USA: Delair Publishing Company Inc.

Shri V.J. Williams is Director (Evaluation), National Institute of Open Schooling, New Delhi.

Dr Savita Kaushal is Academic Officer (Teacher Training), National Institute of Open Schooling, New Delhi.

45

ICT-Enabled School Education: Some Experiences

Jyotsna Dikshit and Santosh Panda

Background

The government aided school education system in India has been highly affected by higher dropout rates, and lower enrolment and retention rates. The formal school system and the non-formal education centres enrol about 150 million children in the non-formal education centres. If those along with the enrolments of all the open schools put together are considered, at least 40 million children are out of the school today. And, if the dropouts are included, the figure reaches about 70 million (Panda & Garg, 2003). Besides the issue of access, as in most of the developing countries, in India too low motivation of teachers, lack of relevant teaching in schools and poor quality of education have been major contributing factors for this statistics. India had earlier been a signatory to the E-9 Summit of 1993 which had resolved to take education to the disadvantaged and the marginalised. Much before that, the Government of India had launched in 2001 the *Sarva Shiksha Abhiyan* (EFA) programme for Universalisation of Elementary Education (UEE) to achieve the following goals:

i) All children should be in schools, education guarantee centres, alternate schools, and 'back-to-school' camps by 2003.
ii) All children must complete five years of primary schooling by 2007.
iii) All children must complete eight years of elementary schooling by 2010.
iv) The focus should be on elementary education of satisfactory quality with emphasis on education for life.
v) All gender and social category gaps at primary stage must be bridged by 2007 and at elementary education level by 2010.
vi) Universal retention should be achieved by 2010.

The task is enormous, and therefore concerted efforts are being made especially through distance learning to achieve the target goals within the stipulated time frame. From 1994, the Government of India with international funding support from the European Union and the World Bank launched the District Primary Education Programme (DPEP) as a comprehensive scheme to improve the quality of school education from all respects. The Distance Education Programme (DEP) was added to it as an integral part for professional development of all the functionaries including teachers in this project. Initially implemented in 18 states, the SSA extended implementation to cover all the 29 states and 6 union territories with DEP again as an integral component. In what will be discussed and focussed in this chapter is a part of the larger SSA formulation. The other aspects of professional development has been discussed in another chapter in this volume.

From Computer Education to Computer-Enabled Education

To create awareness among the school students and teachers about the computer and its usage in the teaching-learning process, the Government of India (GoI) introduced the Computer Literary Awareness in Secondary Schools (CLASS) project, initially as a pilot project during the year 1984-85 in which under the British aid of BBC Microcomputers a total of 12,000 computers were received and distributed to secondary and senior secondary schools through various state governments [source:http://www.education.nic.in/htmlweb/class_02.htm]. Under this project, schools in different parts of the country were provided with school computers, and the teachers were trained at various resource centres identified by the respective state governments to impart computer education to the school children. The CLASS project was again revised in 2002 to accelerate the pace of introduction of IT in schools and create models of school computer education – so as to achieve the goals of universalisation of computer literacy among school graduates within the next five years. The state government of Madhya Pradesh handed the responsibility of project management and implementation of CLASS project to the M.P. Bhoj (Open) University (MPBOU) which completed the project implementation successfully.

ETV

The National Council for Education Research and Training (NCERT) which is the largest national institute dedicated and devoted to school education in India acts as a national-level apex body to provide leadership and guidance in the formulation of programmes and policies for school education including teacher professional development. In order to improve the quality of teaching and learning process using the rapid advancements in educational technology, NCERT's Central Institute of Educational Technology (CIET) telecasts educational TV (ETV) programmes for children and teachers of elementary schools. The programmes have now been stabilised and become an integral part of school culture in the country. The experiences gained from these programmes have been extremely useful in the conception and design of IT-enabled school education in the country.

IT Enabled Education under the Head Start Project

In view of the success achieved under the CLASS projects, the state of MP formed a group known as State-level Task Group to strengthen school education in the state with a new idea of making computer enabled education available at the grass root level through the schools which were already activated under the Education Guarantee Scheme (EGS). The MPBOU which was represented on the Task Group had to play a major role in providing technical inputs required for computer purchase, their installation and providing of basic software. As a pilot project 1000 schools were meant to be activated from the July/August, 1998 session. 2000 teachers, two from each school were called for training on computer operations, use of innovative and interactive software and to build confidence in the teachers in using the computer. Trainings of teachers was conducted at six different regional centres of MPBOU; this resulted in achieving the target of 2000 well trained teachers who were sufficiently motivated to accept the challenge of providing computer enabled education in the 1000 selected schools mostly in the interior areas of the state. When the project was implemented the enormous response and motivation was visible in the students from geographically remote and less developed areas. The key objectives of the project were

- To make learning joyful and interesting to the student through learner centric approach.
- To inspire and support the self learning activities of the students.
- To mobilize academic support for the simplification of difficult concepts.
- To make new resources for learning available to students and teachers.

Computer Based Elementary Education (CBEE)

CBEE is a reformative addition to the DEP-SSA with the prime objective of bringing IT-enabled education to the classroom education so as to improve its quality from all angles. The approach to CBEE is based on the following broad objectives:

- Preparing and empowering learners and teachers for the knowledge-based society.
- Increasing access to quality education.
- Moving towards learner-centred, collaborative learning and fostering creativity.

It was visualised that the CBEE implementation plan includes the following four components:

- Training and capacity building of trainers, teachers, students, other SSA functionaries and the community.
- Development of context-specific, self-learning, interactive multimedia CDs for hard spot areas and other subject areas at upper primary and elementary levels.
- Availability of low cost and user friendly IT infrastructure in the schools.
- Implementation and continuous evaluation of the implementation, including continuous dialogue through ICT and face-to-face modes.

Emerging Scenario

SSA is an initiative of the Ministry of Human Resource Development, Government of India to provide quality education to the primary and upper primary learners. In this background, the government and non-government agencies, and others have formulated a large number of long-term and short-term projects, which have greater focus on the rural, tribal and less developed areas of the country. These agencies are putting massive efforts to provide education, better living conditions, better health care and general awareness for empowering our people living in rural and less developed areas. In this background, IGNOU in collaboration with MPBOU, has also joined hands in taking up the responsibility of training teachers as IT, orienting students on IMM-CD, and development of IMM-CDs on hardspots in subject areas of English, Maths, Science, and Social Studies for grades VI to VII. In this regard, the team has:

- conducted teacher training programme for their IT empowerment in Jharkhand state;
- identified state-wide hardspots in English, Math and Science through workshop mode in Jharkhand state;
- identified state-wide hardspots in English, Math and Science for Punjab state;
- designed and developed interactive multimedia scripting and educational software (IMM-CDs) for Math, Science and English in Gurmukhi for the state of Punjab;
- designed and developed teacher training interactive multimedia educational CDs for Punjab state; and
- conducted needs analysis for the rest of the country.

Thus, the combined strengths of the two open universities briefly outlined below, provide substantive justification for handling of Computer Based Elementary Education under the Sarva Shiksha Abhiyan for teacher training, interactive multimedia CD design and development for both hard spots for upper primary and elementary education, and implementation of the initiative. The collaborating team:

- Has network of expertise in content spread across the country
- Is pioneer in technology mediated education
- Is Centre of Excellence in educational software development
- Has expertise in management and implementation of large country-wide projects
- Has already implemented teacher training programmes such as B.Ed., Certificate in Primary Education, and other teacher training programmes, including training on ICT
- Has devised cost-effective ways to design, develop and deliver technology mediated programmes
- Has proven expertise in designing adaptable learning systems
- Has already successfully undertaken similar projects including HEADSTART, SSA-Punjab etc.

Framework for Successful Integration of Technology into the Learning Environment

Integrating technology into the learning environment is by no means an easy job. Our experiences with the Headstart project in the state of Madhya Pradesh have been unique. Under this project we motivated and involved the community in a big way to expand and strengthen quality education by providing computer-enabled education at the grass root level to a very massive group of students in rural areas through ICT-enabled networks in the state. This initiative received international award for most successful performance and intervention in the area of primary education among all the Commonwealth countries. The state government, and an autonomous organisation under the government called Rajya Shiksha Kendra under the Rajiv Gandhi Shiksha Mission handled the project. With this unique experience, coupled with the long standing experience of IGNOU in multimedia based distance education delivery, and that on interactive multimedia and blended learning designed by the IUC, we had generated enormous capabilities in providing computer enabled education to the primary and upper primary learners by developing interactive multimedia CDs in English, Mathematics and Sciences which are considered to be the hardspots of the learners at these levels. To ensure success, it was necessary to plan clearly each step of implementation and to regiment processes and impose stringent guidelines at every stage and to monitor and track the effectiveness of the model. The four components, which are essential to integrate technology in the learning environment, are shown in Fig. 1.

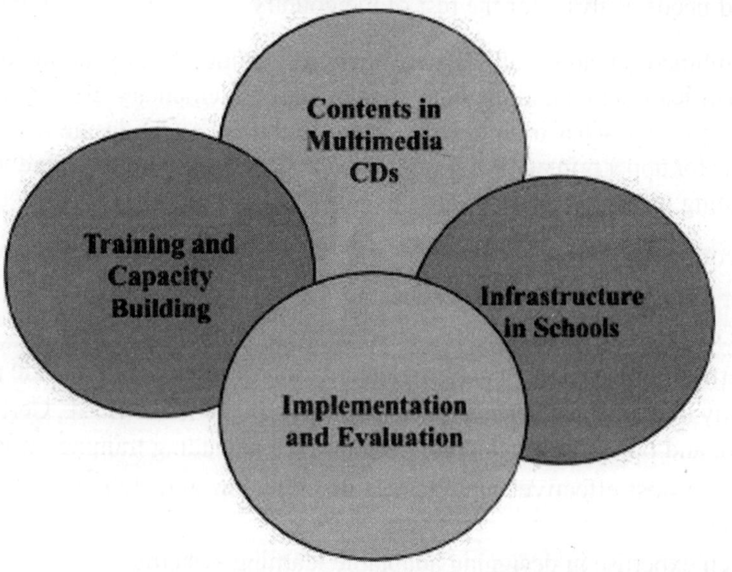

Figure 1: Components to integrate technology in the learning environment

The four components include:

- Development of learner-friendly and contextual interactive multimedia CD-ROMs on hardspots in school subject areas in regional languages as well as in English medium.
- Installation of hardware and software, and their maintenance, in the elementary schools.
- Training and capacity building of teachers, students and other functionaries involved in the SSA on IT-enabled education.
- Implementation, constant monitoring, timely evaluation and follow-up revision of the programme.

The outcomes of integrating technology in schools is show in Fig. 2.

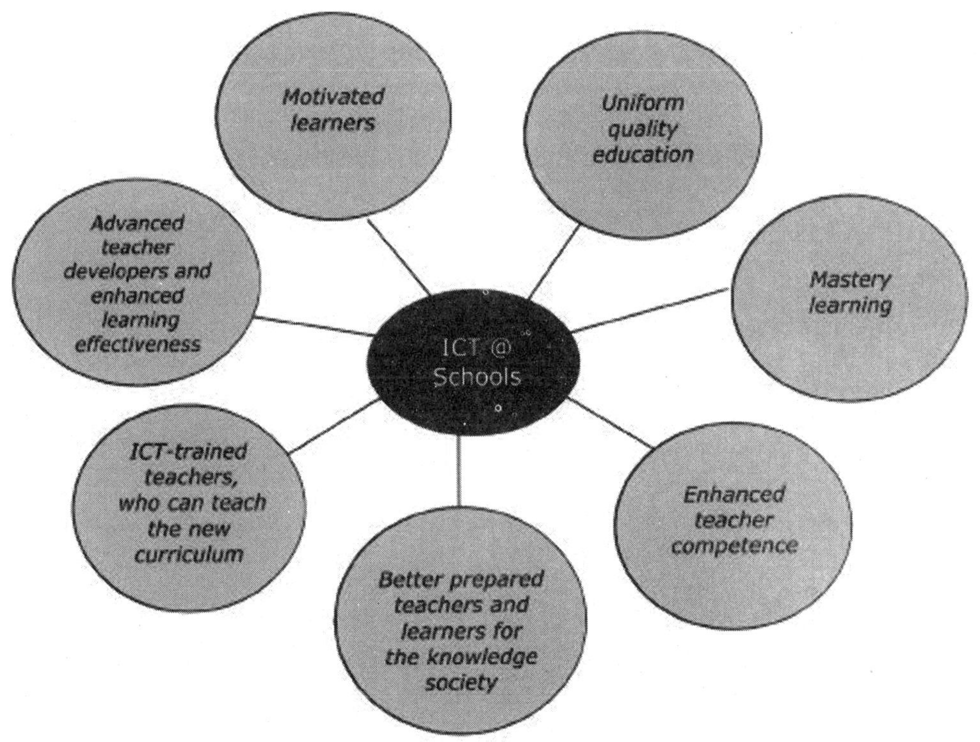

Figure 2: Outcomes of integrating of technology in schools

Our Model

Our model of CBEE as shown in Fig. 3 suggests that there is simultaneous:

- training of trainers for further training in the design and development of interactive multimedia CD-ROM,

- actual development of IMM-CDs,
- orientation of learners through 'colour picture workbook' on how to use the CDs for self learning individually and most importantly in groups,
- teacher orientation through manuals, guides, workbooks, and f2f workshops and teleconferencing on how to use the CDs for further facilitating student learning in individual and group situations (i.e. to contextualise learning and facilitate classroom teaching), as also for developing ability to teach through ICT,
- orientation of various functionaries in the district project offices (DPOs), clusture resource centres (CRCs), block resource centres (BRCs) and village education committees (VECs) to facilitate collaboration, networking and actual implementation of the scheme of CBEE,
- orientation and training of evaluators and researchers to build continuous evaluation, research and improvement into the programme, and
- continuous interaction of state level and central level officers with grass-root functionaries.

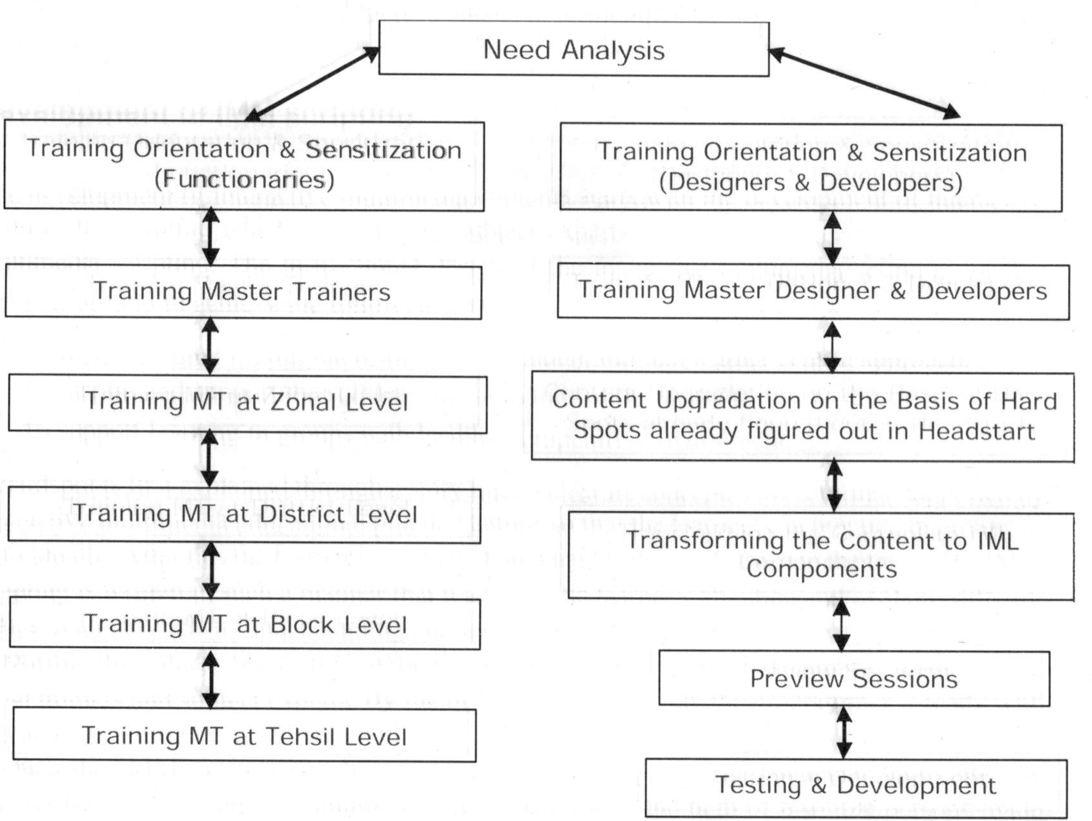

Figure 3: The implementation model

The media to be used for training include: face-to-face interaction, painted workbooks, IMM CD-ROM, teleconferencing (and some web resources and web support). The model suggested for a holistic implementation of the scheme starting from needs analysis (i.e. collation and analysis of the existing data at state level and some additional new data) to pilot run and implementation includes the following:

Learning is visualised to be in regional language, context-specific, activity-based and joyful, in a collaborative group situations, with minimal but guided teacher facilitation, and in an educational system or environment geared towards ICT-enabled education. It is contended that learning can be individualised, but would be enriched for development of individual cognitive structure and for knowledge construction and negotiation in collaborative learning situations in the community, with significant teacher intervention, guidance and facilitation. This is further facilitated, consolidated and integrated by community of teachers and educators and community participation in general. The planned and guided implementation is visualised as follows:

- The IGNOU-MPBOU central team (with guidance and guidelines from the MHRD, GoI) plans the whole scheme in consultation with the state SSA project team (and this interaction is continuous, especially through MPBOU and IGNOU regional centres in the states and union territories); develops training materials; organises training; and oversees implementation.
- The Inter-University Consortium of IGNOU and the R&D Lab of MPBOU provide master expertise in training of trainers and development of IMM CD-ROMs, and for blended learning.
- The IGNOU regional centre in each state in collaboration with the respective state SSA, acts as the nodal implementation agency and for monitoring the implementation from time to time. It also mobilises state experts for training of trainers, design and development of interactive multimedia CDs, training of teachers and learners, and orientation of other functionaries, under the guidance of the IUC.
- The resource persons (master trainers and developers) are drawn from and located at SCERT, DIETs and DPOs, and in selected schools in various clusters.They undertake further training and development of IMM CD-ROMs. The DEP-SSA of IGNOU has its downlinks available at DIETs and this is being extended to DPOs and BRCs. Further, the state level facilities (for instance GramSat of Orissa, conferencing facilities of the Academy of M.P.) can also be utilised for the purpose of orientation, training and continuous interaction. The activities of SSA functions and functionaries are handled by the DEP-SSA.
- Selected functionaries of BRCs and CRCs are trained in content development, ICT-enabled education project management, and monitoring and evaluation of CBEE.
- While selected teachers from clusters of schools are trained as master trainers and content developers, all the teachers of all the schools of each state shall be trained in the use and integration of IMM CD-ROMs (and other ICTs) in instructional design and instructional delivery. Further, all the students need to be oriented/trained on the use of IMM-CDs in individual and group situations, and learning from each other.

Process of Developing IMM-Content

Interactive multimedia courseware development and teacher training is done in collaboration with the respective state governments. The role of IGNOU-MPBOU and the state government is pre-defined. The process of developing IMM content is explained in the following steps:

Identification of hardspots

Workshops are conducted for the identification of hardspots. The state government provides subject-wise two to three teachers from the grass root along with a teacher educator for the hardspot identification along with the hardspots already identified by the state (if any). The central team organises the workshop and provide subject-wise resource persons, and multimedia script writes. After a general introduction a subject-wise team of resource persons, script writers, teacher educators and teachers from grass root level is constituted. These subject-wise groups have discussions, brain storming sessions within themselves and by the end of the workshop produces priority wise hardspots of each subjects. The basic structure of the table of contents of CDs which are to be developed is also recommended for the approval of IMM-CD development.

Development of IMM scripting

The development of interactive multimedia contents starts with the development of interactive multimedia scripting which is written by subject experts who are also experts in the field of multimedia scripting. The instructional design of the interactive multimedia scripting for this revolves around to achieve the following goals:

- To make learning joyful, interesting to the student through learner centric approach.
- To inspire and support the self learning activities of the students.
- To support learning in groups with healthy competitive environment

A hardspot is first explained through a story line to clear its concept. This is further supported by interactive multimedia educational practice games so that the learners can practice in groups or individually. After this the learner is evaluated on what he/she has learned in the topic. The IMM scripting is written in such a manner that it attracts the learner's attention and explains difficult topics in an easy, clear, understanding and interactive manner.

During this phase there are interactions between the graphic designers, scriptwriters, programmers and subject experts. By the time the script is ready the programmer is ready with a demo.

Once the IMM Script is ready it is translated into the regional languages and vetted by experts form the region. The audio is then recorded with the help of resource persons made available by the state and within a month from this the IMM-CD is developed and is made ready for demo to the state government. Also, the testing of CD before the final demo is done on school children their actions on interacting with the IMM-CD is closely observed and the feedback given by them on technical aspects are reviewed and revised. After the demo to the state the IMM-CD is delivered to the state government for its delivery.

The process of IMM-CD Development is shown in Fig. 4.

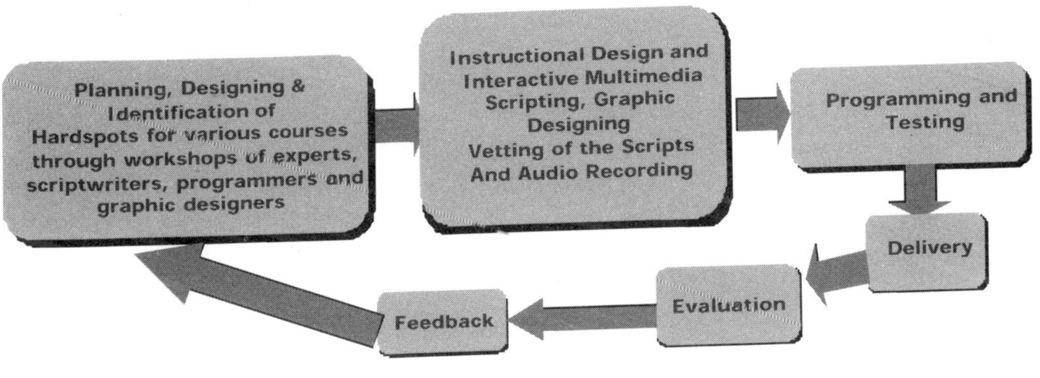

Figure 4: Process of developing, delivering and evaluation process of IMM CDs

This involves an interactive multimedia learning model as shown in the following Fig. 5.

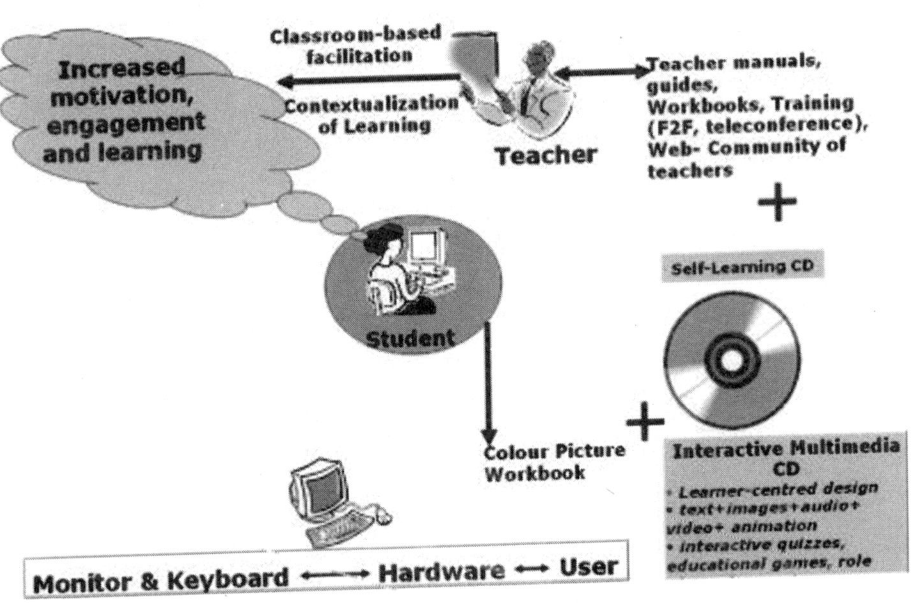

Figure 5: Interactive multimedia learning: a model

The process starts with survey of needs of students and teachers, followed by identification of hardspots in workshop situations, and identification of learning styles and contexual examples and activities; and their collation within a structural-constructivist framework of learning (and teaching). The requirements of the regional language are also taken into consideration. The school teachers are themselves trained to develop scripts for interactive multimedia incorporating all the principles of learner-centred design, text-audio-video-graphics-animation, interactive quizzes, educational games and role plays. Coloured picture books are developed for facilitating the use by students and teachers. The interactive multimedia CD each with 10-12 hardspots (for self-learning as well as group learning) are so designed as to be used by the teacher in the classroom, facilitated further by teacher manuals and guides/workbooks (and teacher capacity building). The CDs are piloted on both teachers, learner and school educators and further revised before large scale use. They are so designed as to contexualise learning and for classroom-based facilitation of learning. These all are supposed to increase motivation and engage students in individual and group learning.

Conclusion

The contents thus developed on hardspots for the SSA project can be adapted to the requirements of schools of each state, and this experience coupled with long term national-level implementation of the Distance Education Programme of earlier DPEP and the present SSA of the MHRD by IGNOU provide confidence and strength to IGNOU-MPBOU to fully implement the CBEE under SSA all over the country. Recently, this team is involved in developing computer text books from class VI-X which will facilitate and cater the computer training needs and requirements of the state government. India has also launched the EduSat in 2004 which will work as a carrier of information up to the grass root level to develop a knowledge India and a knowledge society. These contents can be used through central and regional content repositories and can also be telecast through two-way videoconferencing simultaneously with teacher presentation and interaction. Preliminary experience shows positive impact of these ICT-enabled blended learning experiences within the classroom. What will be further required is quality instructional design and judicious use of ICT for improving the quality of school learning experiences.

References

Panda, S. & Garg, S. (2003). Distance learning in India with open schools. In Bradley, J. (ed.), *the Open Classroom: Distance Learning in and out of Schools*. London: RoutledgeFalmer.

Dr. Jyotsna Dikshit is Reader in M.P. Bhoj (Open) University, Bhopal, India.
Email: jdikshit@hotmail.com

Professor Santosh Panda is Director, Staff Training and Research Institute of Distance Education, & Head of Inter-University Consortium, Indira Gandhi National Open University, New Delhi.
Email: spanda@ignou.ac.in